THE EPIC SAGA BEHIND FRANKENSTEIN: THE TRUE STORY

Rondo Award Winner · Expanded Edition

by
SAM IRVIN

Foreword by
ANNE RICE

Afterword by
GUILLERMO DEL TORO

A Knuckle Samwitch Book

THE EPIC SAGA BEHIND
FRANKENSTEIN: THE TRUE STORY
Rondo Award Winner · Expanded Edition

By SAM IRVIN

Foreword by ANNE RICE

Afterword by GUILLERMO DEL TORO

Cover Artwork by MARK MADDOX

Designed by STEVE KIRKHAM

A KNUCKLE SAMWITCH BOOK

ISBN: 979-8-86462-342-8

Website for graphic designer Steve Kirkham: www.treefrogcommunication.co.uk

Frankenstein: The True Story
The Movie: Copyright © 1973 by Universal Pictures. All Rights Reserved.
Originally broadcast in the U.S. in 1973 on NBC-TV; in the U.K. in 1975 on BBC2; released theatrically in the UK, Mexico and Spain in 1974 by Cinema-International Corporation (a joint venture of Universal Pictures and Paramount Pictures).

Early, shorter drafts of the text and interviews in this book, by Sam Irvin, were originally published in Sam Irvin's *Bizarre* #3 (1974) and *Bizarre* #4 (1975); in Richard Klemensen's *Little Shoppe of Horrors* #38 (2017); in the extras for Shout! Factory's North American Region A Blu-ray of *Frankenstein: The True Story* (2020); and in the extras for Fabulous Films UK Region B Blu-ray of *Frankenstein: The True Story* (2023). Rights to all versions of the text and interviews are reserved and copyrighted by Sam Irvin.

Quotes from the diaries of Christopher Isherwood are used with the permission of Don Bachardy and the Estate of Christopher Isherwood. The diaries were published in three volumes:
Isherwood, Christopher; editor Katherine Bucknell. Book 1: *Christopher Isherwood Diaries Volume 1, 1939-1960*; Book 2: *The Sixties: Diaries Volume 2, 1960-1969*; Book 3: *Liberation: Diaries Volume 3, 1970-1983*. New York: HarperCollins Publishers, 1997, 2010, 2012, respectively. Special thanks to Don Bachardy and Katherine Bucknell.

Photos reproduced herein are for educational purposes and are protected by fair use guidelines. Photos remain the copyright of the various individuals and associated production and distribution companies. The photos have been curated from collections throughout the globe, courtesy of Don Bachardy, Daniel Bouteiller, David Boyce, Jonny Coffin, Del Valle Archives (delvallearchives.com), Steve Gray, Tim Hewitt, Hershenson/Allen Archive, Sam Irvin, Steve Kirkham, Charles Moniz, Gary Parfitt, Terry Pearce, James Anthony Phillips, Russ Raney, Pierre Sarrazin, Alec Smight, Uwe Sommerlad, Philippe Spurrell, John Stoneman, the University of Southern California Cinematic Arts Library (Ned Comstock, curator), and Ava Victoria.

Interior Artwork: All artwork is Copyright © 2023 by each individual artist: Don Bachardy, David Brooks aka Brux, Oscar Calibos, Frederick Cooper, Dan Gallagher, Paul Garner Monster Art, Ron Hezekiah, Daniel Horne, Graham Humphreys, Stefano Junior, Mark Maddox, Dave Matsuoka, Mel Odom, Robert Risko, Adrian Salmon, Greg Staples, Bruce Timm, Neil D Vokes (color by Matt Webb) and Paul Watts.

Above Caricature: Michael Sarrazin chases Sam Irvin, by Dan Gallagher.
Previous Title Page: Mural artwork by Mark Maddox.

TABLE OF CONTENTS

Caricatures by Paul Garner.

Lestat by Mel Odom.

THE EPIC SAGA BEHIND *FRANKENSTEIN: THE TRUE STORY*

FOREWORD BY ANNE RICE

The television production of *Frankenstein: The True Story* directly inspired me to write *Interview with the Vampire*. It contained unforgettable images and ideas. I saw it in my apartment in Berkeley – and seeing this "beautiful monster" swept me off my feet. I got right up from the TV and decided to write something lush and romantic like what I'd just seen – a stunning, sensuous, and thrilling story about gorgeous supernatural beings. In those days, one couldn't get a DVD or a VHS tape even – you saw something once and had to remember it in your heart, until, mercifully, someone reran it. The movie had such a profound influence on my writing that I wonder what I would have written had I not seen this. It was horror the way I longed to see horror done – with depth, dignity, beauty, and seriousness. I highly recommend it.

Anne Rice and Sam holding *Little Shoppe of Horrors*.

Art by Dan Gallagher.
Lettering by Nick Nix.

THE EPIC SAGA BEHIND *FRANKENSTEIN: THE TRUE STORY*

INTRODUCTION

"The greatest fantasy film of all time." That was the delirious declaration I wrote in 1974 about *Frankenstein: The True Story* when I put the movie on the cover of my fanzine *Bizarre* No. 3 a few months after it first aired in the U.S. on NBC-TV. A tad overwrought, I admit. In my defense, I was an impressionable 17-year-old monster kid from North Carolina. But my searing emotional reaction was sincere at the time and ran much deeper than mere adolescent zeal. As a closeted gay teen who felt like an outsider and a freak of nature, the movie spoke to me in profound ways I would not fully comprehend until many years later.

In my travels to England in 1974-75 to meet and interview many of my horror film idols (from Christopher Lee to Terence Fisher – chronicled in my 2022 coming-of-age memoir *I Was a Teenage Monster Hunter!*), I managed to score several members of the *True Story* cast: Jane Seymour, Nicola Pagett, Margaret Leighton and Michael Wilding. I met the editor Richard Marden. I corresponded with the associate producer Ian Lewis.

I also exchanged letters with producer Hunt Stromberg Jr. – though, at the time, I was not fully aware just how deep his love of horror went nor how much we had in common. I didn't even know he had discovered Vampira – much less that he was gay. Yet, instinctually, I knew we were kindred spirits.

In 1972, the very same year I started *Bizarre*, Richard Klemensen founded his own fanzine called *Little Shoppe of Horrors* and we quickly became pen pals over our shared passion for British horror movies. However, while Dick continued producing his magnificent zine for the next half-century-and-counting, I gave up *Bizarre* after 1975 to pursue a career as a filmmaker, beginning as Brian De Palma's assistant (on *The Fury* and *Dressed to Kill*) and eventually directing over 50 projects, including *Guilty as Charged*, *Oblivion*, *Elvira's Haunted Hills*, and the gay horror series *Dante's Cove*.

One of my proudest achievements was co-executive producing Bill Condon's Oscar-winning masterpiece *Gods and Monsters* starring Sir Ian McKellen as director James Whale. It was a dream come true to help recreate Frankenstein's laboratory for a flashback sequence on the set of *Bride of Frankenstein* – my all-time favorite movie.

I was not surprised to learn that *Bride of Frankenstein* was also Hunt Stromberg Jr.'s favorite movie – and that James Mason's Dr. Polidori character in *True Story* was directly based on Dr. Pretorius from *Bride*. It all made such perfect sense.

So, when Dick Klemensen asked if I might be interested in spearheading an issue of *Little Shoppe of Horrors* devoted to the making of *Frankenstein: The True Story*, I didn't just leap at

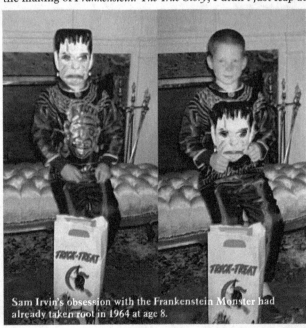

Sam Irvin's obsession with the Frankenstein Monster had already taken root in 1964 at age 8.

Sam holding 2020 Rondo for Best Commentary.

SAM IRVIN
RONDO AWARD
BEST COMMENTARY

2020 RONDO AWARD
FRANKENSTEIN: THE TRUE STORY
SAM IRVIN
BEST COMMENTARY

LITTLE SHOPPE OF HORRORS
Frankenstein: The True Story

RONDO AWARD WINNER
BEST ARTICLE OF THE YEAR

JAMES MASON · LEONARD WHITING · DAVID McCALLUM · JANE SEYMOUR · NICOLA PAGETT · MICHAEL SARRAZIN

FRANKENSTEIN: THE TRUE STORY

Sam's 2017 Rondo for Best Article.

2017 RONDO AWARD
SAGA OF FRANKENSTEIN: THE TRUE STORY
SAM IRVIN
BEST ARTICLE

Below : Rondo Award guru David Colton & Sam with LSoH.

FTTS Blu-ray and LSOH cover art by Mark Maddox.

THE EPIC SAGA BEHIND *FRANKENSTEIN: THE TRUE STORY*

Cartoons by Dan Gallagher, *Little Shoppe of Horrors* No. 39 (2017).

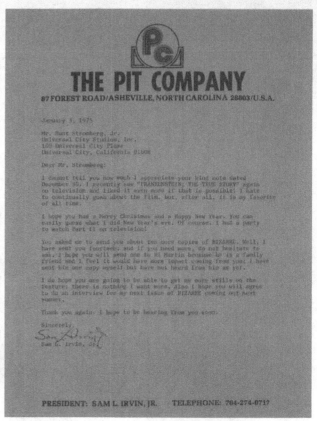

Above Left: Cover of *Bizarre* No. 3. Above Right Sam Irvin letter to Stromberg, 1975.

the chance. l jumped over the freakin' moon!

But then reality hit me. How would I find enough new material to make such an endeavor worthy of the magazine's stratospherically high standard? Then I remembered something. When I was researching my biography book *Kay Thompson: From Funny Face to Eloise* (Simon & Schuster), University of Southern California Cinematic Arts Library archivist Ned Comstock casually mentioned that the Hunt Stromberg Jr. Papers were among the library's Special Collections. 25 boxes of them, no less! I had no use for them at the time, but somehow, I knew that one day they would come in handy.

Well, that day had come. Among the tonnage of material to sift through, there had to be at least a file or two on *Frankenstein: The True Story*. When I came upon three copies of *Bizarre* – and several teenage fan letters I had written to

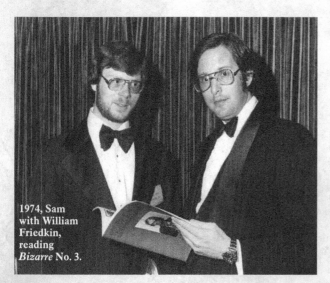

1974, Sam with William Friedkin, reading *Bizarre* No. 3.

Stromberg – it felt like destiny. As I dug deeper, I not only found a treasure trove of *True Story* ephemera, I also came to the seemingly preordained conclusion that Stromberg was just the sort of complicated, colorful character I had been seeking to write about – as a follow-up to my exhaustive, detective-like coverage of Kay Thompson.

But there was more to it than that. The deeper I dug into Stromberg's upbringing, the more I identified with him. Both of us were "Juniors," raised by formidable, controlling fathers who were already successful showbiz executives. We both wanted to be in the movie business – but not on our fathers' coattails. We had dreams of our own. Our dads were ashamed of their queer sons and did everything they could to sway away the gay – including sending us to military institutions in the hopes that it would "butch us up." Under enormous pressure to fit in, both of us married women. Neither marriage lasted, of course. Our queerness won out. All these failed attempts to control us just made us stronger. We had something to prove.

My spirit animal has always been Mr. Toad from *The Wind in the Willows*, the mischievous, freewheeling, extravagant eccentric who becomes obsessed with automobiles. Upon seeing a shiny new red car zooming by, Toad became dazed, eyes spinning, and all he could think about was procuring one for himself. Well, that perfectly describes Hunt's disposition – and mine as well. When we set our sights on something, we are relentless – and we don't give up easily. *Frankenstein: The True Story* never would have happened in such a lavish way were it not for the burning passion and rabid resolve of Hunt Stromberg Jr. I get it. I'm that way, too. And I admire him for it.

What you are about to read has many facets. It is an eye-opening exposé on the movie industry of the early 1970s with an emphasis on Universal Pictures and the horror genre.

Top Left: Peter Fuller, Steve Kirkham, Allan Bryce & Sam at Hammer House. Top Right: Constantine Nasr & Sam. Above: Dan Gallagher, Mark Maddox, Dick Klemensen, Sam and Neil D Vokes. Left: Cover artist Mark Maddox channels Sarrazin, holding Gallagher poster.

But the chronicle also reveals the astonishing courage of a revolutionary group of LGBTQ+ artists securing their place at the table. Despite my own subjective point of view, I did not embark on this project with a "gay agenda" in mind. That agenda was baked in. Even I was taken aback by how daring this whole enterprise was from its earliest inception. How the hell did they get away with it?! To answer that question fully, I had to dig deep into the movie's queer sensibility and the "Lavender Hill Mob" that made it happen. Ultimately, though, the heart of this saga is a triumph of determination – against all odds – that is relatable to us all. The adventure *behind* the creation of *Frankenstein: The True Story* is so astounding, it is an epic unto itself. Prepare to catch your jaw before it drops to the floor.

When my *Frankenstein: The True Story* opus was published in *Little Shoppe of Horrors* No. 38 in 2017 (eternal genuflection to Dick Klemensen), I very proudly won that year's Rondo Award for Best Article. This directly led to me being invited

to create the special features for Shout! Factory's 2020 North American Region A Blu-ray restoration of *Frankenstein: The True Story*, produced by the tireless film scholar Constantine Nasr (consider your feet properly kissed by me and all the rest of us). Amazingly, I ended up winning another Rondo Award – this time for Best Audio Commentary. My extras (including on-camera interviews with Jane Seymour, Leonard Whiting and co-screenwriter Don Bachardy – along with the 3-hour-plus audio commentary) were subsequently licensed for inclusion on Fabulous Films' 2023 UK Region B Blu-ray restoration of *Frankenstein: The True Story*.

And yet, even after all of that, I still had many more fascinating scoops to report – and lots of unpublished photos and artwork languishing in my archive. Could there possibly be another, all-encompassing outlet for my obsession? Bingo! You're holding it! This lavish coffee-table book is the ultimate, massively expanded celebration of *Frankenstein: The True Story* commemorating its 50th Anniversary and the 100th birthday of producer Hunt Stromberg Jr. (1923-1986).

How did this dream-come-true edition come about? Again, it all seemed like fate. In December 2019, I traveled to London to interview Leonard Whiting on camera for the Shout! Factory's Blu-ray extras of *Frankenstein: The True Story*. Three Monster Kids got wind of my visit and suggested we get together for lunch (and a pilgrimage to Hammer House for a photo op). They were Peter Fuller, curator of the Vincent Price Legacy UK; Allan Bryce, editor-

Sam with Shout! Factory U.S. FTTS Blu-ray.

Sam with Fabulous Films UK FTTS Blu-ray & DVD.

publisher of *The Dark Side* and *Infinity* magazines; and Steve Kirkham, graphic designer of *We Belong Dead* magazine and their associated books. Decades earlier, Allan and Steve had actually purchased copies of my fanzine *Bizarre* – which apparently had made quite an impression on both of them.

Allan Bryce recalled, "I will never forget back in 1974 buying that issue No. 3 of *Bizarre* – with the photograph of *Frankenstein: The True Story* glued on the cover – from dear Fred Zentner's Cinema Bookshop at 13-14 Great Russell Street in London. Sam, you are a legend in our small world of genre publishing, and I just pray that your mantelpiece does not collapse under the weight of all those Rondo Awards!" (Oh, Allan. Flattery will get you everywhere! And it did! I accepted Allan's invitation to interview Cassandra Peterson, aka Elvira, for *The Dark Side* No. 222 and won another Rondo for it! Thank you for the platform, my friend!)

At that same fateful lunch, Steve Kirkham brought along his original mint-condition copy of *Bizarre* No. 3 for me to sign – which I was more than delighted to do. Not to mention being astounded and touched that anyone even remembered!

Then Steve pitched the idea of designing a grand-scale book honoring *Frankenstein: The True Story*. Well, you could have knocked me over with a feather. My dream for half a century had always been to do a great big, beautiful book on *Frankenstein: The True Story*, with ample space for extra-large images and no limit on my definitive "making of" text – plus a comprehensive biography of producer Hunt Stromberg Jr. In fact, in 1974, I wrote a letter to Stromberg proposing this very same idea – which still exists among Stromberg's papers archived at the University of Southern California's Cinematic Arts Library. Stromberg loved the idea – but both of us got busy with other projects and we never found the time to bring this to fruition.

Flash forward forty-five years and here was Steve Kirkham reawakening my desire to finally check this off my bucket list. No arm-twisting necessary. Steve and I immediately shook hands on the deal – witnessed by Peter and Allan at that December 2019 lunch – and made a pact to get this done in time for the 50th Anniversary.

Prior to our deep dive into the production of this book, however, I needed a graphic designer for my 2022 memoir *I Was a Teenage Monster Hunter!* Because so much of it centered around *Bizarre*, Steve not only understood and appreciated this niche of fanzine history and the Anglo-centric horror genre interviewees, he was simply *the* ideal person for the job. And wow, he knocked it out of the park! Fortuitously, we didn't kill each other during the process, either. In fact, we had a blast! So, we couldn't wait to get going on our *Frankenstein* monster. And Steve has captured lightning in a

bottle yet again! Thank you, my dear partner-in-crime!

It should be noted that it was the illustrious multi-Rondo Award winning cover artist of this book, Mark Maddox, who first suggested to Dick Klemensen that he should feature *Frankenstein: The True Story* in *Little Shoppe of Horrors* – mainly because Mark is just about as big a fan of the movie as I am; and he was itching to paint the cover! So yes, it really was Mark who ignited this post-modern renaissance of *Frankenstein: The True Story* – and he has outdone himself not once, not twice, but *three* times! First with the groundbreaking triple-foldout mural for *Little Shoppe of Horrors* No. 38 – to date, the largest continuous horror magazine cover image ever. Second, Mark provided all-new artwork for the cover of Shout! Factory's Blu-ray of *Frankenstein: The True Story*. And now, back for Round Three, Mark enthusiastically accepted the challenge to create fresh and fabulous imagery to adorn the cover and back cover of this enormous volume. I don't know how the hell he did it, but he topped himself again! Hats off to you, pal!

I also want to thank the league of extraordinary artists who contributed their own masterpieces featured in the pages of this book: Don Bachardy, David Brooks aka Brux, Oscar Calibos, Frederick Cooper, Dan Gallagher, Paul Garner Monster Art, Ron Hezekiah, Daniel Horne, Graham Humphreys, Stefano Junior, Mark Maddox, Dave Matsuoka, Mel Odom, Robert Risko, Adrian Salmon, Greg Staples, Bruce Timm, Neil D Vokes (color by Matt Webb) and Paul Watts.

And, of course, curating all the photos and posters for this book would have been impossible without the generous support of Don Bachardy, Daniel Bouteiller, David Boyce, Jonny Coffin, David Del Valle and his Del Valle Archives (delvallearchives.com), Steve Gray, Tim Hewitt, Hershenson/ Allen Archive, Charles Moniz, Gary Parfitt, Terry Pearce, James Anthony Phillips, Russ Raney, Pierre Sarrazin, Alec Smight, John Stoneman, the University of Southern California Cinematic Arts Library (Ned Comstock, curator), and Ava Victoria.

I was extremely fortunate to track down many surviving *True Story* cast and crew members, plus a battalion of folks with a variety of connections to the film, who very kindly agreed to be interviewed, including Tony Aitken, Phyllis Allarie, Skye Aubrey, Don Bachardy, Rick Baker, Julian Barnes, David Boyce, Richard Chamberlain, Shonya Lyn Chapmon, Colin Chilvers, Michael Chilvers, Jim Danforth, Joe Dante, Sarah Douglas, Jon East, the late-Robin French, Mark Gatiss, Graham V. Hartstone, the late-William Hobbs, Tom Holland, the late-Geoffrey Holder, Karl Howman, the late-Barry Humphries, the late-Angela Lansbury, the late-Jack Larson, the late-Margaret Leighton, Ian Lewis, the late-Richard Marden, James Duke Mason, Morgan Mason, Pier Mason, David McCallum, Denise Mellé, Peter Melrose, the late-Nicola Pagett, Michael Pharey, Pierre Sarrazin, the late-Sid Sheinberg, Jane Seymour, Alec Smight, Brian Smithies, John Stoneman, Allan Warren, David Weston, Leonard Whiting, the late-Michael Wilding, the late-Christopher Wood, Ava Victoria, and Jon Voight.

I particularly want to thank Third Assistant Director / Pack Rat Terry Pearce who miraculously saved numerous

Top Left: Cassandra Peterson (aka Elvira) & Sam. Top Right: Sam & Julie Brown. Center Left: Sam with Chucky and creator Don Mancini. Center Right: Jane Seymour & Sam. Bottom Left: Sam & RuPaul. Bottom Right: Marina Sirtis & Sam.

Parker Stevenson & Pamela Sue Martin with Sam.

Jonathan Bennett with Sam.

Olivia d'Abo & Sam.

production reports (including a complete set of call sheets) that proved to be invaluable to my research.

A big salute also goes to Katherine Bucknell who meticulously edited Christopher Isherwood's diaries, published by HarperCollins in three massive volumes that I highly recommend. They were invaluable resources for quotes and for establishing an accurate timeline of events.

There is also a battalion of friends, family and film fans who have helped me along the way immeasurably with their kindness, research and support: Nancy Allen, Melinda Angstrom, Anne Irvin Aspinwall, Henry Baker, Simon J. Ballard, James Benge, Wayne Alan Blood, Laurent Bouzereau, Derek Botelho, Julie Brown, Allan Bryce, Katherine Bucknell, Nige Burton, Charles Busch, Darrell Buxton, Jeffrey Cason, Roman Chimienti, David & Eileen Colton, Ned Comstock, Bill Condon, Janet Irvin Crowder, David De Leon, Larry Estes, Eugenio Ercolani, Ansel Faraj, Bryan Fuller, Peter Fuller, John Green, Christopher Gullo, Brendan Haley, Ernest Harris, Sue & Del Howison, David Huckvale, Tim Irvin, John J Johnston, Doug Jones, Stefano Junior, Richard Kraft, Jim Kunz, Dori Legg, Tim Lucas, Jordan Lummis, Paul Magrs, Leonard Maltin, Don Mancini, Darryl Mayeski, James McCabe, Eric McNaughton, Bryan Moore, Jack Morrissey, Stephen R. Myers, Cassandra Peterson, James Anthony Phillips, Lynn Presser, Jan Jones Pulley, Russ Raney, Ben Raphael Sher, Scott Skelton, Uwe Sommerlad, Gregor Spethmann, Philippe Spurrell, Anthony Taylor, James Thompson, Joe Thornton, Tony Timpone, Lisi Tribble, Lee Tsiantis, Moyb Ullah, Michael Varrati, John Weber, Charlotte Westenra, William Wilson, Taylor White, Dave Woodman, and Brock Yurich.

My husband Gary Bowers (together since 1982) should receive some sort of sainthood for putting up with me and my various obsessions. I greatly appreciate your indulgence all these decades, babe.

A very special acknowledgement must be made to the late, great Anne Rice who generously contributed the Foreword because of our shared passion for *Frankenstein: The True Story*. I will never forget personally handing her a copy of *Little Shoppe of Horrors* No. 38 and how excited she was flipping through its pages – literally fangirling – as I was fanboying over her. Anne's eyes would have grown to Peter Lorre proportions had she lived long enough to see this book.

In 2016, I came across a tweet on the Twitter feed of the celebrated director Guillermo del Toro (*Pan's Labyrinth*, *Hellboy*, *Pacific Rim*, *Crimson Peak*) in which he professed his adoration of *Frankenstein: The True Story*. Ever since then, I have dreamed of getting him to elaborate on his thoughts

about the film – but he got a wee bit busy directing a little picture called *The Shape of Water* (2017) for which he won two Oscars – for Best Picture and Best Director – followed by *Guillermo del Toro's Pinocchio* (2022), for which he won a third Oscar for Best Animated Feature Film. Immediately after that, in 2023, it was announced that he was writing, directing and producing his own version of *Frankenstein*. The guy stays busy. And I figured my chances of pinning down one of the world's greatest directors at the very peak of his brilliant career were just getting slimmer by the minute.

Nevertheless, as the deadline for my book drew closer, I decided it was now or never. It couldn't hurt to ask. On Sunday, June 4, 2023, I composed an email to Mr. del Toro, inviting him to please consider writing the Afterword to my labor-of-love. With every ounce of hope, I clicked "send." Finally, the request was out there in cyberspace. I had no idea if he would even receive it, much less have the time to add anything to his very busy schedule. I didn't expect to get a response for days, weeks or even months. If ever.

But then, to my glorious astonishment, a mere seven hours later, I received the most exquisite email imaginable. Not only had Mr. del Toro generously granted my supreme wish, but the eloquence of his Afterword was so profoundly touching and heartfelt, it brought tears to my eyes. There are no words to adequately express the gratitude I feel toward Mr. del Toro for bestowing this honor on me and my book with his exquisite recognition of the poetic beauty to be discovered within *Frankenstein: The True Story*.

FRANKENSTEIN: THE TRUE STORY
(A Universal Presentation)

Principal Photography: March 15 through July 2, 1973
(76 days).
James Mason Introduction filmed August 25, 1973.

Filmed at Pinewood Studios; and at the following UK locations:
Clivedon estate, Taplow, Berkshire; Beachy Head, Eastbourne,
Sussex; Virginia Water Lake, Windsor Great Park, Old Windsor,
Berkshire; Bray Village, Berkshire; St. Mary Abbott's Hospital,
Kensington; Burnham Beeches, Farnham, Buckinghamshire;
Dromenagh Farm, Iver, Buckinghamshire; St. Mary the Virgin
Parish Church, Hedgerley, Buckinghamshire; St. Peter's Church
and Hambleden Village, Hambleden, Buckinghamshire; St. Mary's
Church and Denham Village, Denham, Buckinghamshire.

Budget: $3.5 million

Complete TV Version Running Time: Approximately 180 minutes
(*not* counting commercials, Mason intro, preview of Part 2 at the end
of Part 1,
nor recap of Part 1 at the beginning of Part 2;
counting only one set of opening and closing TV credit sequences;
note that the sequence at the end of Part 1 of
Sarrazin getting up on the beach and walking away
is repeated at the beginning of Part 2.)

Truncated Theatrical Version Running Time:
122 minutes, 39 seconds
(with a few extra seconds of gore; and, longer closing credits)

U.S. Television:
World Premiere on NBC-TV (180-minute version):
Part 1: Friday, November 30, 1973; 9:00-11:00 PM.
(13.3 million viewers; No. 1 for the time slot; No. 27 for the week.)
Part 2: Saturday, December 1, 1973; 9:00-11:00 PM.
(14.6 million viewers; No. 1 for the time slot; No. 15 for the week.)
Repeated on NBC-TV (180-minute version):
Part 1: Monday, December 30, 1974; 9:00-11:00 PM.
Part 2: Tuesday, December 31, 1974; 9:00-11:00 PM.

U.K. Theatrical Distribution:
Distributed by Cinema-International Corporation
Theatrical premiere (122:39 version):
Paramount Theatre, Lower Regent Street, London.
September 19 through October 2, 1974.

U.K. Television:
BBC2 (180-minute version, both parts joined together):
Saturday, December 27, 1975: 8:20-11:30 PM.

France Television:
FR3 (180-minute version, shown in two parts):
Part 1: Saturday, November 20, 1976: 8:30-10:10 PM.
Part 2: Saturday, November 27, 1976: 8:30-10:10 PM.

West Germany Television:
ZDF (180-minute version, shown in two parts):
Part 1: Tuesday, October 21, 1980
Part 2: Friday, October 24, 1980

Japan Television:
CX, Fuji Television, Tokyo, Channel 8
(89-minute version, dubbed in Japanese):
Friday Foreign Movie Theatre: July 27, 1979, 9:00-11:00 PM

The 122:39 version was also theatrically released in
Mexico (Cinema International), Spain (Arte 7),
Lebanon (Sunny Film International, Beirut), Portugal,
Uruguay, and India.

CAST

Dr. Polidori	JAMES MASON
Victor Frankenstein	LEONARD WHITING
Henry Clerval	DAVID McCALLUM
Agatha / Prima	JANE SEYMOUR
Elizabeth Fanshawe	NICOLA PAGETT
The Creature	MICHAEL SARRAZIN
Sir Richard Fanshawe	MICHAEL WILDING
Lady Fanshawe	CLARISSA KAYE
Mrs. Blair	AGNES MOOREHEAD
Dowager Countess Duval	MARGARET LEIGHTON
Lacey	SIR RALPH RICHARDSON
Chief Constable	SIR JOHN GIELGUD
Ship's Captain	TOM BAKER
Baronet's Son (Prima's suitor)	JULIAN BARNES
Impatient Coach Passenger	ARNOLD DIAMOND
Nurse (Mrs. McGregor)	YOOTHA JOYCE
Priest (hears Victor's confession)	PETER SALLIS
Felix (Agatha's husband)	DALLAS ADAMS
William Frankenstein	KARL HOWMAN
Injured Man (arm amputee)	DAVID WESTON
1st Helper (during amputation)	JEREMY YOUNG
2nd Helper (during amputation)	PADDY JOYCE
Police Constable	PETER GLAZE
1st Chinese Manservant	TONY THEN
2nd Chinese Manservant	KIM TEOH
1st Sailor	MICHAEL GOLDIE
2nd Sailor	BARRY LINEHAN
3rd Sailor	TONY AITKEN
4th Sailor	DEREK DEADMAN
Dressmaker	ROSAMUND GREENWOOD
Priest (Clerval & Victor scene)	DERMOT WALSH
Clergyman (Clerval's funeral)	MARTYN READ
Clergyman (William's funeral)	PETER GREENE
Church Organist (hymn service)	KEN BROWN
Mother of Prima's suitor (service)	PATRICIA VARLEY
Footman	NEVILLE PHILLIPS
Usher in Box Seat at Opera	WILLIAM HOBBS
6-Year-Old Girl in Park	PIER MASON
Little Boys in Park	SEAN GUEST
	PETER MARSHALL
Coffin Supplier (at stable)	NORMAN STANLEY
Grieving Mother (of Colin Lewis)	SHEILA FAY
Dancers at the ball	WENDY BARRY/MICHAEL BUCHANAN
	WALTER CARTIER/JAN DARLING
	ANN FROST/JANIE KELLS
	MICHAEL LANDER/PAT LOVETT
	JERRY MANLEY/VICKI MURDEN
	GEORGE SALAVISA/PETER SALMON
	RENE SATORIS/GILLIAN SHEPHERD
	ARTHUR SWEET/SUE WESTON
Ballroom Guest #1	ELIZABETH SPENDER
Ballroom Guest #2	SARAH DOUGLAS
Ballroom Guest #3	DORIS SHELTON
Sailors	KEN BUCKLE/TEX FULLER
	KEN HAYWARD/STEVE JAMES
	BILL REED/JEFF SILK
	GERRY WAIN/PAUL WESTON
Toby (Lacey's dog)	TOBY THE DOG

Thug Scene filmed but dropped from the final cut:

Thug #1	DAVID BOYCE
Thug #2	MICHAEL DA COSTA
Thug #3	MICHAEL WENNINK
Passerby	MARC BOYLE

Creature in Town Square Cage Scene; cast but never shot:

Little Girl Hostage/Cage Scene	CHLOE FRANKS
Little Girl #2 from Cage Scene	SAMANTHA WEYSON
Little Boy #1 from Cage Scene	RICHARD BEAUMONT
Little Boy #2 from Cage Scene	MICHAEL McVEY

Stock footage clip from Universal's
The Phantom of the Opera (1943):
Opera Singer (curtain call bow): SUSANNA FOSTER

Stand-ins (for camera and lighting)

For James Mason	BILL BURNS
	EDDIE MILBURN
	JACK ARMSTRONG
	GERRY PARIS
For Leonard Whiting	DAVID FIELD
For David McCallum	JOHN MOYCE
	TOM BOOTH
For Jane Seymour	JENNIFER PETTICAN
	CHRISTINE SPOONER
	VAL HAYES
For Nicola Pagett	CHRISTINE SPOONER
For Michael Sarrazin	NORTON CLARKE
For Michael Wilding	BOB WRIGHT
	MIKE REYNEL
	JOE PHELPS
For Clarissa Kaye	LIZ COKE
	ERICA SIMMONS
For Agnes Moorehead	CHARLOTTE STECKER
	JOYCE PERKINS
For Margaret Leighton	BLANCHE LOVEDAY
	BUNNY SEMEN
For Ralph Richardson	JOE PHELPS
For John Gielgud	IAN SELBY
For Peter Glaze	JOE TREGONINO
For Julian Barnes	KELLY VARNEY
	WARREN BLACK
For Dallas Adams	JOHN CLIFFORD

On-Screen Doubles

For Michael Sarrazin	NORTON CLARKE
For Jane Seymour	MICHELINE DAVIES
Nude double for Jane Seymour	NICOLA AUSTIN
Severed arm gripping Whiting	ROY ASHTON

Stunt Doubles

For Leonard Whiting	JIMMY LODGE
	GEORGE LEECH
For Jane Seymour	SADIE EDEN
	DOROTHY FORD
For Michael Sarrazin	MARC BOYLE
For Ralph Richardson	GEORGE LEECH
For Tom Baker	JOE POWELL
For Dallas Adams	CLIFF DIGGINS
	PAUL WESTON
	PETER MUNT
For Tony Then	MALCOLM WEAVER
For Kim Teoh / Karl Howman	ROY SCAMMELL

CREW

Producer	HUNT STROMBERG JR.
Director	JACK SMIGHT
Writers	CHRISTOPHER ISHERWOOD
	DON BACHARDY
Based on the novel by	MARY SHELLEY

Production Department

Associate Producer	IAN LEWIS
Production Manager	BRIAN BURGESS
Location Manager	IAN GODDARD
Assistant to the Producer	JACQUE SHELTON
Producer's Secretary	PHYLLIS ALLARIE
Production Secretary	VICKI DEASON
1st Assistant Director	JOHN STONEMAN
2nd Assistant Director	PETER COTTON
3rd Assistant Director	TERRY PEARCE
1st A.D. (last few days)	BRIAN HEARD
Add'l 3rd A.D. (on heavy days)	MICHAEL PHAREY
Continuity	ANGELA MARTELLI
Production Runner	STEVEN RIDGWELL

Casting Department

Casting Director	SALLY NICHOLL

Camera Department

Director of Photography	ARTHUR IBBETSON
Camera Operator	JOHN HARRIS
Focus Puller	STEVE CLAYDON
Clapper/Loader	JONATHAN TAYLOR
Camera Grips	JIMMY SPOARD
	GEORGE BEAVIS
Second Camera Operator	BOB KINDRED
Second Camera Focus Puller	CHRIS MOORE
Helicopter Camera Operator	PETER ALLWARK

Second Unit

2nd Unit Director (Mason intro)	HUNT STROMBERG, JR.
2nd Unit Director (Agatha death)	JOHN STONEMAN
2nd Unit Dir. of Photography	EDWARD "TED" SCAIFE
2nd Unit Camera Operator	FREDDIE COOPER

Electric Department

Supervising Electrician	JOHN SWANN
Chargehand Electrician	HARRY INGLETON
Electricians	R. SAUNDERS
	JOHN HIGGINS
	H. BISSET
	R. TAYLOR
	TERRY GODDARD
	MAX MATTHEWS

Art Department

Production Designer	WILFRID SHINGLETON
Art Director	FRED CARTER
Set Dresser	BRYAN GRAVES
Property Buyer	KEN DOLBEAR
Scenic / Matte / Titles Artist	PETER MELROSE
Scenic Artist	ROBERT SPENCER
Sketch Artist	JACK STEPHENS
Construction Manager	MIKE REDDING
Draughtsman	BRIAN ACKLAND-SNOW
Draughtsman	MICHAEL LAMONT

Special Effects Department

Special Effects Supervisor	ROY WYBROW
Draughtsman / Effects Design	RON BURTON
Special Effects Technician	COLIN CHILVERS
Miniature / Model Effects	BRIAN SMITHIES
Optical Effects	WALLY VEEVERS
Process Projection Effects	CHARLES STAFFELL
Special Effects Assistant	ALAN BARNARD
Special Effects Assistant	BUD ROSSLER
Special Effects Prop Man	BILL LYNCH
Matte Effects	RAY CAPEL

Makeup / Hairdressing Department

Chief Makeup (Sarrazin)	HARRY FRAMPTON
Makeup Artist	ROY ASHTON
Makeup Artist	ALDO MANGANARO
Hairdresser	PATRICIA McDERMOTT
Assistant Hairdresser	CATHY KEVANY

Wardrobe Department

Costume Supervisor	ELSA FENNELL
Wardrobe Mistress	EVELYN GIBBS
Wardrobe Master	MIKE JARVIS

Choreography

Choreographer	SALLY GILPIN

Stunts

Stunt Arranger	WILLIAM HOBBS
Stunt Arranger	RAY FORD
Stunt Consultant	JACQUE SHELTON

Animals

Animal Consultant	JACQUE SHELTON

Editing Department

Editor	RICHARD MARDEN
1st Assistant Editor	NIGEL BATE
2nd Assistant Editor	DAVID BEESLEY

CAST AND CREW

Sound Department

Sound Mixer	GORDON EVERETT
Sound Recordist	KEN BARKER
Sound Boom Operator	STAN HAINES
Sound Camera Operator	MIKE HEAVISIDE
Sound Maintenance	CHARLES VAN DER GOOR

Post Sound Department

Sound Re-recording Mixer	GRAHAM V. HARTSTONE
Sound Editor	DON SHARPE
Dubbing / Footsteps Editor	PAUL SMITH
Dubbing Assistant	ROCKY PHELAN
Assistant Editor	MARY KESSELL
Assistant Editor	RICHARD HISCOTT
Dialogue Editor	ARCHIE LUDSKI
Assistant	ROY BIRCHLEY

Music Department

Composer	GIL MELLE
Music Supervisor / Arranger	PHILIP MARTELL
Additional Arranger	CARLO MARTELLI
Additional Arranger	BERNARD EBBINGHOUSE
Orchestra	LONDON SYMPHONY ORCHESTRA
Recorded at	ANVIL SOUND STUDIOS, DENHAM, BUCKS

Studio Standby Crew

Carpenter	TREVOR NICOL
Plasterer	DAVE BAYNHAM
Plasterer's Labourer	J. FINNEGAN
Stagehand	WILLIAM SMITH
Rigger	MICK KILGANNON
Grip	JIMMY SPOARD
Painter	RON FALLEN
Chargehand Prop	EDDIE FRANCIS
Prop Man	ALF SMITH
Prop Man	KEN WILKS
Chargehand Dressing Prop	BRIAN GAMBY
Unit Drivers	BASIL BROWN
	JIMMY SPILLER
	TOM PRESTON
	REG DAVIES
Studio Driver	PHIL RIDGWELL
Prop Truck Driver	CHARLIE GILL
Wardrobe Van Driver	RAY GIBBS
Unit Nurse	JOYCE PEGLER

Accounts Department

Production Accountant	MAURICE LANDSBERGER
Assistant Accountant	KEITH KNOWLES
Accounts Secretary	JANICE WILLCOX

Vendors

Cameras and Lenses	PANAVISION
35mm Film Stock	KODAK
Color Processing	TECHNICOLOR
Studio Facility	PINEWOOD STUDIOS
Insurance Provider	ANTHONY GIBBS & SONS

Publicity Department

Unit Publicist	LILY POYSER
Stills Photography	GEORGE COURTNEY WARD
	DOUGLAS LUKE

Production and Distribution

Production Company	UNIVERSAL TELEVISION PICTURES LIMITED
U.S. broadcaster	NBC-TV
Foreign theatrical distributor	CINEMA-INTERNATIONAL

Miscellaneous

Titan Camera Crane:
WESTCHESTER PRODUCTIONS (ROGER DOWNLEY)

Hydraulic rocker, wind machines, and other special equipment:
THE TRADING POST (JIM HOLE)

Horses and period carriages:
GEORGE MOSSMAN

Production vehicles and trailers:
JOHN ANDERSON CARAVANS LTD.

Generator:
CINE-MOBILE

Crew buses:
DENHAM COACHES (JACK CRUMP)

TV aerial removal and reinstallation
(for period setting authenticity):
TELEVISION AERIAL SPECIALISTS OF WINDSOR

Helicopters:
Alouette II Helicopter with Typer Mount for 35mm Arriflex
BRITISH EXECUTIVE AIR SERVICES (BEAS), KIDLINGTON,
OXFORDSHIRE

Additional Music Credits:

Opera attended by Dr. Frankenstein and the Creature:
The Marriage of Figaro, K. 492
Composed by Wolfgang Amadeus Mozart
Unknown recording (licensed).

First melody Lacey plays on the violin:
Come Lasses and Lads (Traditional)
Arranged by Philip Martell

Second melody Lacey plays on the violin:
Scenes from the Bavarian Highlands, Op. 27, Lullaby
Composed by Sir Edward William Elgar
Arranged by Carlo Martelli

Hymn sung at church service:
The Church's One Foundation
Composed by Samuel Sebastian Wesley and Samuel J. Stone
Traditional arrangement with church organ and congregational choir

Piano music played by Elizabeth, then mimicked by Prima:
Piano Sonata No. 23 in F minor, Op. 57 Appassionata
Composed by Ludwig van Beethoven
Arranged by Philip Martell

Nursery rhyme sung a cappella by Prima as she tries to strangle a cat:
I Love Little Pussy (Traditional)
Nursery rhyme, with adjusted lyric "I Love Little Kitty"
Performed by Jane Seymour
Pre-recorded at Anvil Sound Studios, March 28, 1973.

First melody heard at Prima's debutante ball:
Mazurka No. 5 in B-Flat Major, Op. 7, No. 1
Composed by Frédéric François Chopin
Arranged by Bernard Ebbinghouse

Second melody heard at Prima's debutante ball:
Eine kleine Nachtmusik
Composed by Wolfgang Amadeus Mozart
Arranged by Philip Martell

Prima's solo ballet at debutante ball:
Introduction and Allegro for Harp, Flute, Clarinet and String Quartet
Composed by Joseph Maurice Ravel
Arranged by Philip Martell

Stock Footage:

Clip of Susanna Foster's curtain call from
The Phantom of the Opera (1943)
Courtesy of Universal Pictures

THE EPIC SAGA BEHIND *FRANKENSTEIN: THE TRUE STORY*

PART ONE
THE MOVIE

Frankenstein
The True Story

JAMES
MASON

LEONARD
WHITING

DAVID
McCALLUM

JANE
SEYMOUR

NICOLA
PAGETT

MICHAEL
SARRAZIN

CHAPTER 1
DEVELOPMENT

THE PITCH

"This isn't going to be a Hammer film!" declared producer Hunt Stromberg Jr., 47, to his new bosses: Lew Wasserman, 57, Chairman of MCA-Universal Pictures; and Sidney J. Sheinberg, 35, President of Universal Television (the man who launched Steven Spielberg). The pronouncement was made in May 1970 when Stromberg was pitching his passion project *Dr. Frankenstein*, an ambitious reimagining of Mary Shelley's classic novel that would eventually premiere in two parts on NBC-TV in 1973 (Friday, November 30, and Saturday, December 1, 9:00 to 11:00 PM each night) under the rather disingenuous title *Frankenstein: The True Story* – a late-in-the-game network renaming.

Though Stromberg's project would eventually become the 40th Frankenstein film (starting with Thomas Edison's version in 1910), there was a time when Universal Pictures seemingly had a lock on Shelley's creature. From 1931 to 1948, unchallenged, Universal produced a series of eight Frankenstein movies, beginning with James Whale's two groundbreaking classics, *Frankenstein* and *Bride of Frankenstein*, then continuing – with ever-diminishing sophistication – through *Abbott and Costello Meet Frankenstein*.

As the post-World War II Atomic Age redefined the horror genre, Universal let its Frankenstein series peter out – leaving the field wide open for anyone with a camera to make a Frankenstein movie without having to compete with Universal's established franchise. The source material – *Frankenstein; or, the Modern Prometheus*, by Mary Wollstonecraft Shelley, published in 1818 – had long been in the public domain, so the only proprietary claim Universal could make would be the unique characters and plot points that originated in their films – and, of course, the iconic high-forehead / flat-top monster makeup design (by Jack Pierce) that was worn by Boris Karloff and his successors in the studio's movie series.

That's why non-Universal entries, such as *I Was a Teenage Frankenstein* (1957) and *Frankenstein 1970* (1958), had monsters that looked nothing like the Universal model.

None of these hokey knockoffs seemed like much of a threat until the independent British firm known as

Hammer Films decided to reboot the franchise in full color, with realism and gravitas, elevated considerably by the authoritative presence of Peter Cushing as Dr. Frankenstein in six of its seven theatrical films, from *The Curse of Frankenstein* (1957) through *Frankenstein and the Monster from Hell* (filmed in 1972, though not released until 1974). There was one fleeting convergence of the two rival studios: *The Evil of Frankenstein* (1964), a Hammer Film Production co-financed and distributed by Universal Pictures. This was a marriage-of-convenience that allowed the monster's makeup design to resemble Karloff's famous head gear.

Common industry wisdom was that Universal had foolishly let one of its most valuable assets flounder – and had carelessly let Hammer Films commandeer and set the new standard for Frankenstein films. So, in 1970, when Hunt Stromberg Jr. waltzed into the corporate Black Tower at Universal City to pitch his *Dr. Frankenstein* project, resentment had festered to the breaking point. Stromberg had no idea that his statement – "This isn't going to be a Hammer film!" – would resonate far beyond its surface implication. He simply meant that he didn't want to make a B-movie.

Stromberg's pitch began with *Dr. Frankenstein* but went on to propose an entire industry of high-class, star-studded horror remakes, including *Dracula*, *The Mummy*, *The Wolf Man*, *The Invisible Man* and *The Phantom of the Opera*. With screenwriter Joseph Stefano of *Psycho* fame, Stromberg was already developing *Dr. Jekyll & Mrs. Hyde* featuring a female

Opposite Page: Modern tribute movie poster art by Frederick Cooper.

Al Lewis, Yvonne DeCarlo and Fred Gwynn in *The Munsters*.

Vampira.

doctor who becomes a homicidal femme fatale, geared to star a major Oscar-winning legend such as Ingrid Bergman (of the 1941 *Jekyll & Hyde* with Spencer Tracy), Bette Davis, Maggie Smith or Sophia Loren – nine months *before* Hammer's *Dr. Jekyll & Sister Hyde* went into production and sucked the wind out of this variant. And, if he could secure the rights from RKO, Stromberg envisioned a state-of-the-art remake of *King Kong*.

Wasserman and Sheinberg were intrigued. They saw this as an opportunity to reclaim their studio's long-lost monsters – and to one-up Hammer at its own game.

To get the ball rolling, Stromberg was convinced that audiences were ready for a fresh take on Shelley's creation – and he was not alone in his thinking. Paul Morrissey's *Flesh for Frankenstein* (released in March 1974), Mel Brooks' *Young Frankenstein* (released in December 1974) and Richard O'Brien's *The Rocky Horror Picture Show* (released in August 1975, based on his 1973 stage production) are but three examples of how the Frankenstein mythos was on the verge of being stretched in new and unexpected directions.

But Stromberg had no interest in sexing up nor sending up the genre. He wanted to make "a prestige picture." *Prestige?* That was a word not commonly associated with Frankenstein movies – which, by then, had been ostensibly ghettoized as either exploitation horror or outright parody. Universal was itself guilty of spoofing its most lucrative monster in *Abbott and Costello Meet Frankenstein* (1948) and then made the visage even sillier with its television series *The Munsters* (1964-1966) featuring Fred Gwynn sporting Universal's signature monster makeup as "Herman Munster."

The Munsters was an ongoing cash cow for Universal – especially in syndication where it was unstoppable. And guess who was responsible for greenlighting the series in the first place? None other than Hunt Stromberg Jr. when he was the all-powerful Vice President of Programming for CBS-TV during the network's Golden Era. In fact, while developing

The Munsters, it was Stromberg who personally cast his pal Yvonne De Carlo as "Lily Munster" and helped hone her creepy look (including the two white streaks in her hair as an homage to *Bride of Frankenstein*).

And this was not Stromberg's first stab at fashioning a goth horror queen, either. Back in 1954, when Stromberg was head of programming for KABC-TV, the local ABC affiliate in Los Angeles, he created, wrote and produced *The Vampira Show*, featuring his discovery Maila Nurmi as "Vampira."

Although Stromberg had grown up on the Metro-Goldwyn-Mayer lot in Culver City where his father was one of the studio's top producers (*The Thin Man*, *The Women*, and Best Picture Oscar winner *The Great Ziegfeld*), he had a particular affinity for Universal because of its classic horror films. Stromberg Jr.'s roots as a horror fan went all the way back to seeing James Whale's *Frankenstein* (1931), starring Boris Karloff as the Monster, when it first opened in theaters—at the impressionable age of 8. His passionate love of *Frankenstein* and Karloff rose to new heights when, just one year later, his after-school hangout was the MGM set of his father's production of *The Mask of Fu Manchu* (1932) starring Karloff as "the Frankenstein of the Orient." It was there that he became a life-long family friend of Karloff who later starred in another one of his father's movies, *Lured* (1947), with Lucille Ball.

In addition to befriending Karloff, Stromberg Jr. also got to meet Kenneth Strickfaden, the wizard who created all the steampunk electrical equipment for *Frankenstein* and *The Mask of Fu Manchu*. He even made a few gizmos himself that prompted his father to joke to a journalist that his son "was turning into a juvenile Frankenstein."

In 1935, at age 11, Stromberg Jr. visited the Universal set of James Whale's *Bride of Frankenstein* as the wide-eyed guest of not only Karloff and Strickfaden, but also a new family friend named Elsa Lanchester, who was, of course, portraying the female creature, while she was

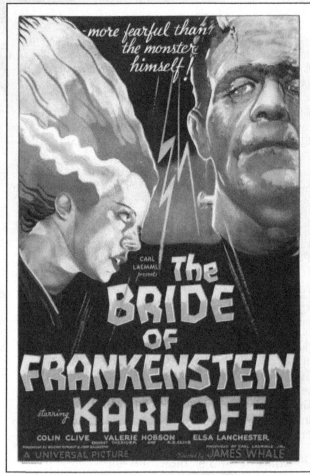

-more fearful than the monster himself!

CARL LAEMMLE presents

The BRIDE OF FRANKENSTEIN

starring KARLOFF

COLIN CLIVE · VALERIE HOBSON and ELSA LANCHESTER

A UNIVERSAL PICTURE   Directed by JAMES WHALE

Karloff & James Whale, *Bride of Frankenstein.*

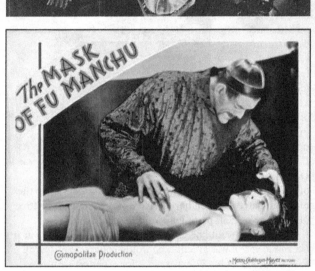

The MASK OF FU MANCHU

Cosmopolitan Production

Lon Chaney Jr., Peter Lorre & Boris Karloff in *Route 66.*

Despite Stromberg's history of poking fun at Frankenstein and grooming iconic camp vamps, he had a serious dramatic vision for his *Dr. Frankenstein* movie and he stuck to his guns.

"*Dr. Frankenstein* will not be a horror film," Stromberg insisted in the *Chicago Tribune*. "There will be horror in it, but, above all, I am creating a romantic, epic melodrama."

Indeed, the outcome would be a sophisticated reconstruction of the Frankenstein story on a grand-scale, populated by A-list actors, with sumptuous settings, lavish costumes, a three-hour running time, and an eye-popping budget of $3.5 million. To put that number in perspective, Hammer's contemporaneous *Frankenstein and the Monster from Hell* was made for little more than $300,000.

Before rampant inflation struck the industry in the late-1970s, the biggest theatrical movies of the early-1970s were still being budgeted in the seven-digit range: *Live and Let Die* – $7 million; *Earthquake* – $7 million; *The Godfather* – $6 million; *The Poseidon Adventure* – $5 million; *Young Frankenstein* – $2.8 million; *The French Connection* – $1.8 million; *Taxi Driver* – $1.5 million; *Murder on the Orient Express* – $1.4 million; and *The Last Picture Show* – $1.3 million. Made-for-television movies during that era were rarely budgeted higher than $450,000 – often considerably less.

So, when Universal committed $3.5 million to make *Frankenstein: The True Story*, it was earth-shaking. Not only was the budget greater than many major studio theatrical releases, it was, by far, the highest budget of any made-for-television movie up to that time. It also happened to be the most money ever spent on a horror movie prior to *The*

simultaneously starring in his father's MGM production of *Naughty Marietta* (1935). *Frankenstein* and *Bride of Frankenstein* would become Stromberg Jr.'s favorite films of all-time, a fanaticism that would fuel a life-long desire to produce his own Frankenstein movie.

In 1962, Stromberg Jr. cashed in his closeness with Karloff when he convinced the reluctant actor to don his Frankenstein monster makeup once again (for the very last time) for a tongue-in-cheek Halloween episode of *Route 66* (CBS) entitled "Lizard's Leg and Owlet's Wing" co-guest-starring Lon Chaney Jr. (who appeared as the Wolf Man, the Mummy and the Hunchback of Notre Dame), Peter Lorre and Martita Hunt (from Hammer Films' *The Brides of Dracula*).

Exorcist (released December 26, 1973, one month after the television premiere of *Frankenstein: The True Story*).

THE LAVENDER HILL MOB

Wheels were set in motion on May 1, 1970, when it was announced in *Daily Variety* that Hunt Stromberg Jr. had signed a nonexclusive development deal to produce theatrical and made-for-television movies for Universal, with an office set up on the lot at Universal City, Building 426, Suite 3.

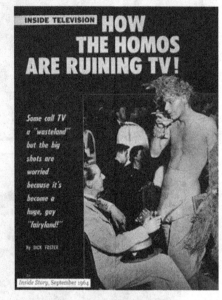

INSIDE TELEVISION **HOW THE HOMOS ARE RUINING TV!**

Some call TV a "wasteland" but the big shots are worried because it's become a huge, gay "fairyland!"

BY DICK FOSTER

Inside Story, September 1964

It wasn't long before the maintenance department received the following love letter from Stromberg: "It is impossible for me to create new versions of *Frankenstein* and *Dracula* in an office that looks like Dr. Frankenstein's laboratory after the monsters have wreaked havoc. Accordingly, could my office please have a small paint job? Menacingly, Hunt."

Stromberg would be paid a weekly salary of $1,000 but if *Dr. Frankenstein* was greenlit, he would collect a producing fee of $57,000 – plus $750 per week for expenses while on location in England. This was chump change compared to the millions he had inherited when his father passed away in 1968. For Stromberg, *Dr. Frankenstein* was never about the money. It was a labor of love.

Stromberg's favorite movies, *Frankenstein* and *Bride of Frankenstein*, were both helmed by gay director James Whale who was something of a hero and role model to the next generation of Hollywood's gay movers and shakers – among whom Stromberg was counted as an unapologetic out-and-proud member.

In *James Whale: A Biography; or the Would-Be Gentleman*, author Mark Gatiss (co-creator of *Sherlock* and the 2020 miniseries *Dracula*) writes that Whale was known within the industry as "The Queen of Hollywood." If the title was up for grabs in the post-Stonewall era, Stromberg was certainly doing everything in his power to claim that throne.

In a 2015 interview for this book, Universal's Sid Sheinberg was asked if it was common knowledge back then that Hunt Stromberg Jr. was gay. Sheinberg, who happened to be straight (married to *Jaws* actress Lorraine Gary from 1956 until his passing in 2019), chuckled and said, "I say this with the greatest admiration and respect for the LGBT community, but Hunt was gay like the sun shines in the tropics. I guess you could walk around with your eyes closed and not know it. Those were the days when it really wasn't talked about. But everybody knew Hunt was gay. It was just a matter of fact, and he did nothing to hide it."

In England, homosexual acts were not decriminalized until 1967. Human rights in the United States took even longer. In 1969, New York's Stonewall Riots ushered in the

Gay Liberation Movement and not until December 15, 1973 (two weeks **after** *Frankenstein: The True Story* premiered) would the board of the American Psychiatric Association vote to remove homosexuality from its list of mental illnesses. Even so, homosexuality remained illegal in the state of California until 1975.

Despite rampant homophobia and persecution, LGBTQ+ characters were being portrayed in movies with increasing regularity, i.e. John Huston's *Reflections in a Golden Eye* (1967), Mark Rydell's *The Fox* (1967), Robert Aldrich's *The Killing of Sister George* (1968), Ken Russell's *Women in Love* (1969), John Schlesinger's *Midnight Cowboy* (1969), Stanley Donen's *Staircase* (1969), William Friedkin's *The Boys in the Band* (1970) and Michael Sarne's *Myra Breckinridge* (1970). Even Roman Polanski's *The Fearless Vampire Killers* (1967) featured a randy gay bloodsucker – and Hammer's *The Vampire Lovers* (1970) was saturated in lesbianism.

Hollywood's "Gay Mafia" (aka "Velvet Mafia" and "Lavender Mafia") were tongue-in-cheek labels that cropped up during this revolutionary period to describe LGBTQ+ people in the arts who were perceived to be subversively masterminding the proliferation of queer subject matter in the entertainment industry. Amused by this conspiracy theory, Stromberg facetiously dubbed himself Kingpin of the "Lavender Hill Mob," co-opting the title of one of his favorite British farces. What started as a wisecrack, however, soon evolved into a genuine crusade – and, like Alec Guinness in that classic 1951 Ealing Studios comedy-caper, the time had come for Stromberg to recruit his own partners in crime.

JAMES BRIDGES & JACK LARSON

Accordingly, when Stromberg opened his office at Universal Pictures in May 1970, his first order of business was to meet with gay writer – and aspiring director – James Bridges who shared a common affinity for *Frankenstein*. The 34-year-old was a veteran writer of sixteen episodes of *The Alfred Hitchcock Hour* (1962-1965), the Universal-produced anthology series that Stromberg presided over at CBS and gotten to know Bridges in the process. Bridges had more recently scripted Joseph Sargent's sci-fi thriller *Colossus: The Forbin Project* (Universal, 1970) and would soon become one of Hollywood's A-list writer-directors – twice Oscar-nominated – for such hits as *The Paper Chase*, *The China Syndrome* and *Urban Cowboy*.

Since the early 1960s, Stromberg had been socially acquainted with Bridges and his longtime companion, Jack Larson, widely remembered as "Jimmy Olsen" on *The Adventures of Superman*

(1952-1958). Following his run on the series, Larson kept getting turned down in auditions and soon it became apparent that he was hopelessly typecast. In 1961, Larson's former boyfriend Montgomery Clift advised him, "Don't put yourself through this humiliation any longer. Give up acting and try something else." So, Larson became a noted playwright and librettist.

From early on, Stromberg was a champion of Larson's writing career. In fact, an advertisement in the *Los Angeles Times*, dated February 10, 1966, listed Stromberg among the benefactors of Larson's new play, *The Candied House*, based on the Hansel and Gretel fairy tale. Also on that endorsement list were future *Frankenstein: The True Story* associates

Christopher Isherwood, Don Bachardy, Margaret Leighton, Michael Wilding and Agnes Moorehead. Birds of a certain feather were already starting to congregate.

In an exclusive July 2015 interview with 87-year-old Jack Larson (two months before he passed away), Larson explained that, around 1970, at the age of 42, he'd been asked by the great Russian composer Igor Stravinsky, 88, to collaborate on an opera. Stravinsky, known among colleagues to be bisexual, took a liking to Larson and asked him to present him with story ideas. Larson quickly became obsessed with the notion of doing an adaptation of *Frankenstein*. He spent time re-reading the Shelley novel, writing a rough outline, and preparing his pitch for

CHAPTER ONE: DEVELOPMENT

Above: James Bridges.
Right Top: James Bridges & John Travolta, set of *Urban Cowboy*.
Right: James Bridges & Debra Winger, set of *Urban Cowboy*.

Stravinsky. While studying Shelley's classic, Larson was surprised by the undercurrent of homosexual desire – and he planned to emphasize those aspects in his libretto.

For instance, in Shelley's book, ship captain Robert Walton recounts Dr. Frankenstein's story in a series of letters to his sister Margaret. Prior to meeting Frankenstein, Walton expresses what many have interpreted as a "coming out" confessional: "I desire the company of a man who could sympathize with me; whose eyes would reply to mine. You may deem me romantic, my dear sister, but I bitterly feel the want of a friend. I have no one near me, gentle yet courageous, possessed of a cultivated as well as a capacious mind, whose tastes are like my own." As if drawn together by fate, Walton finds the companion he has so desired in the form of Dr. Frankenstein.

Every time Larson found another trace of gay subtext in Shelley's novel, he would eagerly report the finding to his partner James Bridges, who, caught up in Frankenstein fever, decided to write his own spec treatment for a film version of *Frankenstein*, the first-ever faithful adaptation of the book.

Stromberg knew of Bridges' passion to bring a literate adaptation of *Frankenstein* to the screen – but once Stromberg actually sat down and read Bridges' slavishly-accurate treatment, it became crystal clear why no other film had ever stuck to the source material.

With all due respect to purists, Shelley's novel may have been groundbreaking in 1818, but by today's standards, it is tediously didactic (with many pages devoted to the monster's repetitive moralistic pontificating) and often plodding (with superfluous subplots that lead nowhere).

For example, in the first half of the book, we learn everything there is to know about a former nobleman named DeLacey who had a checkered past in Paris – but, once the monster crosses paths with him, there is no payoff nor further mention of DeLacey's former life. No wonder DeLacey became simply a poor old blind man in *Bride of Frankenstein* (and many other incarnations). His backstory serves no dramatic purpose whatsoever.

In the second half of the book, considerable anticipation builds toward creating a mate for the monster – yet nothing ever comes of it. This has to be one of the most anticlimactic plot twists in the history of literature.

Reading the book makes one appreciate just how astute James Whale and his adaptors were at stitching together the brilliant *ideas* of the Shelley novel, building upon them, and discarding the dead weight. (It should be noted that Peggy Webling had already executed much of the weed whacking for her stage adaptation which was the basis for the screenplay to the 1931 *Frankenstein*. *Bride of Frankenstein* resurrected fleeting remnants of Shelley's novel but many of the characters and plot points were wholly original. A battalion of writers, credited and uncredited, worked on both screenplays.) Even diehard Shelley fans who are still moved by the book's many prosaic charms must admit that it is not a blueprint for a conventional screen treatment.

Consequently, Stromberg's interest in Bridges' faithful "take" on the material quickly evaporated. Likewise stalled, Larson never got to collaborate with Stravinsky on a *Frankenstein* opera before the composer passed away in 1971.

THE SHELLEYS, BYRON & POLIDORI

Despite these setbacks, Jack Larson did go on to write the libretto for Virgil Thomson's opera, *Lord Byron*, commissioned by the Metropolitan Opera in New York,

THE EPIC SAGA BEHIND *FRANKENSTEIN: THE TRUE STORY*

Lord Byron.

Mary Shelley.

Percy Bysshe Shelley.

Dr. Polidori.

and performed at the Juilliard Theater in 1972 – a performance attended by Stromberg who was intrigued by this subject as well.

Of course, there is a direct connection between *Frankenstein* and Lord Byron – one of the greatest British poets who led a scandalous bohemian lifestyle involving scores of affairs with both sexes and incest with a half-sister. In the summer of 1816, Byron, 28, vacationed at Lake Geneva in Switzerland with his handsome young personal physician / traveling companion / lover du jour Dr. John

William Polidori, 20, and their guests Mary Godwin (soon-to-be-Shelley), 18, and her 23-year-old fiancé Percy Bysshe Shelley (another well-known British poet), whereupon they famously challenged one another to write horror stories. Byron and Percy Shelley came up empty-handed but Polidori – or "Polly Dolly" as Byron teasingly nicknamed him – wrote *The Vampyre* (1819), the first vampire story ever published (pre-dating Bram Stoker's *Dracula* by seventy-eight years), and Mary conceived *Frankenstein; or, the Modern Prometheus* (1818).

CHAPTER ONE: DEVELOPMENT

The prologue from *Bride of Frankenstein*:
Top: Elsa Lanchester (Mary Shelley), Gavin Gordon (Lord Byron), Douglas Walton (Percy Bysshe Shelley), Una O'Connor (housekeeper with dogs). Left Center: Walton, Lanchester, Gordon. Left Bottom: Lanchester, Gordon, Walton. Above: Lanchester.

THE EPIC SAGA BEHIND *FRANKENSTEIN: THE TRUE STORY*

The prologue to *Bride of Frankenstein* presents a dramatization of Mary, Percy and Byron lounging together in an opulent living room by the glow of the fireplace where the gentlemen encourage her to tell them more of the story, beyond the confines of her book. (Oddly, Polidori was left out.) Mary was portrayed by Elsa Lanchester – who, later in the film, turns up as the female creature with the wild beehive updo.

Lanchester explained the director's intent thusly: "James Whale wanted this unusual prologue to show how very pretty people can have very wicked thoughts."

Four years after the publication of *Frankenstein*, Mary's husband Percy drown in a boating accident, a tragic event that would inspire the drowning of Dr. Frankenstein's brother William at the very beginning of *Frankenstein: The True Story* – which becomes the catalyst that motivates Dr. Frankenstein's desire to reanimate life. Conversely, in Shelley's novel, Dr. Frankenstein's brother is killed by the monster much later in the story, so his death is a tragic consequence of the doctor's deed, not the stimulus that prompted it.

All of these components got blended in a whirlwind of cross-pollination between Stromberg, Larson and Bridges over dinners and social gatherings. But, business was business and, despite their friendship, Stromberg was underwhelmed with Bridges' *Frankenstein* treatment and ultimately rejected it.

CHRISTOPHER ISHERWOOD & DON BACHARDY

Stromberg next called upon another writer from the same interconnected gay social circle: Christopher Isherwood, 66, the august British novelist whose autobiographical *The Berlin Stories* had been famously adapted into *Cabaret*, the Tony-winning Broadway musical and soon-to-be Oscar-winning 1972 movie.

His 1945 novel, *Prater Violet*, is a biting satire of London's film industry about the trials and tribulations of a fledgling gay screenwriter named Christopher Isherwood – a thinly-veiled account of his real-life experience as a beleaguered writer on *Little Friend* (Gaumont British, 1934) starring Nova Pilbeam.

Many of Isherwood's novels were autobiographical, dealing quite openly with his own homosexuality, several of which were turned into films, including *Goodbye to Berlin* which was adapted into *I Am a Camera* (1955) starring Laurence Harvey as Isherwood; *A Single Man* (2009) starring Colin Firth (Oscar-nominated for Best Actor); and

Christopher Isherwood & Don Bachardy, circa 1970s.

Christopher and His Kind (2011) starring Matt Smith (*Doctor Who*, *The Crown*).

Isherwood also wrote the screenplays for movies such as W. S. Van Dyke's *Rage in Heaven* (1941) starring Ingrid Bergman; Robert Siodmak's *The Great Sinner* (1949) starring Gregory Peck, Ava Gardner and future *Frankenstein: The True Story* co-star Agnes Moorehead; David Miller's *Diane* (1956) starring Lana Turner and Roger Moore; and, Tony Richardson's *The Loved One* (1965) with future *True Story* cast members Sir John Gielgud and Margaret Leighton.

Aside from knowing each other socially, Stromberg and Isherwood had a professional history. In 1967, when Stromberg was developing projects for Columbia Pictures and its television subsidiary Screen Gems, he had hired Isherwood to write the teleplay for *A Christmas Carol*, based on the Charles Dickens novel, to star Rex Harrison as Scrooge. Jackie Cooper, the *Our Gang* child actor-turned-president of Screen Gems, announced with great fanfare on December 18, 1967, that his company was committing an unprecedented $1 million budget for the two-hour telefilm, to be produced by Stromberg in England at Shepperton Studios. (Cooper and Stromberg had become friends way back when they were elementary students at the Little Red School on the MGM lot – along with Judy Garland and Mickey Rooney.)

In *Christopher Isherwood's The Sixties, Diaries 1960-1969* (Chatto & Windus and HarperCollins, 2010), Isherwood's entry for December 22, 1967, reads as follows: "Hunt Stromberg Jr. seriously believes he can induce Queen Elizabeth to appear as a sponsor on our television movie of *A Christmas Carol*! This he plans to arrange through Douglas Fairbanks Jr.!" No one ever accused Stromberg of thinking small.

As contracted, Isherwood turned in a 102-page draft of *A Christmas Carol: A Ghost Story of Christmas* on January 17, 1968, which everyone seemed to love. However, on February 25, 1968, Screen Gems inexplicably got cold feet and cancelled its commitment – which resulted in Stromberg abruptly cutting ties with the studio (the top front-page headline of *Daily Variety*, March 4, 1968). Isherwood's script for *A Christmas Carol: A Ghost Story of Christmas* remains unproduced to this day.

Nevertheless, the experience strengthened Stromberg's friendship with Isherwood – and, by association, his longtime companion Don Bachardy, 36, the renowned portrait painter (who would soon be collaborating with Isherwood on the teleplay for *Dr. Frankenstein*). Bachardy met Isherwood in 1953, when he was 18 and Isherwood was 48. They settled into a beautiful Spanish Colonial Revival home overlooking the Pacific Ocean in Santa Monica, California, where, fatefully, their next-door-neighbor was none other than Elsa Lanchester. The two men remained together until Isherwood's death in 1986. An award-winning documentary about their 33-year relationship, *Chris & Don: A Love Story* (2007), includes a brief section about *Frankenstein: The True Story*.

JACQUE SHELTON

On March 16, 1968 – just a couple of weeks after *A Christmas Carol* had fallen apart – Bachardy told Isherwood that "the most fun friends" among their "queer social circle" were Truman Capote, Gore Vidal, Tony Richardson, Hunt Stromberg and his companion Jacque Shelton. ("Jacque" is pronounced "Jack" with a soft "J", like "shack.")

Mae West & Jacque Shelton.

Another important member of this clique, Jacque Shelton was born in Texas in 1931 and came to Hollywood in the 1950s in search of fame and fortune. He and Stromberg fell hard for one another in January 1961 when they met on the set of *Rawhide* (CBS, 1959-1965), the Western series that launched Clint Eastwood. An experienced equestrian, Shelton had become a stuntman and wannabe actor who, under Stromberg's regime at CBS, was subsequently given a slew of walk-on parts in the network's shows, from *The Twilight Zone* to *Gunsmoke*. In 1964, when Stromberg got his longtime pal Mae West to guest star on *Mister Ed* (the comedy series about a talking horse), he personally cast Shelton as West's hunky houseboy who helps give the horse a bubble bath. Other than Stromberg, however, nobody else in Hollywood was smitten with Shelton's acting ability.

By the mid-1960s, Shelton gave up dreams of stardom to open an antique shop and to pursue a career as an aviculturist – collecting and raising exotic birds – including the flock of peacocks that roamed the yard of the West Hollywood mansion he shared with Stromberg at 8400 Harold Way (next door to Liberace – who performed at their parties). They also raised a pet woolly monkey named Wilbur (named after the horse owner on *Mister Ed*). He gifted Mae West one of Wilbur's relatives, Tricky. One day, Stromberg brought Wilbur with him on a leash to the set of *The Judy Garland Show*. Miss Garland, who was constantly at odds with Stromberg, was not amused.

In addition to their mansion in West Hollywood, Stromberg and Shelton owned the Double S Ranch (their initials) in Springtown, Texas, where Shelton housed some of his rarest birds in an aviary and, oh yes, was also raising a Bengal tiger. As one does.

Fueled by booze, drugs and more outlandish drama than a telenovela (including temporary breakups, extracurricular affairs, robberies, extortion attempts, death threats, bodyguards, a burned-down ranch house, and a torched Rolls-Royce), Hunt and Jacque led colorful lives, to say the least – and Isherwood and Bachardy were highly amused by the latest tales of their wild shenanigans.

Shelton would eventually be credited on-screen at the conclusion of *Frankenstein: The True Story* as "Assistant to the Producer" – though Isherwood claimed his involvement was far more influential, "playing the role of co-producer."

SID SHEINBERG

In *Christopher Isherwood's Liberation, Diaries 1970-1983* (Chatto & Windus and HarperCollins, 2012), the entry for August 28, 1970, reads as follows: "Hunt Stromberg called up out of the blue and asked if I would be interested in doing 'the definitive *Frankenstein*'?!"

Isherwood knew that James Bridges had submitted his *Frankenstein* treatment to Stromberg, so, before accepting the assignment, he insisted on getting Bridges' blessing.

"Jim was very generous about it," recalled Don Bachardy in a 2015 interview for this book. "He said to Chris and me, 'Use any part of it you like.'"

Cover of *Christopher Isherwood's Liberation, Diaries 1970-1983* (Chatto & Windus and HarperCollins, 2012), edited by Katherine Bucknell.

It took four months for things to get serious, but on January 11, 1971, Isherwood wrote in his diary: "The Frankenstein project now seems to be sanctioned by the head of Universal, Sid Sheinberg, who is not too bright but quite pleasant."

Contrary to Isherwood's first impression, Sheinberg was one of the brightest bulbs in the industry. In *Steven Spielberg: A Biography*, author Joseph McBride wrote, "Sid Sheinberg came to California in 1958 [at age 23] to teach law at UCLA and was hired the following year by the legal department of Revue Productions, the television production arm of MCA, then a leading Hollywood talent agency. After helping negotiate MCA's purchase of Universal in 1962, Sheinberg began climbing the corporate ladder as a TV business affairs executive. He started a new era in television in 1964 when he came up with the idea for the made-for-TV movie (then known as the *NBC World Premiere*). As Universal's TV division thrived, Sheinberg soon became the favored son and heir apparent of MCA president Lew Wasserman."

Sid Sheinberg & Lew Wasserman.

THE EPIC SAGA BEHIND *FRANKENSTEIN: THE TRUE STORY*

James Bridges, Don Bachardy, Jack Larson, Barbara Hershey, on the set of *The Baby Maker* (1970), written and directed by Bridges; produced by Larson.

In 1971, the *Los Angeles Times* reported that Universal Television, under Sheinberg's leadership, was responsible for "one out of every four primetime hours" on all three of the major networks combined (NBC, ABC and CBS) and "the principal supplier of television movies."

Writer-producer William Link (*That Certain Summer*; creator of *Columbo* and *Murder, She Wrote*) said that "story conferences were great with Sid – he would re-plot, he could restructure, and it was a two-way street. He was a sophisticated man."

Sheinberg's latest experiment was *Vanished*, the first-ever two-part television event movie, broadcast on March 8 and 9, 1971, on *NBC World Premiere* – the first prime-time network miniseries. Minus commercials, the film had an unprecedented running time of 196 minutes, with the highest budget yet for a television production: $2.1 million. If that wasn't enough to raise eyebrows, the subject matter of the film certainly did.

Directed by Buzz Kulik (*Brian's Song*) and based on the bestselling novel by Fletcher Knebel (*Seven Days in May*), *Vanished* was a political thriller loosely inspired by the real-life 1964 arrest of Walter Jenkins, President Lyndon Johnson's Chief-of-Staff, who was caught engaging in homosexual activity in a men's bathroom at the YMCA. Married to a woman and the father of six children, Jenkins' double-life as a homosexual flew in the face of President Dwight Eisenhower's 1953 Executive Order that banned homosexuals from working for the federal government due to its inherent "security risk." During the Red Scare of the 1950s, there was a great deal of fearmongering that a closeted homosexual could easily become the target of blackmail and, therefore, a threat to national security – known at the time as the Lavender Scare.

Despite the exploding popularity of gay subject matter in *theatrical* motion pictures, the topic was all-but-taboo on television. But that didn't stop Sheinberg from championing *Vanished*. The movie was a rousing ratings success, received glowing reviews, and won five Emmy Awards.

This success gave Sheinberg and Universal the courage to greenlight what is considered television's first sympathetic portrayal of homosexuality in *That Certain Summer* (*ABC Movie of the Week*, November 1, 1972) starring Hal Holbrook and Martin Sheen as a long-time committed gay couple coming out to Holbrook's 14-year-old son (played by Scott Jacoby) from a previous marriage. The film won the Golden Globe Award for Best Movie Made for TV and was nominated for seven Emmy Awards with Jacoby winning the Emmy for Best Supporting Actor. (The movie also happened to be scored by future *Frankenstein: The True Story* composer Gil Mellé.)

These triumphs belonged to many, but none more crucial than Sheinberg whose audacious trailblazing in television simply had no bounds. It should also be noted that Sheinberg would later be responsible for Universal becoming the first Hollywood studio to offer health care benefits to same-sex partners. Unbeknownst to Isherwood at that time, Sheinberg turned out to be the ideal studio advocate for *Dr. Frankenstein* – a gay-friendly ally who would not redact the queer subtext that would eventually permeate the teleplay.

EUREKA!

As time went on, however, Isherwood's reservations mounted. "Personally I am still doubtful if the story can be written at all," he noted in his diary on January 11, 1971. "Have been reading Jim Bridges' treatment which only shows up its weaknesses. When people say it is a 'classic,' they

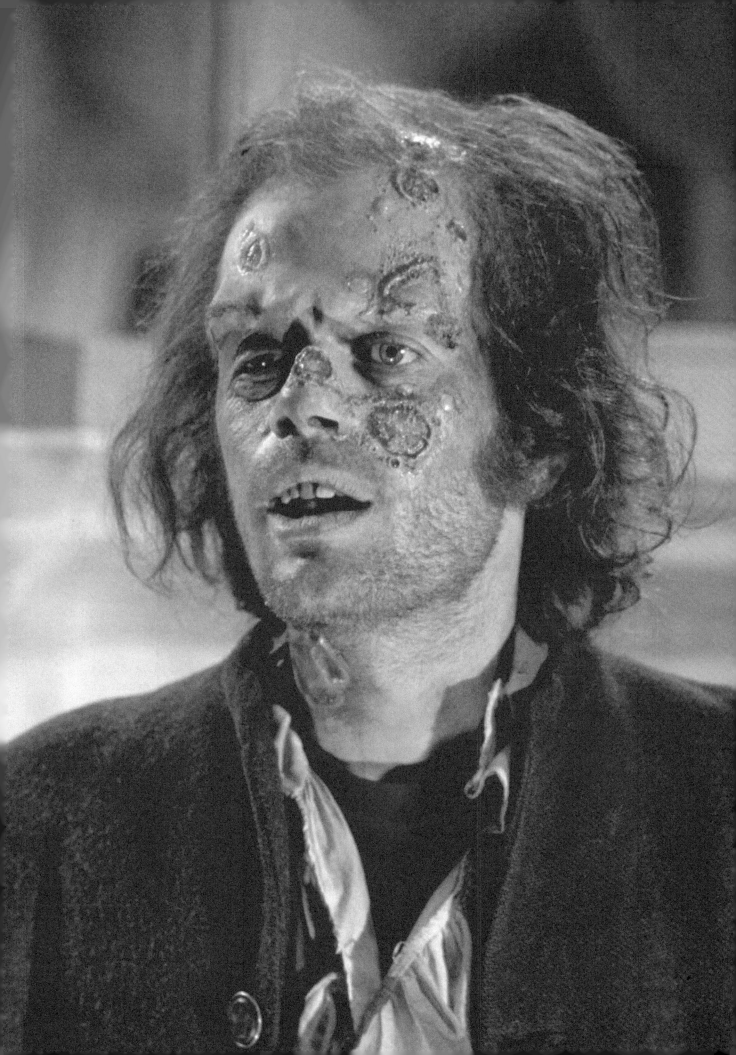

really mean only that the makeup is a classic, as long as Boris Karloff wears it. The Universal people will surely realize that *Frankenstein* is now hopelessly old hat."

Despite his misgivings, Isherwood agonized over how to resuscitate *Frankenstein* for a new generation – until, finally, he was thunderstruck with inspiration.

"The Creature must be *beautiful!*" Isherwood declared, recalling the moment of his epiphany in a 1975 interview for *Radio Times*. "Mary Shelley certainly made an error in making the Creature hideous from the very start. In [our version of] *Frankenstein*, the Creature is first created as a being of great beauty – truly a second Adam. He is perfect... Frankenstein even takes his creation to the opera, everyone admires him. But, gradually, inexplicably, his body deteriorates... It is a tragedy, there's no question. Great poignancy... with Faustian overtones."

Exhilarated by this fresh angle on the material, Isherwood agreed to give it a go. Contracts were drawn up for a flat fee of $40,000 – with the controversial proviso that Isherwood would be collaborating on the script with his partner Don Bachardy.

"No doubt Don is being soundly bitched already as a boyfriend who is being brought along for the ride," Isherwood speculated in his diary.

Nothing could have been further from the truth. The two men had a supportive working arrangement in which they meticulously discussed every plot point, every idea, every line of dialogue – an honest-to-God collaboration. Nevertheless, some of Bachardy's duties were secretarial. Because Isherwood's left hand was afflicted with Dupuytren's contracture (a deforming and disabling condition), Bachardy assumed the responsibility of typing it all out on a Smith Corona electric typewriter.

DR. PRETORIUS

On January 29, 1971, Christopher Isherwood and Don Bachardy met with Hunt Stromberg Jr. at Universal City for the first official story conference on *Dr. Frankenstein*. After watching archival prints of *Frankenstein* and *Bride of Frankenstein* in a private screening room on the lot, Stromberg explained that, rather than trying to dramatize Mary Shelley's novel, he basically wanted to remake both films, combining them into one magnum opus.

For starters, Stromberg wanted to open the film with a prologue much like the one from *Bride of Frankenstein* featuring Mary Shelley, Percy Bysshe Shelley and Lord Byron – with the addition of Dr. John William Polidori who took

Ernest Thesiger as Dr Pretorius in *Bride of Frankenstein*.

part in the real-life horror writing challenge. Not only did Stromberg want to cast an actress to play both Mary Shelley and the female creature (à la Elsa Lanchester in *Bride*), he also wanted Percy, Byron and Polidori played by the same actors who would portray Dr. Victor Frankenstein, Henry Clerval and Dr. Pretorius, respectively.

Pretorius?! Yep. Dr. Septimus Pretorius was, of course, the mad scientist in *Bride of Frankenstein* – unique to that film, nowhere to be found in Shelley's book. A former teacher of Dr. Frankenstein, Dr. Pretorius had become a mysterious outcast who dabbled in the black arts, growing homunculi (miniature living humanoids) in Petri jars – all part of a grand scheme for world domination. One dark-and-stormy night, Dr. Pretorius shows up unannounced and blackmails Dr. Frankenstein into collaborating with him for the making of a full-sized female creature to be a mate for the monster.

With a macabre sense of humor, Dr. Pretorius also had an effeminate demeanor that left little to the imagination, portrayed so deliciously by the great British character actor Ernest Thesiger (who had previously been directed by Whale in *The Old Dark House*). In the movie, Frankenstein's housekeeper Minnie (Una O'Connor) announces his arrival, describing him as "a very queer-looking old gentleman." The insinuation was deliberate.

In *James Whale: A Biography, or the Would-Be Gentleman*, author Mark Gatiss described Pretorius as "a desiccated homosexual imp" with "waspish malevolence" who tempts Dr. Frankenstein "away from all that is safe and natural." In *The Monster Show: A Cultural History of Horror*, author

Ernest Thesiger as Dr Pretorius in *Bride of Frankenstein*.

With Una O'Connor.

David J. Skal reported that Whale instructed Thesiger to play Pretorius as an "over the top caricature of a bitchy and aging homosexual." That he did. And, because of it, according to Vito Russo's *The Celluloid Closet*, Dr. Pretorius is considered one of the earliest examples of a homosexual character in mainstream cinema.

So, in 1971, at the very inception of this new *Dr. Frankenstein* project, Stromberg pledged his allegiance to Dr. Pretorius, demonstrating that he had no interest whatsoever in sticking to Shelley's book, despite what Universal and NBC may have otherwise believed. In fact, as development progressed, this new incarnation of Dr. Pretorius would end up being infused with diabolical elements of Dr. Fu Manchu, Dr. Mabuse, Dr. No and Dr. Strange.

RICHARD BURTON & ELIZABETH TAYLOR

Stromberg considered the role of Dr. Pretorius to be a central component of his master plan – a juicy supervillain that was to be designed specifically to attract a big-league movie star. In a January 1971 memo to Sid Sheinberg, Stromberg confidently wrote, "It is my goal to induce none other than Richard Burton to play the role of the flamboyantly insane Dr. Pretorius." Burton would also be given the role of the real-life Dr. Polidori in the prologue – *if* he could be convinced to come aboard. And that was a big "if."

At that point in his illustrious career, Burton, 46, had been Oscar-nominated a whopping six times (and would later add a seventh nomination for *Equus* in 1978). He had also won a Golden Globe, a BAFTA, a Tony, and countless other accolades.

Furthermore, Stromberg wanted Burton's wife, two-time Oscar winner Elizabeth Taylor, 39, to play Agatha, the farm girl who is killed, then brought back to life as Prima, the evil "bride of the monster" – plus the part of Mary Shelley in the prologue.

"How could Liz resist *three* roles in one?" Stromberg enthused to his bosses. "I have been acquainted with the Burtons for many years and they are intimates of Isherwood so it might not be entirely out of the question."

Stromberg had the added advantage that the Burtons' agent Robin French also represented Isherwood and James Bridges – so was, thusly, a cheerleader of the Frankenstein project. (In 1974, French would become head of domestic production at Paramount Pictures.) In a 2015 interview for this book, Robin French said, "I had known Hunt Stromberg Jr. since his early days at CBS because a lot of

our actor clients got jobs in the shows Hunt was doing. A few years later, we got reacquainted on the *Frankenstein* thing at Universal."

With the endorsement of French, Stromberg sent the *Dr. Frankenstein* treatment to the Burtons, and, on February 1, 1971, he reported encouraging news to his bosses: "My overture has elicited a favorable response, though of course they will want to see the full script when it is completed."

REX HARRISON & ALBERT FINNEY

If Stromberg could reunite Burton and Taylor for what would have been their eleventh film together (*Cleopatra*, *Who's Afraid of Virginia Woolf*, etc.), the sky would be the limit in attracting other stars to the party – like Rex Harrison to play Dr. Frankenstein and Albert Finney to play the Creature, Stromberg's initial dream team.

Because Harrison was so famously associated with his role as Henry Higgins in *My Fair Lady* (for which he'd won both a Tony *and* an Oscar), the notion of him playing Dr. Frankenstein inspired Stromberg, Isherwood and Bachardy to develop a similar mentor-like relationship between the doctor and his creation, à la *Pygmalion* (1913), the George Bernard Shaw play which was the basis for the musical *My Fair Lady*. In the play, language professor Henry Higgins boasts that he can train a low-class Cockney flower girl, Eliza Doolittle, to pass for a duchess at a high society party – but, while teaching the girl, he falls in love with her. The concept of Dr. Frankenstein training the Creature to pass for a high society gentleman had never been done before. And the suggestion that an attraction grows between the doctor and his muse would indeed be daring, virgin territory.

At that time, Albert Finney was best known for playing the leading role in Tony Richardson's *Tom Jones* (1963), the bawdy comedy that had won the Oscar for Best Picture and a Best Actor nomination for Finney. He had more recently teamed with Audrey Hepburn in Stanley Donen's romantic comedy *Two for the Road* (1967). If a vibrant, sexy and

Richard Burton and Elizabeth Taylor.

Rex Harrison.

Above: Rex Harrison & Audrey Hepburn, *My Fair Lady*. Right and Right Center: Finney & Audrey Hepburn, *Two for the Road*. Right Bottom: Finney in *Tom Jones*.

charming leading man like Finney were to take on the role of the Creature, it certainly would make a statement that this was not your father's *Frankenstein*.

"Hunt Stromberg seems slightly insane on the subject of *Frankenstein*," Isherwood pondered in his diary, skeptical that any of these big-name stars would actually sign on. "Casting turns him on like dope."

Although he appreciated Stromberg shooting for the moon, Isherwood felt that Rex Harrison was far too old for the part and wanted the doctor to be much more youthful, fresh out of med school – as he was in Shelley's book. Rather than argue about it, however, Isherwood decided to forge ahead with the treatment, incorporating his own ideas, with the hope that Stromberg would agree once he read everything in context.

"We have given the Creature an extra dimension," Isherwood wrote in his diary on February 1, 1971. "Frankenstein has a rather older college friend named Rudolf, who is the sinister influence [like Mephistopheles in *Faust*, hell-bent on challenging the Gods]. It is Rudolf who

Albert Finney.

THE EPIC SAGA BEHIND *FRANKENSTEIN: THE TRUE STORY*

gets Frankenstein involved in monster making. Then Rudolf dies… and Frankenstein then takes the brain out of Rudolf's corpse and puts it into the Creature. So, Rudolf is imprisoned within the Creature, struggling to communicate… This solves a lot of the problems, right away."

In subsequent drafts, Rudolf's name was changed to Henry Clerval, a character from the novel, though the similarity ends there. (Clerval would be played by David McCallum in the movie.)

FIRST PRESS ANNOUNCEMENT

On February 1, 1971, the front page of *Daily Variety* headlined: "Universal *Frankenstein* By Stromberg To Be Long, Faithful."

The text of the news item read as follows: "*Frankenstein* will be telefilmed by producer Hunt Stromberg for Universal and NBC-TV, although there is a possibility the film – at least four hours long – will go into theatrical release first. Christopher Isherwood has been signed by Stromberg to write the vehicle, planned for four major stars. This is the second ultralong for Universal, first being its four-hour *Vanished*, to be aired as two NBC-TV *World Premiere* shows."

Here's the kicker: "Latest version of tome by Mary Shelley will not be based on the first *Frankenstein* film or its sequels, but will adhere to the book." Little did they know what was *really* afoot.

THE TREATMENT

By early March 1971, Isherwood and Bachardy were knee-deep into mapping out their fanciful treatment, in a tangled web of unresolved issues. "One keeps dismissing ideas because they are 'impossible,' 'too farfetched,' 'unconvincing,' Isherwood updated in his diary. "But perhaps we ought to be wilder and sillier."

They decided that the real-life characters in the prologue would visually assume the characters in the narrative right before our eyes. This resulted in the decision that Mary Shelley would morph into Elizabeth rather than Agatha / Prima since the latter characters would not be introduced until the second half of the film. Percy would become Dr. Frankenstein; Byron would become Clerval; and Polidori would become Pretorius.

They eventually decided to change the name of Pretorius to Polidori, matching his real-life counterpart, because they wanted to accentuate his castrating nickname "Polly Dolly" in both the prologue *and* the main narrative.

With no holds barred, Isherwood and Bachardy labored another month and delivered their completed 77-page treatment on April 13, 1971 (with the project officially assigned the Universal production code number 81454). The plotline basically lays out the film as we know it, with some diversions that would eventually be cut.

QUEER SUBTEXT

Hunt Stromberg submitted the treatment to Sid Sheinberg and his team at Universal and soon received notes for adjustments, most of which were negligible.

There was, however, an early sequence that the bosses felt was far too racy for primetime television – a scene in which Dr. Frankenstein goes to a brothel where Henry Clerval invites him to participate in a three-way with one of the female prostitutes. Frankenstein demurs, preferring to watch from the sidelines so he will retain his virginity for his wedding night with Elizabeth.

Hurt by his rejection, Clerval lashes out, "No man should marry while he still has any genius or ambition left in him. Marriage is fatal to the man of science. What can a wife give you that you can't get from any of these whores? And they never ask questions, never get jealous of your work, never try to make you stay with them longer than you want to. All they require is your money, and they give you good value for it. It's an admirable relationship, with no hypocrisy and no waste of time."

Not only does Clerval share the same brazen sexual fluidity of his prologue counterpart Lord Byron, his petulant and misogynistic outburst is clearly motivated by the fact that he has been jilted by the true object of his desire – Victor Frankenstein.

The rest of the queer subtext was slightly more subtle – yet undeniably present, like a dog whistle for those with gaydar:

a. Clerval and Frankenstein become roommates while they dabble in secret, unorthodox experiments. Clerval remarks to Frankenstein, "It's seldom I meet a kindred spirit." The coded phraseology was ripe with innuendo. (It also sounded like the lovesick words of ship captain Robert Walton, waxing poetic about his desire for Dr. Frankenstein's companionship, in Shelley's novel.)

b. Adding fuel to this fire, Polidori tells Frankenstein that Clerval had "deserted" him – leaving the extent of their former relationship a mystery. Clerval's emasculating nickname for Polidori – "Polly Dolly" – left little room

McCallum & Whiting bond.

for doubt. (Historically, their real-life counterparts, Byron and Polidori, had a tempestuous bond that ended badly. Depressed and penniless after Byron's abrupt desertion,

The only time we see McCallum & Mason together, dropping hints about their former relationship.

Opposite page: Art by Stefano Junior.

Left: The backstory of the relationship between Clerval and Polidori highly suggests they were lovers.

McCallum rudely dismisses Pagett so he can be alone with Whiting.

Polidori died a premature death at the age of just 25 – which the coroner claimed was due to "natural causes," but historians have uncovered strong evidence of suicide by cyanide.)

c. Rhetorically, Polidori ponders, "Why do we take such pains to hide our ugly little secrets." On the surface, he was referring to his disfigured hands hidden by gloves – but practically everything he said was thick with double meaning.

d. When Frankenstein's fiancée, Elizabeth, shows up unannounced, Clerval is extremely rude to her, making it clear that she is not welcome. Like in the excised brothel scene, his contempt is driven by jealousy. Frankenstein does not offer much in the way of solace to his future bride and soon she departs, feeling uneasy and rejected, leaving Clerval and Frankenstein to their own devices.

e. When Clerval dies and Frankenstein decides to put his brain into the Creature, it is a realization of unrequited love – a longing to keep Clerval alive, by whatever means necessary.

f. The Creature (with Clerval's brain) is brought to life by Frankenstein as a "beautiful" specimen of manhood – and he becomes Frankenstein's new roommate and protégé. As Mark Gatiss put it so eloquently in his article "Queer Frankenstein" (*Shivers* No. 30, June 1996), when the landlady (Agnes Moorehead) catches Frankenstein sneaking the hunky barefoot Creature up the stairs to his apartment in the dead of night, it's as though "the Creature were a bit of rough trade he's dragged in off the street." The tables have turned on this mentorship. While living in seclusion together, Frankenstein teaches the Creature everything – table manners, how to speak, crash

Whiting makes final adjustments to Sarrazin.

Pagett & Whiting argue as McCallum guards apartment.

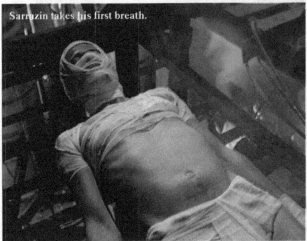

Sarrazin takes his first breath.

THE EPIC SAGA BEHIND *FRANKENSTEIN: THE TRUE STORY*

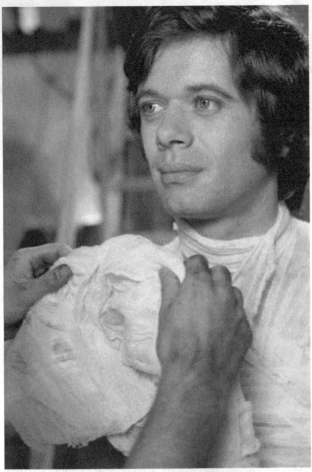

Whiting sneaks Sarrazin into his apartment.

Whiting on bed with Sarrazin.

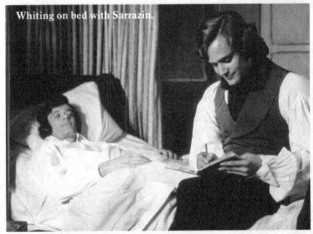

Sarrazin & Whiting dine privately; Agnes Moorehead serves them.

Whiting gifts Sarrazin a tuxedo for their date to the opera.

Whiting & Sarrazin in box seat, watching opera.

Whiting & Sarrazin on date at the opera.

Whiting introduces Sarrazin to Margaret Leighton at opera.

Beautiful Sarrazin sits in contemplation.

courses on art, literature, music – everything he needs to pass as a high society dandy. By the time Frankenstein escorts his sexy beast to a night at the opera (Mozart's *The Marriage of Figaro*), their inseparable bromance has reached its zenith.

g. Dr. Polidori is presented as an older "confirmed bachelor" who, because of his crippled hands, employs two handsome Chinese manservants to facilitate his every need, from chauffeuring to feeding – and anything else one might imagine.

h. When the Creature's skin deteriorates, Dr. Frankenstein cruelly abandons him. "You loved your Creature so long as it was pretty," Polidori scoffs. "But once it lost its looks, that was another matter." Bachardy confirmed this was an intentional, biting indictment on the youth-and-beauty obsessed culture that is so pervasive in the gay community.

i. When the Creature finds a piece of the broken mirror and in its reflection discovers that his skin is deteriorating and becoming ugly, he cries out, "Victor!" In the film, Dr. Frankenstein says nothing. He just stares at the Creature, disgusted by his rotting condition. In the April 13, 1971, treatment, Frankenstein disingenuously tries to console the Creature by saying, "I will never desert you. You must trust me – we will be together always." But the Creature senses that Dr. Frankenstein no longer wants him.

j. When the rejected Creature tries to commit suicide by stabbing himself in the heart again and again, Dr. Frankenstein coldly watches from his chair, doing nothing to stop him. Curiously, the color of the fluid that emerges from the Creature's chest wounds is not

Whiting about to turn and see boils behind Sarrazin's ear.

THE EPIC SAGA BEHIND *FRANKENSTEIN: THE TRUE STORY*

Whiting's point of view of the boils behind Sarrazin's ear.

Whiting sees the boils behind Sarrazin's ear for the first time.

Whiting in tears, cannot bring himself to tell Sarrazin the truth.

Sarrazin's hands cradle Whiting as tears stream down.

Sarrazin does not understand that he is deteriorating.

Sarrazin finally sees his deterioration in a shard of mirror.

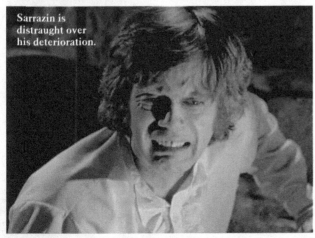

Sarrazin is distraught over his deterioration.

Whiting ignores Sarrazin now that his creation is deteriorating.

CHAPTER ONE: DEVELOPMENT

Whiting turns away from Sarrazin, repulsed by his deterioration.

The Creature (Sarrazin) on mast of ship in the storm – as he taunts Dr. Polidori (Mason) by calling him "Polly Dolly" – but the voice coming out of Sarrazin's mouth is that of Dr. Clerval (David McCallum) whose brain was implanted in Sarrazin's head.

the usual blood red. This was not a technical mistake nor network censorship to tone down the gore. Look again and you will see that the color of the fluid is a pale tint of purple. Lavender. In the published teleplay, no particular color is indicated for the "gluey fluid" – but in the 1971 treatment and several early drafts of the script, the writers' original intent is revealed thusly: "The wounds made by the knife are visible but they are not

Sarrazin tries to commit suicide by stabbing himself. The "blood" that oozes from the wound is purple.

Polidori (Mason) hoisted to the top of the mast by the Creature (Sarrazin).

A lightning bolt has zapped Polidori and fried him to a crispy skeleton – as the Creature (Sarrazin) gleefully watches.

bloody. Only a few drops of gluey purple fluid have oozed from them and immediately coagulated." The choice of the color purple was not random. As previously noted, purple and lavender are colors commonly associated with the LGBTQ+ community and often used symbolically. The call sheet for April 30, 1973, pointedly lists "purple blood" among the special makeup requirements.

k.   When first brought to life, the Creature (with Dr. Clerval's brain) has complete amnesia but, slowly, the mind of Clerval regains consciousness and takes over – with the post-dubbed voice of David McCallum coming out of Michael Sarrazin's mouth (inspired, no doubt, by Ygor's voice coming out of the Monster's mouth, post-brain-transplant, in *The Ghost of Frankenstein*). During the stormy night on the ship, the Creature – with Clerval's brain now fully conscious and in charge – hoists his former mentor Polidori to the top of the mast, then watches gleefully as a lightning bolt literally zaps "Polly Dolly" to a crisp. Was this a sugar-daddy entanglement gone horribly wrong? [Note another connection to *The Mask of Fu Manchu*: When Terry (Charles Starrett) is possessed by Dr. Fu Manchu (Boris

Karloff), there is a haunting shot of him standing in a rainstorm, laughing maniacally – similar to the storm-at-sea sequence in *Frankenstein: The True Story* when the Creature – with the brain and voice of Dr. Clerval – is laughing maniacally as Dr. Polidori is hoisted up the mast and struck by lightning.]

l.   On the ship during the storm, Dr. Frankenstein is climbing the mast when he is accidentally knocked off the yardarm and falls to the deck – unconscious. Elizabeth rushes to his aid, but the Creature – with Clerval's brain calling the shots – brutally tosses her aside, lifts Frankenstein into his arms and lovingly carries him to the cabin below where he gently lays him on the bed. (All that's missing is a cutaway to Hitchcock's *North by Northwest* train penetrating a tunnel.)

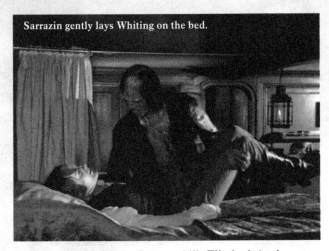
Sarrazin gently lays Whiting on the bed.

m. Later that night, the Creature kills Elizabeth (and her unborn baby) – Clerval's final act of claiming Frankenstein all to himself.

n. At the end, Frankenstein and the Creature come together for one last tearful embrace as the mountain of ice caves-in on them, a tragic penultimate act of double suicide that evokes *Romeo and Juliet*.

RICHARD CHAMBERLAIN

Stromberg must have liked where all this was headed because suddenly he lost all interest in the stuffy 63-year-old Rex Harrison playing Dr. Frankenstein (even Peter Cushing was only 59 when he made *Frankenstein and the Monster from Hell*). Instead, in an April 14, 1971, memo to Sheinberg, Stromberg announced he was shifting his sights onto 37-year-old heartthrob Richard Chamberlain, widely known as TV's *Dr. Kildare* (1961-1966) for which he had won a Golden Globe. More recently, Chamberlain had impressed critics with his portrayal of Pyotr Ilyich Tchaikovsky, the homosexual Russian composer, in Ken Russell's *The Music Lovers* (1970).

Richard Chamberlain, *Lady Caroline Lamb*.

Though publicly closeted at that time, Chamberlain would later "come out" as gay in his 2003 memoir *Shattered Love*, a fact that insiders like Stromberg were well aware of back then.

In August 1971, with only a partially completed script, Stromberg offered Chamberlain the role but, according to Isherwood's diary, the actor demanded "half of the picture's budget! And top billing!!"

Contacted in 2015 for this book, Chamberlain had no memory of it. "I can't remember what I did three days ago," Chamberlain chuckled, "so it doesn't mean it didn't happen. I would have loved doing the film, particularly had I known Margaret Leighton and Michael Wilding were going to be in it. I was a friend of theirs and I adored them."

Instead, with considerable irony, Chamberlain went on to play none other than Lord Byron in Robert Bolt's *Lady Caroline Lamb* (1972) with three future *Dr. Frankenstein* cast members: Margaret Leighton, Michael Wilding and Sir Ralph Richardson.

THE FIRST DRAFT

On August 18, 1971, Isherwood and Bachardy turned in their first draft screenplay for *Dr. Frankenstein*, with a total of 197 pages in standard screenplay format (about a minute per page = 3 hours, 17 minutes).

The following day, Isherwood wrote in his diary, "Hunt called this morning to say he finds it marvelous and that the dialogue has the 'distinction of Shaw or Wilde'! More impressive, businesswise, was a call I got this afternoon from Robin French, telling me he'd met Sid Sheinberg this morning who's said, 'I've got the best script I've ever had!'"

Equally impressed with the teleplay were the top brass at NBC-TV: Herbert S. Schlosser, Executive Vice President (promoted to President of the network in 1974), and Lawrence R. White, Vice President of Programming. Schlosser told Stromberg that *Dr. Frankenstein* would be "biggest production of the year."

FRANCO ZEFFIRELLI

Initially, Stromberg wanted Franco Zeffirelli to direct *Dr. Frankenstein* – and the director was eager to read it. In an August 18, 1971, memo to Sid Sheinberg, Stromberg reasoned, "My representatives also represent Franco Zeffirelli, and I believe he would be ideal for this. As you will recall, he directed the Burtons brilliantly in *The Taming of the Shrew*, and I thought his direction of *Romeo and Juliet* was spectacular – just the sort of style we're seeking for this project."

Another factor that no doubt appealed to Stromberg was that Zeffirelli happened to be gay and, therefore, would likely relish the queer subtext. In the minus column, Zeffirelli wouldn't come cheap – and he would be hard to control.

In the same memo to Sheinberg, Stromberg pleaded, "It is very difficult to actually nail down, even tentatively, the casting of this until we know better whether this first will be a theatrical feature or whether instead it will be made specifically for television. For example, Isherwood feels that Albert Finney would agree to star in the project if this is first a theatrical film, but probably will decline if it is solely for television. I would appreciate knowing as soon as possible which direction we are taking."

Despite Stromberg's preference to turn *Dr. Frankenstein* into a major theatrical release, Sid Sheinberg firmly believed

Franco Zeffirelli.

Boris Sagal.

the film should be made for television – with costs under tight control and the project under his purview.

Zeffirelli made it clear that he was not at all interested in directing a made-for-television movie – but even if the film were to be elevated to theatrical status, the director had many other projects on his radar that were more to his liking. So, it was a polite pass.

MERVYN LEROY

Two days later, on August 20, 1971, Stromberg sent the treatment of *Dr. Frankenstein* to 70-year-old veteran director and honorary Oscar recipient Mervyn LeRoy (*Little Caesar, Little Women, The Bad Seed, Mister Roberts, Gypsy*). LeRoy was most famous, though, as the producer of *The Wizard of Oz* for which he was also an uncredited director. LeRoy had been a friend of Stromberg's father since the 1920s and had known Hunt Jr. since the day he was born – so he was practically an extended family member. LeRoy liked the *Dr. Frankenstein* outline but explained that he was busy developing a Western and just couldn't take on another project at that time. In truth, his career was behind him. He never made another movie. It is possible that early symptoms of Alzheimer's were already disabling his mojo. He died of the disease in 1987.

BORIS SAGAL

Growing impatient, Sid Sheinberg made a sudden utilitarian choice of director for *Dr. Frankenstein* – Boris Sagal whom he had personally signed to a long-term contract with Universal Television beginning in 1969. Born in the Ukraine, Sagal was a seasoned TV director with credits that included two episodes of *The Twilight Zone* (1961), four episodes of *Alfred Hitchcock Presents* (1961-62), and a two-part *Man from U.N.C.L.E.* that was released theatrically in Europe as *The Helicopter Spies* (1968). One of his daughters, Katey Sagal, born in 1954, would grow up to star in *Married with Children* and *Sons of Anarchy*.

What made Boris Sagal a bit more interesting than ever before, though, was his latest theatrical movie, released that very same month of August 1971: *The Omega Man*, starring Charlton Heston, based on Richard Matheson's 1954 science fiction novel *I Am Legend*. On loan out to Warner Bros., Sagal had directed *The Omega Man* on a large scale, yet with precision and efficiency. The movie's big box-office reception had springboarded the director to flavor-of-the-moment status in Hollywood.

"Sid plans to have Boris Sagal direct *Frankenstein*," Stromberg informed Isherwood on September 21, 1971. "Boris and I have worked together in the past and he is an extremely practical man."

After a meeting with the director, Isherwood noted that Sagal was "very pleasant, even charming, but he is definitely a second-string workhorse type of director; the type which is called in when costs have to be cut and the show gotten on the road... and he is accustomed to work in England."

In fact, Sagal had just recently directed a TV movie in the UK for Universal Television and NBC called *Destiny of a Spy* (1969), an espionage thriller starring Lorne Greene, Anthony Quayle, Rachel Roberts and Harry Andrews, shot at Pinewood Studios and associate produced by Ian Lewis – who would repeat the duty on *Dr. Frankenstein*.

POLANSKI'S PRODUCTION DESIGNER

At that time, MCA-Universal's top executive in the UK was Brian Brolly, 35, who had been Vice President of MCA Television, London, since 1962. Immediately after *Dr. Frankenstein* would complete production, Brolly would become managing director of Paul and Linda McCartney's MPL Communications (the *Band on the Run* era), and then of Andrew Lloyd Webber's Really Useful Theatre Company (where he shepherded *Cats, Starlight Express* and *The Phantom of the Opera*).

The first person Brolly recruited from the UK to join the *Dr. Frankenstein* team was the renowned production designer Wilfrid Shingleton, 57, who had won an Oscar for David Lean's *Great Expectations* and a BAFTA for John Guillermin's *The Blue Max*. His other impressive credits

Stromberg & Brian Brolly.

included John Huston's *The African Queen*, David Lean's *Hobson's Choice*, Jack Clayton's *The Innocents*, and two of Roman Polanski's most visually lavish films: *The Fearless Vampire Killers* and *Macbeth*.

At the age of 18, Shingleton began his career as a junior assistant in the art department at Ealing Studios which happened to be located near his family's home. He quickly worked his way up the ranks and became head of the art department from 1938 to 1941, designing such films as Carol Reed's *Penny Paradise* and Marcel Varnel's *To Hell with Hitler*. His job was interrupted by military duty during World War II for which his experience was put to good use designing naval camouflage.

"Precise models of the naval vessels to be camouflaged were made by carpenters," explained historian Kristie Naimo. "The models were then observed in the water tank under different lighting and sea conditions. This is where Wilfrid Shingleton's skills as a film set designer and lighting technician helped."

For *Dr. Frankenstein*, Shingleton was asked to create preliminary concept sketches for the various sequences outlined in the script – and to recommend what might be shot on locations versus custom-built sets at Pinewood Studios.

On November 5, 1971, Shingleton wrote the following letter to the *Dr. Frankenstein* contingent in Universal City, including Stromberg, Boris Sagal, Sid Sheinberg and Universal Television's head of production George Santoro (Sheinberg's right-hand man): "I have suggested that the end 'ice' sequence should be designed as a studio interior set. I hope you will find interesting the suggestions for the difference in the creation of Prima from that of the Monster. I feel they emphasize the [oriental] influence which Dr. Polidori has on the experiments, and visually could be very exciting."

THE LIZ & DICK DEMANDS

Meanwhile, on August 18, 1971, Stromberg officially offered the dual role of Dr. Polidori ("the maimed and hair-raisingly insane scientist" *and* the real-life doctor in the prologue) to Richard Burton and the role of Agatha / Prima (wench slash female creature) to Elizabeth Taylor. Thrillingly, they both agreed to star in the film *if* the studio would meet their demands.

"I remember when Liz and Dick were considering doing the picture for Universal," recalled their agent Robin French. "I had to go to [MCA-Universal Chairman] Lew Wasserman

and explain that if he wanted them, they were each going to get a million dollars and ten percent of the gross, which in those days was the top dollar. And I remember Wasserman saying to me, 'Nobody is worth that. Even Bette Davis, who was my client when she was in her prime, wasn't worth that. So, sorry but no I can't.'"

OLIVER REED & VANESSA REDGRAVE

Wasting no time, Stromberg immediately set his casting sights elsewhere – zeroing in on Oliver Reed and Vanessa Redgrave, the two leads from Ken Russell's scandalous new movie *The Devils* (1971).

Reed was being wooed to play Polidori but the offer got speed bumped. In a December 2, 1971, memo to Stromberg & Co., Brian Brolly reported, "Reed has agreed to play in an Andrew Sinclair film entitled *Byron's Evil* which inter-knits Lord Byron's evil life with the Shelley family and the Frankenstein story." No one knew at the time that *Byron's Evil* would never get made.

This Picture and Above: Oliver Reed & Vanessa Redgrave, *The Devils*.

Richard Burton & Elizabeth Taylor.

Vanessa Redgrave was offered Agatha / Prima – which she quite liked and wanted to do – but she was committed to the six-part BBC series *A Picture of Katherine Mansfield* and would follow that with Sidney Lumet's *Murder on the Orient Express*.

MARLON BRANDO

In December 1971, Stromberg announced that, for the role of Dr. Polidori, he wanted none other than Marlon Brando who had won an Oscar for *On the Waterfront* (1955). Brando

Coppola directs Brando in *The Godfather*.

had recently finished filming Francis Ford Coppola's *The Godfather* in August 1971 but the picture would not be released until March 1972, so no one knew if it was going to be successful. Rumors had been swirling around Hollywood that Brando had become difficult and relied heavily on cue cards. His last few films had not done well at the box office and the general perception was that his career was in the toilet. In fact, he was originally offered only Screen Actors Guild minimum scale to play Don Corleone in *The Godfather* – though Paramount production chief Robert Evans finally agreed to pay Brando $50,000 plus points – which he sold back to the studio, prior to the release of the movie, for $100,000, because he needed emergency cash "to settle some sort of female trouble that had erupted."

As insiders, Stromberg and Isherwood knew all this gossip – and it didn't hurt that Isherwood's agent, Robin French, just so happened to represent Brando, too. So, in December 1971, Stromberg offered Brando the role. The timing was not ideal. The actor was prepping for Bernardo Bertolucci's *Last Tango in Paris* which would begin shooting in January 1972. Notoriously indecisive, Brando did not give them an immediate answer, preferring to think it over and let the character of Polidori percolate in his mind for a while. He also may have been gambling that when *The Godfather* opened in four months, the tide might turn in his favor. Delay, delay, delay.

FRANCIS FORD COPPOLA

Three months earlier, Francis Ford Coppola had gotten wind of *Dr. Frankenstein* and enthusiastically appealed to Stromberg to let him read it. Up until then, though, the director's resume was littered with box-office duds like *Finian's Rainbow* (1968) and *The Rain People* (1969).

In a September 23, 1971, memo to Sid Sheinberg,

Stromberg reported, "Francis Coppola who, as you know, has just finished *The Godfather*, heard about the project from Gore Vidal, and contacted me to say that for years he has himself been planning the classic version of *Frankenstein* and, accordingly, is most anxious to see the script."

Sheinberg instructed Stromberg to politely explain to Coppola that Boris Sagal was already set to direct *Dr. Frankenstein* and that was that.

JOHN BOORMAN

Despite everyone being told that Sagal was "definitely in," vultures circled the studio. In addition to Coppola and Jim Bridges, John Boorman suddenly entered the fray.

A friend of Isherwood and Bachardy, Boorman was mainly known for directing the crime thriller *Point Blank* (1967) starring Lee Marvin. Boorman was currently in post-production on his latest film, *Deliverance*, which would not be released by Warner Bros. until July 1972.

Seven months prior to that, on January 19, 1972, Boorman wrote an impassioned letter to Sid Sheinberg, Lew Wasserman and Hunt Stromberg, which read as follows:

Gentlemen:
You know of my interest in your *Dr. Frankenstein* project. It is simply the best piece of film material I have ever read. I believe its commercial potential as a theatrical film would be prodigious. I know you have planned it all along for television, but I urge you to reappraise it at this time. If you allowed me to direct it as a theatrical feature I could attract an important cast: Jon Voight would play the Monster; Oliver Reed or Paul Scofield [as] Dr. Polidori; etc. This could be achieved for very little extra cost. As a British director I know how to save money on a picture shooting in England, and my nationality would help qualify it for Eady [the Eady Levy, a rebate for films with primarily British cast and crew]. I have just <u>directed</u> and <u>produced</u> an extremely difficult

THE EPIC SAGA BEHIND *FRANKENSTEIN: THE TRUE STORY*

John Boorman on *Emerald Forest*.
Below: Directing *Excalibur*.

the Best Actor Oscar-winner for *Coming Home*; the Golden Globe-winner as the father in *Ray Donovan* (2013-2017); and as the real-life father of Angelina Jolie, Voight hit it big in 1969 playing the hustler in John Schlesinger's *Midnight Cowboy* that had won the Oscar for Best Picture plus Golden Globe and BAFTA awards for Voight.

Isherwood and Bachardy loved the idea of Voight – with whom they had become social friends. (Voight would later sit for a Bachardy portrait on September 20, 1973; see page 279.) Privately, Voight told Isherwood he wanted to be in the movie so badly, he'd play *either* of the leading roles.

This intel intrigued Stromberg who responded to Isherwood thusly: "Since you have indicated to me that Jon Voight might be just as interested in playing Victor Frankenstein, we might want to consider this casting route, particularly if we then could induce Warren Beatty to play the Creature. Knowing Warren as we do, he certainly enjoys flamboyant roles, and where could he ever find a better one?"

With this configuration in mind, Stromberg sent the script to Beatty – whose career was red hot on the basis of *Bonnie and Clyde*, for which he had been Oscar-nominated, and *McCabe & Mrs. Miller*. Beatty ended up passing – but then, out of the blue, Stromberg got a call from Richard Chamberlain's agent explaining that the actor had re-read the script and now preferred to play the Creature, if the part was still available.

In a memo to Sid Sheinberg, Stromberg wrote that with the combination of Voight and Chamberlain, they would have "two of the best young actors in the world."

On March 1, 1972, Isherwood reported, "Boorman has left and is in New York, on his way back home to Ireland. Hunt is now on his side, or says he is; Wasserman and

Jon Voight.

Voight & Director John Boorman.

picture, *Deliverance*, for Warners, bringing it in more than $100,000 under budget. I quote this as a credential for my claim that *Dr. Frankenstein* could be converted from an excellent TV Special into an epic blockbuster for just a little more than you are contemplating spending. I have never written such a letter, but then I have never responded so positively to a script. Whether or not I am finally included in your plans, I beg you to do full justice to this magnificent material. Meanwhile, congratulations on being responsible for such a script. Like Dr. Frankenstein, you have made something so powerful that you must expect repercussions, like being haunted by me! Yours sincerely,
John Boorman

JON VOIGHT & WARREN BEATTY
The idea of Jon Voight playing the Creature was not a fantasy; Boorman had just directed the actor in *Deliverance* and had already shown him the script. Known today as

Warren Beatty.

Roman Polanski – *The Fearless Vampire Killers.*

Coppola & Brando.

Brando in *Last Tango in Paris.*

Sheinberg haven't seen Boorman's film [*Deliverance*] yet, so don't have an opinion. And meanwhile, Warners [the studio that made *Deliverance*] is trying to buy the project away from Universal!"

Then, on March 25, 1972, Isherwood added the following: "Hunt Stromberg called me yesterday, saying that he will never employ John Boorman now because Boorman has lied to him. He has discovered that Boorman's commitment [to write, direct and produce *Zardoz* – at that time, for Columbia Pictures] is and always has been firm, and that he can't possibly get out of it to do *Frankenstein*, even if asked by Universal. We don't know whom to believe… but the fact remains that Boorman is almost certainly out of the picture. Now Hunt talks about Polanski!"

ROMAN POLANSKI

After his tremendous breakthrough success with *Rosemary's Baby* (1968), Roman Polanski was riding high until August 9, 1969, when his wife, actress Sharon Tate, their unborn baby, and four other people were brutally murdered by followers of Charles Manson. After mourning this heinous tragedy for two years, Polanski finally reemerged with *Macbeth* (1971), which was named Best Picture of the Year by the National Board of Review – but few went to see it. By 1972, his career was in a slump – and the new picture he was working on, *What?*, was not about to reverse that downward spiral. Stromberg knew that Polanski needed a hit. The director also had "experience doing a period horror film in the UK," namely *The Fearless Vampire Killers*, which looked exquisitely sumptuous thanks to production designer Wilfrid Shingleton who was already on the *Dr. Frankenstein* payroll.

Augmented with a note of recommendation from Shingleton, Stromberg couriered the screenplay to Rome where Polanski was directing *What?* It joined a large pile of scripts that were awaiting Polanski's consideration – including *Chinatown* by Robert Towne, which, of course, became his next project and resuscitated his career.

THE BRANDO/COPPOLA RECIPE

Meanwhile, on March 14, 1972, *The Godfather* opened to glowing reviews and huge box-office business. On April 18, Stromberg wrote the following memo to Sid Sheinberg: "If there's a chance in hell of getting Brando, we should hire Francis Coppola as our director – and we best get moving. Coppola obviously is very hot now because of *The Godfather*, and of course as you know he was pouncing on me several months ago asking to direct this. However, there certainly is nothing to stop him from doing his own version of this, which is completely similar to our approach, and this would kill us."

Brando as Dr. Moreau.

Sheinberg, however, was not so gung-ho. Brando was considered hopelessly unmanageable. And, despite the huge box-office success of *The Godfather*, Coppola had defiantly gone $1 million over the movie's $5 million budget – a transgression that might be forgiven on a blockbuster hit but would be apocalyptic on anything less. The whole package was viewed as a recipe for disaster.

PETER BOGDANOVICH

Stromberg then met with Peter Bogdanovich, 33, whose breakthrough film *The Last Picture Show* (1971) had been nominated for eight Oscars including Best Picture and Best Director – and had won Supporting Actor Oscars for both Ben Johnson and Cloris Leachman. His most recent film, *What's Up Doc?*, starring Barbra Streisand and Ryan O'Neal, had just been released in March 1972 and was already a smash.

On April 19, 1972, Stromberg updated Sheinberg thusly: "Peter Bogdanovich has just committed to prepare a story treatment for his next picture and will not now know for another month whether or not that project will proceed. Hence, it would be silly to count on him." The treatment was for *Paper Moon* – which did move forward and won an Oscar for Tatum O'Neal.

PETER YATES

Stromberg also approached British-born Peter Yates, 43, mainly known for directing the Oscar-winning action picture *Bullitt* (1968) starring Steve McQueen. His latest picture, *The Hot Rock*, starring Robert Redford, had just been released in January 1972.

"Peter Yates has just committed to directing a Robert Mitchum crime picture for Paramount," Stromberg wrote to Sheinberg on April 19, 1972. The movie would turn out to be *The Friends of Eddie Coyle*.

"There are, however, two other outstanding candidates still readily available," Stromberg continued in his memo. "1.) Francis Ford Coppola. He is dying to do this and, whether we ultimately want him or not, I am now letting him read the script on an informal basis; and, 2.) James Bridges. Both Isherwood and I feel he is a brilliant, imaginative young talent. He already has read the script and wants to do it. Meanwhile Isherwood and I keep receiving missives from Ireland from John Boorman. Even though he has closed a deal with Columbia [to do *Zardoz*], his most recent dispatch assures us he will get out of this commitment if only we will let him do our project."

BUMPED UP TO THEATRICAL

Three days later, on April 22, 1972, Isherwood reported: "*Frankenstein* is now declared a feature film – after

Wasserman finally got around to reading it. We at once cabled Boorman, asking him if he was free to direct it. Boorman hasn't replied yet."

With *Dr. Frankenstein* officially bumped up to theatrical film status, Universal wanted Isherwood and Bachardy to cut the script down from 197 pages to a more manageable 140 pages, which would translate to an approximate running time of 2 hours and 20 minutes. So, the writers dutifully tightened and streamlined the material, turning in what Stromberg referred to as "the svelte draft" on June 1, 1972. The most noticeable thing missing was the prologue; no longer would Mary Shelley and her compadres set the scene.

Never a "yes" man, Sid Sheinberg was not in complete agreement with Wasserman about turning *Dr. Frankenstein* into a theatrical release – and he did not shy away from expressing his reservations.

And then there was NBC to consider. Both Herb Schlosser and Larry White loved the project and had been counting on it to be one of the network's biggest events. It was Sheinberg's responsibility to deliver the blow to them – and to take the heat for it.

Now that the film was going the theatrical route, Boris Sagal was justifiably miffed when he heard that other directors were being considered – especially in light of his big-screen success with *The Omega Man*. In a curt letter to Sheinberg, Sagal's agent demanded a firm commitment for his client to direct *Dr. Frankenstein*, one way or the other. Sheinberg promptly obliged by taking Sagal off the project and reassigning him to direct an episode of *Columbo*. Ouch.

No one was happy. Yet nothing was etched in stone. Wasserman's decision to turn *Dr. Frankenstein* into a theatrical film was exhilarating in theory, but, in truth, was entirely contingent on attaching a *trustworthy* A-list director and big "name" stars for a budget that made sense – none of which had happened yet.

As far as Sid Sheinberg was concerned, nothing was off the table – including *Dr. Frankenstein* returning to the television division where he was convinced it belonged. As weeks went by with no theatrical deals struck, everyone could plainly see the writing on the wall.

On July 8, 1972, Isherwood reported: "Jon Voight has written Sid Sheinberg a very pompous letter, saying that he won't do *Frankenstein* if it's going to be for television, and continuing: 'I must terminate my interest at this time…' He ends by saying that he would like to buy the script if Universal ever wants to sell it."

Then John Boorman complicated matters further by adding to his demands. On July 15, 1972, Isherwood wrote, "Boorman's science fiction story [*Zardoz*] has been turned down at Columbia. His agent wants to make a deal with Hunt; Boorman will direct *Frankenstein* if Universal will buy the sci-fi story as well."

Stromberg and Sheinberg were extremely irritated that Boorman was trying to leverage a second movie out of the deal – especially after they read his script for *Zardoz*, which neither liked. They were on the verge of kicking Boorman to the curb when, just two weeks later, on July 30, 1972, Boorman's new film *Deliverance* (starring Voight) opened and was an immediate hit with critics and audiences alike. Success changes everything in Hollywood. Overnight. Well, in this case, three days.

On August 2, 1972, Isherwood got an urgent call from his agent Robin French telling him that Sid Sheinberg was jumping on a plane to Europe to personally meet with Boorman about directing *Dr. Frankenstein*. And despite the insulting letter that Voight had written to Sheinberg, if Boorman still wanted Voight to play the Creature *or* Dr. Frankenstein, he was willing to let bygones be bygones. But, no matter how much Boorman's stock had risen with the success of *Deliverance*, Sheinberg flatly refused to add *Zardoz* to the pact – which ultimately proved to be a deal breaker.

Which also meant that Voight was out. Contacted in 2016 for this book, Jon Voight remembered very little about the day-to-day skirmishes on the development of *Dr. Frankenstein* – other than having responded very favorably to the script and his desire to do the film if Boorman had directed it. Incidentally, Bachardy, Boorman and Voight have all remained friends over the years and had dined together as recently as 2015.

LINDSAY ANDERSON

With Boorman off the list, Sid Sheinberg immediately set up a meeting in London with Lindsay Anderson. The 49-year-old British director was widely revered for *If…* (1968), winner of the Cannes Film Festival Palme d'Or. But there was, perhaps, an underlying reason why Stromberg and Isherwood deemed Anderson "a perfect fit" for *Dr. Frankenstein*. Though not publicly "out", insiders knew that Anderson was gay and therefore might identify with the subtext of the material. Discussions did not go very far, however, because Anderson was knee-deep in post-production on his latest picture, *O Lucky Man!* (1973), and was simply not available.

JOHN SCHLESINGER'S CONTRIBUTION

In September 1972, the next director to be approached for *Dr. Frankenstein* was Oscar, BAFTA and Golden Globe winner John Schlesinger, 46, one of the foremost filmmakers of the era. His movie *Midnight Cowboy* (1969) had won three Oscars including Best Director and Best Picture; he had also been Oscar-nominated twice more for *Darling* (1965) and *Sunday Bloody Sunday* (1971). Like Lindsay Anderson, Schlesinger also happened to be gay and was a close friend of Isherwood and Bachardy. (In fact, Schlesinger and his longtime partner, fine art photographer Michael Childers, vacationed together with Isherwood and Bachardy at California's Yosemite National Park.)

Much to Stromberg's chagrin, however, the timing was off. Schlesinger was busy rehearsing *I and Albert*, a musical about Queen Victoria and Prince Albert, which would open at the Piccadilly Theatre in the West End on November 6, 1972. Beyond that, the director was already committed to his next film, *The Day of the Locust* (Paramount, 1975), which was set to start pre-production in Hollywood at the same time *Dr. Frankenstein* would begin shooting in England.

Even so, Schlesinger eventually got around to reading the script and, in an October 14, 1972, letter to Stromberg, wrote, "The writing is terrific. I wish you the best with it. Though I am regrettably unavailable to direct, I would highly recommend Dickie Marden to edit the film. He is an Oxford chum of mine who has become, in my humble opinion, one of the best in the business."

Richard "Dickie" Marden had been Schlesinger's editor on one of the great milestones in queer cinema, *Sunday Bloody Sunday* – for which Marden had won the BAFTA Award for Best Editing. There is a kiss in that film between Daniel (Peter Finch) and Bob (Murray Head)

Jon Voight & Director John Schlesinger, *Midnight Cowboy*.

that caused quite a commotion in its day. Even before that landmark, Marden had already dealt with frank gay subject matter when he edited Stanley Donen's *Staircase* (1969) starring Richard Burton and Rex Harrison as longtime lovers. His resume also included such impressive titles as *Two for the Road*, *Bedazzled*, *Anne of the Thousand Days* and *Mary, Queen of Scots*.

At Schlesinger's behest, Stromberg got in touch with Marden who was, at that time, busy editing Joseph L. Mankiewicz' *Sleuth*, based on the whodunit by Anthony Shaffer, starring Laurence Olivier and Michael Caine, to be released in December 1972. Marden read the script and immediately agreed to edit *Dr. Frankenstein* as his next project.

JULIE CHRISTIE

On the casting front, Stromberg was busy wooing Julie Christie, one of the top female stars in the world, with a string of hits including Schlesinger's *Darling* for which she had won both an Oscar *and* a BAFTA for Best Actress; David Lean's *Doctor Zhivago* which had won five Oscars; and, most recently, Robert Altman's *McCabe and Mrs. Miller* for which she was Oscar-nominated for Best Actress.

On July 20, 1972, Stromberg had written a letter to Christie, stating, "I am hoping against hope that you will like the role of Elizabeth. If not, how about Prima?"

Two agonizing months later, on September 20, 1972, Stromberg finally received the following handwritten response from Christie: "Dear Hunt, I'm sorry I haven't replied to your note before. I read the script immediately, and really liked it. But just getting down to writing a letter is always an enormous endeavor for me. The film is probably all cast by now, but if it's of any consequence I think I'd really enjoy being in it. I think

THE EPIC SAGA BEHIND *FRANKENSTEIN: THE TRUE STORY*

Julie Christie.

Bo Svenson as the Creature in Dan Curtis' *Frankenstein* (ABC-TV, 1973).

Julie Christie with Michael Sarrazin.

I would rather play Prima – I guess we'd need to talk about it. But even if it's not cast, my schedule will probably be all wrong for the film. I'm working till about July next year. So, there we are. Over to you. With love, Julie."

Indeed, she was committed to Nicholas Roeg's *Don't Look Now*, among other projects. But despite scheduling conflicts, Stromberg was quick to point out to his bosses that nothing in the business of making movies is ever rock solid. So, he steadfastly clung to the slim hope that Christie might miraculously become available at precisely the time they would need her – whenever that might be.

DAN CURTIS

In the meantime, the unthinkable happened. For its late-night anthology series, *The Wide World Mystery*, ABC-TV announced its own two-hour production of *Frankenstein*, to be presented in two parts, on January 16 and 17, 1973, produced

by Dan Curtis of *Dark Shadows* fame, starring Robert Foxworth, Bo Svenson and Susan Strasberg. Naturally, the news spooked Isherwood and Bachardy but they were relieved to learn that it "didn't seem to worry Hunt a bit." A little reconnaissance had revealed that the production was being hastily produced on a shoestring budget, shot soap-opera style with three cameras on videotape, utilizing many of the same flimsy sets and canned score cues from *Dark Shadows*. Nevertheless, it was a threat – just, thankfully, not a primetime one.

COPPOLA'S RETRIBUTION

No sooner had they recovered from this sucker punch, however, word leaked that an impatient Francis Ford Coppola had decided to move forward with his own faithful version of Mary Shelley's novel as a big budget theatrical feature film he would write and direct for Paramount. On September 30, 1972, Isherwood gravely reported the following: "Hunt Stromberg has heard that a first-draft screenplay has been completed by our rival, Coppola!"

This blow below the belt – in addition to the loss of Boorman and rejections from other A-list directors – caused Lew Wasserman to throw in the towel, abandoning the notion, once and for all, of turning Stromberg's *Dr. Frankenstein* into a theatrical feature.

Though hindsight is twenty-twenty, the studio acquiesced prematurely. No one knew then that Coppola would soon shift gears in favor of *The Conversation* and *The Godfather: Part II*, both of which would be Oscar-nominated for the Best Picture the very same year – with *The Godfather: Part II* taking home the gold.

Even so, Coppola's passion for Frankenstein never died. Two decades later, in the wake of his success directing *Bram Stoker's Dracula* (1992), Coppola would produce *Mary Shelley's Frankenstein* (TriStar Pictures, 1994), at first to be directed by Roman Polanski starring Willem Dafoe, but ultimately directed by Kenneth Branagh starring Robert De Niro. Scripted by Steph Lady and Frank Darabont, the movie was no more faithful to Shelley than any other production, before or since – and many critics compared it unfavorably to *Frankenstein: The True Story*.

THE EGO HAS LANDED

Luckily, NBC's Herb Schlosser and Larry White had never wavered in their desire to present *Dr. Frankenstein* as a two-part, primetime event – and Sid Sheinberg was just as eager to reignite Stromberg's project through Universal's television division where he had more autonomy to get things done his way. Now that the grandiose fantasies of Zeffirelli, LeRoy, Boorman, Coppola, Polanski, Bogdanovich, Yates, Bridges, Anderson and Schlesinger had been put to rest, Sheinberg began looking from within the studio's own roster of contract talent for an economical, disciplined director who, like Boris Sagal, could be trusted to stick to the budget and schedule.

A more controllable director would also be a better fit for Stromberg who clearly saw himself as the captain of this ship. With jolting candor, Stromberg told a reporter that *Dr. Frankenstein* "is not a director's picture. It is a producer's picture. Think about it. The great movies were made in the days of the great producers. Hal Wallis, Irving Thalberg, my

father... to name a few."

Well, alrighty then. The ego has landed.

STEVEN SPIELBERG

One of Universal Television's contract directors under consideration was 25-year-old Steven Spielberg. This was hardly unusual since Sid Sheinberg had famously required every producer on the lot – including Stromberg – to screen Spielberg's impressive 1968 short film *Amblin'*. Despite some initial resistance among the troops, the crusade eventually gained traction. From 1969 to 1972, Spielberg had directed eleven projects for Universal Television – from Joan Crawford in Rod Serling's *Night Gallery* to Dennis Weaver in Richard Matheson's *Duel*.

In a 2015 interview for this book, Sheinberg couldn't recall if the notion of Spielberg directing *Dr. Frankenstein* had gone any further than a name on a list of ideas – or if he had actually been given a script to consider. Spielberg

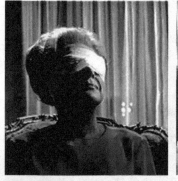 

Top: Spielberg early headshot. Center: Spielberg directs Joan Crawford, *Night Gallery*. Bottom: Spielberg & Sid Sheinberg.

Jack Smight teasingly points a finger at Hunt Stromberg Jr., perhaps calling him out for calling the movie "a producer's picture."

himself has, as of this writing, been unavailable for comment. In any event, in the fall of 1972, Spielberg was preparing to direct his first theatrical feature film, *The Sugarland Express*, scheduled to shoot January 15 to June 1, 1973, precisely the same time period that Sheinberg now wanted *Dr. Frankenstein* to be in production in the UK.

GEORGE SEATON

On November 10, 1972, Hunt Stromberg had dinner with George Seaton, 61, the beloved writer-director of *Miracle on 34th Street* and *The Country Girl*, both of which had earned him Oscars. On contract to Universal since 1968, Seaton completely revitalized the studio and his own career by adapting and directing *Airport* (1970) which became the highest-grossing and most profitable Universal movie up to that time, nominated for 10 Academy Awards including Best Picture – and winning Best Supporting Actress for Helen Hayes.

Prior to the meeting, Seaton had read the *Dr. Frankenstein* script and, over dinner, pitched his directorial ideas to Stromberg. Shortly thereafter, however, either Seaton or Stromberg must have had a change of heart. The "comeback kid" was not hired for *Dr. Frankenstein* and he never directed another picture. (Seaton died of cancer in 1979.)

JACK SMIGHT

Winds change direction in Hollywood all the time but this turnabout was faster than most. By mid-November 1972, just a few days after Stromberg's dinner with Seaton, Jack Smight was suddenly confirmed to direct *Dr. Frankenstein* for the flat rate of $74,000. Bada bing, bada boom! Universal was highly confident in its choice and Stromberg was greatly relieved.

Jack Smight with *Dr. Frankenstein* clapper board.

The writers? Not so much.

On Thanksgiving Day, Isherwood vented his anger thusly: "Hunt has double-crossed us and signed Jack Smight, a C director, behind our backs, and this will almost certainly mean a C grade cast for the picture."

This was, of course, an irrational assessment of Smight who had a very impressive resume and had frequently worked for Stromberg at CBS way back in the 1950s.

In a 2016 interview for this book, Jack Smight's son Alec Smight recalled, "My father flew in World War II in the Pacific as a 17-year-old navigator on B24 bombing missions. After the war, he graduated from the University of Minnesota – his home state – on the G.I. Bill. While there, he discovered a love of the theatre and became an actor. He also met and fell in love with actress Joyce Cunning, his future wife and my future mother. At the time, theatre was such an all-consuming endeavor that, in the late 1940s, he decided to move to Los Angeles with close friend and fellow aspiring actor, Peter Graves – of future *Mission: Impossible* fame. When my dad and Peter finally arrived in L.A., Peter's brother, actor James Arness – later famous for *The Thing from Another World* and *Gunsmoke* – met them at Union Station and told them the town was a bust, said they should save their energy and go back home. Of course, the two of them thankfully decided to stick it out. So, after a brief attempt at a career in radio and in front of the camera, my father soon discovered his passions were better suited to being behind it. The crucial moment came when he happened to rub shoulders with a high-level NBC executive. So, Jack got in the habit of coming by his parking place at NBC and leaving his business card on said executive's windshield every day – for weeks – until, finally, he called Jack and agreed to give him a job, just to get him off his back. Soon thereafter, my dad started working nights in the basement of the old Radio City West building on Sunset and Vine, maintaining NBC's vast troves of film and TV titles, waiting for an opportunity for something better. It wasn't long before he rose through the ranks to become a stage manager, working on a series of live teleplays and soap operas, even the Academy Awards broadcast. His big chance came when he was called to assistant direct a live version of the hit radio play *One Man's Family* by Carlton E. Morse. The day of the first broadcast in 1949, Carlton froze up and Jack, who was sitting right next to him in the control booth, jumped in to direct the episode, on the spot. He did such a stellar job that right after they went off the air, he got bumped up to full-time director. You couldn't write a better story."

From there, Jack Smight went on to direct dozens of NBC episodes of TV. Alec further explained, "In 1955, my father replaced his friend and fellow former stage manager, Arthur Penn, on *The Philco-Goodyear Television Playhouse* in New York."

When Hunt Stromberg Jr. was head of programming for CBS-TV, he hired

Smight to direct a slew of installments for the network's anthology series, including two episodes of *General Electric Theatre* (1956-1958); three episodes of *Studio One* (1958); thirteen episodes of *Climax!* (1956-1959), including *Avalanche at Devil's Pass* starring Vincent Price; four episodes of *The Twilight Zone* (1959-1961); and four installments of *The Alfred Hitchcock Hour* (1963)

The peak of Smight's early career in TV came in 1958 when he won an Emmy for *Eddie*, an installment of NBC-TV's *Alcoa Theatre*, starring Mickey Rooney, followed by an Emmy nomination in 1961 for *Come Again to Carthage*, an installment of CBS-TV's *Westinghouse Presents*, starring Piper Laurie.

For the stage, Smight directed a Broadway comedy *The 49th Cousin* (Ambassador Theatre, 1960-1961) starring Oscar nominee Martha Scott and Marian Winters, the Tony Award winner for Christopher Isherwood's *I am a Camera*.

In the mid-1960s, Smight graduated to major studio theatrical movies, including *I'd Rather Be Rich* starring Sandra Dee, Robert Goulet and Andy Williams; *Harper* starring Paul Newman and Lauren Bacall; *Kaleidoscope* starring Warren Beatty, *The Travelling Executioner* starring Stacy Keach, *Rabbit, Run* starring James Caan, and *No Way to Treat a Lady* and *The Illustrated Man*, both starring Rod Steiger.

When asked to sum up his father's directing style, Alec Smight concluded, "He had an innate sense for storytelling, a musician's ear for dialogue, and, as always, a great rapport with his actors; he started his career wanting to be one after all. His style was clean, subtle, never one to interfere with the basic mechanics of a good story, always seeking to be more efficient, more economical, letting the content come to the fore, keeping the formal tricks to an absolute minimum."

In 1971, Sid Sheinberg had signed Smight to an exclusive contract with Universal Television where, in the two years leading up to *Dr. Frankenstein*, he had directed no less than six made-for-TV movies (with such stars as Olivia de Havilland, Joseph Cotten, Ernest Borgnine,

Richard Crenna and Lee J. Cobb), plus seven episodes of its four top-tier mystery series: *Columbo* (Peter Falk), *McCloud* (Dennis Weaver), *Banacek* (George Peppard) and *Madigan* (Richard Widmark).

One of the primary reasons Smight came to mind was because he had just recently directed a special episode of *Madigan* that was filmed in London – guest starring Fiona Lewis and Arnold Diamond (who would appear in *Dr. Frankenstein* as an impatient coach passenger). It was broadcast on NBC on November 8, 1972 – just a few days before Smight was assigned *Dr. Frankenstein*.

Once the writers met Smight face-to-face over lunch at Universal Studios (on December 5, 1972), the ice began to melt. "We both liked him and doubtless he is competent," Isherwood conceded in his diary. "He is more than ready to be our ally and said at once that of course we must come to England and work with him there on the script. He called Hunt about this, while we were in his office, and Hunt agreed – if Universal would agree."

Sid Sheinberg *did* agree – and ordered that the condensed 140-page theatrical screenplay be expanded to a 180-page teleplay for a three-hour movie (to fill four-hours of broadcast time, including commercials, spread over two nights). Isherwood and Bachardy were delighted that they could restore much of their lost material – including the Mary Shelley prologue.

FRANK LANGELLA & LAURENCE OLIVIER

Casting was not going nearly as well, so, in late-November 1972, Stromberg met with Sid Sheinberg, George Santoro and Jack Smight where, together, they devised the following wish-list: Frank Langella or Edward Albert as Dr. Frankenstein; Albert Finney as the Creature; Laurence Olivier, Burt Lancaster, Orson Welles, Anthony Quinn, Rex Harrison, Paul Scofield or Peter Ustinov as Dr. Polidori; Mia Farrow, Tuesday Weld or Candice Bergen as Prima; Anthony Perkins or Alan Bates as Henry Clerval; Olivia Hussey as Elizabeth; and, Ingrid Bergman or Bette Davis as Mrs. Blair, the landlady.

First to bite the dust was Laurence Olivier who had decided to star in two ITV productions during 1973: *Long Day's Journey into Night* and *The Merchant of Venice*. Perhaps the seed of making an upscale horror film was planted, though. Olivier would eventually play Dr. Van Helsing in Universal's 1979 production of *Dracula*.

Likewise, Frank Langella – known back then for his Golden Globe-nominated performance in *Diary of a Mad*

Smight reacts to Rod Steiger covered in tattoos for *The Illustrated Man*.

THE EPIC SAGA BEHIND *FRANKENSTEIN: THE TRUE STORY*

Housewife – would pass on the role of Dr. Frankenstein but end up an "overnight sensation" as Dracula on the Broadway stage (1977-78) and in Universal's 1979 production.

INGRID BERGMAN & BETTE DAVIS

The next to get scratched from the list was Ingrid Bergman who, instead, chose *Murder on the Orient Express* – and, in doing so, won her *third* Oscar. Likewise, Albert Finney chose *Orient Express* (as Belgian detective Hercule Poirot) for which he would be Oscar-nominated for Best Actor. Anthony

Perkins decided to board that train, too.

Even though Lew Wasserman had agented Bette Davis throughout the height of her career (two Oscars and another nine nominations), she respectfully passed on the part of the landlady, preferring to play a meatier role in Universal Television's *Scream, Pretty Peggy* (ABC-TV, 1973), directed by Gordon Hessler (*Scream and Scream Again*) and written by Jimmy Sangster (*The Curse of Frankenstein, The Nanny, The Anniversary*).

And so it went. Long story short, *none* of the above casting choices would pan out. Not a single one.

Bette Davis.

Ingrid Bergman with her Oscar for *Murder on the Orient Express*.

Several cast members in *Murder on the Orient Express* (1974) turned down offers to be in *Dr. Frankenstein*: Albert Finney, Sean Connery, Anthony Perkins, Vanessa Redgrave, Jacqueline Bisset and Ingrid Bergman. Only Sir John Gielgud accepted offers to appear in both.

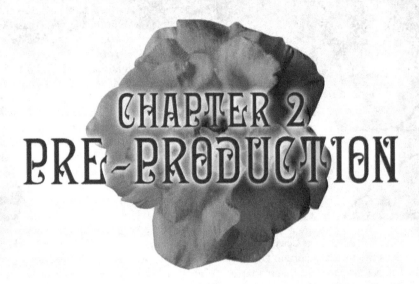

CHAPTER 2
PRE-PRODUCTION

THE SCENIC ROUTE

As you may have gathered by now, Stromberg thrived on chaos – and his journey to London to start pre-production on *Dr. Frankenstein* was especially turbulent. Even for him. Because of his phobic fear of flying, Stromberg decided on a five-week scenic route that became almost as death-defying as the movie he was planning.

On December 6, 1972, Stromberg – along with his partner Jacque Shelton, Shelton's 75-year-old mother Doris, and 32 pieces of luggage in tow – took a train from Los Angeles to New York; then, on December 10, sailed out of New York Harbor bound for Italy.

"Had a very rough crossing in the SS Cristoforo Colombo," Stromberg wrote in a letter to Charles F. Engel, Universal's Executive VP Creative Development. "In fact, the ship had its entire upper deck bashed in by a hurricane-force wave which, in turn, completely flooded the lower deck quarters of the tourist passengers, causing seventy-five injuries. For precautionary reasons, they lowered the lifeboats."

When they docked in Naples on December 20, labor strikes were so bad the intrepid travelers sailed on to Venice, arriving Christmas Eve. A rainy side-trip to Trieste was further dampened by the news that train service had been cancelled. So, they made the 150-mile return journey to Venice via a caravan of taxicabs (to carry all their suitcases) and caught the night train to Paris.

"This was the famous Orient Express," Stromberg noted, conjuring up images of old-world glamour and Agatha Christie-like intrigue. He went on, however, to clarify that the current state of the luxury train was "the dirtiest, most uncomfortable, nightmarish conveyance to be found on the face of the earth."

After a brief sojourn in the City of Lights, they continued on to Calais where, on December 28, they boarded the commuter boat to Dover, England.

Stromberg wrote, "In the dead of winter, the ferry ride was freezing cold, choppy and windy and we all got seasick

but as land became visible through the fog, it was the sight of the majestic White Cliffs of Dover that made the frantic travails of our entire journey worth every minute."

It was also the inspiration that led to the Creature throwing himself off a chalky cliff – but more on that later.

From Dover Eastern Docks, they took a train to London's Victoria Station. Then, a studio car (chauffeured by one of Pinewood Studio's regular drivers Tom Preston) delivered them to the elegant Dorchester Hotel where they collapsed in a heap of exhaustion. But this would only be a temporary base of operation until a suitable apartment could be scouted and rented for the long haul. On January 8, 1973, the motley crew moved into the sprawling Flat No. 4 at 8 Grosvenor Square, London W.1., overlooking the American Embassy. This would be their home-away-from-home for the nine-month gestation of *Dr. Frankenstein*.

Now, it was down to the business of getting *Dr. Frankenstein* up and running. With an official start date of March 15, 1973, looming heavy on the horizon, there was much prep left to be done – with less than 9 weeks to do it.

COURTESY OF ALFRED HITCHCOCK

Universal and Stromberg needed a British associate producer to spearhead the production in the UK, to hire the local crew, and, most importantly, to make sure the project qualified for the Eady Levy, a rebate on box-office receipts in the UK. To qualify, at least 85% of the budget had to be spent in the UK and the vast majority of cast and crew had to be British.

With this in mind, Universal Television's head of production George Santoro hired London-based Ian Lewis to

Opposite Page: Blu-ray cover art with grizzlier deterioration, by Mark Maddox.

Hitchcock on Universal Tour bus with Frankenstein Monster.

When Stromberg found out about Lewis' prior association with Hammer Films, he voiced his disapproval to Santoro. "*Dr. Frankenstein* must have the look and feel of a big-budget romantic epic, like *Doctor Zhivago*," Stromberg declared. Santoro reassured him that Lewis was the right man for the job.

Consequently, when Lewis hired a production manager to be his right-hand man, he knew he needed someone with credentials that would pass the Stromberg litmus test. The person who fit the bill was Brian Burgess, 31, who had production managed *Journey to the Far Side of the Sun* (Universal, 1969) produced by Gerry and Sylvia Anderson (of *Thunderbirds* fame, for which Burgess had directed two episodes) and had just returned from Israel where he had production managed the big-budget Gregory Peck Western *Billy Two Hats* (United Artists, 1974) produced by Norman Jewison. Most impressively, though, Burgess had recently production managed *Frenzy* (Universal, 1972) for director Alfred Hitchcock. (The fact that Burgess had been the second assistant editor on Hammer's *The Curse of the Mummy's Tomb* was simply not discussed.)

Stromberg knew Hitchcock very well, having worked closely with him on *The Alfred Hitchcock Hour* at CBS. And ever since becoming a producer on the Universal lot, Stromberg often had lunch with Hitchcock and regularly fed movie proposals to the director (who was likewise based at Universal City). All it took was one inter-office memo to Hitchcock for Stromberg to receive the thumbs-up he needed to bring Brian Burgess on board.

In that same response, Hitchcock also recommended five other *Frenzy* crew members – all of whom were promptly hired:

1. Script supervisor Angela Martelli (Hitchcock's *Stage Fright*, *The Bridge on the River Kwai*, *You Only Live Twice*). "Angela was quite a character," recalled Alec Smight, son of Jack. "She was feisty and a lot of fun. I vividly remember she always had a cigarette dangling from her mouth with ashes falling into her typewriter."
2. Casting director Sally Nicholl (*The Road to Hong Kong*, *The Spy Who Came in from the Cold*, *Becket*, *Anne of the Thousand Days*, *Mary, Queen of Scots*, *The Abominable Dr. Phibes*). "Sally was a very precise older lady," recalled Stromberg's secretary Phyllis Allarie. "What you might call 'old school.' Small, petite. Good fun. She and Hunt hit it off terribly well."

be the associate producer of *Dr. Frankenstein*. Lewis had been a freelance production manager on such important Universal projects as François Truffaut's *Fahrenheit 451*. Before that, Lewis had worked as Michael Carreras' assistant at Hammer Films, from 1959 to 1964, and then production managed *Frankenstein Created Woman*, *Quatermass and the Pit* and *The Devil Rides Out*. Although no one knew it at the time, following the success of *Frankenstein: The True Story*, Lewis would be appointed Managing Director of Universal Pictures Ltd – the British arm of MCA-Universal – the corporation's top executive in London, a post he held until 1989. [See Chapter 16 for my extensive interview with Ian Lewis.]

Associate Producer Ian Lewis.

McCallum, Smight, Hitchcock's *Frenzy* script supervisor Angela Martelli.

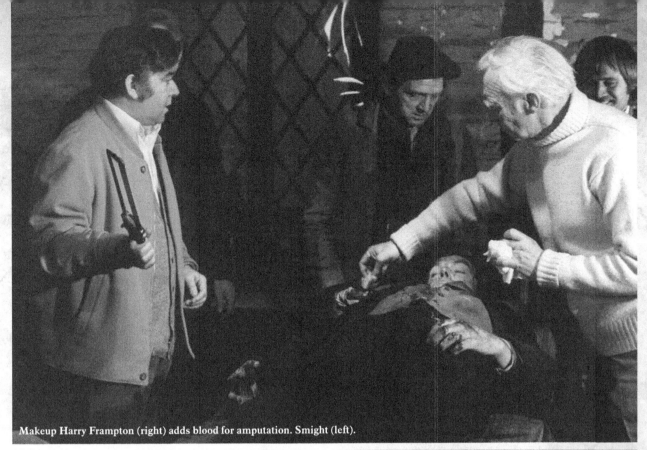

Makeup Harry Frampton (right) adds blood for amputation. Smight (left).

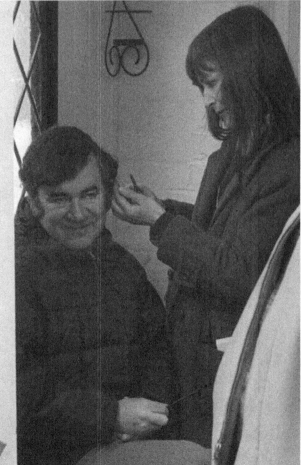

Above Left: Hairstylist Patricia McDermott & Stromberg hold Seymour's severed head. Left: McDermott on the set of *Star Wars*. Above: Patricia McDermott gives Jack Smight a haircut during a break.

3. Head makeup artist Harry Frampton (*Kind Hearts and Coronets*, *Straw Dogs*, *The House That Dripped Blood*, *I, Monster*; *The Last of Sheila*, and, later, several *Pink Panther* sequels and *Victor Victoria*). Actor David Weston, who had his arm cut off in *Dr. Frankenstein* and had previously starred with Leonard Whiting in Disney's *The Legend of Young Dick Turpin*, worked with Harry Frampton on both projects. "Harry was one of the best makeup artists in the business," Weston recalled in 2016, "and he was quite a character, too. A red-hot Communist with a great sense of humor."

4. Hairstylist Patricia McDermott (*The Devil Rides Out*, *Frankenstein Must Be Destroyed*; and, later, *Raiders of the Lost Ark* and the first two *Star Wars* films. According to *The Princess Diarist* by Carrie Fisher, McDermott designed the iconic "cinnamon buns / earphones" hairstyle for Princess Leia, affectionately nicknamed "The Buns of Navarone." "Pat was from Ireland," Fisher wrote, "and spoke with a lovely Irish brogue—causing her to refer to a movie as a 'fill-um.'"

5. Location manager Ian Goddard (assistant director on *Witchfinder General* and, later, *Mad Max*).

CREAM OF THE CROP

Additionally, the following top-drawer crew members were engaged for *Dr. Frankenstein*:

Director of photography Arthur Ibbetson (Oscar-nominated for *Anne of the Thousand Days*, *Willie Wonka and the Chocolate Factory*, *A Countess from Hong Kong*, *Die! Die! My Darling*, *The Chalk Garden*, *The Horse's Mouth*).

Second unit director of photography Edward "Ted" Scaife (camera operator on *Black Narcissus* and *The Third Man*, both

D.P. Arthur Ibbetson (left) & Jack Smight on FTTS set.

Ibbetson (standing in front of camera), 1st A.D. John Stoneman seated cap.

of which won Oscars for Best Cinematography; second unit DP on *The African Queen*; and the director of photography on *The Captain's Paradise*, *Curse of the Demon*, *The Dirty Dozen*).

Costume supervisor Elsa Fennell (*Lolita*, *Goldfinger*, *The Abominable Dr. Phibes*, *Diamonds Are Forever*, *O Lucky Man!*). Elsa also had two brothers in the business: Albert Fennell, producer of *The Avengers* TV series, *The Innocents*, *Dr. Jekyll and Sister Hyde*, *Captain Kronos: Vampire Hunter*; and, Jack Fennell, studio manager of Pinewood Studios.

In addition to lead makeup artist Harry Frampton, another makeup wizard would join the team: the great Roy Ashton (thirty-five-plus Hammer Film credits, *2001: A Space Odyssey*, *The Private Life of Sherlock Holmes*).

The assistant director team would be a force to be reckoned with: First assistant director / second unit director John Stoneman (*Casino Royale* with David Niven, *Sympathy for the Devil*, *If…*, *When Dinosaurs Ruled the Earth*); second assistant director Peter Cotton (*Jabberwocky*, *Saturn 3*, *Rosencrantz & Guildenstern Are Dead*); and, third assistant director Terry Pearce (*Lust for a Vampire*, *Tales from the Crypt*, *The Ghoul*, and, later, *Quest for Fire*, *Willow*).

THE ART DEPARTMENT

Under production designer Wilfrid Shingleton would be the following members of the art department:

1. Art director Fred Carter (*The Fearless Vampire Killers*, *Macbeth*, *The House That Dripped Blood*; and, later, *Robin Hood: Prince of Thieves*).

2. Set dresser Bryan Graves (*Macbeth*; and, later, *The Duellists*, *Excalibur*, *The Bride*).

3. Matte, scenic, forced-perspective, storyboards and titles artist Peter Melrose (*Evil of Frankenstein*; *Dracula, Prince of Darkness*; *Dracula Has Risen from the Grave*; Polanski's *The Fearless Vampire Killers* and *Macbeth*; and, later, *Blakes 7*, *The Trail of the Pink Panther*, *Superman III*, *Aliens*).

4. Sketch artist Jack Stephens (*Chitty Chitty Bang Bang*; and, later, *Murder on the Orient Express*, *The Man Who Would Be King*, *Tess*, *Octopussy*, *The Mission*).
5. Draughtsman Brian Ackland-Snow (*2001: A Space Odyssey*, *Battle of Britain*; and, later, Badham's *Dracula*, *The Dark Crystal*, *Superman III*, *The Doctor and the Devils*). Brother of renowned production designer Terry Ackland-Snow.
6. Draughtsman Michael Lamont (*The Day of the Triffids*, *Tales That Witness Madness*; and, later, *The Shining*, *Star Wars: Episode V – The Empire Strikes Back*, *Star Wars VI – Return of the Jedi*, *Raiders of the Lost Ark*, *Aliens*, *Harry Potter and the Sorcerer's Stone*, plus nine James Bond films – from *Octopussy* through the 2006 *Casino Royale*). Brother of Oscar-winning production designer Peter Lamont (*Titanic*, *Aliens* and numerous Bond films).

THE SPECIAL EFFECTS TEAM

The eight-man special effects team assembled for *Dr. Frankenstein* was particularly formidable:

1. Emmy-nominated special effects supervisor Roy Whybrow (*Help!*, *Casino Royale* with David Niven, *The Dirty Dozen*, *2001: A Space Odyssey*, *The Legend of Hell House*; and, later, *The Adventures of Sherlock Holmes' Smarter Brother*, *The Boys from Brazil*).
2. Academy Award-winning special effects technician Colin Chilvers (*She*, *2001: A Space Odyssey*, *Thunderbird 6*, *Inspector Clouseau*, *The Battle of Britain*, *200 Motels*, *Moon Zero Two*, *The Legend of Hell House*; conceptual effects development on Hammer's unproduced *Vampirella*; and, later, *The Rocky Horror Picture Show*, *Barry Lyndon*, *Lisztomania*, *Tommy*, *Sinbad and the Eye of the Tiger*, the first three *Superman* movies, *Saturn 3*, *Clash of the Titans*, *Bride of Chucky*, *X-Men*, and director of Michael Jackson's music video *Smooth Criminal*). In a 2016 interview for this book, Chilvers explained, "At that time, I was working as a special effects assistant to Roy Whybrow. Roy would go out and get the movie contracts – then myself and the rest of the crew would be the ones that would actually do the practical aspect of it. I was the floor supervisor. Roy would deal directly with the producers, making sure they were happy. I would work closely with the director. Roy had a lot of good contacts. He had been in the business for many years and worked for another effects guy named Cliff Richardson who did *Lawrence of Arabia*. When Cliff's son John came up and entered the business with his father, Roy went out on his own. At that time, I was working with an effects company called Bowie Films – headed by the amazing Les Bowie – that did all the Hammer horror films. After *Frankenstein: The True Story*, in 1974, I went out on my own as a special effects supervisor starting with *The Rocky Horror Picture Show*."
3. Two-time BAFTA-nominated model effects artist Brian Smithies (*Thunderbird 6*; and, later, *Superman*, Badham's *Dracula*, *Clash of the Titans*, *The Great Muppet Caper*, *Dark Crystal*, *Octopussy*, *Amadeus*, *Dune*, *Aliens*, *Harry Potter and the Sorcerer's Stone*, *Die Another Day*).
4. BAFTA-winning optical effects artist Wally Veevers (*Lawrence of Arabia*, *Dr. Strangelove*, *2001: A Space*

Brian Smithies painting glass shot of planet Arakis for David Lynch's *Dune*.

David Lynch, Brian Smithies, during production of *Dune*.

Brian Smithies showing young fans the model spaceship he created for *Thunderbird 6* at the premiere.

Odyssey, Diamonds Are Forever; and, later, *The Rocky Horror Picture Show* and *Superman*).

5. Academy Award and Emmy Award-winning process projection effects artist Charles Staffell (*Fahrenheit 451, Barbarella, 2001: A Space Odyssey, Diamonds Are Forever, Live and Let Die, Zardoz*; and, later, *Murder on the Orient Express, Superman, Octopussy, War and Remembrance, Dune, Aliens, Eyes Wide Shut*).

6. Draughtsman / special effects designer Ron Burton (*Battle of Britain*; and, later, *Superman, Brazil, Aliens, Batman*).

7. Engineering effects assistant Bud Rossler (*Battle of Britain, Le Mans*).

8. Special effects assistant Alan Barnard (*Lawrence of Arabia, Doctor Zhivago, The Dirty Dozen, Battle for Britain*; and, later, *Octopussy, Moonraker, Superman I, II & III, Gandhi, Dragonslayer, Full Metal Jacket, Indiana Jones and the Last Crusade*). Barnard specialized in making and operating machines to create fire, wind, rain, snow, waves and smoke.

STUNT COORDINATION

The stunt coordinator would be William Hobbs who had done the same job on Polanski's *Macbeth* and Hammer's *Captain Kronos – Vampire Hunter* (in which he also portrayed Hagen). In *Dr. Frankenstein*, Hobbs would also appear on-screen as a blink-and-you'll-miss-him usher standing in the box seat at the opera house when Dr. Frankenstein takes the Creature to see *The Marriage of Figaro*.

In a 2016 interview for this book, Hobbs said, "I must have only worked a day here and a day there on the *Frankenstein* film because I only have very vague memories of doing it."

Multitasking, Hobbs was simultaneously prepping the sword fights for Richard Lester's *The Three Musketeers* and *The Four Musketeers* and would later be the fight arranger for *The Duellists, Flash Gordon, Excalibur*, Monty Python's *The Meaning of Life, Brazil*, Polanski's *Pirates, Willow, Dangerous Liaisons, Robin Hood: Prince of Thieves* and *Shakespeare in Love*. In 2011, at age 72, Hobbs was a stunt performer in an episode of *Game of Thrones*, his last professional gig. He passed away at age 79 in 2018.

On days when Hobbs was not available, he was replaced by Ray Ford (*The Assassination Bureau, When Dinosaurs Ruled the Earth,*

William Hobbs in *Captain Kronos: Vampire Hunter*.

and, later, *Lifeforce, Young Sherlock Holmes*). And, completely against UK union rules, Stromberg's partner Jacque Shelton would apply his former stunt experience and occasionally "consult" when needed.

CREATURE COMFORTS

The director's journey to the UK was less eventful than that of the producer. On Saturday, January 6, 1973, a week after Stromberg's arrival, Jack Smight, his wife Joyce, and their teenage son Alec, simply took a plane to London. And therein lies the stratospheric difference between these two men. Functionality Vs. Flights of Fancy.

Joyce Cunning often acted in her husband's projects, though, surprisingly, she would not appear in *Dr. Frankenstein*. Alec would grow up to be the three-time Emmy-nominated director-producer-editor of *CSI: Crime Scene Investigation* (2000-2015).

For the next seven-and-a-half months, Smight and his family had agreed to relocate themselves to London for pre-production, shooting and editing of *Dr.*

William Hobbs in doorway as usher; Whiting, Stromberg, Sarrazin.

Jack Smight.

Alec Smight, Agnes Moorehead, Jack Smight.

Alec Smight and mother Joyce Cunning (Mrs. Jack Smight).

Frankenstein, with young Alec enrolled for a semester at the American Community School. They took up residence at an apartment on Cadogan Lane in the Sloane Square neighborhood of central London – not far from the flat at 4 Cadogan Lane where Judy Garland died in June 1969 from a barbiturate overdose.

"When we arrived in January 1973," Alec Smight recalled, "they were well into prep and getting ready to start production at Pinewood Studios, home to the James Bond franchise and many other wonderful films. I was only 14 years old at the time and had just discovered a love of theatre myself in school, so I struggled with leaving my friends behind and going to a foreign country. On a personal level, I always felt the Frankenstein film was some of my dad's best work, and for me, nothing rivals the experience of getting to live in London for seven-and-a-half months during its production. Of course, there were many highlights throughout the entire journey, but it wasn't until Sam Irvin so kindly reached out to me to exhume my memories of *Frankenstein: The True Story* that I even began to recall what a fun and utterly magical set it was, and how much of an influence it really had on me – and my future career as a director myself."

Not long after arriving in England, one of Jack Smight's most recent TV movies, *The Screaming Woman*, had its UK broadcast premiere on ITV. Based on a story by Ray Bradbury, the mystery-thriller starred Olivia de Havilland and Joseph Cotten. Ernest Harris, who had formally worked in the publicity and advertising departments of the London office of Columbia Pictures and had served as Director of

Publicity for Miracle Pictures, happened to be watching the film that evening. "Two of the reels were in the wrong order," Harris recalled. "There was a scene where Olivia de Havilland is being helped by some guy and then, sometime later, she meets the guy and asks for his help – so it was obvious that it was in the wrong order. I was one of only two people who phoned the broadcaster to complain. The other person got my phone number from the TV people and called me the next day. It turned out to be the director Jack Smight himself! He was in England to make *Frankenstein: The True Story*. As I knew a bit about his career, it was easy enough to chat about his movies. He was horrified that nobody but us had noticed that the reels were out of order. One surprising thing Jack told me was that he preferred making TV films to cinema. He thought he had more freedom and less interference."

Clearly, Smight had never worked for a producer as authoritarian as Hunt Stromberg Jr. – and the complexity and duration of the production of *Dr. Frankenstein* would exceed any television or theatrical movie the director had ever undertaken.

Location scouting began immediately. Stromberg, Jack Smight and Wilfrid Shingleton were taken by associate producer Ian Lewis, production manager Brian Burgess and location manager Ian Goddard on a recce to various sites around the UK, trying to stay within a reasonable radius of Pinewood Studios where stage work would be done. In the final movie, there would be an inside joke aimed at their tour guides. When Clerval and Frankenstein inspect the corpses that have perished in a mining accident, the toe-tags for three men are labeled "Lewis," "Burgess" and "Goddard."

McCallum lifts tarp to show Whiting the toe-tagged corpse.

Toe-tag name: "Goddard" after location manager Ian Goddard.

Deciding which limbs will be used to build their Creature, Clerval remarks, "It's between Goddard and Burgess for the legs and Lewis for the arms." (This sequence was filmed at Pinewood Riding School at the stables on the Pinewood Studios lot.)

Meanwhile, on January 22, 1973, writers Isherwood and Bachardy traveled from America to the UK on a Pan Am jumbo jet in first-class seats. "Universal is being unexpectedly generous with our expense allowance," Isherwood noted in his diary. "In addition to the first-class ticket we get $600 a week each. Hunt himself is getting $750 a week, but with that he has to pay for Jacque Shelton and Jacque's mother."

The writers accepted the invitation of David Hockney, the illustrious painter of the pop art movement, to reside at his Powis Terrace flat in the Notting Hill district of West London while he was away for several weeks.

Isherwood explained, "We were met at London Airport by our production manager Brian Burgess, with two envelopes full of pound notes, the first installment of our expense money. And then a studio-provided limousine [chauffeured by Tom Preston] drove us into London. We were all aware that our driver was shocked by the squalor of Powis Terrace. What were we doing there, when that bulging envelope of notes entitled us to stay at the Connaught or the Dorchester?"

LORD BYRON'S CRIB
The next day, January 23, 1973, Isherwood and Bachardy reported for work. "That first morning, we had a meeting with Hunt Stromberg, who is installed in an office on Piccadilly, quite near Hyde Park Corner," Isherwood wrote in his diary.

Stromberg's office was inside the headquarters of Universal Pictures Ltd at 139 Piccadilly, the building that had once been the grand mansion of none other than – I kid

THE EPIC SAGA BEHIND *FRANKENSTEIN: THE TRUE STORY*

you not – Lord Byron. (The building was recently restored to its former glory as an eight-bedroom mansion, listed on the open market for sale in April 2023 for £35 million.)

"I was the one who told Hunt about 139 Piccadilly being the home of Lord Byron," recalled Ian Lewis. "I knew about it because the Frankenstein / Mary Shelley Society used to come to our office and tour the place."

For Stromberg, this was no coincidence. The space was practically sacred – and he bragged to everyone who came for a meeting that the spirit of Lord Byron was watching over them. Okay, so the blaring rock 'n' roll tunes emanating from the nearby Hard Rock Café (the new "kid" on the block) may have detracted from the historic mystique Stromberg was trying to cultivate, but let's not burst his bubble.

Whiting & McCallum with telescope.

SCRIPT REVISIONS

Mary Shelley's book never explains how Dr. Frankenstein brings his Creature to life. Electrical charges generated from lightning originated in James Whale's *Frankenstein* – and became the standard for nearly every Frankenstein movie since.

Stromberg strived to avoid the obvious tropes of the genre, especially this one. "Frankenstein was a challenge because it had been done so much," Stromberg explained to *The Hollywood Reporter* in November 1973. "I wanted to do several firsts. I didn't want the Creature created at midnight with lightning in a storm because we've seen all that before." Once the writers were settled in London, Stromberg invited them over for dinner to discuss this and other script revisions he and Jacque had been brainstorming.

Stock footage of eclipse of the sun.

Rays of the sun reflected by mirrors in a zigzag pattern throughout the laboratory, collected in giant solar energy storage batteries.

"The chief recommendation," Isherwood wrote in his diary, "was that the Creature shouldn't be created by means of lightning, with a kite used for a conductor, because 'that was in the original Frankenstein film.' Hunt and Jacque suggested solar energy. This seemed an idiotic notion for England, where the weather is so unreliable, but we said, 'Sure, sure.'"

In spite of their misgivings, Isherwood and Bachardy met with production designer Wilfrid Shingleton at Pinewood Studios on January 24, 1973, to discuss what might feasibly be done.

"At the end of two hours," Isherwood reported, "we had recklessly and shamelessly invented the whole process of conveying solar energy to storage batteries by means of mirrors, and also the accident which causes the mirrors to burn each other up and crash down upon Frankenstein and the Creature. After which Mr. Shingleton said he would produce sketches of all this – we never saw these – and we parted with utmost politeness." (Stock footage would be utilized for inserts of the eclipse, telescopic surface of the sun, and various POV's of the daytime sky.)

The writers also received suggestions from Shelton. "Jacque said the Creature couldn't carry Polidori right up the mast," Isherwood continued. "No actor could manage such a feat. Therefore, he should be hoisted up on a hook, which happens to be hanging down from the mast at the end of a rope. Okay, okay." As a former stuntman, Shelton had reason to think about these things.

Loaded down with script notes, Isherwood and Bachardy had their work cut out for them. "January the 25th was the first of our stay-at-home working days on the rewriting of the script," Isherwood noted in his diary. "Luckily, David [Hockney] has a Smith Corona electric typewriter of the same model as ours, so Don felt at home with it."

Young Pagett.

NICOLA PAGETT ON THE TELLY

On January 26, 1973, Isherwood noted, "We went to the Universal office and met Nicola Pagett, whom Hunt and Jack Smight fancy to play either Elizabeth or Prima. She is impressive and not, thank God, very nice. Then I realized that she is the actress I so much admired in 1970 as Blanche in *Widowers' Houses*."

Nicola Pagett, 27, had been seen in such films as Hammer's *The Viking Queen* and as Princess Mary in *Anne of the Thousand Days*. She had also guest-starred on *Danger Man*, *The Avengers* and *The Persuaders!* But it was her role as Elizabeth Bellamy on the first two seasons of *Upstairs, Downstairs* (1971-1973) that had made her a recognizable star in England. The *Downton Abbey* phenomenon of its day, *Upstairs, Downstairs* would eventually be broadcast in the United States on PBS' *Masterpiece Theatre*, but that wouldn't happen until January 1974, a few weeks after *Frankenstein: The True Story* had aired. [See Chapter 10 for my interview with Nicola Pagett.]

As luck would have it, Jack Smight happened to catch an episode of *Upstairs, Downstairs* shortly after arriving in England and was immediately taken with Pagett. He grabbed the phone, called Stromberg, got him to turn on his TV and soon the producer was equally intrigued.

At first, Pagett was skeptical. "I thought it was another Hammer Horror, but couldn't have been more wrong," she recalled when I met her in 1975. "When I read the script, I wanted to be in it so badly, I persuaded Robin Phillips to let me go. I had promised to be in a play he was directing at the

Viking Queen.

Greenwich Theatre in London." (That play happened to be Tom Stoppard's *The House of Bernarda Alba*; Mia Farrow took over the role of Adela when Pagett bowed out. Coincidentally, Farrow had just turned down the role of Prima in *Dr. Frankenstein*.)

In *Dr. Frankenstein*, Pagett would ultimately be cast as Elizabeth Fanshawe (fiancée of Dr. Frankenstein) and as

Pagett in FTTS.

Mary Shelley in the prologue. She would work 36 days of the 76-day shoot, spread nonconsecutively from the first day to the very last, March 15 through July 2, 1973.

DOCTOR WHO?

In late-January 1973, Tom Baker's name came up as a possible Creature. At that time, Baker, 39, was still one year away from taking over the lead in *Doctor Who* (1974-1981), so was then-known for his stage work as a member of the National Theatre Company headed by Laurence Olivier. In fact, it was Olivier who had recommended Baker to portray Rasputin in Franklin J. Schaffner's Academy Award-winning movie *Nicholas and Alexandra* (1971) which had earned Baker *two* Golden Globe Award nominations for Best Supporting Actor and Most Promising Male Newcomer.

In late-January 1973, Stromberg and casting director Sally Nicholl rang up Baker and explained, "Christopher Isherwood has written the script, Tom, and we'd like to think about you for the part of the monster."

Tom Baker as Rasputin in *Nicholas and Alexandra*.

Tom Baker as *Doctor Who.*

"I was bowled over at the prospect," Baker recounted in his autobiography *Who on Earth is Tom Baker?* "'And who is going to direct it?' I asked, as if that mattered to me who was out of work. So they said 'Jack Smight,' and I said 'Ah,' as if that meant something to me."

Stromberg & Co. met with Baker and gave him a copy of the script. "I've never really had the chance to play monsters," Baker told them, dryly adding, "except of course in my private life." Stromberg liked his sense of humor.

"I left the meeting," Baker recalled, "thinking about being a darling monster and how my performance might get me another Golden Globe award [nomination]."

But nothing was definitive – and Isherwood was dead set against it. He appreciated Baker's abilities as an actor – and his towering height of 6' 3" was a plus –but the part of the Creature had been written for someone younger and, frankly, better looking. Isherwood reminded Stromberg that when the Creature first comes to life, Dr. Frankenstein takes one look at him and calls him "Beautiful" – and that the relationship between them hinges on an undercurrent of attraction. Stromberg agreed to keep their options open for a more ideal Creature.

THE DAME EDNA CONNECTION

On January 27, 1973, Isherwood and Bachardy had dinner with one of Britain's most acclaimed artists, Francis Bacon, and a few other friends including writer Stephen Spender and his 23-year-old daughter Elizabeth Spender – who would later appear in Terry Gilliam's *Brazil* (1985) and would become the spouse of Australian comic genius Barry Humphries aka Dame Edna Everage. Isherwood noted, "On impulse, I told Lizzie I would try to get her a part in

Elizabeth Spender (future wife of Barry Humphries) screams!

Spender faints.

Doris Shelton, mother of Jacque Shelton (Stromberg's lover).

Frankenstein; she belongs to Equity and she really is very good-looking."

That's how Dame Edna's future wife ended up as one of the ballroom guests – afforded two memorable reaction shots when the Creature decapitates Prima. In the first close-up, Spender shrieks in horror; the next time we see her, she faints.

Curiously, Sarah Douglas, 20, who, later that same year, played a vampire bride in Dan Curtis' *Dracula* and went on to fame as Kryptonian villainess Ursa in *Superman I & II*, is listed on the call-sheet as a "Ballroom Guest" for the first of the five days it took to shoot the party sequence – and also appears on the cast list with accurate contact and representation information. Upon close scrutiny of the ball sequence, however, Douglas is not readily discernible among the 150 revelers. When contacted in 2016 by her friend Eli Cameron, Douglas responded, "I only have a vague stirring of a memory."

Prominent among the extras at the ball was Jacque Shelton's mother Doris Shelton (1897-1979) – seen in her own medium shot, seated, in a blue gown and black chiffon cape, with a woman-in-red standing behind her. Doris has the appearance of a sweet little old lady – but looks can be deceiving. In a letter to a friend named Helen, dated February 1, 1971, Doris Shelton (who, in real-life, wore rhinestone-cat-eye-style glasses à la Dame Edna; see photo on page 210) reveals just how adventurous she was during an earlier trip to visit her son and his boyfriend:

Dear Helen,
Jacque and Hunt have been so sweet to me here in California and have been taking me just everywhere.

Last night, we saw a new version of that sweet little cartoon *Pinocchio*. When it plays in Fort Worth, you and Juanita must dash to see it. Pinocchio's nose doesn't grow, but something else sure does. It's hilarious. [NOTE: Doris is referring to the pornographic film *The Erotic Adventures Of Pinocchio* (1971).] Last week they took me down to Tijuana where we watched a stag movie being made. I'll tell you all about it when I get home. However, I only stayed for the first half hour just to see what it was all about and then I indignantly left. Next, we are going to one of those new European films entitled *Sexual Practices in Denmark*. Jacque and Hunt also took me to see *Myra Breckinridge* and there was a wonderful little scene where Mae West got laid in the back of her limousine by a big stud policeman. By the way, you'll think I'm crazy, Jacque gave me a see-through blouse for Christmas, and I wore it for the first time to a party last week. It may sound silly for a woman my age to wear a see-through blouse, but I caused a sensation at the party. Tell Nita that I am bringing her one as a gift. We'll probably never get her to wear it but I'm going to wear mine to the next garden club meeting. I really feel it's about time we all woke up and realized that this is 1971 and let's all agree to screw the Victorian past.
Love, Doris
P.S. Had my first stick of pot last week and am bringing some home to you.

On January 31, 1973, Isherwood and Bachardy completed the final 176-page revised draft of the teleplay. With their work officially done, the writers partied with Ingrid Bergman (who had starred in Isherwood's *Rage in Heaven*); dined with John Schlesinger and his companion Michael Childers; visited screenwriter Paul Dehn (*Goldfinger*, *Murder on the Orient Express*) and his longtime companion James Bernard (the Hammer Film composer); then vacationed in Switzerland and Italy (where they visited Gore Vidal) before returning to Los Angeles on February 15, 1973 – two days after it was announced that *Cabaret*, based on Isherwood's *The Berlin Stories*, had been nominated for 10 Academy Awards.

Basking in the glow of this success, Isherwood and Bachardy completed the first draft of their Mummy script for Stromberg, *The Lady from the Land of the Dead*, on March 1,

1973, for which Universal Television assigned the production number 81570. With the Writers Strike commencing March 6, it was imperative that they beat the clock.

INFLUX OF HUNKS

In the interim, Sally Nicholl was busy arranging auditions with practically every thespian in London to read for 40-some-odd available parts down to the one-liners. Held in a conference room at Lord Byron's former bachelor pad, there was a notable influx of handsome young blokes – no doubt instigated by the Lavender Hill Mob. One example was the casting of Julian Barnes, 23, as the dashing son of the local Baronet who first notices Prima (Jane Seymour) at a church service and subsequently dances with her at the ball. As they waltz, he tells Prima, "I love your cool hands."

In a 2015 interview for this book, Julian Barnes (who, incidentally, identifies as straight) recalled, "I met Hunt Stromberg socially through Allan Warren, an actor-photographer chum of mine who happened to be gay. Stromberg must have fancied me because I was summoned to audition for the role." [See Chapter 12 for my interview with Barnes.]

Another example was the casting of gay actor Dallas Adams as Felix, the strapping farmer-husband of Agatha (Jane Seymour). Like Barnes, Adams had also gotten to know Stromberg and Shelton socially before auditioning for the role. Among the screen titles for *True Story*, he was awarded the special credit "Introducing Dallas Adams" – even though he had previously appeared in at least seven television

Dallas Adams in FTTS.

Julian Barnes greets Margaret Leighton (in Bo Peep costume). Inset: Julian Barnes, *Horror Hotel*.

Seymour, Dallas Adams, Stromberg.

Above: Dallas Adams Left: Dallas Adams & Jane Seymour, candlelight. Below Left: Seymour & Adams frolicking. Below Center: Adams & Seymour listening at the door. Below Right: Seymour discovers Adams is dead.

THE EPIC SAGA BEHIND *FRANKENSTEIN: THE TRUE STORY*

programs and movies, including *The Abominable Dr. Phibes* as "2nd Police Official."

Years later, Adams gained notoriety among *Doctor Who* enthusiasts for portraying Professor Howard Foster in the 4-part *Doctor Who: Planet of Fire* (1984). According to *Doctor Who* producer John Nathan-Turner, in the early 1980s, Adams was "the first man to win a gay palimony case in UK legal history." Tragically, Adams would succumb to AIDS in 1991 at age 44.

A great deal of attention was also given to casting the brief role of William Frankenstein, the younger brother of Dr. Frankenstein, who would appear shirtless in a rowboat before diving into the water and drowning. The part went to a strikingly handsome 20-year-old actor named Karl Howman who had recently appeared in the BAFTA-nominated film *That'll Be the Day* (1973) with David Essex and Ringo Starr; and, soon after *Dr. Frankenstein*,

Karl Howman.

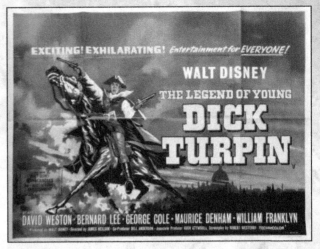

would go on to co-star in Michael Apted's BAFTA-nominated sequel *Stardust* (1974) as Stevie, the keyboardist, for the Stray Cats, the fictional rock 'n' roll band led by Jim MacLaine (David Essex). Howman later became well-known to British audiences for *Brush Strokes* (1986-1991), *Mulberry* (1992-1993) and *EastEnders* (2014-2016).

In a 2016 interview for this book, Howman recalled, "The director and the producer said, 'You're the reason that Frankenstein creates the monster because when you die, he wants to bring you back to life.' They gave me a big build up. But, truthfully, it really wasn't about who could act the best. I got the part because I slightly resembled Leonard Whiting – more so than the other candidates they were seeing at the time."

Unbeknownst to Howman, there was another factor in his favor. Stromberg had admired the actor in the role of the "1st Homosexual Lover" in Pasolini's *The Canterbury Tales* (1972) and had requested that Sally Nicholl bring him in for an audition.

The accident victim who has his arm amputated was played by a handsome chap named David Weston, 34, who had previously co-starred with Richard Burton, Peter O'Toole and Sir John Gielgud in *Becket* (1964); with Lon Chaney Jr. in *Witchcraft* (1964); and with Vincent Price

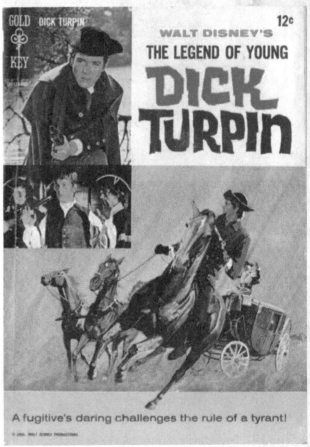
A fugitive's daring challenges the rule of a tyrant!

and Jane Asher in Roger Corman's *The Masque of the Red Death* (1964). He played Romeo opposite Jane Asher's Juliet in an ITV production of *Romeo and Juliet* (1962). And, in 1966, Weston played the title role in Walt Disney's *The Legend of Young Dick Turpin* which co-starred 15-year-old Leonard Whiting as an Artful Dodger-like pickpocket named Jimmy

David Weston in *Witchcraft*.

the Dip. Weston also played Jane Seymour's husband in *The Pathfinders: Fly There, Walk Back* (Thames Television, October 18, 1972).

In a 2016 interview for this book, Weston recalled, "The casting director Sally Nicholl had cast me in *Becket*, you see. She remembered me and had me come in to meet the director and producer on *Dr. Frankenstein*. It was a very small role but a very well-paid job because we first shot the interior scene when I'm having my arm cut off by David McCallum [filmed April 5-6, 1973]; and then, later, we shot the outdoor scene where Leonard Whiting sees that my arm is injured and takes me to the hospital in his coach [filmed June 6, 1973]. There were two months between those scenes and I was paid the whole time to be on hold, so it was a very good salary by the end."

Mainly a stage actor for the Royal Shakespeare Company for which he has starred in 29 productions, Weston has

Whiting and Peter Sallis in church.

Stromberg (left) confers with David Weston (right) at the amputation table; McCallum is in the background.

Yootha Joyce talks to Whiting in hospital.

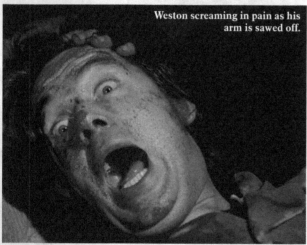

Weston screaming in pain as his arm is sawed off.

Arnold Diamond complains to Whiting in coach.

authored five books, including the humorous memoir *Covering McKellen: An Understudy's Tale* (2011) recounting his chaotic experiences as understudy for Sir Ian McKellen on a tour of *King Lear*; and two fictional accounts of the further adventures of Charles Dickens' the Artful Dodger: *Dodger Down Under* and *Dodger Treads the Boards*.

NO PART TOO SMALL

Also joining the supporting ranks of the cast would be:

Tony Then in FTTS.

1. Peter Sallis (*The Curse of the Werewolf*, *Taste the Blood of Dracula*, the voice of Wallace in *Wallace & Gromit*) as the priest to whom Dr. Frankenstein confesses.
2. Yootha Joyce (*Die! Die! My Darling!*, *Our Mother's House*) as Mrs. McGregor, the head nurse at the hospital.
3. Arnold Diamond (*The Revenge of Frankenstein*, *Paranoiac*, *Maniac*) as the impatient coach passenger.
4. Tony Then (*The Rocky Horror Picture Show*, *Doctor Who:*

Kim Teoh in FTTS.

Stromberg & Kim Teoh on location for FTTS.

Michael Goldie as workman in *Horror of Frankenstein*.

Derek Deadman.

Pier Mason meets Sarrazin in park.

Pier Mason talks to Sarrazin & Whiting in the park.

Left: Headshot of Pier Mason. Right: Pier Mason (right) with colleague at the Corona Stage School. Below: Trade ad.

The Talons of Weng-Chiang, and *The New Avengers*) as Polidori's Chinese Servant #1.

5. Kim Teoh (*Doctor Who: The Talons of Weng-Chiang*) as Chinese Servant #2.

6. Michael Goldie (his third Frankenstein credit following *Frankenstein Must Be Destroyed* and *The Horror of Frankenstein*; plus *Doctor Who: The Wheel in Space*; *Robin Hood: Prince of Thieves*) as the 1st Sailor on the ship.

7. Tony Aitken (*Jabberwocky*, *Agatha Christie: Poirot*, *The Remains of the Day*, *Coronation Street*) as the 3rd Sailor. Contacted in 2016, Aitken recalled, "*Frankenstein* was my very first film, though I had done a few guest roles on television, including an episode of *Upstairs, Downstairs* [London Weekend Television, November 4, 1972] when I first met Nicola Pagett. Nicola and I got on very well and we were pleasantly surprised when we were reunited on the *Frankenstein* set to do this scene together on the deck of the ship."

PIER MASON

Television:
LITTLE GIRL   —Thames
 ('Armchair Theatre')
Jane in
 INHERITORS   —Harlech
DIXON OF DOCK GREEN   —BBC

Film:
SAVAGE MESSIAH   —Russ Films
DR. FRANKENSTEIN   —Universal Pictures
SPECIAL BRANCH   —Euston Films
ARMCHAIR CINEMA   —Euston Films
COMMERCIALS

Ron Howard

3278

8. Derek Deadman (*Jabberwocky*, *Doctor Who: The Invasion of Time*, *Time Bandits*, *Never Say Never Again*, *Brazil*, *Robin Hood: Prince of Thieves*, *Harry Potter and the Sorcerer's Stone*) as the 4th Sailor.

9. Pier Mason (no relation to James; 6-year-old student from the Corona Stage School who later appeared in *Savage Messiah*, *The Mirror Crack'd*, *Pink Floyd The Wall*) as the Little Girl in the Park who speaks to the Creature. Contacted in 2016, Pier Mason recalled, "I was accompanied to the set by a chaperone from Corona, which was standard practice." For her one day of shooting on April 9, 1973, she earned £10.00 British Sterling, minus 25% commission for the school.

10. Peter Glaze of *Crackerjack!* fame as the Police Constable assisting Sir John Gielgud.

11. Rosamund Greenwood (*Curse of the Demon*, *The Prince and the Showgirl*, *Village of the Damned*, *The Witches*) as Prima's dressmaker.

Peter Glaze in FTTS.

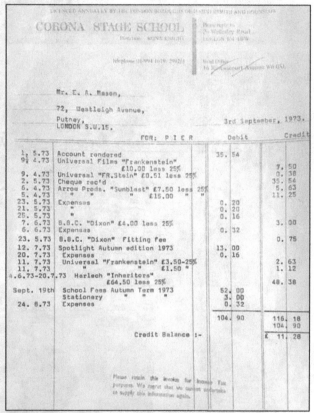

Above: Accounting sheet for Pier Mason's fees. This picture: Grown-up Pier Mason in 2017 holding LSoH issue devoted to FTTS!

Nicola Pagett and Peter Glaze.

Rosamund Greenwood tries to remove Seymour's choker.

THE EPIC SAGA BEHIND *FRANKENSTEIN: THE TRUE STORY*

Dermot Walsh with his real-life wife Hazel Court.

12. Dermot Walsh (top-billed star of *Ghost Ship* and *Undercover Agent*, both co-starring his real-life wife Hazel Court) as the priest giving the service when Clerval follows Frankenstein into the church.

PAGING QUEEN ELIZABETH

But what about those illusive big-league "names" Stromberg was determined to get? Once his feet were firmly planted on British soil, he resurrected a fanciful idea he'd put aside years ago when his project of *A Christmas Carol* was sidelined. He got in touch with his lifelong family friend Douglas Fairbanks, Jr., with two proposals: One was an offer to play the part of Sir Richard Fanshawe, father of Elizabeth and future father-in-law of Dr. Frankenstein. More pointedly, however, Stromberg wanted Fairbanks to extend an invitation to Queen Elizabeth to appear in a special introduction for *Dr. Frankenstein* since, after all, Mary Shelley and her novel were two of England's proudest national treasures.

Daniel Craig as James Bond escorts the real-life Queen Elizabeth to the 2012 Olympics in a comedy sketch directed by Danny Boyle.

Stromberg's colleagues thought he was crazy to think that the Queen would actually endorse a movie – and yet, thirty-nine years later, she was persuaded to film a sketch for the 2012 Olympics, directed by Danny Boyle, featuring Daniel Craig as James Bond, as a cross promotion for *Skyfall*.

In any event, Fairbanks' royal request was respectfully declined and the actor passed on the role of Sir Fanshawe.

THE JAMES MASON EFFECT

Stromberg's unlucky streak was finally broken when he traveled to Switzerland to the home of 63-year-old James Mason (1909-1984), who, by then, had been Oscar-nominated twice – for *A Star Is Born* and *Georgy Girl* – and later receive a third nomination for *The Verdict*. His other credits included Disney's *20,000 Leagues Under the Sea*, Hitchcock's *North by Northwest* and Kubrick's *Lolita*. When Stromberg approached Mason, he had recently completed filming Herbert Ross' all-star whodunit *The Last of Sheila* (written by Stephen Sondheim and Anthony Perkins) and John Huston's *The MacKintosh Man* opposite Paul Newman.

Even though Stromberg had known Mason socially for years, he very carefully strategized his approach. "I purposefully left the title page off," Stromberg explained, "because I was afraid he would turn it down as just another Frankenstein movie."

Stromberg *did* mention that the writers were Isherwood and Bachardy, knowing full well that the actor knew them socially. In fact, Mason had done a sitting with Bachardy in 1962 for a portrait that can be seen in the artist's 2014 coffee-table book *Hollywood* (and in this book on page 280).

It was also incredibly coincidental and fortuitous that the setting of the prologue was Switzerland's Lake Geneva – the very spot where Mason had been residing since 1963, in the foothills of Mont-Pèlerin. Standing with Mason by that very lake, Stromberg slathered on the flattery by stating, "You are my first and only choice to play the grandiloquent Dr. Polidori."

The young James Mason.

Mason headshot FTTS.

First and only choice? *Seriously?!* Stromberg was gambling that Mason would not be in communication with the hordes of luminaries who had already turned down the role, including Richard Burton, Marlon Brando, Laurence Olivier, Burt Lancaster, Orson Welles, Anthony Quinn, Rex Harrison, Paul Scofield, Peter Ustinov, Oliver Reed… and perhaps even Colonel Sanders, for all we know.

Stromberg conveniently failed to mention that *Dr. Frankenstein* was a TV movie – though, technically, it would be released theatrically in Europe where Mason lived. What concerned Stromberg more was the fact that Mason had mixed feelings about playing villains – and did not want to be typecast as such.

In a 1973 interview for *Photoplay Film Monthly*, Mason said, "When I went to Hollywood, I was always trying to get away from sinister characters. If you have a truly romantic image, it gives you a very strong position in the movies. You're leading man material, and from that you can go on to whatever parts you wish to play. Sometimes, I'll admit, in an ordinary straightforward drama, the villain is more interesting than the hero. But only sometimes. When I was cast as a villain in some of those Hollywood pictures, the dice were loaded to such an extent that the character had no chance of winning in any sense at all. He was not only the villain – he was also the loser. Now, losers are not good to play from a career point of view. And I always resent being asked to lose. Then, even in roles which I thought were sympathetic, like those I played in *A Star Is Born* and *Lolita*, my performance was generally regarded as the portrayal of a rather sinister individual."

Agnes Moorehead, Jacque Shelton, Stromberg, Mason.

THE EPIC SAGA BEHIND *FRANKENSTEIN: THE TRUE STORY*

Smight, Mason and wife Clarissa Kaye.

McCallum, Mason, Stromberg (on day they shot the aborted prologue).

20,000 Leagues Under the Sea: **Above Left: Mason as Captain Nemo. Above Center: UK quad poster. Above Right: With the giant squid** in *20,000 Leagues Under the Sea.* **Below Left: Mason & Judy Garland,** *A Star Is Born.* **Below Right: Cary Grant, Eva Marie Saint, Hitchcock & Mason,** *North by Northwest.*

To Stromberg's great relief, however, Mason cottoned to Polidori immediately. "When I was offered the part," Mason recalled in 1973, "I was fascinated because I was so struck by the quality of the script. Since I have played one or two sympathetic parts recently, I can afford now to play a few heavies. At any rate, I no longer fear the typecasting syndrome."

Nonetheless, Mason drove a hard bargain. He demanded $300,000 – which Stromberg and Universal were forced to relinquish, given that time was running out and so were name star candidates. When shooting on locations away from Pinewood Studios, he would be provided with a luxurious 20-foot Double Century dressing room trailer. And, as an added perk, his wife, Australian actress Clarissa Kaye, 42, would also be granted a supporting role in the movie with featured billing among the other guest stars and a commensurate salary.

Still in the honeymoon phase of their 1971 marriage, Mason was anxious to promote the acting career of his new bride – known for playing the mother of Mick Jagger in Tony Richardson's *Ned Kelly.* Mason and Kaye met while appearing together in Michael Powell's *Age of Consent* and Mason pulled strings to share the screen with her again in *The MacKintosh Man.* Following *Dr. Frankenstein,* the nepotism would continue on Tobe Hooper's 1979 miniseries of Stephen King's *Salem's Lot* in which Mason played "Richard K. Straker" and Kaye played "Marjorie Glick" (who becomes a ferocious vampiress).

"I'm in love with my husband and I enjoy working with him," Kaye explained. "I prefer to work only when it is something we can do together."

Kaye was granted the role of "Lady Fanshawe," mother of "Elizabeth," and future mother-in-law of "Dr. Frankenstein." (At 42, she would only be fifteen years older than her daughter in the film, played by 27-year-old Nicola Pagett.)

During the shooting of *Dr. Frankenstein,* Mason and his wife were given $1,500 per week for living expenses out of which they would pay for their own accommodations. Instead of a fancy hotel in the hubbub of London, the Masons opted to rent a bucolic country home near Pinewood Studios. Built in 1690, the historic residence was The White Cottage on Village Road in Denham Village, Buckinghamshire. (This same village was the location for several sequences in *Dr. Frankenstein.*)

Clarissa Kaye recalled, "We didn't realize that we would become, with the signing of our lease, foster parents to at least five-hundred birds! I've never been much of a bird fancier – or watcher, but they are indeed fascinating creatures with definite personalities, and some of them are quite mesmerizing."

Being an authority on birds, Stromberg's boyfriend Jacque Shelton came over often to share his knowledge – resulting in the Masons developing a lasting passion for winged creatures. In fact, the following year, when Mason was in Louisiana shooting *Mandingo,* he and Kaye visited Stromberg and Shelton at their Double S Ranch in Texas to see for themselves the menagerie of birds and other wildlife.

During my research, I befriended James Duke Mason, grandson of James Mason, a writer, activist and politician. Born in Los Angeles in 1992, Duke is the only child of Belinda Carlisle (lead vocalist of the Go-Go's) and Morgan Mason (son of James Mason and his first wife Pamela Kellino Mason; Morgan was a former White House aide and

THE EPIC SAGA BEHIND *FRANKENSTEIN: THE TRUE STORY*

executive producer of *sex, lies and videotape*). Duke is the only grandchild of James Mason.

As an advocate for the LGBTQ+ community of which he himself is an out and proud member, Duke served as an official surrogate for the Presidential campaigns of Barack Obama in 2012 and Hillary Clinton in 2016. In 2015, at the age of just 23, he was appointed to the West Hollywood Lesbian & Gay Advisory Board.

I asked Duke about his grandfather and his fierce portrayal of "Dr. Polidori" in *Frankenstein: The True Story*. He was eager to help but had never actually seen the film – so I gave him a DVD with high hopes that he would respond favorably.

"I absolutely loved watching it," Duke later told me. "I watched it with my Dad, who hadn't seen it since it was

Clarissa Kaye as a vampiress in *Salem's Lot*.

Top Left: Clarissa Kaye & Mason peruse script for *Salem's Lot*.
Top Right: Mason in *Salem's Lot* (with kid and vampire).
Above: Mason with vampire, *Salem's Lot*.

Mason, Kaye, Wilding, Pagett, Stromberg at Cliveden.

Two headshots of Mason in FTTS.

first aired! It was a great, entertaining and enlightening experience for both of us."

Duke was kind enough to write a brief essay for this book about James Mason: "Over the course of my life, I've had an unusual relationship with my grandfather. Sadly, we never actually met – he died eight years before I was born. But I remember, going back to when I was a kid, getting to know him by watching his films. First I saw him as Captain Nemo in *20,000 Leagues under the Sea*, a constant staple of my childhood. As I got older, my parents showed me some of his more mature fare such as *A Star Is Born* and *Lolita*. It wasn't until recently that I actually got to 'meet' the real-life James Mason through an interview compilation that was posted on YouTube. Until then, I only really knew my grandfather through the various characters he portrayed – and, for me, the character of Dr. Polidori in *Frankenstein: The True Story* is among his most fascinating and revealing. As a gay man, I often wondered growing up what my grandfather would've thought of my sexuality. My Dad assured me that James would've had no problem with having a gay grandson. After all, he reminded me, my grandfather had many close friends who were prominent openly gay men, including Christopher Isherwood and Don Bachardy. In fact, my grandfather sat for a Bachardy portrait in 1962 and, to this day, my father has on the wall a series of portraits that Don painted of my grandmother (James' first wife Pamela) and my aunt Portland. It was also interesting to hear from my father how much James truly loved Hunt Stromberg Jr. who produced *Frankenstein: The True Story* and was also gay. It's clear from watching *Frankenstein: The True Story* that my grandfather totally understood and appreciated the queer subtext. Not only is his performance whimsical and even, you might say, a little camp, but I am sure he had conversations with Christopher and Don about the true story behind the character and his motivations. It comes through in the way

John Tristram. (Alleged lover of James Mason.)

Top: Mason with son Morgan Mason. Center: Grown up Morgan Mason, wife Belinda Carlisle, son James Duke Mason. Bottom: James Duke Mason & Sam with LSoH.

CHAPTER TWO: PRE-PRODUCTION

he plays the role, and it was incredibly enlightening for me to see that. I only wish I had seen the movie sooner, as it truly is groundbreaking and way ahead of its time! I now count it among my favorite films that my grandfather made, and there were many of them!"

Because of the proliferation of queer folk among the cast and crew of this movie, it is my duty to point out that in the book *Male Beauty, Postwar Masculinity in Theater, Film, and Physique* (State University of New York Press, 2014), author Kenneth Krauss reported the claim that John Tristram, the openly-gay British-born bodybuilder, Mr. America contestant, hardcore porn model for Colt Studio, and later a professor of French at UCLA, "was the longtime lover of actor James Mason." There is no way to definitively corroborate this assertion but, quite curiously, among Hunt Stromberg Jr.'s papers, John Tristram's name appears several times on party guest lists and Christmas card lists. When I asked a gay friend of James Mason about it, the person (who wished to remain anonymous) responded, "Publicly, James had an eye for the ladies but privately he was less discriminating." I tend to believe that where there's smoke, there's a flame or two.

Mason would end up shooting 37 nonconsecutive days out of the 76-day schedule, from March 20 through June 24. (He would later shoot an introduction as himself, upping his day-count to 38.) His wife went in front of the camera 14 days, spread from March 20 through May 25.

"I used James Mason as my bell cow," Stromberg told a reporter. "I knew if he said 'yes,' the others I wanted would likely say 'yes,' too."

ELIZABETH TAYLOR'S SECOND EX

That bell cow tactic was immediately put to the test upon Stromberg's return from Switzerland when he happened to run into British actor Michael Wilding, star of two Hitchcock films – *Under Capricorn* and *Stage Fright*. They had met on many prior occasions, including the time Wilding had guest-starred on *The Alfred Hitchcock Hour* in 1963 when Stromberg was a bigwig at CBS – and in 1966 when both men were benefactors of Jack Larson's play *The Candied House*. Despite his many credits, however, Wilding was perhaps most widely recognized as having been the second of Elizabeth Taylor's five husbands-and-counting (she would end up marrying eight times – twice to Richard Burton).

On the spot, Stromberg offered Wilding the part of Sir Richard Fanshawe, husband of Lady Fanshawe (Clarissa Kaye) and father of Elizabeth (Nicola Pagett).

Michael Wilding in FTTS.

Wilding & Stromberg, coach outside Cliveden.

The Fanshawe Family: Wilding, Clarissa Kaye & Nicola Pagett.

84   THE EPIC SAGA BEHIND *FRANKENSTEIN: THE TRUE STORY*

"Who is the star of the picture?" Wilding inquired. Nonchalantly, Stromberg replied, "James Mason." Taking the bait, Wilding said, "Count me in."

He would work 12 days, spread from March 20 through May 25.

SEXY BEAST

Michael & brother Pierre Sarrazin.

Sarrazin with soulful eyes.

The next star to join the party was Michael Sarrazin, 32, who had received wide acclaim for his breakthrough role as a marathon dancer opposite Jane Fonda in Sydney Pollack's *They Shoot Horses, Don't They?* (1969) – for which he had been nominated for a BAFTA Award. The film had been nominated for eight Academy Awards and won an Oscar for Gig Young. The movie's success elevated Sarrazin to A-list status and he was considered one of the industry's top young leading men.

In the audio commentary of the Kino Lorber Blu-ray of *They Shoot Horses, Don't They?*, Jane Fonda remarked, "Michael Sarrazin was just perfect for the part. He reminded me of my dad when he was young. Soft eyed. Gentle, lonely, sad, beautiful. That's what he was, and that's what the character was, and it was very easy to care for him deeply, both as the character, in the character, and in real life."

On the same audio commentary for *They Shoot Horses, Don't They?*, Michael Sarrazin recalled, "For the first ten days of shooting... everyone was coming up to me and saying, 'You look like Hank Fonda in *Grapes of Wrath*,' which made me very nervous because I thought... maybe I'll get up to Jane [Fonda] and she'll say 'I don't want to deal with him. He looks too much like my father.' So, on the day when... we did the first little rehearsal... she said 'I'm glad to meet you. You look just like Bambi.'"

That radiant vulnerability was Michael Sarrazin's stock-in-trade. In a 2016 interview for this book, his brother Pierre Sarrazin remarked, "People always said Michael had the most soulful eyes of any actor in Hollywood."

Born in Québec, Canada, Michael Sarrazin grew up in Montreal. He dropped out of high school to become an actor,

gaining local fame in 1965 on *Festival*, the anthology series on the CBC, starring opposite Geneviève Bujold in *Roméo and Jeannette*. That same year, a Universal Pictures talent scout spotted him in the Toronto stage production of *Silences of Love* and he was signed to a seven-year contract with the studio, prompting his relocation to Los Angeles.

In a 1965 interview for the *Montreal Gazette*, Sarrazin seemed a bit trepidatious about the long-term commitment, saying, "Lots of actors – and starlets – go to Hollywood, get a contract and are never heard from again. I expect I'll be put to work on TV films like the Hitchcock show or even *The Munsters*." (Oddly enough, *both* examples he randomly mentioned in jest happened to be shows that Stromberg had shepherded at CBS; and, of course, *The Munsters* was a distant relative of the Frankenstein movie he would eventually do for Universal.)

Initially, his worst fears came true. During the first three years of the deal, Universal assigned him small roles in only four TV shows (most notably Rod Serling's *Doomsday Flight*, a 1966 TV movie) and a forgettable part in his first theatrical film *Gunfight in Abilene* (1967), a routine Western starring Bobby Darin.

His first major role wasn't even for Universal. On loan-out to 20th Century-Fox, Sarrazin was cast opposite George C. Scott in Irvin Kershner's *The Flim-Flam Man* (1967), about a veteran con artist who takes on a young Army deserter as his protégé. Sarrazin got rave reviews – which woke up the folks at Universal City, resulting in second-billed roles in two Universal Westerns: *A Man Called Gannon* and *Journey to Shiloh*.

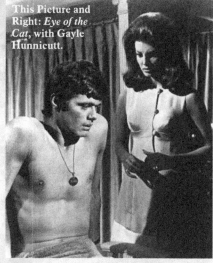

This Picture and Right: *Eye of the Cat*, with Gayle Hunnicutt.

Sarrazin & Jane Fonda, *They Shoot Horses, Don't They?*

This Picture and Right: Sarrazin & Ursula Andress

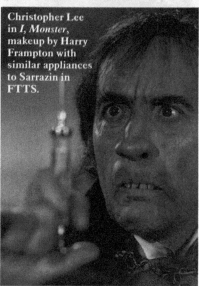

Christopher Lee in *I, Monster*, makeup by Harry Frampton with similar appliances to Sarrazin in FTTS.

20th Century-Fox borrowed Sarrazin again for *The Sweet Ride* (1968) which earned him a Golden Globe nomination. Accordingly, Universal awarded Sarrazin his first top-billed lead in the thriller *Eye of the Cat* (1968) from a script by Joseph (*Psycho*) Stefano. Then, Universal cast him opposite Julie Christie for *In Search of Gregory* (1969).

Next, director John Schlesinger screen-tested Sarrazin for the role of Joe Buck, the hustler, in United Artists' *Midnight Cowboy* (1969), and decided to cast him opposite Dustin Hoffman – but once negotiations got serious for a loan-out agreement, Universal got greedy. Suddenly, producer Jerome Hellman was informed by an unnamed Universal executive that the studio's price tag for Sarrazin's services had tripled since Hellman's first inquiry a week earlier. In an interview in *Vanity Fair*, Hellman recalled, "I said to John [Schlesinger], 'I want to hang up on that prick.' And John said, 'Go ahead.' So I slammed the fucking phone down." Instead, Jon Voight got the part and the movie went on to win Oscars for Best Picture, Best Director and Best Screenplay, not to mention Oscar nominations for Hoffman and Voight – who won a Golden Globe.

Making amends for its egregious miscalculation, Universal decided to loan Sarrazin at a reasonable price for *They Shoot Horses, Don't They?* (1969), which finally solidified his place at the A-list table. Universal next assigned him major parts in Paul Newman's *Sometimes a Great Notion* (1970)

and Lamont Johnson's *The Groundstar Conspiracy* (1972) – in which Sarrazin played a modern variant on Frankenstein's Creature, disfigured and suffering from amnesia. Then, Universal loosened its hold on the actor for several more loan-out agreements with other studios.

When Voight turned down *Dr. Frankenstein*, Universal's George Santoro immediately thought of Sarrazin as an alternate casting choice. Santoro also knew that Sarrazin's seven-year contract with Universal was coming to an end in 1973 so, if the studio planned to use the actor for anything else, it was now or never. After deliberating with Stromberg, Smight and Sheinberg on the matter, it was decided to give Sarrazin the choice of playing either Dr. Frankenstein *or* the Creature.

"When I was first offered the movie," Sarrazin recalled, "I said 'Forget it!' I didn't want to make a standard horror film."

They sent him the material anyway and pointed out the name of the author. Sarrazin did a double take: "How often do you get a Christopher Isherwood script? I thought it was one of the best scripts I've read since I've been in Hollywood."

The question now was which part did Sarrazin prefer to play? Creator or creation? Though, given his towering stature of 6' 2", it seemed obvious he should play the manmade giant.

"The most challenging part was the Creature," Sarrazin concluded. "Isherwood and his collaborator Don Bachardy

Above: Artwork of beautiful Sarrazin by Frederick Cooper.
Far Left: Artwork of Sarrazin in lab, by Dave Matsuoka.
Left: Artwork of beautiful Sarrazin & deteriorated Sarrazin, by Dave Matsuoka.

CHAPTER TWO: PRE-PRODUCTION

took a very realistic approach, bordering on the plausible. There was nothing evil about the Creature. He was somehow touching. Very interesting part, a complex kind of thing."

Nevertheless, Sarrazin was apprehensive about what sort of makeup they had in mind for the Creature: "The character created by Karloff, who was an excellent actor, was a mechanized monster, complete with nuts, bolts and encased in makeup. This was one of the facets that most concerned me, for in this version of the story, the Creature is a young man with great expressiveness."

"Michael was scared to do it," Stromberg told a reporter, "because he thought he would be in a rubber suit."

Sarrazin was worried the monster makeup might turn out like Kiwi Kingston in Hammer Films' *The Evil Of Frankenstein* which had been financed and released by Universal Pictures the year before Sarrazin had been put on contract at Universal.

Stromberg was not about to let that happen. "When I was a kid, my father produced a couple of Lon Chaney pictures," Stromberg Jr. recalled. "I was already mesmerized by him as the Phantom of the Opera and the Hunchback of Notre Dame. When I met him, I was quite young and curious about his makeup kit. He was very kind and patiently showed me some tricks he used. He told me he never wanted his makeup to cover too much of his face. The camera had to see his facial expressions. I never forgot it – and, of course, that's exactly what I wanted for Michael Sarrazin, too."

Sarrazin recalled, "I was assured by producer Hunt Stromberg Jr. not to worry, that Harry Frampton, who had been signed to devise the makeup, was an expert. Among Harry's credits is *Kind Hearts and Coronets*, the film in which Alec Guinness had played eight roles, including a dowager Duchess!"

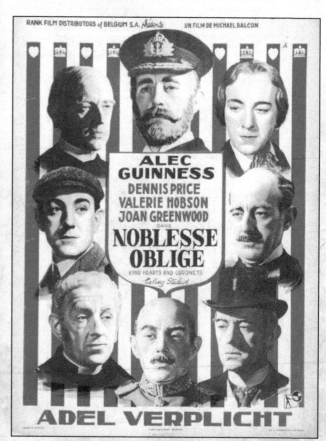

Above Top: Artwork of deteriorated Sarrazin by Brux. Above: Artwork of beautiful Sarrazin in bandages, by Ron Hezekiah.

Frampton had more recently transformed Christopher Lee into a Mr. Hyde-like character for *I, Monster* – with appliances that resembled the ones he would create for Sarrazin.

Stromberg added, "Once Michael understood the concept, he agreed."

There was one awkward issue to clear up, however. Tom Baker was under the false impression that he had bagged the role of the Creature. "And then, you've guessed it, the phone rang," Baker recalled. "It was Hunt Stromberg, the producer. The studio wanted a 'name' for the monster and also Christopher [Isherwood] would prefer somebody who was er, well, handsome. There was nothing I could say to that, except as far as I knew Dr. Frankenstein was not a plastic surgeon and the monster had never been beautiful before. Hunt Stromberg is a prince of a man, and he was sympathetic, very sympathetic, to my point but the studio was the studio, 'you know'. So that was that. I would not get to meet James Mason after all."

That's what Tom Baker thought at the time. But the fat lady hadn't sung just yet.

In a 1973 interview for the *San Francisco Chronicle*, Michael Sarrazin recalled, "I went to England five weeks ahead of the company to work on the makeup with Harry Frampton."

Leaving behind his home in Los Angeles, Sarrazin arrived in London the first week of February 1973. While in the UK for the next five months (required for 50 days of the 76-day shoot), Sarrazin was put up at Blakes Hotel, 33 Roland Gardens, in South Kensington – a 5-star luxury hotel that later, in 1978, would be completely revamped by acclaimed interior designer Anouska Hempel – the vamp from *Scars of Dracula*.

HOW ABOUT JACQUELINE BISSET?

Reveling in the news about Sarrazin, Stromberg saw this as an auspicious opportunity to go after Sarrazin's real-life movie-star girlfriend, Golden Globe-nominated actress Jacqueline Bisset, 28, to play Agatha / Prima. Sarrazin and Bisset met in 1966 while shooting *The Sweet Ride*, fell in love, and starred together again in *Believe in Me* (1971). Stromberg had every reason to believe that Bisset, born and raised in England, would jump at the chance to return to her motherland to play the female creature opposite her real-life beau.

Well, that was the wishful reasoning, at least. Sarrazin was not so gung-ho to do a third film with Bisset. "We are not a

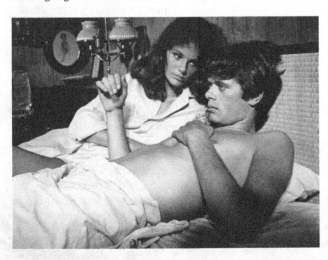

Leonard Whiting as Dr. Frankenstein, FTTS.

Whiting in lab, FTTS.

team," he told a reporter. "We are not a vaudeville act. I bust my tail twelve hours a day, and do you think I want to come home and meet the person I've been working with all day?"

Bisset was not so opposed to the idea, responding, "I love acting so much that it's not like work anyway. I guess the truth is I love it more than Michael. Lucky for me, he understands the drive, although it isn't a quality in me he loves."

Regardless, the proposal was moot since she was already committed to star in *The Man from Acapulco* to be followed by *Murder on the Orient Express*. Unbeknownst to all, however, she would eventually become indirectly involved – for better or worse.

THE ROMEO COMPLEX

Up until then, the two youngest actors to play Dr. Frankenstein were Colin Clive, 31, and Ralph Bates, 30, in *Frankenstein* and *The Horror of Frankenstein*, respectively. Inspired by the direction Isherwood and Bachardy had taken with the character in their script, Stromberg was sold on the idea that Frankenstein's inexperience was vital to the story and, therefore, he became determined to cast the youngest actor ever to play the part.

"I felt that a creature should be created out of the madness of youth," Stromberg was quoted in *The Hollywood Reporter*, "and that Dr. Frankenstein should be young."

So, while reviewing Sally Nicholl's list of available young hunks, the name Leonard Whiting practically leapt off the page. The 22-year-old actor had become world-famous five years earlier starring in Zeffirelli's *Romeo and Juliet*, which was Oscar-nominated for Best Picture and Best Director. Whiting himself had *won* the Golden Globe Award for Most Promising Male Newcomer. The film was also noted for casting the youngest actors ever seen in the

leading roles: Whiting was 17 and Olivia Hussey was only 15. What really grabbed headlines, though, was that both appeared nude on-screen – fleetingly – with Whiting butt-naked on the bed the morning after they had consummated their relationship. It was tastefully done, mind you, but highly provocative considering their ages. Amazingly, because the movie was Shakespeare, many schools across America took students in groups to see the film (yours truly among them, at age 12) – despite its brief nudity which was deemed academically artistic.

Hormones raged from coast-to-coast and abroad, resulting in relentless coverage in teen magazines, whipping up Beatles-like hysteria. In addition to hordes of screaming girls, Whiting was also worshipped from afar by certain male admirers – becoming an unintentional, underground gay icon. This Romeo baggage was precisely what Stromberg wanted for his younger and sexier Dr. Frankenstein. Stromberg also liked the fact that Whiting's height was just 5' 8" which would allow Sarrazin to impressively tower over him by half-a-foot. A meeting was arranged with Whiting and they gave him a copy of the teleplay.

"I took the script home, read it the same afternoon," Whiting said in 1973. "I couldn't put it down. I think it's one of the best scripts I've read."

Stromberg insisted on a screen-test before making a final decision. Directed by Jack Smight outside St. Mary the Virgin Church (in Hambleden Village, Buckinghamshire, near Pinewood Studios), Leonard Whiting performed a scene with Nicola Pagett (as Elizabeth) following the funeral of Dr. Frankenstein's brother William. Stromberg

This Picture and Below: Leonard Whiting & Nicola Pagett in scene that had previously been filmed as their screentest.

McCallum, Robert Vaughn, Leo G. Carroll, *The Man from U.N.C.L.E.*

and Shelton were on the sidelines, scrutinizing the actor. When it was done, Stromberg made up his mind that Whiting was perfect for not only Dr. Frankenstein, but also Percy Shelley in the prologue. He would work 69 days out of the 76-day schedule, far more than any other actor in the cast. [See Chapter 7 for my interview with Whiting.] (Fortuitously, *Romeo and Juliet* would be given a nationwide theatrical re-release by Paramount in the fall of 1973, bolstering Whiting's stardom in the weeks leading up to NBC-TV's premiere broadcast of *Frankenstein: The True Story* in November 1973.)

THE SCOT FROM U.N.C.L.E.

For the role of Henry Clerval / Lord Byron, Stromberg needed someone more confident and experienced than Frankenstein, someone who would be a credible mentor to the young doctor – and, at the same time, a believable former protégé of Polidori. His age had to lie somewhere between Leonard Whiting and James Mason. After Anthony Perkins and Alan Bates had passed on the role, Stromberg decided to offer it to Sean Connery, 42, who had recently said, "Never again," after six turns as James Bond – until, of course, he later returned to the role in *Never Say Never Again* (1983). At the time, however, Connery was trying to break away from typecasting and so, with a choking dose of irony, he had just committed to star in John Boorman's *Zardoz* for the exact same time period at the surprisingly-economical rate of only $200,000 – considerably less than the $1.25 million he commanded as Bond in *Diamonds Are Forever* (1971). Following *Zardoz*, he accepted a mere $100,000 to be

among the all-star ensemble of *Murder on the Orient Express* – demonstrating he may very well have been affordable for *Dr. Frankenstein* had he been available.

Universal's head of production George Santoro recommended another handsome Scotland-born actor who was similarly famous for playing a secret agent: three-time Emmy nominee David McCallum, 39, widely known as Russian spy Illya Kuryakin in 105 episodes of NBC's *The Man from U.N.C.L.E.* (1964-1968). In fact, those very same teen magazines that turned Leonard Whiting into a pop culture phenomenon had, just a few years earlier, turned up the heat on McCallum.

"David McCallum was to espionage what Paul McCartney was to pop," wrote Brian Pendreigh in *The Sunday Times*. "He used to receive more than 30,000 fan letters a month when he appeared in the television spy series." Not long after *U.N.C.L.E.* had been on the air, McCallum came to New York and, without a second thought, decided to take a stroll in Central Park. Bad idea. Within minutes, he was mobbed by fans, like a scene right out of *A Hard Day's Night*. "It took two police on horseback to rescue me," McCallum recalled.

Previously, McCallum had made his mark in a number of major motion pictures, including Roy Ward Baker's *A Night to Remember* (1958), John Huston's *Freud* (1962), John Sturges' *The Great Escape* (1963), and George Stevens' *The Greatest Story Ever Told* (1965) – but his role in *The Man from U.N.C.L.E.* had eclipsed all that.

Just as Connery was trying to shed his association with Bond, McCallum was now trying to shake his typecasting as Kuryakin. Much of the work he had been doing since *U.N.C.L.E.* was for Universal Television, including a guest spot on *Night Gallery* (1971) and a starring role opposite Robert Wagner in *Colditz* (1972-1974), a prisoner-of-war series filmed in England.

In a 1973 interview, McCallum explained, "Hunt Stromberg telephoned and said they were doing another

Frankenstein and I laughed heartily and said, 'Not again!' I had no intention of doing it, but when I read Christopher Isherwood's script, I changed my mind. In fact, I jumped at the part. It's a wonderful script."

McCallum would work 16 days, spread from March 15 through May 16. [See Chapter 9 for my interview with McCallum.]

THE BOND GIRL

Seymour in *Live and Let Die*.

As it happened, the latest James Bond movie, *Live and Let Die* – Roger Moore's first round as 007 – was shooting at Pinewood Studios throughout pre-production of *Dr. Frankenstein*. Around the Pinewood lot, Stromberg had spotted an extraordinarily captivating Bond girl whom he thought would be perfect for the dual role of Agatha / Prima.

"Hunt wanted to meet her," recalled *Dr. Frankenstein* production manager Brian Burgess in a 2016 interview for this book. "So, I went into the Pinewood restaurant and went

Harry Saltzman, Seymour, Albert R. Broccoli, signing for *Live and Let Die*.

up to Harry Saltzman, the producer of the Bond pictures. I introduced myself and said, 'We'd like to meet the actress in your movie.'"

"No!" Saltzman barked like a rabid dog. "She's *our* star! You can't come anywhere near her!"

Burgess reported to Stromberg that his overture had been summarily brushed off. Of course, that just made the actress all the more intriguing.

Then one day in late-February, Stromberg was eating lunch in the Pinewood restaurant at a table with Jacque Shelton, Jack Smight and Ian Lewis. He kept looking across the room where several *Live and Let Die* teammates were clustered – sans guard dog Saltzman. Stromberg turned to his comrades and said, "Excuse me a moment. I'll be right back." He walked straight over to the 007 table and re-introduced himself to Roger Moore – they'd met socially on previous occasions – and explained he was producing *Dr. Frankenstein* at Pinewood.

"The script is written by Christopher Isherwood," Stromberg name-dropped, trying to impress the table.

"Oh yes," Moore replied, with a sly grin. "He wrote a picture I did at MGM called *Diane*. It bombed so badly, the studio dropped me. I hope you'll have better luck with this one."

"Well, we have better actors, so that's a start," Stromberg dryly retorted, getting a rise from the table, Moore included. "And while we're on that subject, I wonder if you would do me the honor of introducing me to your enchanting co-star."

"Why, of course, my good fellow," Moore said, turning to the ravishing 22-year-old actress seated beside him with hair down to her waist. "This is Jane Seymour. And mark my words. She's going to be a major star."

Stromberg & Seymour (ballroom sequence).

THE EPIC SAGA BEHIND *FRANKENSTEIN: THE TRUE STORY*

Seymour smiled and said, "A pleasure to meet you, Mr. Stromberg."

"The pleasure is all mine," Stromberg replied. "I understand that your picture wraps just before my picture starts, which is extremely fortuitous, don't you think?"

"Why's that?" the actress asked.

"Because, Miss Seymour, you are going to be in my picture," Stromberg announced with utter confidence.

Seymour laughed. "You can't be serious."

"I'm dead serious," Stromberg replied. "I want you to play not one, but two parts. An innocent farm girl named Agatha who dies in an accident and is brought back to life as an evil female creature named Prima."

Not sure what to make of this peculiar man, Seymour politely said, "I look forward to reading the script."

"That's not necessary," he replied. "I want your commitment, here and now, before I return to my table for dessert."

Taken aback, Seymour asked, "Have you ever seen me act?"

"Roger thinks you're going to be a major star," Stromberg said. "That's all I need to know. And did I mention your co-stars will be James Mason, Michael Sarrazin, Leonard Whiting and David McCallum?"

Seymour's jaw dropped. "Well, then, how can I say 'no'?"

"You can't," Stromberg replied. "I'll have my people talk to your people and we'll see you at the read-through." With that, Stromberg turned on his heel and marched back to his table in a blaze of glory.

"That's a glaring example of how Hunt refused to take 'no' for an answer," observed Brian Burgess. "He was very smooth at manipulating people to get what he wanted."

Eventually, Seymour was given the opportunity to read the teleplay. "I loved the script immediately," she recalled, "but I must confess the idea of playing two entirely different

Top left: Seymour as Agatha, the innocent farmgirl.
Top right: Seymour as Prima, the evil female creature.
Above: Sarrazin cradles Seymour as dead Agatha.

characters was the main attraction." When asked to describe them, Seymour replied, "Agatha is very ordinary and very human. On the other hand, I see Prima as an animal-like character, because she acts entirely on her instincts with an extraordinary directness in everything she does."

In an interview for *Radio Times*, Isherwood revealed that the inspiration for Prima was "the beautiful automaton in the opera *Tales of Hoffmann*."

In this 1881 French *opéra fantastique*, the protagonist falls in love with a ravishing beauty named Olympia, not knowing that she is a mechanical doll created by an inventor.

In his 2013 review of *Frankenstein: The True Story* (on the Collinsport Historical Society website), Ansel Faraj noted that Prima "has a scar around her neck, which she hides with a choker – à la the classic tale *The Green Ribbon*, which is only fitting considering what she's got coming to her."

The Green Ribbon, from the 1984 book *In a Dark, Dark Room and Other Scary Stories*, by Alvin Schwartz, is a tale about a girl named Jenny who wears a green ribbon around her neck but refuses to take it off or reveal why, not even to her husband Alfred. After reaching old age, she finally lets Alfred untie the ribbon, causing her head to fall onto the floor. According to Wikipedia, "The story was inspired by a French tale of unknown origin, and several variations of the story have appeared in print." These include Washington Irving's 1824 short story *The Adventure of the German Student* (in which the woman with the choker turns out to have been beheaded via guillotine); Alexandre Dumas' 1851 story *The Woman with the Velvet Necklace*; and Ann McGovern's 1970 short story *The Velvet Ribbon* (in the collection of stories titled *Ghostly Fun*). Given the tale's ubiquity through the ages, it does seem quite plausible, if not probable, that Isherwood and Bachardy were at least partly inspired by this when they decided to disguise Prima's neck scar with a choker. The scene in which Elizabeth enters Prima's bedroom late at night to uncover what lies beneath the ribbon feels like a sequence right out of this grim fairy tale.

Stromberg felt that the contrast between Agatha and Prima should be heightened with opposing hair colors: innocent blond for Agatha and a darker, malevolent brunette for Prima.

Geoffrey Holder, *Live and Let Die*.

Geoffrey Holder, the towering Trinidadian-American actor-dancer-choreographer-designer-director (and the "uncola nut" pitchman in 7-Up commercials), was co-starring in *Live and Let Die* as a henchman who tries to sacrifice Solitaire (Jane Seymour) in a voodoo occult ceremony. Holder was also serving as choreographer on the movie and had discovered during rehearsals that Seymour was a trained dancer.

In a May 2014 phone interview with Holder (five months before he passed away), he recalled, "When Jane told me she'd been cast as 'the bride of Frankenstein' and that the monster was going to tear off her head at a dance, I said, 'My dear, that sounds lovely – but have you told them what a great dancer you are?' Of course, she hadn't. So I took it upon myself to corner Hunt Stromberg Jr. – who was quite a character as you know – and I said, 'Hunt, my dahling! You have noooo idea what Jane is capable of doing. She is a prima ballerina! When the monster comes calling, she should be performing Salome's *Dance of the Seven Veils*! She must liberate her body before the monster liberates her head!' At first, Hunt just stared at me like I'd lost all my marbles – but then he smiled wickedly and said, 'You may be right.' I knew I'd struck a chord."

In the original script, the party was a masquerade ball – and when the Creature arrived, the guests thought he was just another partygoer in a monster get-up. It was a clever idea but Stromberg was worried it "would resemble the ball from *The Fearless Vampire Killers*." He felt the actors would look silly in costumes – particularly Dr. Frankenstein as the harlequin jester that Isherwood and Bachardy had scripted him to be. Stromberg wanted the scene to be elegant and sophisticated, in stark contrast to the horror that was about to happen. So, he changed it to a formal dance and, taking

Geoffrey Holder & Seymour, *Live and Let Die*.

Seymour dancing at ball in FTTS.

Two closer shots of Seymour dancing at the ball, FTTS.

Holder's recommendation to heart, he added a solo ballet for Prima – set to the music of Maurice Ravel's *Introduction and Allegro for Harp, Flute, Clarinet and String Quartet*. It worked perfectly for the character because Prima was a supreme mimic; all it took was one viewing for her to master anything. And, the Creature's arrival would come at the climax of this ballet – which proved to be a much more dramatic disruption than merely interrupting a conversation.

To choreograph, they hired Sally Judd Gilpin (1938-2008), former leading ballerina for the London Festival Ballet, who had recently directed the dances in Polanski's *Macbeth* and Carol Reed's *The Public Eye*. Gilpin had previously appeared on-screen as a dancer in *The Masque of the Red Death* and *Half a Sixpence*. From 1960 to 1970, she was married to John Brian Gilpin (1930-1983), lead dancer and artistic director of the London Festival Ballet (from 1962-1968). It was widely known in the dance community that their marriage ended when Sally discovered that her husband was the longtime lover of Sir Anton Dolin (1904-1983), founder of the London Festival Ballet.

Dance rehearsals for *Dr. Frankenstein* were held in the Band Room at Pinewood Studios on sporadic days throughout the first three weeks of May 1973 – whenever Jane Seymour was not otherwise engaged in shooting – in preparation for the grand ballroom scenes that would be shot May 21-25. Aside from makeup tests and dance rehearsals, Seymour went before the cameras for 26 days, spread from April 4 through June 21.

Stromberg was so impressed with Seymour's abilities and star potential that, immediately following the shoot,

he announced that he had chosen her to star with David McCallum in his Mummy spectacular for Universal Television, *The Lady from the Land of the Dead*, scripted by Isherwood and Bachardy. Stromberg fawned, "Only once or twice in each decade does a young girl appear on the show business horizon who combines both great beauty and superb acting ability. Vivien Leigh, Jean Simmons and Julie Christie are past examples. This decade belongs to Jane Seymour!" Though *The Lady from the Land of the Dead* never did come to life, Stromberg's prediction was right on the money. Seymour went on to win an Emmy, two Golden Globes and a star on the Hollywood Walk of Fame. [See Chapter 8 for my two interviews with Seymour.]

WRITERS' STRIKE

On March 6, 1973, nine days before *Dr. Frankenstein* began shooting, the Writers Guild of America declared a Writers' Strike against TV and movie producers. Isherwood noted in his diary, "Hunt had the gall to suggest that we should write an extra scene for Mason, in which Polidori denounces Henry [Clerval]. I told him we aren't about to strike break – there are too many spies around."

On March 7, Stromberg assuaged Sid Sheinberg's concerns with the following missive: "I will personally 'manicure' the script as necessary."

Don Bachardy & Christopher Isherwood.

THE READ-THROUGH

On March 8, 1973, Stromberg hosted an intimate script read-through of *Dr. Frankenstein* in London. In attendance were Jack Smight, Jacque Shelton, and cast members James

Mason and wife Clarissa Kaye (Stromberg far right) at FTTS read-through.

Mason, his wife Clarissa Kaye, Michael Sarrazin, Leonard Whiting, David McCallum, Jane Seymour, Nicola Pagett and Michael Wilding. The other guest roles had not yet been cast. In addition to reading the script aloud, the gathering also served as an early birthday celebration for Smight who would turn 48 the following day.

Six-thousand miles across the globe, from his home in Santa Monica, Isherwood reported the details secondhand: "Hunt rang up very drunk to tell me that the cast had just read through the script and that David McCallum is sensational as Henry Clerval and that James Mason had said that Leonard Whiting is so great that he'll steal the show and that every time Michael Sarrazin (as the Creature) had said 'Victor' he (Hunt) had felt tears come into his eyes, etc. etc. They have got an incredibly beautiful girl named Jane Seymour to play Prima."

THE ELSA LANCHESTER CRISIS

On a roll, Stromberg set his sights on collecting guest stars to play the various featured roles in the film. For the part of Mrs. Blair, the nosy landlady of Dr. Frankenstein – which Ingrid Bergman and Bette Davis had already turned down – Stromberg wanted a "Una O'Connor type," referring to the quirky Irish character actress who played Minnie, the mettlesome and skittish housekeeper, in *Bride of Frankenstein*.

In 1942, when Universal released *The Ghost of Frankenstein*, critics noted that certain actors in the movie, such as Lionel Atwill and Dwight Frye, had portrayed different characters in earlier *Frankenstein* films, prompting the studio to issue a press release stating that it was "the custom of the studio" to bring back some of "the same faces in each succeeding feature of the *Frankenstein* series."

Inspired by this hallowed tradition, Stromberg suddenly became obsessed with the idea of Mrs. Blair being portrayed by Elsa Lanchester, 70 – next-door-neighbor of Isherwood and Bachardy – who had so memorably played Mary Shelley and the female creature in *Bride*.

As mentioned earlier, Stromberg met Lanchester in early 1935 when he was just 11 years old – when she was simultaneously shooting his father's movie *Naughty Marietta* at MGM and *Bride of Frankenstein* at Universal – and, from then on, she had remained a family friend. In the 1960s, Stromberg personally cast her as a guest star on a number of CBS shows – and, impishly, he made a habit of ending letters with this tongue-in-cheek wrap-up: "Must close now, as Elsa Lanchester has just arrived to show off her new wart."

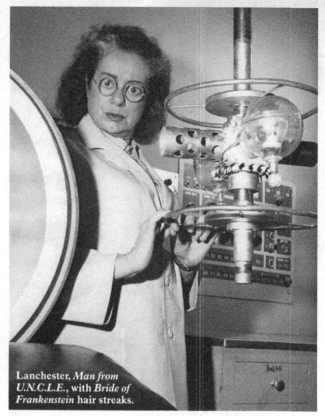

Lanchester, *Man from U.N.C.L.E.*, with *Bride of Frankenstein* hair streaks.

Though she occasionally grumbled about her fame as the Bride, in truth, Lanchester basked in the glory of her most famous role – and, in the autumn of her career, she did not shy away from spooky projects that played upon that image, including *Blackbeard's Ghost* (1968), *Willard* (1971) and an episode of *Night Gallery* (1972). And she certainly had no problem adding those two familiar wavy white streaks to her frizzy mane when she guest-starred as a mad scientist on *The Man from U.N.C.L.E.: The Brain-Killer Affair* (1965) – a shameless sendup of her electrifying coiffure in *Bride*. That gig also introduced Lanchester to *U.N.C.L.E.* series regular David McCallum who would work with her again in *Dr. Frankenstein* if Stromberg had his way.

Lanchester truly wanted to do it – but, alas, she was already committed to shoot a low-budget horror film in Hollywood at the very same time – *Arnold* for Bing Crosby Productions. Gnashing his teeth, Stromberg offered to personally buy out Lanchester's contract, but the producers

Above Left: Elsa Lanchester in *Terror in the Wax Museum*, wearing bonnet similar to what Agnes Moorehead would wear in FTTS. **Above Centre:** Elsa Lanchester wore another bonnet in *Murder by Death*. **Above Right:** *Murder by Death* with James Coco, James Cromwell, Eileen Brennan, Peter Falk, Richard Narita, Estelle Winwood, Elsa Lanchester, Peter Sellers, David Niven, Maggie Smith.

held firm. Then, he turned to his associate producer Ian Lewis and said, "My father managed to work around *Bride of Frankenstein* in order to get Elsa into *his* movie. Why can't we figure out a way to do the same?"

"I remember 'the Elsa Lanchester crisis' very well," recalled Ian Lewis. "Hunt damn near drove us crazy but, ultimately, she just couldn't be reasonably scheduled."

Heartbroken, Lanchester honored her contract and remained Stateside to perform in one of the most forgettable films on her resume. What's even sadder is that, after finishing *Arnold*, she didn't work again for two-and-a-half years (until her comeback in the all-star spoof *Murder by Death*).

BEWITCHING AGNES MOOREHEAD

For the role of Mrs. Blair, Stromberg finally landed Agnes Moorehead, 72, who had won an Emmy, two Golden Globes, and four Oscar nominations – not to mention her iconic role as Endora, Samantha's bitchy-witch mother, in *Bewitched* (1964-1972).

According to her *Bewitched* co-star Dick Sargent, Moorehead was a devout Christian, often arriving on set "with the *Bible* in one hand and her script in the other." Nevertheless, she was twice divorced and often socialized with a fiercely-protective coterie of gay friends – many of them outrageously irreverent, including Stromberg and *Bewitched*'s Paul Lynde who, after her death, said, "Well, the whole world knows Agnes was a lesbian – I mean classy as hell, but one of the all-time Hollywood dykes."

Some have challenged that claim but, in 1992, when I directed Dick Sargent in the Showtime thriller *Acting on Impulse* (his last film before his 1994 death from prostate cancer), he had recently gone public about his own homosexuality and confided to me that Moorehead had never officially "come out" but, privately, would "let her guard down when she felt safe among likeminded friends."

As luck would have it, Moorehead knew Una O'Connor quite well, having worked with the actress in RKO's *Government Girl* (1943). So, Stromberg's directive to play Mrs. Blair as "a Una O'Connor type" was taken to heart – resulting in Moorehead affecting a thick Irish accent and hamming it up for all it was worth.

All of her scenes were shot on E Stage at Pinewood Studios, completed in six days, spread sporadically from March 19 through March 29, 1973.

Stromberg treated her like a queen during her stay in London and she loved his wicked sense of humor. Whenever her chauffeured car came to pick her up, Stromberg would always say, "Dahling, your broom has arrived." It was a playful nod to *Bewitched*, of course, and it never failed to crack her up.

Sadly, it would turn out to be one of Moorehead's final roles. Later that year, she would portray Aunt Alicia in a new stage adaptation of Vincente Minnelli's 1958 hit musical film *Gigi* (winner of 6 Academy Awards including Best Picture) which opened on Broadway on November 13, 1973. A few weeks into the run, Moorehead became ill and had to be replaced by Arlene Francis. Diagnosed with uterine cancer, she passed away April 30, 1974, at the age of 73.

Curiously, Moorehead was among the unusually high number of cast and crew members from *The Conqueror* (1956) who died of cancer, including John Wayne, Susan Hayward and director Dick Powell. Dr. Robert Pendleton,

Agnes Moorehead in *Bewitched*.

This Picture and Right: Agnes Moorehead in FTTS.

Above Left: Una O'Connor, *Bride of Frankenstein.* **Above Center and Right: Ernest Thesiger & O'Connor,** *Bride of Frankenstein*

Moorehead & Stromberg.

Above: Valerie Hobson & John Profumo. Below: Hobson & Karloff, *Bride of Frankenstein.*

Moorehead & Mason.

Sarrazin is distraught that Moorehead is dying.

professor of biology at the University of Utah, and other investigators, have concluded that the "epidemic outbreak of cancer cases" was likely due to radiation exposure while filming in the Utah desert downwind from a nearby Nevada nuclear testing site.

THE PROFUMO AFFAIR

Still intoxicated by the idea of casting a living connection to *Bride of Frankenstein*, Stromberg was then inspired to offer a role to Valerie Hobson who played Elizabeth Frankenstein in the 1935 classic. Stromberg wanted Hobson to portray the Dowager Countess Françoise Duval, the flirtatious French lady who encounters Dr. Frankenstein and his beautiful Creature during sintermission on their night at the opera.

A native of England, Hobson came to Hollywood in 1934 at the age of 16 and was promptly signed by Carl Laemmle Jr. to an exclusive contract at Universal where she starred in eleven movies, including *Bride of Frankenstein* and *Werewolf of London.* Abruptly dropped from her contract during Universal's mid-1930s financial crisis, she returned to the UK in 1936 where she continued making movies, including *Kind Hearts and Coronets* – one of Stromberg's favorite Ealing comedies from which he had already engaged makeup artist Harry Frampton.

Stromberg had an intimate connection to Hobson through James Mason who had been a friend of the actress ever since they had starred together in the 1936 spy thriller *The Secret of Stamboul,* based on the novel by Dennis Wheatley.

Jack Larson recalled, "Jim [Bridges] and I had dinner with Hunt after he returned from London and he told us the funniest story about meeting Valerie Hobson. He said, 'James Mason warned me that she'd retired from acting [in 1954] when she'd married a British politician, but that just made me want her all the more, to promote her comeback.'"

Stromberg asked Mason, "What does she do now?"

Mason paused, took a deep breath and said, "Val and her husband devote their lives to charity work."

Stromberg replied, "Well, then perhaps she'll play the role for charity."

Above: James Mason & Valerie Hobson, *The Secret of Stamboul*.

Resolute, Stromberg persuaded Mason to arrange a meeting and, the next day, the two men were chauffeured to the stately Dower House in Hertfordshire where Hobson resided. Armed with a chilled bottle of Dom Perignon – Hobson's poison of choice – the men were warmly greeted by the actress who, at the age of 55, was still a stunningly beautiful woman.

After a tour of the premises, Stromberg launched into a passionate proposal for her to join the stellar cast of *Dr. Frankenstein* for the one-day guest cameo appearance as Countess Duval – for which she would be paid handsomely, the proceeds of which, he benevolently suggested, could be donated to her favorite charity.

"I am flattered to be remembered so fondly," Hobson told the producer, "but I am content to remain out of the public eye."

During the drive back, a defeated Stromberg shook his head, mystified. "I can't understand why she wouldn't jump at the chance for a comeback. Do you think she still holds a grudge against Universal?"

Looking away, Mason smirked and began to giggle.

"What's so funny?" Stromberg asked.

"You have no idea who her husband is, do you," Mason said, stifling his amusement.

"No," Stromberg replied. "Who?"

Mason looked at Stromberg and said two words: "John Profumo."

Stromberg's eyes narrowed. "*The* John Profumo?"

Mason nodded knowingly – then burst out laughing.

"You might have told me earlier, you shit," Stromberg sputtered, realizing he had been punked from the get-go. "I'll get you for this. Just you wait!"

There was baggage to this story. Heavy baggage. In 1963, John Profumo, Britain's Secretary of State for War, was caught having an affair with Christine Keeler, a 19-year-old wannabe model, who was also having an affair with Yevgeni Ivanov, senior naval attaché at the Soviet Embassy and a spy for the Soviet Union. The repercussions of "the Profumo Affair" led to the resignation of Prime Minister Harold

Macmillan and the defeat of the Conservative Party during the 1964 elections – one of the most infamous political scandals of the twentieth century. It would later be the subject of the film *Scandal* starring Ian McKellen as Profumo and Deborah Grant as Valerie Hobson.

Though humiliated by her husband's infidelity and the relentless media scrutiny, Hobson stood by her man and remained married to him (until her death in 1998). Understandably, she never, *ever* wanted to be in the public eye again. And Mason knew it – but he relished catching up with an old friend while mercilessly pranking a newer one.

The addendum to this story was Stromberg's payback. Instead of sending a welcoming fruit basket or flowers to Mason for Day One, the producer mischievously stocked the actor's dressing room with a decorative conversation piece – of the Charles Addams variety.

Photoplay Film Monthly journalist Gordon Gow was one of the privileged few who got to experience the gag, up close and personal: "Although it was mid-morning, and bright daylight shone through the windows of James Mason's dressing room [No. 148] at Pinewood Studios, nevertheless I experienced a spooky shiver the moment I entered the place. The first thing to command my eye was an inert and naked body lying on the floor against the wall. Mason himself was nonchalant about it. 'Interesting, isn't it? A life-size replica of Michael Sarrazin, you know.' At second blink, I could see it was a dummy – but a very convincing one."

Mason thought it was the most hilarious gift he had ever received – and derived immense pleasure from spooking visitors with it. The tongue-in-cheek one-upmanship between Mason and Stromberg would thrive throughout the rest of their lives.

SIMONE SIGNORET, S'IL VOUS PLAÎT?

On March 8, 1973, Isherwood reported in his diary that "the part of the foreign lady at the opera is to be offered to Simone Signoret – wow!"

Signoret was, of course, a huge star in France and the first French actor to win an Academy Award – for Best Actress in Jack Clayton's *Room at the Top*. Also on her mantle were a César, three BAFTAs, and an Emmy. Since 1951, she had been married to French star Yves Montand. Like seemingly every other celebrity on the planet, Stromberg had met Simone and Yves socially – and it also helped that she had co-starred with James Mason in not one, but *two* Sidney Lumet films: John le Carré's *The Deadly Affair* and

James Mason & Simone Signoret, *The Deadly Affair*.

Chekhov's *The Sea Gull*. So, Stromberg sent an impassioned letter to Simone inviting her to play Countess Duval. "If we are fortunate enough to have you," Stromberg wrote, "we intend to improve even further this guest-star cameo part." Nevertheless, it was no dice. Signoret passed.

DAME ANGELA LANSBURY

Next, Stromberg offered the role of Countess Duval to Tony Award winner and three-time Oscar nominee Angela Lansbury (*Gaslight*, *The Picture of Dorian Gray*, *The Manchurian Candidate*) whom he had known since 1950 when he and Lansbury's husband, Peter Shaw, partnered to form a short-lived literary agency in Hollywood – before Shaw went off to become a major talent agent at William Morris (representing Elvis Presley among others) and Stromberg hit it big as a television executive. (Contrary to a wildfire of erroneous claims on the Internet, Lansbury's husband was definitely *not* the same Peter Shaw who played Dr. Pretorius' miniature Devil in *Bride of Frankenstein* – though the connection would have been delicious had it been true.)

Lansbury in *Death on the Nile*.

Lansbury garnered her third Oscar nomination for *The Manchurian Candidate*.

Lansbury at the *Psycho* house on the Universal lot.

Lansbury was in London that spring rehearsing *Gypsy*, a revival of the musical that would open at the Piccadilly Theatre on May 29, 1973.

Contacted for this book in 2015, Dame Angela Lansbury fondly recalled, "Everybody knew Hunt Stromberg, Jr., and they certainly knew his dad. He was a great friend of ours and it was through Hunt that my twin brothers, Bruce and Edgar, got executive jobs at ABC and CBS." When asked about being offered a role in *Dr. Frankenstein*, she said, "I would love to have worked with Hunt but I was so involved with what I was doing in *Gypsy*, I couldn't think about anything else."

Gypsy went on to become a massive hit – and when the production was transferred to Broadway, Lansbury won *another* Tony (her second of five).

TRAPPING MARGARET LEIGHTON

Still in search of a star to play Countess Duval, Stromberg hosted a dinner party with several of the *Dr. Frankenstein* cast members – including Michael Wilding who brought along his current wife Margaret Leighton whom he had met in 1949 when they had starred together in Alfred Hitchcock's *Under Capricorn*. Leighton had won two Tony Awards for Best Actress in *Separate Tables* and *The Night of the Iguana*;

Margaret Leighton (in opera costume) in FTTS.

Michael Wilding & Leighton (in Bo Peep getup) in *FTTS*.

Borgnine in *Torpedo Run*.

an Emmy Award for Best Supporting Actress as Gertrude in *Hamlet* opposite Richard Chamberlain; and a BAFTA Award for Best Supporting Actress in *The Go-Between* for which she was also Oscar-nominated.

Having struck out with Hobson, Signoret and Lansbury, Stromberg decided to offer the role of Countess Duval to Leighton – and for all we know, the dinner party may very well have been set up as a trap to snag her.

"Why don't you come and play something in it?" Stromberg asked her in front of everyone at the table.

"Yes, certainly I will," Leighton responded.

The only scene of the Countess in the script was the encounter at the opera in Part 1. But Stromberg promised to sweeten the deal by creating another scene later in the story, so she could also appear in Part 2.

Due to the ongoing Writers Strike, Hunt wrote the new scene himself – a comical moment when the Countess arrives at the ball in costume as Little Bo Peep – only to discover the formal dance is not a masquerade.

Leighton would only work two days on the film: May 22, 1973 (the Bo Peep scene), and June 2, 1973 (the opera intermission).

Although Isherwood and Bachardy were annoyed by Stromberg's script tampering, this brief addition to the ball proved to be a memorable moment of comic relief. When the film was broadcast, the *Los Angeles Times* raved that Leighton's "jewel-like bits as a nitwit noblewoman must literally be seen to be believed."

[See Chapter 11 for my 1974 interview with Margaret Leighton, with a cameo appearance by her real-life husband / *Frankenstein: The True Story* costar Michael Wilding.]

AHOY ERNEST BORGNINE

As originally scripted, the guest role of the American Captain of the ship had a few juicy scenes, including one meaty tête-à-tête with Polidori as they are being chased by the coastguard. Jack Smight, who had just directed Oscar winner Ernest Borgnine, 56, as Vince Lombardi in the ABC made-for-television movie *Legend*

Borgnine in *McHale's Navy*.

in *Granite: The Vince Lombardi Story* (Universal Television, 1973), suggested that Borgnine would be ideal for the Ship Captain. It would have been a bit of typecasting given Borgnine's many maritime credits, including *Torpedo Run*, *Ice Station Zebra*, *The Poseidon Adventure*, *The Neptune Factor* and the series *McHale's Navy*. Stromberg loved the idea and promptly offered Borgnine the part – which the actor readily accepted. For now, at least, he was committed.

BAGGING TWO KNIGHTS

Then, just when everyone thought Stromberg couldn't possibly stuff another star into this constellation, he defiantly bagged not one, but *two* knights: Sir Ralph Richardson *and*

Above: Artwork of Richardson by Frederick Cooper.
Right: Artwork of Sarrazin & Richardson, by Dave Matsuoka.

THE EPIC SAGA BEHIND *FRANKENSTEIN: THE TRUE STORY*

1. CHESTER TERRACE.
REGENT'S PARK.
N. W. 1.

Perhaps he could have a rocking chair? Easily upset and a blind person would feel a lack of much movement that can take?

Something like this? Try to make the eyes large. Lot eyebrows ..

Left: Richardson self-portrait for FTTS. This Picture: Direct match of Richardson in FTTS

Richardson touching Sarrazin.

Richardson as blind fiddler.

Richardson plays fiddle for Sarrazin.

Sir John Gielgud, both considered to be among the greatest actors of their generation.

Richardson, 70, had been nominated for three Tony Awards for his work on Broadway. In movies, he had been Oscar-nominated for *The Heiress* and later would be posthumously Oscar-nominated again for *Greystoke: The Legend of Tarzan, Lord of the Apes*. He had won Best Actor at the Cannes Film Festival for *Long Day's Journey into Night* and a BAFTA Award for *The Sound Barrier*. His very first movie was *The Ghoul* (1933) starring Boris Karloff and Ernest Thesiger. Other genre credits included *Things to Come*, *Whoever Slew Auntie Roo?* and *Tales from the Crypt* in which he played the Crypt Keeper.

In *Dr. Frankenstein*, Richardson would play Lacey, the blind fiddler who is the grandfather of Agatha (Jane Seymour) – filmed over the course of four days, May 29-June 1, 1973, in Burnham Beeches (exteriors) and Pinewood's F Stage (interiors). The character was loosely based on DeLacey from Shelley's novel but more closely follows the interpretation of the character as played by O. P. Heggie in *Bride of Frankenstein* (1935). Gene Hackman would soon have a field day spoofing the character in *Young Frankenstein* (1974).

"It was a remarkably good script," Richardson said at the time, "but only what one would expect from Isherwood."

Richardson had a very specific look in mind for the character and took it upon himself to draw a sketch with detailed notations. He sent this to Stromberg for approval and ended up looking exactly like the drawing in the final film.

The role of the Chief Constable in *Dr. Frankenstein* would be played by Sir John Gielgud, 68, who had been Oscar-nominated for *Becket* and would later win an Oscar for *Arthur*. He had won a BAFTA for *Julius Caesar* and would soon win a second BAFTA for *Murder on the Orient Express*. He would go on to win two Golden Globes, one for *Arthur* and the other for Dan Curtis' miniseries *War and Remembrance* (also starring Jane Seymour); and an Emmy for *Summer's Lease*. One of Gielgud's earliest screen roles was in Alfred Hitchcock's *Secret Agent* (1936) alongside Peter Lorre.

When Stromberg was wooing Gielgud to come aboard, associate producer Ian Lewis warned that they were in danger of going over budget. Without blinking, Stromberg simply said, "Relax. I'll pay for him out of my own pocket." It is a bit of an unsolved mystery whether Universal or Stromberg picked up the tab, but I have a feeling it was probably both. Universal likely paid what was allocated in the budget and Stromberg greased Gielgud's palm under the table with a sizable cash bonus or lavish gift.

Gielgud's guest cameo appearance consisted of just one scene, filmed on May 18, 1973, at Pinewood Studios in Heatherden Hall's Pine & Green Rooms. Jack Smight was a bit intimidated to be directing a legend as formidable as

Stromberg, Richardson & Sarrazin (in full makeup) on set for the ballroom scene. Richardson does not appear in that sequence, so was just a visitor that day.

Richardson & Smight.

Richardson with Sarrazin & Stromberg.

THE EPIC SAGA BEHIND *FRANKENSTEIN: THE TRUE STORY*

Above: Mason & Gielgud at lake location. Gielgud was only visiting. He and Mason did not share a scene in the film.

Gielgud (left) with Whiting, Smight, Stromberg, Pagett.

Peter Glaze, Nicola Pagett, Leonard Whiting, John Gielgud.

THE EPIC SAGA BEHIND *FRANKENSTEIN: THE TRUE STORY*

Gielgud – but the actor knew how to put his director at ease. Smight's son Alec recalled, "Gielgud walked right up to my dad and said, 'My dear fellow, I'm often very bad and I'd appreciate it if you'd tell me so.'"

Though Gielgud never publicly "came out," everyone knew he was gay. In 1953, he had been scandalously arrested and fined for lewd conduct in a men's lavatory, but his fans stood by him, and the brouhaha eventually blew over.

Say what you will about Stromberg but the cast for *Dr. Frankenstein* was nothing short of sublime and, for that, he deserves a hell of a lot of credit. If there had been more available parts, who knows what might have happened? In a November 1973 interview for the *Los Angeles Times*, Stromberg lamented, "I later ran into Alec Guinness and Robert Morley, after they heard Mason was to star, and they both asked why didn't I call them?"

On June 13, 1975, backstage at the Apollo Theatre on the West End, following a performance of *A Family and a Fortune*, the play's leading lady Margaret Leighton introduced me to her leading man Sir Alec Guinness. I quoted this claim made by Hunt Stromberg Jr. and asked him if it was accurate. Alec laughed and said, "Yes! It seems everybody who is anybody was in that picture, and I felt as though my invitation must have been lost in the post." As Guinness examined the cover of my *Bizarre* No. 3 fanzine with the color photo of Michael Sarrazin in full deterioration mode as the Creature, I told Alec, "I believe you know the makeup artist who did this. Harry Frampton."

"Ah, yes indeed," Alec responded. "Harry is a genius. All nine of my characters in *Kind Hearts and Coronets* were done by him."

BASE OF OPERATION

During pre-production, Stromberg divided his time between Universal's headquarters in London (where casting sessions

continued) and an office space he had been assigned at Pinewood Studios. His secretary Phyllis Allarie recalled, "In the center of Pinewood is H Stage where some of the sets would be constructed [including the cellar underneath Frankenstein's laboratory for the acid bath sequence]. The building would also house our production offices – a section known as H Block. It was on the ground level and had a long hallway with several offices, one after the other. First, there was Hunt's office, then mine, then the main production office which housed production manager Brian Burgess, production secretary Vicki Deason and the production runner Steven Ridgwell. Next to them was the accounts office headed by Maurice Landsberger, followed by an office for the assistant directors. Further down was the art department where Wilfrid Shingleton and his staff were based."

Asked where the special effects department was located, modeler Brian Smithies recalled, "In an old wooden shed – just in front of where the current Bond stage is. We were always put out in sheds as far away as possible from anything that mattered. I think they were worried that something would catch fire or blow up, but we never had any accidents."

The wardrobe department was based in the main building on the lot devoted to costuming; and, the editing suite – equipped with upright 35mm Moviolas – was located in the Cutting Room Block near the main entrance of the studio.

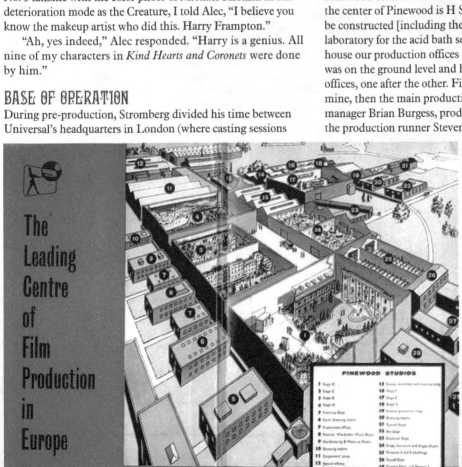

The Leading Centre of Film Production in Europe

PINEWOOD STUDIOS

THE RANK ORGANISATION

Iver Heath, Buckinghamshire (Iver 700)

PINEWOOD STUDIOS

1 Stage D.
2 Stage C
3 Stage B
4 Stage A
5 Publicity Dept.
6 Stars' dressing rooms
7 Production offices
8 Medical, Wardrobe, Plans Dept.
9 Hairdressing & Make-up Dept.
10 Dressing rooms
11 Carpenters' shop.
12 Special effects. Still photograph laboratories
13 Boiler house
14 Plasterers' shop

15 Stores, wardrobe and machine shop
16 Stage F
17 Stage E
18 Stage G
19 Process projection stage
20 Dressing rooms
21 Tunnel Stage
22 Art Dept.
23 Electrical Dept.
24 Props, furniture and drapes Dept.
25 Theatres 1 and 2 (dubbing)
26 Sound Dept.
27 Camera Dept. and Theatre 5 (projection)
28 Cutting rooms
29 Theatres 3 and 4 (viewing)

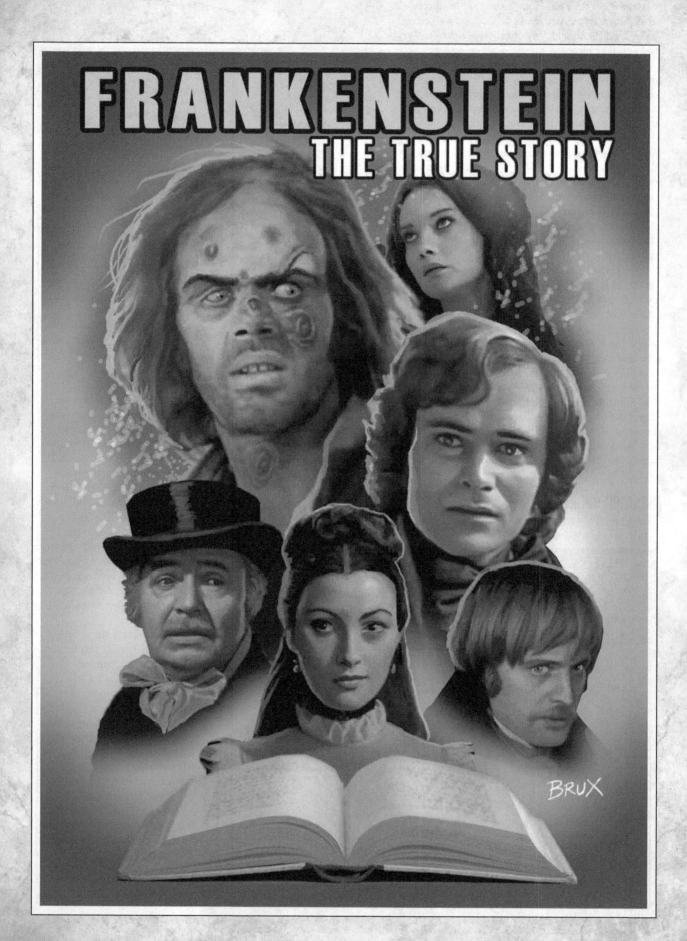

CHAPTER 3
FILMING

LET THE GAMES BEGIN

Dr. Frankenstein began shooting on Thursday, March 15, 1973, on E Stage at Pinewood Studios where a composite of interior sets for Dr. Frankenstein's lodging house had been constructed – foyer, stairwell, living room and bedroom.

Entrance to Pinewood Studios.

McCallum, Pagett & Whiting, Day 1 of filming FTTS.

Isherwood's diary entry for that date reported the following: "Hunt called today to tell me that they have just finished their first day's shooting – Nicola [Pagett] and Leonard Whiting and David McCallum in the scene of Elizabeth's visit to the lodgings and her hostility toward Henry Clerval. Everybody had been terrific, and McCallum terrific-terrific. (Hunt was drunk again; it's very tiresome that he calls at eight in the evening, their time.) However, he let slip some ominous hints. They have altered the period costumes quite a bit, because Hunt thinks the Regency clothes look unattractive on women. They have also altered 'a few words' in the script. Also, on this first day, they were ahead of schedule by midday – which sounds like quickie filming."

Anxious and cynical, Isherwood was clearly suffering from separation anxiety – yet, in the long run, it was probably for the best that he was not there. One can easily see why Isherwood preferred writing novels and Bachardy favored painting portraits; these were mediums that were better suited to autonomous sensibilities.

In general, writers are rarely encouraged to be on set because the process is often riddled with compromises and on-the-spot adjustments. It can become soul crushing for scribes who are married to every word of their script. I know very well what it is like myself – which is why in recent years, I have refused to write screenplays. I am only a director-for-hire. To preserve my sanity. Between directing gigs, I write books like this one because I can do it my way. So, I can fully identify and empathize with Isherwood's emotional reaction to the progress report from Hunt. But at the same time, I can put it into perspective and judge it a bit more objectively. Things were not as bad as it sounded.

THE DAILY ROUTINE

The work schedule was five days per week, with three paid holiday breaks for Good Friday, April 20; Easter Monday, April 23; and, Spring Bank Holiday, Monday, May 28.

When shooting took place at Pinewood Studios, the typical workday lasted eight hours, plus one hour break for lunch. The call time was usually 8:30 A.M.; lunch was from 1:00-2:00 P.M.; and wrap was at 5:30 P.M. There were two 15-minute "tea and biscuit" breaks at 11:00 A.M. and 4:00 P.M. Dailies were screened at 5:30-6:30 P.M. in Theatre 1.

When location shoots were nearby, the cast and crew would report to Pinewood at 7:00 A.M. and be driven in cars and vans to the location by 8:00 A.M. and returned to the studio by 6:00 P.M. Special arrangements were made for Beachy Head, the one distant overnight location.

The only sequence shot at night was the burning of Dr. Frankenstein's laboratory – on a slightly later "split call," from 9:30 A.M. to 9:30 P.M. All other exterior nighttime sequences were shot day-for-night.

No shooting was done on weekends – with the exception of Saturday, June 2, (when the opera box-seat set and opera

Michael Pharey.

Michael Pharey in 2017 holding LSoH #38.

lobby staircase were shot) to make up for the prior Monday Spring Bank Holiday – so, it still amounted to a five-day work week. (Also, in order to be less disruptive utilizing the actual lobby staircase inside Pinewood's administration building, weekend shooting was preferred when most offices were closed.)

Studio chauffeurs were assigned to pick-up and return the producer, director, and the main cast members according to their individual call and wrap times. Dressing rooms were assigned to each cast member inside various studio buildings.

Michael Sarrazin and his makeup artist Harry Frampton would often start earlier than the rest of the cast and crew on days when the Creature makeup was needed to be camera-ready. The scheduling of this overtime was customized accordingly.

The cast and crew averaged about 65 people per day, plus extras, stand-ins, and stunt doubles as needed. For the week that the ballroom sequence was being filmed, the headcount bloated to 230 people per day.

On the heavier days, Michael Pharey was brought on as an additional third assistant director to help with crowd control. "I would corral all the extras and tell them things like when they were permitted their lunch and tea breaks," Pharey recalled in a 2016 interview. "My other duties included organizing a ham sandwich for James Mason and a chicken sandwich with black coffee for Agnes Moorehead." Well, someone had to do it.

Given that the "above the line" VIPs included a sizable number of LGBTQ+ folk, one might assume that the "below the line" rank and file of the crew would be just as diverse. Not necessarily.

"I think I was the only gay person on the entire shooting crew," Pharey confided. "It was my first job right out of film school. I was there to get a union ticket. I had no idea if being gay in this industry would be a problem or not, so, naturally, I was fascinated that the producer and his partner were so open about being a couple. It made a huge impression and gave me a great deal of courage and pride. Even so, I was very discreet and careful about my sexuality at that time. It was a macho industry."

After *Dr. Frankenstein*, Pharey went on to work as a sound camera operator on three Ken Russell movies: *Mahler*, *Tommy* and *Lisztomania*. Subsequently, he joined Thames Television as a film cameraman for international news and documentaries, including the controversial *This Week: Death on the Rock* about the 1988 deaths of three IRA members in Gibraltar that rocked the Thatcher government.

HISTORIC LOCATIONS

The exterior of Dr. Frankenstein's lodging house was shot March 23, 1973, at the Lych Gate, the fifteenth-century gatehouse of Vicarage Walk at St. Michael's Church in Bray Village, the civil parish bordering the Thames in Berkshire – near Bray Studios where many a Hammer film had been shot.

Another historic location was St. Mary Abbott's Hospital in Kensington which had "a perfectly preserved gem of a Dickensian ward" – a wing that had been closed off for decades that proved ideal for several scenes involving Frankenstein and Clerval, filmed April 5-6, 1973.

"It had been closed up for years," recalled Alec Smight, "but the old gas lamps were still there, and after special effects got them up and running again you really felt transported through time. Of course, that's one of the

Lacey's farmhouse erected in Burnham Beeches.

Blind Lacey welcomes the Creature to farmhouse.

Bride of Frankenstein, blind fiddler at cabin about to meet Monster.

spying on Agatha and Felix; and Agatha's death when the stagecoach runs over her.

On June 6, twenty-four miles from Pinewood Studios, Hambleden Village in Buckinghamshire was used for the crossroads sequence where Dr. Frankenstein insists on taking the injured man to the hospital in his carriage; and the coach encounter with Polidori when Dr. Frankenstein is taken away from Elizabeth on their honeymoon night.

THE MARY SHELLEY PROLOGUE

On May 16, twelve miles from Pinewood Studios, Virginia Water Lake in Windsor Great Park, Old Windsor, Berkshire, stood in for Lake Geneva, Switzerland, in the prologue featuring Mary Shelley, Percy Bysshe Shelley, Lord Byron and Dr. Polidori. This sequence was, of course, inspired by a similar prologue in *Bride of Frankenstein* featuring Elsa Lanchester as Mary Shelley, introducing her story to Percy Shelley (Douglas Walton) and Lord Byron (Gavin Gordon).

In the early stages of writing *Dr. Frankenstein*, Christopher Isherwood and Don Bachardy seriously considered bookending the movie with an epilogue featuring these same real-life characters established in the prologue.

On October 27, 1971, Isherwood wrote this in his diary: "Just after Don and I left the gym, two days ago, we saw a small man who looked a bit crazy and who limped. His hands were covered in small bags of cellophane; he was wearing them like gloves. They were very red, so they may have been burnt and therefore sensitive. But the thought struck me that maybe he had a neurotic fear of contamination. This naturally made me think of Dr. Polidori in our *Frankenstein* script. I said to Don: 'Suppose we have an epilogue at the end of the picture? Mary has just finished telling her story and they are all about to begin the picnic. Polidori is there, too; he has forgotten them… Some of the picnic food is sticky, so Mary says, 'Dr. Polidori, I fear you will have to take off those elegant gloves of yours, you'll spoil them, otherwise.' And Polidori does so. They all watch him – they are still under the spell of the story and half expect to see that his hands really *are* crippled. Polidori realizes what they are thinking. When the gloves are off, he holds up his hands to show them that they are perfectly formed. He smiles. The others all laugh. End of picture. Now—here's the synchronicity: Immediately after seeing the man with the cellophane bags, we went to Columbia Studios, where they were showing *The Shooting* [(1966)], a Western made by Monte Hellman, who directed *Two-Lane Blacktop*. (It's one of the best Westerns I've ever seen.) In it, Jack Nicholson plays a hired gunman *who wears gloves all the time*; it is said of him that he never takes his gloves off, 'even with a woman.' At the end, he and Warren

wonderful things about shooting a period piece in the UK; there are so many amazing places that seem almost untouched by time."

The farmhouse where Lacey (Sir Ralph Richardson) lives with his granddaughter Agatha (Jane Seymour) was prefabricated at Pinewood, then erected six miles away at Burnham Beeches, a nature preserve in Farnham, Buckinghamshire – frequently used for film productions, from *Goldfinger* to the *Harry Potter* franchise. Due to inclement weather conditions, these exterior cottage sequences could not be filmed on consecutive days which is why they started on May 29 and returned on June 1. On June 5 and 7, the same wooded area was utilized for the Creature

McCallum as Lord Byron in aborted FTTS prologue.

This Page: Super-rare photos of the aborted FTTS prologue; all that survives

Pagett, Whiting, Smight, McCallum, at location for aborted prologue.

Oates have a fight. Oates wants to put Nicholson out of action as a gunman, so *he cripples Nicholson's hand* by beating on it with a rock!"

Nonetheless, Isherwood and Bachardy never included this – nor any version of an epilogue featuring Mary Shelley & Co. – in any of their drafts of the script. But the idea is intriguing – and would have been a fascinating denouement for the movie, as well as a pay-off for what is set-up in the intended prologue. In fact, the more I've thought about this, the more I've wondered if James Whale had ever considered an epilogue for *Bride of Frankenstein*, as an extension of *his* prologue with Mary Shelley & Co. It makes perfect sense. Since the story is being told by Mary Shelley, why not give her the last word at the end?

During my deep dive into comparing various drafts of the *Dr. Frankenstein* script, I did come across one unique example of an epilogue that *did* make it into a draft. However, it was not written by Isherwood and Bachardy – due to the WGA Writers Strike, from March 6, 1973, through June 24, 1973, which prohibited their involvement. Since the filming began during the strike, on March 15, 1973, all necessary adjustments, cuts or embellishments had to be written by a non-WGA member. That's why the producer Hunt Stromberg Jr. took upon himself to make a number of changes on his own.

STROMBERG'S EPILOGUE

Two script revision pages, dated April 2, 1973, written by Hunt Stromberg Jr., added an Epilogue featuring Mary

Shelley & Co. Immediately after the avalanche occurs, crushing Dr. Frankenstein and the Creature, this is what was intended to follow:

(We cut to a block of ice being cracked with a pick. Camera pulls up to reveal Dr. Polidori, back at the picnic, preparing his lemonade.)

Polidori:
Well, so much for Mary's little story. I frankly doubt she will get anyone to publish it.

(We see Mary overhearing this but for now says nothing in response. Her eye is suddenly fascinated by the Brazilian butterfly circling above her.)

(Another angle Shelley and Byron.)

Shelley:
(pleased) Isn't my wife extraordinary? I was frightened almost to death by her story. (glancing at watch) My goodness, it's already after four o'clock and I'm famished.

Bryon:
Well, I'm not. Mary's story has caused me to <u>lose</u> my appetite.

Shelley:
You have lost your appetite my dear Byron because you <u>know</u> Mary's story of horror is much better than the one you tried.

(Byron gives him a cutting look.)

Shelley:
Actually, Mary has beaten us all, and she will probably become even more famous than you, Lord Byron.

Byron:
My dear Shelley, let us not get carried away.

(Cut to Mary. The butterfly has by now alighted on her shoulder.)

Mary:
(delighted) From the jungles of the Amazon, Brassolis Astyra. How beautiful it is. I wonder what it is doing here?

(She gently motions to the butterfly and it flies from her shoulder into the skies.)

Mary:
Oh, by the way, Dr. Polidori, I overheard your remarks. Not only shall my story be published but immodest though I may seem, I believe my Frankenstein will live forever.

The rest of the script resumes with the original Coda (Scene 263B) as previously written by Isherwood and Bachardy (never actually filmed). "It is the beginning of the Arctic summer. The great iceberg formed by the avalanche breaks away from the shore and slides down into the water. The whole ice floe is now cracking; open channels appear in it. Down one of these channels, the iceberg starts to drift. Days pass. The berg is now out at sea, in sunshine, drifting steadily southward. Gulls circle and land on it. Suddenly, the ice gives forth a strange high-pitched grinding sound.

A crack appears in it. The gulls take flight. Working its way up through the crack, the Creature's hand appears. Its fingers open as it feels the sunlight. FADE OUT. THE END." [NOTE: With considerable irony, the Creature's hand reacting to the sunlight takes on new meaning with this draft since Stromberg's insistence on changing the creation sequence from electricity (generated by lightning on a stormy night) to solar energy (collected in broad daylight).]

By the time the prologue with Mary Shelley & Co. was about to be shot on May 16, 1973, Stromberg had come to the logical and economical conclusion that the movie had far too many endings and the avalanche was powerful enough to stand on its own. Stromberg also feared that the coda might seem like a set-up for a sequel that was not intended. Consequently, the epilogue (written by Stromberg) and the coda (written by Isherwood & Bachardy) were cut from the script and never filmed.

Nevertheless, the prologue with Mary Shelley & Co. (written by Isherwood and Bachardy) was indeed filmed on May 16, 1973, and included in early rough cuts of the movie. It featured Nicola Pagett (as Mary Shelley), Leonard Whiting (as Percy Bysshe Shelley), David McCallum (as Lord Byron), and James Mason (as Dr. Polidori).

NBC executives decided it was too esoteric for the masses and replaced it with the Introduction featuring James Mason as himself in modern-day London (filmed August 25, 1973).

THE DROWNING SEQUENCE

On the same day that the prologue was shot (May 16), Virginia Water Lake in Windsor Great Park was also the body of water used when William Frankenstein (Karl Howman) dives out of a rowboat and drowns.

Karl Howman recalled, "In the scene, we were meant to be having a picnic by the lake and I go out on a rowing boat and shout, 'Come on, Victor! Come on in!' I dive off the boat into the water and never surface – supposedly having hit my head on a rock at the bottom of the lake. Victor comes charging into the water trying to save me but he can't find my body and it's too late. I've drown. The director wanted me to dive off the boat, then swim underneath the boat, come up the other side, out of shot, so they can't see me, and wait for him to yell, 'Cut!' That was the idea. Now, I wasn't a great swimmer but when you are starting out in the acting business, you agree to anything. (laughs) They row me out to the boat. I have britches on and a wig similar to Leonard Whiting's hair so we'd look like siblings. Everything went according to plan. I stood in the boat, yelled, 'Come on,

William Frankenstein (Karl Howman) wobbling in the boat.

CHAPTER THREE: FILMING

Victor Frankenstein (Whiting) wades into the lake toward boat.

Whiting can't find his drowned brother.

Open Clerval grave with Mason & Whiting, used for cover of teleplay book. (The Parish Church of St. Mary the Virgin in Hedgerley, Buckinghamshire).

Victor! Come on in!' I dove into the water, clawed my way under the boat – which was quite terrifying – but I finally made it and came up the other side, listened, and I heard Leonard screaming and splashing about. And then I *thought* I heard, 'Cut!' So, I climbed back in the boat. But, as I was climbing, I noticed that Leonard was still shouting and searching for me. Oh my God. The shot was still in progress and I'd ruined it. The director called, 'Cut!' I was all wet. My wig was coming loose, and they had to bring me back in. The director said, 'We'll have to do it again.' And I said, 'I can't do that again. That petrified me.' So, they used a stunt double [Roy Scammell] for the second take. In the film, you only see me in one shot, when I am standing in the boat, waving and shouting 'Come on, Victor!' And I'm quite sure they dubbed me as well. They wanted a posher voice. It's the smallest part in the history of cinema, I guess. (laughs) And I actually made it even smaller because of what happened when we were shooting."

THE HOLY TRINITY
Three historic churches appear in *Dr. Frankenstein*:

1. St. Mary's Church in Denham, filmed on April 3, 1973. "There is a scene in which McCallum follows Whiting into St. Mary's Church in Denham Village," recalled third assistant director Terry Pearce who was 24 years old when the movie was being shot. "I remember it quite well because, as an infant, I was actually christened there. Next door to the church, Whiting walks by an A-frame house that, in real-life, was the home of Sir John Mills."

The interior of the church was used for the daytime scene when Clerval sits behind Frankenstein. This church also appeared in *Kind Hearts and Coronets* and the series of Miss Marple movies starring Margaret Rutherford. Sections of the structure date back to the fourteenth century.

2. The Parish Church of St. Mary the Virgin in Hedgerley, Buckinghamshire (built in 1852), filmed on March 30, 1973. The cemetery outside this church was used for the nighttime grave-robbing scene with Frankenstein and Clerval. It was also used for Clerval's gravesite for the daytime encounter between Polidori and Frankenstein (as seen on the cover of the published teleplay). The interior was the setting for the nighttime confession scene between Frankenstein and the priest (Peter Sallis).

3. St. Mary the Virgin Church in Hambleden Village, Buckinghamshire, filmed on April 4, 1973. This twelfth-century cruciform church was the exterior and interior location for the funeral of William Frankenstein as well

St. Mary the Virgin Church in Hambleden Village, Buckinghamshire.

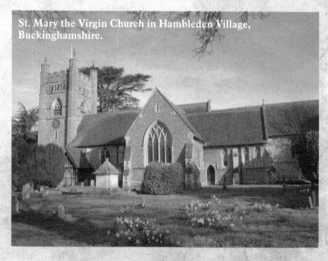

This Picture and Below: Church service. (St. Mary the Virgin Church in Hambleden Village, Buckinghamshire).

Across the aisle, Julian Barnes flirts with Seymour. Next to him is his mother (Patricia Varley) singing a hymn.

Cliveden aerial view.

Cliveden driveway view.

Titan crane in driveway at Cliveden, with Stromberg, director of photography Arthur Ibbetson in foreground; crew behind them.

as the sequence when Prima attends a church service with Victor, Elizabeth and her parents as the aristocrat (Julian Barnes) notices her from across the aisle. This church was also used as a location in *Chitty Chitty Bang Bang* and *Sleepy Hollow*.

THE PROFUMO LOVE NEST

The most lavish location in the movie was Cliveden, a ginormous mansion in Taplow, Berkshire, that portrayed the exterior of the Fanshawe estate, home of Elizabeth and her parents. Several carriages and horses from Cliveden's stables were also employed for the film – majestically photographed from a Titan crane. These sequences were completed in two days, March 20-21, 1973.

Built in 1851, Cliveden became the residence of Lord and Lady Astor and their descendants in 1893. For movies,

Cliveden had been used to double Buckingham Palace in the Beatles' film *Help!* and was featured in *The Yellow Rolls-Royce* and *The Promoter* starring Alec Guinness and, quite ironically, Valerie Hobson. Why? Because in 1963, Cliveden became notorious as the setting for "the Profumo Affair" where Hobson's husband John Profumo carried on his tryst with Christine Keeler. Though it will forever be infamous as "the Profumo love nest," Cliveden is now a world-famous resort hotel under managing director Johan Tham, husband of actress Jenny Agutter (*Logan's Run, Captain America: The Winter Soldier*).

CLIFFHANGER

At the half-way point in the original script, the Creature tries to commit suicide by walking into a river with rushing rapids that wash him downstream. Stromberg nixed that and came up with a far more visually stunning idea.

"The Creature should hurl himself off the White Cliffs of Dover," Stromberg announced at a production meeting. He

Beachy Head, aerial view of chalk cliffs.

The cast and crew stayed nearby at Grand Hotel, Sea Front in Eastbourne.

Helicopter with aerial camera operator Peter Allwark & Stromberg.

Stromberg at helicopter, looking through the eyepiece of the camera.

Associate Producer Ian Lewis, Production Manager Brian Burgess, Stromberg & Smight on the shore at the base of Beachy Head (where Sarrazin comes ashore after throwing himself off the cliff).

explained how this breathtaking panorama was the first sight of British land he had beheld during his ferry boat passage to England. "It made the hair on the back of my neck stand on end," Stromberg added. "I want that kind of impact when the Creature tries to end his life. As the climax of Part 1, it will literally be a cliffhanger."

The sequence was gut wrenching, played almost entirely without dialogue. Dr. Frankenstein chases the Creature to the edge of the cliff, begging him to stop. But, when the Creature turns to face Frankenstein, the doctor cannot express in words his true feelings. He does not have to. The Creature can see from his creator's expression nothing but revulsion, pity and regret. The Creature makes it easy for him by leaping from the precipice and plunging to what he hopes will be his death.

When Boris Karloff and James Whale were making *Frankenstein* in 1931, they shared the opinion that abandonment was central to the tragedy. In Denis Gifford's *Karloff: The Man, The Monster, The Movies*, Karloff himself is quoted as follows: "The most heartrending aspect of the creature's life, for us, was his ultimate desertion by his creator."

Many people – Stromberg included – have identified the cliff that was used for the Creature's attempted suicide as being the White Cliffs of Dover. Not true. After failing to

secure the White Cliffs of Dover for filming, the substitute location was, in fact, Beachy Head, another equally stunning chalk bluff in Eastbourne, Sussex. The precipice is the highest chalk sea cliff in Britain, rising 531 feet above sea level – and one of the most notorious suicide spots in the world. Shooting this sequence turned into one of the more elaborate undertakings of the production.

When asked about the dummy of Sarrazin that falls from the cliff, special effects artist Colin Chilvers recalled, "We built four identical dummies for multiple takes. The skeleton was made out of steel. We made sure that the arms would only bend like human arms. The weight was made to be roughly the same as Sarrazin so when it hit the water, it would be lifelike. Each dummy was dropped by helicopter near the cliff."

Stromberg explained, "For a shot that lasts about 30 seconds on film, it took two-and-a-half months of preparation, four dummies that had to be tested to fall like a human, seven cameras, four helicopters and two boats."

Whiting chasing Sarrazin in the distance.

Sarrazin stops in foreground. Whiting stops several feet behind.

Sarrazin turns (to face Whiting).

Whiting just stares (as Sarrazin).

Rejected by his creator, Sarrazin runs to the cliff, Whiting follows.

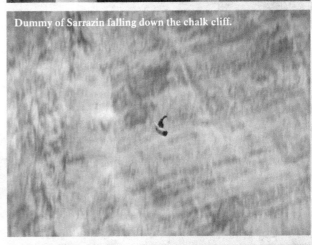

Dummy of Sarrazin falling down the chalk cliff.

Sarrazin's dummy splashes into the ocean.

Whiting arrives at the cliff's edge, looks down.

CHAPTER THREE: FILMING

Gaff: As Whiting retreats, a white car crosses in the distance.

Sarrazin's body washed ashore.

Wait! He's still alive!

Sarrazin gets up and heads off in search of someone who will love him. 'END OF PART ONE' title card.

Gaff Squad Alert: In the final helicopter shot when Leonard Whiting is walking away from the edge of the cliff, a white car can be briefly spotted scooting between two little hills in the distance – just before the image dissolves into the next sequence.

The two-day shoot, June 26-27, 1973, was the movie's only distant, overnight location – 124 miles from Pinewood Studios. As a result, a slightly reduced cast and crew of 50 people were transported by chauffeured cars, vans and buses and put up for one night at the Grand Hotel, Sea Front in Eastbourne. The call sheet noted, "This is a five-star hotel and… anyone eating in the hotel dining room should be formally dressed."

Other films that have used Beachy Head as a location include *Battle of Britain*, *Chitty Chitty Bang Bang*, *Quadrophenia*, *The Living Daylights*, *Harry Potter and the Goblet of Fire*, *Robin Hood: Prince of Thieves* and *Atonement*. For television, it has served as a location for *Monty Python's Flying Circus*, *The Prisoner*, *Luther* and *Black Mirror*.

IN AND AROUND PINEWOOD

The park where Frankenstein first sees boils starting to form behind the Creature's ear was filmed on April 9, 1973, at Pinewood Garden on the grounds of the studio behind Heatherden Hall where there is an ornamental balustraded bridge that spans a lake.

That same day, inside Heatherden Hall, the dinner scene (when Prima suddenly feels faint) was staged in the wood-paneled Boardroom (also used for scenes in Jack Clayton's *The Great Gatsby*, Harvey Dent's office in Tim Burton's *Batman*, and many a Bond film).

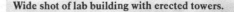

Wide shot of lab building with erected towers.

Roof detail of the lab building .

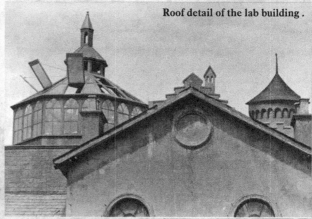

THE EPIC SAGA BEHIND *FRANKENSTEIN: THE TRUE STORY*

Left: Young Alec Smight on FTTS set.
Below: Young Alec Smight with fake moustache slates the burning of Frankenstein's laboratory building.
Inset: Slate held by Alec Smight, burning of building.

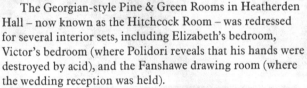

A series of pictures showing the burning of lab building.

The Georgian-style Pine & Green Rooms in Heatherden Hall – now known as the Hitchcock Room – was redressed for several interior sets, including Elizabeth's bedroom, Victor's bedroom (where Polidori reveals that his hands were destroyed by acid), and the Fanshawe drawing room (where the wedding reception was held).

On June 4, the exterior of Frankenstein's laboratory was shot near Pinewood at a derelict barn at the Old Stable Block, Dromenagh Farm, Seven Hills Road, Iver, Buckinghamshire.

Jack Smight's son Alec remembered this particular location in great detail. "On a regular basis," Alec recalled, "my mom would take me out of the American Community School I was attending and let me visit my dad on set. Week after week, we'd dart off to some distant historical site or ancient location, watching the production take shape. I was beginning to explore and have fun, but… once summer kicked in and the production was in full swing, it was one of the most amazing experiences I have ever had, and one that catalyzed my own nascent passion for filmmaking and set me on my future path in the entertainment industry."

Alec confirmed that the foreground building of Frankenstein's laboratory was an existing edifice and that the skylight tower that rises up from the rear was constructed by set builders.

"The torching of Victor Frankenstein's laboratory is an indelible memory," recalled Alec Smight. "There was no way I was going to miss it. By then, I had become friends with the crew, so the make-up people put a fake mustache on me, and the camera crew let me slate the shot! In fact, my dad kept a clip from the 35mm dailies of me in front of the lab, slate in hand – which I still have as a cherished memento."

When the complex goes up in flames and explodes, it was a controlled blaze that burned the abandoned building to the ground. This was executed under the tight supervision of Langley's Fire Brigade and Police Department.

Nearly everything else in the movie was shot on custom-built sets, including the interiors of Frankenstein's lodging house (E Stage), the cavernous laboratory and its adjacent

Whiting & Smight make fun of Sarrazin's height; Pinewood Garden, bridge in background.

Sarrazin hides behind curtain in cabin of ship.

Set of interior cabin on ship. Sarrazin surprises Mason.

Wide shot of balustraded bridge with Sarrazin & Whiting.

3rd Assistant Director Terry Pearce with clapper board on the set of interior cabin on ship.

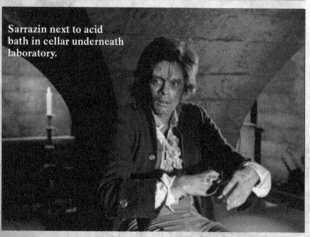

Sarrazin next to acid bath in cellar underneath laboratory.

study (F Stage), the cellar underneath the laboratory (H Stage), the interior of Lacey's farmhouse (F Stage), the box seat at the opera (F Stage), Prima's bedroom (G Stage), the grand ballroom where Prima's head gets plucked (B Stage), the deck of the schooner (A Stage), the schooner's interior cabins and hallway (F Stage), the massive Arctic wasteland with the schooner stuck in the ice floe (J Stage) and the ice grotto (studio backlot).

MONSTROUS MAKEUP

The haunting makeup for Michael Sarrazin's deteriorating Creature in *Dr. Frankenstein* has often been misreported as the work of Roy Ashton, the man behind many of Hammer Films' greatest monsters, including Christopher Lee in *The Mummy*, and Oliver Reed in *The Curse of the Werewolf*.

Above Top: Sarrazin with full-deterioration makeup at map to North Pole, art by Frederick Cooper. Above Left: Lee, Sarrazin, Cushing face masks by Ashton. Above Center: Ashton & Harry Frampton. Above Right: Ashton. Right: Frampton making up Christopher Lee for *I, Monster*.

Somewhat controversially, Ashton had also done the Creature (Kiwi Kingston) in *The Evil of Frankenstein* – but Stromberg and Sarrazin felt that design was too heavy for the actor's expressions to be discernible. This was the reason why Ashton was very specifically *not* assigned Sarrazin's Creature in *Dr. Frankenstein*. In an interview conducted by Jan Van Genechten and Gilbert Verschooten for *Little Shoppe of Horrors* No. 14, Ashton set the record straight: "I did *Frankenstein: The True Story* for Universal Television, which was produced by Hunt Stromberg Jr., whose father was a Hollywood celebrity. That was a lengthy film, I was there for six months! Harry Frampton made up Michael Sarrazin as the Monster, while I took care of all the others: James Mason, David McCallum, Leonard Whiting, and Sir Ralph Richardson."

Even so, Ashton *was* responsible for making a cast of Sarrazin's face to create a life-size plaster bust which Frampton used as a model to develop the prosthetics that would be applied during the shoot.

"There were six stages of makeup," producer Hunt

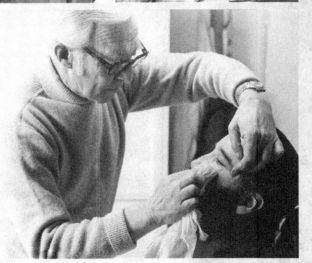

Stromberg Jr. explained. "It was a terrifically precise and difficult thing to do. The Creature had to look burned and then the burns had to begin healing. We had to make sure the makeup never immobilized Sarrazin's face. By the time the fourth stage was reached, the task of applying his makeup took five hours to complete."

Three pieces of Dave Matsuoka artwork – Left: Sarrazin holds Seymour's dead body. Center: Whiting examines Seymour's head in jar. Right: Sarrazin holds Seymour's decapitated head at ball.

Whiting with brain in jar.

Seymour head as Agatha, in jar.

"It was essential the Creature would not look grotesque," Sarrazin insisted. "The change had to be gradual. First growths, like warts, behind the ear; then a slight bulging of the forehead, a coarsening and thickening of the skin, the head growing slightly lopsided."

These six distinct stages of the Creature's deterioration had to be carefully mapped out for continuity purposes, scene by scene.

"I was in that makeup for ten weeks of the five months we spent on the film," Sarrazin recalled, "starving through lunch because I couldn't go into the commissary looking like that."

The Creature's deterioration, however, was not the only gruesome requirement of the makeup department. Other grim curios included a dummy of Sarrazin's entire body to drop off the cliff; a cast of Jane Seymour's face for her severed head; a body cast of Seymour to submerge in water; a scar around Seymour's neck; an acid-scarred stump at the end of

THE EPIC SAGA BEHIND *FRANKENSTEIN: THE TRUE STORY*

McCallum picking up crawling arm from floor.

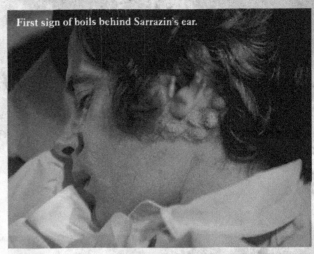

First sign of boils behind Sarrazin's ear.

Whiting starts to remove glove of Mason's right hand.

Whiting's hands remove Mason's back glove.

Stromberg with Sarrazin in early stage of deterioration; as a joke, Sarrazin lets his fake teeth denture hang loose from his mouth.

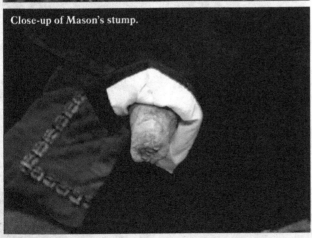

Close-up of Mason's stump.

James Mason's right arm; a shriveled and scarred hand at the end of Mason's left arm; and Mason's burnt skeletal corpse (post lighting strike). Ashton concluded, "We might hold the record for the number of damaged limbs, diseased faces and general oddities made for any one production."

THE CRAWLING ARM

"The crawling arm in the picture was actually cast from mine," explained makeup artist Roy Ashton in *Little Shoppe of Horrors* No. 14.

The interior mechanics of the arm were devised by special effects technician Colin Chilvers: "I wanted control over the fingers of the arm which was how the arm was going to move, so I used radio control servos. The arm had batteries and a radio control receiver inside of it – which allowed me to move each finger separately. The outer skin of the arm was made of rubber and so when we added the mechanics inside, the weight of the arm was fairly substantial. I didn't want to use wires to pull it along. I wanted the fingers to actually crawl and be able to pull the weight of the arm themselves. When we first tested it, the fingers didn't have enough traction on the floor. They just scratched and didn't move the arm at all. So, we had to embed into the fingertips little tiny pins that were sticking out so when the fingers scratched at the floor, the pins dug into the surface like little ice picks and were able to pull the weight along."

Ashton remarked, "That was really a most eerie sort of effect, turning out much more convincing than the hand we previously used in *Dr. Terror's House of Horrors*."

Stromberg was so impressed with the arm, he boasted to

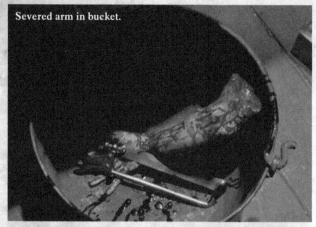

Severed arm in bucket.

Makeup artist Roy Ashton's real arm was drafted into service to grab Leonard Whiting's hand.

Whiting with severed arm in open doctor's bag.

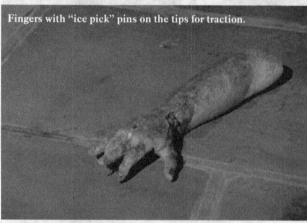

Fingers with "ice pick" pins on the tips for traction.

Styrofoam arm disintegrates with acetone.

Whiting & McCallum with severed arm.

THE EPIC SAGA BEHIND *FRANKENSTEIN: THE TRUE STORY*

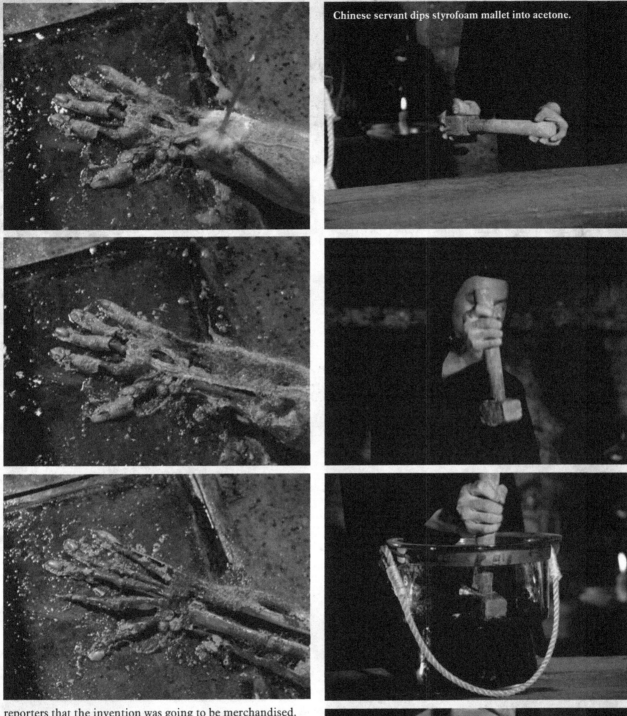

Chinese servant dips styrofoam mallet into acetone.

reporters that the invention was going to be merchandised. Sadly, that novelty never crawled onto store shelves.

There is one moment when the amputated arm / hand grabs Leonard Whiting's hand and David McCallum has to pry it off. This was shot in close-up in order to use a real forearm and hand for the action. Roy Ashton's own arm was drafted into service for this gripping moment. Since he had molded the fake version from his own arm – and he had shaved the hair off his arm for the molding process – it was a perfect match in every way.

Winner of seven Academy Awards, makeup artist extraordinaire Rick Baker watched the premiere broadcast of *Frankenstein: The True Story* in 1973 at the age of 22 — the same year he received his first screen credit as the makeup artist on John Landis' *Schlock*. "*Frankenstein: The True Story* made a huge impression on me," Baker explained in a 2018

interview for this book. "There were so many memorable moments but the one that intrigued me the most was the crawling arm. When Dr. Frankenstein poured acid on that arm and it disintegrated right before our eyes, I thought, 'How the hell did they do that?!' I was mesmerized."

The answer to Baker's question comes directly from the creator of this effect, Colin Chilvers: "We started with a plastic skeleton and added fake blood vessels and muscles. Then we made the exterior skin out of styrofoam because it quickly melts when you pour acetone onto it."

Similarly, the iron mallet that Polidori's Chinese servant dissolves in acid was made of styrofoam and dipped in acetone.

BEETLE MANIA

Special effects technician Brian Smithies created the large black beetle that is brought to life by Clerval. "I only had about three weeks to make the beetle," recalled Smithies in a 2016 interview for this book. "It was a very large species of beetle called the *Goliathus goliatus* which was the biggest one

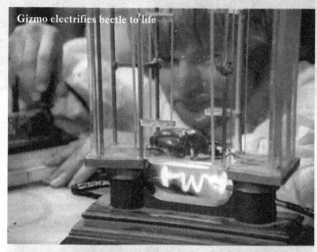
Gizmo electrifies beetle to life

Brian Smithies.

McCallum holds beetle as Whiting observes.

McCallum shows Whiting the contraption to revive beetle.

McCallum's finger nudges the resurrected beetle to crawl.

we could get at the time. I made a fiberglass cast of it and created all the internal mechanics. We managed to find these absolutely miniscule electric motors from Swiss Medical Engineering [SME]. They were very powerful little motors with tiny little gear boxes. I had to build everything around that. There was a train of gears and levers that operated so that the legs moved back and lifted and came forward."

THE BUTTERFLY EFFECT

Smithies also created the mechanized butterfly that comes to life and flutters around Elizabeth until she smashes it with a Bible. "I cast a butterfly body and then obtained some real butterfly wings," Smithies recalled. "Little spring metal supports went up the wings. These were hinged at the

Butterfly on Bible.

Pagett with butterfly.

Whiting tries to console Elizabeth after butterfly scares her.

bottom. Coming off the hinge was a tag that I connected with another tag using a tiny little homemade rubber band. It was fairly intricate. To get it airborne, I mounted it on the end of a very thin wire on a fishing rod. It was tungsten wire – the wire they use in lightbulbs. It's so thin, the camera lens doesn't see it. Then I had to operate it with the feeling of a butterfly flitting about the room."

STEAMPUNK GIZMOS

Designed by Wilfrid Shingleton, Frankenstein's steampunk laboratory was something to behold, the largest ever constructed for a Frankenstein film up to that time, filled to the brim with Rube Goldberg-like mechanical gizmos.

When Dr. Frankenstein is gathering rays of the sun to power up the solar batteries, he adjusts a circular series of solar panels that light up with a brilliant, almost blinding white light. When asked if this was a post-production optical effect, Brian Smithies said, "No. We covered those panels with a material called Scotchlite. It was new at the time, made

Wide shot of lab, with Scotchlite reflector.

Whiting next to Scotchlite reflector.

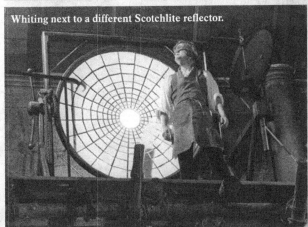

Whiting next to a different Scotchlite reflector.

Wide low angle of lab.

Reflector explodes.

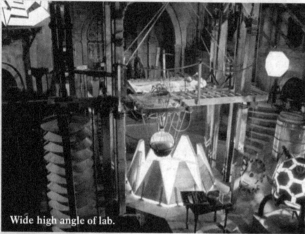
Wide high angle of lab.

Explosion in the laboratory.

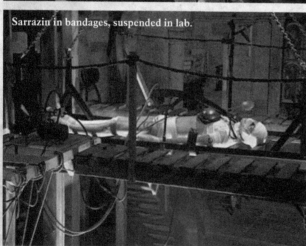
Sarrazin in bandages, suspended in lab.

by 3M. It's a highly reflective, retroreflective material that is now used for movie theatre screens. It is a cloth material coated with millions of tiny glass beads. You shine a light at it, and it will send a reflection straight back at the source. It's the principal of the headlights of a car hitting the eyes of a cat in the road. You know how it makes the eyes glow? That's what happens with each bead. It was the same material they used for the front screen projection shots that Wally Veevers and Charlie Staffell created for the film." Scotchlite was also used for Polidori's glowing hypnosis locket.

Additionally, the special effects department created all of the laboratory chemical potions and pyrotechnics. Colin Chilvers recalled, "We had Leonard Whiting toss a spoonful

Sarrazin's body glowing with solar power.

Scotchlite was used to illuminate Mason's glowing hypnosis locket.

Lab set on fire, later in the film.

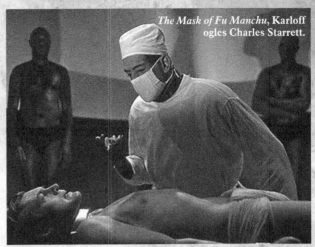
The Mask of Fu Manchu, Karloff ogles Charles Starrett.

of sulfur into the vat of liquid that created fireworks and smoke. We also pumped petroleum up from the bottom of the vat to burn on the surface of the water."

"During the scene when the Creature is made," Hunt Stromberg Jr. explained to a reporter, "there were six locked-off cameras, meaning that they weren't being run by cameramen, and only Roy Whybrow was on the set – it was that dangerous to do."

Besides the explosives in the creation sequence, the lab is also set on fire later in the film – another controlled blaze that had to be extinguished after each take.

All of the laboratory sequences involving the Creature being brought to life took ten days, spread from April 16 through May 2, 1973. Then, the crew moved to another stage while the art department transformed the laboratory set for its next inhabitant.

The Mask of Fu Manchu: Loy, Karloff in throne, Starrett with pith helmet.

FU MANCHU MAKEOVER

By the time Prima is brought to life, Frankenstein's lab has undergone an extreme makeover instigated by Dr. Polidori whose taste in decorating and fashion has the lush flamboyance of Dr. Fu Manchu – directly inspired by *The Mask of Fu Manchu*, the 1932 Karloff movie produced by Hunt Stromberg Jr.'s father.

Having commandeered the laboratory, Polidori surrounds himself in opium-den chic and gets more comfortable sporting a smart black kimono robe – à la Dr. No, the Chinese arch villain from the James Bond novel and movie of the same name, who likewise had artificial hands disguised in black gloves; with shades of Dr. Mabuse, the criminal mastermind of three Fritz Lang movies, who hypnotized victims with Chinese glasses and Chinese incantations; and a dash of Marvel's Dr. Strange, Master of Black Magic, the surgeon with injured hands, mystic powers of persuasion and a Chinese manservant named Wong.

Polidori one-ups Dr. Strange with *two* Chinese houseboys who obediently spruce up the lab with wall-to-wall Chinese décor – including silk screens, lanterns, chandeliers, urns, potted plants, a chaise lounge, silk pillows, a giant fireplace bellows with golden dragon ornamentation, and a pagoda-shaped

Thesiger as Pretorius in *Bride of Frankenstein*.

Dr. No – one of many influences.

CHAPTER THREE: FILMING

129

Two Chinese servants: Kim Teoh & Tony Then.

Left: German poster for Fritz Lang's *The Testament of Dr. Mabuse* (1933). Right: Dr. Strange comic book from 1973; first cover appearance of servant Wong. (Courtesy of Marvel Comics)

birdcage with live pheasants (supervised by bird expert Jacque Shelton – who also helped wrangle swans for lakeside scenes).

Even the exterior of Polidori's carriage is decked out in red and green Chinese symbols with winged-dragon gargoyles jutting out from the corners. Embellishing the upper rim of the coach are thirty golden jingle bells to announce his arrival from a mile away.

Unapologetically, Polidori explains to Frankenstein, "The day after you left rather abruptly, I moved in. Being a confirmed traveler, I've learned to make myself at home wherever I go." Isherwood's use of the phrase "confirmed traveler" was a sly play on words: "confirmed bachelor" is a polite euphemism for a gay man – and Polidori fit the bill on all counts. After all, as delineated earlier, the character was primarily based on the overtly queer Dr. Pretorius from *Bride of Frankenstein*. But the addition of Chinese servants, mysticism and imagery is clearly rooted in Stromberg's seminal fascination with *The Mask of Fu Manchu* in which Karloff's portrayal of the supervillain was blatantly homosexual.

In the article "Queer & Now & Then: 1932" for *Film Comment*, journalist Michael Koresky wrote that it was "perhaps the queerest version" of all Fu Manchu characterizations, "presented as a dandyish, Harvard-educated aesthete. The famously lisping Karloff delights not only in threatening and enacting terrible violence but

also in his own glittering fineries and elegantly manicured long fingernails, not to mention his cadre of muscled Asian and African slave boys, rarely dressed in more than skimpy underwear. Of particular interest here is the fact that the most elaborate, most explicit, and sexualized tortures is not of the main explorer's fetching daughter Sheila, but of her strapping, dopey, and equally dull husband Terrence 'Terry' Granville. Played by former Dartmouth footballer Charles Starrett, the alarmingly square-jawed 6-foot-2-incher, was one of those early sound actors hired for his deep voice as much as his ability to look pretty. The film's queered gaze is first revealed when Fu Manchu hands Starrett over to his wicked, nymphomaniacal daughter (Myrna Loy, shockingly), who proceeds to have two of her father's underwear-clad

Sarrazin brings the corpse of Agatha (Seymour) to the laboratory hoping they can bring her back to life.

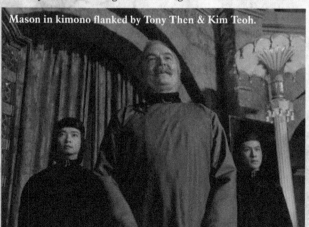
Mason in kimono flanked by Tony Then & Kim Teoh.

THE EPIC SAGA BEHIND *FRANKENSTEIN: THE TRUE STORY*

Laboratory with Chinese makeover.

Tony Then, Kim Teoh, Mason & Sarrazin with corpse of Seymour.

Mason shows off the madeover lab to Whiting; Sarrazin behind mask.

Mason tells Sarrazin to take off that silly mask. We see more Chinese décor around them.

Sarrazin lowers mask.

Whiting & Mason mix chemicals for the creation of Prima.

Mason shows Whiting the tank with Prima's dummy under water.

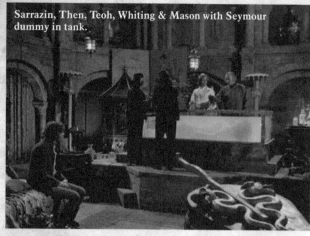

Sarrazin, Then, Teoh, Whiting & Mason with Seymour dummy in tank.

Whiting & Mason over tank. Whiting pours chemical into fluid.

Whiting & Mason pour chemicals as Sarrazin observes.

Teoh, Whiting and Then drop chemicals into tank as Mason observes.

Whiting adds more chemicals. Mason observes.

Rainbow of colors begin to appear in the bubbling tank of fluid.

Chemicals spark and combust in the tank.

Fire erupts in the tank of fluid.

THE EPIC SAGA BEHIND *FRANKENSTEIN: THE TRUE STORY*

Colorful lava lamp-style blobs form in the tank.

Prima (Seymour) is seen through the lava lamp-style blobs with hair blown in slow motion to make it seem that she is under water.

Dressed and dry, Prime (Seymour) sleeps after her chemical birth. Mason and Whiting discuss their success.

Sarrazin, Mason and Tony Then.

In 1972, MGM re-released three classic horror films: *The Mask of Fu Manchu*, *Mark of the Vampire*, and *Dr. Jekyll and Mr. Hyde*. This is a press-kit cover for the triple bill. There were protests about offensive depictions of Asians in THE MASK OF FU MANCHU — which fueled its notoriety.

slaves chain him up, rip his shirt off, and whip him, while the young woman looks on with frenzied sexual excitement ('Faster, faster!'). Afterward she asks, 'He is not entirely unhandsome is he, Father?' Daddy's response: 'For a white man, no.' The homoeroticization becomes truly unambiguous in a later, far more extended scene in which Fu Manchu himself delightedly hovers over the prone body of the man, clad only in a loincloth and manacled to a table, and proceeds to drag his nails over his heaving, sweaty chest."

Reinforcing Stromberg's formative childhood memories of that production was a controversial national theatrical re-release of *The Mask of Fu Manchu* by MGM in 1972, just a few months before *Dr. Frankenstein* went into production. The reissue was met with heated protests from the Japanese-American Citizens League. Activists demanded, unsuccessfully, that MGM halt the release, complaining that it "was offensive and demeaning to Asian-Americans."

One criticism was that Caucasian actors (Boris Karloff and Myrna Loy) played the two leading Chinese characters. Though this casting practice is now deemed racist, it was standard operating procedure back then – and would continue to be quite common for at least another decade after this 1972 protest, as evidenced by *The Fiendish Plot of Fu Manchu* (1980) starring Peter Sellers as Fu Manchu, and *Charlie Chan and the Curse of the Dragon Lady* (1981) starring Peter Ustinov as Charlie Chan.

Aside from this legitimate concern, however, the group's other main objection focused on Fu Manchu being portrayed as "an ugly evil homosexual." Fighting racism with homophobia was perhaps not the best way to get their message across.

In any event, this timely reexamination of *The Mask of Fu Manchu* instigated the infusion of Chinese elements into *Dr. Frankenstein*.

LEARNING CURVES

Colin Chilvers explained, "When the girl monster is being made, they had hired a nude body model [Nicola Austin, the Playboy Bunny in *Old Dracula*] to stand-in for Jane Seymour – and she was being brought to life in this giant vertical test tube. Our job in the special effects department was to fill this tube with liquid. So, we conducted a test and as the water began to rise around this nude model, no one had anticipated that the water in a circular tube would act as a magnifier. Suddenly, this beautiful woman's body looked like an American football player, twice the width that she was high."

"That was quite funny," Brian Smithies agreed. "The most magnificent torso you'd ever seen… quite

Brian Smithies.

Rubenesque… but no arms. Over lunch, we had to quickly create a thin cutout out of plywood and painted Jane Seymour as very thin and skinny. We used that as the figure in the test tube."

In addition to the vertical test tube, a dummy of Jane Seymour's body was also submerged in a horizontal tank of liquid. "For that, we had a metal-framed tank with half-inch-thick glass," Smithies recalled. "In those days, we used putty as a sealant. But, of course, putty always gets pushed out by the weight of the water and the water runs all over the place. Well, they'd just invented this wonderful stuff called silicone rubber and it sticks glass to itself so we thought this would be ideal. We set up a tank, filled it with water and it was wonderful. Not a leak anywhere. Then we added liquid paraffin wax for this sort of lava lamp effect [mineral oil and paraffin wax of various colors]. What we didn't know is that silicone rubber dissolves in petroleum-based products. So, the water leaked even worse than before. There was a learning curve."

To simplify matters, Jane Seymour was filmed in certain shots with no water at all, in slow motion, with fans blowing her hair to simulate underwater movement. Foreground

This Picture: Rare nude version Nicola Austin stand-in for Seymour. (Never in a release print of the movie.) Inset: Sheet-covered alternate version Nicola Austin. (Release version)

THE EPIC SAGA BEHIND *FRANKENSTEIN: THE TRUE STORY*

Giant phallus with nude Nicola Austin (Seymour's double) inside.

Sarrazin fears fire that has erupted in the tank holding Seymour.

glass tanks of liquid with bubbles and undulating blobs of lava lamp goop added to the illusion. Or, as critic Ansel Faraj amusingly called it in his review, "lava lamp mysticism."

There is a brief sequence when Dr. Frankenstein stitches the head of Agatha onto a female body under Dr. Polidori's supervision – as the Creature watches from the sidelines. The only version that made it into the U.S. television cut and the international theatrical cut was the one in which Jane Seymour's body double, Nicola Austin, is lying horizontally on a slab, on her back, with her torso politely covered by a white sheet. There was, however, an alternate version in which there is no white sheet at all – with Austin's full-frontal naked body exposed. Obviously, nudity would never have been allowed on NBC-TV. This alternate nude footage was intended for a sexier international theatrical cut. When this more explicit version was submitted to the British Board of Film Classification (BBFC) for release in the UK, it was going to receive an X certificate which, in 1974, meant that no one under 18 would be admitted. By substituting the version in which the body was covered with the sheet, the board awarded the film an AA certificate, which lowered the age restriction to no one under 14. The powers-that-be at Universal decided there was not enough nudity to warrant limiting the age of the audience, so the nude footage was never released for any version of the film. Nevertheless, a color photo of the nude version has survived and can be seen on page 134.

All these scenes of the Chinese-decorated laboratory – involving the creation of Prima and the aftermath – were shot in eight days, spread from May 4-15, 1973.

POACHING THE PHANTOM OF THE OPERA

The sequences at the opera house were not as complex nor as expensive as they might seem. There are several isolated shots of Frankenstein and the Creature sitting in a box seat inside the opera house auditorium watching *The Marriage of Figaro* – as we hear the opera being performed off-camera (a licensed recording, by the way). These are merely tight shots of an isolated box-seat set constructed on F Stage at Pinewood, filmed on June 2, 1973.

Artwork by Adrian Salmon.

Giant phallus with painted wooden cutout of thin Seymour.

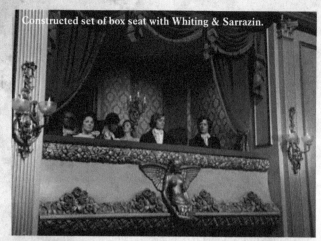
Constructed set of box seat with Whiting & Sarrazin.

Borrowed footage of Susanna Foster's curtain call in *The Phantom of the Opera* (1943).

Various Peter Melrose matte paintings

Aliens.

Aliens.

Dracula Has Risen from the Grave, plus two castle mattes below.

Melrose painting matte for *The Fearless Vampire Killers.*

The one-and-only wide shot of the entire auditorium – when we see the audience applauding the diva's curtain call – is actually a clip from Universal Pictures' *The Phantom of the Opera* (1943). The diva onstage is actress Susanna Foster – though she is very tiny in the frame and not easily recognized. Because the footage came from Universal's film library, it was repurposed free of charge.

There was also a sequence around the stairs in the lobby of the opera house that takes place during the intermission – when the Creature is introduced to Countess Duval – and then a brief bit when Frankenstein exchanges glances with Dr. Polidori on his way back to his seat. Third assistant director Terry Pearce confirmed, "This was 'cheated' on the back staircase of Heatherden Hall at Pinewood Studios – with fifty-four extras employed as atmosphere. At the top of those stairs were the offices of producer Peter Rogers and director Gerald Thomas, the team that made all the *Carry On* pictures." In fact, their latest film, *Carry On Girls*, was shooting at Pinewood the same time that *Dr. Frankenstein* was in production there.

THE GRAND BALLROOM

The opulent grand ballroom for Prima's debutante ball was constructed on B Stage, with faux marble columns, gold trim, elaborate floor design and wall murals intricately painted by the art department in pale hues of pink and green. A white sculpture of a nude woman was displayed on a revolving pedestal.

Contacted in 2017, matte painter Peter Melrose recalled, "Back in those days, a lot of my work was 'topping up' sets. For instance, for Terence Young's *The Amorous Adventures of Moll Flanders* [starring Kim Novak, 1965], a ballroom set was

THE EPIC SAGA BEHIND *FRANKENSTEIN: THE TRUE STORY*

Various Peter Melrose mattes for *The Fearless Vampire Killers*.

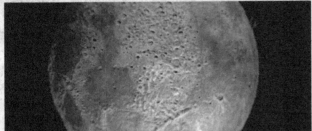

Polanski waving to Melrose painting backdrop *Fearless Vampire Killers*.

Veronica Carlson with Melrose matte in *Dracula Has Risen from the Grave*.

Ballroom set with painted wall and floor designs by Peter Melrose.

Whiting dances with Seymour.

built up to a certain height and then, beyond that, I created a matte painting on glass that extended the height of the walls and finished off the ceiling and the chandeliers. I did that sort of thing all the time – but, oddly enough, *not* on *Dr. Frankenstein*. The producer, Hunt Stromberg Jr., wouldn't have it. He insisted on the real thing."

So, the walls of the ballroom set for *Dr. Frankenstein* rose a precipitous 25-feet – and had practical ceiling extensions when briefly needed for the widest angles. A giant chandelier was hung in the center of the room. Nevertheless, authenticity could only go so far. A double-door opened at

CHAPTER THREE: FILMING

137

Smight with bullhorn to communicate with large crowd of ballroom extras.

Smight and Mason check out the nude statue that gets knocked over during the chaos at the ball.

Sarrazin throws pedestal.

In the aftermath of the chaos at the ball; Smight directs Whiting & Sarrazin.

one end of the ballroom. This is where Margaret Leighton arrived in her Little Bo Peep getup – and where the Creature makes his startling entrance. Beyond that, a long hallway is visible in the background. Or so it appears.

"The producer wanted a hallway extension to be built full-scale," Melrose explained, "but there was simply not enough room left on the stage to do it. So, on canvas, I painted a large forced-perspective hallway backdrop that you see outside those double doors. I also painted the doors and some other embellishments for the ballroom set in the French baroque style. Stromberg's aide, Jacque – who was always by his side – came over to me and I thought to myself, 'Uh-oh. They must not like it.' I braced myself for the worst. Then Jacque opened his mouth and said, 'Hunt loves your decoration so much, he'd like you to come over to America and paint some of that in our house.' I was very relieved – and very flattered. However, I politely declined."

For five consecutive days of shooting, May 21-25, 1973, 150 extras were hired as atmosphere to populate the ballroom.

MAURICE JARRE & MICHEL LEGRAND

Eight weeks into the fourteen-week shoot, Isherwood reported in his diary, "Maurice Jarre, who composes music for films, called to say he had been in England and had seen an hour-and-a-half of *Frankenstein* footage, because Hunt wants him to do the *Frankenstein* music. He said that he had been greatly impressed by what he had seen."

By then, Jarre, 48, had already won two Oscars for *Lawrence of Arabia* and *Doctor Zhivago* – and would later win a third for *Passage to India*. Not to mention six Oscar nominations on top of that.

Isherwood explained that Jarre ultimately decided to pass because "he didn't want to do the music if the film is to be only for TV." Jarre's snobbery didn't last long. The following year, he scored the television production of *Great Expectations* that, ironically enough, featured two cast members from *Frankenstein: The True Story*: James Mason and Margaret Leighton. A dozen years later, Jarre would finally get to score a theatrical Frankenstein film: *The Bride* (1985).

According to Phyllis Allarie, Stromberg then approached two-time Oscar winner Michel Legrand (*The Thomas Crown Affair*, *The Summer of '42*, Robert Fuest's *Wuthering Heights*, *The Go-Between*, *Lady Sings the Blues*) but the composer was committed to score Richard Lester's *The Three Musketeers* which was being rushed for European release dates in December 1973.

MID-LIFE CRISIS

On April 18, 1973, *Daily Variety* published a report from London about the shoot-in-progress. Refreshingly honest, Stromberg told the trade paper, "Anyone looking for the remake to be a gothic monster yarn can forget it. While the new edition retains the spirit and theme of the original novel, it's otherwise a total invention based on a romantic conception in which, for one thing, the manmade creature is a beauty and not horrific."

The network had a completely different impression of what was being made. NBC VP of Programming Larry White issued the following statement on June 28, 1973: "Isherwood wanted to tell the Mary Shelley story just as she told it, and has used most of her material." Clearly, White never read the Shelley novel and seemed oblivious to the contradiction Stromberg had been telling reporters.

As the Creature enters the ballroom, we see Peter Melrose's forced-perspective backdrop painting of the hallway outside the double-doors.

The film was being edited by Richard Marden as they went along and, about halfway through the shooting schedule, it became apparent that the running time was turning out to be much longer than the page-count of the script had indicated. Due to the Writers' Strike, Stromberg had to abbreviate the remaining material to avoid excessive footage being left on the cutting room floor – and to curtail the budget overrun.

In a memo recommending cuts, Stromberg wrote, "Instinct tells me we should find a way to go straight from the mayhem at the ball to the ship, omitting the whole jail sequence, the rooftops, etc."

Smight, Marden and their bosses at Universal agreed. With all those sequences tossed out, a new scene was devised by Stromberg as a bridge between the catastrophe at the ball

– when Prima is beheaded by the Creature – and the ship-at-sea with Frankenstein, Elizabeth, Polidori and the Creature on board. This connecting thread involved Elizabeth manipulating the Chief Constable into dropping charges against Dr. Frankenstein.

Isherwood later grumbled about this scene – causing many to assume that every word of dialogue spoken between the Chief Constable (Sir John Gielgud) and Elizabeth (Nicola Pagett) came from Stromberg. The truth, however, is that the dialogue is largely a cut-and-paste pastiche of lines from an excised scene (written by Isherwood and Bachardy) at the police station during which Dr. Polidori manipulates the Chief Constable into dropping charges against Dr. Frankenstein – which, by the way, had a fatal flaw in logic. Earlier in the story, it had been established time and again that Polidori possessed hypnotic powers and, therefore, could have just hypnotized the Chief Constable into releasing Dr. Frankenstein from custody. So, despite Isherwood's objections, it made much more sense for Elizabeth to manipulate the Chief Constable using her own verbal powers of persuasion – which, at the same time, made her character less passive.

Whenever inspiration struck, Stromberg would scribble down ideas and lines of dialogue on the backs of envelopes, matchbooks, napkins or whatever he could find at any given moment. At the end of each week, those notes would be gathered and transcribed.

"Hunt was forever tweaking the script," recalled Stromberg's secretary Phyllis Allarie who was 24 years old in 1973. "On most Saturdays, Hunt would have his driver, Tom Preston, pick me up at home at around 10 o'clock in the morning and drive me to Grosvenor Square. Hunt would dictate his revisions while I took shorthand on my notepad. Sometimes Jacque would come in and give a little aside. But primarily it was just Hunt and myself. I remember Hunt would pace back and forth in the room as he dictated to me, all the while chain smoking. Each time he passed by, I noticed the length of the ashes at the end of his cigarette growing precariously longer and longer, fearful they would fall on me. They never did – but I was always wary of that. Once we were done, we would all gather in the dining room for a lovely luncheon: Hunt, Jacque, Jacque's mother Doris

Little Maria by the lake, played by Marilyn Harris.

Son of Frankenstein – Peter von Frankenstein (Donnie Dunagan).

Ghost of Frankenstein – Monster throws man off roof. Inset: *Ghost of Frankenstein* – Monster incarcerated at the police station, chained to a chair; Gallow visits him, unafraid.

Ghost of Frankenstein – Chaney holds Janet Ann Gallow on roof.

THE EPIC SAGA BEHIND *FRANKENSTEIN: THE TRUE STORY*

and myself. Hunt always had food brought in from a very swish French restaurant. The waiter in his uniform would ring the bell and it would arrive the good old-fashioned way. Huge, huge platters with these silver domes. It was fantastic. The driver would take me home late afternoon and then, on Monday morning, I would go into the production office, type up the new pages and have them distributed. Normally, I didn't like working on weekends, but Hunt was so much fun, I didn't mind it one bit."

Ultimately, when compared to Isherwood and Bachardy's authorized published teleplay, Stromberg's embellishments to the final film were not as numerous as one might suspect – and were far outweighed by the trims he had to make in order to reign in length and budgetary concerns.

One of the scenes that was dropped was a lynch mob sequence in the town square (originally scheduled to be filmed on location in Haddenham Village, Buckinghamshire) with the Creature on display in a cage – after being captured for murdering Prima. The script reads: "People crowd around its barred cell... the Creature entertains the onlookers. It is clowning, playing the monster, a monster that is really harmless... The onlookers are puzzled by its behavior at first, but then they are amused. Children begin to laugh. The grown-ups begin to tease it... They have moved in close and are pressing against the bars. This is the opportunity for which the Creature has been waiting. Still clowning, it sidles up near to the bars, then suddenly grabs a tiny girl from her father's arms. Instantly, its manner changes. It becomes ferocious

Chloe Franks with voodoo doll in *The House That Dripped Blood*.

and terrifying. It holds the child – who is still laughing and thinking this is all a game – threatening to dash her against the bars. Then it points to the gate of its cage, demanding to be let out... A constable unlocks the gate of the cage... The Creature comes out still holding the child in front of it like a shield... The others watch in tense silence but the child laughs... When it has reached the other side of the square, it carefully puts the child down. Then it turns and dashes off. Little Girl (beginning to cry): 'Take me with you!'"

This sequence of the Creature interacting with an innocent child who is not afraid of him was directly inspired by similar scenes in the original *Frankenstein* (Little Maria by the lake, played by Marilyn Harris), *Son of Frankenstein* (Peter von Frankenstein played by Donnie Dunagan) and *Ghost of Frankenstein* (Cloestine Hussman played by Janet Ann Gallow).

An April 13, 1973, production memo announced that 9-year-old horror film veteran Chloe Franks (*Trog, The House That Dripped Blood, I, Monster, Tales from the Crypt, Whoever Slew Auntie Roo?*) had been officially contracted from the Corona Stage School to play the Little Girl Hostage in the cage sequence – but ultimately the scene was never shot.

Other scenes that were dropped included interior police station and jail sequences (where Dr. Frankenstein was going to be incarcerated after Prima's murder at the ball); exterior police station sequences (including the Creature's jailbreak when he climbs to the top of a building and throws a policeman off the roof – à la *Ghost of Frankenstein*); a seaport dock (where the ship is loaded and launched); and several ship sequences (including a coastguard boat chasing the galleon to the outer waters of its jurisdiction).

Another sequence that was jettisoned from the shooting schedule was a gypsy encampment fracas before the Creature stumbles upon the old blind man. This was inspired by the scene in *Bride of Frankenstein* when the hungry Monster smells a chicken roasting over a fire at a gypsy campsite. He emerges from the shadows to beg for food but inadvertently frightens the gypsies who all run away. Left alone by the fire, the Monster reaches for the roasting chicken and burns himself from the heat of the flames. From that moment on, the Monster would always be fearful of fire. Because the scene was so well-known, Stromberg insisted that Isherwood reverse the outcome in *Dr. Frankenstein*. Instead of a roasting chicken, Isherwood substituted a big pot of boiling soup. The Creature is hungry, he emerges from the shadows, the gypsies are frightened and hide. This time, however, the gypsies watch in horror as the Creature picks up the boiling pot of soup and drinks from it without any reaction to the searing heat, no sense of pain whatsoever. The scene was originally scheduled to be shot on location in Black Park with a caravan of carts and 12 horses – but was dropped from the script before it ever got shot.

And, as mentioned earlier, the coda – with the Creature's hand emerging from an iceberg – was discarded.

SARRAZIN GOES AWOL

Pruning the script turned out to be the least of their worries. In mid-May 1973, completely without warning or permission, Michael Sarrazin suddenly disappeared from the production, nowhere to be found. At first, there were fears for Sarrazin's well-being. Even his representatives had no clue of his whereabouts. Eventually, it was discovered that he had gone to France to see his girlfriend Jacqueline Bisset – and had apparently forgotten to tell anyone. Or so it seemed.

Sarrazin & Smight.

Sarrazin & Streisand, *For Pete's Sake. Inset:* Streisand & Jon Peters.

Bisset & Truffaut.

Truffaut & Bisset at Cannes, May 1973.

Bisset.

Truffaut.

"It was extremely unprofessional," first assistant director John Stoneman recalled. "And because my job was creating and overseeing the shooting schedule, I am the one who had to scramble to find scenes we could shoot without Michael. But even *that* was difficult because we had no idea when – or even *if* – he was coming back. It was a catastrophe."

"Hunt Stromberg was spitting nails," recalled the producer's secretary Phyllis Allarie. "The entire production was on the brink of collapse."

So, too, was the relationship between Sarrazin and Bisset. Trouble in paradise had actually begun eight months earlier during the September-November 1972 filming of *Day for Night* when Bisset engaged in an affair with her director / co-star François Truffaut which became an international tabloid scandal. Despite the firestorm of publicity, Bisset and Sarrazin managed to reconcile and seemed to be back on solid ground. Then, while Sarrazin was toiling away on *Dr. Frankenstein* in the UK and Bisset was filming *The Man from Acapulco* in France, the world premiere of *Day for Night* was held on Monday, May 14, 1973, at the Cannes Film Festival, where Bisset unexpectedly showed up to walk the red carpet arm-in-

arm with Truffaut – the photo op of all photo ops – sparking a tsunami of paparazzi pictures that were splashed in newspapers all over the world the following day. Even if nothing was going on between them, the appearance of impropriety was enough to send Sarrazin through the roof. That's why he did not show up for work on Wednesday, May 16.

Rushing to France that day to confront Bisset, Sarrazin was astounded to discover that his girlfriend's affections were leaning in another, altogether unexpected direction. Hairdresser-to-the-stars Jon Peters, then-husband of actress Leslie Anne Warren, happened to be in France to style hair for various fashion shows. Peters had crossed paths with Bisset during a photo shoot for *Paris Vogue* (published November 1973) and, according to *Vanity Fair*, had begun an affair with her.

Peters was well-known throughout Hollywood and had the reputation of being a notorious womanizer – the direct inspiration for Warren Beatty's Casanova-like hairdresser character in *Shampoo*. In the bestselling book *Hit & Run: How Jon Peters and Peter Guber Took Sony for a Ride in Hollywood* (Simon & Schuster), authors Nancy Griffin and Kim Masters reported that, during Peters' 1973 Parisian

Artwork by Frederick Cooper.

Sarrazin enters ballroom.

Guard shots Sarrazin with rifle; doesn't stop him.

liaison amoureuse with Bisset, he received a transatlantic phone call out of the blue from Barbra Streisand about potential employment. Peters immediately flew back to Los Angeles and drove to Streisand's mansion in Beverly Hills where a flirtatious "job interview" took place. "You've got a great ass," Peters boldly stated to Streisand – and from that moment on, Bisset was a fling of the past. Streisand promptly hired Peters as her "hair and wardrobe consultant" on *For Pete's Sake* which would begin shooting in September 1973 in New York – where they would share a suite at the Plaza Hotel.

Streisand's leading man in the movie would be… drum roll please… Michael Sarrazin! Boy, there must have been some icy stares between Peters and Sarrazin on *that* set. (Adding to this series of incestuous coincidences, the director of *For Pete's Sake* happened to be Peter Yates who had turned down *Dr. Frankenstein*.)

Jon Peters eventually divorced Leslie Anne Warren; was Streisand's lover and manager for several years; and became a top Hollywood producer of such major studio movies as *A Star is Born* (starring Streisand), *An American Werewolf in London*, *Flashdance*, *The Color Purple*, *The Witches of Eastwick*, *Rain Man*, *Gorillas in the Mist*, *Batman*, *Batman Returns*, *Wild Wild West*, *Superman Returns*, *Man of Steel* and the latest version of *A Star is Born* (starring Lady Gaga).

But in May 1973, it was the electricity between Peters and Bisset that nearly short-circuited *Dr. Frankenstein*.

"It was a terrible predicament for all concerned," Phyllis Allarie confirmed, "and Hunt was absolutely beside himself.

Sneering Seymour – sees Sarrazin.

Sarrazin – sees Seymour.

Seymour hissing at Sarrazin.

Sarrazin reaches for Seymour.

Sarrazin rips choker off Seymour's neck.

Sarrazin enraged at Seymour, hands on shoulders.

Seymour with Sarrazin's hands grabbing her by the neck.

Sarrazin holding severed head with entrails dangling.– NOT in the TV version.

Sarrazin gives the head of Seymour to Mason.

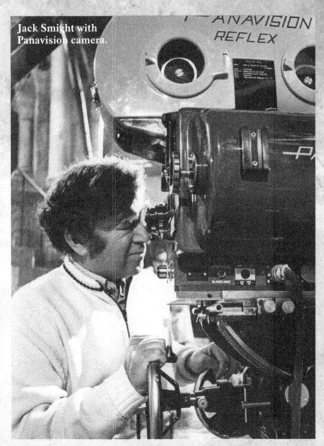
Jack Smight with Panavision camera.

Crowd flees in horror from ballroom.

Mason stands on sofa as the crowd tries to escape through window.

John Stoneman & Jack Smight with Seymour dummy in tank.

The production had to shoot around Michael's absence."

A week later, on Wednesday, May 23, Sarrazin finally returned to work. "I don't remember any chastisement when Michael came back," Allarie added. "There was just general relief that the movie could be completed. Nobody dared say anything that might have resulted in Michael leaving again."

With excruciating irony, Sarrazin resumed shooting *Dr. Frankenstein* with the scene in which the enraged Creature bursts into the ballroom and yanks off the head of Prima. Method acting was never put to better use.

THE FALL GUY

In addition to the panic Sarrazin was causing at the Black Tower in Universal City, there were also top-secret discussions among the upper echelon about the possibility of replacing director Jack Smight.

"I was called for a meeting with Hunt Stromberg, Jacque Shelton, Ian Lewis and Brian Burgess," recalled first assistant director John Stoneman. "I was asked if I would take over directing for a few days until a new director could be hired and flown in from Hollywood."

When asked why Smight was on the chopping block, Stoneman said, "I was not given any specific reasons other than the production was falling behind schedule and in danger of going over budget. From what I'd seen, though, none of the problems were due to Jack. Stromberg had spent crazy amounts of money on the 'name' actors in the cast; Sarrazin had gone AWOL; and the script was overly ambitious for the time and money at our disposal."

"There were times when Hunt and Jack didn't see eye-to-eye," recalled production manager Brian Burgess. "They were total opposites. That may have had something to do with it."

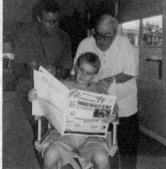

Left: Smight with Charlton Heston during the shooting of *Midway*. Right: Many years later: Alec Smight (left), Alec's 10-year-old son Danny Smight, and 75-year-old Jack Smight.

Stoneman was not told whom they had in mind to replace Smight, but the most likely candidate was Boris Sagal who was already well-versed about the project and still under contract to Universal Television. Declaring his loyalty to Smight, however, Stoneman refused to act as an interim director. Eventually, the decision came down to keep Smight for the rest of the movie.

"The production was too far along to reasonably replace a director," explained Brian Burgess. "You can't. That's what you *don't* do. Luckily, cooler heads prevailed, and everyone came to their senses."

Instead, however, they let Stoneman go – replaced by Brian Heard (location manager on the ITC series *The Protectors* starring Robert Vaughn). When asked why the higher-ups had turned on him, Stoneman reasoned, "It was my loyalty to Smight that did me in. First and foremost, they felt I should be loyal to the production. So, that was that." [See Chapter 15 for my interview with Stoneman.]

Whatever complaints Stromberg and/or Universal may have had with Smight, they were soon forgiven and forgotten. Stromberg attached Smight to direct *The Lady from the Land of the Dead* for Universal TV and NBC (though it never got made) and Universal confidently assigned Smight to such important, big-budget theatrical films as *Airport 1975* and *Midway*.

NEIL DIAMOND

Even with Sarrazin back and Smight firmly planted in the director's chair, the production had a few more wrinkles that had to be ironed out. Originally in the script, when the Creature returns to the opera house by himself to see *The Marriage of Figaro* again, he encounters three thugs who taunt him in a dark alley behind the theater, hoping to rob what appears to be a vulnerable, well-dressed gentleman. The leader of the gang breaks a bottle over the Creature's head without any discernable effect. Then, when the Creature steps into the light, revealing his gnarly face, the thugs get spooked and run away. Afterwards, Dr. Frankenstein finds the Creature there and takes him home.

Stromberg tried to convince music superstar Neil Diamond, 32, to do a guest cameo appearance as the leader of this gang but he turned it down. Instead, Stromberg cast gay actor David Boyce, 28, former drummer for the Roadrunners, the 1960s Liverpool rhythm and blues band which famously played the Cavern Club in 1963 with the Beatles. [See Chapter 13 for my interview with Boyce.]

The original plan was to shoot the sequence in central London outside the Royal Opera House in Covent Garden – while also filming establishing shots of this historic building's façade with period carriages and extras. However, by the time they got around to shooting these bits on June 25, 1973, the movie was running over schedule and over budget. So, the establishing shots were omitted, and the thug scene was economically "cheated" in an existing alley on the backlot at Pinewood. Sadly, the attempted mugging never made the final edit of the film, left on the cutting room floor. However, we do get a glimpse of that alley when Dr. Frankenstein locates the Creature and leads him away.

CALLING TOM BAKER

In the process of truncating the scripted scenes for the ship sequences, the role of the American Captain had been drastically reduced. Stromberg informed Ernest Borgnine that, with fewer shooting days and less screen time, they were going to have to renegotiate his fee accordingly. Borgnine respectfully bowed out. Stromberg was very sad to lose one of his big-name Oscar-winning stars, but it saved the production money, and it gave him the opportunity to make nice with an actor he had kind of screwed over when they were casting the Creature: Tom Baker.

In a 2014 interview for *Hollywood News*, Baker recalled, "They ended up giving the role of the monster to a very good-looking actor. Instead, they gave me the part of the Ship's Captain."

Tom Baker & Stromberg, during a break on deck of ship.

THE EPIC SAGA BEHIND *FRANKENSTEIN: THE TRUE STORY*

Pagett & Baker deluged in the storm.

Derek Deadman, Stromberg, Tom Baker, Tony Aitken, on the ship deck.

Baker in storm.

Tony Aitken, Nicola Pagett, Derek Deadman, Michael Goldie, Tom Baker, on ship, below deck.

Tom Baker tries to shoot the Creature to no avail.

Baker was pleased to take on the consolation prize if for no other reason than he would get to meet James Mason after all. Stromberg decided to make the captain British so that Baker would not have to fake an American accent. He would end up shooting 6 days, spread nonconsecutively from June 8-20. (Replacing an American actor with a British one also helped the production qualify for the Eady rebate.)

Seven years later, Stromberg would hire Baker again to play the villainous Hasan in *The Curse of King Tut's Tomb*. [For details of that cursed production, see Chapter 17, my biography of Stromberg.]

THE LA-DI-DAS

The main sailors on the ship were played by up-and-coming character actors Derek Deadman, Michael Goldie, Barry Linehan and Tony Aitken. Contacted in 2016, Aitken remembered, "There was a big demarcation in those days between extras – the guys who didn't have a line – and the actors who had been engaged to speak. Extras thought actors were posh or 'la-di-das.' But, because this was my first film, I was completely unaware of any class structure. I remember one chap turned up in a red Jaguar XK-E. I thought, 'Oh, he must be a star.' I sidled up to him and said, 'What a beautiful car.' I was driving a yellow Mini Moke or something terribly unimpressive. He said, 'Oh yeah, you've got to make an impression, laddie. If you turn up at Pinewood Studios in an E-type Jaguar, you get VIP treatment and a good parking spot. Remember that.' He was a lovely man, but it turned out he was an extra and so once he figured out I had speaking lines in the movie, he didn't talk to me again. I would have happily chatted with anybody, but I was shown to the changing room where Tom Baker and the other actors were putting on sailors' uniforms for the scene and became one of the 'la-di-das.'"

ROCKING THE BOAT

As written, the ship-at-sea sequences were going to break the budget – but Stromberg, having witnessed boats being filmed on his father's movies, knew exactly how to solve the problem. In a memo to his troops, Stromberg instructed, "Please delete the lifeboats surrounding the vessel near the end of the script, as these lifeboats would entail us actually being on water. Minus the lifeboats, it is my personal feeling that the ship sequence can be done on a sound stage in the atmosphere of a densely foggy and stormy night."

He was dead right. So, the deck of the schooner was erected inside A Stage at Pinewood Studios. Colin

Artwork by Frederick Cooper.

Mason (note hands), Whiting, Pagett, Sarrazin on deck.

On deck of ship, Mason (with acid-ravaged hand), Sarrazin, Smight.

Deluge of water dumped on deck.

Mason (with stump and acid-ravaged hand), Derek Deadman, Pagett.

Artwork by Adrian Salmon.

Chilvers recalled, "The boat was on a hydraulic rocking gimbal that was rented from Jim Hole's company called The Trading Post."

Actor Tony Aitken (Sailor #3) added, "There was this Merlin engine – a beautiful ex-World War II Supermarine Spitfire or Avro Lancaster bomber engine – which was mounted on a scaffold. They would fire it up and the eight-foot propeller would drive out this huge amount of wind. Dump tanks dropped water in front of it which resulted in this sideways spray at eighty miles-per-hour coming at you. So, Tom Baker, myself and the other sailors were out on this deck with passengers including Nicola Pagett. Tom got a bit grumpy about it because, as the Captain, he had to do an awful lot of shouting while this Merlin engine was blowing gallons of water in his face. Well, as you can imagine, every time he opened his mouth, it immediately filled up with water, and he'd be choking from it, unable to breathe – much less talk."

About halfway through shooting the storm sequence, the rocking mechanism broke, and the rest of the shots had to be "cheated" with a handheld camera and the actors simulating the rocking movement – "poor man's process," as it is commonly called, like the actors frequently did on the original 1960s *Star Trek* series.

"In synchronization, we would sway from one side to the other as though the ship was moving," Aitken recalled, "rocking from side to side like a bunch of goons. It was very funny."

It took six days to shoot these complex sequences: four on deck (June 8, 11-13) and two for the action on the mast (June 21-22) where Polidori gets struck by lightning.

In the wide establishing shots, the ship-at-sea was a model traversing rolling waves in a huge tank of water. These

3rd Assistant Director Terry Pearce helps Mason as he is hoisted up mast.

Sarrazin hoists Mason up the mast.

Sarrazin hoisting Mason (off-camera) up the mast as Whiting and Pagett look up in horror.

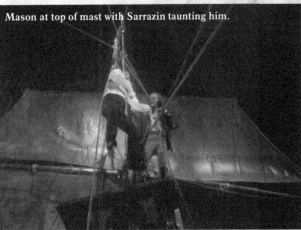

Mason at top of mast with Sarrazin taunting him.

Tom Baker, Whiting, Pagett and crew looking up mast at Mason & Sarrazin (both off-screen).

Cutaway of the ship in storm.

are exactly the kinds of shots Brian Smithies would later craft for other films, so the assumption has been that Smithies must have created these shots for *Dr. Frankenstein*, too.

"When I recently rewatched the film," Smithies explained, "those shots reminded me of the model ship shots I created of the Demeter for *Dracula* with Frank Langella. In fact, the shots were so similar, at first I thought they must have added those shots to *Frankenstein* at a later date for the DVD release or something, borrowed from *Dracula*. But then, when the ship nearly tips over, I knew it wasn't anything I had done."

Asked if it was possible that someone else on the *Dr. Frankenstein* effects team might have created these model shots without his knowledge, Smithies said, "No. Anything involving models, I would have known about it."

A clue to this mystery was discovered in a pre-production memo dated February 27, 1973, recommending that, to save money, the "schooner at sea" shots could be stock footage

CHAPTER THREE: FILMING

149

Cutaway of the ship in storm.

Sarrazin covered in snow, steers the boat.

Below: Brian Smithies' model ship of the Demeter for John Badham's *Dracula*.

borrowed from an earlier movie. If that was indeed the case, I am still trying to pinpoint the film in question. It would most likely have come from a Universal picture, like the curtain-call footage borrowed free-of-charge from Universal's 1943 version of *The Phantom of the Opera*. If anyone manages to find a match, I'd love to hear about it.

ARCTIC MAJESTY

The Arctic climax for *Dr. Frankenstein* was the first time the icy northern wastelands of Shelley's novel had ever been depicted in a Frankenstein film. These sets were perhaps the most challenging to pull off because they appear in broad daylight which is not very forgiving.

When Frankenstein regains consciousness in his cabin aboard the ship, the boat is dead still, having been embedded in ice. He climbs on deck to find everything covered in snow and frost – including the frozen corpse of Elizabeth (and their unborn child).

Colin Chilvers recalled, "To achieve the look of a frozen corpse, we used a Venturi spray gun to spray hot paraffin

wax over Nicola Pagett. The same principal as a sandblasting gun. The wax beads up like the inside of a freezer after it has frosted up."

This scene was shot on the same A Stage where the ship deck was erected. Only now, instead of the black void of night that was seen during the storm, the art department had to create a daytime backdrop for the vast oceanic ice shelf and distant glaciers.

"Unfortunately, the artificial snow we initially used for the deck of the ship was a substance called urea-formaldehyde foam insulation [UFFI]," Brian Smithies remembered. "With hoses, they used to spray it into the walls of homes to create insulation. It was two liquids sprayed together that then produced this white foam like shaving crème that stank. It was horrible. The vapors irritated the actors' eyes. We had to stop shooting." (Due to fears that the insulation product was

Smight directs Sarrazin covered in snow, steering the boat.

Whiting on snowy deck spots dead/frozen Pagett.

150   THE EPIC SAGA BEHIND *FRANKENSTEIN: THE TRUE STORY*

"Arctic Majesty" by artist Bruce Timm.

a carcinogen, UFFI was banned in the U.S. by the Consumer Product Safety Commission in 1982. However, decades of testing have proven that the substance is relatively harmless and unfairly stigmatized. It is still used in Europe where it has never been banned and is considered one of the better "retrofit" insulations.)

What they began filming on June 21 had to be postponed until June 22 so that the effects crew could sweep clean the irritating UFFI and re-spray the scenery with hot paraffin wax and spread mounds of salt on the deck.

"Of course, the salt dries your skin and stings like hell," Smithies added. "Either way, it wasn't pleasant."

In one shot of Frankenstein on the deck of the ship, the Creature can be seen in the deep background trudging toward a grotto in a faraway mountain of ice. This was accomplished via chroma key compositing with a blue screen backdrop.

Once Frankenstein has left the ship and is walking

toward the grotto, the art department created an expansive set on J Stage with the vast snow shelf and the schooner stuck in the ice floe. Front projection shots were created by Wally Veevers and Charles Staffell, the world's foremost pioneers of this technology, who had previously worked their magic on such films as *2001: A Space Odyssey* and *Diamonds Are Forever*. Unlike rear projection, which projects footage onto a screen behind the performers, front projection has the pre-filmed material projected over the performers and onto a screen made of Scotchlite, the highly reflective glass-beaded material used for the solar panels in the laboratory scene.

"We later used front screen projection on *Superman* and *Dune*," Brian Smithies recalled. "Quite a lot of it. The image that is projected does not need to be very powerful. It reflects very powerfully off of the glass beads of the Scotchlite material – but it doesn't show up on the actor. It is so much sharper and vibrant than rear screen projection."

Dead/frozen Pagett..

Whiting's hand touches dead/frozen Pagett.

Stromberg & Whiting on deck of ship, with fake snow.

Whiting on deck with chroma key / blue screen backdrop. The speck in the distance is the Creature heading to the grotto.

Whiting walking away from false-perspective model ship.

Reverse angle of Whiting approaching grotto.

Whiting further away from false-perspective model ship.

Whiting arriving at grotto in the distance.

On the ice shelf, a quarter-size ship was constructed. Smithies explained, "When Leonard Whiting is walking away from the boat on the ice – and you see the entire ship behind him – we made a model ship for the false perspective background. The hull was a painted cutout which then had realistic masts and rigging added on top. Colin Chilvers and I worked on the rigging."

"I painted the cutout of that hull," confirmed scenic artist Peter Melrose. "I also painted the sky backdrop and matte paintings of the Arctic wasteland for perspectives in both directions – angles looking toward the ship stuck in the ice and the reverse angles looking toward the snowy mountain with the grotto at its base where the Creature was heading."

It took weeks for the special effects unit to prepare for these front projection shots but only one day, June 14, 1973, to shoot them in-camera with the live actors.

Once Frankenstein reaches the Creature, they stand inside the icy grotto that was built outside on Pinewood's backlot as a full-scale set – shot June 28-29.

Stromberg on the snowy grotto set.

Sarrazin puts his hand on Whiting's shoulder in forgiveness.

Stock footage of iceberg collapsing.

Not In Movie: Two shots of the manufactured avalanche-in-progress on the grotto set at Pinewood Studios. This footage did not make the final cut of the movie. Ironically, the photos were published in *TV Guide*.

Sarrazin close-up in the snowy grotto.

CHAPTER THREE: FILMING

"The ice cave set was huge," recalled Colin Chilvers. "It was approximately 60-feet wide, about 30 feet high and at least 30 feet deep. The construction and plastering department had carved the ice walls out of styrofoam. I remember one funny thing that happened. We had just finished preparing the collapsing ice cave. Everyone in the effects department had been working on it all day long. Toward the end of the day, Roy Whybrow [head of the SPFX department] walked out from the studio to the backlot to see how we were doing. Just then, this limo pulled up and Stromberg and the director and a couple of other executives got out and congratulated Roy on how wonderful it looked. He hadn't done anything at all! But that's what Roy was there for. To be the figurehead."

Asked about the collapsing ice cave, Chilvers elaborated thusly: "Inside the grotto, I built a rig whereby wire cables were anchored to the ground and to the top of the rig – at different angles. Fixed onto those wires were huge styrofoam 'ice rocks' ready to fall on cue. When Michael Sarrazin and Leonard Whiting entered the cave, there was a safe area where they were instructed to stand. When the director cued for the avalanche to begin, I just cut the wires so that the styrofoam ice collapsed in on itself."

This manufactured collapse was not as realistic as everyone had hoped so the footage did not actually make the final cut of the film – but color photos of it were published in *TV Guide* the week of the movie's premiere.

Many stock footage shots of the Arctic were licensed, including the giant glacial cliffs collapsing into the ocean at the movie's conclusion. Curiously, some of these same exact stock shots appeared many years later in the Academy Award-winning documentary *An Inconvenient Truth* (2006), former United States Vice President Al Gore's treatise on climate change.

LET THEM EAT CAKE!

During the latter weeks of the shoot, there was an outbreak of birthdays. James Mason turned 64 on May 15, 1973; Stromberg turned 50 on May 16; Sarrazin turned 33 on May 22; Nicola Pagett turned 28 on June 15; and Leonard Whiting turned 23 on June 30. Each milestone was celebrated on set with cake and refreshments for the entire cast and crew.

Jane Seymour didn't have a birthday to celebrate but, nonetheless, she served cakes to her colleagues on a weekly basis. It seems a loyal group of admirers from Holland would send a special cake each week addressed to "Miss Jane Seymour, c/o Pinewood Studios."

"It was always one of the richest of Dutch concoctions – a Deventer Koek," Seymour recalled. "But I must confess, sharing it with the cast and crew wasn't really a sign of my unselfishness. Without sharing it, I would have gained pounds and pounds of unwanted weight."

On the subject of guilty pleasures, Stromberg was known to be a heavy drinker. When asked if this was evident during production, his secretary Phyllis Allarie replied, "Nights and weekends were the only times I saw Hunt drink alcohol. I know he drank a lot, but to my knowledge, Monday to Friday at the studio, he did not touch alcohol – but, my word, he consumed liters of Coca-Cola. And he smoked, smoked, smoked. He always had a Salem cigarette in one hand and a can of Coke in the other." (Stromberg also happened to be one of the largest shareholders in the world of Coca-Cola stock – with over 1 million shares inherited from his father.)

On days off, many of the cast and crew socialized together. Jack Smight's son Alec recalled, "I became friendly with the cast, especially with Leonard Whiting and his wife, who took me out on numerous occasions to get dinner and sightsee. One of the most memorable field trips we had was going to the Odeon in London to see Lindsay Anderson's classic *O Lucky Man!*, still one of my favorite movies of all time." (*O Lucky Man!* also happened to co-star Sir Ralph Richardson who was co-starring in *Frankenstein: The True Story*.)

Other than a couple of rough patches, the shoot was generally a very happy one. "With all the time I spent on set," Alec Smight observed, "I distinctly recall the sense of earnest camaraderie, natural rapport, and die-hard work ethic you don't find anywhere else but on a well-functioning film set."

Cake for Jack Smight, either for his birthday on March 9, or to celebrate the start or end of production.

Stromberg's birthday: Mason, Stromberg, Smight and camera operator John Harris.

Gag image of Sarrazin giving a birthday cake to Mason, instead of Seymour's severed head. Photoshop by Tim Hewitt.

THE EPIC SAGA BEHIND *FRANKENSTEIN: THE TRUE STORY*

Pagett & Whiting cut the cake in the wedding scene of Dr. Frankenstein and Elizabeth Fanshawe.

Nicola Pagett birthday cake, with Smight & Stromberg.

A young Stromberg with a cigarette in his mouth, standing in front of a huge "NO SMOKING" sign.

Hunt offering McCallum a Salem cigarette, set of FTTS the day they were shooting the aborted prologue.

Smight directs Sarrazin, as Hunt hovers between them, with his pack of Salem cigarettes on display in his pocket.

and Chief Operating Officer of MCA-Universal, to serve alongside Chairman Lew Wasserman. He would now oversee all the studio's projects, television *and* theatrical. This promotion boded well for Stromberg who was developing a number of follow-up projects for the studio. Or so he hoped. [See Chapter 17, my biography of Stromberg.]

PICTURE WRAP

The last day of principal photography was on Monday, July 2, 1973. In the morning, they filmed the brief sequence of Dr. Frankenstein (in a fake goatee applied by Roy Ashton) and Elizabeth lounging outdoors on their honeymoon. This was shot by the lake in Pinewood Garden behind Heatherden Hall – with swans wrangled by Jacque Shelton. They finished by lunch, after which the cast and crew were invited to attend

Whiting (fake goatee) on honeymoon. FTTS.

Mason, Kaye, Wilding & Seymour welcome Pagett & Whiting (fake goatee) home from their honeymoon.

On May 23, 1973, Stromberg sent a memo "to all members of cast and crew" that read, "Universal is a conservative company, highly circumspect, not given to lavish praise. Accordingly, I was both amazed and obviously very pleased (for <u>ALL</u> of us) when, last night, I was told that the one hour and twenty-five minutes of the film which we recently sent to Universal Studios in California is described by the key Universal executives in one word – 'FANTASTIC.' Everyone connected with the picture, obviously, shares in this one-word comment."

Exactly two weeks later, triggered in part by the extraordinary buzz *Dr. Frankenstein* was generating throughout the industry, the project's godfather, Universal Television President Sid Sheinberg, was elected President

156
THE EPIC SAGA BEHIND *FRANKENSTEIN: THE TRUE STORY*

Whiting (fake goatee) & Pagett honeymoon, with swans. Pinewood Garden.

Stromberg's lover Jacque Shelton wrangling swans on the last day of the shoot, July 2, 1973, at Pinewood Garden.

Roger Moore, Michael Attenborough & wife Jane Seymour, Princess Anne, premiere *Live and Let Die*, July 5, 1973. Also attended by Smight & Stromberg (FTTS had just completed shooting).

a 3:00 P.M. screening in Theatre 7 of the movie's rough cut-in-progress, followed by a wrap party in the Pine & Green Rooms of Heatherden Hall.

"A few days later, Hunt hosted a celebratory lunch for about ten of us on the crew who were still wrapping out at Pinewood," recalled Stromberg's secretary Phyllis Allarie. "He had requested that the chef make steak and kidney pudding for the occasion. The recipe was made in two very large basins. When the chief waiter, Chris, walked through the Pinewood restaurant with these two massive puddings on a salver, some wag at the next table said, 'Good Lord, they look like two enormous breasts!' And Hunt, quick as a flash, turned 'round and replied, 'I've never seen any *that* big.' We all fell about laughing." (That "wag" at the next table turned out to be Terry Lens, the second assistant director of Hammer's *Scream of Fear* and *Maniac* and production manager of Tobe Hooper's *Lifeforce*; he became Allarie's partner from 1975 until his passing in 2008.)

With a total of 76 days of shooting, *Dr. Frankenstein* had gone 11 days over schedule. It is a state secret how much the picture went over budget, but Ian Lewis recalled, "Enough corners had been cut to keep the overage relatively minor."

Three days later, on Thursday, July 5, 1973, Stromberg, Smight and a few other *Dr. Frankenstein* V.I.P.s were guests of Jane Seymour at the Royal World Premiere of *Live and Let Die* at London's Odeon Leicester Square Cinema in the presence of Princess Anne.

CHAPTER 4
POST-PRODUCTION

PRIMA 11

Shortly after picture wrap, Stromberg received an amusing letter from James Mason – but to fully appreciate its contents, a little bit of backstory is required. Throughout the shooting of *Dr. Frankenstein*, Mason had been obsessively following the Watergate scandal as it unfolded, dramatically reciting newspaper reports during breaks to a captive cast and crew – whether they were interested or not. Some joked that Mason's ambitious and scheming interpretation of Dr. Polidori must be based on President Richard Nixon – which is an intriguing and altogether plausible theory to consider.

However, the contents of the letter Mason sent to Stromberg may point to another, perhaps even slimier role model: John Dean, White House Counsel for Nixon, who was described by the FBI as "the master manipulator of the Watergate cover-up" and later authored a bestselling memoir entitled, appropriately enough, *Blind Ambition* (1976). Cutting a deal to reduce his jail time to just four-and-a-half months, Dean pled guilty to a single felony count in exchange for becoming a key witness for the prosecution. His incriminating testimony was largely responsible for Nixon's ultimate resignation. Everyone involved in Watergate had blood on their hands,

Maureen Dean and John Dean.

Nixon included, but Dean's Machiavellian treachery was nothing short of Shakespearean. Or Polidorian, as the case may be.

Having lived through Mason's Watergate mania, Stromberg was not at all surprised when he opened the envelope to find a newspaper clipping of John Dean's dazzling wife Maureen, under the headline: "The Mysterious Mrs. John Dean."

G. Gordon Liddy (convicted of conspiracy, burglary and illegal wiretapping in the Watergate case) and other insiders alleged that Maureen was involved in a sophisticated prostitution ring that had infiltrated the highest ranks of government – though denials were fast and furious, and nothing was ever proven. Sound familiar?

In the movie, Polidori confesses to Dr. Frankenstein his true motivation behind creating his reptilian Prima: "Our dear girl must be married as soon as decently possible. An unmarried woman has no freedom of action. Once she has entered society with a husband, I shall find her a lover. She must become the mistress of someone in the ruling class – a great banker, a cabinet minister, maybe even a Royal prince."

Frankenstein interjects, "And then you'll begin pulling the strings."

Polidori replies, "Then I shall proceed to make her the most famous woman in Europe – the instrument of my power."

Mason's tongue-in-cheek letter to Stromberg read as follows: "When you get around to making *Prima II*, don't you think that Maureen Dean would be the perfect casting? Jane Seymour will be far too expensive. I look forward to hearing all the gossip so I'll give you a ring some night soon. Don't forget we are quite close – should you feel the urge to communicate. Love from both of us (& to Jacque & Doris), James."

QUEER SENSIBILITY

Post-production for *Dr. Frankenstein* took place in London with producer Hunt Stromberg Jr. and director Jack Smight collaborating with John Schlesinger's recommended editor Richard "Dickie" Marden whose most recent film *Sleuth* had received four Oscar nominations that year.

"Richard Marden was a funny character," recalled Alec Smight. "His editing room was an explosion of film clips. He had stuff all over the place. He was one of those guys who would reach into a pile and pull out the exact frame he wanted. I remember thinking, 'How did you know that's in there?'"

Along with Stromberg & Shelton, Isherwood & Bachardy, James Mason, Agnes Moorehead, Sir John Gielgud, Dallas Adams, David Boyce and Michael Pharey, Marden was another key conspirator among *Dr. Frankenstein*'s burgeoning Lavender Hill Mob.

"Everyone knew Dickie was gay," Phyllis Allarie confirmed. "He was a charming man – absolutely one of the loveliest people. He was a bit 'old school' – always nattily dressed, always wore a jacket and tie – but he had a fantastic sense of humor. Hunt was terribly camp so between the two of them, there was a lot of laughter."

If Stromberg had any concerns that his straight director might not instinctively identify with the nuances of the gay subtext in *Dr. Frankenstein*, the hiring of Marden to edit the film was an effective insurance policy.

Indeed, the sequence in which the beautiful Creature is brought to life and comes face-to-face with his equally handsome Creator was conceived with arresting sensitivity. In 1974, *Cinefantastique* critic Daniel Masloski was so moved by it, he waxed poetic: "This young Victor Frankenstein is not a mad doctor. He is us. And when he decides to 'join the brotherhood of Prometheus' and defy the gods, we join and defy with him. And when man takes fire from heaven, we are excited and elated as we have never been watching other Frankenstein movies. The second Adam breathes his first breath. He looks down at us from high above, he comes down to us… the bandages fall from his face, he smiles. We know what the grandeur of man can be… but what is most important is that we feel."

After *Dr. Frankenstein*, Marden would be sought to collaborate with such iconic gay directors as George Cukor (on *The Corn is Green*), Franco Zeffirelli (on *Hamlet*, *Sparrow* and *Jane Eyre*) and Clive Barker (on *Hellraiser* and *Nightbreed*) while continuing his alliance with Schlesinger (on *The Falcon and the Snowman* and *The Innocent*).

ROUGH CUT

Seven weeks after picture wrap, the director's cut was completed. Jack Smight (and his family) returned to Los Angeles to personally deliver a copy print to be screened at Universal City on August 13, 1973, by Universal executives Lew Wasserman, Sid Sheinberg, George Santoro, Charles F. Engel and Frank O'Connor (VP in Charge of Specials), plus a heavyweight contingent from NBC headed by Herb Schlosser and Larry White. Also invited were Christopher Isherwood

and Don Bachardy since they were local and anxious to see it. Stromberg and Marden stayed behind in London, hoping for the best. To their great relief, everyone loved the cut of the movie – with the exception of two people: the writers.

"Am not so joyful today," Isherwood lamented in his diary on August 14, 1973. "Yesterday we saw an untitled, undubbed print of *Dr. Frankenstein* (the cut they're going to show on TV) and today I had to [telephone London to] tell Hunt Stromberg in no uncertain language what we thought of it. God knows we went (to the projection room at Universal) with no great expectations, but this was worse than anything I'd expected. … No, I don't want to write any more. I feel really sick to my stomach."

With all due respect, Isherwood's objectivity must be called into question. He was *never* able to impartially judge movies based on his writings because he could only see what was missing and/or changed.

For instance, John Schlesinger's biographer William J. Mann reported that shortly after *Cabaret* (based on Isherwood's *The Berlin Stories*) had won a staggering haul of *eight* Academy Awards, including Best Director, Isherwood marched right up to the film's director Bob Fosse at a party and shouted, "You fucked up my book, my classic! You ruined the integrity of my piece, turned it all into surface!"

Accustomed to Isherwood's irascibility, Stromberg wasn't about to let the writer rain on his parade. Isherwood noted in his diary that Stromberg "refused to listen" and "just kept repeating that he was sure we would get an Emmy!"

Over the next several months, however, Isherwood would often voice his displeasure about *Dr. Frankenstein* to show business colleagues and, in some cases, to the press – which is simply not how the Hollywood game is played. Nor an Emmy Award campaign.

Dismissing Isherwood's criticisms, Universal's head of production George Santoro reassured Isherwood's agent Robin French that the studio and the network were "absolutely delighted" with the picture – unanimously in agreement that it was going to be "the must-see television event of the season."

Naturally, however, there was some polishing left to be done – standard operating procedure before locking the final cut of any picture. Universal and NBC executives powwowed and came up with a set of unified, constructive notes for the producer and the editor in London. Most were relatively minor nips and tucks. A few were more substantive, like the consensus that Michael Wilding's voice needed to be replaced.

Preemptively downplaying the substitution, Stromberg spoke openly about it in a *Los Angeles Times* interview published two weeks before the movie was broadcast: "If fans wonder why Michael Wilding doesn't sound like himself, it's because he's never gotten over the habit of talking fast in that clipped, British way. So we dubbed his voice with another actor's voice that Americans can understand."

In truth, Wilding was suffering from early signs of a disorder that impaired his vocal cords. Nicola Pagett, Phyllis Allarie and other witnesses recalled that, at times, it sounded as though Wilding had laryngitis. This was certainly the case when I met him in 1974 – though, at the time, I assumed the condition was a temporary ailment.

Contacted in 2017, Graham V. Hartstone, sound re-recording mixer for *Dr. Frankenstein*, recalled, "Michael Wilding's voice was post-dubbed by Robert Rietty, known in the business as 'the man with a thousand voices.' He dubbed

Sarrazin with map to North Pole.

Sarrazin is happy to see his creator again.

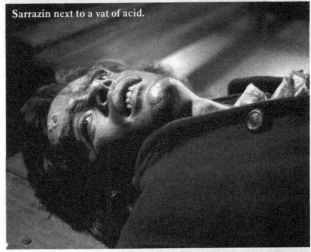

Sarrazin next to a vat of acid.

Sarrazin fuming at the ball.

Sarrazin early deterioration.

Sarrazin hides by a huge jar of green fluid.

Sarrazin tries to commit suicide.

Sarrazin holds the family dog of Agatha (Seymour) and her grandfather (Ralph Richardson).

Sarrazin removes masquerade mask.

THE EPIC SAGA BEHIND *FRANKENSTEIN: THE TRUE STORY*

Michael Wilding converses with Leonard Whiting.

Wilding & Clarissa Kaye.

voices on all the James Bond pictures, including the entire role of the main villain, Largo, in *Thunderball* because Adolfo Celi's Italian accent was too thick." (Hartstone and assistant sound editor Richard Hiscott worked on so many sound mixes together, they were nicknamed "the Sprocketeers.")

THE BIG LIE
Regrettably, NBC made the dubious decision to retitle the film *Frankenstein: The True Story* – an egregious development that was first reported in the *Los Angeles Times* on August 29, 1973.

In protest, Isherwood and Bachardy released the following statement: "We would like to put it on record that neither of us are in favor of the subtitle: *The True Story*. It wasn't our idea. How can one claim that one version is 'truer' than the others?"

They were right, of course. And NBC should have known better. The disastrous side effect was that critics would forever be saddled with the journalistic responsibility of pointing out the lie. Decades later, the problem still persists. For instance, in *The Stranger* (Seattle's alternative arts and culture newspaper), DVD reviewer Bret Fetzer defended Mary Shelley's honor thusly: "While a subtitle like *The True Story* might make you think this 1970s TV production hews close to Mary Shelley's classic novel, it's safe to say that Shelley's opus did not include crawling disembodied arms,

sinister Chinese coolies, solar power, or the flabbergasting paisley dressing gown that Dr. Frankenstein wears for one brief but startling scene. In fact, this version deviates from Shelley's story in almost every detail." And that's just one example of how off-putting the title is to anyone who has bothered to crack open Shelley's novel.

TURNING IN HER GRAVE
The biggest change made to the film was the elimination of the Shelley / Byron / Polidori prologue. It is hardly surprising that it was nixed by NBC. In the world of network television, there is one golden rule: It is imperative to hook the audience before the first commercial break; otherwise, viewers will channel surf to the competition.

Spectators were expecting a Frankenstein movie, not a history lesson about nineteenth-century poets on a picnic by Lake Geneva. Sure, James Whale had gotten away with a similar conceit in *Bride of Frankenstein* but there were fundamental differences, too. The *Bride* prologue was only four minutes; the *True Story* prologue was double that. The *Bride* intro was set on a spooky, stormy night; the *True Story* intro was set in tranquil, broad daylight. Most important, the *Bride* prelude served as a recap of the first *Frankenstein* movie, with scary clips of the horror film interspersed. In the *True Story* prelude, there was nothing creepy at all. In fact, eighteen minutes would go by before the first grisly moment in the movie occurred – when Clerval amputates the arm of the wounded patient.

Dropping the prologue did, however, cause two major problems:

1. The opening would now begin abruptly with the drowning of William Frankenstein – a terribly awkward and choppy commencement with a peculiarly misplaced reaction shot of Elizabeth (Nicola Pagett) whose devious expression seems to suggest she telepathically willed the tragic accident to happen. Of course, she didn't. This close-up appears to be a remnant of Pagett in character as Mary Shelley – who *did* will the incident to happen because she supposedly wrote it (though the drowning was, in truth, an Isherwood-Bachardy invention). Are you with me? Marden did the best he could editing the material at hand. Nevertheless, I think we can all agree, it is a bit cringe worthy. Interestingly, in the shorter

Reaction shot of Pagett that seems to have been a leftover from the aborted prologue. Her cold, dispassionate expression does not match the moment of William Frankenstein's drowning

Mason at fake tombstone of Mary Shelley.

The real tombstone of Mary Shelley.

Wollstonecraft Shelley, 1797-1851" and explains that she was the author of *Frankenstein*. Then Mason narrates a lengthy montage of rousing clips from the movie (spoilers be damned!). Mission: accomplished. No one would dare change channels after seeing such an enticing barrage of footage.

There was, however, one deplorable sham that most viewers never questioned. In fact, Mary Shelley was *not* buried at the cemetery at St. John's Wood Church. And the bogus vertical tombstone – fabricated by Wilfrid Shingleton's art department – is not even remotely similar to the authentic horizontal tablet that marks Mary Shelley's real resting place (alongside her parents) next to St. Peter's Church, on Hinton Road, in Bournemouth. *Frankenstein: The True Story* was no more true to the Mary Shelley novel than the introduction was to her grave. There must have been some mighty desperate extenuating circumstances to have warranted such madness.

GIL MELLÉ

Meanwhile, post-production of the film itself proceeded and the pressure was mounting to hire a composer. Sid Sheinberg wanted someone British, partly to ensure the film would qualify for the Eady subsidy, but also to save on travel expenses.

Stromberg met with British composer Richard Rodney Bennett (*Far from the Madding Crowd*, *Nicholas and Alexandra*, *Lady Caroline Lamb*) but, like early candidates Maurice Jarre and Michel Legrand, Bennett was reluctant to work in television. Instead, he scored *Murder on the Orient Express* which earned him his third Oscar nomination and won the BAFTA Award for Best Film Music.

Stromberg even met with John Barry, famous for his James Bond scores, whose job that year on *Live and Let Die* had been usurped by Paul McCartney's wingman George

theatrical version, the movie begins with the funeral – which is still quite brusque but somewhat less clumsy.

2. Dropping the prologue also meant that the top-billed star, James Mason, would not make his entrance until forty-five minutes into the movie – for only a thirty-second snippet.

To solve the latter problem, NBC decided to replace the prologue with a five-and-a-half minute preview hosted by James Mason – as himself – hastily organized by production manager Brian Burgess and shot on Saturday, August 25, 1973, with a crew of 30 people.

The sequence would be directed by Hunt Stromberg Jr. because Jack Smight had already returned to California to immediately direct three back-to-back movies for Universal: *Linda* (ABC-TV – broadcast November 3, 1973, nearly a month *before True Story*) starring Stella Stevens; *The Man from Independence* (ABC-TV, March 11, 1974) starring Robert Vaughn as President Harry S. Truman; and then, for the theatrical division, *Airport 1975* (released October 18, 1974) starring Charlton Heston, Karen Black, Linda Blair, Myrna Loy, Gloria Swanson and a parade of other familiar faces.

The introduction's director of photography was veteran Edward "Ted" Scaife (who had shot the second-unit death of Agatha) with the camera mounted on a Titan crane for certain shots.

In present-day London, we see Mason taking a stroll through St. John's Wood Church cemetery (on Lord's Roundabout, between Lord's Cricket Ground and Regent's Park) where he shows us the tombstone of "Mary

Gil Mellé and synthesizer.

Gil Mellé.

NO SMOK

CHAPTER FOUR: POST-PRODUCTION

Gil Mellé.

Broadway actor Howard Hall, Gil Mellé's father who abandoned him at age 2.

Martin. Unfortunately, Barry was already set to score the ABC-TV production of *The Glass Menagerie*, starring Katharine Hepburn, that would be broadcast two weeks after *Frankenstein: The True Story*.

With the clock ticking, Universal Television's head of production George Santoro recommended 41-year-old composer Gil Mellé, born in New Jersey, but, by then, based in California. Both Santoro and Stromberg were big fans of the musician's work and concurred he would do a terrific job with *Dr. Frankenstein* – but Sid Sheinberg was still determined to hire a Brit.

Refusing to take 'no' for an answer (as usual), Stromberg took it upon himself to telephone Mellé at his home in Los Angeles and pitched him the movie – which the composer loved and wanted to do – if only they could figure out a way to get Sheinberg to agree. And that's when Stromberg hatched a plan. "Why don't you and your wife take a vacation to London," Stromberg suggested to Mellé. "Right *now*. Once you're here, Sid won't have any more excuses *not* to hire you." (On the down-low, Stromberg personally covered some of those travel expenses.)

The scheme worked like a charm. Mellé got the gig.

Mellé was widely acclaimed for his jazz albums and his innovative electronic score to Universal's sci-fi thriller *The Andromeda Strain* (1971) – for which he had been nominated for a Golden Globe. On contract to Universal, Mellé had served the studio well on a multitude of television series, from Rod Serling's *Night Gallery* to *Columbo*. From 1971 to 1973, the composer had been assigned to eleven TV movies, including *The Six Million Dollar Man* (ABC-TV, 1973) and *Savage* (NBC-TV, 1973), starring Martin Landau and Barbara Bain, directed by Steven Spielberg.

Although initially known for jazz and electronica, Mellé was classically trained and eager to stretch those muscles on a full-bodied orchestral score. In "The Gil Mellé Chronicles" by James Anthony Phillips, published

Philip Martell & James Bernard.

in *Little Shoppe of Horrors* No. 38, Mellé is quoted thusly: "My main influence at that time was Edgard Varèse for the philosophy and poetics of music; Béla Bartók for his sonorities and innovative orchestrations; and, Miklós Rózsa for his melodies."

In a 2017 interview, Mellé's widow Denise told me, "Upon our arrival at the airport in London in early-August 1973, we saw a large sign that read 'Gil Mellé' and there was Hunt Stromberg and his chauffeur to greet us. Producers may have done that sort of thing for movie stars, but it was quite unexpected for a composer. Hunt was an extraordinary person and he treated us like royalty."

Stromberg and *Frankenstein*'s director Jack Smight met with Mellé for the "spotting session" – dissecting the movie scene by scene, deciding exactly when each music cue would begin and end, and discussing the style of music needed for every occasion. Shortly thereafter, however, Smight left for Hollywood to direct another picture, leaving Stromberg in charge of all the remaining artistic decisions.

"Luckily, Hunt and Gil were in perfect sync," Denise Mellé confirmed to me. "For the rough cut's temporary score, Hunt had used lush orchestral cues from movies like *Doctor Zhivago* – about as far removed from *Andromeda Strain* as you can get. Despite Gil's reputation as an electronic composer, he agreed one-hundred percent that the music for *Frankenstein* must be a purely symphonic orchestral score."

Stromberg told the composer to emphasize the romantic melodrama of the movie, including a searing, emotional love theme between Dr. Frankenstein and his Creature.

In his article on the composer, James Anthony Phillips observed, "Mellé was quick to grasp the parallels between the characters in the Frankenstein movie and the writing team of Christopher Isherwood and Don Bachardy – gay partners wrestling with their own emotions over lost beauty and aging."

It should also be noted that Mellé was no stranger to queer subject matter having recently scored *That Certain Summer* (Universal / ABC-TV, 1972), the groundbreaking TV movie, mentioned earlier in this book, with Hal Holbrook and Martin Sheen as a gay couple.

"After Gil had begun writing the music," recalled Denise Mellé, "Hunt made an appointment to come to our rented flat at Ossington Street and Moscow Road, near Notting Hill Gate. He wanted to hear a sample composition which, of course, made Gil very nervous. When Hunt arrived, Gil sat down at the piano and played 'Prima's Theme' which Hunt immediately adored. From that moment on, Hunt trusted Gil implicitly and never asked to hear another note until the recording session."

James Anthony Phillips noted, "Using the leitmotif style advocated by Golden Age composers such as Erich Wolfgang Korngold, Max Steiner and Miklós Rózsa, Mellé developed recurring themes for all of the main characters in *Frankenstein: The True Story*."

Denise Mellé explained that Gil did not use an orchestrator. In just six weeks, he would not only compose the music but would write out the entire score himself, by hand, for one-hundred players.

Even with traditional acoustic instruments, Mellé would be as inventive as ever. He had a special set of orchestra bells built for the recording. "I wanted to use these bells in the final scenes of the picture when they're sailing to the Arctic Circle," Gil Mellé explained in a 2002 interview. "The three bells that I designed and built for the score were the D, the D-flat, and the low C in the bass cleft. These bells were enormous, I'm telling you! That bell that went down to the low C must have been twenty-six feet long. At that time, the lowest bell ever made was the low E-flat bass bell made for Richard Strauss for *Don Quixote*."

"I can assure you, Universal did not want to spend the extra money on those bells," Denise Mellé stated. "It was Hunt Stromberg who went to bat for Gil and got it approved. Hunt believed in Gil, and he wanted everything in the movie to be special."

By then, the movie was on the verge of going over budget – if it hadn't done so already. I do wonder if Stromberg actually got Universal to foot the bill for those custom bells – or if perhaps Hunt quietly paid for them himself, but pretended he'd charmed his bosses once more.

When the composer was asked to describe his *Frankenstein* music, he said, "The score was in the early Romantic idiom, and I wanted to reflect the time that the poets like Shelley, Keats, Byron and Mary Shelley all lived and where the literary influence laid. I tried to write a beautiful score and didn't try to write 'monster music.' Everyone approached *Frankenstein*, *The Wolf Man* and all that in such a heavy-handed manner. Discordant, loud, frightening music. It's been done."

Asked if horror movies were genuinely in his wheelhouse, Mellé explained, "I happen to love science and horror fiction and *Frankenstein* is one of my favorite stories. I can relate to being an outcast. I was abandoned by my biological father at the age of 2 and raised by an Irish neighbor. The Creature in *Frankenstein: The True Story* is just like every person sitting in the audience. He didn't ask to be here, but he *is* – despite his limitations, whatever the flaws in his physical and his mental

Cover and back cover art for bootleg soundtrack for FTTS.

makeup. He's trying to do the best that he can with his own personal situation. Once I realized that, I could make a way for the audience to relate to this Creature on an interpersonal level. *That* was the ticket on how to write the score. That's what the main theme of *Frankenstein* is saying. It's soulful. You have to get down to the heart of the monster. Really get into the character."

In a 2018 profile in *JazzTimes*, journalist Aaron Steinberg wrote, "When Mellé turned two, his mother abandoned him as well. They didn't have contact again until Mellé was 32 when his mother told him that Howard Hall, his biological father, was the first person to play Dracula in a stage production; Bela Lugosi was his understudy. Hall's love of scotch trumped his career, however, and he had to give up his role to Lugosi; the rest is history." Fascinating family lore, but according to David J. Skal, who chronicled the first stage productions of *Dracula* for his book *Hollywood Gothic*, "The name Howard Hall appears nowhere in connection with the 1927 Broadway production, though it's possible he auditioned for the part. Lugosi was the only actor billed from the very beginning, including out-of-town tryouts, and certainly was never an understudy. Hall had his first Broadway credit in 1929. This story has all the signs of a sour-grapes anecdote

from a failed performer who may have missed out on a part that later became world-famous."

Scott Skelton, co-author of *Rod Serling's Night Gallery: An After-Hours Tour,*

observed, "One of Mellé's cues for *Night Gallery,* entitled 'I Sell Faith,' from the segment *Dr. Stringfellow's Rejuvenator* starring Forrest Tucker (NBC, November 17, 1971), became the kernel for the main theme of *Frankenstein: The True Story.* To hear this antecedent online, go to nightgallery.net/music-in-the-gallery. 'I Sell Faith' begins about 38 seconds into the excerpt with a solo piano. An oboe or English horn states the theme clearly about 53 seconds in. It's a mournful little phrase, and Gil developed it rather brilliantly into something more grand and sweeping to serve the score of *Frankenstein: The True Story.*"

The *Frankenstein* score was recorded from late-September through early-October 1973 at Anvil Studios in Denham (where later scores for *Star Wars* and *Alien* would be recorded) by the prestigious London Symphony Orchestra, the 100-piece ensemble considered by many to be the finest in England (founded in 1904, the oldest of all London orchestras).

In my interview with associate producer Ian Lewis, he explained that Mellé and music supervisor Philip Martell (who had supervised a multitude of Hammer Film scores) took turns conducting the orchestra and sitting in the control booth. Martell believed that it was the composer's job to write quiet music when the scene called for it and not the job of the sound engineer to turn down the dial. Lewis witnessed

moments of temperament that flared up between the two musicians over this and other issues.

Amusingly, Mellé defended his reputation by saying, "I have heard that I have an abrasive personality like Bernard Herrmann and have had disagreements with producers, music directors and film directors in the past, but it would take one-hundred Gil Mellés to make one Bernard Herrmann."

James Anthony Philips explained that Mellé had first-hand knowledge of Herrmann's volatile temperament because Mellé happened to be on the Universal lot within earshot of the recording stage where Herrmann had his infamous blow-up with Hitchcock over the score to *Torn Curtain* (1966) that resulted in John Addison replacing Herrmann as the composer on the film.

Denise Mellé added, "When *Frankenstein: The True Story* was broadcast, Gil was upset that the wonderful prologue featuring Mary Shelley had been dropped from the final cut of the film. And he was not pleased that a few of his cues ended up being edited and repositioned. Yet, despite these minor disappointments, Gil considered the music that he composed for *Frankenstein: The True Story* to be his finest and one of the happiest experiences of his career."

In 1974, *Cinefantastique* critic Daniel Masloski acknowledged that Mellé's music "plays a large part in the effectiveness of the film. The entire score is memorable (and should be released on record); particularly, I shall never forget Mellé's Creation theme, his music for the Creature's attempts to destroy itself and his truly awe-inspiring sounds for the climax in the Arctic wastes."

In 1975, when Stromberg was developing *The Legend of King Kong* as a big-budget theatrical spectacle for Universal Pictures, Mellé was his composer of choice – until producer Dino De Laurentiis and Paramount got into the *King Kong* business and stopped Stromberg's project dead in its tracks.

Instead, Mellé went on to score Stromberg's production of *The Curse of King Tut's Tomb* (NBC, 1980) plus thirty-nine other TV movies. He also scored the beloved television series *Kolchak: The Night Stalker* (ABC-TV, 1974-1975). His many theatrical feature film credits included *Embryo, The Sentinel* and *The Ultimate Warrior.* Mellé would die of a heart attack on October 28, 2004, at the age of 72.

ROSE OF WINTER

For the main titles, Stromberg decided to start with the opening of a red leather-bound book to a page where there are several pressed flowers. The center one, seemingly dried and dead, comes to vibrant life again via time-lapse photography – beautifully designed and executed by Peter Melrose (known for his complex opening moonscape in *The Fearless Vampire Killers*). The bloom was a pale pink and white Japanese camellia known as "the Rose of Winter." As we all know, a cut flower rapidly wilts. When placed in a vase of water, though, it can be revived to its former beauty but only for a brief period of time before it will eventually wither to the point of no return – an arresting metaphor for the resurrection and inevitable deterioration of the Creature.

Headshots of each star fade up in the center of the camellia as their credits appear, with the exception of "and Michael Sarrazin as the Creature" which is superimposed over the flower, with no accompanying image of his face, keeping his look a mystery. After all, the Creature *is* the efflorescence of this story.

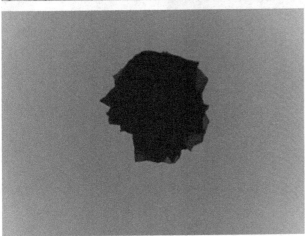

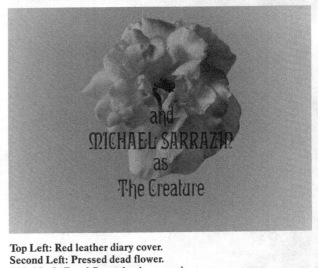

Top Left: Red leather diary cover.
Second Left: Pressed dead flower.
Third Left: Dead flower begins to revive.
Bottom Left: Flower revives to full bloom.
Above Top: FTTS title over bloom.
Above Center: James Mason headshot and credit over bloom.
Above Bottom: "and Michael Sarrazin as The Creature" credit over bloom.

ISSUE NUMBER THREE

BIZARRE

THE CONNOISSEUR'S MAGAZINE OF THE GROTESQUE

TWO DOLLARS

FRANKENSTEIN:
THE TRUE STORY

Cover of *Bizarre* No. 3. (August 1974), edited and published by Sam Irvin.

CHAPTER 5
BROADCAST & RELEASE

READY FOR PRIMETIME

The first press screening was held in Los Angeles on November 1, 1973. Defying the network's embargo, *San Francisco Examiner* columnist Dwight Newton simply could not contain his enthusiasm for the film, leaking the following "first review" on November 7: "In a Hollywood screening room last week, my wife was not the only viewer to wince, gasp or even shriek. Her reaction was typical. We were watching the forthcoming *Frankenstein: The True Story*. NBC-TV restrictions prohibit an advance critique but I can tell you that the audience was left limp. Horror fans take note. What happens to Frankenstein's exquisite female creation is, to put it mildly, electrifying. The Creature is played by 32-year-old French-Canadian, Universal contract actor Michael Sarrazin. He'll be the talk of television when *Frankenstein* is released. The casting is inspired, with big 'name' stars brought in to enhance minor roles."

Exultant industry buzz spread like wildfire, with expectations reaching stratospheric heights. The combined marketing machines of Universal and NBC went into overdrive.

Universal Television issued a deluxe press kit featuring a sumptuous blood-red faux suede presentation folder with gold embossed lettering. Contained within its interior pockets were a set

of twenty-eight 8x10 black-and-white stills and twenty-two separate press releases highlighting behind-the-scenes anecdotes and interview quotes from the cast and filmmakers. Additionally, full-color transparencies were provided to magazines. Theatrical feature films rarely got this kind of special treatment, much less made-for-TV movies.

PUBLISHING THE TELEPLAY

With great pride – and with every intention of campaigning for an Emmy nomination for Best Teleplay Adaptation – Universal, NBC and Stromberg agreed to the highly unusual move of publishing the Isherwood-Bachardy script, in its entirety. Back then, movie tie-in novelizations (prosaic adaptations of screenplays) were a frequent marketing tool for new motion pictures, but mass-market publishing of actual scripts in *advance* of a movie's premiere was extremely rare. There are

only four known precedents (all paperbacks): *Butch Cassidy and the Sundance Kid, Joe!, Sunday Bloody Sunday* and *Young Winston*, all of which would go on to be Oscar-nominated for Best Screenplay – with *Butch Cassidy* awarded the statuette. It appears that no teleplays of made-for-television films had ever been published prior to broadcast.

Breaking new ground, Universal struck a deal with a major publisher, Avon Books, a division of the Hearst Corporation, to rush-release a paperback edition of the *Frankenstein: The True Story* teleplay to hit bookstore shelves the week of the film's premiere.

The wraparound cover of Avon Books' FTTS script.

In 2015, Don Bachardy recalled, "We were delighted when we learned that our script would be published until we realized that it was going to be the shooting draft – which had been altered by Hunt Stromberg. I immediately got on a plane, flew to New York, and literally stormed the offices of Avon Books. I told them that Chris and I would take our names off the publication if they went ahead with the shooting draft. I gave them the draft that Chris and I approved and, lo and behold, that's what they ended up publishing. Thank heavens!"

In a letter to Isherwood dated November 12, 1973, Avon's Senior Editor Judith Webber wrote, "I'm delighted that we were able to coordinate with you and Mr. Bachardy to verify that our edition will represent the final version of the screenplay, exactly as you wrote it."

Because the teleplay was owned by Universal, Isherwood and Bachardy were not entitled to any royalties from the sale

Isherwood & Bachardy.

of the book. Hollywood super-agent Irving "Swifty" Lazar, who had just become Isherwood's new agent, felt differently. Isherwood reported in his diary, "Swifty has called Universal and they have agreed in principal that Don and I should get some money from the sales of the paperback."

In the haste to get the book to press, an introduction written by Isherwood and Bachardy did not make the deadline and subsequently remained dormant, tucked away in Isherwood's files. During my research of the Christopher Isherwood Papers archived at the Huntington Library in San Marino, California, I stumbled across this essay and my heart leapt. Would it be possible to publish this extraordinary discovery? I asked Don Bachardy and, to my great delight, he gave me his blessing. I am honored and extremely grateful. I would also like to acknowledge and thank Sara S. Hodson, Curator of Literary Manuscripts at the Huntington Library, and her associates, Catherine Wehrey, Natalie Russell and Michael Fish, for their invaluable assistance and support.

ABOUT OUR *FRANKENSTEIN* SCREENPLAY
by Christopher Isherwood & Don Bachardy

When Universal asked us to write a new version of *Frankenstein*, set in the period (around 1820) at which Mary Shelley wrote her novel, we decided that we were chiefly interested in the character of Dr. Frankenstein himself. Why does a brilliant young doctor want to make a creature? What does he imagine he is going to do with it when he's made it? How far will he feel himself responsible for its behavior? As we asked ourselves these questions, we began to invent those parts of our story which aren't in the novel.

According to us, the making of the Creature is an act of protest and defiance by Frankenstein – protest against the cruel accident of his brother's early death; defiance of the teachings of contemporary religion ("your brother's death was God's will, you must accept it without question") and contemporary science ("you mustn't try to make a copy of a human being, it's against the laws of nature").

Frankenstein is terrified at the thought of what he is about to do, but, encouraged by Henry Clerval, he thinks of himself as Prometheus, the mythical hero who defied the gods by stealing their fire and giving it to mankind. (Shelley, Mary's husband, did in fact produce a verse-drama about Prometheus in 1820, only two years after Mary published *Frankenstein*, and she was well aware of his interest in this subject when she was writing her novel.)

It was here that we departed from the original *Frankenstein* story. Our Dr. Frankenstein is making his Creature as a monument to his dead brother; he intends it to be "The Second Adam," a being who will be physically and spiritually superior to ordinary humans. Addressing it, he says, "You who know nothing of greed or hatred –you will show us how to live. Wherever you go, you will bring happiness."

So now it seemed to us necessary that the Creature should start its life beautiful, good-natured and intelligent; not appear immediately as a hideous freak which scares everybody – as it does in almost every other version of the story, including Mary Shelley's original. According to our version, the process by which the Creature is made is *apparently* successful. Only the audience knows that Frankenstein's method is at fault and that the Creature is doomed to deteriorate. This situation is not only more dramatic, it allows time for a stronger, more "human" relationship to develop between Frankenstein and the Creature.

When the Creature does begin to deteriorate, it is Frankenstein who behaves the worse of the two. The Creature,

Isherwood & Bachardy.

even when it has become dangerous to others, goes on trusting Frankenstein and feeling attachment to him; but Frankenstein can't overcome the disgust and shame which the Creature now causes him. At last, he has a chance to get rid of the Creature altogether; he would like to, but he can't quite bring himself to do the deed. Polidori says to him contemptuously: "It pleased you as long as it was pretty. Then you wanted to be rid of it – but someone else had to do it for you! So much for your dainty conscience!" Parents of problem children should be able to sympathize with Frankenstein, even though they will probably condemn his behavior!

Dr. Polidori also creates a creature – an exquisite young girl, intelligent, charming, heartless – who isn't about to deteriorate. His motives for making her are the worst possible; she is to be the instrument of his insane ambition. It is a paradox of our story that Frankenstein's misshapen murderous Creature seems ultimately noble, while Polidori's remains a mere beautiful reptile, and gets killed like one.

At the end of the story, Frankenstein can't evade his responsibility any longer. He has lost everything. He is all alone with the Creature he has made, on the Arctic ice. And now he does out of compassion what he couldn't do out of fear; he destroys the Creature at the cost of his own life. Or, at least, he tries to.

This is the text of the final draft of our screenplay, exactly as we wrote it. Before the film was shot, many cuts were made, some speeches were altered and some new scenes were written by other people. The subtitle of the film, *The True Story*, was not invented by us.

THE ADDENDUMS

In addition to the missing introduction, a page of the script was inadvertently left out – a section that Christopher Isherwood referred to as "Byron and the Butterfly" (from the prologue that was filmed but didn't make the final cut). When Isherwood spotted the mistake in the galley proof, he called Avon Books' Senior Editor Judith Weber, but, alas, it was too late. The book had already gone to press. Weber offered some consolation by stating that, if the book was a big enough success to warrant a second printing, the missing section could potentially be added at that time. This potential "second chance" got Isherwood thinking about *another* scene from an earlier draft, referred to as "Polidori and the Captain," that he lamented losing and hoped might *also* be added to a second printing of the book.

In a letter to Weber, dated November 17, 1973, Isherwood wrote, "Following our telephone conversation of yesterday, I am sending you the additional material for your edition of our *Frankenstein* screenplay. We realize that it won't be used in the first printing, so let's hope there's another soon! The insert scene with Byron and the Butterfly is, as I'm sure you'll agree, really valuable. It announces the butterfly theme which twice reappears. The other scene, between Polidori and the Captain, is one which we like very much and it nearly went into the finished picture."

In Isherwood's diary entry, dated November 17, 1973, he wrote: "When the schooner is being chased by the British coastguard cutter, Polidori says, 'God bless America!' – which now seems amusingly topical, because it sounds like that other crook, Nixon, in his first statement about Watergate."

Little did Isherwood know that James Mason was so obsessed with the Watergate scandal, some of the cast and crew genuinely suspected that he based his interpretation of Polidori on Nixon.

Although the first printing of the teleplay sold moderately well, demand was not high enough to warrant a second printing – so these inserts were never published. Herewith are Isherwood and Bachardy's two desired additions, published here by special permission from Don Bachardy:

BYRON AND THE BUTTERFLY

On page 10 of the Avon Books edition, Byron says, "In *your* eyes, my dear Mary, I see myself more clearly than I like. I doubt if they miss a single fault." Immediately following this speech, the subsequent missing material should be inserted. The script formatting has been adapted to match that of the paperback book.

(As Byron says these words, a butterfly starts to flutter around him. Finally, it flies right into his face.)

Byron.
(striking at it) Devil take it!

(The butterfly flutters away from him and settles on the table cloth. Byron irritably picks up a plate to crush it.)

Shelley.
(with dismay) Don't.

(Shelley stoops down, carefully catches the butterfly in his cupped hands, takes it down to the water's edge and gently releases it. Byron finds this funny.)

Mary.
(defensively) Shelley cannot endure to see any creature harmed.

Byron.
And you?

Mary.
I make certain exceptions.

(She looks straight at him. There is a certain half-joking hostility between them. Byron recognizes this, then dismisses it with a shrug, smiles, picks up a leg of chicken and sniffs it.)

Resume script on page 10 with Byron's speech: "But now, I am ravenous! Shelley, be a good fellow and call Dr. Polly. He won't deign to listen to Mary or me."

POLIDORI AND THE CAPTAIN

On page 196 of the Avon Books edition, the description reads: "The schooner is leaving the dock. We see its stern with the name Ariel. The Chinese stands on the dock, looking after it.

He smiles sweetly." Immediately following this passage, the subsequent additional material should be inserted.

(EXTERIOR. DECK OF SHIP – NIGHT.)

(The ship is now several miles out at sea. It is becoming foggy, and the shore is no longer visible. Polidori and the Captain stand at the rail. A light appears, flashing dimly through the fog.)

Captain.
That's the coastguard cutter. They're signaling that we should heave to.

Polidori.
(very nervous) What can they possibly want?

Captain.
(watching his face with amusement) You tell *me*, Doctor. Looks like it's you, or your friends.
(meaningly) Maybe I'm carrying cargo that's more valuable than I was given to understand –

Polidori.
If it's a question of – additional charges – I'm sure we can arrange that between us –
(a pause) Do you *have* to stop for them?

Captain.
(teasing him) I could tell you were in a hurry, the first minute you came aboard.
(patting him familiarly on the shoulder) Don't you worry about those limeys – they won't follow us much farther – there's fog ahead. Why should we kowtow to *them*? This ship is a one-hundred-foot piece of the United States – the land of the free!

Polidori.
God bless America!
Captain.
(laughing) You're going to feel right at home in our country, Doctor! Over there, a man like you can go a long way.

Resume script on page 196 with the scene header: "INTERIOR. FRANKENSTEIN'S CABIN – NIGHT."

NATIONAL COVERAGE IN *TV GUIDE*

THE EPIC SAGA BEHIND *FRANKENSTEIN: THE TRUE STORY*

'Frankenstein'
Literature's most celebrated monster is revived for another airing

By Samuel Rosenberg

BACKGROUND

[On Friday and Saturday, Nov. 30 and Dec. 1, NBC will present "Frankenstein: The True Story," a new two-part version of the literary classic. To add to your understanding and enjoyment of the film, we are here providing two views of Frankenstein: a portrait of Mary Shelley, whose novel started it all (by a literary scholar, Samuel Rosenberg); and, just for amusement, an irrelevant and irreverent view of the new TV monster, with apologies to the producers of the film, who have approached the subject with much more respect than the writer of our captions, TV GUIDE's Laddie Marshack. (See Sports and Specials column in program section for time and channels.)—Ed.]

I remember that fateful night perfectly: at 1 o'clock, I awakened from a deeply troubled sleep, staggered to my nightmare-dispelling TV set, and hastily switched it on. There was a seemingly endless wait and then *The Late Late Show* began: "Bride of Frankenstein."

I was delighted and relieved. Many of the movies given to us "night people" are real clinkers: but this . . . this was director James Whale's brilliant 1935 sequel to his classic 1931 "Frankenstein" and, critics agree, the masterpiece among horror films.

Yes, a wonderful film, and I settled back happily to watch its pseudo-documentary prologue. First we see a beautiful long shot of a Gothic castle silhouetted against an El Greco cloudscape. With the cameraman's magic→

Dr. Frankenstein's laboratory, of course.

He turns on the super-duper cosmic machine, and it makes a terrible noise. . . .

TV GUIDE NOVEMBER 24, 1973   29

However, he begins to deteriorate.

He gets downright scabrous.

It's enough to make him mean, and he turns somebody into a skeleton. . . .

continued

When the future authoress of "Frankenstein" was 16, her nearly bankrupt father appealed to his ardent young disciple Percy Bysshe Shelley for financial help, and the gullible young aristocrat immediately left his young wife Harriet and their infant son in a Welsh village to gallop to rescue Godwin in London.

There Shelley was not only bilked by Godwin out of £4700 (worth about $50,000 today) but was entrapped by Mary and her stepsister Jane Clairmont into making love to Mary on her mother's grave.

Bedazzled by the combined intellectual and sexual charms of William Godwin and his daughter, Percy Shelley abandoned Harriet to live with Mary Godwin. After trying vainly to win him back, Harriet finally committed suicide in the Serpentine Lake in London's Hyde Park, not far from the spot where the grown-up Shelley frequently sailed little paper boats made of bank notes.

The writing of "Frankenstein," two years after the elopement, was the accidental by-product of the "long enchanted summer" of 1816, which Shelley and Mary spent in Switzerland in the company of her sister Jane, Lord Byron, and the latter's personal physician-in-attendance, John Polidori.

When the Shelleys arrived in Geneva at the end of May 1816 with their infant son, William, and Jane Clairmont, they found that their scandal had preceded them. The story was gleefully spread by English tourists that the "aristocratic renegade" Shelley had purchased the two beautiful daughters of the godless Godwin for £1500 (£800 for Mary, £700 for Jane) and was now living with them in a pashalike state of binominal hanky-panky.

But when the infamous Lord Byron suddenly appeared in Geneva a few days later in the company of the handsome young Dr. Polidori (whom he called Polly-Dolly) and moved into the Hotel d'Angleterre, already occupied by Shelley and his bartered brides, →

TV Guide – 5-page FTTS spread.

32

It's such a terrible noise, Dr. F. falls down, in fear of what he hath wrought.

What he hath wrought turns out to be a very stunning fellow.

The wraps off, stunning fellow smiles demurely. . . .

30

continued

we are wafted through castle walls into a sitting room where Lord Byron is conversing elegantly with Percy Bysshe Shelley and Mary Shelley about the great success of her new novel "Frankenstein, or The Modern Prometheus."

Then Lord Byron performs his famous limp over to Mary (Elsa Lanchester) and says, in a Warner Bros. version of high-class English English: "It is a pitteh, my deah Mary, thet you disposed of your Mawnstah so ahterly and irrevocably. The pahblic are clemerring for a see-quell." And Mary looks up from her embroidery of cupids and roses and says sweetly: "Baht, your Luddiship, the Mawnstah is not dead. He is alive end well, thenk you, end I hev jahst written a see-quell for him, to be called 'Bride of Frankenstein.'"

At this moment a strange thing happened. Though this was my fifth or sixth viewing of the film, for the first time I suddenly became aware of the image of the charming and shy young authoress presented by James Whale. Had Mary Shelley really been like that, so young (about 25), so pretty and wholesome-looking? And if she was, out of what strange psychic cupboard had she taken the ingredients to fashion the most successful horror tale of all time? Where did that terrifying yet touching Monster come from?

Seated before my television set, my intuition told me that there had to be something very strange and remarkable in the story of pretty Mary Shelley and how she came to write about Frankenstein's Monster. So, during the first round of commercials—beer, bad breath, cake mix, athlete's foot, dog food, and hair spray—I lunged at my encyclopedia and learned that though Mary Shelley had never written a sequel to her novel, she had actually begun writing Frankenstein at the age of 18!

Mary Shelley was the child of the radical philosopher, novelist and publisher William Godwin and the great pioneer feminist Mary Wollstonecraft, who died giving birth to Mary. →

TV GUIDE NOVEMBER 24, 1973

It's lonely being mean, hard to make friends. And so he sails to Antarctica to get away from it all.

Antarctica's no bargain either. He gives it all up and enters an ice cave.

He's too noisy, and the blocks come tumbling down. . . .

34

continued

Geneva's gossips really had a field day.

Byron's scandal was far greater than that of the Shelleys. After several years of the most spectacular literary, social and amorous successes, the 28-year-old Byron had been ostracized by English society and violently attacked in the press for his brutal treatment of his bride Annabella. After a marriage that lasted only one year, Annabella told one and all that, in addition to his sadism, Byron had repeatedly boasted to her of his homosexual affairs and his love for his half sister, Augusta.

Now every brassbound telescope in Geneva was sharply focused on the doors and windows of the Hotel d'Angleterre. To get away from all this goggle-eyed attraction, Shelley and Byron rented adjacent villas on the perimeter of Geneva and settled down for the summer.

Mary Shelley's journal tells us that the summer of 1816 was exceptionally rainy and dreary, and forced the young social outcasts to spend a great deal of their time indoors. Byron and Shelley quickly formed an advanced seminar in poetry and philosophy and read aloud and discussed an enormous number of books, all dutifully listed in Mary's journal.

Daytimes the ambitious young intellectuals wrote seriously and read and discussed and laughed at the outside world of ordinary people. But at night it was different. Subdued, they clung together by candlelight at Byron's Villa Diodati and relaxed by telling the most horrifying ghost stories they could remember.

At first it was great fun, but then a strange obsession seized them and they became compulsive talkers and listeners whose Scheherazade lives seemed to depend upon their nightly storytelling, and for weeks they descended deeper and deeper into the inferno of the tormented dead who come back to haunt the guilty living.

Then, on June 16, at Villa Diodati, the developing macabre drama sud- →

TV GUIDE NOVEMBER 24, 1973

CHAPTER FIVE: BROADCAST & RELEASE

175

And the ice seals him up—until Hollywood is ready to thaw him out again.

denly reached its high climax. The evening began with Byron reading a German ghost story about a man who kisses his bride in their wedding bed and sees to his horror that she has been transformed by his Judas kiss into the dreadful moldering corpse of the woman he had deserted. The choice of that particular story, so evocative of the tragic, deserted Harriet in the Shelley-Harriet-Mary triangle—had to be Byronic mischief.

It was then that Byron made his historic suggestion that each of them should try to write a ghost story. He began a story about a vampire but soon gave it up because he and Shelley were working on a much higher intellectual plateau, and gave his story idea to Polidori. It became the famous "The Vampire," direct ancestor of all vampire tales, including Bela Lugosi's "Dracula."

According to Mary's account, she could not at first think of an idea for the group's supernatural parlor competition, but just two evenings later (June 18), the idea of Frankenstein came to her as a result of an excited discussion between Byron and Shelley about the possibility of emulating the Greek god Prometheus (he made men from clay) and creating men by scientific means.

"That night," wrote Mary, "when I placed my head upon my pillow, I did not sleep. My imagination possessed and guided me, gilting the images that arose in my mind with a vividness far

36

beyond the usual bond of reverie. I saw—with shut eyes, but acute mental vision—I saw the pale student of unhallowed arts beside the thing he had put together. I saw the hideous phantasm of a man stretched out and then, on the working of some powerful engine, show signs of life and stir with an uneasy half-vital motion.

"I have found it!" continued Mary. "What terrified me will terrify others; and I need only describe the spectre which haunted my midnight pillow."

The question: "What sort of person was this teen-aged creator of the world's most beloved Monster?" is best answered, I think, by two comments made about her by Jane Clairmont and Percy Shelley.

Eleven months after Percy Shelley and Mary met, Mary became mildly ill. "Dr." Percy Shelley, who was extremely perceptive in his saner intervals, wrote the following "comic" prescription for his ailing soul mate in her journal: "9 drops of human blood, 7 grains of gunpowder, ½ oz. of putrefied brains, 13 mashed grave worms."

But perhaps the most revealing clue to the personality of this juvenile Monster-creator may be seen in the recently published diary of Mary's closest friend and constant companion, Jane Clairmont, who wrote:

"I can never help feeling horror even in looking at her—the instant she appears I feel, not as if I had blood in my veins, but in its stead the sickening motion of the Death Worm.

"What would one say of a Woman . . . who would go and gaze upon the spectacle of a Child led to the scaffold. One would turn from her in horror—yet she did so, she looked coolly on, rejoiced in the comfortable place she had got in the shew, chatted with her neighbors. Never once winced during the exhibition; and, when it was all over, went up and claimed acquaintance with the executioner and shook hands with him." (END)

TV GUIDE NOVEMBER 24, 1973

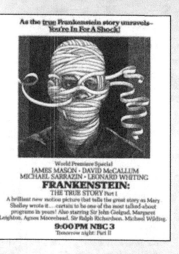

As the true Frankenstein story unravels—
You're In For A Shock!

World Premiere Special
JAMES MASON • DAVID McCALLUM
MICHAEL SARRAZIN • LEONARD WHITING
FRANKENSTEIN:
THE TRUE STORY Part I
A brilliant new motion picture that tells the great story as Mary Shelley wrote it . . . certain to be one of the most talked-about programs in years! Also starring Sir John Gielgud, Margaret Leighton, Agnes Moorehead, Sir Ralph Richardson, Michael Wilding.
9:00 PM NBC 3
Tomorrow night: Part II

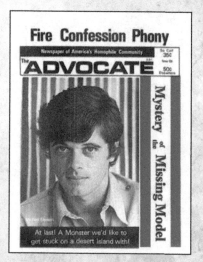

WORLD
PREMIERE
SPECIAL!
JAMES MASON
DAVID McCALLUM
MICHAEL SARRAZIN
LEONARD WHITING

FRANKENSTEIN:
THE TRUE STORY
Part I

If you think you know Frankenstein,
get set for a shock!

Also starring Sir **John Gielgud,**
Margaret Leighton, Agnes Moorehead,
Sir Ralph Richardson & Michael Wilding.
(Tomorrow night: Part II)

9:00 PM NBC 3

The week of the movie's premiere, *TV Guide* (then the most-read magazine in America with a weekly circulation of 19 million) published a breathtaking five-page spread, featuring twelve full-color photos from the film. Unfortunately, *TV Guide*'s resident critic, Judith Crist, had missed the advance screening of the movie, so, her "review" amounted to nothing more than an ill-informed preview, stating that the script had "returned to the Mary Shelley original that got lost along the Karloff-monster-movie way." Which just goes to prove that you cannot judge a movie by its title – nor its press release.

NBC bought a half-page advertisement in *TV Guide* for the movie, featuring artwork of Sarrazin hidden behind bandages that were beginning to swirl off his head, and the copy line: "If you think you know

Frankenstein, get set for a shock!"

And, finally, amid the program listings for Friday, November 30, *TV Guide* devoted a half-page "Close-Up" sidebar to *Frankenstein: The True Story*, with a photo of Whiting and Sarrazin, and a more accurate description of the movie that included the following: "With an accent more on character than terror, the drama revolves around the 'father-son' rapport between Dr. Frankenstein and his creation, a relationship that takes a dark turn when the creature's body begins to deteriorate."

BLINDSIDED

"Father-son" was the safe, traditional way to construe the relationship between Dr. Frankenstein and the Creature – a perfectly viable interpretation ascribed by many, including network censors and Leonard Whiting himself. [See Chapter 7 for my interview with Whiting.]

The fact that Whiting was unaware of the writers' subtextual intent echoes a similar blindside that occurred with Charlton Heston on *Ben-Hur*. According to Gore Vidal, who was an uncredited Metro-Goldwyn-Mayer staff writer on *Ben-Hur*, he "infused a subtle yet clear gay subtext into the screenplay." In a 1996 interview for *The Advocate*, the national gay news magazine, Vidal explained, "Over the years I have told the funny story of how I wrote a love scene for Ben-Hur [Heston] and Messala [Stephen Boyd] and how *only* the actor playing Messala was told what the scene was about because, according to director William Wyler, 'Chuck will fall apart.'"

Many years after the fact, Heston got wind of this subterfuge and fired off several vitriolic attacks against Vidal in the *Los Angeles Times*, but nothing he could say changed the way the scene had been written, no matter how Heston may have unwittingly played it.

COVER OF *THE ADVOCATE*

When *Frankenstein: The True Story* first aired, many journalists turned a blind eye to its suggestive homoeroticism. There was one rather rebellious exception to that tacit gentleman's agreement. Emblazoned on the cover of its December 5, 1973, issue (which hit newsstands ten days earlier), *The Advocate* (back then, a bi-weekly tabloid subtitled "Newspaper of America's Homophile

Fire Confession Phony

Newspaper of America's Homophile Community

The **ADVOCATE**

Mystery of the Missing Model

At last! A Monster we'd like to get stuck on a desert island with!

Community" with a national circulation of 40,000) featured a large, dreamy headshot of Michael Sarrazin with the cheeky headline: "At Last! A Monster we'd like to get stuck on an island with!" Inside, entertainment critic Harold Fairbanks (an intimate of Isherwood and the former lover of German novelist Klaus Mann) penned an article entitled "Big Talents Assemble Unusual Frankenstein" that left nothing to the imagination, including the fact that writers Isherwood and Bachardy were "lovers."

LOCAL NEWSPAPER COVERAGE

Throughout the country, *Frankenstein: The True Story* received quite a bit of editorial space in television supplements of local newspapers. The most lavish example was New York's *Newsday* which put *Frankenstein* on the cover of *TV: Newsday's Weekly Guide to Television* (November 25-December 1, 1973) featuring an original full-color portrait of Sarrazin by the renowned sci-fi book jacket artist Gary Viskupic. With a circulation of 450,000 copies, there were a lot of fans in the New York area that clipped this cover and kept it as a collectible mini-poster.

FRANKENSTEIN MEETS MAE WEST

A few nights before the broadcast, a swanky premiere/dinner party was hosted on the lot at Universal City. Nancy Anderson, West Coast editor of *Photoplay* magazine, reported, "Jacqueline Bisset is so proud of Michael Sarrazin's performance in *Frankenstein: The True Story*, she was beaming at him throughout the invitational screening."

Mae West.

Mae West and Jacque Shelton (Hunt's boyfriend and later Assistant to the Producer for FTTS) in *Mister Ed* (1964).

Mae West visits the set of Jack Smight's *Midway* (1976), seen here with actor Kevin Dobson. (Stromberg arranged for this photo op.)

Back together, Sarrazin and Bisset had managed to weather the storm of her short-lived affair with Jon Peters – but the reconciliation didn't last. In 1974, the two would break up again, once and for all.

Denise Mellé, wife of the movie's composer, was there that evening and vividly recalled, "Gil and I couldn't believe our eyes when Hunt and Jacque walked in with none other than Mae West and her coterie of four young studs in tuxedos. This was a few years after *Myra Breckinridge* so she was no spring chicken. But she was dressed head-to-toe in glitter and glam and made quite an entrance, let me tell you."

Holding court, Hunt explained to the thongs of agog onlookers, "Mae and I go way back. She used to bounce me in her lap when I was a little boy."

With one hand on her swiveling hip and the other plumping her bouffant, Mae deadpanned, "He wasn't so little."

TELEVISION APPEARANCES

On Friday, November 30, 1973, the day that *Frankenstein: The True Story*, Part 1, would have its primetime premiere broadcast on NBC, Michael Sarrazin appeared that morning on NBC's *The Today Show* to plug the movie in an interview conducted by Barbara Walters (who, at that time, co-hosted the program with Frank McGee).

Left: Two of several station break title cards that were sent to all local NBC-TV affiliates to use during commercial breaks. In case of any dead air, instead of cutting to black, these images would appear. They were sent in the form of 35mm slides.
Above: Actual vintage packaging of the station break slides.

"I remember the *Today Show* hosts talking about the upcoming telecast," recalled John Weber, a longtime fan of the film. "They showed a clip that began with the heavily bandaged creature rising from the life-giving scaffold, and him walking towards Victor, who then removed his facial covering, and Victor exclaiming 'You. Are. Beautiful.' Seeing that clip – and reading the article about the film in that week's issue of *TV Guide* – had me all psyched up to watch it that night."

The day before, on November 29, 1973, Hunt Stromberg Jr. was interviewed by newscaster Roy Eaton on WBAP-TV Channel 5, the local NBC affiliate in Fort Worth, Texas – 27 miles from the Stromberg and Shelton Double S Ranch in Springtown, Texas. Clearly, after spending the bulk of the year in the UK and then escorting Mae West to the screening party in Los Angeles, Stromberg and Shelton had retreated to their Double S for some R & R.

THE RATINGS

Ratings-wise, *Frankenstein: The True Story*, Part 1, won Friday night viewership for NBC nationwide, ranking No. 27 for the week on the Nielsen Ratings Chart, with 13.3 million viewers. CBS counterprogrammed Richard Brooks' acclaimed, theatrical true-crime thriller *In Cold Blood*; and, ABC ran its popular Friday night comedy lineup, including *Room 222*, *Adam's Rib* and *Love, American Style*.

Goosed by positive word-of-mouth, Part 2 did even *better* on Saturday night, ranking No. 15 for the week, with 14.6 million viewers – competing against CBS' formidable juggernaut of *The Mary Tyler Moore Show*, *The Bob Newhart Show* and *The Carol Burnett Show*; and on ABC, a college football game.

THE AFTERGLOW

When the dust settled, Isherwood wrote in his diary, "Many people called us about it, all professing to have enjoyed it despite its faults – no, not quite all. Cukor was frank."

Isherwood should have known not to take George Cukor seriously. By then, the 75-year-old Hollywood director (known as the "unofficial head of Hollywood's gay subculture") had become a notorious curmudgeon. And, who knows? Since he had won an Oscar for directing *My Fair Lady*, maybe he was not amused by the scenes in which Dr. Frankenstein mentors the Creature à la Henry Higgins and Eliza Doolittle.

On the other hand, Oscar-nominated screenwriter Calder Willingham (Stanley Kubrick's *Paths of Glory*, Mike Nichols' *The Graduate*, Arthur Penn's *Little Big Man*) was so moved by the film, he composed the following personal letter to Isherwood: "My wife Jane and I liked your *Frankenstein* show a great deal. I felt it was undoubtedly, by far, infinitely, the best variation on this theme, really an original work with little debt to the long-ago authoress. It seemed to me much more than an unconscious homosexual *Pygmalion* parable (surely, conscious and unconscious homosexual tension did play a part in this drama?), it seemed to me a dream-drama of this entire whole sad modern world itself. Off into 'the northern wastes,' now that truly was haunting. There were many moments of real superiority in this work."

RAVE REVIEWS

What took Isherwood by surprise the most, however, was the plethora of positive reviews. In his diary, Isherwood noted: "Hunt Stromberg called from Texas, trying to placate me by quoting from various 'rave' notices, including one by Cecil Smith in the *Los Angeles Times*."

No exaggeration, Smith's praise was unqualified: "Splendidly endowed... a remarkably literate script... admirably translated to film by director Jack Smight... a total triumph, superbly mounted and beautifully played, properly terrifying yet accomplished with rich wit and polish."

And the gushing didn't end there. In the *New York Daiy News*, Kay Gardella wrote: "A splendid job... a remarkable production. Never in our wildest dreams could anyone tell us we'd be riveted to a television set for four hours to watch this chilling take unfold... but the Stromberg production has been put together with such care and with such sensitivity to the

real meaning of the classic, it was hard to pass up. The entire cast was impressive, but it was the two leading men – Leonard Whiting as Dr. Frankenstein and Michael Sarrazin as the Creature – and their pathetic relationship to one another that was the most absorbing element in the drama. Sarrazin was unquestionably the most sympathetic creature we've ever seen."

That unusual relationship between Frankenstein and the Creature also caught *Dallas Times Herald*'s critic Bob Brock off guard: "Viewers will be enthralled by the sensitive mounting of this love story. That's right, love story."

The review in the *Christian Science Monitor* agreed: "There is not only romance and heartbreak in the literate script, but also an uncanny degree of clever humor, thanks to James Mason as Dr. Polidori."

In the *San Diego Union*, Don Freeman enthused: "The ultimate in horror films with a superbly assembled cast to chill the marrow – my marrow, anyway. I salute Mr. Stromberg for his foresight in hiring Christopher Isherwood, the novelist, to handle the adaptation, which was literate, forceful and richly detailed. You don't, in fact, very often encounter horror yarns with such a high degree of craftsmanship. The whole cast was splendid. It was an enterprise with a lot of scope and very scary, too."

Terence O'Flaherty wrote the following in the *San Francisco Chronicle*: "Stunning. The production was just short of Biblical in its theatrical effects and the acting was flawless."

Syndicated Copley News Service columnist Nancy Anderson wrote, "In my opinion, this television *Frankenstein* is of such superior quality it should have been a theatrical release."

The review in *Variety* raved: "Appropriately monster-sized, lavishly budgeted, and loaded with guest stars, the production achieved production qualities rarely seen on TV except when theatrical movies are shown. The four hours encouraged a leisurely pace, but the stage was quickly set and the tale never dropped its gruesome fascination. Whiting, McCallum and Sarrazin all played with great style, and Mason was appropriately slimy as the evil Dr. Polidori. As Prima, the she-monster, Jane Seymour was superb. Aside from the ample budget, much of the success of the show can be traced to the respectful but literate and imaginative treatment accorded Mrs. Shelley's novel by Christopher Isherwood and Don Bachardy. They did a first-rate job. The highlight for horror freaks comes when the male creature decapitated the female creature with his bare hands. The entire scene in a crowded ballroom was one of the most successful segments in the program."

And, for *The Hollywood Reporter*, Sue Cameron wrote: "Bravo. *Frankenstein: The True Story* was literate, entertaining, fascinating, suitably scary and a real treat. Aside from Christopher Isherwood's script, Michael Sarrazin as the Creature should receive an Emmy nomination. It is the finest work he has ever done. He instills humanity, warmth, compassion and all sorts of emotions we don't usually see in a creature. He was fabulous."

Renowned critic Leonard Maltin declared that the movie was "a Frankenstein film for the thinking man."

The 1974 edition of Steven H. Scheuer's *Movies on TV* awarded the film three out of four stars (the same review rating it gave the original 1931 *Frankenstein*), stating, "Despite its over three-hour length, the quality of performance is so uniformly high that it holds your interest and casts a tantalizing spell of horror, mixed with wonder and suspense."

To be fair and balanced, an exhaustive search was made among the major media outlets of the day to find dissenting opinions – but only one mixed review was found in *The New York Times* by television critic Howard Thompson. On the upside, he conceded that the film was "lavish and beautiful" with "fine performances by Leonard Whiting and Nicola Pagett." On the downside, he grumped that the second half "broadened into a lurid, wildly flapping adventure-thriller" with "a suave, lunatic surgeon (James Mason) straight out of a hokey 'Late, Late Show.'"

To each his own. But, for many viewers (present company included), the gonzo twists and turns of Part 2 – fueled by Mason's ferocious depravity – are precisely what helped make the film so exhilarating.

Michael Sarrazin was very proud of his work. In an interview in the *San Francisco Chronicle* on December 3, 1973, he said, "The thing about the Creature that is most challenging is that he should evoke sympathy, you should care about him, and to make this happen without dialogue. I think we brought it off. Jack Smight did a marvelous job. Somehow, no matter how hideous the Creature becomes, it doesn't repulse you."

Many years later, Montreal organizer of Le Cinéclub, Philippe Spurrell, met Michael Sarrazin and asked him about his legacy in cinema: "Michael said that of all the films he's done, *Frankenstein: The True Story* is the one that he is asked about the most. He said that when he was making the movie, he was in awe of all the talented people around him – and he felt a bit inferior by comparison."

Because Michael Sarrazin passed away in 2011 at age 70, I was not able to interview him for this book. However, I contacted his brother Pierre Sarrazin who said, "Thank you for remembering Michael for his role in *Frankenstein: The True Story*. At the time, he had been offered the choice of playing either Dr. Frankenstein or the Creature. He obviously chose the latter. He was very proud of his performance, and it ranks up there with his finest work. Michael was a wonderful actor but more importantly he was a kind, gentle man. I am comforted that he is remembered this way."

FAN REACTION

Fanboys-and-girls from coast-to-coast, often the hardest to please, were absolutely enthralled by what they saw. One such viewer, who posts blogs under the name "bipolarber" on the Classic Horror Film Board, recalled his experience as a kid seeing the film for the first time in 1973: "This film was one of the first great horror movie experiences of my life. I relish the memories of getting to school the next day and talking with my friends about the scenes from the previous night's viewing: The 'sawbones' amputation, and the arm coming back to life, the absolutely STUNNING lab... Jane Seymour getting her head popped off like a cork, the lightning blasting James Mason, the servant falling into the acid bath, the final scene in the Arctic... Yep, a definite favorite!"

If success can be gaged by watercooler moments, this movie delivered them by the 5-gallon tank load on both nights. For *Time Out New York*, the most talked-about sequence was the "glorious moment of delirium when the monster disrupts a society ball to collect his bride, ripping off her pearl choker to reveal the stitched neck, then annexing her head as his property." The national conversation, at least among fans of the genre, was dominated by this film for weeks.

Horror fan magazines had little forewarning – so reaction in print did not begin to appear until early 1974 when *Castle*

of Frankenstein No. 21 presented a major spread on the movie. Editor-publisher Calvin T. Beck wrote, "Reaching more people in two evenings than any genre entry's done before, NBC-TV's airing of *Frankenstein: The True Story* excited the whole world! Time and again, TV has proved an extraordinary ability of accepting challenges and scaling great heights. But so far, nothing has aroused so much sensation as NBC's monumental two-part production of *Frankenstein*. The face of entertainment history is now radically altered – it will never be quite the same."

He was right. In hindsight, a case can be made that *Frankenstein: The True Story* proved to be seismic in the way that Universal's back-to-back *Dracula* (1931) and *Frankenstein* (1931) redefined horror; and, in the way that Hammer's *Curse of Frankenstein* (1957) and *Horror of Dracula* (1958) revitalized the genre. Just as *2001: A Space Odyssey* (1968) and *Planet of the Apes* (1968) suddenly made sci-fi respectable and *Rosemary's Baby* (1968) elevated modern-day horror to Oscar-winning heights, *Frankenstein: The True Story* helped to revolutionize the industry's way of thinking about Gothic horror films. This overall trend directly led to major financial risks being taken on such 1970s game changers as *The Exorcist*, *Jaws*, *Star Wars*, Badham's *Dracula* – subjects that heretofore would have been relegated as B-movies.

In that same 1974 issue of *Castle of Frankenstein*, Beck invited a panel of four knowledgeable film journalists to submit their own diverse critiques of the movie – including frequent *Little Shoppe of Horrors* contributor Bruce Hallenbeck who opined, "*Frankenstein: The True Story* is a very fine film... McCallum shines... Mason is a standout as Polidori. Yet the most deliciously evil character in the film is Jane Seymour as Prima. Miss Seymour can do more with a certain look than most actresses with mountains of dialogue, and hers is perhaps the most sinister and perverted female characterization I have ever seen."

Another panelist, Paul Roen, bravely acknowledged the elephant in the room: "The strongest human relationship is essentially homosexual: the bond between creature and creator. Sarrazin is more pathetically lovable than was Karloff."

The lone female critic on the panel, Belinda MacEvoy, had some quibbles but conceded, "I cannot recall when TV has ever produced anything as opulent or as expensive looking."

The fourth and final panelist, Richard Barstow, concluded, "*Frankenstein: The True Story* was one of the damned best things in my 25 years of TV watching. Any way you look at it, it's a classic!"

In a 1974 issue of *Cinefantastique*, Vol. 3, No. 2, critic Daniel Masloski wrote, "It is a film of rare beauty... an epic

FTTS spread in *Castle of Frankenstein* No. 21.

Sam Irvin holds copy of *Bizarre* No. 3.

in the true sense of the word."

I was so blown away by the film, I put a color photo of Sarrazin as the Creature on the cover of my fanzine *Bizarre* No. 3, published in the summer of 1974. I devoted seven pages to the film, plus I conducted in-person interviews in London with Margaret Leighton and Jane Seymour – the latter subsequently published in *Bizarre* No. 4 (1975). In my review of the movie, I boldly stated it was "the greatest fantasy film of all time."

In *Bizarre* No. 3, *Frankenstein: The True Story* was showered with 9 Bizarre Awards (out of 22 nominations), including Best Picture of the Year (Hunt Stromberg Jr.), Best Supporting Actress (Jane Seymour), Best Cameo Actress (Margaret Leighton), Best Adapted Screenplay (Christopher Isherwood & Don Bachardy), Best Score (Gil Mellé), Best Cinematography (Arthur Ibbetson), Best Costuming (Elsa Fennell), Best Art Direction & Set Decoration (Wilfrid Shingleton & Fred Carter), and Best Editing (Richard Marden).

My teenage reaction was, admittedly, over-the-top – but it legitimately demonstrates the kind of spell the film cast over its many passionate enthusiasts. A spell that clearly has not dissipated in the last half-century.

Stromberg was so proud of the movie's success, he thought the sky was the limit. "It's the definitive *Frankenstein*," he boasted in the *New York Daily News*. "I want it to become an annual television attraction like *Wizard of Oz* – maybe to be shown around Halloween."

THE TIDE TURNS

With reviews, ratings and audience reaction as positive as it was, many expected the film to sweep the Emmy Awards – especially an optimistic Hunt Stromberg Jr. who convinced Universal to host a special free screening for members of the Academy of Television Arts & Sciences and the Directors Guild of America. A large display ad (6 x 11.5 inches) was taken out in *Daily Variety*, Wednesday, January 30, 1974, announcing the screening to be held the following evening on Thursday, January 31, 1974, at Universal Studios, Room 1. The "for your consideration" style ad listed the names of thirteen stars of the movie, the producer (Stromberg), the director (Smight) and the composer (Mellé).

Glaringly absent from this advertisement were the writers (Isherwood and Bachardy) who had committed the unforgiveable sin of publicly badmouthing the film. For those keeping tabs on this feud, a high-profile omission like this was a dire warning to anyone else who might dare to bite the hand that fed them.

An Invitation
to the Members of the
DIRECTORS GUILD OF AMERICA
and the
ACADEMY OF TELEVISION ARTS & SCIENCES
To A Special Screening
A Universal Studios Presentation
of the
NBC World Premiere Movie

Starring

JAMES MASON • LEONARD WHITING

DAVID McCALLUM • JANE SEYMOUR • NICOLA PAGETT

and

MICHAEL SARRAZIN
as "The Creature"

Guest Stars
(In order of appearance)
MICHAEL WILDING • CLARISSA KAYE • AGNES MOOREHEAD
MARGARET LEIGHTON • SIR RALPH RICHARDSON
TOM BAKER • SIR JOHN GIELGUD

| Produced by | Directed by | Music Composed by |
| HUNT STROMBERG, JR. | JACK SMIGHT | GIL MELLE |

"Admirably translated to film by director Jack Smight, a total triumph, superbly mounted and beautifully played, properly terrifying yet accomplished with rich wit and polish."
— *Cecil Smith, L.A. Times*

"Never in our wildest dreams could anyone tell us we'd be riveted to a television set for four hours to watch this chilling tale unfold . . . It was a splendid job."
— *Kay Gardella, N.Y. Daily News*

THURSDAY, JAN. 31 • 7:30 P.M. • UNIVERSAL STUDIOS, Room 1
R.S.V.P. 985-4321, Ext. 2495
Admission by Directors Guild or TV Academy Card

Daily Variety FTTS ad, January 30, 1974, with stunning snub of writers!

When the Emmy nominations were announced, the movie was unceremoniously ignored. Not a single nomination. Zilch. The five nominees for Best Special, Comedy or Drama, were: *The Autobiography of Miss Jane Pittman* (CBS) – which won this category; *The Execution of Private Slovik* (NBC); *The Migrants* (CBS); *6 Rms Riv Vu* (CBS); and *Steambath* (PBS).

Was the film handicapped by Isherwood's vocal objections? The ugly feud that this prompted? Snobbery against the horror genre? Homophobia? An overly broad category? Or just the capricious vagaries of awards? Whatever the case, *Frankenstein: The True Story* proved to be far more impactful, influential and enduring than its Emmy snub would suggest.

The Isherwood-Bachardy script was nominated for a Nebula Award (from the Science Fiction and Fantasy Writers of America) but, disappointingly, lost out to Woody Allen for *Sleeper*.

MUTILATION

The next indignity the film had to suffer was being slashed from three hours to two for the international theatrical release, starting with the UK where it premiered in London at the Paramount (a first-run cinema in the West End on Lower Regent Street) on September 19, 1974, distributed by Cinema-International Corporation (the joint venture of Universal and Paramount to handle foreign territories on all their films). As mentioned earlier, the movie received an AA certificate (suitable for ages 14 and over) from the BBFC – with the running time documented precisely as 122 minutes and 39 seconds. The recut and theatrical delivery elements had been created in London at a cost of $33,500.

Philippe Spurrell, founder of Le Cinéclub in Montreal, acquired 16mm prints of both the television and theatrical cuts and verified that the shorter theatrical version actually contains a few added seconds of uncensored and miscellaneous footage.

Here are the differences in order of appearance:

a. When Dr. Frankenstein is listening to Dr. Clerval for the first time in Clerval's office, he gazes downwards to see an empty bloodied bucket then gazes back up at Clerval. Three shots. In the TV version, Dr. Frankenstein merely fixes an attentive gaze on Clerval as he speaks.

b. When Dr. Frankenstein pours acid on the crawling arm to destroy it, it is held for a few seconds longer.

c. When Agatha is run over by the wagon, a key shot is held for a few frames longer.

d. When the Creature removes Prima's head from her body, the shot is wider and it is held for a few seconds longer, allowing us to clearly see the bloody entrails hanging below her neck. There is another 2.5-second shot added of the Creature holding her head where, again, it is wide enough for us to see the bloody entrails dangling below her neck.

e. Another fan of the movie, Andy MacDougall, noted that in the aftermath of the decapitation, there are additional fleeting glimpses of partygoers making a mad dash for the exit.

f. The end titles contained many more credits than the television version – including makeup credits for Harry Frampton and Roy Ashton; a first assistant director credit for John Stoneman; and Sally Nicholl is correctly credited as the casting director – whereas on the television cut, she erroneously shares credit with Jacque Shelton as "assistants to the producer." The theatrical cut correctly isolates Shelton as the sole "assistant to the producer."

The 1974 British quad poster and newspaper ads featured the copy line: "He created the perfect man – then something went wrong." Something went wrong, all right. Losing a third of the movie was, to borrow a phrase from Isherwood's *Prater Violet*, a theatrical misstep "beside which the slaughter of Rasputin is just a quick breakfast."

How did it do? In an October 9, 1974, letter to Stromberg, Ian Lewis delivered the blow thusly: "I am sorry to say that *Frankenstein* did not do very well in the West End. It only played for two weeks and did not attract the numbers for which we had all hoped. Unfortunately, our critics over here do not like the idea of films that are made for television in the States being cut and shown in the theatres. They tend to think that a fast one is being pulled on them."

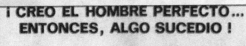

¡CREO EL HOMBRE PERFECTO...
ENTONCES, ALGO SUCEDIO!

Universal Presenta

FRANKENSTEIN
SU VERDADERA HISTORIA
(FRANKENSTEIN THE TRUE STORY)

Estelarizada por

JAMES MASON · LEONARD WHITING
DAVID McCALLUM · JANE SEYMOUR
NICOLA PAGETT y MICHAEL SARRAZIN como
"EL MONSTRUO"

Estelares Invitados

MICHAEL WILDING · CLARISSA KAYE · AGNES MOOREHEAD · MARGARET LEIGHTON
RALPH RICHARDSON · JOHN GIELGUD · TOM BAKER · Producida por HUNT STROMBERG JR.
Guión de CHRISTOPHER ISHERWOOD y DON BACHARDY · Basado en la novela clásica de MARY W. SHELLEY · Dirigida por JACK SMIGHT · Música de GIL MELLE
Una Película Universal · TECHNICOLOR® · Distribuida por Cinema International Corporation

Opposite Page: UK quad. Above Left: Spanish poster.
Above: Lebanese poster. Below: Newspaper ad for FTTS
premiere at Paramount Theatre in London.

JAMES MASON   LEONARD WHITING   DAVID McCALLUM   JANE SEYMOUR   NICOLA PAGETT   RALPH RICHARDSON   JOHN GIELGUD

He created the
perfect man –
then something
went wrong.

Universal presents

FRANKENSTEIN ▫ the true story AA

starring JAMES MASON
LEONARD WHITING · DAVID McCALLUM · JANE SEYMOUR · NICOLA PAGETT and
MICHAEL SARRAZIN as THE CREATURE   Guest stars MICHAEL WILDING, CLARISSA KAYE, AGNES MOOREHEAD
MARGARET LEIGHTON, RALPH RICHARDSON, JOHN GIELGUD, TOM BAKER
Produced by HUNT STROMBERG JR. Screenplay by CHRISTOPHER ISHERWOOD and DON BACHARDY From the Classic Novel by MARY W. SHELLEY Directed by JACK SMIGHT Music Composed by GIL MELLE
A UNIVERSAL PICTURE "TECHNICOLOR" DISTRIBUTED BY CINEMA INTERNATIONAL CORPORATION

FROM THURSDAY
PARAMOUNT
LOWER REGENT STREET
Programmes: Weekdays 1.30, 3.45, 6.10, 8.35.
Late Show Friday & Saturday 11.15 p.m.
Sunday 3.45, 6.10, 8.30.

THE EPIC SAGA BEHIND *FRANKENSTEIN: THE TRUE STORY*

He created the perfect man—
then something went wrong.

A UNIVERSAL PICTURES PRESENTS

FRANKENSTEIN:
THE TRUE STORY

starring JAMES MASON

LEONARD WHITING · DAVID McCALLUM
JANE SEYMOUR · NICOLA PAGETT and
MICHAEL SARRAZIN as THE CREATURE

Guest stars MICHAEL WELDING · CLARISSA KAYE
AGNES MOOREHEAD · MARGARET LEIGHTON · RALPH RICHARDSON
JOHN GIELGUD · TOM BAKER

Produced by HUNT STROMBERG, JR. Screenplay by CHRISTOPHER ISHERWOOD and DON BACHARDY
Directed by JACK SMIGHT From the Classic Novel by MARY W. SHELLEY
A UNIVERSAL PICTURE TECHNICOLOR®

Opposite Page:
Mexican poster.
This Page: Bombay,
India three-sheet
poster. Notice
"Michael Wilding"
is mispelled as
"Welding".

In the November 1974 issue of the British Film Institute's *Monthly Film Journal*, critic Tony Rayns wrote that the movie "centres on the bond between creator and his creature, who are given a symbiotic, quasi-homosexual relationship. The creature's physical degeneration then becomes a matter of narcissism betrayed (cf. Dorian Gray)." He concluded, however, that the "two-hour digest" cut of the original three-hour broadcast was "an almost unqualified disaster," resembling "the butchered English version of Melville's *Le Cercle rouge*."

Other reviews were mixed, like *Time Out* (London): "Whiting is a weak Frankenstein, but more than made up for by Mason, first cousin to Fu Manchu as Polidori;" *Film Review*: "Editing for the big screen makes it seem a bit jumpy in places but the film nevertheless remains a considerable achievement, superbly acted in every role;" and *Films Illustrated* (October 1974): "This version, at two-hours-plus, is a mightily disorganized movie. It is nevertheless Michael Sarrazin's fiercely sympathetic portrayal of the Creature that holds the film together."

UK horror fan magazines were a bit more tolerant of the hatchet job. *World of Horror* (No. 3, 1974) declared that the theatrical cut was "excellent" and gave the movie a three-page spread; and, in *Monster Mag* (No. 12, 1974), editor Jan Cook urged readers: "Go and see it!"

The cheerleading did not make much of a difference, though. With lackluster box-office receipts, Cinema-International quickly lost interest in the movie, which is why it received belated, spotty theatrical releases in only a handful of other territories around the world, including Mexico, Spain, Lebanon, Portugal, Uruguay, and India (see super-rare three-sheet poster from the release in India, rated A, no one under 18 admitted).

Above: Two Adverts from release in Spain.

FRANKENSTEIN: the true story

In 19th century England, Dr. Victor Frankenstein, his fiancee, Elizabeth, and her parents, Lord and Lady Fanshawe, are attending the funeral of Victor's brother, William, who was accidentally drowned.

Young Victor, a recent medical school graduate, is bitter over his brother's fate and voices aloud his wish that men could have power over life and death.

Later, on his way to Edinburgh by stagecoach, Victor witnesses the aftermath of an accident involving a ploughboy. He accompanies the youth to a hospital where the latter's arm is amputated by a surgeon, Henry Clerval.

Victor sees Clerval deposit the arm in a black leather bag, and later the surgeon tells him that a new era in science is emerging that will enable men to have power over death.

Victor's reaction is mixed, but he eventually joins Clerval in his research and later learns that the ploughboy's arm has been preserved.

When a number of local men are killed in a quarry accident, Frankenstein and Clerval appear on the scene, ostensibly to aid the injured, but in reality to choose parts of bodies for their next major experiment – the creation of a living creature............

Advertising Promotion Guide ⑤ **Cinema International Corporation**

Would all exhibitors please note that accessories and blocks must be ordered from National Screen Service Ltd. 15 Wadsworth Road, Greenford. Middlesex UB6 7JN Tel: 01-998 2851

FTS8 1' Single Column 75p

FTS3 1' Double Column 75p

FTS10 2' Single Column 75p

FTS6 2' Double Column 75p

Editorial Blocks

FTS1 Sir Ralph Richardson and Michael Sarrazin in a scene from Universal Pictures' "Frankenstein, The True Story."

Adapted from the classic novel by Mary Shelley. The film stars James Mason, Leonard Whiting, David McCallum, Jane Seymour, Nicola Pagett and Michael Sarrazin in the creature.

Accessories

36 x 40" Quad Crown Posters 28p each
10 x 8" Coloured stills at 67p per set.
(hire fee only)

When used for publicity there must not be any express endorsement linked to the players in "Frankenstein, The True Story."

All prices are subject to VAT, with the exception of Blocks, which have been Zero-rated.

Display Stills

Prices are:—
11 x 14	26p
20 x 16	78p
22 x 28	£1.08
30 x 20	97p
40 x 30	£1.84
60 x 40	£3.76
72 x 40	£4.80

The stills illustrated here should be used on your front-of-house and for any other promotional displays. They are available from N.S.S. 15 Wadsworth Rd., Perivale, Greenford, Middx., UB6 7JN. (TEL: 01-998 2851)

Left and Above: UK Pressbook. Below: Two German programs.

FILM-PROGRAMM DER KINO-SZENE
Leonard Whiting · James Mason
Michael Sarazin · David McCallum
62

FRANKENSTEIN WIE ER WIRKLICH WAR

Retro Filmprogramm 48

FRANKENSTEIN WIE ER WIRKLICH WAR

Cast
Dr. Polidori	JAMES MASON
Victor Frankenstein	LEONARD WHITING
Henry Clerval	DAVID McCALLUM
Agatha/Prima	JANE SEYMOUR
Elizabeth Fanshawe	NICOLA PAGETT
The Creature	MICHAEL SARRAZIN
Sir Richard Fanshawe	MICHAEL WILDING
Lady Fanshawe	CLARISSA KAYE
Mrs. Blair	AGNES MOOREHEAD
Foreign Lady	MARGARET LEIGHTON
Lacey	SIR RALPH RICHARDSON
Chief Constable	SIR JOHN GIELGUD
Sea Captain	TOM BAKER
Felix	DALLAS ADAMS
Young Man	JULIAN BARNES
Passenger in Coach	ARNOLD DIAMOND

Credits
Producer	HUNT STROMBERG JR
Screenplay by	CHRISTOPHER ISHERWOOD and DON BACHARDY
From a Classic Novel by	MARY W. SHELLEY
Director	JACK SMIGHT
Associate Producer	IAN LEWIS
Music Composed by	GIL MELLE
Musical Supervisor	PHILIP MARTEL
Director of Photography	ARTHUR IBBETSON B.S.C.
Production Designer	WILFRID SHINGLETON
Film Editor	RICHARD MARDEN
Production Manager	BRIAN BURGESS
Special Effects Supervisor	ROY WHYBROW
Costumes by	ELSA FENNELL

Certificate 'AA' Length 11,056 ft. Running Time 123 mins.
A UNIVERSAL PICTURE DISTRIBUTED BY CINEMA INTERNATIONAL CORPORATION.

FRANKENSTEIN: the true story AA starring JAMES MASON

LEONARD WHITING · DAVID McCALLUM · JANE SEYMOUR · NICOLA PAGETT and MICHAEL SARRAZIN as THE CREATURE Guest stars MICHAEL WILDING, CLARISSA KAYE, AGNES MOOREHEAD MARGARET LEIGHTON RALPH RICHARDSON JOHN GIELGUD TOM BAKER

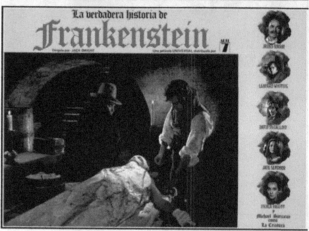

THE EPIC SAGA BEHIND *FRANKENSTEIN: THE TRUE STORY*

Full-color lobby cards from the release in Spain.
One of the lobby cards (see above) actually shows the entrails hanging from Jane Seymour's severed head. This was censored from the U.S. TV broadcast by cropping out the entrails. The theatrical releases in foreign territories show this full-frame image with the entrails.

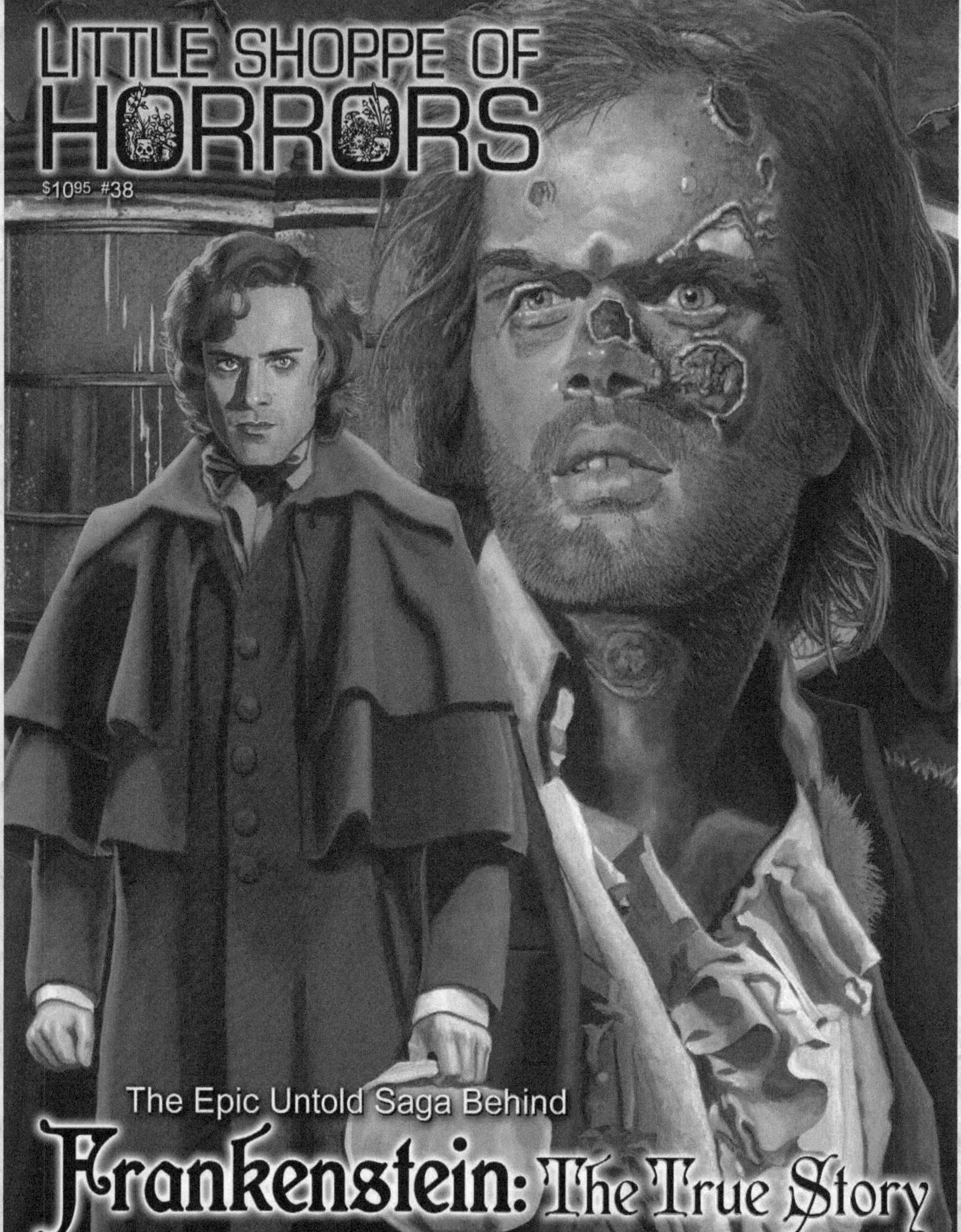

LITTLE SHOPPE OF HORRORS

$10⁹⁵ #38

The Epic Untold Saga Behind

Frankenstein: The True Story

by Sam Irvin

Cover of *Little Shoppe of Horrors* No. 38 (June 2017), art by Mark Maddox

CHAPTER 6
THE LEGACY

FLEETING REPRIEVES

Back in the U.S., thirteen months after its debut, the movie was encored on December 30 and 31, 1974 – but things got off to a rocky start. "I thought I was going to have a stroke when NBC started repeating it in the wrong order," recalled film buff Martin Allen. "They got about a minute into the re-cap when the screen went black and cut to commercials. It was fixed by the time the break was over." Despite the hiccup, ratings were solid, and many more converts were initiated.

Fan mail poured into the Universal City mailroom, much of it forwarded to Stromberg who kept a bulging file of the most interesting examples. One charming standout was a January 1975 letter from an enterprising 12-year-old girl named Pam Wachter of Vancouver, Washington, who wrote, "After two airings, movies usually go on the late show or are not played again. I hope you don't do this to *Frankenstein: The True Story*. I enclose with this letter a list of people who would like to see the movie a **third** time." Attached to the note was a petition signed by twenty-five devotees.

Presently living in Seattle, Pam Wachter Martorano was amazed to learn that her grass-roots campaign had survived all these years in Stromberg's archive. "The decaying arm crawling across the floor still haunts me to this day," Pam stated in 2016. "As an adult, I've indoctrinated my husband and son – and now they are fans, too."

Coming to the film's rescue in the UK, BBC2 broadcast the full three-hour version (the same cut that had aired in two parts in the U.S., joined together as one) on Saturday, December 27, 1975, from 8:20-11:15 PM. That week, UK's *Radio Times* reported the following: "Although made for television, this film was released in the UK for cinema distribution, not only heavily cut, but with several scenes disastrously out of sequence. The BBC is showing the most complete version it can lay its hands on." [See sidebar "Home Alone with Frankenstein" on page 117.]

Then, in 1976, the complete three-hour version was publicly screened in Paris at the Fourth Annual International Festival of Fantastic and Science-Fiction Films where it

received a five-minute standing ovation and *won* the Best Scenario Award. This buzz resulted in the broadcast of the three-hour version on France's FR3, the cultural public television network, shown in two parts on November 20 & 27, 1976, with two separate full-page spreads devoted to the film in consecutive issues of *Télé 7 Jours*, the French equivalent of *TV Guide*. The recognition, however, was too little, too late. As far as Universal was concerned, the movie was old news.

TELEVISION SYNDICATION

In 1977, the film went into syndication in the U.S., occasionally popping up on local independent channels.

Netherlands VHS, 1990s.

Above: CK Entertainment, USA VHS, 1st release, 1993, – with random cover models. Right: GoodTimes Home Entertainmnt USA VHS, 1995.

For instance, in 1980, San Francisco's KTVU Channel 2 (later, a Fox affiliate) presented *True Story* in two parts on Thursday and Friday, October 16 & 17, at 8 P.M. both nights. *San Francisco Chronicle* TV critic Terrence O'Flaherty wrote, "Seven years ago on NBC, Hunt Stromberg Jr. and Universal Studios gave *Frankenstein* the most lavish production of all… and it is still the best. Stromberg went first class all the way."

In most cases, though, the film was relegated to the late-night graveyard – and because the excessive running time did not fit comfortably into standard time slots, Universal offered stations an alternate 89-minute cut, the most reprehensibly mangled version yet.

One could sense that a general dismissal of the film was mounting – partly based, one must assume, on the antiquated snobbery that made-for-TV movies were of lesser importance than theatrical ones. Despite all the accolades the film had generated in 1973, there were no websites or search engines to keep those opinions alive.

It also didn't help that nearly every *new* mention of the film started off by discounting the misleading title and clarifying that the film was not at all faithful to the Shelley novel. It's hard to recover from such negativity and explain that, on its own terms, the film has merits – especially if all the editorial space allotted is a one-sentence blurb in local TV listings.

Most damaging to the film's stature, however, was the simple fact that it was so rarely available – and almost never in its uncut form. In the late-1970s, when films started being manufactured on videocassette for the burgeoning home entertainment market, made-for-TV movies were seldom deemed worthy of release, especially with such a vast number of classic theatrical films yet to be mined. As a result, *Frankenstein: The True Story* was completely ignored by the videocassette market until 1993 when the 20-year-old movie was licensed from Universal by CK Entertainment, a minor independent distributor, for its inauspicious debut on

VHS. To economically fit the film on one standard 2-hour cassette (in SP mode), the appallingly truncated 89-minute syndication cut was used. No sales figures are available – but it is safe to assume it wasn't a chartbuster. Two years later, GoodTimes Home Video issued the 122-minute theatrical cut on VHS (in the lower-resolution LP mode) but fans of the original full-length airing were still left unsatisfied.

Responding to a groundswell of discontent, the Sci-Fi Channel (then-owned by Universal and Paramount) resurrected the complete NBC broadcast version and presented the film on its afternoon "Moonlight Matinee" series in two parts on August 4 & 5, 1993 – three months shy of the film's 20th Anniversary. Then the channel encored the film twice in 1995 (with both parts joined together as one) for weekend afternoon showings on May 6 and July 23. And, in 1997, the complete NBC broadcast version was presented on AMC (American Movie Classics), then-owned by General Electric / NBC.

SCULPTED CREATURE

Given the endless number of models kits and figures that have been produced of various incarnations of the Frankenstein Monster, it is kind of astounding that – as of this writing – I know of only one model kit of Michael Sarrazin as the Creature in *Frankenstein: The True Story*. It was produced by Russ Raney and his Model Prisoners company.

"When I started Model Prisoners in August of 1997," Russ told me in 2016, "I decided to only produce kits I would buy myself and not the same subjects that everyone else was popping out. Don't get me wrong. I love Karloff. But there are literally over one-hundred versions of Boris as Frankenstein's Monster. While sitting behind my table at WonderFest 2003 in Louisville, Kentucky, my son Kevin and I started that all-too-familiar conversation that always begins with, 'You know what would be cool?' To our knowledge, the Creature from *Frankenstein: The True Story* had never

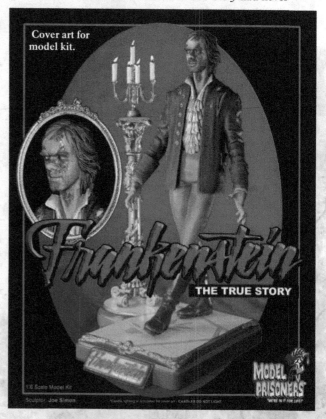

Cover art for model kit.

THE EPIC SAGA BEHIND *FRANKENSTEIN: THE TRUE STORY*

Russ Raney of Model Prisoners.

Sculptor Joe Simon.

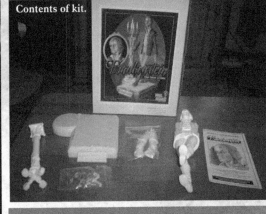

Contents of kit.

Sarrazin model kit, built and painted by Michael Reagan.

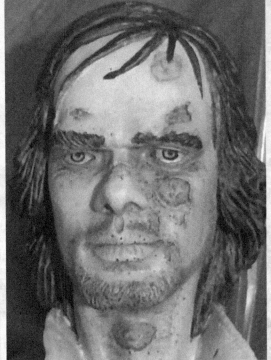

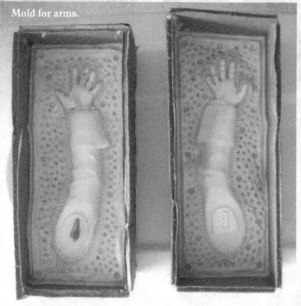
Mold for arms.

Mold for Creature.

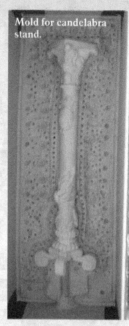
Mold for candelabra stand.

Model displayed with autographed photo of Sarrazin & Blu-ray.

been done and we agreed that it would be a sure-fire winner with fans around the world. Then, my son started up a conversation with a sculptor next to us at the GEOmetric Designs table. We brought up our *True Story* idea. We expressed that the likeness and texture had to be absolutely top notch. He then reached into a box at his side and pulled out a sculpture he had just finished, a female Tusken Raider character from *Star Wars* (cut from the film). She was exquisite. We knew right then and there that we'd found the man for the job – 30-year-old Joe Simon, from Minnesota, who now has become legendary in the field of 'garage-kit sculptors.'"

I asked how they decided what pose to sculpt. Raney responded, "One of the most memorable scenes in the movie

was when the Creature disrupts the debutante ball to rip off Prima's head – so we agreed to capture the moment the Creature enters the ballroom, in mid-stride, stalking his prey."

To suggest the ballroom setting, they added a faux marble floor base and an ornate pedestal with a candelabra perched on top (which Jimmy Flintstone molded for white metal castings). Graphic designer and cartoonist Nick Nix of Cartoon-Ups designed the logo lettering for the nameplate line art that is attached to the front of the base. (Through this connection, I later got Nick to design the title logos for my book *I Was a Teenage Monster Hunter!* and my convention appearance poster *The Fearless Frankenstein Scholar*.)

Meanwhile, Joe Simon got to work on sculpting the Creature. "Within a few weeks," Raney recalled, "I

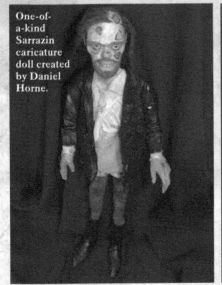

One-of-a-kind Sarrazin caricature doll created by Daniel Horne.

Horne's doll on Sam Irvin's desk, with LSoH #38.

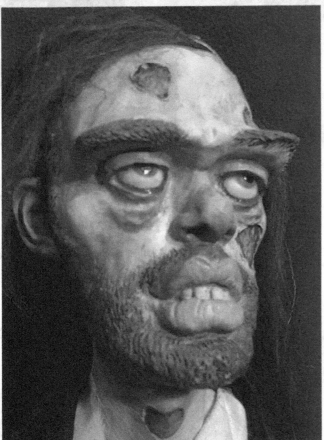

Caricature art of Sarrazin by Daniel Horne.

started getting email progress updates from Joe. From past experience, I expected to see a wire stick figure with clay stuck on it. What I got were photos of a skinless man straight out of an anatomy book – every muscle and tendon, from head to toe. Joe actually sculpts from the inside out, then covers all that precise layering and detail with skin and finally clothes on top of that. It's his way of achieving accurate proportion and flow – but all that meticulous work ends up being covered. It was just amazing to witness the effort he put into this thing. But, at the same time, I couldn't help but be a little bit creeped out. The more I thought about it, the more I realized Joe was our very own Dr. Frankenstein, building our Creature with such realism, I almost feared that, with one misplaced spark, the thing might just come to

life and walk right out the door. Luckily, it stayed inanimate long enough for us to mold all the pieces for a *really* cool kit. Only Gods and Monsters know what happened to the original sculpture after that. Muahahahahaha! Okay, in reality, it went on my shelf and collected dust – but that's the boring version of the story."

Raney promoted a special pre-order price of $76 that would rise to $95 once the kit was available. "Girding ourselves for the expected avalanche of orders," Raney explained, "we ended up selling only ten. But, by then, we were obligated to the guaranteed delivery date and had to fulfill these orders. So, going deeper into debt, we proceeded to cast them up using Randy Guthrie of Lil' Monsters Productions."

Everyone seemed extremely happy with the result, so they expected word-of-mouth to spread like wildfire. "And then nothing," Raney lamented. "I mean, absolutely *nothing*. No orders for a year. I hadn't even recouped the cost of the sculpt. So, I had the caster ship all the molds back to me."

The molds deteriorated and when an occasional "on demand" order did surface, they had to recreate molds using one of the existing kits. In 2015, the kit got quite a boost when it appeared in *Amazing Figure Modeler* magazine, No. 40. In the "New Product Releases" section, editor/publisher Terry J. Webb wrote, "Proving you can't keep a good man down, Model Prisoners resurrects the Creature from the 1970s television classic *Frankenstein: The True Story*, finally available again."

I spotted the coverage of the kit in *Amazing Figure Modeler* and immediately contacted Russ to buy one for myself – and I hired legendary model finisher Michael Reagan to custom build and paint it. The result is pictured here in all its glory. Among the lucky few who have this in their collections is Michael Sarrazin's brother Pierre.

As of 2023, this *Frankenstein: The True Story* model kit has officially been retired. Good luck finding one of the few that escaped into the world.

The dearth of Sarrazin-as-the-Creature figures on the market prompted me to commission artist Daniel Horne to create a one-of-a-kind caricature doll – and a caricature portrait to go along with it. Aren't they to die for?

GLIMMERS OF HOPE

In 2004, using his two 16mm prints of the television and theatrical versions of *Frankenstein: The True Story*, Canadian cinéaste Philippe Spurrell combined the three-hour broadcast with extra seconds of gore found in the shorter theatrical cut, resulting in a 16mm master print of all available footage. This unique version was screened that year to rapt audiences at Montreal's FanTasia International Film Festival and Vancouver's CineMuerte Horror Film Festival. It may have made Universal sit up and take notice of the fan interest in this movie.

Finally, on September 26, 2006, Universal deemed its 33-year-old property worthy of release by its own Universal Studios Home Entertainment division. By then, the popular format had shifted to DVD which could fit the full three-hour NBC broadcast (along with Mason's introduction). A few foreign DVDs of the three-hour version followed, including a 2014 DVD release in the UK by Second Sight Films.

Above Left: Japanese DVD. Above Right: UK DVD Below: Front & back of UK DVD.

In 2015, a two-disk Japanese release from Fieldworks presented a Blu-ray of the three-hour cut (from a DVD-quality master) including, for the first time, the preview clips for Part 2 (shown at the conclusion of Part 1), narrated by James Mason; as well as the recap clips of Part 1 (shown at the beginning of Part 2), narrated by Leonard Whiting. The second disc contained the 89-minute syndication cut badly dubbed in Japanese.

Because *Frankenstein: The True Story* had such sketchy availability over the years, many had never seen it – especially the unadulterated three-hour version. Consequently, the tarnished legacy of *Frankenstein: The True Story* was in dire need of rehabilitation.

The great horror cover artist Mark Maddox, who has won multiple Rondo Awards for Artist of the Year, has always been a fan of *Frankenstein: The True Story*. He wanted to paint a magazine cover for the movie, so he told Richard "Dick"

Canadian cinéaste Philippe Spurrell's unique 16mm print of FTTS that includes censored footage – like the entrails dangling from Seymour's neck. Inset: From the monitor: Sarrazin holding severed head; entrails dangling.

Phillippe Spurrell.

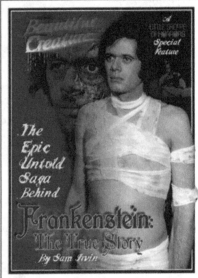

Top: Foldout mural cover of LSoH #38, by Mark Maddox. Center Row, Left: Pre-publication ad for LSoH with rare temporary Maddox cover. Center Row, Center: Publication ad for LSoH with final Maddox cover. Center Row, Right: Interior title page. Bottom Row, Left: New York 2017 screening sponsored by Forbidden Planet & Dread Central. Bottom Row, Right: U.S. DVD from Universal.

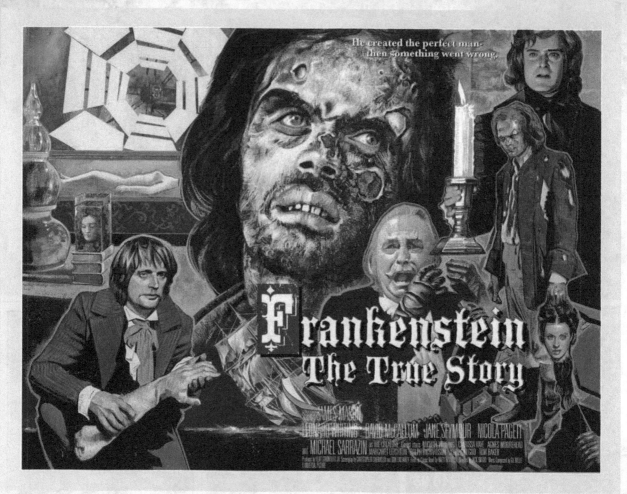

He created the perfect man—
then something went wrong.

Frankenstein
The True Story

Starring JAMES MASON

LEONARD WHITING · DAVID McCALLUM · JANE SEYMOUR · NICOLA PAGETT

and MICHAEL SARRAZIN as the Creature

Top: UK quad style tribute poster by Graham Humphreys. Above: Spanish DVD; German DVD; U.S. Shout! Factory Blu-ray (art by Mark Maddox); and UK Fabulous Films Blu-ray (art by Graham Humphreys).

Klemensen, editor-publisher of *Little Shoppe of Horrors*, that he should do a cover story on the film in a future issue.

Dick knew of my keen interest in the film dating back to the 1974 cover story I had done in my own fanzine *Bizarre* No. 3. He offered me the opportunity to write a "making of" article for *Little Shoppe of Horrors* No. 38 which evolved into me guest-editing the issue which was entirely devoted to the movie. I wanted the cover to be as spectacular as the film itself, so we decided to make it a three-panel foldout, the largest cover of any horror magazine in history. And Mark painted the most exquisite mural for that wraparound.

To celebrate the publication of the special issue, I organized events in Los Angeles and New York. First, on June 18, 2017, Taylor White's Creature Features Store & Gallery in Burbank, California, unveiled a month-long exhibit of *Frankenstein: The True Story* art and memorabilia; and, I moderated a panel discussion of the film featuring Julian Barnes (who played the aristocrat who dances with Jane Seymour), Denise Mellé (widow of the composer Gil Mellé), and artist Bruce Timm (*Batman: The Animated Series*) who had painted the inside front cover of the issue. The event was standing-room-only, with over 150 spectators – including Cassandra Peterson aka Elvira, Mistress of the Dark, Nancy

THE EPIC SAGA BEHIND *FRANKENSTEIN: THE TRUE STORY*

This Page: Creature Features FTTS event, June 18, 2017 – Poster in window.

Panelists Julian Barnes, Sam Irvin, Denise Mellé, Bruce Timm.

Cassandra Peterson aka Elvira dropped by.

Crowd watching panel.

Glass case with FTTS memorabilia.

Sam Irvin shows off Mark Maddox' FTTS mural.

Creature Features Art Gallery exhibit.

3rd Assistant Director on FTTS, Terry Pearce, and Sam Irvin, holding LSoH mag, 2017.

Allen (*Carrie, Dressed to Kill, Robocop*) and Julie Brown (*Earth Girls Are Easy, Medusa: Dare to be Truthful*).

Then, on June 27, 2017, I hosted a free screening of Philippe Spurrell's unique 16mm print of *Frankenstein: The True Story* at the Quad Cinema in New York City, co-sponsored by Dread Central and Forbidden Planet Comic Book Store, with a panel discussion afterwards moderated by Tony Timpone of *Fangoria* magazine, featuring panelists Alec Smight, Philippe Spurrell, James Anthony Phillips, and yours truly.

In 2018, the 45th anniversary of *Frankenstein: The True Story*, and the 200th anniversary of Mary Shelley's novel, I very proudly won the Rondo Award for Best Article of the Year for "The Epic Untold Saga Behind *Frankenstein: The True Story*" published in *Little Shoppe of Horrors* No. 38.

Appallingly, in April 2018, a French distributor named Seven7 tried to take advantage of the renewed interest in

Left: Quad Cinema panel: Tony Timpone, Sam Irvin, Alec Smight, James Anthony Phillips & Philippe Spurrell. Right: Quad Cinema group shot in lobby: Spurrell, Timpone, Smight, Irvin, Phillips.

Frankenstein: The True Story by releasing a so-called "Blu-ray" of the film – but the result was a rip-off in more ways than one. First of all, they used just a DVD-quality master of the television cut, with no upgrade in resolution. Secondly, they inexplicably dropped the James Mason prologue. And, thirdly, without authorization, the company brazenly stole Mark Maddox's artwork from the cover of *Little Shoppe of Horrors* No. 38 for the cover of the Blu-ray. When objections were raised by Maddox and the owner of the original artwork itself (yours truly), after-the-fact promises of compensation were never fulfilled. It left a very bad taste in many mouths, including Blu-ray critics who were harsh in their assessment of this bogus enterprise.

Finally, Shout! Factory in the United States stepped up to the plate for a proper Blu-ray (Region A for North America) of *Frankenstein: The True Story*, released in March 2020, featuring a gorgeous 2K remaster of the complete 3-hour-plus NBC-TV premiere (including the James Mason introduction; the preview of Part 2 and the recap of Part 1). An exquisite

new cover painting was done by none other than Mark Maddox. For the special features, produced by indispensable cinephile Constantine Nasr, I interviewed on camera Leonard Whiting, Jane Seymour and Don Bachardy – plus I wrote and narrated the wall-to-wall 3-hour-plus audio commentary – for which I very proudly won the 2020 Rondo Award for Best Audio Commentary.

In 2023, Fabulous Films in the UK released a Blu-ray and DVD (both for Region B players in Europe) of the same 2K remaster and all my extras, with new exclusive cover art by the wonderful Graham Humphreys – with a folded doubled-sided poster of his artwork

From 2020: Alec Smight holding LSoH No. 38 and FTTS Blu-ray.

Sam with Jane Seymour, holding *Bizarre*, FTTS script book, LSoH; the day we filmed Seymour's interview for Blu-ray extras.

Sam with Leonard Whiting, holding *Bizarre* & LSoH; the day we filmed interview for Blu-ray extras.

THE EPIC SAGA BEHIND *FRANKENSTEIN: THE TRUE STORY*

in every case. Since I pretty much hoard all *Frankenstein: The True Story* artwork, I added Graham's original art to my collection, and it is on display in the pages of this book.

And now, with the invaluable help of graphic designer Steve Kirkham and cover artist Mark Maddox (who jumped at the chance to do a *third* round), I am very proud to present this lavish book in your hands to honor *Frankenstein: The True Story* on the occasion of its 50th Anniversary – for posterity.

THE RIPPLE EFFECT

For those of us who saw *Frankenstein: The True Story* when it first premiered, a lasting impression was made that has been hard to shake.

For many aspiring writers and filmmakers, it proved to be inspirational.

Sarrazin tattoo art by Steve Bejma; tattoo on Beth Stelter.

Elements unique to *Frankenstein: The True Story* resonate in numerous descendants. For instance, in Mel Brooks' *Young Frankenstein* (1974), Dr. Frankenstein (Gene Wilder) dresses his Creature (Peter Boyle) in a tuxedo and presents him to high society at a theater where, instead of watching an opera, they provide the entertainment themselves by performing "Puttin' on the Ritz."

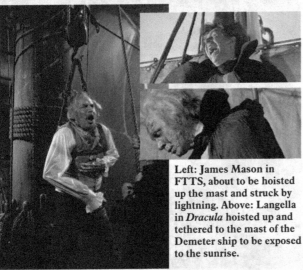

Peter Boyle and Gene Wilder in Mel Brooks' *Young Frankenstein* (1974).

Left: James Mason in FTTS, about to be hoisted up the mast and struck by lightning. Above: Langella in *Dracula* hoisted up and tethered to the mast of the Demeter ship to be exposed to the sunrise.

Video Watchdog critic Kim Newman believes that Badham's *Dracula* (Universal, 1979) drew inspiration from *Frankenstein: The True Story* by the way in which Dracula (Frank Langella) was violently hoisted up the mast of the ship to be burned by sunrise – in the strikingly similar way in which Dr. Polidori was violently hoisted up the mast of the ship to be struck by lightning. For *Little Shoppe of Horrors No. 36*, Constantine Nasr asked director John Badham and screenwriter W.D. Richter about this supposition, but they "didn't specifically recall even seeing the film or intentionally swiping the concept." Nevertheless, both films were produced in England by Universal under the studio supervision of Ian Lewis with a few other crossover crew members. It seems unfathomable that there could have been collective amnesia.

In *The Bride* (1985), Dr. Frankenstein (Sting) teaches the female creature (Jennifer Beals) how to be a lady just as Whiting taught Sarrazin how to be a gentleman; and, the Monster (Clancy Brown) describes the female creature as "beautiful" – echoing Whiting calling Sarrazin "beautiful." Casting iconic heartthrob Sting as Dr. Frankenstein certainly paralleled the Romeo prototype of Whiting.

Sting as Dr. Frankenstein and Jennifer Beals as the Bride of Frankenstein in *The Bride* (1985).

Clancy Brown as the Monster in *The Bride* (1985).

But when it came to turning Dr. Frankenstein into a sex symbol, *Mary Shelley's Frankenstein* (1994) took matters to an extreme with a buffed-up Kenneth Branagh strutting around shirtless for what seemed like half the movie. A big-studio budget, director Kenneth Branagh, producer Francis Ford Coppola, and Oscar winner Robert De Niro (as the Creature) couldn't breathe life into the overheated proceedings. In *Newsweek*'s scathing review, critic David Ansen compared Branagh's performance to Jon Lovitz' "Master Thespian"

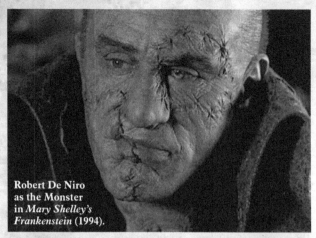

Robert De Niro as the Monster in *Mary Shelley's Frankenstein* (1994).

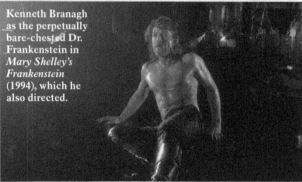

Kenneth Branagh as the perpetually bare-chested Dr. Frankenstein in *Mary Shelley's Frankenstein* (1994), which he also directed.

Luke Goss as the Monster in Hallmark's *Frankenstein* (2004).

sketches on *Saturday Night Live* and advised his readers, "For a much more provocative, original retelling, someone should resurrect the 1973 TV movie *Frankenstein: The True Story*, written by Christopher Isherwood. In that version, the monster comes out perfect, beautiful – and then, to his enamored creator's horror, slowly begins to rot."

In 1992, a 117-minute TNT Network version of *Frankenstein* featured derivative sequences of the Creature (Randy Quaid) jumping off a cliff and a ship locked in the Arctic ice. In 2004, a 177-minute Hallmark Channel adaptation included a scene in which the youthful Dr. Frankenstein (Alec Newman) witnesses his dog being run over by a coach (à la Agatha); the ship in the Arctic is likewise stuck in the ice; and the sequences between the Creature (Luke Goss) and the old blind man (Jean Rochefort) are liberally pilfered.

In *Victor Frankenstein* (2015), starring James McAvoy (as Dr. Frankenstein) and Daniel Radcliffe (as Igor), the death of

Randy Quaid as the Monster in TNT's *Frankenstein* (1992).

Sir John Mills as the blind hermit and Randy Quaid as the Monster in TNT's *Frankenstein* (1992).

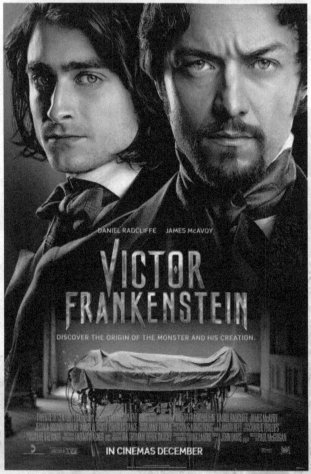

DANIEL RADCLIFFE JAMES McAVOY

VICTOR FRANKENSTEIN

DISCOVER THE ORIGIN OF THE MONSTER AND HIS CREATION.

IN CINEMAS DECEMBER

THE EPIC SAGA BEHIND *FRANKENSTEIN: THE TRUE STORY*

Scenes from Bernard Rose's *Frankenstein*: Carrie-Anne Moss & Xavier Samuels.

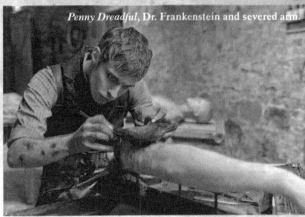

Penny Dreadful, Dr. Frankenstein and severed arm.

Xavier Samuels as the beautiful Creature.

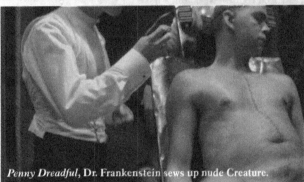

Penny Dreadful, Dr. Frankenstein sews up nude Creature.

Xavier Samuels, Carrie-Anne Moss, Danny Huston.

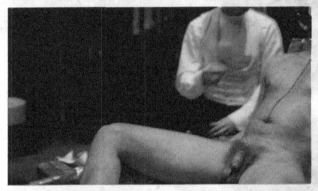

Frankenstein's brother is the underlying driving force behind his quest to create a man.

And, in *Frankenstein* (2015), a modern-day reboot, scientist Victor Frankenstein (Danny Huston) and his wife Elizabeth (Carrie-Anne Moss) create a flawless human specimen named Adam (Xavier Samuels). When he is brought to life, Elizabeth cradles him in her arms and whispers gently, "Beautiful. You are so beautiful." But, like the Creature in *True Story*, Adam's physical perfection soon deteriorates, beginning identically with a boil behind his ear.

Perhaps the most moving homage to *Frankenstein: The True Story* was contained in Showtime's series *Penny Dreadful* (2014-2016). In the first two episodes of Season 1, directed by J. A. Bayona (*The Orphanage, The Impossible, A Monster Calls, Jurassic World: Fallen Kingdom*), the handsome young Dr. Frankenstein (Harry Treadaway) brings to life a beautiful, innocent and heartbreakingly endearing creature named Proteus (Alex Price) – who, upon his "birth," was shown full-frontal naked – an unabashedly homoerotic advancement that the Lavender Hill Mob would certainly have applauded. On the *TV Guide* website, blogger Chappy Quiddick commented, "As a fan of the TV movie *Frankenstein: The True Story*, I liked where this story seemed to be heading."

The end of Season 2 and the beginning of Season 3 features John Clare (Rory Kinnear), another one of

Penny Dreadful, beautiful nude creature is confronted by Dr. Frankenstein.

CHAPTER SIX: LEGACY

Frankenstein's creatures, stranded in the Arctic aboard a galleon imbedded in the ice.

Penny Dreadful had an impressive pedigree, including Oscar-winning executive producer Sam Mendes (director of *American Beauty, Skyfall, Spectre*). But, the connection to *Frankenstein: The True Story* is most directly linked to the series' creator and writer, three-time Oscar nominee John Logan (*Gladiator, The Aviator, Star Trek: Nemesis, Sweeney Todd, Hugo, Skyfall*) – who would have been 12-years-old when the movie was first shown in 1973.

Logan explained in a 2014 interview in *Adweek*, "When I was a teenager in the 1970s, I built models in my bedroom and I watched horror movies and read horror comic books. I've always loved monsters. Only as I've grown up have I realized that the affection I have for them is a kinship. Growing up as a gay man, before it was as socially acceptable as it might be now, I knew what it was to feel different from other people, to have a secret and to be frightened of it – even as I knew that the very thing that made me different made me who I was. I think all the characters in *Penny Dreadful* grapple with a version of that... It was very personal to me."

In 2016, Tony DiSanto, MTV's former president of programming and executive producer of *Teen Wolf* and *Scream: The TV Series*, said, "I remember seeing the 1973 Michael Sarrazin TV movie adaptation *Frankenstein: The True Story*... [which] was a huge departure from the Frankenstein 'monster movie' I grew up on, and inspired me to discover and understand the depth of the story... [with its] timeless, fantastic themes that are universally relatable on a primal level." As a result, DiSanto has developed Chandler Baker's *Teen Frankenstein* (2016), the first in a new young adult book series.

In a 2014 interview for *USA Today*, Steve Niles (creator and screenwriter of *30 Days of Night*) talked about his regard for *Frankenstein: The True Story*: "While it strayed wildly from Shelley's novel, it did a great job of catching the emotion of the story. Plus, you get to see James Mason blasted into a skeleton."

Contacted for this book in April 2016, writer-director Tom Holland (*Fright Night, Child's Play*, Stephen King's *The Langoliers*, Stephen King's *Thinner*; and screenwriter of *The Beast Within* and *Psycho II*) recalled, "I have vivid memories of *Frankenstein: The True Story* having seen it [at the age of 30] when it first came on NBC in 1973. A two-parter, with huge production values for TV of that time. The shock that still stays with me is the reveal of the Creature, played by Michael Sarrazin, as the bandages are taken off him for the first time. He was beautiful. The second image that stays with me is the ship locked in Arctic ice at the end. The writing was excellent and the acting even better. It's a who's who of the best of the actors from the classical studio period, led by James Mason. Also, the subtext is the love between Victor Frankenstein and his Creature. Both male actors were gorgeous to begin with, but the creature regresses, turning into a physical nightmare, which might have been a comment on relationships. They found the true tragedy in the original story. It has size and impact, but it is finally about love – gone terribly wrong."

Mark Gatiss, co-creator of the miniseries *Sherlock* and *Dracula*, is another

Mark Gatiss' article "Queer Frankenstein" in *Shivers*.

aficionado of *Frankenstein: The True Story*, proclaiming it to be "one of the most successful versions of Shelley's tale, handsomely mounted and authentically filthy in all the right areas. Sarrazin is inexpressibly moving as he first catches sight of his beautiful features in decay. His haunted vulnerability takes the acting honours."

One of the biggest devotees of *Frankenstein: The True Story* was the late, great bestselling author Anne Rice (1941-2021). Upon seeing the original 1973 broadcast at the age of 32, she was directly inspired to write *Interview with the Vampire* (published in 1976), taking its lush homoerotic romanticism to a whole new level. "The movie had such a profound influence on my writing that I wonder what I would have written had I not seen this," Rice rhapsodized. "It was horror the way I longed to see horror done – with depth, dignity, beauty and seriousness." [See Rice's Foreword in this book.]

But that's just the tip of the iceberg.

The movie has been the most influential on none other than three-time Oscar winner Guillermo del Toro (*Pan's Labyrinth, Hellboy, Pacific Rim, Crimson Peak, The Shape of Water, Nightmare Alley, Pinocchio*). He feels that *Frankenstein: The True Story* "has nothing to do with Shelley's novel and yet is the one that gets the closest to it." His admiration for the film is immense, calling it a "quirky, brilliant and moving masterpiece." [See del Toro's Afterword in this book.] As of this writing in the summer of 2023, del Toro is prepping his own version of *Frankenstein* for Netflix, to star Oscar Isaac, Andrew Garfield and Mia Goth.

Hopefully, my proselytizing will continue to bolster the reputation of *Frankenstein: The True Story* and introduce its wonders to a legion of new fans.

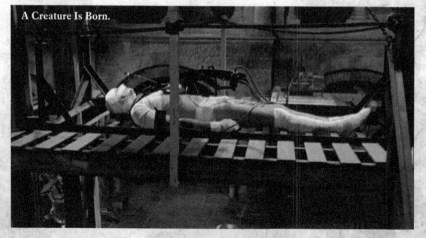

A Creature Is Born.

PART TWO
INTERVIEWS
WITH THE CAST

CHAPTER 7
LEONARD WHITING

Leonard Whiting was born in London on June 30, 1950. At the age of 12, while performing the song "Summertime" from *Porgy and Bess* at a wedding, Whiting was spotted by a talent scout who cast him in the smash hit West End production of *Oliver!* as the Artful Dodger (replacing original cast member – and future member of The Monkees – Davy Jones). Whiting played the part for eighteen months.

His first international exposure came with Walt Disney's *The Legend of Young Dick Turpin* (1966) in which he played an Artful Dodger-like pickpocket named Jimmy the Dip, broadcast in the U.S. on *Walt Disney's Wonderful World of Color* (NBC-TV) and theatrically released in Europe. The leading role of Dick Turpin was played by David Weston who would later reunite with Whiting for *Frankenstein: The True Story* as the accident victim whose arm is amputated.

"Then I was sent around to the National Theatre to audition for Sir Laurence Olivier," Whiting explained in a 1968 interview for *Seventeen*. "I sang 'Love is the Sweetest Thing' for him. He listened for a minute and said, 'All right, he'll do,' and that was it. I was signed on for William Congreve's restoration comedy *Love for Love* as a singing page."

When Italian director Franco Zeffirelli was casting his film *Romeo and Juliet*, the legendary theatrical designer Lila de Nobili recommended that he see Whiting in *Love for Love*. "I did so," Zeffirelli explained in his autobiography, "and, sure enough, he seemed ideal. His looks were perfect for the role; he was the most exquisitely beautiful male adolescent I've ever met."

At the age of 17, Whiting was cast opposite 15-year-old Olivia Hussey in *Romeo and Juliet* (Paramount, 1968), which became a massive international phenomenon, propelling Whiting to teen idol status on par with the Beatles. He won the Golden Globe Award for Most Promising Male Newcomer and the movie was Oscar-nominated for Best Picture and Best Director and won two Oscars for Cinematography and Costume Design.

The film was also controversial because its young

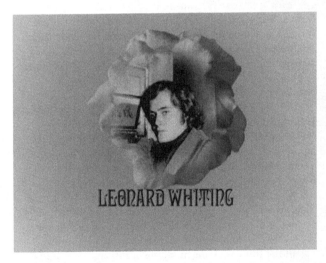

LEONARD WHITING

stars briefly appeared nude on screen. In a 1969 interview conducted by Rex Reed, Whiting said, "Now suddenly I'm in a business I used to respect for its art and I'm doing a nude scene. I don't think they put that nude scene in the movie for any other reason but money and publicity, and that bothers me. So I don't know if I can become an actor like Orson Welles and Marlon Brando, because you have to do a lot of things you don't believe in to get anywhere. I don't want to be a star."

Whether he liked it or not, he already was one – and his fans were clamoring for more. Despite his reluctance, Whiting, still just 17, went on to star opposite Robert Shaw and Christopher Plummer in Peter Shaffer's *The Royal Hunt of the Sun* (1969); at the age of 18, played the title role in

Whiting & Mason, FTTS.

Whiting with reflection of Mason in the mirror.

Right: Clipping of 12-year-old Whiting as the Artful Dodger in *Oliver!*
Above: Whiting in *The Legend of Young Dick Turpin*.

This is the way I looked when I played the part of the "Artful Dodger" in *Oliver!* at the New Theatre in London. I was 12 years old—and happy as a king!

Casanova (1969); at 19, romanced Jean Simmons, 41, in *Say Hello to Yesterday* (1971); and, at 20, starred opposite Curd Jürgens in *War is Hell* (1972). He also starred in *Love Story: My Brother's House* (ITV, 3/28/1973) with Arnold Diamond – who would be reunited with Whiting for a brief appearance in *Frankenstein: The True Story* as the impatient coach passenger.

In February 1973, at age 22, Whiting accepted producer Hunt Stromberg Jr.'s offer to play Dr. Frankenstein in *Frankenstein: The True Story*. In the prologue of the movie, he would also portray poet Percy Bysshe Shelley, husband of *Frankenstein* author Mary Shelley – a sequence that was filmed but, sadly, left on the cutting room floor.

When all was said and done, Stromberg sent Whiting a thank-you note that read, "Of all of the very important stars we had in *Frankenstein*, I think by now you know you are my favorite, both professionally and personally. Frankly, I wouldn't think of doing anything in England that didn't contain a major role for you."

The following interview was conducted by phone on February 26, 2016.

THE INTERVIEW

SAM IRVIN: How did you get involved with *Frankenstein: The True Story*?
LEONARD WHITING: My name may as well have been Romeo at the time. That's what I was famous for – it was still pretty much foremost in the public's mind. My agent [Jimmy Fraser, Fraser & Dunlap Ltd.] called and said they wanted me for the lead in a *Frankenstein* movie. He set up a meeting for me with the producer Hunt Stromberg Jr. I read the script,

which I liked very much, and then they had me do a screen test with Nicola Pagett who I got on with tremendously well. A marvelous actress. It was shot at a church [St. Mary the Virgin Church in Hambleden Village, Buckinghamshire] near Pinewood Studios with Jack Smight directing.

SAM: Was Hunt Stromberg Jr. there?
LEONARD: Oh, absolutely. Hunt was omnipresent. He'd be at the opening of an envelope. (laughs) And, his partner Jacque was there, too.

SAM: Jacque Shelton.
LEONARD: Yes, that's right. One day, I asked Hunt, "How did you meet your partner?" He said, "On the set of *Rawhide*." Now, I don't know whether that was a joke or what.

SAM: It wasn't a joke. A little correction, though. Jacque was a stuntman. Hunt met him on the set of *Have Gun— Will Travel* in 1961 when Hunt was Vice President of Programming for CBS-TV. After they became lovers, Hunt gave Jacque small parts on four different episodes of *Rawhide* – and a slew of bit parts on at least fifteen other CBS shows, including *The Twilight Zone*, *The Wild Wild West* and *Gunsmoke*.
LEONARD: Now it makes sense. During the screen test for *Frankenstein*, Hunt and Jacque were there together. They were *always* together.

SAM: What happened after the screen test was done?
LEONARD: When we finished shooting the test, they didn't say anything. They just looked at me, smiled and nodded.

Whiting in *Romeo & Juliet*.

Whiting in tights climbs tree in *Romeo & Juliet*.

Whiting, *The Royal Hunt of the Sun*.

Olivia Hussey & Whiting, *Romeo & Juliet*.

Poker faces. But I felt good about what I'd done and I thought I've got a good chance of getting in here. Then, Hunt came to me and said, "Would you mind awfully, darling, if we dye your hair reddish blond?" I said, "Why is that, Hunt?" He said, "Because it's beginning to look like a Sicilian movie." (howls with laughter) Because, you see, Nicola had dark hair and so did Michael Sarrazin and some of the others they were casting. But Hunt never failed to crack us all up.

SAM: Once filming was underway, how would you describe Jacque Shelton's function on the film?
LEONARD: He was there to take care of Hunt and to make sure that Hunt's power structure wasn't compromised by anybody else.

SAM: Tell me more about Hunt.

CHAPTER SEVEN: LEONARD WHITING

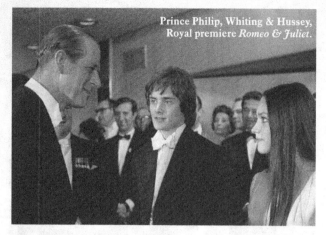
Prince Philip, Whiting & Hussey, Royal premiere *Romeo & Juliet*.

Heartthrob Whiting.

LEONARD: Oh my God. I tell you, Hunt was *outrageous*. I know some wonderful stories about him, but they are all rather risqué!

SAM: We're all adults here. Do tell!
LEONARD: Okay, so Hunt's partner Jacque had brought along his mother to England for the duration of the production, a lady from Texas called Doris who wore these huge flyaway diamond monkey glasses.

SAM: Like a Texan version of Dame Edna Everage?
LEONARD: Bingo. But Hunt used to be extremely, absolutely *unbelievably* rude to her in front of everybody. I mean, we'd be having a really posh sort of cocktail party and

Scene that Pagett & Whiting performed for screen-test.

suddenly he'd shout over the room, "Doris! You know what you are, Doris?" And she'd say, "No, Hunt. What?" And he'd call her something extremely vulgar – the "c" word that rhymes with Hunt. And then she'd say, "That's what they call *you*," and start laughing. Hunt had an absolutely *wicked* sense of humor.

SAM: What was the relationship like between Doris and her son Jacque?
LEONARD: It was kind of strange. A combination between, "I love you because you're Mom," and "Please don't say anything to upset Hunt." But I quite liked her. She was a cheerful little thing. Quite cute. And no matter how rude Hunt would be to her, she thought it was *hilarious*. Didn't phase her one bit. I know a few other stories that are even more vulgar but my wife Lynn is listening and doesn't approve. For the sake of peace and decorum, I think I should try to be a little bit more charming.

SAM: (laughs) Okay, if we must move on, I guess we must. What was Jack Smight like as a director?
LEONARD: Jack was very charming and down to earth. He

Doris Shelton and son Jacque Shelton.

had a workman-like attitude towards making pictures. He was very easy to work with and very nice, so that was a really, really good experience.

SAM: How did being directed by Jack Smight compare to being directed by Franco Zeffirelli?
LEONARD: Completely different attitudes. Jack was very much old school Hollywood in the sense that he always was aware of keeping everything coming in under budget and had a very workman-like attitude towards filming. Franco was more like a Renaissance Italian painter. Jack came on the set knowing exactly what he wanted versus Franco who would come on set, work with the actors and figure things out. Franco always wanted things to look as beautiful as they possibly could which was the embodiment of romance – the ideology and the beauty of the old masters in Italy.

SAM: Jack Smight brought his wife Joyce and their 14-year-old son Alec to the UK during filming. Do you remember them?
LEONARD: Yes. I liked them very much. Joyce was a charming woman and Alec was a very nice, precocious young man.

SAM: I interviewed Alec Smight, who, for many years, has been a very big director and producer of *CSI: Crime Scene Investigation*. He fondly remembered you and your first wife Cathee Dahmen.
LEONARD: Well, how nice of him to remember us so well and also to be remembered by somebody in such a positive, lovely way. Please say to him that's so lovely to hear. I look forward to meeting him again sometime.

SAM: What locations stand out in your memory?
LEONARD: Well, of course, the stage work was done at Pinewood but we had a few locations that were very impressive. There was quite an elaborate bit by the White Cliffs of Dover where the Creature jumps off the precipice.

SAM: A lot of people think it's the White Cliffs of Dover but the location was actually a similar-looking chalk cliff at Beachy Head.
LEONARD: Beachy Head. Well, that shows how clever you are. You know this and I didn't. (laughs) But, as you may know, the script did not have anything as grand as this.

SAM: That's right. The original script had the Creature walking into the rapids of a river and getting washed down stream. Not nearly as dramatic.
LEONARD: The cliff was Hunt's idea. He was always thinking big. The script might read, "The Creature goes past a window of a cottage in the country," but Hunt's idea of a "cottage in the country" was one of the greatest stately homes of England, you know? (laughs) That was just the way his mind worked.

SAM: The residence of Dr. Frankenstein's fiancée was shot at Cliveden.

Alec Smight, Joyce Cunning Smight, Hunt Stromberg Jr. & Jack Smight.

Whiting & Mason at FTTS ball.

Sarrazin & Whiting giggling over a private dinner.

Stromberg, Whiting & Smight.

LEONARD: Exactly! Cliveden. One of the biggest estates in all of England – where all the Profumo scandal was based. Mandy Rice-Davies and Christine Keeler and all that. Well, anyway, Cliveden was kind of big for a "small country cottage." And knowing Hunt, it probably wasn't his first choice. He probably first tried to get Buckingham Palace and would have probably said, "Well, I've talked the Queen into doing a nice little cameo."

SAM: Funny you should say that. Hunt actually tried to get Queen Elizabeth to film a special introduction for *Frankenstein: The True Story*. She was friendly with Douglas Fairbanks Jr. and Hunt knew Douglas, so he was pressuring him to twist her arm into doing it.
LEONARD: Exactly my point. Hunt always thought big. Everything with Hunt was on the far side of excess. He was quite wealthy because of his father. He spent money like it was nothing. He was very extravagant – but very generous, too, I must say. Beyond the money and gifts and generosity, though, the great thing about having Hunt around on the set was that he really could make you laugh. And he had such a love for actors – and he made us all feel like kings and queens. He really was a total pleasure.

SAM: From what I gather, Hunt was very creatively involved on the production.
LEONARD: Yes, very much so. One time, Hunt came in and had sort of a script meeting with me and James Mason, who was playing Polidori. He said to James, "Look, I have an idea. After the Creature comes in and rips Prima's head off, we never show what happened to the head. So, what about this? When you are on the ship traveling up to the North Pole, the

Creature comes to you and gives you a hat box. You open the hat box, grab hold of what's inside and pull out the head of Prima." I looked at James. There was this very long pause. Then, very calmly, in that marvelous James Mason voice, he said, "Well, Hunt, I'm not going to do that." (laughs) That was such a funny moment because, I mean, this is James Mason! Somebody who was so known and famous. I wish you could have met him. He had the most extraordinary sense of humor where he'd say something and then about five minutes later, when it sunk in, it would make you roll up with laughter.

SAM: Do you recall any other funny stories?
LEONARD: Hunt was trying to hire various American stars, which, of course, is frowned on by British Actors Equity. So, Equity was giving Hunt a very hard time about it, threatening to shut down the production. So, the following day, Hunt marched onto the set and announced, "Okay everybody! We're gonna finish shooting the movie in Hollywood!" If Hunt felt like he was being pushed around, he wouldn't tolerate it. Then [associate producer] Ian Lewis came in and said, "Oh, don't worry. I've got lots of contacts. Just leave it up to me and I'll clear it all through." Which is what happened. So we happily finished shooting it in England.

SAM: So, I take it there was a lot of drama with Hunt.
LEONARD: Never a dull moment with Hunt. But he was such good fun. I don't know if anybody mentioned it to you but his breakfast every day was liquid, if you know what I mean. (laughs) By the time he got to the set, he was already three sheets to the wind.

SAM: I'm not surprised. Tell me about Michael Sarrazin.
LEONARD: Well, the whole cast was very nice, *especially* Michael Sarrazin. He was a tremendously underrated actor, don't you agree? He did that part very, *very* well. We were all very impressed with him.

SAM: What was your working relationship like with Sarrazin?
LEONARD: Very, *very* friendly. But he was sort of kooky in a way. He was very American in the sense that he almost behaved like a cartoon. Like *Tom and Jerry*, or something. Which was very new to me. But I thought that some of the scenes he did have such tremendous pathos. He was an extremely intelligent guy.

THE EPIC SAGA BEHIND *FRANKENSTEIN: THE TRUE STORY*

SAM: Who else do you recall from the cast?
LEONARD: Well, I remember meeting the great Sir Ralph Richardson, though I didn't have any scenes with him. But that's typical of Hunt's casting, isn't it? "Who shall we get for the blind guy in the cottage? Uh… Sir Ralph Richardson!" Well, why not?

SAM: He learned all that from hanging around his father's film sets at MGM during the Golden Age of the Hollywood Studio System. His father told him, "The man who watches Clark Gable walk down the street is, at that moment in the film, as important as Gable himself."
LEONARD: Really? Well that explains it. Having grown up in Hollywood like that, I'm sure Hunt knew where all the bodies were buried.

SAM: Right. He knew everybody.
LEONARD: And he had a ranch in Texas. What was the ranch called? The Double S?

SAM: Good memory! Yes. The Double S Ranch. Named after Stromberg and his partner Jacque Shelton.
LEONARD: Of course! He invited me there once and I said to my first wife, Cathee [Dahmen], "Would you like to go and spend some time with Jacque and Hunt at the Double S Ranch in Texas? And she said, "Sure. I'll be the Indian and you can be the cowboy." (laughs) Because, as you probably know, she was part Chippewa Indian from the Great Lakes.

Whiting & Sarrazin at the moment of "birth."

Whiting & Sarrazin at the opera.

Sarrazin grasps Whiting's hand, as Mason observes.

[NOTE: Cathee Dahmen (1945-1997), was half German, half Native American Chippewa, born and raised in Minnesota. She became a major fashion model with the Ford Agency and appeared on the covers of *Harper's Bazaar* (1968) and *Vogue* (1971). She was married to Whiting from 1971 to 1977 and they had a daughter named Sarah.]

SAM: In the fall of 1974, a year after *Frankenstein* was completed, James Mason was in Louisiana shooting *Mandingo* and decided to visit Hunt and Jacque at the Double S Ranch in Texas. He brought along his wife Clarissa Kaye.
LEONARD: Did they really? Oh my God. I wish I'd have gone, actually, because I'm sure they would have taken care of us beautifully. You know, they should have made a movie of Hunt's life. It should start with Sinatra's "One For My Baby (And One More For The Road)" – (sings) "It's quarter to three, there's no one in the place except you and me; So, set 'em up, Joe, I got a little story you oughta know…" – with Hunt, pushing his nose and his nervous tick and dancing away on his tap-dancing heels. That would have been really funny, you know? I'm sure there's a script there for one of your movies. Keep that in mind as you continue researching his life.

SAM: I'm certainly fascinated by Hunt. He's such a character.
LEONARD: Absolutely. If I had to sum him up in just one word, I'd say "outrageous." I mean that in the most positive way. I liked him very much and I thought Jacque was very sweet, too.

SAM: How did people react to Hunt being gay at that time?
LEONARD: Hunt seemed to be so sure of his own sexuality that he would have gotten irritated if anybody made him feel uncomfortable about it. So, therefore, people felt that energy and they respected him for it. Whether it was just pure respect – or fear because he was the boss and could fire you – I don't know. But people just accepted it. It was like coffee and cream, you know? It was just something that was there. And he felt no need to apologize or anything. He was very outlandish and, as you know, very camp with it. So, it didn't really worry him what other people thought. And nobody would get in his way in terms of what he felt was the artistically correct thing to do.

SAM: There has been a great deal of discussion over the years about the gay subtext in *Frankenstein: The True Story*.

McCallum & Whiting.

Whiting & McCallum.

Elsa Lanchester terrified!

Whiting, Sarrazin & Leighton at opera.

LEONARD: To be honest with you, I never felt it when we were shooting, and I never thought it when I saw the movie.

SAM: It was certainly not overt but more on a subconscious level.
LEONARD: It's probably more subconscious of the viewer than subconscious of the writers, don't you think?

SAM: Well, no, that's not quite the case. Don Bachardy told me himself that he and Christopher Isherwood discussed the homoeroticism and gay subtext at length when they were writing the screenplay and that it was consciously laced into their work – an intentional gay subtext between Dr. Frankenstein and the Creature.
LEONARD: Really? Well, I never knew anything about it. The producer didn't sit down with me and the director and Michael and say, "Listen, you know, this is obviously a homoerotic thing."

SAM: I'm not surprised, considering the timeframe. This was 1973, after all. And the film was being made for American television at a time when gay subject matter was still fairly taboo.
LEONARD: Yes, perhaps. But, to be honest with you, I like to think of myself as being quite bright, but I never ever, *ever* thought that that was the intent. I mean, to me, it was just sort of a Gothic kind of story, you know? I'm afraid that this sort of homoerotic stuff honestly wasn't talked about.

SAM: I don't think Isherwood and Bachardy made their

intentions known, though Stromberg certainly knew what they were up to – and encouraged it. But it may never have been discussed with the director Jack Smight or any of the actors. And certainly the powers-that-be at Universal and NBC would never have approved anything blatant. Whatever came through, simply came through as subtext, in a subtle way.
LEONARD: If it came through as a positive subtext, then good enough, you know?

SAM: Right. Now, tell me about David McCallum.
LEONARD: Well, it was a thrill meeting him because I'd always been very fond of the stuff that he did for telly, like *The Man from U.N.C.L.E.* He played Illya Kuryakin.

SAM: The fact that we remember his character's name in that series, after half a century, tells you something right there, doesn't it?
LEONARD: Indeed it does. And, I must say, when I met him, I did find him to be – in the most pleasant way – an

Leighton being flirtatious at opera.

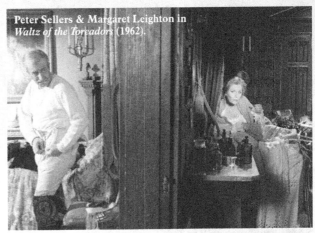
Peter Sellers & Margaret Leighton in *Waltz of the Toreadors* (1962).

Whiting & Sarrazin, nervous that Leighton is too inquisitive.

Whiting & Pagett on deck of ship, deluged with water.

extremely eccentric guy. Very quiet. Very on his own, you know? Kind of enigmatic. I've never ever met anybody like David. But, like with Michael Sarrazin, we got on very well. I can't think of anybody who didn't get on with anybody in that film. It was a very pleasant and happy experience. So many wonderful actors. Mason, Richardson, Gielgud... even Agnes Moorehead. I mean, to actually be on the same set as the great Agnes Moorehead was really quite something. She was very confident about what she was doing and very, *very* lovely. You've seen the movie, how well she does. Brilliant.

SAM: Did you know that Hunt originally wanted Elsa Lanchester for that role?
LEONARD: Really? That would have been very interesting. But, that's what I've been talking about. That's Hunt being creative again, isn't it?

SAM: Yes. What about Margaret Leighton?
LEONARD: Oh, I especially liked her. Just splendid. She was married to Michael Wilding at the time, who was in the picture, too. Well, on the first day, she came to me and knocked on the door and she said, "Darling, can I ask you a great favor?" And so I said, "Yes, what's that?" She said, "I'd like to swap dressing rooms with you. Mine's on the first floor and yours is on the ground floor – and because I'm such a charming old lady, I don't want to make the steps every day, so would you mind changing?" So I said, "Of course, darling." So I gave her my dressing room, went upstairs and the following day I got sent two rather nice, freezing-cold bottles of Dom Perignon. I thought that was jolly nice. She was a real classical

English beautiful actress. I don't want to sound overly effusive, but, you know, she was even darling as an old lady as well.

SAM: I thought her scene during the intermission at the opera was so richly realized. It was wickedly funny and yet suspenseful at the same time. Was the Creature going to say or do something wrong? And Leighton kept interrogating him, relentlessly. And you – stuck in the middle as mediator – trying to remain nonchalant on the surface while being a nervous wreck on the inside. It was a classic Hitchcockian situation.
LEONARD: Absolutely. She was one of those kind of actors who, in the old days, like with Ealing comedies, just managed to get so much out of a part when they were playing it. I love all those classic British comedies, like *I'm All Right Jack* with Peter Sellers and Terry-Thomas. I don't think Peter Sellers has ever been better.

SAM: I love that film. There was another very good Peter Sellers comedy from around that same period called *Waltz*

of the Toreadors with Margaret Leighton as his leading lady.
LEONARD: All those comedies are golden because the
actors used to get such elegant energy out of their parts,
didn't they?

SAM: **Yes. Very much so. Tell me about the scenes on the
ship with Tom Baker as the Captain.**
LEONARD: Tom is a big, tall guy with curly red hair. I
remember him well. And the art department did a beautiful
job with all that rear screen, blue screen or whatever it was
called. I thought all that looked really, really believable. And
also that water stuff was good, too, wasn't it? It was supposed
to be a storm at sea and they poured thousands of gallons of
water on our heads.

SAM: *Frankenstein: The True Story* **made a huge
impression on so many of us who saw it when it originally
aired. A lot of famous people, too. For instance, Anne Rice
was so moved by the movie, it directly inspired her to write**
Interview with the Vampire.
LEONARD: Well, how lovely. How lovely. Sounds like she's
a very intelligent woman, huh? That is really lovely to hear.
I'm so glad that everybody speaks so well about the film.

POSTSCRIPT

Shortly after filming *Frankenstein: The True Story*, Leonard
Whiting went on to star as Nicholas Nickleby in *Smike!*
(BBC, 12/26/1973), a pop musical loosely based on Charles
Dickens' *Nicholas Nickleby*, with Andrew Keir and Beryl
Reid. Then, he starred as Jacob in the Biblical film *Rachel's
Man* (Allied Artists, 1975) co-starring Mickey Rooney and
Rita Tushingham. In the fall of 1974, in Scotland, Whiting
played Feste, the jester, in a stage production of Shakespeare's
Twelfth Night.

Upon Whiting's
return to London
in December 1974,
Frankenstein producer
Hunt Stromberg Jr.
offered him the role
of Charles Darnay in
Universal Television's
2-part NBC miniseries
remake of Charles
Dickens' *A Tale of
Two Cities*, adapted by
Herb Meadow, to star
Sean Connery (Sydney
Carton), Geneviève
Bujold (Lucie),
Alec Guinness (Dr.
Manette), Cantinflas
(Barsad), James
Mason (Marquis St.
Evrémonde), Faye
Dunaway (Madame
Defarge), Margaret
Leighton (Miss Pross)
and Laurence Olivier
(General Lafayette).
Whiting was game to
do it but, sadly, the
movie never got made.

Whiting & Hussey reunite in
Social Suicide.

Hussey & Whiting.

After that, Whiting
virtually disappeared
from movies and television, preferring to live a private life. In
an interview with *People* in 1992, Whiting explained, "I was
thrust for a long moment into international stardom. When
that happens, people want to see you in that same persona
again and again. Orson Welles once said 'I started at the top
and worked my way downward.' I can identify with that."

Whiting & Irvin.

The Dreamstone, mad scientist Urpgor (right)
voiced by Leonard Whiting.

THE EPIC SAGA BEHIND *FRANKENSTEIN: THE TRUE STORY*

Irvin & Whiting during filming of interview for the Blu-ray.

Whiting being filmed for Blu-ray.

After Whiting split with his first wife Cathee Dahmen in 1977, he fathered his second daughter, Charlotte Westenra, with her mother Valerie Tobin. (In 1982, Valerie Tobin married William Warner Westenra, 6th/7th Baron Rossmore of Monaghan.) Charlotte has become a prolific stage director in London – and was a very supportive conduit in helping to arrange this interview with her father. (Thank you, Charlotte!)

In 1995, Whiting married his manager Lynn Presser and they are still together today. Lynn was also very generous in helping to coordinate this interview. (Thank you, Lynn!)

The reluctant star does occasionally dip his toe back into show business when a project catches his fancy. From 1990 to 1994, Whiting was the voice of the mad scientist Urpgor on three seasons of the popular British animated series *The Dreamstone* (ITV, 1990-1994). And, in 2015, Whiting reunited with Olivia Hussey to portray the parents of Julia (played by India Eisley, Hussey's real-life daughter) in the British independent film *Social Suicide*, a modern, social-media-influenced take on *Romeo and Juliet*.

On December 15, 2019, I interviewed Leonard Whiting again, this time on camera in London, for a special feature among the extras included on an exquisite new 2K restoration Blu-ray of *Frankenstein: The True Story* (Shout! Factory, Region A, 2020; and Fabulous Films, Region B, 2023).

Whiting & Mason.

CHAPTER 8
JANE SEYMOUR

On February 15, 1951, Jane Seymour was born in Hillingdon, England. Her birth name was Joyce Penelope Wilhelmina Frankenberg, the oldest child of John and Mieke Frankenberg. Two younger sisters, Sally and Anne, would eventually be added to the family. Jane was a prodigy ballet dancer who began training at three and, at thirteen, made her debut with the London Festival Ballet. At the Arts Educational Trust in London, she furthered her training in dance, music and theatre.

"As a girl I was determined to become a dancer," Jane told me. "I had danced at the Kirov Ballet at Covent Garden, London's Royal Opera House. Then I did a jazz class and damaged the cartilage in my knees. Consequently, I realized, a.) I wasn't built for ballet – I have a long back and shorter legs, whereas ballerinas need the reverse; and, b.) I had an injury which meant I could never do classical ballet. It was probably the best thing that ever happened to me because it led to becoming an actress."

Shifting gears to focus on an acting career, Jane became disenchanted with her last name. "Frankenberg sounded too much like Frankenstein," she recalled. "At first, I shortened it to 'Joyce Frank' but then my agent suggested 'Jane Seymour' and I went with it."

Little did she know then that the Frankenstein name would come back to haunt her in the most exquisite way.

Jane's movie debut was as an uncredited chorus girl in Richard Attenborough's *Oh! What a Lovely War* (1969) which prophetically featured two future *Frankenstein: The True Story* co-stars Sir Ralph Richardson and Sir John Gielgud. Through this association, she met the director's son, Michael Attenborough, the renowned theatre director later appointed Commander of the Order of the British Empire (CBE); they married in 1971. Richard Attenborough then cast his new daughter-in-law in his next picture, *Young Winston* (1972), in the role of "Pamela Plowden," the first great love of Winston Churchill (Simon Ward). This led to high-profile, 10-episode arc in the long-running BBC television series *The Onedin Line* that brought Jane to the attention of producers Albert R. Broccoli and Harry Saltzman who cast her as "Solitaire,"

JANE SEYMOUR

their latest Bond Girl, in *Live and Let Die* (1973), starring Roger Moore in his first turn as "James Bond."

Before that film assignment was even completed, Jane was spotted at the Pinewood Studios commissary by producer Hunt Stromberg Jr. who decided, right then and there, that she was perfect for the dual role of "Agatha," the innocent farm girl, and "Prima," the evil female creature, in *Frankenstein: The True Story* (1973) – and he refused to take "no" for an answer.

On Friday, May 30, 1975 (the day after my adventures with Donald Pleasence), I had the enormous pleasure of dining with Jane at the White Elephant Club, a trendy showbiz hangout on Curzon Street in the Mayfair district of

Seymour as Prima.

Pagett investigates what Seymour's choker is hiding.

Seymour as Prima, giggling that she faked being faint?

Seymour as Agatha.

West London. For *Bizarre* No. 4, I had requested a sit-down interview to discuss her career and, in particular, her role in *Frankenstein: The True Story*.

Jane was shorter than I had imagined, but her hair was the longest I'd ever seen. Straight and silky, it fell all the way down to her waist. She was very charming and talkative. We had a wonderful dinner with my cassette tape recorder running. I ordered shrimp cocktail and was astounded when the shrimp arrived with their shells intact – eyeballs and all! I had never seen them served this way and I had no idea how to eat them. So, Jane taught me. It was hilarious watching her demonstrate, knife in hand. She really got into it – like a female "Dr. Frankenstein," dissecting body parts for her next creation. I was a little woozy by the time she completed slicing and dicing.

I will also never forget her saying, "It was in Michael Carreras' office at Hammer Films that I first saw your magazine *Bizarre*. It was on his desk – so you *do* get around."

She had me at "hello," but this endeared her for life. Afterwards, I escorted Jane to her car where she discovered that she'd inadvertently locked her keys inside. We went back to the restaurant so she could call a friend to bring her the spare set. While we waited, we had a night cap at the bar and continued chatting up a storm. She was lovely.

Forty years later (to the month!), on May 19, 2015, I reconnected with Jane to expand on her memories of making

THE EPIC SAGA BEHIND *FRANKENSTEIN: THE TRUE STORY*

Cartoon of Jane teaching Sam how to de-shell shrimp, by Dan Gallagher.

Exotic Seymour, *Live and Let Die.*

Frankenstein: The True Story for *Little Shoppe of Horrors #38* (June 2017). It was as if not a day had gone by since our first meeting. We picked up where we left off and continued our discussion.

Herewith are *both* of my Jane Seymour interviews, May 1975 and May 2015.

THE 1975 INTERVIEW

SAM IRVIN: What did you think of doing *Live and Let Die*?

JANE SEYMOUR: I think everyone knows that Bond films are great fun but don't give any of the players much chance to act. Everyone always remembers me as "The Bond Girl" and that can be both good and bad. People stop me in the streets, practically anywhere in the world, point and then try to remember where they saw me. I'm sure half of them think I must be a long-lost cousin. No, seriously though, it was great fun of course. And it leads on to so many interesting things. This last year I travelled from Amsterdam to Paris to London to Greece to the States, London, States again, India, Ireland. Oh yes, and then to Corfu for a holiday. And now I am about to go to Spain for location shooting on this new Sinbad film of mine. And my favorite food stopped being fish and chips. One gets used to the good life. On the other hand, it is annoying that people forget the other films, TV and theatre that I do.

SAM: What have thought about *Frankenstein: The True Story*?

JANE: It was great fun doing it, but it was a lot of hard work, too. I particularly liked my role, which had many dimensions

Roger Moore & Jane Seymour, *Live and Let Die.*

Christopher Lee, Jane Seymour, Simon Ward, *Orson Welles' Great Mysteries*.

Sinbad and the Eye of the Tiger.

Patrick Wayne & Seymour, *Sinbad and the Eye of the Tiger*.

to it. Nicky Pagett was not as pleased with her role, and she told me one day that she wished she had gotten mine. I made good friends on that film with the cast. In fact, I bought a house around the corner from Nicky, and I see Leonard Whiting from time to time.

SAM: What have you done since *Frankenstein: The True Story*?
JANE: Sulked because they cut the film down from four hours to two hours for this country! I was intact but it ruined the continuity. Nowadays, I find I'm getting more particular about the end products. I have stacks of scripts in my living room that I've had to turn down because they just aren't right. This last year, I've been doing good roles in the theatre – I've done "Lady Macbeth", "Nora" in Ibsen's *A Doll's House*, "Bathsheba" in Thomas Hardy's *Far From The Madding Crowd*, as well as some interesting bits for the BBC and the commercial stations here. I did one of the *Orson Welles' Great Mysteries* with Christopher Lee and Simon Ward called "The Leather Funnel" based on the Arthur Conan Doyle story, and it was directed by Alan Gibson. Ken Russell offered me a huge part in his newest film *Lisztomania*, with Roger Daltrey and Ringo Starr. I turned it down because

there were many scenes in which I would have had to appear nude, and I didn't find much point in it. I don't know who they ended up getting for the part, but I do know that Sara Kestelman and Fiona Lewis are both in it. Now I am doing *Sinbad and the Eye of the Tiger* which stars Patrick Wayne who is John Wayne's son, and Taryn Power who is the daughter of Tyrone Power. Patrick Troughton is also in the cast. I play a beautiful princess, and my wardrobe for the film is going to be a sight to behold. It is going to be great fun, I can already tell. I know that it must sound crazy that I turned down a Ken Russell film for a Sinbad movie, but I do not want to get into a situation where I am remembered for nudity.

SAM: Have you been offered other roles that called for nudity?
JANE: Oh yes! I have had several nudie ones offered. Not that I mind nudity but there has got to be some point. Otherwise, it is boring. Well, it is boring for the female half of the audience anyway, and I suspect for many of the fellas, too – only they have to pretend to be wildly fascinated.

[NOTE: This last comment, delivered tongue-in-cheek, seemed to be gently and affably aimed at closeted gay men – no malice intended whatsoever. I suspect that Jane was on to my secret, giving me a little knowing wink.]

SAM: Do you like doing horror films?
JANE: It depends. Provided they are not grisly ones. It is not that I get frightened or anything. I am just terribly vain, and I wouldn't like to end up looking like a zombie or something. Unless it was a good-looking zombie! (laughs) Oh, I suppose if they paid me enough I wouldn't mind being a bad looking zombie! (more laughs) Hammer Films seemed to be interested in me, and I expect they will offer me a few parts when they get back to making films. They haven't started one in so long. It was in Michael Carreras' office that I first saw your magazine *Bizarre*. It was on his desk, so you *do* get

THE EPIC SAGA BEHIND *FRANKENSTEIN: THE TRUE STORY*

around. Who knows? It may have been your magazine that drew his attention to me.

[NOTE: Two weeks after this interview, on June 15, 1975, Peter Sykes, who was busy prepping to direct Hammer's *To the Devil a Daughter* (shot September-October 1975), told me, "Jane Seymour was being discussed for a part in *To the Devil a Daughter*, but the German partners have insisted that a German actress play the part. Klaus Kinski might be in it as well." Klaus Kinski did not end up in the cast but his daughter, Nastassja Kinski, did. At just 14 years of age, Nastassja played the "daughter" of the title instead of Jane Seymour, 24.]

SAM: Thank you for your time – and especially for teaching me how to deshell shrimp! I wish you great luck on *Sinbad and the Eye of the Tiger* and hope that we will be seeing much more of you in the near future.

THE 2015 INTERVIEW

SAM IRVIN: Is it true that producer Hunt Stromberg Jr. cast you in *Frankenstein: The True Story* at the Pinewood Studios commissary?
JANE SEYMOUR: Yes! When I was working on *Live and Let Die*, I was having lunch one day in the commissary with Roger Moore – and Hunt Stromberg came over to the table and said, "We want you to do *Frankenstein*." I didn't go in for a casting or anything. He saw me at lunch and cast me on the spot.

SAM: What was it like working with director Jack Smight?
JANE: I remember it being pretty good. Of course, I was in my comfort zone because I was dancing a lot. *Frankenstein:*

The *True Story* was one of the first things I did after being a ballet dancer.

SAM: Do you remember Julian Barnes who danced with you in the ballroom scene?
JANE: Yes, he was a really nice guy. We got along quite well.

SAM: I interviewed Julian last week and he had his date book from back then. He said he had two days of dance rehearsal with you and the choreographer Sally Gilpin.
JANE: Ah! Sally Gilpin. She'd been married to the famous ballet dancer John Gilpin – but he was gay, so their marriage didn't last. I loved working with Sally. She was a terrific choreographer. That's one of the things I loved most about doing *Frankenstein* because my life back then was dance. In

Seymour & Smight. Michael Wilding in background.

Seymour dancing solo at the ball

Whiting, Seymour & choreographer Sally Gilpin on ballroom set.

Stromberg & Seymour (needlepointing).

Jane Seymour & Joyce Cunning (Mrs. Jack Smight) needlepoint on the set.

fact, do you remember the sequence in *Live and Let Die* where I'm carried to the stake? Well, that all came out of my doing improvisational dance on the beach with Geoffrey Holder – which had nothing to do with Guy Hamilton's direction. Geoffrey realized I was a dancer, so he used me that way. Then, I came into *Frankenstein* and was delighted that I had a big dance scene to do in this one – with a partner and then a solo bit on my own.

SAM: Did you know that it was Geoffrey Holder who told Stromberg that you were an accomplished dancer – and that they should give you a solo dance in *Frankenstein: The True Story*?

Jane Seymour, Dallas Adams, Sir Ralph Richardson.

JANE: No, but I'm not surprised. Geoffrey was so marvelous and supportive of me. As you can tell, I've always been very happy to be dancing in any film. One day, somebody will put all my dance scenes together into a montage. (laughs) The other funny thing I do is, if I ride a horse, I am so nervous, all I can do is smile with all my teeth showing. Whenever they hire a double for me, it doesn't work because they aren't smiling. That'll make a funny montage, too, someday.

SAM: There are behind-the-scenes photos on the set of *Frankenstein: The True Story* showing you and Joyce Cunning, the wife of director Jack Smight, engaged in needlepoint. Their son, Alec, told me that his mother was a rabid needlepoint aficionado. Did Joyce indoctrinate you?
JANE: No, no. It was a wonderful coincidence. I was a major needlepoint person myself. Aside from dance, needlepoint was my *other* obsession. I'd been sewing all my life. In fact, when I was 15, I had my own company selling embroidered blouses – which I embroidered myself. So, Joyce and I bonded over our mutual passion.

SAM: What do you recall about playing Agatha, the country farm girl?
JANE: Well, the thing I remember most is that my grandfather was played by Sir Ralph Richardson, which was very exciting but also quite intimidating. I had gone and done my research of how someone would speak from that part of the world. When we began the scene, I spoke my lines with an accent so thick, nobody understood a word I said. The response from Sir Ralph was, "What did you say, my

Seymour about to strangle cat.

Pagett catches Seymour just as cat has run away.

Whiting and Mason hover over tank with Seymour dummy.

Artwork of Jane Seymour licking hand from cat scratch, by Frederick Cooper.

CHAPTER EIGHT: JANE SEYMOUR

dear?" And I thought, oh, gosh, here I am, an actress, I'm trained, I'm trying to do the correct accent, and play this country girl authentically – and my grandfather is speaking Royal English.

SAM: What else do you recall about working with Sir Ralph Richardson?
JANE: On my first day, I didn't know that you weren't supposed to sit in whatever chair was available. Well, I sat in Sir Ralph's chair, and he just walked around the chair five times until I realized that I was sitting in his chair. He didn't tell me to not sit in his chair. He just kept walking round and round – like a dog circling around its prey. And I kept thinking, "Why is he walking round and round? He's an old guy." Then, suddenly, I realized, "Oh my God, I'm in his chair!" I literally leapt out like a rocket ship, and I ran. I don't think I ever talked to him again. I was mortified. "Oh my God, I have really screwed up now."

SAM: When "Agatha" is brought back to life as the female creature, "Prima," you had to be naïve but also conniving and wicked.
JANE: It was a very seductive role. She was very innocent but at the same time she was a monster. I'd played a lot of virgins. That's what I'd just played in the James Bond film as well. I'd had my fill of proper ladies, so this part was much more fun because she had an evil side to her. When I compare pictures of myself in *Frankenstein: The True Story* and *East of Eden* [for which Seymour won the Golden Globe Award as Best Actress], I see a lot of similarities. The character of "Cathy Ames" [from John Steinbeck's Pulitzer-prize winning novel *East of Eden*] had that same, "Oh, I'm very innocent, *but…*"

SAM: In one of your scenes as "Prima," you start to strangle a cat – until you are caught red-handed by "Elizabeth Frankenstein," played by Nicola Pagett. How did you manage to pretend to strangle the cat without really hurting him?
JANE: Well, it wasn't easy – and the cat also managed to put his claws right through my costume and left nasty claw marks on my thighs. And the cat wasn't keen on doing more than one take. There was something else quite memorable about that bit, too. You're not going to believe this, but, in the scene, I sang, "I love little pussy, her coat is so warm…" That's how I learned the song as a child. In England, it was an innocent lullaby about a pussy. Well, needless to say, when I sang that, everyone on the set fell apart. It was hilarious – only I was devastated because I had no idea what "pussy" meant. So, they let me finish it singing "pussy" while they were all chortling and peeing themselves laughing. And then Jack Smight, the director, came over to me and very politely said, "I'd like you to sing it again, dear, only this time, if you'd be so kind, please transpose the word 'pussy' to 'kitty.'"

SAM: You lose your head twice in this film – first as "Agatha," after her neck is broken, "Dr. Polidori" grafts her head onto "Prima," his female creation; and then as "Prima," "the Creature" plucks off her head at the ball. Did you have to do a face mask for these severed heads?
JANE: Yes, I did. I did a death mask. They put straws up my nose so I could breathe. It was very claustrophobic, but pretty cool.

SAM: Do you remember if it was Roy Ashton who did your

death mask? Or Harry Frampton?
JANE: No, sorry. But I got the mold, I think. I'm pretty sure I have that death mask somewhere. That's something I should find. [Unfortunately, as of this writing, Jane had not been able to locate the mask.]

SAM: In the tank of water, they used a full-body dummy of you. Did they also make a cast of your entire body to create that dummy?
JANE: No. But I was invited to look at a line-up of naked women and pick one as my stand-in. It was the first time that had ever happened to me. It was quite uncomfortable, staring at these poor naked women, judging them, and finally deciding, "That one looks the most like me naked." [Seymour chose Nicola Austin who, shortly thereafter, appeared as a Playboy Bunny in Clive Donner's *Old Dracula* starring David Niven.]

SAM: When Michael Sarrazin starts to pull off your head in the ballroom sequence, you rise up slowly in the frame. Was this simply you rising up on your tiptoes, or was there a seesaw or some elaborate elevator rig?
JANE: I just rose up on my tiptoes. Nothing fancy.

SAM: Tell me about working with James Mason.
JANE: James Mason made sure that his wife Clarissa Kaye got a part in the movie as well. In make-up and hair, James and Clarissa would be there together, and he would read the *London Times* out loud to her with his very plummy voice. It was cool at first, but it became very distracting because I was trying to learn my lines
.
SAM: And what about David McCallum?
JANE: I was particularly excited about meeting David McCallum because I was a huge *Man from U.N.C.L.E.* fan. I didn't have any scenes with him, but I got to meet him at the table-read when all the actors were gathered, before we started shooting, to read through the script. I was sitting at the table across from him and it was just more than I could bear. To be perfectly honest, I was more excited about meeting David McCallum on *Frankenstein* than meeting Roger Moore on *Live and Let Die*. At that time in my life, my three favorite idols were Roger Moore because of his TV series *The Saint*, David McCallum of *The Man from U.N.C.L.E.*, and, of course, Paul McCartney of The Beatles. So, with *Live and Let Die* and *Frankenstein: The True Story*, I managed to meet my fantasy trifecta.

SAM: How was it working with Nicola Pagett?
JANE: We became friends, actually. We were very competitive after that, I think, because we were both going up for the same jobs all the time. She's a terrific actress. And she ended up living one street away from me in Barnes, Mortlake. So, we did actually know each other a little bit.

SAM: You told me in 1975 that Nicola would have preferred to have played your part in the movie.
JANE: Yes. I think she might have been a little bit jealous. You know, I'd just come off the Bond film and now I was doing this. She'd obviously gotten her career going before I did, so I could understand that she might have felt that way. She had the bigger role, though.

SAM: But I think she felt your role was juicier.
JANE: Maybe. But she had a lot more scenes.

Jane Seymour pretends to be pregnant to mock Nicola Pagett.

SAM: Tell me about Michael Sarrazin.

JANE: I'd seen Michael Sarrazin in *They Shoot Horses, Don't They?* so I was incredibly impressed to be working with him. Unfortunately, I didn't get to work with him much. I do remember he was very uncomfortable and grouchy about having to be in that monster make-up all day.

SAM: And Leonard Whiting?

JANE: We actually became pretty good friends. A few years ago, I saw him in England. I could hardly recognize him. He's a carpet salesman. He's older and he's put on a bit of weight. He's not Leonard Whiting as you remember him at all. But he's such a dear guy. I was so excited to be working with him on *Frankenstein* because, of course, I'd seen him in *Romeo and Juliet*. That whole thing of *Romeo and Juliet* resonated with me enormously because I'd always wanted to play "Juliet" when I was in ballet school. Olivia Hussey was terrific, but we all were so jealous of her good fortune. I finally met the director Franco Zeffirelli on the day that it opened, at the premiere. And he said, "How come I never met you for 'Juliet'? You would have been perfect." That's what he said to me.

SAM: Wow. You must have died.

JANE: Yeah, I was really upset. But then he tested me to do *Roman Holiday*. They were going to do a remake of it – and I did a screen test. But sadly, the film never got made. I have another story that has a connection to Olivia Hussey. Not long after *Romeo and Juliet* had been such a huge hit, I did a film called *The Only Way* [1970] with Martin Potter, who'd just come off *Fellini Satyricon* [1969]. It was my first substantial movie role. I played a dance teacher. It was a Danish-British co-production. Anyway, I met the producer for it and he said, "I don't know if you're aware of this but you look enormously like Olivia Hussey." And I said, "Really?" He said, "Yes. But you know, I've decided to hire you over her." And I thought, "Well, that's kinda crazy. She's just done one of the biggest movies of all time." And then he showed me two photographs and said, "See for yourself. This one is Olivia and this one is you." He was right. We looked *exactly* alike – because both pictures were of me! In the same outfit – but from slightly different angles, from the same photo shoot. Well, Olivia and I had the same agent and the agent had accidentally written "Olivia Hussey" under one of my photographs. Years later, I told Olivia this story and we had a good laugh about it because, clearly, she didn't need to do that movie. She was doing much bigger and better things at that time.

SAM: That's hilarious.

JANE: Another time, I got really close to playing "Juliet" at the Shaw Theatre [in Somers Town, in the London Borough of Camden, in 1971, opposite Simon Ward as "Romeo"]. Sinéad Cusack [who later married Jeremy Irons] and I kept going through audition after audition and I got closer and closer, and she kept saying to me, "How's it going? Are you gonna get it?" And I said, "Oh, Sinéad, I'm so excited. I can't believe it. They've had to offer it to a "name," but they know the "name" probably won't do it because she's got plenty of other stuff to do, so I'm expecting to get an offer any minute." And you know what? You know who this "name" was? Sinéad Cusack. And she took the role."

SAM: Do you remember producer Hunt Stromberg Jr. being a forceful presence on set? He actually said in the press that *Frankenstein: The True Story* was "a producer's picture," not "a director's picture." Did you get the feeling that director Jack Smight was less in control?

JANE: I didn't know any better at that time, you know? I'd just done the Bond film and was used to the producer Harry Saltzman telling the director Guy Hamilton what he did and didn't like, so… this just seemed like the same thing, business as usual.

POST-SCRIPT

After *Frankenstein: The True Story*, Jane Seymour went on to even greater fame in theatre (Broadway's *Amadeus*), movies (*Somewhere in Time*) and television (*Dr. Quinn, Medicine Woman*, for which she won Emmy and Golden Globe Awards), with over 150 credits-and-counting. She has been immortalized with a star on the Hollywood Walk of Fame and, at the age of 56, rekindled her love of dance as a contestant on the fifth season of *Dancing with the Stars* (ABC-TV, 2007).

Seymour with Golden Globe Award for *Dr. Quinn, Medicine Woman.*

Seymour on *Dancing with the Stars.*

Jack the Ripper.

Battlestar Galactica.

War and Remembrance.

Phantom of the Opera.

Severed head of Jane Seymour for FTTS.

THE EPIC SAGA BEHIND *FRANKENSTEIN: THE TRUE STORY*

Seymour holding copy of FTTS Blu-ray.

Sam & Jane Seymour, September 6, 2022.

Her genre-related projects have included *Sinbad and the Eye of the Tiger* (1977), *Battlestar Galactica* (1978), *The Phantom of the Opera* (TV movie, 1983, opposite Maximilian Schell), *Jack the Ripper* (TV mini-series, 1988, opposite Michael Caine who won the Golden Globe for Best Actor), and Dan Curtis' *War and Remembrance* (TV mini-series, 1988, opposite Robert Mitchum and her former *Frankenstein: The True Story* co-star Sir John Gielgud, for which she was nominated for an Emmy and a Golden Globe).

Frankenstein: The True Story would not be the last time Jane met her fate via decapitation. In *La Révolution Française* (1989), she played "Marie Antoinette" who was sent to the guillotine. The all-star cast included Klaus Maria Brandauer, Peter Ustinov, Claudia Cardinale, Sam Neill and Christopher Lee – the latter reunited with Seymour for the first time since they co-starred in *Orson Welles' Great Mysteries: The Leather Funnel* (1973).

"I adored working with Christopher again," Jane said. "Very much so. He was such a character. He played the man who invented the guillotine. So, I guess you could say I've lost my head to Michael Sarrazin *and* Christopher Lee. Not too shabby."

Believe it or not, I ended up interviewing Jane for a *third* time, on November 24, 2019 – this time on camera for a special feature among the extras included on an exquisite new 2K restoration Blu-ray of *Frankenstein: The True Story* (Shout! Factory, Region A, 2020; and Fabulous Films, Region B, 2023).

And then, when I was producing the audiobook edition of my coming-of-age memoir, *I Was a Teenage Monster Hunter! How I Met Vincent Price, Christopher Lee, Peter Cushing & More!*, Jane agreed to re-record the answers to our two print interviews as a guest-star voice, recorded at her home in Malibu on September 6, 2022. Jane was just as gracious as ever – and freakin' ageless!

Crew for FTTS Blu-ray extra: David De Leon (make-up), Garry Allyn (hairstylist), Jane Seymour (interviewee), Sam Irvin (interviewer), Jim Kunz (cameraman), Malibu, California, November 24, 2019.

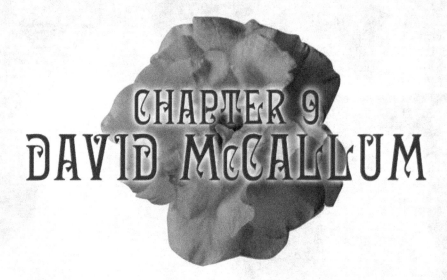

CHAPTER 9
DAVID McCALLUM

Born in Glasgow, Scotland, on September 19, 1933, David McCallum is most iconically known as Russian secret agent Illya Kuryakin on *The Man from U.N.C.L.E.* (NBC-TV, 1964-1968) and the eccentric medical examiner Dr. Donald "Ducky" Mallard on *NCIS: Naval Criminal Investigation Service* (CBS-TV, 2003-2023-and-counting).

His movie credits include Roy Ward Baker's *A Night to Remember* (1958), John Huston's *Freud* (1962), John Sturges' *The Great Escape* (1963), George Stevens' *The Greatest Story Ever Told* (1965), Ivan Tors' *Around the World Under the Sea* (1966), Harry Alan Towers' *King*

McCallum as "Gwyllm" in *The Outer Limits*.

Solomon's Treasure (1979), John Hough's *The Watcher in the Woods* (1980), and Jim Wynorski's *The Haunting of Morella* (1990).

He was also a series regular on the following television shows: *Colditz* (1972-1974) opposite Robert Wagner; *The Invisible Man* (1975-1976) in the title role; *Kidnapped* (miniseries 1978); *Sapphire and Steel* (1979-1982) opposite Joanna Lumley; *Cluedo* (1990-1993) as Professor Plum; *Trainer* (1991-1992) opposite Susannah York; *VR.5* (1995-1997) opposite Lori Singer; *Team Knight Rider* (1997-1998); and, *The Education of Max Bickford* (2001-2002) opposite Richard Dreyfuss.

His made-for-TV movies include: *The Six Million Dollar Man: Wine, Women and War* (1973), *Screaming Skull* (1973) and *The Return of the Man from U.N.C.L.E.: The Fifteen Years Later Affair* (1983) with Robert Vaughn, Patrick Macnee and George Lazenby.

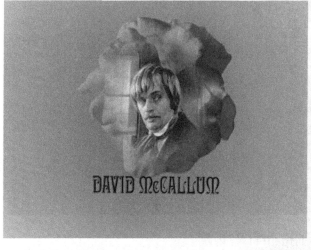

DAVID McCALLUM

McCallum has guest-starred on a plethora of series, including *The Outer Limits* (as "Gwyllm," the super-evolved man with six fingers), *Night Gallery*, *Hammer House of Mystery and Suspense*, *Alfred Hitchcock Presents*, *Monsters*, *SeaQuest DSV*, and *Babylon 5*.

He is also the author of the acclaimed crime novel *Once a Crooked Man* (Minotaur Books, 2016).

In *Frankenstein: The True Story*, McCallum plays Dr. Henry Clerval, a former protégé – and ex-lover – of Dr. Polidori (James Mason) and, as the film begins, the mentor of Dr. Frankenstein (Leonard Whiting). After his death, Frankenstein transplants Clerval's brain into the Creature (Michael Sarrazin). When first brought to life, the Creature has complete amnesia but, slowly, the mind of Clerval regains consciousness and takes over – with the post-dubbed voice of McCallum occasionally coming out of Sarrazin's mouth (inspired, no doubt, by Ygor's voice coming out of the Monster's mouth, post-brain-transplant, in *The Ghost of Frankenstein*). McCallum also played Lord Byron in the filmed-but-aborted prologue.

Jill Haworth & McCallum, *The Outer Limits*.

McCallum and Sam, at McCallum's home in Santa Monica, July 27, 2015.

The following interview was conducted on July 27, 2015, at McCallum's home in Santa Monica, California.

McCallum in *NCIS: Naval Criminal Investigation Service*.

Jack Smight & McCallum in lab set of FTTS.

Jack Smight and Henry Fonda on the set of *Midway*.

THE INTERVIEW

SAM IRVIN: Thank you very much for inviting me to your home to talk about *Frankenstein: The True Story*.
DAVID McCALLUM: My God, it was quite a cast, wasn't it? I remember Agnes Moorehead – she was wonderful. Nicola Pagett was a lovely lady. And Jack Smight, of all people, directing us. When I think of Jack, I think of *Midway*, the World War II movie with Charlton Heston and Henry Fonda. Anybody who can direct *that* movie the way he did can do anything in this world. I always liked Jack. He was very workman like. Very practical. He didn't waste a lot of time like so many other directors. He knew what he was doing. He was wonderful.

SAM: What do you recall about Leonard Whiting?
DAVID: He was very pleasant, very professional. We did our

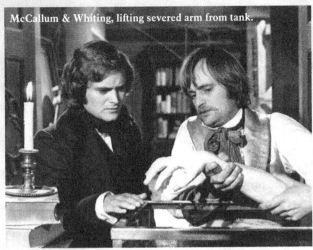
McCallum & Whiting, lifting severed arm from tank.

Karloff with mirror, *Mask of Fu Manchu*.

McCallum & Whiting graverobbing.

McCallum reflected in giant distorted mirror.

McCallum & Whiting, with beetle.

McCallum with mirror.

work. But that's really all I can remember. As you know, I died very early in the story.

SAM: Michael Sarrazin played the Creature – with your brain in his head. During the climax, your voice can be heard coming out of Sarrazin's mouth. These bits were obviously post-dubbed. Do you recall going into the ADR studio to do that?
DAVID: Only very vaguely. I've done so much ADR in my lifetime, it all blends together.

SAM: What stands out most in your memory of playing Clerval?

DAVID: I remember the script was very good – and it called for a lot of mirrors. I'm looking in a mirror at myself in one of the early scenes when I've stolen the severed arm. My character was a narcissist, so the mirrors were a recurring theme. When we got to the laboratory scene, I was supposed to hold up a mirror and gaze at myself while giving a speech. So, I went to the prop room and found this huge, round mirror that would blow-up and distort my face, like a giant fisheye lens. I showed it to Jack Smight and he loved it, so we put it in the scene.

SAM: The associate producer Ian Lewis was there when you were shooting this mirror sequence. He told me that when Hunt Stromberg walked on set and saw you holding the big round fisheye mirror, he gasped! Ian thought, "Oh

no. He must hate it. Here we go." But, quite the contrary, Hunt loved it and exclaimed, "My God! That's exactly how Boris Karloff was introduced in my father's production of *The Mask of Fu Manchu*!"

DAVID: Now that you mention it, I do vaguely remember Hunt going on about something to that effect, but I've never seen that film, so the reference was coincidental on my part. In any event, after we did a couple of takes, I said to Jack, "I can go this far. Or I can go further. What do you want me to do?" He said, "Oh, what you're doing is fine. We've got it." So, they moved on to the next bit. But he was wrong because, in my gut, I think I could have taken it another step and it would have been much more wonderful.

SAM: What more would you have done?

DAVID: (laughs) I wish I could remember. I just remember I wanted to try something wild and never got to try it. The scene cried out for my character to kind of lose his mind in that moment. And I wasn't sure if we'd really gotten it right.

Stromberg startles McCallum as a joke on set.

Joan Collins & David McCallum in *The Man from U.N.C.L.E.* ("The Galatea Affair," Season 3, Episode 3, September 30, 1966). Years earlier, David and Joan studied at RADA together.

Jack sat me down and he said, "No, no, no. We got it. Don't worry."

SAM: Let's go back to the beginning. It is my understanding that the producer Hunt Stromberg Jr. called you out of the blue and convinced you to do the film.

DAVID: That's true. And I needed some convincing to do a Frankenstein movie. But, once I read the script, there was no question. Christopher Isherwood is a brilliant writer, and this wasn't going to be an exploitation horror movie.

SAM: So, you were just offered the role? You didn't have to audition for it?

DAVID: That's right. At that point in my career, I didn't really have to go to auditions anymore. I was just offered parts because they knew my work. I remember we shot *Frankenstein* at Pinewood Studios. I started my career there. I was under contract with the Rank Organisation for several years – and they owned Pinewood Studios and made all their pictures there. I had done a lot of acting in school and, as a teenager, did voices on BBC radio. Then I went in the Army for two years, based in North Africa. When I came out, I studied at the Royal Academy of Dramatic Arts (RADA).

SAM: Where Joan Collins was one of your classmates.

DAVID: You did your homework. Very good. So, eventually, there was this photograph taken of me that looked like James Dean. In 1956, someone at the Rank Organisation saw this photo and hired me to be in a film called *The Secret Place* with Clive Donner directing – and from that I was asked to go under contract.

SAM: Your second film for Rank was *Hell Drivers* (1957) starring Stanley Baker, Herbert Lom, Patrick McGoohan and some unknown guy named Sean Connery.

DAVID: (laughs) Yes, *that* guy. Wonder what became of him.

SAM: They could have re-released it in the 1960s as *Hell Drivers* starring James Bond and Illya Kuryakin!

DAVID: Luckily, no one did that. But I also met an actress in that cast named Jill Ireland who, as you know, became my first wife in 1957. We did another picture together that same year called *Robbery Under Arms* with Peter Finch.

SAM: The next picture you did for Rank was *Violent Playground* (1958) with Stanley Baker and Peter Cushing. What was Peter like?

Connery, McCallum with unidentified woman.

THE EPIC SAGA BEHIND *FRANKENSTEIN: THE TRUE STORY*

The Rank Organisation presents

Stanley BAKER
Peter CUSHING
Anne HEYWOOD
David McCALLUM

Michael Relph and Basil Dearden's production

VIOLENT PLAYGROUND

Original Screenplay by James Kennaway
Produced by Michael Relph
Directed by Basil Dearden

Sharon Tate & McCallum in *The Man from U.N.C.L.E.*

McCallum, his real-life wife Jill Ireland, Robert Vaughn, *The Man from U.N.C.L.E.*

McCallum & Cushing in *Violent Playground*.

DAVID: A true gentleman. Very good actor, too. Then I did a very big picture for Rank called *A Night to Remember* (1958), about the Titanic – which is still the best Titanic movie. The director was Roy Ward Baker, a lovely man.

SAM: You then did a lot of British television, including Thornton Wilder's *The Skin of My Teeth* (1959) with Vivien Leigh; Noël Coward's *The Vortex* (1960) with Ann Todd; and Emily Brontë's *Wuthering Heights* (1962) with Claire Bloom. Those are some amazing leading ladies.
DAVID: I was very lucky. All this led to my role as Carl van Schlossen in *Freud*, directed by John Huston, which we shot in Germany. It starred Montgomery Clift as Sigmund Freud and Susan Kohner as his wife. Susan happened to be the daughter of Paul Kohner, the big talent agent, who signed

me up and brought me over to America to play Judas in *The Greatest Story Ever Told*.

SAM: Before you made the move to Hollywood, though, you starred with Steve McQueen and Charles Bronson in *The Great Escape*, shot in West Germany.
DAVID: Yes. I made the mistake of introducing my wife Jill Ireland to Charles Bronson and, well, you know what happened after that.

SAM: Ouch. Okay, moving right along... of course, once you were in Hollywood, this led to *The Man from U.N.C.L.E.* which turned you into a teen idol of Beatles-like proportions, receiving 30,000 fan letters a month. They called you "the blond Paul McCartney."
DAVID: Yes, well, we've heard all those stories.

SAM: One of the things I didn't know, though, is that you met your second wife, Katherine Carpenter, because of *U.N.C.L.E.* I read that on a weekend in New York in 1965, you and Robert Vaughn were doing a photo shoot with several high fashion models at various landmarks in the city – and that one of those models happened to be Katherine. Is that true?
DAVID: Yes. Well, you see, at that point, my wife Jill Ireland, unbeknownst to me, had taken up with Charles Bronson. Jill and I split up. I met Katherine on that photo shoot and we've been together for fifty years.

SAM: Congratulations. Getting back to *Frankenstein: The True Story*, when Clerval first meets Dr. Frankenstein, he's been called upon to amputate the arm of a wounded man. That was shot at St. Mary Abbott's Hospital in Kensington which had a perfectly preserved wing that looked like a vintage Dickensian ward.

CHAPTER NINE: DAVID McCALLUM

235

McCallum as Illya Kuryakin in *U.N.C.L.E.*

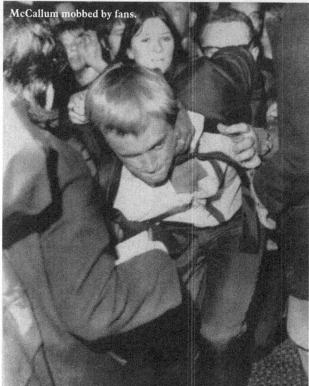
McCallum mobbed by fans.

DAVID: That's right. The attic. When they refurbished the hospital in the 1930s or whenever they redid it, they just closed off the attic as such and left it as it was. For the movie, they just opened it up again. And we went into this amazing location. It was a remarkable place. Like a time capsule. It felt like we were stepping back in time. I sawed off someone's arm. I wanted the amputation to be believable so I got them to get a piece of wood and nail it to the operating table where the man's arm would be, out of sight of the camera. So, when they shot the scene, I sawed through that piece of wood – and it fell on the floor. The resistance made it believable. And all it took was a piece of wood and a saw.

SAM: Do you recall the set of the boarding house where Clerval and Dr. Frankenstein rent lodgings from a nosy landlady played by Agnes Moorehead. The interiors were constructed at Pinewood Studios.
DAVID: I only have vague memories of that. What I remember most is the giant laboratory at Pinewood. It was a very impressive set. And they must have spent a fortune constructing it.

SAM: Do you remember the prologue in which you played Lord Byron – Nicola Pagett played Mary Shelley, Leonard Whiting played Percy Shelley and James Mason played Byron's physician Dr. Polidori. It was cut from the movie but here are photos I have, proving it was filmed. What can you tell me about it?
DAVID: (looking at photos) I vaguely recall shooting by that lake but, unfortunately, I don't remember anything specific.

SAM: Were you aware at the time of the subtext of homosexuality in Isherwood and Bachardy's script? For instance, the way your own character of Clerval reacts so rudely and dismissively to Dr. Frankenstein's fiancée can, on one level, be interpreted as jealousy – that Clerval's interest in Dr. Frankenstein goes beyond just mentorship.
DAVID: I'm sure I must have thought about those things, especially since I knew Isherwood was gay and much of his

McCallum right after cutting off arm.

McCallum as Lord Byron, Mason as Dr. Polidori, Smight & Stromberg; the day they shot the aborted prologue.

236   THE EPIC SAGA BEHIND *FRANKENSTEIN: THE TRUE STORY*

Above: Pagett as Mary Shelley, Whiting as Percy Shelley, Smight, McCallum as Lord Byron; the day they shot the aborted prologue. Below: McCallum, Mason & Stromberg.

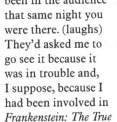

Above Top: Keith Jochim as the Monster and John Carradine as the blind hermit. Above: Keith Jochim as the Monster – Broadway flop in 1981.

writing dealt with that subject matter. But I'm afraid it has been so long, I simply don't remember any details. I'm sorry.

SAM: Were there any difficulties during the shooting that you recall?
DAVID: One of the things I found hard with this film – and others like it – was that we had actors with very different acting styles from very, very different fields. The theatre, major motion pictures, British television, American television. It was challenging. Michael Sarrazin was in his world, which was more realistic than, say, Agnes Moorehead who was very theatrical. I'm not saying it was a negative. They both were wonderful. But when you blend actors, it helps to have a lot of rehearsal so it all comes together, so it all fits. When you get to play a well-written part like Henry Clerval, if you don't have that rapport with everybody, you come away slightly dissatisfied. With more time and more rehearsal, I think a number of moments could have been better. That's not a criticism. I tend to be a very harsh critic of my own work. They were quite happy with what they got. And it had some absolutely beautiful things.

SAM: Does anything else come to mind?
DAVID: I afraid not. They took my brain out and put it into Michael Sarrazin's head. Maybe he got all my recollections. I do remember something about *another* Frankenstein project, though, that might interest you. Years later, I got a call. They were doing *Frankenstein* on Broadway. And it was a big, *big* production – and the organs were playing and the whole thing.

SAM: That would have been in 1981. There was a notoriously expensive production of *Frankenstein* at the Palace Theatre on Broadway that had 29 preview performances, then officially opened, got trashed by the critics, and closed after just one night. I saw it during previews. The cast included David Dukes as Dr. Frankenstein, Keith Jochim as the Creature, John Carradine as DeLacey, the blind hermit, John Glover as Henry Clerval, and Dianne Weist as Elizabeth. It was directed by Tom Moore who did *Grease* (1972-1980).
DAVID: That's the one. I may have been in the audience that same night you were there. (laughs) They'd asked me to go see it because it was in trouble and, I suppose, because I had been involved in *Frankenstein: The True Story* and, therefore, familiar with the subject. So, I went and it was as spectacular. Gorgeous sets, amazing pyrotechnics, beautiful music and bombastic sound effects. But they'd forgotten to write a book. The book was very weak. The actors did the best they could. But it just didn't work. After the performance, I talked to somebody involved with the production and I said, "You know, two or three changes in the cast would really strengthen the performances all around. Plus, one week of rewrites to get the story in shape." I'm sad that that didn't happen because it had a lot of potential – and certainly enough money was at their disposal to have made it better.

SAM: Tell me about your father, David McCallum, Sr., the great violinist and orchestra conductor.
DAVID: When I was growing up, my father was the concert master of the Scottish Orchestra in Glasgow. Then, about 1936, he became the concert master of the London Philharmonic Orchestra. During the War, he was the concert master for the National Symphony Orchestra and played violin for the BBC's Overseas Music Unit. After the War, he became the concert master of the Royal Philharmonic Orchestra.

CHAPTER NINE: DAVID McCALLUM

237

SAM: Is it true that he played violin with the string section on The Beatles' recording "A Day in the Life"?
DAVID: Yes, that's true.

SAM: During the height of the popularity of *The Man from U.N.C.L.E.*, you recorded two albums, which you arranged and conducted yourself. Was your father involved in those?
DAVID: Yes. He played violin on several of those tracks. He was an adviser and mentor to my career as a musician.

SAM: I've read that Led Zeppelin guitarist Jimmy Page credits your father with giving him the idea of playing guitar with a violin bow.
DAVID: Absolutely true. My father died March 21, 1972. I was doing the *Colditz* series with Robert Wagner.

SAM: According to the cast contact sheet for *Frankenstein: The True Story*, during the shoot, you were residing at 28a Dawson Place, London W.1.
DAVID: Yes. Then we bought a little house up in

McCallum, Melinda O. Fee, and Craig Stevens (of *Peter Gunn* fame) in *The Invisible Man* series (1975-76).

Staffordshire and I did the pilot of *Six Million Dollar Man*.

SAM: *The Six Million Dollar Man: Wine, Women and War* (Universal Television / ABC-TV, 10/20/1973) was the second of three TV-movies before it went to series in 1974. In it, you played another Soviet agent Alexi Kaslov, not too far removed from Illya Kuryakin, with a sexy assistant played by Britt Ekland.
DAVID: By then, I'd played so many parts since *The Man from U.N.C.L.E.*, I wasn't worried about typecasting.

SAM: It also kept you in good standing with Universal which eventually gave you your own series, *The Invisible Man* (NBC-TV, 1975-76).
DAVID: I did do quite a lot of work for Universal in those days. Paid a lot of bills. I agreed to do *The Invisible Man* with the impression it was going to be a serious update of the H. G. Wells novel about a man who desperately wants to be normal again. Well, Universal decided to turn it into a light comedy. We had fun making it, but I still wonder if it might have been better as a drama.

SAM: You starred in the series *Sapphire and Steel* with Joanna Lumley.
DAVID: Well, now there is a fantastic woman. Joanna and I are still friends to this day. We exchange Christmas cards and I try to see her every time I'm in London.

Joanna Lumley & McCallum, *Sapphire and Steel.*

Belgian poster for *The Spy in the Green Hat*.

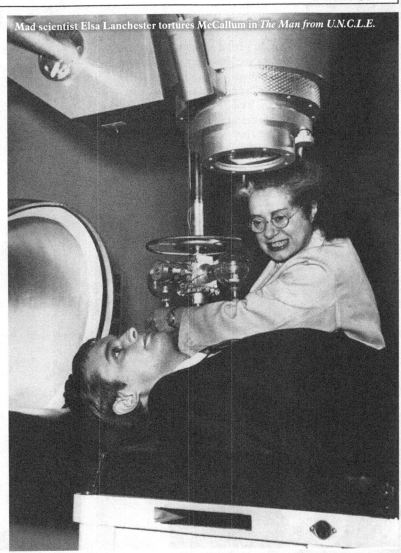

Mad scientist Elsa Lanchester tortures McCallum in *The Man from U.N.C.L.E.*

SAM: What are some of your favorite movies?

DAVID: Well, *Casablanca* comes to mind. Humphrey Bogart and Ingrid Bergman are sublime. I have the soundtrack of *Casablanca* on my iPhone. When I go to bed at night, I've been listening to the last scene, the plane taking off.

SAM: That's fantastic. I also love Bogart in *The Maltese Falcon*.

DAVID: That's a great one, too. Back in the days of *The Man from U.N.C.L.E.*, we did one episode where all of the gangsters from the Warner Brother's pictures were guest stars. And they're all in it! Elisha Cook Jr. from *The Maltese Falcon*... Maxie Rosenbloom...

[*Author's Note: The Man from U.N.C.L.E.: The Concrete Overcoat Affair* (NBC, 11/25/1966 & 12/2/1966) was directed by Joseph Sargent, with guest stars Jack Palance, Janet Leigh, Joan Blondell and a gallery of gangster-types, including Elisha Cook Jr. (*The Maltese Falcon*), Slapsy Maxie Rosenbloom (*Mr. Moto's Gamble*), Eduardo Ciannelli (Hitchcock's *Foreign Correspondent*), Allen Jenkins (*The Falcon Takes Over*), Jack La Rue (*The Story of Temple Drake*) and Vince Barnett (*The Killers*). This two-part episode was released outside the U.S. as a feature film entitled *The Spy in the Green Hat*.]

SAM: A guest star I remember so vividly from another episode was Elsa Lanchester as a mad scientist with terrible vision. I'll never forget the moment she's lost her

Coke-bottle-glasses, can barely see anything, and walks straight into the empty elevator shaft. Every time I'm waiting for an elevator, I think about that moment.

DAVID: Elsa Lanchester was such a marvelous actress. It was such a thrill to work with her.

SAM: I loved how she allowed them to spoof *Bride of Frankenstein* by adding two white streaks to her frizzy mane of hair.

DAVID: That was very clever. There were many nods to old movies in that series.

SAM: What do you think about the new *Man from U.N.C.L.E.* movie? [This interview was conducted eighteen days before Guy Ritchie's *The Man from U.N.C.L.E.* opened in U.S. theaters on August 14, 2015.]

DAVID: Actually, I just saw it at a private screening a couple of nights ago. To my great surprise, it is very good. Excellent, in fact. I can honestly say that the director Guy Ritchie and his co-writers have written an excellent screenplay which, in many ways, is a wonderful tribute to what Bob and I and the others did back in the sixties. They have used a little bit of the camp, but they haven't overdone it. It's a great action movie and it's beautifully cast. There is a woman in it who is remarkable. I told my wife I could fall in love again.

SAM: Alicia Vikander.

DAVID: Yes. Alicia Vikander. Now there's a star-in-the-making. I'd love to shake her hand. She is a superb actress. And also, she gets to wear the period 60's clothes – and she knows how to wear them. As you know, my wife Katherine was a very big fashion model back then and she is always highly critical of movies that try and fail to capture the period fashions of the 1960s. Well, she thought that this new *Man from U.N.C.L.E.* movie captured the style perfectly. She turned to me and said, "They got it right!" And Alicia Vikander got it right, too.

[*Author's Note:* A few months after this interview took place, Vikander would win the Academy Award for Best Supporting Actress for *The Danish Girl*; and receive two Golden Globe nominations for her work in *The Danish Girl* and *Ex Machina*.]

SAM: Were you and Robert Vaughn asked to do cameo appearances in the film?

DAVID: No, and I'm glad they didn't try to do that. It would have been a distraction for the sake of a silly gag.

SAM: Aside from your ongoing role as Ducky on *NCIS* and the voice of Alfred in a number of animated *Batman* adventures, what else do you have cooking these days?

DAVID: I'm glad you asked. I have just written a book. It's a crime novel called *Once a Crooked Man*. It will come out in January [2016] from Minotaur Books, a division of St. Martin's Press. I have the mockup. I've just gotten some advance notices which are quite encouraging. They'll put a blurb or two on the jacket.

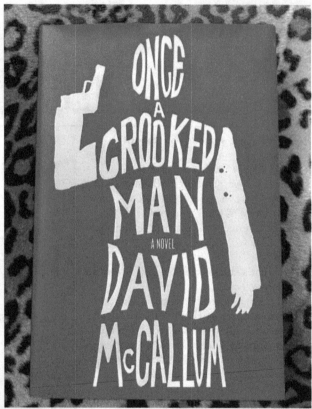

McCallum voiced Alfred Pennyworth in the animated *Batman* television series. (Courtesy of DC Comics and Warner Brothers).

THE EPIC SAGA BEHIND *FRANKENSTEIN: THE TRUE STORY*

David McCallum and Sam Irvin, Jan 21, 2016, book signing event for McCallum's *Once a Crooked Man*.

SAM: (reading one of the rave advance reviews) **These notices are fantastic. This one calls you "a tremendous novelist." How much did you pay that guy?**
DAVID: Nothing. I promise.

POSTSCRIPT

At the time of this interview, September 19, 2016, McCallum was 84 years old. He explained that he was the father of five children: three sons with Jill Ireland (Paul and Val; a third adopted son Jason died of an accidental drug overdose in 1989) and a son and daughter with Katherine Carpenter (Peter and Sophie). He is also the proud grandfather of eight. "We have six grandsons in New York and two granddaughters in Los Angeles," explains McCallum. "We keep the boys and the girls on different coasts so we can keep them straight."

His first novel, *Once a Crooked Man*, was published in January 2016 to rave reviews. The protagonist, Harry Murphy, is an actor who gets sucked into international intrigue. On January 21, 2016, following a signing event for the book at the Barnes & Noble at the Grove in Los Angeles, I asked David if there would be further adventures of Harry Murphy. With a twinkle in his eye, he replied, "Well, I like to spend as much of my free time as possible with my grandchildren, but my publisher is asking for more. So, we'll see."

Art by Frederick Cooper.

CHAPTER 10
NICOLA PAGETT

Born June 15, 1945, in Cairo, Egypt, Nicola Pagett grew up in Hong Kong, Cyprus and Japan, moving with her British family wherever her father's job as an executive for Shell Oil dictated. At age 17, Nicola came to London where she studied acting for two years at the Royal Academy of Dramatic Art (RADA). In 1964, Nicola appeared in several stage productions with the Worthing Repertory Company. Then her television debut performance in *Armchair Theatre: The Girl in the Picture* (1964) caught the attention of director Sir Robert Helpmann (the evil Child Catcher in *Chitty Chitty Bang Bang*) who cast her to tour with Vivien Leigh in his stage play *La Contessa* (1965).

From there, Nicola guest-starred on such series as *Danger Man* (known in the U.S. as *Secret Agent*), *The Spies, The Avengers, The Persuaders!* and *The Rivals of Sherlock Holmes*. Her early movie roles included Talia in Hammer's *The Viking Queen*; the bride in *There's a Girl in My Soup* starring Peter Sellers; and Princess Mary in *Anne of the Thousand Days* starring Richard Burton.

Her biggest break came, however, when she was cast as Elizabeth in *Upstairs, Downstairs*, the smash hit television series that was the *Downton Abbey* of its day. Upon his arrival in the UK in January 1973 to prep *Frankenstein: The True Story*, director Jack Smight spotted Pagett on an episode of the series and called producer Hunt Stromberg Jr. to turn on his TV. Stromberg was equally intrigued. At first, the two men were undecided if she should play the dual roles of Agatha / Prima or Mary Shelley / Elizabeth Frankenstein. They ultimately went with the latter.

In the summer of 1975, I was in London collecting interviews for my fanzine *Bizarre* No. 4. A year earlier, I had already met and interviewed Margaret Leighton about her role in *Frankenstein: The True Story* but she knew I was on the prowl to meet anyone else involved in the movie. So, on Friday the 13th of June 1975, I was invited by Margaret to a performance of her new play at the Apollo Theatre on Shaftsbury Avenue near Piccadilly Circus. It was called *A Family and a Fortune*, by Ivy Compton-Burnett, a drawing room dramedy examining how inheritance brings out the worst among relatives. The cast included the great Alec Guinness, whom I idolized (as did everyone). But Margaret thought this would be a marvelous opportunity for me to

NICOLA PAGETT

meet one of the other cast members, Nicola Pagett.

After the show, I went backstage armed with copies of *Bizarre* No. 3 featuring *Frankenstein: The True Story* on the cover. When I was introduced to Nicola, Margaret opened the magazine to point out the various photos of the cast, including both of them.

"Nicola, darling," Margaret intoned, "you must do an interview with this young man for his magazine."

Sheepishly, Nicola looked at me and said, "I'm sorry to disappoint you but I am embarrassed about that film. I saw it at the Paramount last year when it opened – and they've cut it to shreds."

Pagett as Mary Shelley, aborted FTTS prologue.

Pagett, Patrick McGoohan, *Danger Man* (1965). Stromberg imported this series to the U.S. for CBS-TV, renamed *Secret Agent*.

"Yes, it is a disaster," I agreed. "The editor Richard Marden arranged a screening of that god-awful 2-hour cut for me at Pinewood Studios. It's missing a third of the original film that was shown on television in America. You shouldn't judge it on that. You must see the full 3-hour version."

"But I've also heard that Christopher Isherwood is not happy with that one, either," Nicola countered, unwavering in her stance.

"Well, I beg to disagree," I said. "I think it is one of the very best Frankenstein films ever made. And you are wonderful in it. I understand that the BBC will be broadcasting the complete 3-hour version later this year [December 27, 1975] and I encourage you to keep an open mind and see it for yourself."

"We'll see," Nicola said, skeptically. Other friends were there waiting to see her, so she politely excused herself.

Sympathetically, Margaret shrugged and whispered, "Well, it's her loss. At least we tried."

It only took forty years for me to convince Nicola to discuss her role in *Frankenstein: The True Story*. The following interview was conducted by phone on Nicola's 70th birthday, June 15, 2015.

THE INTERVIEW

NICOLA PAGETT: So, I understand from your emails that we've met before.

SAM IRVIN: Yes, very briefly, forty years ago this very month – June 1975. While I was visiting London that month, I came to see you, Margaret Leighton and Alec Guinness in a play called *A Family and a Fortune* at the Apollo Theatre. I had already met Margaret Leighton the year before to interview her about her role in *Frankenstein: The True Story*. She invited me backstage and introduced me to you – which was very exciting because I was such of fan of your work in the *Frankenstein* film, too.

Unfortunately, a butchered, two-hour theatrical version of the movie had recently been released in the UK and you were very upset about it. I urged you to see the three-hour version shown on American television before discounting the whole thing but you didn't seem eager to discuss it. So, it's only taken me four decades to convince you to open up.

NICOLA PAGETT: (laughs) Well, you certainly are persistent.

SAM: Early in your career, you appeared on an episode of *Danger Man* with Patrick McGoohan.

NICOLA: I couldn't hit my mark. I had to come twirling in through a door and I couldn't hit the exact spot I needed to land for the camera to be focused. And you can't look down, searching for your mark on the floor. I got it wrong maybe eight times and then, on the ninth take, I finally got it right – but Patrick got it wrong. I think he got it wrong on purpose, which wasn't very kind of him.

The Viking Queen.

THE EPIC SAGA BEHIND *FRANKENSTEIN: THE TRUE STORY*

Pagett and Andrew Kier in *Viking Queen*.

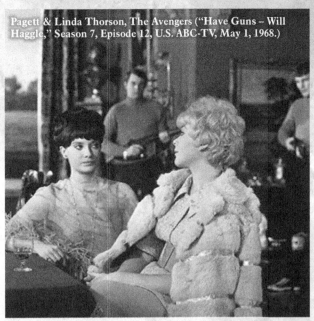
Pagett & Linda Thorson, The Avengers ("Have Guns – Will Haggle," Season 7, Episode 12, U.S. ABC-TV, May 1, 1968.)

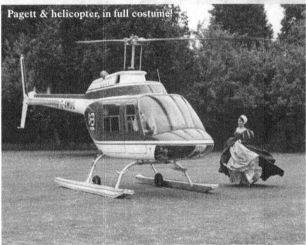
Pagett & helicopter, in full costume!

SAM: You did a Hammer Film called *The Viking Queen*. What was that like?
NICOLA: It was, you know, one of those situations when they ask you if you can drive a chariot – and you say, "Of course I can drive a chariot." (laughs) It was quite an experience. I also remember Wilfrid Lawson was the King in that. The great drunk English actor. We were in Ireland for eight weeks. I nearly went mad, actually. My part wasn't very big, so I ended up just getting fat because there was nothing else to do but eat.

SAM: Don Chaffey directed this movie not long after he did *One Million Years B.C.* which turned Raquel Welch into an international sensation. Was there an expectation that being in *The Viking Queen* was going to propel your career in a similar fashion?
NICOLA: No, because I wasn't the female lead. That part was played by Carita. Maybe she had high hopes of being the next Raquel Welch – but lightning rarely strikes twice. It's such an extraordinary phenomenon, isn't it? Hits. You can't legislate for them. They just happen. Carita was lovely. A very sweet girl. But she had no experience. None at all. And they didn't treat her very nicely. They didn't have a stand-in and she used to stand there for hours in the boiling heat while they set up the shots. She never complained, though. Not once. I admired her patience.

SAM: Do you remember working with Andrew Keir on that film?
NICOLA: Yes, yes, of course. I remember being *very* impressed at the time because he'd worked with Elizabeth Taylor on *Cleopatra*.

SAM: Adrienne Corri was in that film as well.
NICOLA: Yes, indeed. Adrienne was a ball of fire. So alive. Very intense, very high octane. Fun to be around. We all adored her.

SAM: You also did an episode of *The Avengers*.
NICOLA: I looked ridiculous in that. My wardrobe was very weird. But it was kind of a mad show, really.

SAM: Then you did a very big film, *Anne of the Thousand Days*, with Richard Burton. I have a press photo dated August 1969 of you, in full costume, racing across the lawn to board a helicopter. What was that all about?
NICOLA: Oh, that was quite something. I was doing a play called *Widowers' Houses* at the Nottingham Playhouse at the same time I was shooting *Anne of the Thousand Days* at Shepperton Studios – which was about a hundred miles apart. Literally. So, they had to give me a helicopter at the end of each shoot day to make my 7:30 curtain in Nottingham.

SAM: Arthur Ibbetson was the Director of Photography on *Anne of the Thousand Days* as well as *Frankenstein: The True Story*.
NICOLA: Yes, I remember him well. A very nice man. And very good at his job. He made everything look so beautiful.

SAM: The producer of *Frankenstein: The True Story*, Hunt Stromberg Jr., specifically wanted Arthur Ibbetson because of the work he'd done on *Anne of the Thousand Days*. I wonder if that's how he knew your work.

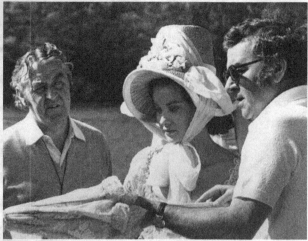

Above: Director of Photography Arthur Ibbetson, Pagett, Smight, on day the aborted prologue was shot for FTTS. Ibbetson was also Pagett's DP on *Anne of the Thousand Days*.

Ian Ogilvy & Pagett in *Upstairs, Downstairs* (1971-73).

NICOLA: Hunt and the director Jack Smight had seen me in *Upstairs, Downstairs*. That's how I got the part in *Frankenstein*. I remember they were a bit surprised that my hair was black because, apparently, the television made my hair look brown.

SAM: What did you think of Hunt?
NICOLA: With Hunt, I felt like I was standing on an electric cable, on the verge of being shocked at any moment. (laughs) I remember several of us were invited to have lunch at a flat he was sharing with his partner Jacque [Shelton]. They were renting it from some woman who owned it. Well, in the middle of eating lunch, the phone rang, so Hunt Stromberg took the call and put on a woman's voice and pretended to be the landlord – saying the most outrageous and embarrassing things to this poor unsuspecting person on the other end of the line. Hunt thought it was the

funniest thing in the world – but, of course, he was a bit drunk, which wasn't unusual for him.

SAM: Hunt and Jacque were renting Flat No. 4 at 8 Grosvenor Square, overlooking the American Embassy.
NICOLA: It was a spacious flat in a very smart part in London and there was a very nice older Englishman who was cooking lunch in their kitchen. Roast beef, Yorkshire pudding and everything.

SAM: Do you remember other stories about Hunt?
NICOLA: (laughs) Hunt nicknamed me Nanook – after *Nanook of the North*, the old movie about the family who lived in the Arctic. Remember those popular 1970s winter coats that were white and looked like they came from Tibet? I wore mine all the time. Hunt took one look at me in that old dirty flea-bitten white coat – because I didn't look very smart – and he called me Nanook of the North. And the nickname stuck. I must say, Hunt was very affable, and he was absolutely dedicated to treating all of us extremely well. He wined and dined us, gave us gifts. He wanted everyone to be happy and did everything in his power to make us laugh. He could be crass at times – but I knew his heart was in the right place.

SAM: What do you recall about his partner Jacque Shelton?
NICOLA: Jacque was completely different – kind of big and burly and easy to talk to. The one thing that pops into my mind was that Jacque kept trying to diet. The rest of us were eating this rich, fancy meal but Jacque was sitting there with a rather sad dietary plate of cold chicken. He peeled the skin off and said, "Oh, that bit's fattening. I can eat the rest."

SAM: Did you get to know Michael Sarrazin well?
NICOLA: Every now and then, you do something wrong that haunts you for the rest of your life. Well, with Michael Sarrazin, I'd seen *They Shoot Horses, Don't They?* and I thought that was a fantastic movie. Absolutely brilliant. And I thought of him as a *huge* Hollywood movie star. Untouchable. But, of course, in reality, he wasn't like that at all. I just *thought* he was because he never used to come to lunch with the rest of us in the dining room. He seemed like a loner to me – and not very sociable. And then, after work one day, I gave this laid-back kind of party at my little house. I didn't think Sarrazin would want to come, so I didn't ask him – because he was "too important." Well, Leonard Whiting was sharing a car with Sarrazin and the driver stopped at my house to drop off Leonard. When Leonard got out, I saw Sarrazin sitting in the back of the car. I remember the lonely look on his face. And as the driver drove off, this terrible feeling of regret crept over me. "What have I done?!" As the years went on and I got over being star stuck by Hollywood movie stars, I understood how I had completely misinterpreted everything about Sarrazin. He didn't come to lunch with us in the dining room because he didn't want everyone to see him looking so ugly in his monster makeup. I hoped I would someday run into him and I would have the opportunity to apologize to him and explain what a fool I'd been. Then, a few years ago, I read that he died of cancer and I thought, "Oh my God." It just broke my heart. And it haunts me that I never got the chance to tell him how brilliant he was and to apologize for my insensitive behavior. It haunts me. It really does.

THE EPIC SAGA BEHIND *FRANKENSTEIN: THE TRUE STORY*

Pagett, Stromberg & Sarrazin in chairs on church lawn.

Michael Wilding & Pagett at the ball.

Clarissa Kaye (Mason's wife) and Nicola Pagett.

SAM: Do you have other regrets?
NICOLA: I have so many regrets. I mean, there was Agnes Moorehead, who was completely approachable and wonderfully ordinary and sweet and unthreatening. And when I think of all the things I could have asked her about Orson Welles and didn't, you know? And now, of course, it's just too late. Why did I waste my youth?

SAM: Of course, there was also James Mason in the movie, who was quite a legend himself.
NICOLA: James Mason was wonderful. I've never known anyone more honest than James – to the point of complete tactlessness. You know his wife Clarissa Kaye was in the

Whiting as Lord Byron & Pagett as Mary Shelley, filming the aborted prologue, with Stromberg posing with them between set-ups.

CHAPTER TEN: NICOLA PAGETT

movie playing my mother. Well, one time on the set, James was watching her perform a scene and he leaned over to me and said, "Gosh, she's a terrible actress. Look at her. She can't act at all, can she?" (laughs) He was *terrible*!

SAM: Tell me about Margaret Leighton.
NICOLA: Well, Maggie was dying but she wouldn't admit it. She was unbelievably uncomplaining because she was in a lot of pain. Her eyes used to glitter with pain. When we did that play together *A Family and a Fortune* – the one you saw – the guy that played my brother in the play was my now ex-husband Graham Swannell. Graham and I got quite friendly with Maggie and her husband Michael Wilding. We saw them socially quite a bit. And then there was a phone call from her. We were going to go down to the country to have lunch but she couldn't breathe. She was gasping on the phone and said, "I'm awfully sorry, darling. I'm having an awful trouble breathing now. I think we better cancel." And not long after that, she died. I've never known anyone so brave and upbeat about everything.

SAM: Did you keep in touch with Michael Wilding?
NICOLA: Michael used to phone, but he had this peculiar illness where you couldn't hear what he was saying. It was very sad.

SAM: I would have loved to have seen you play Mary Shelley in the prologue that never made it into the final cut. Do you remember shooting that scene? I sent you photographs.
NICOLA: I do remember the four of us being by the lake, but the rest is a blur. Of course, I remember reading about these poets and how they had a bet with Byron to see who could write a really scary story. Maybe I'm remembering what I read in the script rather than what I might have learned in school.

SAM: Do you have any recollections of working on the sets?
NICOLA: I particularly remember the sequences on the deck of the ship – and the rocking mechanism underneath us broke. That was very funny – and if you look closely, I am trying desperately not to laugh because we had to pretend it was rocking. So instead of the ship moving, we moved. And we nearly got the giggles because we felt so stupid. We just managed to hold on till they said, "Cut!" Then we all burst out laughing. The fake snow wasn't funny at all. They put this artificial snow down on the huge studio floor. The smell of it was terrible and the chemicals got in our eyes. Our eyes were crimson. It was a disaster. They had to shut it down and start over with a safer kind of fake snow.

SAM: How was Jack Smight as a director?
NICOLA: Jack Smight was lovely. He just made you feel like you could do your job. I can't remember details exactly, but it was a very happy film to make in that regard.

SAM: He brought his wife Joyce Cunning and their 14-year-old son Alec. Do you remember them?
NICOLA: I only have a vague memory of Alec but I remember Joyce vividly. I remember she said, "There is no such thing as catching a cold. It just means you're feeling sorry for yourself." She was always sewing with Jane Seymour. Jane did a lot of *beautiful* embroidery.

Nicola Pagett and Tom Baker getting drenched on the deck.

SAM: What else do you recall about Jane?
NICOLA: Jane always wanted to pursue her acting career in America. That's where her heart was. Even though she was English, *emotionally* she was American and that's where she was heading. I'm such a home bird. So we weren't alike at all in that way. One day she said, "I'm going to Hollywood," and I said, "Well, I'm going to Cricklewood" – which is about as down market as you can get in London, you know? (laughs) Hollywood has always scared me a little bit. The stakes are so high. And they don't let you get old in America. I knew that the theatre in England would allow me to continue to work.

SAM: Do you prefer stage to television and movies?
NICOLA: Well, the stage is back-breakingly hard work. Eight performances, six days a week. You live your life from eight o'clock in the morning to six o'clock at night when you hit the road, face the traffic, do the play, then come home and not be able to sleep because you're still high from the play. I needed all that when I was younger – but it becomes exhausting. I remember when I was working with Alec Guinness in *A Family and a Fortune*, he said, "After this, I don't think I can do it anymore." What I love about the theatre, though, is that once you're on stage, they can't edit you. On the other hand, I love film sets, too – but for entirely different reasons. I love the fact that it's all collaborative in that moment. Like when you do a sex scene, you say, "Listen, I'm gonna do two little gasps, then I'm gonna put my head back and then I'm gonna lower my body." And the camera

Seymour, Pagett and Whiting (with goatee post-honeymoon).

THE EPIC SAGA BEHIND *FRANKENSTEIN: THE TRUE STORY*

Pagett & Sir John Gielgud, FTTS.
Peter Glaze in background.

operator says, "Thank you," because now he knows how to follow the movement and pull focus correctly. There's something really extraordinary about that.

SAM: Tell me about Leonard Whiting.
NICOLA: It had been a few years since he'd done *Romeo and Juliet*, but we all still looked at him as Romeo. It was such a defining role for him. I don't know what's happened to him since. He was still successful, I think, at least for a little while, but then it all faded away, didn't it? But he's a sweet, sweet man. Really lovely. Very easy and nice to be with. Same with David McCallum. Lovely man.

SAM: How was Sir John Gielgud?
NICOLA: Frightening, but wonderful. One is so in awe, you know? I couldn't think of things to say. I remember doing an odd line of dialogue and it didn't really work. He said, "Oh, you aren't going to do it like that, are you?" I tried to say the line more naturally, the way I would say it. Gielgud said, "It's a bit cheesy but it works." (laughs)

SAM: You didn't have scenes with Sir Ralph Richardson but did you get to meet him?
NICOLA: I did meet him, yes. But I didn't have much to do with him. You know, Hunt sent me a letter he'd received from Ralph Richardson, in his own handwriting in black ink, on beautiful thick paper, copper plate letterhead, expensive stuff. And it said something about how he'd liked my work. And Hunt said, "I thought you might like to have this." And he gave it to me, which was very sweet. Even then, at that age, I thought, "Well now, *this* is an honor."

SAM: Why have you been so reluctant to talk about *Frankenstein: The True Story*?
NICOLA: Because it was a tragedy, the whole venture. The Christopher Isherwood script was wonderful when we started but, of course, they changed everything he did. As you know, I was very unhappy with the version they released to theaters here. But they were making changes the whole time we were shooting, too. Sometime afterward, I saw Christopher Isherwood and he was distraught. The only one of us he really admired was Jane [Seymour]. He was furious with all the rest of us. But what do you do when the producer hands you his blue pages? You just had to do it.

SAM: Are you referring to the scene Hunt wrote for you and Sir John Gielgud as the Chief Constable?
NICOLA: Yes.

SAM: But, you see, even that situation has been blown way out of proportion. The scene that Isherwood and Bachardy wrote was Dr. Polidori persuading the Chief Constable to ignore Dr. Frankenstein's confession. But there is an inherent problem with the scene as originally written. It was previously established that Polidori has the power to hypnotize people in order to get what he wanted. So, why doesn't he just use hypnosis to change the Constable's mind? The scene made no sense. So, Stromberg switched the characters so that Elizabeth Frankenstein is the one who must persuade the Constable not to press charges against her husband.
NICOLA: I didn't know that. I must confess that I don't think I've ever really seen the film. I don't know that I've actually seen it. I just remember Isherwood's face. Did he have his name taken off?

SAM: No. He and Don Bachardy are fully credited. And the authorized teleplay that they wrote, before the various cuts and changes, was published the same month the film was broadcast. So, it is easy to compare what they intended versus the result. Quite frankly, I don't feel that the three-hour movie deviates that drastically from what Isherwood and Bachardy wrote. Sure, there are some regrettable changes – such as the Mary Shelley prologue being cut out. That change, however, was instigated by NBC, not Stromberg. The changes that Stromberg made were, in some instances, quite clever. For instance, it was Stromberg's idea to have the Creature throw himself off a cliff into the ocean – which was so much more dramatic than the Creature walking into a river.
NICOLA: So, you think Isherwood was wrong to feel the way he did?

SAM: I believe that Isherwood's negative reaction was an overreaction. It was an emotional reaction from a writer of novels whose work was normally published with little or no interference. For example, *Cabaret* was based on Isherwood's *The Berlin Stories* and it is a wonderful film that won eight Oscars including Best Actress for Liza Minnelli and Best Director for Bob Fosse. And yet Isherwood wrote in his own diary that he hated Minnelli's performance and he publicly chastised Fosse for ruining his book. Taking this into account, it certainly puts his criticism of *Frankenstein* in perspective. I just don't think he was capable of being objective.
NICOLA: Maybe so. I haven't read the Mary Shelley book. Is Isherwood faithful to Shelley?

SAM: Not at all. It is almost entirely an original script.
NICOLA: Really? Because when I read the script, it was riveting, and I thought that it was straight from Mary Shelley.

SAM: That's what a lot of people thought – especially when it was released with the title *Frankenstein: The True Story*.
NICOLA: The title was very misleading, then.

SAM: Yes. Isherwood *hated* the title, and, in this particular case, his anger was entirely justified. His title – and the working title when you were shooting it – was simply *Dr. Frankenstein*. Unfortunately, "*The True Story*" part of the title was added by NBC a couple of months before it was broadcast. It had nothing to do with Stromberg or even Universal.

NICOLA: Well, all I can tell you is that Isherwood is a hell of a writer because I loved the script. I couldn't put it down.

SAM: I agree with you. Isherwood and Bachardy's script was superior to the book in a number of ways. First of all, they have the Creature start off beautiful, then slowly deteriorate, which is far more poignant. The monster in Shelley's book is hideous-looking from the get-go and he's a giant, over eight-feet tall – which would be very hard to faithfully dramatize. The screenwriters also bring to life the female creature Prima, a subplot that Mary Shelley starts to set-up, but then abandons.

NICOLA: I greatly respect Isherwood's writing. He's not quite Tolstoy, but, you know, the billing is a couple down from that. He's one of the greats. I felt very privileged to have been cast in an Isherwood script.

SAM: I really do recommend that you see the three-hour version. I think you would be pleasantly surprised. Your performance is nothing short of luminous.

NICOLA: You flatter me – and I am very touched. Thank you.

POSTSCRIPT

Following *Frankenstein: The True Story*, Nicola went on to play the title role in the Emmy-nominated miniseries *Anna Karenina* (BBC, 1977) after Diana Rigg turned it down; co-starred with Ryan O'Neal in *Oliver's Story* (1978), the sequel to *Love Story*; co-starred with John Cleese in *Privates on Parade* (1983); and, co-starred with Hugh Grant and Alan Rickman in *An Awfully Big Adventure* (1995).

In 1995, while appearing in *What the Butler Saw* at the National Theatre, Nicola began suffering from erratic behavior that was later diagnosed as acute manic depression. Under the UK's Mental Health Act, Nicola was "sectioned" (admitted, detained and treated) in a psychiatric ward five times. Her frank, first-hand account of the harrowing ordeal was chronicled in her 1998 memoir *Diamonds Behind My Eyes*.

"It was very traumatic at the time," Nicola said, "but I'm very proud of it now because everything in this country is changing. My struggles – and the struggles of many others – have shed light on the government not helping people; they're very chastened by it. I wrote my book because I wanted to expose all of this, to blow it all up – but, of course, as a result, I haven't worked. Mind you, I don't think I could have worked."

Pagett & Ryan O'Neal in *Oliver's Story* (1978), sequel to *Love Story*.

Privates on Parade.

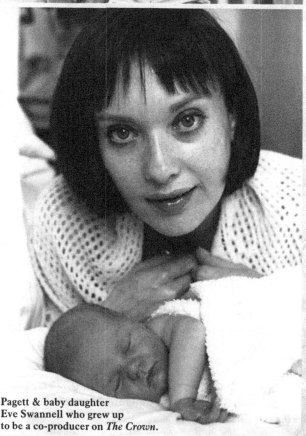
Pagett & baby daughter Eve Swannell who grew up to be a co-producer on *The Crown*.

Pagett in *Anna Karenina* (1977).

June 4th '17

Dear Sam,

I do hope this reaches you. Thank you so very much for sending me 'Little Shop of Horrors' — what a great gossipy read. I would have enjoyed it nearly as much even if I hadn't been in it. You've done Mary Shelley a great service and you write beautifully.

My daughter Eve was delighted to see her name in print in the credits.

I hope all goes well and there's lots more writing — So Merry Christmas a bit early!

Yours,

Nicola Pagett.

From 1975 to 1997, Nicola was married to actor-turned-playwright Graham Swannell – who shared the stage with her in *A Family and a Fortune* (1975), the play I saw them in with Alec Guinness and Margaret Leighton. The couple had a daughter, Eve, born April 16, 1979.

Now in her forties, Eve Swannell works behind the camera on movies and television. She was the Production Coordinator on such major films as *Great Expectations*, *Les Misérables* and *Kick-Ass 2*. Eve moved up to be the Unit Production Manager of Hammer's *The Woman in Black 2: Angel of Death* and has most recently been co-producer/line producer on over 40 episodes of the celebrated Netflix miniseries *The Crown*. A special thank you goes out to Eve for helping to coordinate this interview with her mother.

Nicola turned out to be a wonderful interview subject and, I am very happy to report, she was pleased with the result. Upon receiving a copy of *Little Shoppe of Horrors* No. 38 – in which a shorter version of this interview was first published – Nicola wrote the following letter, dated June 4, 2017: "Dear Sam, I do hope this reaches you. Thank you for sending me *Little Shoppe of Horrors*. What a great gossipy read. I would have enjoyed it just as much even if I hadn't been in it. You've done Mary Shelley a great service and you write beautifully. I hope all goes well and there's lots more writing. So, Merry Christmas a tad early. Yours, Nicola Pagett."

Sadly, four years later, on March 3, 2021, Nicola died suddenly from a brain tumor. She was 75.

Director Jack Smight & Nicola Pagett, FTTS.

CHAPTER TEN: NICOLA PAGETT

251

CHAPTER 11
MARGARET LEIGHTON

On Tuesday, July 9, 1974, I traveled to EMI Elstree Studios in Borehamwood, Hertfordshire, to interview the great 52-year-old classical stage and screen actress Margaret Leighton (1922-1976) over lunch at the studio commissary. I had just turned 18 and was in England gathering interviews for my fanzine *Bizarre* No. 3 (August 1974) that would feature *Frankenstein: The True Story* on the cover. (Please take my youthful age into account; some of the questions I ask are rather naïve.)

I was especially interested in chatting with Leighton about playing the small but important guest role of the Dowager Countess Françoise Duval (the French lady at the opera and later costumed as "Little Bo Peep" at the ball) in *Frankenstein: The True Story* – for which I was giving her a Bizarre Award for Best Cameo Actress in my forthcoming issue. I wasn't the only one impressed. In its review of the film, the *Los Angeles Times* had raved that Leighton's "jewel-like bits as a nitwit noblewoman must literally be seen to be believed."

Margaret costarred in another horror film, *From Beyond the Grave* (1974), with Peter Cushing and Donald Pleasence.

Leighton had won two Tony Awards for Best Actress in the Broadway plays *Separate Tables* and *The Night of the Iguana*; an Emmy Award for Best Supporting Actress as "Gertrude" in *Hamlet* opposite Richard Chamberlain; and a BAFTA Award for Best Supporting Actress in Joseph Losey's *The Go-Between* for which she was also Oscar-nominated.

Margaret appeared in 25 other movies, including Alfred Hitchcock's *Under Capricorn* (1949) with Ingrid Bergman, Joseph Cotten and her future real-life husband Michael Wilding; John Guillermin's *Waltz of the Toreadors* (1962) opposite Peter Sellers; Tony Richardson's *The Loved One* (1965) featuring Rod Steiger, James Coburn, Sir John Gielgud, Liberace, Roddy McDowall and Robert Morley; John Ford's *7 Women* (1966) with Anne Bancroft; Bryan Forbes' *The Madwoman of Chaillot* (1969) with Katharine Hepburn, Yul Brynner, Richard Chamberlain, Donald Pleasence and Danny Kaye; Brian G. Hutton's *X, Y and Zee* (1972) starring Elizabeth Taylor and Michael Caine; Robert Bolt's *Lady Caroline Lamb* (1972) starring Sarah Miles, Jon

MARGARET LEIGHTON

Finch, Richard Chamberlain, Sir John Mills, Sir Ralph Richardson, Lord Laurence Olivier, and her then-husband Michael Wilding; and James Cellan Jones' *The Nelson Affair* (1973) starring Glenda Jackson and Peter Finch.

Her television credits included guest-starring in episodes of *Alfred Hitchcock Presents, Suspicion, Burke's Law, The Alfred Hitchcock Hour, Dr. Kildare, The Girl from U.N.C.L.E.* and *Space: 1999*.

On the day I met Margaret, she was currently playing Miss Havisham in Joseph Hardy's new production of Charles Dickens' *Great Expectations* (1974) – a film to be premiered on television in the U.S. and released theatrically in the UK and other countries around the world. It boasted an impressive

Peter Sellers & Margaret Leighton in *Waltz of the Toreadors* (1962).

Margaret Leighton as Miss Havisham in *Great Expectations*.

Richard Chamberlain & Margaret Leighton, *Lady Caroline Lamb* (1972).

Leighton in *Alfred Hitchcock Presents* ("Tea Time," Season 4, Episode 10, December 14, 1958) for CBS-TV when Stromberg was calling the shots.

Leighton & York, *Great Expectations*.

Leighton & Michael York on set of *Great Expectations*. (Photo by Sam Irvin).

Leighton in *Space: 1999*.

Cartoon of Sam interviewing Leighton & York, by Dan Gallagher.

all-star cast including her *Frankenstein: The True Story* co-star James Mason (as Magwitch), plus Michael York (as Pip), Sarah Miles (as Estella), Robert Morley, Anthony Quayle, Rachel Roberts, Heather Sears, Joss Ackland, and Ben Cross.

We were having a wonderful chat over lunch when a gentleman asked if he could join us. I looked up and, to my great surprise, it was none other than blond, blue-eyed dreamboat Michael York, 32-years-young back then. I had to contain my excitement because not only was I a huge fan of his work in such hit movies as Franco Zeffirelli's *Romeo and Juliet*, Bob Fosse's *Cabaret* and Richard Lester's *The Three Musketeers*, I also had a major crush on him – like any closeted gay 18-year-old would! I composed myself with thoughts like, "I must remain professional. And butch."

Wise old Margaret could see right through it. She insisted that Michael should do a horror film so he could be interviewed by me for my fanzine. He laughed and said, "Well, to be honest, I would very much like to be in a horror film. I just haven't been asked."

I pointed out that he should have solicited advice from Christopher Lee when they were working together on *The Three Musketeers* and *The Four Musketeers: Milady's Revenge.* "You're right, I should have," Michael replied. "I adored working with Christopher Lee and I'm a big fan of his Hammer films."

I knew that Michael was a member of the all-star cast for the forthcoming production of Agatha Christie's *Murder on the Orient Express* (Royal World Premiere, November 21, 1974), directed by Sidney Lumet, also starring Albert Finney, Ingrid Bergman, Sean Connery, Lauren Bacall, Anthony Perkins, Vanessa Redgrave, Richard Widmark, Jacqueline Bisset, Wendy Hiller, Martin Balsam, Rachel Roberts and Sir John Gielgud (who also had a cameo role in *Frankenstein: The True Story*). I asked Michael how the shooting had gone. He replied,

"Marvelously. In fact, all the studio work was done right here at Elstree. We just wrapped in May."

After dessert, Margaret and Michael invited me to come with them to the set of *Great Expectations* and watch the afternoon shooting. It didn't take the slightest bit of arm-twisting. With a twinkle in her eye, she asked Michael to set up three director's chairs on the edge of Miss Havisham's dining room set – one for each of us. Margaret took her place in the center chair so she would be flanked by me and Michael.

As luck would have it, the scene they were shooting was the pivotal and terrifying moment when Miss Havisham's musty old wedding dress catches on fire and Pip must heroically put out the flames. Enthralled, I watched Margaret play the scene up until the moment of the fire. Then, a stunt woman, dressed identically, stepped in and Margaret sat next to me, gripping my arm in suspense, as the double's dress went up in flames.

Michael also had a stunt-double on standby, wearing the exact same costume, but he insisted on doing his own stunt work – rushing in to try to smother the growing inferno with his overcoat and a throw rug. It was all tightly controlled and safely done – but unnerving, nonetheless.

Margaret whispered to me, "Michael likes you. He's showing off by doing that stunt himself."

The main wide shot was extremely frightening as the seated stunt woman went up in more flames than imaginable – and once Michael York smothered most of the flames out with the coat and rug, we all watched in horror as a remnant ember of the fire ignited anew on the floor, just underneath the edge of the rug at Michael's feet. Firemen raced into the shot with extinguishers and blasted the fire out. But they kept the footage in the movie right up until the firemen entered the scene – so, if you watch closely, you can see those unplanned flames dangerously licking at Michael's feet.

THE INTERVIEW

SAM IRVIN: When did you get started in films?
MARGARET LEIGHTON: Around 1947 or 1948. I had previously done much work on stage. I started acting when I was 15 years old. The first film I ever did was called *Bonnie Prince Charlie* (1948) with David Niven; and then I did *The Winslow Boy* (1948) with Robert Donat. I did many *many* more. There were *so* many in those days that I forget. My most famous films over the years have been *Under Capricorn* for Hitchcock, *The Astonished Heart*, *The Elusive Pimpernel* with David Niven again, *The Waltz of the Toreadors*, *The Third Street*, *The Madwoman of Chaillot*, *The Go-Between*, and *Lady Caroline Lamb*. I, of course, did a lot of stage work all during my film career. I have been in such plays as *The Cocktail Party*, *Three Sisters*, *Night of the Iguana* and I did a television production of *Hamlet* with Richard Chamberlain in the lead. I played "Gertrude."

SAM: Have you won awards?
MARGARET: Yes. I was voted Best Actress for *The Night of the Iguana* in the Antoinette Perry Awards [aka the Tony Awards]. Variety Club of Great Britain gave me an award for Best Actress in Theatre for my performance in *Antony and Cleopatra*. I was nominated for an Academy Award for *The Go-Between*, which I lost. And I have received several others like the award your magazine is giving me this year. Very recently I was honored by the Queen with the C.B.E. award.

Stromberg & Leighton.

Leighton in opera house costume.

This Picture and Right: Stromberg playing around with Leighton's scarf and wrapping it around himself.

SAM: Please explain to my American readers what the C.B.E. award is.
MARGARET: It means Commander of the British Empire and the initials becomes part of my name: "Margaret Leighton C.B.E."

SAM: How were you cast in *Frankenstein: The True Story*?
MARGARET: My husband Michael Wilding was in it. In fact, a lot of friends of mine were in it. A bunch of us were having dinner together and the producer [Hunt Stromberg Jr.] said, "Why don't you come and play something in it?" I said, "Yes, certainly I will." Well, there was this small part for a French woman, and I played it. That is all that happened. I really did not think they were serious when they asked me to do it. But they were serious, and I rather enjoyed it. It was great fun.

SAM: When you agreed to be in *Frankenstein: The True Story*, did they expand your part at all?

MARGARET: Yes. The part at the opera was in the original script. It was a very important role, fundamental to the development of the story. The producer Hunt Stromberg Jr. came to me and told me that the film would be shown in America in two parts on television. He said that he would hate to see me only in one part of the film. He wanted to put me in both parts so that audiences could see me both nights. So, they added in my favorite part at the ball when I come dressed up as Little Bo Peep. I like the Little Bo Peep bit the best. That was very funny.

[NOTE: With the Writers' Strike ongoing (March 6-June 24, 1973), Stromberg took it upon himself to write the Little Bo Peep bit – inspired by the masquerade ball that had originally been scripted but had evolved into a formal dance. The handsome aristocrat (Julian Barnes) – who had been courting Prima – greets the Countess at the door and they discuss the dilemma of her costume while she

Leighton in Bo Peep costume at ball.

undresses the young man with her roving peepers.]

SAM: Your character seems quite flirtatious in both scenes – with Leonard Whiting and Michael Sarrazin at the opera, and, later, with the handsome young aristocrat (Julian Barnes) at the ball.
MARGARET: (with a flirtatious smile and twinkle in her eye) Flirt or not, the foreign lady is still a lady.

SAM: How many days did it take to film your part in *Frankenstein: The True Story*?
MARGARET: It was about a day for each of the two bits I did.

[NOTE: Leighton's two days on *Frankenstein: The True Story* were: May 22, 1973 (the Bo Peep scene), and June 2, 1973 (the opera intermission).]

CHAPTER ELEVEN: MARGARET LEIGHTON

Michael Wilding and his real-life wife Margaret Leighton (in Bo Peep costume) during a break shooting the ballroom sequence.

SAM: Did you visit the set when your husband Michael Wilding was shooting his scenes.

MARGARET: I did not come to the set to visit. I was only there for filming my own scenes. My husband might have sometimes brought people home for a drink after a day of shooting.

[NOTE: Immediately following *Frankenstein: The True Story*, Leighton accepted the offer to play Madame Orloff, the eccentric clairvoyant, in Amicus Productions' anthology film *From Beyond the Grave* which began filming at Shepperton Studios on June 4, 1973.]

SAM: After *Frankenstein: The True Story*, you went on to

appear in another horror film called *From Beyond the Grave*? What did you think of that?

MARGARET: Oh, I enjoyed doing that very much indeed. I read the whole script and thought that the third segment, "The Elemental" – and, in fact, the character that I chose to play Madame Orloff – was the most amusing of them all. I was also intrigued by the last tale about the door where the closet would change into that great room. I enjoyed reading that very much.

SAM: Were you approached by the producers Max Rosenberg and Milton Subotsky, the heads of Amicus Productions, to be in *From Beyond the Grave*?

MARGARET: I don't know who wanted me to be in that picture. My agent just rang me up and said that they wanted me for it.

SAM: Did you meet Peter Cushing on *From Beyond the Grave*?

MARGARET: No. All of his scenes were in the antique shop. We had nothing together. But I have met Peter before. He is a charming man. Very nice.

SAM: What did you think of the other stars of that film that you met?

MARGARET: I thought Ian Carmichael was really good and so was Nyree Dawn Porter. Nyree told me that she had done another one of these horror films where they have four or five tales. I forget the name of the one she did, but I know the title was absolutely hilarious. The titles they think up are unbelievable!

SAM: That film would be *The House That Dripped Blood*.
MARGARET (laughs): Yes! That's it. Don't you think that is the most hilarious title? I almost died when she told me!

SAM (laughs): I agree – and it certainly is memorable.

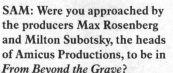
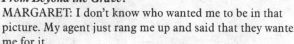

Leighton on paperback book of *From Beyond the Grave*.

Leighton and Elizabeth Taylor in *X, Y and Zee* (1972). Leighton's real-life husband Michael Wilding had previously been married to Taylor!

Ian Carmichael and Margaret Leighton in *From Beyond the Grave*.

Michael Wilding drops by set of *Great Expectations* to drive wife Margaret Leighton home. Photo taken by Sam Irvin the day he visited the set.

MICHAEL YORK (interjecting): I hate to cut this short, but I think it is time for us to be back at the set.

SAM: Oh, goodness. I don't want you to be late because of me! I've got all I need. Thank you very much for answering these questions.

POSTSCRIPT

At the end of the day, Margaret Leighton's husband dropped by the set to pick her up and drive her home. He was actor Michael Wilding – who played Elizabeth Frankenstein's father in *Frankenstein: The True Story* but was perhaps best known as one of Elizabeth Taylor's former husbands. This was such an unexpected treat. I hadn't counted on meeting *two* stars of *Frankenstein: The True Story* that day. I was thrilled to meet him.

Wilding told me about his friendship with *Frankenstein: The True Story* producer Hunt Stromberg Jr. and how he had bumped into him in London and was offered the part on the spot.

Then, Leighton and Wilding politely said their goodbyes and off they went. After Michael York very kindly drove me to the train station, I was pinching myself all the way back to London, in awe of my good fortune.

This glorious day in 1974 would not be the last time I saw Margaret. The following summer of 1975, we would meet up again backstage at *A Family and a Fortune* on the West End – and, astonishingly, she would introduce me to yet another star of *Frankenstein: The True Story*: Nicola Pagett. [See Chapter 10 for my interview with Pagett.]

Margaret went on to star in two more movies: Joseph Losey's *Galileo* (1975) with Topol, Edward Fox, Sir John Gielgud, Michael Gough, Patrick Magee and Madeline Smith; and Kevin Connor's *A Dirty Knight's Work* aka *Trial by Combat* aka *Choice of Weapons* (1976) co-starring Sir John Mills, Peter Cushing, Donald Pleasence and Barbara Hershey.

Seven months after I last saw Margaret, she died of multiple sclerosis on January 13, 1976, at the age of just 53. She was survived by her husband Michael Wilding.

I should note that Wilding, was quite raspy that day in 1974, as though he were recovering from laryngitis. I later found out he was suffering from a disorder that impaired his vocal cords. In fact, his dialogue in *Frankenstein: The True Story* had to be post-dubbed by Robert Rietty, known in the business as "the man with a thousand voices." Rietty dubbed many characters in James Bond pictures, including the entire role of the main villain, Largo, in *Thunderball* because Adolfo Celi's Italian accent was too thick. Wilding was also afflicted with lifelong epilepsy which was worsening as he got older. Sadly, *Frankenstein: The True Story* would turn out to be his final screen appearance. He died in 1979 from a fall caused by an epileptic seizure.

CHAPTER 12
JULIAN BARNES

Julian Barnes was born November 8, 1949, in London. "My stepfather Kenneth Shipman owned Twickenham Studios," Barnes explained, "so I grew up during my teenage years tripping over cables and trying not to get in the way. Both the Beatles' films, *A Hard Day's Night* and *Help!*, were made there and I got to watch some of the filming of those." Becoming a professional actor in 1968, Barnes has divided his time between theatre, films and television ever since. He spent a year at the Royal Shakespeare Company with Sir Ian McKellen. Eventually, in 1981, he relocated to the United States and continued his acting career in Hollywood.

Barnes cuts in between Whiting & Seymour for a dance.

Seymour & Barnes dance at ball.

His many film credits include *Horror House*, *The Devil's Widow* aka *Tam Lin*, *The Rocketeer*, *Mars Attacks!* and *Pacific Rim*.

In *Frankenstein: The True Story*, Julian plays the wealthy son of a baronet who first spots Prima (Jane Seymour) at a church service, then dances with her at her debutante ball. He also greets Dowager Countess Françoise Duval (Margaret Leighton) when she shows up at the ball in costume as Little Bo Peep.

The following interview was conducted by phone on May 9, 2015.

THE INTERVIEW
SAM IRVIN: What can you tell me about your experience

appearing in *Frankenstein: The True Story*?
JULIAN BARNES: I don't want to contradict Stanislavski who said, "There are no small parts, only small actors," but let's be realistic. I had a relatively small part. (laughs) Nevertheless, I have a few memories that might be of interest. In the scene at the ball when Margaret Leighton shows up in costume as Little Bo Peep, I have a few lines with her in the doorway. Well, she was not a young woman by then and she was a little unsteady and maybe a little nervous. I remember helping to steady her and sort of being her "rock" in that scene.

Barnes & Margaret Leighton (dressed as Bo Peep) in ballroom.

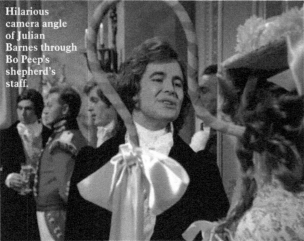

Hilarious camera angle of Julian Barnes through Bo Peep's shepherd's staff.

SAM: When I met Leighton in 1974 on the set of *Great Expectations***, she was not terribly mobile. In fact, her role as Miss Havisham was mostly done in a chair. Between set ups, Michael York was her "rock," helping her to her chair on the sidelines.**

JULIAN: That's exactly what I mean. She had a pretty good grip on my arm as we entered the ballroom. I could tell she needed me to steady her, so I did.

SAM: Her husband Michael Wilding was also in the movie – and was in the ballroom scenes as well.

JULIAN: Yes, I remember him hovering about, making sure that she was okay.

SAM: What else do you recall?

JULIAN: My strongest memory is learning about Watergate. (laughs) Between set ups for the ballroom sequence, James Mason would hold court with all the other movie stars in the scene. The actors sat in this circle around him and James – in his very distinctive timbre – would read the articles from the *Herald Tribune* about the Watergate scandal, from start to finish. (laughs) So, there I sat, along with this amazing cast, being educated about Watergate by James Mason. It was wonderful.

SAM: How did you get the part in the movie?

JULIAN: I first met the producer Hunt Stromberg Jr. socially through Allan Warren, an actor chum of mine who happened to be gay. Allan was very social and he knew a lot of celebrities – like Judy Garland, Liberace and Noël Coward. He became a very famous photographer. But anyway,

Stromberg must have fancied me because I was summoned to audition for the role in *Frankenstein*.

SAM: I assume you are aware that Hunt Stromberg Jr. was gay.

JULIAN: Yes, of course. I was going to mention that in as tactful a way as possible, but you beat me to it.

SAM: And, for the record, I assume you are straight.

JULIAN: Yes. I married a very sweet girl from Wisconsin in 1992. I was 42 at the time. Never had any kids. I've maintained the gypsy life of an actor. But, of course, I've always been around gay people and I'm completely open-minded about all that. I've always had many close friends who are gay.

SAM: Great. It makes this situation with Stromberg all the more amusing. So, when you got this invitation to audition for his movie, did you get the impression he might be a little bit smitten with you?

JULIAN: Well, you see, when I was twenty-three, I got all kinds of offers, Sam. (laughs) But Hunt was a gentleman. All strictly business. Luckily, I kept my date book from that time, and I can give you a few specifics. I auditioned for Hunt and the director Jack Smight on February 6, 1973, at 139 Piccadilly. At 2:35 in the afternoon.

SAM: Wow. That *is* specific. 139 Piccadilly was the headquarters of Universal – and, by the way, the former house of Lord Byron.

JULIAN: What a curious coincidence. Then I saw them again at that same office the following Friday, February 9, at noon. A "call back." Then they officially offered me the part. The next notation I have is on April 4 – "One day, *Dr. Frankenstein*."

SAM: According to the call sheet, that was the day you shot the church service sequence at St. Mary the Virgin Church in Hambleden. Jane Seymour is standing at a pew in the front of the church with Clarissa Kaye and Michael Wilding. Leonard Whiting and Nicola Pagett are in the pew behind her. You are across the aisle, in the front row, observing Jane, obviously enamored with her from afar. Patricia Varley is standing next to you, playing your mother.

JULIAN: Yes, that's exactly right. It was very straight forward. Nothing unusual comes to mind. Then, at the top of

In church, while singing a hymn, Julian Barnes flirts with Seymour as his mother (Patricia Varley) glances over.

the page for the week of April 23, I've made a note to myself that reads: "Call Hunt Stromberg." And then, on Friday, April 27, it reads: "Lunch at Pinewood." I had lunch with Hunt that day.

SAM: One of the things Stromberg probably wanted to talk to you about was expanding your role at the ball. He had just written a new scene for Margaret Leighton to show up at the party under the misconception that it is a costume ball. So, she's dressed as Little Bo Peep. He wrote you into that scene as the gentleman who greets her at the door and tries to comfort her during her embarrassment.
JULIAN: Yes, I do remember he added extra bits for me. It was very nice of him. Then, we jump ahead to May 17 and 18 – "dance rehearsals at Pinewood Studios [in the Band Room] for *Dr. Frankenstein* with Jane Seymour." [Production reports indicate that Barnes also rehearsed with Seymour on May 10.] I had to learn how to do the waltz properly. We had a choreographer named Sally Gilpin. Then, the following week, Monday, May the 21st through Friday the 25th, we filmed the ballroom sequence.

SAM: Did you get to know Jane Seymour well?
JULIAN: Actually, Jane and I ran in the same social circle for a while. There were several sons of famous people in that social circle. I used to call them "the sons of 'names.'" There was Sir Donald Sinden's son Jeremy. Peter Bridge, who was a very successful theatre impresario at the time, had a son named Andrew [three-time Tony Award winning lighting designer for *Phantom of the Opera*, *Fosse*, and *Sunset Boulevard*]. And then I was also a friend of Michael Attenborough, son of Lord Richard Attenborough. Jane and Michael were married back then. [Seymour was married to Michael Attenborough from 1971 to 1976.]

SAM: What do you recall about the director Jack Smight?
JULIAN: I remember him being quite energetic and very amenable. Never abrasive or anything of that nature. He just seemed to be very efficient. I always appreciate that in a director.

SAM: Did you get to know Leonard Whiting?

Frankie Avalon & Julian Barnes, *Horror House*.

CHAPTER TWELVE: JULIAN BARNES

JULIAN: Yes. We ran with the same crowd for a while. And I ran into Lenny years later and we had a laugh. I remember sharing a pint with him and, you know, exchanging stories. It was a riot. We talked about Franco Zeffirelli who, as you know, had directed Lenny in *Romeo and Juliet*.

SAM: I discovered in my research that Zeffirelli was Hunt Stromberg Jr.'s first choice to direct *Frankenstein: The True Story*. How did you know Zeffirelli?
JULIAN: When Zeffirelli was auditioning actors for *Brother Sun, Sister Moon*, I was summoned to an office behind the Dorchester and, as I walked in, there was Franco's casting director – and later his producer – Dyson Lovell. Dyson looked like Bob Guccione of *Penthouse* magazine fame. He had his shirt open to his waist and bunches of gold chains around his neck. He leaned back in his chair, looked me up and down, and finally said, "Where were you when we were casting Romeo?" (laughs) My agent had given me a heads up about Mr. Zeffirelli's preferences and, after this opening comment, it appeared to me that Mr. Lovell might be gay as well. The "gay Bob Guccione." So anyway, I was sort of on guard a little bit. And his next line was, "You *must* meet Franco." I walked into a huge conference room and there was Franco sitting at the end of the table and he said, "Sit down," and he asked me a few questions. He had a still photographer with him at the time and he had him take some pictures of me. Then Franco stood up, took the camera and took a few pictures himself. He said, "Oh, Julian. I'd like to do a session with you in the park." He was staying at what was then the Carlton, on Sloan Street. So, at a later date, we went down into the park and he took some more pictures. It got a little bit obsessive. (laughs) I remember him saying, "Oh, Julian, you look so pale. Come to Italy and let me put some color in your cheeks." And, of course, I'm thinking to myself, "Which cheeks, dear?" (laughs) Bruce Robinson who wrote the screenplay of *The Killing Fields* and directed *Withnail & I*, is also an actor and he played Benvolio in *Romeo and Juliet*. When we got to talking about our experiences with Zeffirelli, he said, "Julian, you have no idea. Because I wouldn't play around with him, he made my life an absolute misery on that film."

SAM: Did you meet Bruce Robinson on *The Devil's Widow* aka *Tam Lin*?

Color lobby card *The Haunted House of Horror*, aka *Horror House*.

JULIAN: Yes. The cast was pretty astonishing – starting with Ava Gardner. Aside from being a ravishing older woman with *enormous* poise and grace, she was an absolute sweetheart. Sinéad Cusack – you know, Jeremy Irons' wife. Ian McShane, who was arguably one of the greatest joke tellers I've ever met. Joanna Lumley who is just sublime. There's a famous classical guitarist called Julian Bream – and, from the very first day we met, Joanna decided that she was just gonna call me "Bream." I have no idea why, but it was her own special nickname for me. Then there was Stephanie Beacham who was right up there with the Julie Christies of the world. A world-class beauty. Stephanie and I became good friends. In fact, I got married to my sweet girl from Wisconsin in Stephanie's house in Malibu. Jenny Hanley became a pal and we'd go for rides in her sports car. And last, but not least, Madeline Smith. An absolute sweetheart. She was ethereal, like an angel. With those amazing eyes.

SAM: You were also in *Horror House*.
JULIAN: Yes. Frankie Avalon, Jill Haworth, myself, Richard O'Sullivan, Mark Wynter, who was kind of a pop star at the time, and, of course, the great Dennis Price. It was filmed in the deserted Birkdale Palace Hotel in Southport, Lancashire. It was pretty weird. Apparently, when the hotel was about to be built, the architect left the design plans with the builders, then went away to do some other job. He came back only to discover that his hotel had been built the wrong way around. The front entrance was supposed to face the sea. Instead, it faced inland. He was so distraught, he went to the top of the hotel and threw himself off. Well, of course, there were legends that the architect haunted the place. So, naturally, to save money, the production had us all staying there – in this obviously haunted hotel. None of us were very happy about that.

SAM: Shortly after *Frankenstein: The True Story*, you were the top-billed star in *Mistress Pamela*.
JULIAN: It was a bawdy costume romp in the vein of *Tom Jones*. I was supposed to be the next Albert Finney – but lightning didn't strike twice. It looked very expensive, though, thanks to our director of photography – the great Arthur Ibbetson whom I had just met on *Frankenstein: The True Story*. He'd been Oscar-nominated for *Anne of a Thousand Days*.

SAM: Since then, you have appeared in many big studio films, like your role as Charlie, the movie actor, in *The Rocketeer* starring Bill Campbell.
JULIAN: That film was a lot of fun to make. I remember Bill being an absolutely charming young man. He was great.

SAM: Yes, I couldn't agree more. I was lucky enough to direct Bill in a sci-fi comedy for Showtime called *Out There*. You were also in Tim Burton's *Mars Attacks!* What did you do in that?
JULIAN: I was the White House waiter in that one. I walk into a bedroom and and it's the President's daughter in bed. I'm bringing her pizza under a sterling silver dome cloche. And then I think I die shortly thereafter. (laughs) A woman came up to me and said, "You realize who is playing the President's daughter in your scene, don't you?" I said, "No." She said, "That's Natalie Portman." I went, "Really?" (laughs) Unbelievable. I was very embarrassed I hadn't recognized her.

SAM: You were the "British UN Representative" in Guillermo del Toro's *Pacific Rim*. What was that like?
JULIAN: Oh, that was terrific. Guillermo was such a nice man.

Barnes brings pizza to Natalie Portman in *Mars Attacks*.

Barnes in *Mistress Pamela*.

Barnes in Guillermo del Toro's *Pacific Rim*.

Sam & Barnes, follow-up interview 2015.

SAM: Del Toro is a huge fan of *Frankenstein: The True Story*, by the way. He called it "quirky, brilliant and moving."

JULIAN: Really? That's nice to hear. I should have brought it up. I'm sure he had no idea I'd been in it.

POSTSCRIPT

On June 18, 2017, Julian Barnes graciously agreed to be on my Q&A panel at Taylor White's former Creature Features Store & Gallery in Burbank for the publication celebration of *Little Shoppe of Horrors* No. 38 devoted to *Frankenstein: The True Story*. He was still acting at the time, particularly his recurring role as "Harold the Butler" on the soap opera *Days of Our Lives* (78 episodes, 1992-2018). I spoke to Julian by phone in May 2023 and, at the age of 73, he is now mostly retired from acting but doing well. He was very happy to hear about this book to celebrate the 50th Anniversary of *Frankenstein: The True Story* and sends his best wishes to all the fans of the film.

Sam & Barnes, June 18, 2017, for FTTS celebration panel at Creature Features.

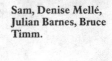

Sam, Denise Mellé, Julian Barnes, Bruce Timm.

Comic strip art by Neil D Vokes; lettering by Nick Nix; color by Matt Webb.

CHAPTER 13
DAVID BOYCE
THE THUG WHO GOT CUT

"What about Neil Diamond?" producer Hunt Stromberg Jr. postulated. "He'd be perfect for the leader of the thugs."

Director Jack Smight and casting director Sally Nicholl glanced at each other, wondering if it was finally time to have Stromberg taken away in a straitjacket.

"No, I'm serious!" Stromberg implored. "I met Neil backstage last year at one of his concerts and he told me he wants to get into movies. So, here's his chance!"

What could this possibly have to do with *Frankenstein: The True Story*, you ask? Well, in May 1973, two months after the film had been shooting, the decision had been made to eliminate several action sequences due to budgetary and running time concerns. Stromberg's boyfriend Jacque Shelton, a former stuntman by trade, who was working on the film as Assistant to the Producer, voiced his opinion that the movie was becoming too talky, with not enough excitement. Shelton had a point – and Stromberg agreed.

Due to the ongoing Writers' Strike (March 6-June 24, 1973), screenwriters Christopher Isherwood and Don Bachardy could not help remedy the situation, so Stromberg took it upon himself to write a new sequence (revision pages dated May 10, 1973) that would be inserted when the Creature decides to go back to the Opera House to see *Marriage of Figaro* once more:

110 EXT. THEATRE – NIGHT
We see a sign that says "No Performance Tonight." The Creature reads it but apparently either ignores it or doesn't understand it. He is intent upon hearing Figaro music again and begins banging the entrance door. When no-one appears, his *frustrations* become more intense. It is by now late at night and the streets apparently are deserted.

Across the street, three Thugs suddenly loom up near a streetlamp. They cannot see the Creature's face, but of course they can see that he appears to be an expensively dressed gentleman.

FIRST THUG (with ominous interest): Look over there!

SECOND THUG: Must be a right rich bloke!

THIRD THUG (menacingly): And all *alone*.

FIRST THUG: Let's go.

They stealthily move off to begin to surround the Creature. Two of the thugs have coshes (dangerous looking clubs). The Third Thug has a mean looking dagger.

The Creature, by now starting to leave the theatre and even more frustrated, is suddenly pounced upon by the Thugs.

At this precise moment Victor appears, and sees what is happening. He starts to run toward the Creature to offer help against the Thugs. But before Victor can get there the Creature has sprung into action, after first being clubbed on the head by the two thugs behind him. (The clubbing has no effect on him whatsoever).

The Third Thug with the dagger appears in front of the Creature and sees its face. The Thug freezes in terror at the sight he sees.

What follows is a *spectacular* and *terrifying* fight.

The Creature lifts one of the Thugs (the one in front of him, with the dagger) into the air and slings him through the glass door of the theatre entrance.

Then it grabs the other two Thugs, one in each of its arms, and crashes their heads together, either killing them or certainly rendering them totally unconscious.

Victor is helpless to do anything about the situation. He can only watch with dismay.

When the melee is over the Creature, now completely calm having vented his frustrations, turns woefully to Victor.

CREATURE (sadly): No Figaro?

VICTOR: Come. We must leave here before anyone arrives. Mrs. Blair is dead – (indicating bodies of three Thugs, sadly) and now this.

The Creature looks forlornly at Victor.

VICTOR: I know it wasn't your fault.

As Victor leads the Creature away, he looks back sadly at the theatre.

Although the sequence never made it into the final cut of the film, it turns out that it was actually shot, albeit simplified from the original concept. Always reaching for

Prop poster for *Marriage of Figaro* were plastered on the wall of this stage door alley of the Opera House.

Stromberg and Sarrazin (in early-deterioration make-up and tuxedo with white gloves) on the exterior backlot set at Pinewood Studios that was dressed to look like the rear alley stage door entrance to the Opera House. This is where Dr. Frankenstein (Whiting) finds the Creature (Sarrazin) dressed in formal attire, trying to attend the opera again. The thug scene took place in this same alley but was cut from the final film.

THE EPIC SAGA BEHIND *FRANKENSTEIN: THE TRUE STORY*

Series of shots that made it into the film that show off the set where the cut thug scene took place: Sarrazin in alley headed to the stage door area.

Sarrazin arriving at the stage door area. Note sign over door "STAGE DOOR" and poster on the wall for *Marriage of Figaro*.

Sarrazin turns to face camera.

Whiting arriving from alley, looking for Sarrazin.

Sarrazin and Whiting come together to talk by the stage door.

Neil Diamond & Lord Laurence Olivier in *The Jazz Singer*.

the moon, Stromberg did indeed offer the role of Thug 1 to 32-year-old Neil Diamond – which the entertainer promptly turned down. As bonkers as this sounds, Diamond was genuinely trying to break into movies. Three years later, he was the frontrunner to star in Martin Scorsese's *Taxi Driver* (1976) until Robert De Niro nabbed the role. Diamond finally landed his first and only movie role-to-date in *The Jazz Singer* (1980) for which he was paid $3.5 million, the highest sum ever paid for an acting debut – and his co-star was Lord Laurence Olivier, no less.

Back on planet Earth, Sally Nicholl dutifully set up an audition for non-superstars to try out as thugs. One of the candidates was gay actor David

Boyce, 28, the former drummer for the Roadrunners (August 1962-August 1965), the Liverpool rhythm and blues band that famously played the Cavern Club in 1963 with the Beatles. George Harrison once stated that the Rolling Stones were "almost as good as the Roadrunners." Boyce and his mates may have been a wee bit outdistanced by the Beatles and the Stones, but they are fondly remembered today as one of the best bands to emerge from Liverpool during that era. Once the group disbanded, Boyce put aside his drumsticks to study acting at the Rose Bruford College of Theatre and Performance. The following interview with Boyce was conducted in January and March 2016.

CHAPTER THIRTEEN: DAVID BOYCE: THE THUG WHO GOT CUT

Above: The Roadrunners, David Boyce (far left).
Right: The Roadrunners with Little Richard; David Boyce (second from left).

Headshot of David Boyce, 1972. (Photos by Rosalind Mann)

THE INTERVIEW

SAM IRVIN: Had you auditioned for any movies prior to *Frankenstein: The True Story?*

DAVID BOYCE: No. It was the first movie casting I had been to. Having left drama school at the end of the summer term 1972, I spent a season doing badly-paid – but artistically satisfying – repertory work at the Crucible Theatre in Sheffield until May 1973. The casting for *Frankenstein* came up right after that in June. It was a cattle market job out at Pinewood Studios. I remember the day very well. It was unusually hot. I was pretty broke and the tube fare from my shared house in Chelsea to Uxbridge nearly cleaned me out so I had to walk the three-and-a-half miles from the station to Pinewood. Can you believe that in those days young broke actors could live in Chelsea on social security? We lived a couple of doors down from David Bowie in Oakley Street.

SAM: But you made it to the casting on time?

DAVID: Yes. I arrived sweaty and grumpy only to be herded into a small room with about twenty other actors. Enter Stromberg and Smight. They silently walked up and down the line, staring at us in turn. After a long pause, Stromberg

– in thick American accent – said, "OK guys, I want ya to say sumt'n so I can hear your accents." Stunned silence. My anger broke through and, in rather grand Shakespearean tones, I shouted, "My name is David Boyce and it took me a very long time to get here this afternoon." Emboldened by my interjection, some of the others introduced themselves. Without comment, Stromberg and Smight left the room and I walked and tubed my way home. The next day I got a call from my agent telling me that I'd been offered the job. Some pages arrived which contained cod cockney dialogue along the lines of – Thug 1: "Gor blimey 'e looks like a right rich bloke." Thug 2: "Yer let's do 'im." Didn't sound very Christopher Isherwood to me. More Dick Van Dyke in *Mary Poppins*. But, what the hell. I was skint and it was a Hollywood movie.

SAM: Then what happened?

DAVID: About a week later we shot the scene, day-for-night, on an exterior set on the Pinewood backlot which looked as though it had been left over from a Mexican Western. The director introduced me to Michael Sarrazin who was very polite. A big deal was made about how I was never to refer to Sarrazin as "The Monster" but always "The Creature"

David Boyce on stage in *Hamlet*.

David Boyce on stage in *Bertolt Brecht*.

Headshot of David Boyce, 1972.
(Photos by Rosalind Mann)

David Boyce as Og in *Blake's 7*

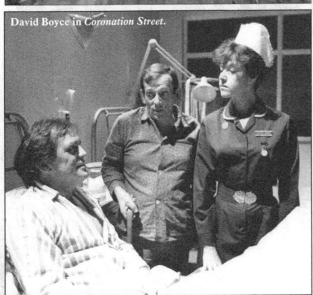

David Boyce in *Coronation Street*.

David Boyce as the Clown in *The Rainbow Thief*.

David Boyce as the Clown in *The Rainbow Thief*.

Christopher Lee in *The Rainbow Thief*.

which seemed somewhat pedantic as the denouement of our little scene was me hitting him over the head with a bottle; he revealing to me his hitherto hidden features; and, my running away screaming in terror. And here again, there was a disconnect because, in fact, he looked rather attractive.

SAM: The call sheet for June 25, 1973, lists you and two other actors as the thugs – 31-year-old Michael Da Costa (*Steptoe and Son*) and 22-year-old Michael Wennink (*Davy Jones' Locker*).
DAVID: I remember Michael Da Costa, a Mediterranean-looking cove, who, unlike me, seemed to know his way around. He also seemed determined to try to corpse me by whispering camp obscenities into my ear whilst we were doing our day-for-night, nosing about, lurking acting. Remember, this was my first time on a film set and I didn't know a long shot from a hole in the ground. The Rose Bruford College had only prepared its students for a life in THE THEATAH, DAHLING!

SAM: Was there a coordinator for the stunt?
DAVID: Yes. The producer's boyfriend instructed me on how to smash the fake bottle over Sarrazin's head. We blocked the scene, ran through it a couple of times without breaking the candy-glass bottle, then shot a master. Sarrazin had no lines so all he had to do was approach a door – looking very elegant in a high-collared evening cape which obscured his face. Da Costa, Wennink and I crept up on him, I broke the bottle over his head, at which point Sarrazin turned to face me, unhurt. I screamed and ran away. One take. Then they shot a close up of Sarrazin's turn, after which he left the set. Then they did a three-shot of Da Costa, Wennink and me delivering our introductory dialogue, and it was all over. My travelling expenses were paid, and they provided a car to drive me back to London.

SAM: Did you continue your acting career after that?
DAVID: Yes. I also did a lot of theatre and TV – like Og in *Blake's 7*. My favorite movie role was playing the Clown in *The Rainbow Thief* starring Peter O'Toole, Omar Sharif and Christopher Lee. By 1997, thanks to a small inheritance, I went back to the north of England, where I came from, settled in a little village close enough to Liverpool so I could study philosophy at the University – and play drums in a semi-pro blues band, just for fun.

POSTSCRIPT

For more on David Boyce's years as the drummer for the Roadrunners, read his account at http://sixtiescity.net/LRR/runners.htm

Sarrazin as the Creature, early stage of deterioration.

THE EPIC SAGA BEHIND *FRANKENSTEIN: THE TRUE STORY*

PART THREE
INTERVIEWS
WITH THE
CREATIVE TEAM

BIZARRE

FRANKENSTEIN

YWOOD   Don Bachardy

CHAPTER 14
CO-SCREENWRITER
DON BACHARDY

Born May 18, 1934, in Los Angeles, portrait artist Don Bachardy met British novelist Christopher Isherwood on Valentine's Day 1953 and instantly became lovers. Bachardy was 18 and Isherwood was 48. They remained together 33 years until Isherwood's death in 1986. Bachardy still lives and conducts portrait sittings in the home they shared in Santa Monica overlooking the Pacific.

Bachardy studied at the Chouinard Art Institute in Los Angeles and the Slade School of Art in London. His first one-man exhibition was held in October 1961 at the Redfern Gallery in London, with subsequent one-man exhibitions in Los Angeles, San Francisco, Seattle, Houston and New York.

His portraits can be found in the permanent collections of the Metropolitan Museum of Art in New York, Harvard University, Princeton University, the Smithsonian Institute, the National Portrait Gallery in London, among many other major institutions. Bachardy painted the official gubernatorial portrait of Jerry Brown that hangs in the California State Capitol Museum.

Eight coffee-table books have been published of his work, the most recent of which was *Hollywood* (Glitterati Inc., 2014) with over 300 portraits culled from six decades of sittings with famous actors, directors and writers, featuring forewords by Armistead Maupin and Tom Ford.

His notoriety as a portrait artist landed him a gig on Bryan Forbes' *The Stepford Wives* (1975), based on the Ira Levin novel. In the movie, William Prince plays an artist who draws portraits of Katharine Ross and Tina Louise. What you see in the film are Bachardy's illustrations – and it is Bachardy's hands, doubling for Prince, in the insert shots (filmed in June 1974).

Bachardy made a cameo appearance in Tom Ford's *A Single Man* (2009) based on Isherwood's novel of the same name, starring Colin Firth (Oscar and Golden Globe nominee) and Julianne Moore (Golden Globe nominee). Bachardy portrays a professor in the teacher's lounge to whom Firth says "Hello, Don."

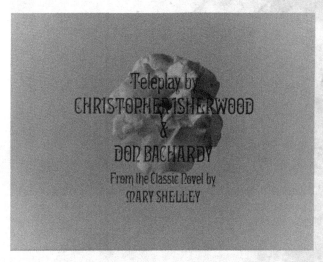

Two documentary films have been made about his life and work: *The Eyes of Don Bachardy* (2004) and *Chris & Don: A Love Story* (2007).

In 1968, Bachardy's first collaboration with Isherwood was on the stage play *A Meeting by the River* (based on Isherwood's 1967 novel) which had several tryout runs in New York, Los Angeles and London before finally opening on Broadway in 1979 at the Palace Theatre, starring Keith Baxter, Simon Ward and Sam Jaffe. Their screenplay adaptation of *A Meeting by the River* remains unproduced.

In 1969, Bachardy collaborated with Isherwood on the screenplay adaptation of *I, Claudius*, based on the 1934 novel by Robert Graves, for director Tony Richardson – but the project never got off the ground.

Opposite Page: Don Bachardy holding *Bizarre* No. 3. (Photo by Sam Irvin)

Original screenplay and published paperback script.

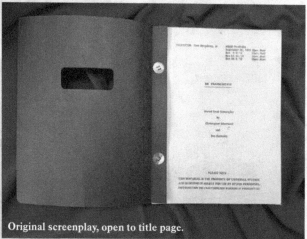

Original screenplay, open to title page.

Bachardy & Isherwood in the 1950s.

Isherwood posing for Bachardy.

Bachardy standing beside portrait of Isherwood.

Isherwood & Bachardy in the 1960s.

Chris & Don: A Love Story (2007) documentary; DVD box cover.

Isherwood portrait by Bachardy.

Bachardy self-portrait.

Above Top: From *Stepford Wives*: Katherine Ross by Don Bachardy. Above Center: Bachardy's hand on-screen drawing Katherine Ross. Above Bottom: Tina Louise by Don Bachardy.

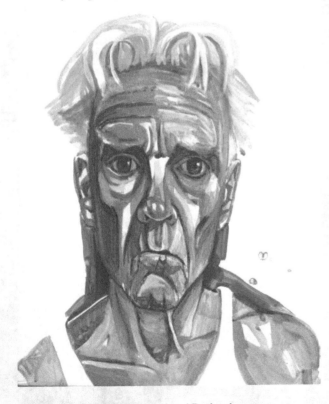

Bachardy in his art studio.

That same year, Isherwood and Bachardy wrote a treatment for the movie version of *Cabaret*, based on Isherwood's *The Berlin Stories* (1939). Ultimately, however, Jay Allen ended up writing the screenplay for the film.

For producer Hunt Stromberg Jr. on behalf of Universal Television, Bachardy collaborated with Isherwood on two teleplays: *Frankenstein: The True Story* (NBC, 1973) and *The Lady from the Land of the Dead*, the first draft of which was completed in March 1973 though it was never produced. (See Chapter 16 for my biography of Stromberg.)

In 1975, Bachardy collaborated again with Isherwood on *The Beautiful and Damned*, a teleplay adapted from the book by F. Scott Fitzgerald, to be produced for NBC by Douglas S. Cramer (*Wonder Woman*, *Love Boat*, *Dynasty*) and his then-companion Wilford "Bud" Lloyd Baumes (*Love Boat*) – though it was never made.

The following interview was conducted over the course of several sessions, from March 2015 through January 2016. A very special thanks goes to the late, great Mart Crowley, playwright of *Boys in the Band*, for introducing me to Don.

THE INTERVIEW

SAM IRVIN: How did the project of *Frankenstein: The True Story* come about? Whose idea was it?
DON BACHARDY: It originated with Hunt Stromberg Jr. He approached Chris to write the script – and Chris asked me to collaborate with him.

SAM: I understand that James Bridges (writer-director of *The Paper Chase*, *The China Syndrome*, *Urban Cowboy*) did a treatment for *Frankenstein* before you and Chris were hired.
DON: Yes. Jim was very generous about it. He said to Chris and me, "Use any part of it you like." But we didn't use any of it. Chris did not like it at all.

SAM: Bridges' longtime companion Jack Larson (Jimmy Olsen from TV's *The Adventures of Superman*) told me that Bridges' treatment was very faithful to Mary Shelley's book.
DON: That's right. I never read Mary Shelley's book until this project came up and, I must say, I was appalled. The book is totally undramatic. She never explains anything. How did it ever happen? From the very beginning, she sets up this mystery and then never answers any of the questions she raises. I was stunned. It was a very weak inspiration for us. We discarded almost all of it. Of course, the basic idea of a doctor reanimating a creature made of human body parts is hers, but we took much more inspiration from the James Whale movies *Frankenstein* and *Bride of Frankenstein*. Mostly, our script is original.

SAM: The title of your script was always *Dr. Frankenstein*. What did you and Chris think when NBC changed the title to *Frankenstein: The True Story*?
DON: Well, as soon as we heard it was going it be called *The True Story*, we were very upset. What's "true" about it? It's a total misrepresentation. Completely misleading. It wasn't a "true story" and it wasn't "true" to the Mary Shelley novel. So, it made absolutely no sense – and we were very angry about it. But we couldn't stop it.

SAM: On February 1, 1971 – two years before *Dr. Frankenstein* went into production – there was a front-page report in *Daily Variety* that read as follows: "*Frankenstein* will be telefilmed by producer Hunt Stromberg for Universal and NBC-TV, although there is a possibility the film – at least four hours long – will go into theatrical release first." You were already writing the first draft script at that time. Did you suspect it was going to be a two-part NBC-TV presentation?
DON: No. The original concept was to make a theatrical movie – at least that's what Stromberg told us, and I believe that's what he wanted as much as we did.

SAM: Did James Bridges want to direct the movie?
DON: In the early days, yes. Jim Bridges was interested in directing the movie. We would see Jim and Jack Larson

socially and talk about it. We were very good friends. And I remember our very first work on the *Frankenstein* script was with Jim in mind as the director. It was always easier for us to have a person to write for. And then, after Jim, it was John Boorman whom we both admired. He would have made a wonderful *Frankenstein* film. That was just right up his alley. His movies always looked so good. The production values were so good. We were friends of John Boorman. He read the script and loved it. He was very keen on directing it but Hunt Stromberg didn't want him. He was worried that he'd have no control over Boorman. Stromberg considered it his own project and he did not want to relinquish control to a powerful director. We were very disappointed when he dropped out of the *Frankenstein* project.

SAM: Do you also think that Stromberg was worried about the budget? Boorman would have been quite expensive, especially having just directed and produced *Deliverance* (1972) which had been Oscar-nominated for Best Director and Best Picture.
DON: No, I never heard Stromberg express concern about money. I don't think that was his reasoning at all. It was power. Boorman was too powerful at that time and Stromberg wanted to control everything.

SAM: Stromberg ended up hiring Jack Smight.
DON: Yes. We'd seen a couple of Smight's films, *Harper* and *No Way to Treat a Lady*, neither of which particularly impressed us. He was a very nice man. He treated us very kindly, with the utmost respect. He did the best he could. But he certainly did not have the capacity to stand up to Stromberg on any decision.

SAM: So, if this was originally intended to be a theatrical

John Boorman portrait by Bachardy, 1994.

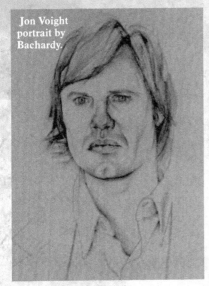
Jon Voight portrait by Bachardy.

release, did you and Chris write the script with a three-hour-plus running time in mind?
DON: Yes. We always envisioned the movie to be a three or four-hour epic, with a "roadshow" style theatrical release.

SAM: Regarding casting, is it true that Jon Voight was being considered for the role of Dr. Frankenstein?
DON: Yes. Chris and I loved Jon's work in *Midnight Cowboy* and, of course, he had just worked with Boorman in *Deliverance,* so we were all friends. Jon read it and was quite keen about the idea. I think he may have also thought about playing the Creature but, of course, that would have been up to Boorman and he agreed with us that Jon was perfect for Dr. Frankenstein. We've all remained friends ever since then and, coincidentally enough, I just had dinner a few nights ago [in March 2015] with John Boorman and Jon Voight.

SAM: Voight would have been interesting as Dr. Frankenstein but, at that time, he was a very big star and would have cost a lot of money. Stromberg would have had budget constraints to consider.
DON: Yes, but I don't think Voight would have done the film with Jack Smight directing. He wanted to work with Boorman again. And if Boorman had done the movie, he would have insisted on teaming Voight with a more interesting actor for the Creature than Michael Sarrazin.

SAM: For the cast of *Frankenstein: The True Story*, Hunt actually made bona fide offers to Jon Voight, Marlon Brando, Richard Burton, Elizabeth Taylor, Rex Harrison, Albert Finney, Oliver Reed, Vanessa Redgrave, Julie Christie, Warren Beatty, Richard Chamberlain, Frank Langella, Laurence Olivier, Burt Lancaster, Orson Welles, Anthony Quinn, Paul Scofield, Peter Ustinov, Mia Farrow, Tuesday Weld, Candice Bergen, Olivia Hussey, Edward Albert, Sean Connery, Anthony Perkins, Alan Bates, Ingrid Bergman, Bette Davis, Simone Signoret, Angela Lansbury, Elsa Lanchester, Valerie Hobson, Douglas Fairbanks Jr., Ernest Borgnine... even Neil Diamond!
DON: Yes, yes. Well, that's the way Hunt's mind worked. He was always coming up with wild inventions of casting. Very grand fantasies. He imagined the script would just be easily written to fit in a part for so-and-so, whomever it was.

SAM: At what stage of development did this project transition from a theatrical movie to a two-part NBC-TV movie?
DON: Before shooting began. I don't recall how much in advance, but we were aware of the change. We were very disappointed by the turn of events and very distressed by the changes Stromberg was making to our script. The film was

released theatrically outside the United States. I know it was released to theaters in the UK.

SAM: Yes, indeed. I was mortified when I saw that version. The editor Richard Marden arranged a screening for me in 1975. It had been butchered from 180 minutes down to 123 minutes and was virtually incomprehensible. A third of the movie was gone.
DON: Neither Chris nor I saw the theatrical version. From what you say, it would have upset us even more. We saw the three-hour version at a screening at Universal. We were so depressed, all we could say to Stromberg was, "Congratulations on finishing the movie."

SAM: I must say, though, in defense of the final film, I think it was very hard for you and Chris to be objective. Yes, some scenes were cut and others altered – and I completely understand how bitter a pill that was for you and Chris to swallow at the time. But, as an objective viewer, I thought the movie was extraordinary, loaded with so many wonderful ideas.
DON: Yes, there were some wonderful ideas. They just weren't executed to the full extent we had intended.

SAM: In writing the script, you were obviously influenced by James Whale's *Frankenstein* and, in particular, his sequel *Bride of Frankenstein*.
DON: Yes, both Chris and I are very big fans of those movies and of James Whale. In fact, Chris knew James Whale.

SAM: Did you ever meet Whale?
DON: Sadly, no. I just missed meeting James Whale. When I first got together with Chris in 1953, they'd recently had a meeting. Chris told me what a nice man he was and how much he liked him. I wanted to meet him but, sadly, it never happened before he died.

[NOTE: The meeting between Isherwood and Whale was perhaps not quite as idyllic as Bachardy was led to believe. The fateful dinner took place on November 18, 1949, at Whale's home in the Pacific Palisades at 788 South Amalfi Drive. As detailed in *Christopher Isherwood: Lost Years, A Memoir, 1945-1951*, in attendance were five of the most iconic gay figures of the era: Whale, 60; his longtime partner David Lewis, 45 (producer of *Dark Victory*); underground filmmaker Kenneth Anger, 22 (who later authored the bestseller *Hollywood Babylon*); director Curtis Harrington, 23 (who later directed *What's the Matter with Helen?*); and Isherwood, 45. After dinner, Anger showed his short film *Fireworks* in which he portrayed a teenager brutally tortured and raped by a group of sailors. Isherwood hated it and, "aggressively drunk on Whale's strong martinis," he voiced his disdain unapologetically. Then, Harrington showed his surreal short film, *Fragment of Seeking*, in which he plays a young man obsessed with a woman he can never manage to reach. Again, Isherwood was unimpressed – and joked that Harrington should rename it *Fragment of Squeaking*. To Isherwood's "great regret," these rude outbursts offended Whale and his guests. In an interview conducted by David Del Valle for *Films in Review*, director Curtis Harrington recalled his version of the events that night: "They were talking about me and my short experimental films, and Isherwood said to Whale, 'I want to write one and you should be in it. I see a scene where they open a manhole and you creep out of it.' I was just sinking into my chair."]

James Whale mischievously entering a door marked "Keep Out".

James Mason portrait by Bachardy, 1962.

DON: I very much liked *Gods and Monsters*, the movie you produced with Ian McKellen as James Whale.

SAM: Thank you. I was a co-executive producer on that. Very proudly so. The director Bill Condon won an Oscar for his brilliant screenplay adapted from the book *Father of Frankenstein* by Christopher Bram.

DON: A wonderful film. I did a portrait of Bill Condon a few years ago. A very nice man. Very talented. Anyway, Chris and I greatly admired Whale's movies. Much like the prologue in *Bride of Frankenstein*, we wrote a prologue in our script that featured Mary Shelley, Percy Bysshe Shelley, Lord Byron and Dr. Polidori that was lost in the final cut of the film.

SAM: It also seems that you were influenced by the Frankenstein movies made by Hammer Films, the ones with Peter Cushing as Dr. Frankenstein.

DON: No. The only Hammer film that Chris and I saw was *The Horror of Dracula* which we quite liked. I don't know why we didn't see the Frankenstein ones but we didn't.

SAM: There has been speculation that you or Chris may have been influenced by *The Revenge of Frankenstein* in which the creature starts off somewhat "normal" looking – though scarred, but slowly deteriorates and his posture contorts.

DON: No, as far as I know, neither one of us saw that film. It was Chris' idea that the creature should start off beautiful, then deteriorate as the story progressed.

SAM: Coincidentally, in June 1973, the very same month that *Frankenstein: The True Story* completed filming, the first stage production of Richard O'Brien's *The Rocky Horror Show* opened in the West End with a very sexy Creature brought to life by Dr. Frank-N-Furter. And shortly thereafter, Paul Morrissey's *Flesh for Frankenstein* went into production with a sexy Creature. Perhaps the idea of a repulsive creature had been done so often, it was time for a fresh approach.

DON: Yes. To have the Creature go from beautiful to horrible, it made the character so much more poignant and tragic.

SAM: I couldn't agree more. There was also a considerable amount of gay subtext in *Frankenstein: The True Story*.

DON: Yes. Very much so. We were amusing ourselves. We worked those elements into the script the way we wanted

to. Luckily, we had a very intelligent producer in Hunt Stromberg.

SAM: You mean, because Hunt was also gay, he recognized the gay subtext and didn't object to it.

DON: That's right. He was all for it. Yes, indeed.

SAM: The relationship between Dr. Frankenstein and the Creature reminds me of *Pygmalion* – Professor Henry Higgins mentoring Eliza Doolittle and slowly falling in love with her. Was this an inspiration?

DON: Yes, of course. That's exactly what Chris and I had in mind.

SAM: In early drafts of your script, the character of Dr. Polidori played by James Mason was actually called Dr. Pretorius.

DON: Yes. He was based on Dr. Pretorius from *Bride of Frankenstein*.

SAM: Why did you change his name to Dr. Polidori?

DON: I don't recall.

SAM: Of course, Dr. Pretorius is considered one of the first gay characters in mainstream cinema – so deliciously played by Ernest Thesiger.

DON: Yes, we thought he was wonderful in that film.

SAM: So, your version of the character was also intended to be gay, I am assuming.

DON: (laughs) Isn't it obvious?

SAM: I also got the distinct impression that Dr. Clerval, played by David McCallum, is another gay character in your script. His jealousy and disdain of Elizabeth is so pronounced – and his desire to monopolize Victor Frankenstein verges on obsession.

DON: You are not mistaken.

SAM: But all of this gay subtext must have flown right over the heads of network executives and censors, don't you think? If they'd known what you were up to, I don't think they would have allowed it for a primetime television presentation.

DON: We never discussed it with anybody, so I don't know if it was recognized or not. We just put it in there and hoped for the best.

SAM: Practically all of Chris' writing deals with gay subject matter, much of it autobiographical. It seems odd to me that the people in charge would not be on high alert for anything that might be remotely construed as gay.

DON: Hunt Stromberg was very much aware of what we were doing in the script and he supported every bit of it. We only dealt with him so I really don't know what anyone else thought.

SAM: So, if there were any network concerns, they would have been voiced to Hunt?

DON: I assume so, yes. But I never heard of any objections whatsoever. We certainly were never told to tone it down.

SAM: Did you and Chris have any discussions about the gay subtext with director Jack Smight?

DON: Not that I recall. It just wasn't talked about openly.

SAM: But surely Jack must have been aware of the gay subtext, especially when his producer was openly gay and his two writers were openly gay.

DON: It had to cross his mind. He wasn't blind.

SAM: Were you aware that Hunt wanted Elsa Lanchester to play Mrs. Blair, Dr. Frankenstein's landlady?

DON: Yes. Elsa lived next door to us. She loved Chris – absolutely *adored* him. But she regarded me as her rival. She put up with me.

SAM: (laughs) Her late husband, Charles Laughton, was gay – and she knew it. He told her so. Was she ever in love with anyone who wasn't gay?

DON: No. Can you believe it? How many gay men does she think she can have in one lifetime? And she always complained that she was the martyred one. She'd say, "Oh, Charles was so cruel. He never told me until after we were married." I think she knew from the very beginning. I think she was wise to his proclivities right away. She preferred nothing but queer friends her entire life. (laughs) We had a sitting together. I did some drawings of her. She was one of my first celebrity sitters and I couldn't please her. The closer I got to capturing her, the less she liked it, until finally she took me downstairs in order to set me on the right path. And what was the right path? She showed me a picture that she'd done herself of what she thought she looked like – as instructions for me, a poor, struggling novice in the business of portraiture. She was an egomaniac and she thought she could push me around. I realized in those early days that she and I would never be friends.

SAM: During the development of *Dr. Frankenstein*, Hunt hired you and Chris to write what was intended to be his follow-up *Mummy* project.

DON: Yes. We titled it *The Lady from the Land of the Dead*. We had a lot of fun writing it, but it never got produced.

SAM: How did you and Chris work together as writing partners?

DON: Chris encouraged me to be as wild and as inventive as possible. Often, I would have an idea, but I'd say, "Oh, Chris, it's too silly. I don't even want to tell you." He'd say, "No! Tell me." And I would tell him. And he'd say, "Well, you know, that really won't work quite right, but it suggests something to me." And he would then start elaborating and go from there. By the time the idea was in the script, it was transformed. He just loved that collaborative aspect. He loved discussing everything with me. Whenever I got discouraged, I'd say, "Oh, I'm just a typist." But he'd say, "No! You're wrong. You help me enormously." That was who he was. He really wanted my company and the suggestions I made.

SAM: But sometimes when you're partners in all aspects of your life, it can be hard to collaborate on a creative project. Tastes are different. Art is so subjective. Feelings can so easily be hurt.

DON: Yes, but, you see, I had my own profession. I'm an artist. We collaborated on writing *Dr. Frankenstein* in the mornings. In the afternoon, I was always busy doing a sitting. So, I didn't have any temperament to defend any of the ideas I suggested. Chris was free to take what he liked and discard what he didn't like. I wasn't invested in it to the degree he was. He was the writer by profession, and he ultimately decided what was best. I had no ego about it. I had my artwork to do. We established me at the typewriter with him dictating. We discussed ideas back and forth until we finally got something he liked. Then, I took my place at the typewriter and got it down on paper. He would encourage me if I had ideas along the way and I would speak to him freely if I didn't like something. He would always take my ideas seriously. But I was smart enough not to interfere with him when it came to final decisions – because he was a wonderland of inventions. Participating with him was fascinating, witnessing how his mind worked. He always made it fun. That man was just a real entertainer.

SAM: Did Chris enjoy writing screenplays as much as he liked writing novels?

DON: He preferred writing novels. But we needed money and writing scripts was lucrative. He didn't really want to sit down and write screenplays but that's how we supported ourselves. If I helped him write scripts, it made it so much more agreeable for him to do the work. We made it a fun thing to do together. There was never any pressure on me because my whole participation was just to lubricate the procedure. I didn't expect anything for myself. I didn't need it. It didn't have anything to do with my career as an artist.

SAM: Tell me about your trip to London to do the final rewrite on *Dr. Frankenstein*.

DON: We stayed at David Hockney's studio. It wasn't very comfortable there. It was largely one big room, like a loft, and in the center of the room, there was a mountain of crap. In those early years, David was a slob. Chris and I were both very tidy people. Very orderly.

SAM: What were script conferences like with Hunt Stromberg Jr.?

DON: I knew that Chris liked to have me present, but I kept a very low profile and always avoided any direct participation. I just sat and listened – and never interfered. Chris encouraged me to have input and insisted that my ideas were very helpful, but, during those kinds of meetings, I always tried to keep out of it. Socially, I enjoyed Hunt but when it came to business and script conferences, Hunt was a tedious person to be around. Chris got along very well with him – but then he just had that knack of dealing with all sorts of people. He was naturally interested in people; he had a writer's interest. He probably could have written a whole book about Hunt if he'd wanted to. I loved hearing stories about Hunt when Chris would come home from meetings with him or when they would talk on the phone. We did have many social evenings together and it was perfectly relaxed. I behaved myself and Hunt behaved himself.

SAM: Did you ever do a portrait of Hunt?
DON: No. Can you imagine Hunt sitting still? Or even understanding what I wanted from him? He simply wasn't that kind of personality.

SAM: Did you witness Hunt's heavy drinking?
DON: Oh yes. In the evenings, he would get quite drunk, but he never behaved badly. The drinking would get worse as the night went on. We would often excuse ourselves early before he got too drunk. I remember at some of our meetings during the day, he would be dazed with a major hangover.

SAM: After a November 1972 script conference with Hunt, Chris wrote in his diary that Hunt seemed "dazed and not with it, like a dope taker." Others have told me that he was a heavy pill-popper. Did you get that impression as well?
DON: Yes, I believe he was.

SAM: Your *Frankenstein* script was published by Avon Books in November 1973, the same month the movie premiered on NBC.
DON: Yes. I have a story to tell you about that. When Chris and I heard that Avon was going to be publishing the script, it was news to us. We were delighted until we realized that it was going to be the shooting draft – which had been altered by Stromberg. I immediately got on a plane, flew to New York and literally stormed the offices of Avon Books. I told them that Chris and I would take our names off the publication if they went ahead with the shooting draft. I gave them the draft that Chris and I approved and, lo and behold, that's what they ended up publishing. Thank heavens! Only there was one terrible mistake.

Paperback book cover of published script to FTTS.

There's one page missing – and somehow no one noticed it until it was too late. But I have the missing page. Chris and I put it in our copy of the book and that's where it is on the shelf today. (See Chapter 5 for the missing text.)

POSTSCRIPT

In July 2017, I sent Don Bachardy a copy of *Little Shoppe of*

Horrors #38, devoted entirely to the making of *Frankenstein: The True Story*, including my interview with him. A few days later, he called and said, "I enjoyed the magazine very much and I am very pleased with it. I was really quite surprised by how elaborate it is. I'd never seen so many production stills and exploration of various scenes. The detail of it was remarkable. It's so thorough. I didn't know publications existed examining a particular production so carefully and extensively. It was a real enjoyment for me. I got a lot out of it. I hope it gets a lot of attention. It deserves it."

On December 4, 2019, I interviewed Don Bachardy again, this time on camera for a special feature among the extras included on an exquisite new 2K restoration Blu-ray of *Frankenstein: The True Story* (Shout! Factory, Region A, 2020; and Fabulous Films, Region B, 2023).

Over the years, Don and I have become good friends and, on several occasions, he has invited me to his art studio in Santa Monica to pose for paintings.

Sam & Don Bachardy on the day of the interview filming for the Blu-ray.

Sam, Don Bachardy, holding FTTS Blu-ray (portrait of Isherwood in background).

Portrait 1 of Sam by Don Bachardy.

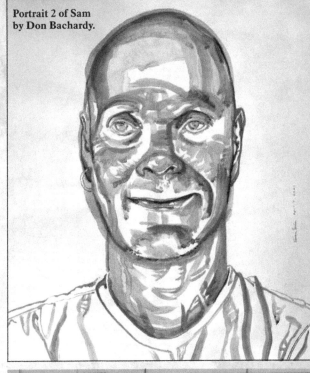

Portrait 2 of Sam by Don Bachardy.

Portrait 3 of Sam by Don Bachardy.

Don Bachardy holding Portrait 4 of Sam.

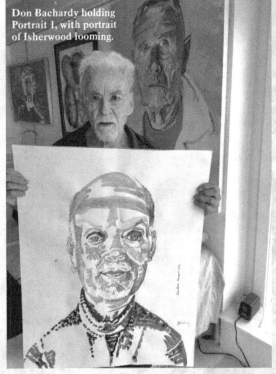

Don Bachardy holding Portrait 1, with portrait of Isherwood looming.

Sam with Don Bachardy in his art studio.

CHAPTER 15
FIRST ASSISTANT DIRECTOR
JOHN STONEMAN

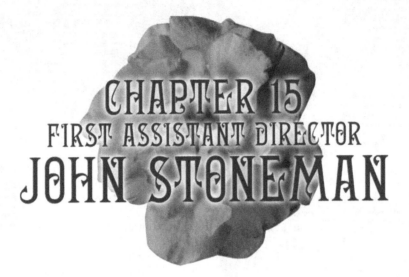

John Stoneman was born in 1939 along England's southwest coast in the Devonshire fishing village of Brixham. During his boarding school days, he became disenchanted with formal education. "I saw an advertisement for an assistant art director at Pinewood Studios which later turned out to be the coffee boy," John recalled. "I applied for it and got it."

Working his way up through the ranks at Pinewood, John eventually became one of the top assistant directors in the UK film industry for such directors as John Huston, Jean-Luc Godard, Lindsay Anderson, Val Guest, Terence Young, John Guillermin, Don Chaffey, Ken Hughes, Freddie Francis and Cornel Wilde. His most famous credit is also his most notorious: *Casino Royale* (1967), the out-of-control James Bond spoof that boasted five credited directors and an entire galaxy of stars. Stoneman was also the First A.D. on *If…* (1968), *Sympathy for the Devil* (1968), and Hammer's *When Dinosaurs Ruled the Earth* (1970). The following interview was conducted March 21, 2016.

This Picture and Left: Stoneman with Titan Crane at Cliveden for FTTS.

THE INTERVIEW

SAM IRVIN: What do you recall about your work as First Assistant Director on *When Dinosaurs Ruled the Earth*?

JOHN STONEMAN: (laughs) After the first week, the director Val Guest said, "I think I may have made a mistake." The poor actors were running around fighting off dinosaurs

that they couldn't see. We had long poles with the heads of dinosaurs as representations for their eyeline. It worked as well as it could in those days but it's a terrible film. Val never had any problems with Hammer over it, though. In fact, I think they offered him another one, but he said, "Once was enough."

SAM: Do you remember any funny stories about *Dinosaurs*?
JOHN: I'd always heard stories about Hollywood studios sending one of their "heavies" to the set to fix a problem. I'd never actually witnessed it until it happened on *Dinosaurs* when a Warner Brothers "heavy" turned up. Remember the girl that appeared in it, Victoria Vetri? During the shoot, her boyfriend came to see her and she got deep into cocaine. About a week later, this gentleman turned up in a trenchcoat and, if you can believe it, with a trilby hat on. He was a "heavy" from Hollywood and he looked like a mobster. He had words with Ms. Vetri, let's put it that way. About her drug use.

Victoria Vetri and director Val Guest on the set of *When Dinosaurs Ruled the Earth*.

Victoria Vetri and Sam Irvin pointing to poster from *When Dinosaurs Ruled the Earth*; Monster Bash, October 2021.

SAM: They were hoping she would be the next Raquel Welch.
JOHN: *That* she wasn't.

SAM: How did you get involved with *Frankenstein: The True Story*?
JOHN: While I was directing second-unit action sequences for a Canadian film in 1971, I fell in love with Canada and a Canadian girl named Sarah Libman and decided to move to Toronto permanently. So I was in Canada in 1973 when I got a call from a great friend of mine, John Palmer, one of the top production managers in the UK, who had done huge films like *Lawrence of Arabia* and *Doctor Zhivago*. He recommended me to associate producer Ian Lewis to do *Frankenstein* as the First Assistant Director. John seemed concerned that the American producers were overly impressed by star "names" – and that casting was perhaps getting a little bit out of hand. I had the somewhat dubious honor of being the assistant director on one of the most star-studded movies ever made in the UK – *Casino Royale*, the one with Peter Sellers, David Niven, Woody Allen, Orson Welles, Ursula Andress, and so on. The American producers on *that* picture did exactly the same thing. They just kept adding big "names" to it, in the hope that the starry cast would offset all the problems.

SAM: Which directors did you work with on *Casino Royale*?
JOHN: I worked with at least three directors on that. I was the First A.D. for John Huston, Ken Hughes and, of course, Val Guest with whom I'd worked on many movies. So, when he asked me to work on *Casino Royale*, I agreed. But, as you know, the project was just a nightmare. I remember David Niven coming onto the Ken Hughes set once with totally the wrong costume on. He said, "Oh, this is not Shepperton Studios, is it. It's MGM Studios." He was a great sport about it. It wasn't his fault. Characters would be written-in virtually day-by-day. A lot of problems were caused by Peter Sellers who wanted to be a director and a writer – and he eventually walked off the film. I never worked on anything like it before or after.

SAM: So, when you arrived in the UK to interview for the job on *Frankenstein: The True Story*, with whom did you meet?
JOHN: Oddly enough, my interview was conducted by

THE EPIC SAGA BEHIND *FRANKENSTEIN: THE TRUE STORY*

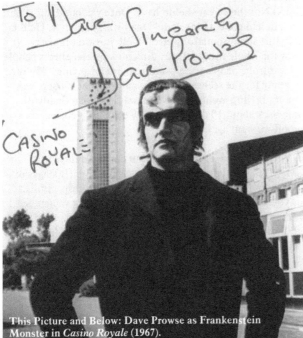

This Picture and Below: Dave Prowse as Frankenstein Monster in *Casino Royale* (1967).

Jacque Shelton, the partner of the producer Hunt Stromberg Jr. I thought it was quite strange because Jacque didn't seem like a producer to me. It was at Pinewood Studios and I remember I met Hunt Stromberg about a week later. After that, Hunt and Jacque were always together. Hunt wanted all these "name" stars and Ian Lewis' job was to keep that under control. (laughs) Well, Ian certainly had his hands full.

SAM: How did things go on *Frankenstein*?
JOHN: Well, I'm afraid I must confess that it was not a happy tale for me. I've never had such a bad time on a film. There was a very dramatic conclusion to my role on it, which I will get to. But first, let me give you a rough overview of the film. Jack Smight, the director, was very qualified, particularly in the area of films for television. I got on extremely well with him and his wife, Joyce. They brought their son Alec with them to England, too. He was just a boy back then but he's gone on to be a very big director-producer in television. I'm delighted when I see Alec's name as a director on *CSI* because it is a program I particularly like. I remember I took Alec to a couple of auto races so that Jack and Joyce could have a weekend free. Anyway, I had a really excellent relationship with Jack and his family.

SAM: Had you worked previously with any of the actors on the film?
JOHN: I knew David McCallum from 1957. He was in a film called *Robbery Under Arms* and he recognized me immediately. In fact, I asked him if he'd phone my then fiancée, Sarah. She'd always loved him as the Russian spy Illya Kuryakin on *The Man from U.N.C.L.E.* He called her and said, "I'm David McCallum." And she said, "Oh, you mean Illya Kuryakin?" (laughs) She was blown away with it. And then she visited the set one day and got to meet David in person.

SAM: Is it true that you directed second unit shots for the film?
JOHN: Yes. Only a few sequences with carriages going through the forest, and so forth, like the carriage that runs over Jane Seymour. I didn't deal directly with the actors, of course. That was Jack's domain. I would work with stunt doubles. They provided me with a major cinematographer for the second-unit shots – Edward "Ted" Scaife who had shot very big pictures like *The Dirty Dozen*.

McCallum, Sarah Libman (fiancée of Stoneman), production manager Brian Burgess.

2nd Unit Director John Stoneman with camera (center); 2nd Unit Director of Photography Edward "Ted" Scaife (right). Coach driver on left.

Stoneman with Jack Smight. Far right, almost cropped out, is young Alec Smight.

SAM: So, what went wrong on the production?
JOHN: We started drifting behind schedule which, of course, Ian Lewis was extremely concerned about, as was the production manager Brian Burgess. And one evening, when we'd finished shooting, I was asked if I'd go to a meeting with the producers – Hunt Stromberg, Jacque Shelton, Ian and Brian. I could sense that something serious was going on. Then, in this bizarre meeting, I was asked if I would be prepared to take the film over and become the director for a matter of three or four days while they brought in another director because they were unhappy with Jack Smight. It was entirely wrong because it wasn't Jack that had put the movie behind schedule, so, I said, "No. I won't do it. That would be extremely disloyal of me to do to Jack – and I don't think you've got the right impression why we are behind schedule."

SAM: Why were the producers blaming Jack Smight?
JOHN: Unfortunately, Jack got a couple of minor things wrong. We were shooting a scene in one particular direction on quite a large set. As you know, generally, you shoot all the stuff in one direction and then change the lighting around so that you then shoot everything else you need in the opposite direction. Jack either forgot a shot or decided to add a shot from the direction we'd already completed – which meant that we had to go back and re-light the direction we'd already done. It was further complicated because walls of the set had to be removed and that sort of thing. It wasn't the most efficient use of time, but it's something that often happens on a film shoot. It's not unusual. But the incident was blown out

of proportion as one of the reasons why the film was behind schedule.

SAM: Were there other problems that caused delays?
JOHN: Yes. A very big one. Michael Sarrazin disappeared – without telling anybody where he'd gone. It was a catastrophe. We were all worried he might have been in an accident or something. Nobody could find him. His agents didn't know anything. It turned out that Michael was worried about his girlfriend, Jacqueline Bisset. She was shooting another picture on location somewhere.

SAM: In France. *The Man from Acapulco*. According to *Vanity Fair* and many other sources, Bisset was having an affair with hairdresser-to-the-stars Jon Peters – the future mega-movie producer. Sarrazin apparently got wind of those rumors.
JOHN: I didn't know the details, but clearly Michael was upset about something going on with his girlfriend. He just up and left – leaving the production high and dry. Our worst nightmare. If you get behind on studio stages, you're in big trouble because other films are coming in to use those stages. So Jack wound up in an unenviable position, to say the least. What was he supposed to shoot? And, to make matters worse, we had no idea where Michael was or how long he was going to be away – or even if he would ever return.

SAM: Didn't the disappearance of Sarrazin freak out the producers and Universal?
JOHN: Not the way it should have. Once we found out where Sarrazin had gone, Hunt said, "Don't worry about it. He'll be back. Just shoot something else." Well, it wasn't that easy. It threw the whole thing off. Art directors, special effects people and wardrobe people were coming to us and saying, "We're not ready for the scenes you *now* want to shoot." There was a lot of juggling around to do. Anyway, Sarrazin finally did come back about 10 days later and we got our acts together and off we went again.

SAM: Were there other things that caused delays?
JOHN: Yes. Sir Ralph Richardson was in the early stages of Alzheimer's or something like that. I say this respectfully, but you almost had to prop him up. He couldn't remember his dialogue, so we had to make cue cards. And then we had James Mason who was his usual arrogant self – always wanting to discuss and change scenes to his liking.

SAM: So, why would the powers-that-be suddenly turn on Jack Smight – and make him the scapegoat?
JOHN: Somebody had to take the fall, I guess, and it wasn't going to be Michael Sarrazin. Politically, it was probably the worst thing that I could have done to say my loyalty has to be with the director – but I have no regrets about that. It's a bit like being the first officer on a ship. If I had agreed to take over, I would have been undermining the captain of the ship. That's why I was so strongly opposed to it.

SAM: So, then what happened?
JOHN: The following week, I was asked not to come into the studio. For all intents and purposes, I was fired. But not officially fired. They simply said, "Don't come to work." It was bizarre. I contacted ACTT [Association of Cinematograph Television and Allied Technicians, 1933-1991], the technicians union. They said, "John, don't make a

fuss because you could stop the whole film's production and we don't want to get into a big fight with Hunt and his gang." So I thought, "Well, that's it. I just don't like the politics of feature films anymore."

SAM: How far along was the production when you left?
JOHN: At least halfway through, maybe a little further. I know that the next sequence was going to be Frankenstein at sea and I was very well known for my work with large special effects of that sort. There was a movie called *A Twist of Sand* [1968], directed by Don Chaffey, that had a lot of ship-at-sea sequences. On that film, I handled it all, and I think that was probably another reason why John Palmer recommended me for *Frankenstein*. Anyway, I didn't quite reach that point on *Frankenstein* – which was too bad. I was looking forward to those scenes.

SAM: I know the ship-at-sea sequences were filmed during the latter part of the shoot. Were you around when they burned down the exterior of Frankenstein's laboratory?
JOHN: Yes. I was still there for that. They attached a tower and things to an old, abandoned warehouse near Pinewood. We had three or four cameras shooting that sequence when it went up in flames. Roy Whybrow was in charge of the special effects and it was perfectly done – as one would expect from somebody like him.

SAM: That was shot on June 4, 1973 – and the picture wrapped on June 22. So, you only missed the last week or two of the 14-week shoot.
JOHN: I don't think I am credited on the film, though, am I?

SAM: The credits for the television broadcast version are minimal – there are no credits at all for any assistant directors. However, you are credited as the First Assistant Director on the theatrical cut of the film. After you left the production, who took over your position?
JOHN: Peter Cotton, who was the Second A.D., moved up. And the Third A.D., Terry Pearce, moved up to Second. The ACTT told me they were going to bring on a new Third A.D. but I don't remember who it was. I remember the location manager was Ian Goddard whom I'd known for years. In fact, I was actually renting a house with Ian when I came back to the UK to work on *Frankenstein*.

SAM: The crew list has both you and Ian Goddard living at 8 Brands Hill Avenue, High Wycombe, in Buckfordshire.
JOHN: That's it. Ian Goddard was very surprised by what happened. He said to me, "I will try and find out what's going on," but he couldn't find out anything. Everybody shut up like a clam.

SAM: Were you still working on the production when Sir John Gielgud did his one day of shooting as the Chief Constable?
JOHN: Yes. John Gielgud had a glorious time that day. He thought the whole thing was a crazy jaunt. I remember him coming onto the set dressed in a cape – which, of course, must have been his idea. We set up one complex tracking shot of Gielgud interviewing Leonard Whiting and Nicola Pagett. He had to walk over to a junior policeman, then to Leonard and, finally, to Nicola. The camera started tracking back with him and – I'll never forget it – he threw his cape out in

John Gielgud hands his cape to Peter Glaze.

this very flamboyant way and said to the junior policeman, "Are you doing anything later tonight?" (laughs) I mean everybody, from the electricians to the camera grips, we all fell apart.

SAM: Peter Glaze played the "Police Constable" in that scene with Gielgud. He was a well-known comic actor who was a regular on the long-running comedy sketch series *Crackerjack!*
JOHN: Yes, that's him. He was rather chubby and short – and I remember the look on his face was so funny. The more experienced actors treated it as great fun.

SAM: How were the other actors to deal with?
JOHN: My wife became great friends with Jane Seymour. Leonard Whiting was very nice young man. We had absolutely no difficulties with him. I think he was a bit overpowered by all these enormous sets and this big movie feel that it had. But once Jack called, "Action!", he did his job to the best of his ability. We had no other problematic actors that I can recall.

SAM: Tell me about Hunt Stromberg Jr. and his partner Jacque Shelton.
JOHN: They were a little, um, flamboyant. That's a nice word for it. I remember one very funny thing they did. One day we were shooting a coach on a cobblestone street on the backlot at Pinewood. Hunt and Jacque were delighted with this coach and they both climbed inside it. Hunt closed the door and pulled down a little blind that came down over window. We all thought, "Huh. That's a weird thing to do." But we went on about our business. Then, a couple of minutes later, the closed carriage started rocking backwards and forwards. Everybody on the crew knew that these two guys were, uh, just a bit light in the loafers – and that something unspeakable was going on inside that coach! (laughs) Suddenly, the door flung open. Hunt and Jacque were standing there, laughing hysterically, looking at all our shocked expressions. It was quite obvious they set the whole thing up as a prank. It was really cute – once we all realized it was a joke.

SAM: Do you remember any other pranks that Hunt did?
JOHN: We were shooting a scene with Leonard Whiting and Michael Sarrazin sitting in this box seat – only we weren't shooting in a real theater. We just had the box seat

Sarrazin pranks crew and pretends to yank off Stromberg's head!

Stromberg stands up as Sarrazin laughs.
(NOTE: Usher on left in doorway is stuntman William Hobbs of *Captain Kronos: Vampire Hunter*.)

Infamous coach where Stromberg & Shelton pranked crew. Here helping Agnes Moorehead inside to repeat the "rocking backwards and forwards" prank.

THE EPIC SAGA BEHIND *FRANKENSTEIN: THE TRUE STORY*

Stoneman & Smight ponder plastic dummy of Seymour. Pubic hair, perhaps?

John Stoneman in more recent years.

constructed as a set at Pinewood. We rehearsed the scene with Whiting and Sarrazin four or five times and then we actually got to the point of doing a take. The camera rolled. Jack called "Action!" Then, all of a sudden, Michael Sarrazin bent down, almost like he had dropped something. Jack was about to say, "Cut!", but before he did, Sarrazin brought up Hunt Stromberg's head in his hands – as if he was in the process of pulling off Hunt's head.

SAM: Like Sarrazin yanking off the head of Jane Seymour at the ball?
JOHN: Yes! Exactly. Hunt had been hiding out of sight inside that box seat set all the time we were rehearsing. And then suddenly Sarrazin had his hands around Hunt's neck. He dragged him up into view of the camera – and the entire crew fell apart. And they got it on film. The camera didn't cut. I'm sure Hunt got that piece of film and would run it all the time at home for friends.

SAM: I have pictures of it! Do you recall any other funny incidents that happened on set?
JOHN: At one point, we had a plastic dummy of Jane Seymour that was in a bath in Frankenstein's laboratory. She was below the water. Jack said to me, "It doesn't really look like a woman, does it? I think we should send it back to the makeup department and ask them to put some pubic hair on it." (laughs) I said, "Well, *I'm* not doing it." (laughs) Anyway, off goes my second assistant Peter Cotton with a soaking wet dummy to take it to the makeup department, and yes, it came back with pubic hair on it – which, of course, could never have been shown on a television movie! It was hilarious.

SAM: After *Frankenstein: The True Story*, were you offered other First Assistant Director jobs?
JOHN: If I had stayed in England, I think I would have probably found difficulty carrying on working in features. I still heard from Val Guest, of course. He used to call me every

time he started a new project – but, by then, I was usually committed to something else. Even when he moved to Palm Springs, he and I stayed in contact right up until he died. He wasn't what I would call a great artistic film director – we're not talking about Lindsay Anderson or Jean-Luc Godard – but Val was a terrific, professional film director. He gave me so much knowledge and experience that had a tremendous influence on how I would later handle my own productions. I'm grateful to him for that.

POSTSCRIPT

Following *Frankenstein: The True Story*, John Stoneman went back to his adopted home of Toronto and, in 1974, married his Canadian sweetheart Sarah Libman. They formed a company called Mako Films Ltd. to pursue John's love of underwater documentary filmmaking. He directed and shot the humpback whale documentary *Nomads of the Deep* (1979), the first underwater IMAX film. He was also the director-producer-cinematographer-host of over one-hundred episodes of the acclaimed undersea documentary series *The Last Frontier* (1987-1990). "I just about saturated the world market with my underwater footage," John added. "I sold my films to nearly 80 countries around the world, which is not bad for a Canadian documentary company." Today, John is still recognized on the streets as "the Jacques Cousteau of Canada."

CHAPTER 16
ASSOCIATE PRODUCER
IAN LEWIS

Ian Lewis began his motion picture career at Hammer Films, first as Michael Carreras' assistant (1959-1964), and then as the Production Manager of *Frankenstein Created Woman* (1967), *Quatermass and the Pit* (1967) and *The Devil Rides Out* (1968). For Universal Pictures, Lewis was the Production Manager of François Truffaut's *Fahrenheit 451* (1966) and the Associate Producer of Jack Smight's *Frankenstein: The True Story* (1973) – the success of which resulted in his appointment as Managing Director of Universal Pictures Limited – the British arm of MCA-Universal – a post he held through 1989. Of particular interest, one of the films he supervised was John Badham's *Dracula* (1979).

Given the breadth of that resume, I had a ton of questions to ask. Luckily, Ian Lewis graciously submitted to being interrogated by me over the course of four lengthy telephone sessions in the fall of 2015. 82-years-young at that time, Ian was full of great humor and happy to reminisce about the old days. His charming wife Ann (married since 1962) was occasionally called upon to help remember a name or detail. My sincerest thanks go out to both of them.

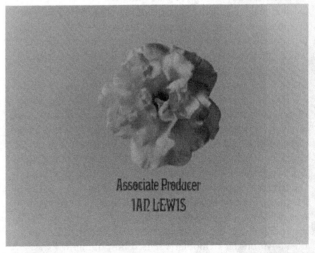

Associate Producer
IAN LEWIS

IN THE BEGINNING

SAM IRVIN: When and where were you born? And tell us about your family and upbringing.
IAN LEWIS: I was born the 23rd of November, 1932, in Clapham Common in London. My father worked in Covent Garden. It was a family business – the foremost fruit and vegetable market in the U.K. with a warehouse and everything. My great grandfather founded the business and it had gone down all through the family.

SAM: Were you raised to take over the family business?
IAN: No. My father never wanted me to go into it, and I must admit I don't think I wanted to. I certainly didn't want to have to get up at four o'clock in the morning as he did and get back about four o'clock in the afternoon.

SAM: Did you have siblings?
IAN: No, I was an only child. I did have a brother, but he was born dead.

SAM: I'm sorry to hear that. Where did you go to school?
IAN: When I was 14, I went to Cumnor House, a prep school. And then I moved on to Bradfield College. I spent five years there and I left at the end of the winter term in December 1951. I had Christmas at home and then the second of January 1952, I was called up on National Service. I spent two-and-a-half years in the Royal Artillery.

SAM: After your National Service, what did you do?
IAN: My father was determined that I would go into Lloyds, the famous insurance company. So, when I had done my National Service, I came out and I went to work for Adam

Brothers, a firm of insurance brokers. My father knew one of the senior directors and had arranged a job for me there. I spent about five years with them learning the insurance business. I disliked it. In fact, I hated it.

SAM: Where did you go after that?
IAN: I was still living at home and we had a neighbor named Jack Goodlatte who was the head of ABC Cinemas.

[NOTE: Associated British Cinemas (ABC) was a chain of cinemas in the UK, a subsidiary of Associated British Picture Corporation (ABPC), founded in 1927, "a consortium of British film producers and theater companies, including Pathé News, whose director, Norman Thomas, became head of the company. A large portion of the shares of ABPC was owned by the American film studio Warner Bros." (SOURCE: Hilmes, Michele. *Network Nations: A Transnational History of British and American Broadcasting*. London: Routledge, 2012, E-book.) ABPC owned ABPC Elstree Studios and had a distribution arm called Warner-Pathé Distributors. MGM owned *another* studio in Elstree called MGM-British Studios. ABPC was absorbed into EMI in 1969. ABPC Elstree Studios then became known as EMI-Elstree Studios. Later, Thorn Electrical Industries took over EMI and the studio was renamed Thorn-EMI Studios (the *Star Wars* movies and the *Indiana Jones* franchise were shot there). After further ownership twists and turns, in 2000, the studio became an independent company was renamed Elstree Film & Television Studios, Ltd. – which, as of this writing, is still its moniker. We will refer to MGM-British Studios as MGM Studios; we will refer to ABPC Elstree Studios as Elstree Studios.]

IAN: Jack and his wife were great, great friends of my mother and father. They would see each other I suppose twice a week at least. Jack was in charge of booking movies for the cinemas, so he would get prints of all the new films coming out – because he had to see them to determine whether he was going to book them or not. He would run movies at his home and we'd be invited to come over and see them. Plus, my mother and father went to the cinema quite often when I was young and if I could be taken, I'd be taken – because, of course, I could only be taken to a U-certificated film. But anyway, I saw an awfully large number of films. When I was working with Adam Brothers, I would see sometimes two or three movies a week. But I was a really unhappy bunny at Adam Brothers. I could see myself with no future because the firm was run by two people. They had two sons in the business. They were allowed to go out and get business in. I was not. And it looked to me as though I would have to sit around and wait for one of the top to die and then I'd move up a position. Jack Goodlatte sensed how unhappy I was. And one night when I was at his home watching a movie, he took me aside and said, "You're very unhappy in your work, aren't you?" And I said, "Yes. I'd do anything to get out of it, but I don't know what I could do." And he said, "Would you like to come and work in the studios?" At that time, ABC Cinemas was part of ABPC Studios at Elstree. And I said, "Yes, I would." Then he said, "Leave it with me. I'm going to bring it up with your mother and father sometime soon and we'll see what we can do." And he manufactured a job for me in the studios.

SAM: What did you do at Elstree Studios?

IAN: I went in as the assistant to their best producer, a man called Bill Whittaker. When I say they manufactured the job for me, it's because there really was not enough for me to do to warrant a full-time position. I used to go in there and whatever Bill wanted me to do, I'd have it done by about 11 o'clock. And I had a choice of either sitting around or trying to find something else to do. So, I took to going off and working with each one of the departments in the studio and learning how they worked – like the sound department or the editing department – because everything was done in-house in those days. For instance, I'd go to the construction department, and I'd just sort of attached myself to somebody in that department and say, "Look, show me what you do and how you do it and all the rest of it." So, I had about three years doing that at ABPC.

SAM: What films did you observe being made there?
IAN: A lot of films. All sorts of funny films were going on at the time, like *Tommy the Toreador* for example.

[NOTE: *Tommy the Toreador* (1959) was a musical-comedy starring Tommy Steele, Janet Munro, Bernard Cribbins, Ferdy Mayne and Charles Gray; produced by George H. Brown; and directed by John Paddy Carstairs.]

IAN: *Tommy the Toreador* was directed by John Paddy Carstairs, the brother of Tony Nelson-Keys. He changed his name because he had a row with his father Nelson Keys.

[NOTE: John Paddy Carstairs' birth name was Nelson John Keys. His father's name was Nelson Keys. Carstairs was his mother's maiden name. John had three brothers, all in the movie business: Anthony "Tony" Nelson-Keys (of Hammer fame); Basil Henry Keys (assistant director of Jacques Tourneur's *Curse of the Demon*; associate producer of Terence Fisher's *The Phantom of the Opera* and Freddie Francis' *Paranoiac*); and Rod Nelson-Keys (editor of several "Carry On" comedies, including *Carry On Screaming!*).]

IAN: Anyway, I wasn't working on these films as such. I didn't have anything to do with production whatsoever. I only basically saw or learned what was going on in the studio to feed those productions. ABPC was a very funny company to work with.

SAM: In what way?
IAN: (laughs) Well, there was a man called Vaughn Dean who ran Elstree Studios. He was very, very strict and conservative – which could be very amusing at times. Are you are familiar with the book *Lady Chatterley's Lover* by D. H. Lawrence?

SAM: Yes. It was kind of the *Fifty Shades of Grey* of its era. Quite scandalous.
IAN: Exactly. Well, I was on the set one day when Vaughn Dean saw an electrician up in the gantry reading a book. Like a schoolmarm, he made him come down and show him what his was reading – and the book turned out to be *Lady Chatterley's Lover*. Now, in the eyes of Vaughn Dean, that book was *highly* offensive, but making matters even worse, the book had a piece of paper inside it designating all the pages where the word "fuck" appeared and it was being passed around the crew. Well, he was furious. He confiscated the book, then called a meeting of all the crew and said, "If I ever find anybody else reading a book like this ever again, I'll have you thrown out!"

SAM: Hilarious.

IAN: Yes, but you see, that was the era we were in.

HELL IS A CITY

SAM: How did your work for Associated British Picture Corporation lead you to Hammer Films?

IAN: In 1959, ABPC was financing a Hammer Film called *Hell Is a City* – and as they were financing it, they wanted somebody to go on the picture to overlook their money. There was a man named Gordon Scott who was going to be ABPC's rep on the picture, co-signing the checks and making sure that they made the picture properly. But suddenly I was asked to go and do the job – to oversee the money.

[NOTE: *Hell Is a City* was a crime-thriller starring Stanley Baker, Donald Pleasence and Billie Whitelaw; directed by Val Guest; produced by Michael Carreras; a Hammer Film Production, filmed in 1959, released in the UK by Warner-Pathé Distributors in April 1960; it was released in the United States by Columbia Pictures in November 1960.]

IAN: Having done what I'd done at Elstree Studios by attaching myself to all the various departments, I had a very good grounding – a solid understanding of how each department worked. So, when I suddenly got thrust into the financial side on *Hell Is a City*, I knew exactly what to do. I looked where they were spending money and made sure they were not going over budget.

¡CRISOL PASIONAL DE POPULOSA URBE!

HELL IS A CITY

COLUMBIA PICTURES presenta el emotivo

VERDE ES LA EVIDENCIA

estrellas STANLEY BAKER JOHN CRAWFORD DONALD PLEASENCE
Argumento de VAL GUEST - Basado en una novela de MAURICE PROCTER
Producida por MICHAEL CARRERAS - Dirigida por VAL GUEST
UNA PRODUCCION HAMMER FILM

en sistema HAMMERSCOPE

SAM: Val Guest directed *Hell Is a City*.

IAN: Yes. Val Guest directed a lot of Hammer pictures. I didn't have a lot to do with him, though. The only person I had anything to do with was Michael Carreras because he was the producer – and, of course, the son of James Carreras who was the head of Hammer. Michael also had the title of Managing Director of Hammer. So, we did that picture, things went smoothly, and afterwards I came back to ABPC and resumed working for Bill Whittaker, doing the usual things I had been doing.

SAM: Did you have a particular genre of film that you liked a lot?

IAN: I've always liked the "feel good" films. I don't really like films that you come out of thinking, "God, why did I go to see that?" Personally, I think film is an incredible medium and, unfortunately, sometimes we have some people who use it the wrong way. I think it's a great shame. It's there to entertain. It's there to teach. It's there to help people. But to go and just make films that satisfy your own ego is the wrong use of it.

SAM: Would you consider yourself a fan of horror films before you got into the business?

IAN: No, no. Not at all.

SAM: At that time, had you seen Hammer Films' big breakthrough hits, like *The Curse of Frankenstein* (1957) or *Dracula* (1958)?

IAN: To be quite honest, I doubt if I'd seen a Hammer Horror before I went to work for them.

SAM: So, once you were back at ABPC working for Bill Whittaker, how did you end up working for Hammer again?

IAN: A few weeks later, Michael Carreras suddenly came to me and said, "Would you like to come and join us at Hammer

Michael Carreras.

Films? I'd like you to be my assistant."

SAM: Didn't Michael Carreras already have an assistant?
IAN: Yes. He had a lady named Jean Hamilton who was basically his assistant, which was a bit of a problem. I had one or two run-ins with her because she felt that I was trying to take her job on *Hell Is a City*. I knew if I took the job, I would have to make my peace with her, which wasn't going to be easy. And I also had to go and see Jack Goodlatte and say to him, "Do you think this is a thing I should do?" And he said, "Well, I'll talk to his father, Jimmy Carreras, who is the head of Hammer. But I think it's almost certainly the right thing for you to do." Jack came back and said, "It's the right thing for you to do, so you should go and do it." And that's when I really broke with ABPC to become Michael Carreras' assistant at Hammer Films.

SAM: Was it an easy transition?
IAN: I have to say I had quite a lot of problems.

SAM: Making peace with Jean Hamilton?
IAN: Yes. She remained working for Michael Carreras, so I had to be very careful to get on her good side. We basically had to call a truce. I did my job and she did her job.

SAM: What were your duties?
IAN: Hammer used to make about six, seven or eight pictures a year. First, there was the development and pre-production period which could go on for however long it took. Then, there was the shooting period which was five or six weeks. And finally, there was the post-production period which was never more than six weeks. What I ended up doing for Michael was work on scripts during the development period.

SAM: Were you a script reader? Evaluating potential scripts for Hammer to consider making?
IAN: Sometimes I'd be a reader. Sometimes Michael would hand me a script and say, "This is too long. Where can we cut it?" So, I'd read it and I'd have to think about where we can cut it.

SAM: So, in some cases, you were a script doctor?
IAN: I wouldn't do any re-writing, but I'd make recommendations. I would be in on script meetings. I'd be sitting with Michael Carreras, Jean Hamilton, and nearly always Jimmy Sangster – who was the writer on a lot of Hammer films. It would be an open discussion about what we thought should happen with the script. I was very inexperienced, but I was asked for my opinion and often gave my opinion.

SAM: When revisions were made and a new draft of the script was delivered, would Michael have you comment on that as well?
IAN: Yes. I'd read it first and comment to him if it worked or hadn't worked. Then he would ask me, "Should I read it?" And I would nearly always say, "Yes, you should read it." And we'd go from there. Once the script problems were repaired, I'd hand the script over to the production manager two or three weeks before the shoot. Then I'd take over the previous picture, which was in post-production, and watch what was happening there. Jimmy Needs was the supervising editing. I'd see if there were any problems that needed to be ironed out, and basically feed that information back to Michael.

SAM: Were you also doing preliminary schedules and budgets?
IAN: Yes, I certainly did – in conjunction with their accountant.

SAM: When you say that the shooting schedules at Hammer were around five or six weeks, how many days per week were they shooting?
IAN: Five days per week, Monday through Friday.

SAM: Would they ever do six days per week?
IAN: No.

SAM: Because the sixth day would have triggered overtime?
IAN: That's right.

SAM: Were there any exceptions, like if a location was only available on a weekend?
IAN: Possibly, but it would have been extremely rare.

SAM: Or if an actor was only available on a weekend?
IAN: I don't think recall that ever being done.

SAM: Aside from Jean Hamilton, were there other employees at Hammer who had to be navigated carefully?
IAN: Well, you see Tony Nelson-Keys ran the studio – Bray Studios – which was owned by Hammer back then, and they shot most all their pictures there. On just about every one of their productions, Tony was credited as the associate producer. To a certain extent, I was beginning to encroach on his turf, so he wasn't very happy about that. So life got quite tricky at times. Tony, one has to admit, could lose his rag very easily and that could end up in a rather nasty session sometimes. But I learned how to handle it and we made it work. In the end, we became great friends.

SAM: What was the corporate structure at Hammer back then?
IAN: It was very much a family affair. It was a terrific family affair because the same crew were on all the pictures. They were family. As an example, at Christmas time we'd stop production. There would be three long tables put in one of the stages at Bray Studios. Michael Carreras, Tony Hinds and Jimmy Carreras would sit at the head of each table. Everyone would bring their wives and children – and every child would get a present. The turkey would be carved. It would be a wonderful meal. As Christmas bonuses, most of the work force got two weeks' money, tax paid. Unfortunately, the Christmas parties and bonuses ended abruptly.

[NOTE: James "Jimmy" Carreras was co-founder and Chairman of Hammer. (In 1970, he was knighted by the Queen.) His son Michael produced many of Hammer's movies – and occasionally directed. Anthony "Tony" Hinds was the son of the late William Hinds, co-founder of Hammer Films; Tony Hinds produced many Hammer films and occasionally wrote Hammer scripts under the pseudonym John Elder. The two producing teams – led by Michael Carreras and Tony Hinds respectively – worked independently of each other. The crew was mostly the same group of people who would go from film to film, no matter which team was producing it.]

SAM: What happened?

THE EPIC SAGA BEHIND *FRANKENSTEIN: THE TRUE STORY*

IAN: It was when the workers started to unionize. I don't remember what year it was, but one March, one of the workers went to see Michael and said, "We want to know whether we're getting our bonus at Christmas time." And Michael said, "You're not entitled to a bonus. That is given by us to say thank you for all the hard work. We're not going to tell you whether you're going to get it at this stage of the year. And he said if you persist in asking us and want us to tell you, then I'm afraid I shall have to most likely say there will be no bonus." And there was no bonus and no Christmas party after that. Very silly. The unions basically cut their hands off. It's just one of those things that happened and, from then on, the family atmosphere at Hammer deteriorated except for the old people who had been with Hammer for quite a long while. It was a shame, a great shame.

SAM: How was catering done on Hammer films?
IAN: We used outside caterers when we were on location. When we were in the studio at Bray, we had a marvelous lady who ran the kitchen there. The food was wonderful, really wonderful. We very seldom had any complaints about the food. The best thing at Bray in the morning was, when you first got there, there was sausage in a roll. Wonderful sausages she had made – and everybody had one of those the moment they arrived. And if you could get a second one off her, you would, but she would only give you one.

SAM: Did you have tea breaks?
IAN: Yes. Tea breaks in the morning and tea breaks in the afternoon. You had to have those. Union rule.

SAM: What times were the tea breaks? Give me the rundown of a typical shoot day.
IAN: Well, we started at half past eight, so the tea break in the morning was about 11, quarter to 11, and the trolley would come on the set.

SAM: Wasn't there a craft service table with snacks and beverages throughout the day?
IAN: No. It was only later in my career that we started doing that, running buffet catering throughout the day, so, at any time of the day or night, you could go and get something to eat, which is what it is now.

SAM: In America, we call that the craft service table.
IAN: Yes.

SAM: So, getting back to the old days, how long would the tea breaks last?
IAN: A quarter of an hour. You had to queue up at the trolley and, until Hammer was unionized, the crew got it for nothing. But once Hammer was unionized, the crew had to pay for it.

SAM: Pay for the tea?
IAN: Yes – and pay for the buns or whatever they had with it.

SAM: Wow. That's surprising. What about lunch?
IAN: You had an hour off for lunch – and it was paid by the production. There was a rule that you could call what's known as "the quarter," which at the end of shooting in the morning or at the end of shooting at night, you could call "the quarter" and you were allowed to keep shooting an extra 15 minutes in order to complete the setup – then break for

lunch, or, if it was at the end of the day, call it a wrap.

SAM: In America, instead of calling "the quarter," the term we use is to call "grace" – which is basically a grace period to finish the set-up.
IAN: Yes.

SAM: So, if you started at 8:30 in the morning, what time was lunch?
IAN: I believe from one till two. And you went back on the floor. You had a tea break that's about half past three and you wrapped at 5:30. Unless you called "the quarter."

SAM: So, we're talking a nine-hour day.
IAN: With an hour off for lunch. Yes.

SAM: So, the union rates were based on eight hours, plus one hour for lunch?
IAN: That's right.

SAM: What happened if you went beyond that? I mean, beyond "the quarter" grace period?
IAN: You had to apply for overtime. You had to go to the shop stewards by four o'clock and ask for an hour's overtime.

SAM: That's fascinating to me because in all my experience directing low budget films in America, the standard has always been twelve hours of shooting, plus a half-hour lunch. So, our days are usually twelve-and-a-half hours. If the crew is union, and certainly the actors are almost always union, there is overtime after eight hours, but that is just factored into the budget.
IAN: There was no overtime on Hammer films unless there were extraordinary circumstances. Terry Fisher and the other directors knew that from the start.

SAM: Wow. That completely changes my understanding of the typical Hammer schedule of "five or six weeks of shooting." Compared to the tight schedules I usually have on the films I direct, I always thought Hammer's schedules were a wee bit on the luxurious side. But if you were only shooting eight hours a day, that's four hours less than what I normally get out of a day. It's a huge difference.
IAN: Yes. Those eight-hour days sped by very quickly.

SAM: Were you and Michael Carreras based at Bray Studios?
IAN: No. Our offices were at Hammer House [113-117 Wardour Street, London], not down at Bray Studios [near Maidenhead, Berkshire, England]. I spent most of my time at Hammer House because development was done there, and then, after the films were shot, they were edited at Hammer House where I was involved in the post-production.

SAM: Take us on a tour of Hammer House.
IAN: It was six floors. The first floor was occupied by Anglo-Amalgamated [a film production and distribution company]. The second floor were the offices of Jimmy Carreras and Brain Lawrence [Hammer's business manager]. The third floor was Tony Hinds and his team. The fourth floor was Michael Carreras and his team. The fifth floor was the editorial floor for Hammer. And the six floor was occupied by Anglo-Amalgamated again, the office of Nat Cohen [co-owner of Anglo-Amalgamated].

SAM: So, you were on Michael Carreras' floor?
IAN: Yes. The fourth floor.

SAM: And how many people would have had offices on that floor?
IAN: Michael, Jean Hamilton, me, and Michael's secretary. That would've been it on our floor.

SAM: How many editors would've been working on the fifth floor?
IAN: Well, when I first started there, Jimmy Needs was editing the pictures and he edited all of them. Then he became supervising editor, which basically meant that he still edited most of the pictures, but he had another editor working under him.

SAM: Like Bill Lenny?
IAN: Yes, he was one of the editors. There were several of them. I think Bill started off by being more of a sound editor, then went on to picture editing.

SAM: So, basically, Michael Carreras and Tony Hinds produced Hammer films independently of each other.
IAN: That's right. At the time, Tony Hinds cranked out the standard Hammer Horrors while Michael was trying to make movies that weren't Hammer Horrors.

SAM: Anthony Nelson-Keys was the producer on a number of Hammer films. Did he run a third producing team?
IAN: No, he was employed by Hammer. He ran Bray Studios and, as part of his contract, he got a credit as the associate producer on all the pictures.

SAM: On a lot of pictures, Anthony Nelson-Keys was credited as the associate producer. But occasionally he received credit as the producer.
IAN: Later on, he got producer credits.

SAM: I noticed that on a lot of these pictures, Michael Carreras would get an executive producer credit – even on some of the Tony Hinds pictures. Was that in name only?
IAN: If Tony Hinds was producing, yes. Michael did nothing with Tony Hinds at all. They ran very separate groups. And stayed out of each other's way. They never worked together.

THE TWO FACES OF DR. JEKYLL

SAM: So, when you came back to work full-time at Hammer as Michael Carreras' assistant, was he producing The Two Faces of Dr. Jekyll starring Paul Massie, Dawn Addams and Christopher Lee. It was filmed from November 23, 1959, through January 22, 1960.
IAN: Yes, I believe that's the

one. It was directed by Terry Fisher – who was a lovely man. He was almost a mechanical director, if you know what I mean.

SAM: How so?
IAN: Well, he knew exactly what shots he needed. He needed the master shot and he needed the two close shots. He very seldom experimented with anything. He knew what he had to get and he got them – and he very seldom went over schedule. He was a lovely man. Everybody loved working for him. He was never difficult. Never unpleasant.

SWORD OF SHERWOOD FOREST

SAM: The next film that Michael Carreras did was Sword of Sherwood Forest. The producer credits went to Sidney Cole and Richard Greene – who also played the leading role of Robin Hood. Michael was credited as executive producer on this one. It was shot on location in Ireland and at a studio in Dublin that also happened to be called Bray Studios – even though it had no affiliation or connection with the Bray Studios that Hammer owned in London. The filming dates were May 23 through July 8, 1960.
IAN: Quite right. I worked on that. I was in Ireland the whole time. Michael put me on the picture to watch over the money. In fact, I caught the Irish production manager stealing film stock. That's really what enabled me to get into the union.

SAM: Please explain.
IAN: I actually found out that the Irish production manager was being very, very clever. He was buying film stock on

Bray Studios Ireland and all our film stock came from Bray Studios in London. And he was selling it off. So, we had to get rid of him and that meant I had to take over the picture.

SAM: So, you became the production manager?
IAN: More or less. I was doing it unofficially at first because I wasn't in the union. Sid Cole was the producer on the movie *and* the Vice President of ACTT [Association of Cinematograph Television and Allied Technicians, the trade union in the UK, 1933-1991]. The union was very difficult to join at that time but Sid pulled some strings and got me in. Got me my card and everything. After that, I could legally be a production manager.

SAM: Aside from Richard Greene, the cast also included Peter Cushing as the Sheriff of Nottingham. Tell me about Peter.
IAN: Well, he was a lovely man, too. Just like Terry Fisher, he knew what he had to do and he did it. He was very good. A damn good actor. Somehow, he got stuck with Hammer. It wasn't until much later that he got appreciated outside of Hammer. But he was a very lovely man. Never any trouble. Never *ever* any trouble. Whereas Christopher Lee could be quite difficult at times.

SAM: In what ways?
IAN: Chris was known as "Nasty" by certain people. And they called him "Nasty" to his face, so he knew he was called that, which was very funny. If he got out of bed on the wrong side, he took it out on people. Most people do that anyway.

SAM: You mean he could just be in a grumpy mood sometimes?
IAN: Yes. But people like Terry Fisher and Peter Cushing? I never saw them grumpy. Not once. Never. But most normal people can get grumpy at times. So, I think you could say that Christopher Lee was a bit more normal in that way. He didn't let it get out of hand, though. He knew what side his bread was buttered on. At that time, he wasn't a big draw. It was only later in his life that he actually became an actor that other people wanted outside of horror films.

SAM: When I met Christopher Lee, he was funnier than I had imagined.
IAN: He had many sides that most people didn't know about. He used to sing opera! Seriously belt out opera in his dressing room. We often had to go and shut him up because we could hear it on the stage he was making so much noise.

SAM: It sounds like you all were having a lot of fun.
IAN: We were. The whole thing about Hammer – it was a family. Everybody who worked there knew each other. We had so many lovely people. Bernie Robinson – he was a wonderful art director. Very, very, *very* clever. Jimmy Needs, the supervising editor – incredible. He could rescue a Hammer Horror very quickly. With Terry Fisher, you knew he never missed a shot that he needed. Rosie Burrows was the head of wardrobe. She became a very, very senior wardrobe mistress in the business. One of the best. I don't even know if she's still alive, actually, but she was a lovely lady. Pat McDermott was a hairstylist, one of the best in the business.

SAM: You later hired Patricia McDermott as the hairstylist for *Frankenstein: The True Story* (1973).

IAN: Yes. When you're in charge of a picture, you like to get people you know and trust can do the job well. By then, I was no longer with Hammer. Pat was still around and working very well, so that's why I got her on that picture.

PASSPORT TO CHINA

SAM: The next picture Michael Carreras produced was *Passport to China* (1961; also known as *Visa to Canton*), which Michael also directed. It starred Richard Basehart.
IAN: That was a picture nobody wanted to make. Michael got

very set on it – and no one could talk him out of it. The thing about Michael is he always wanted to do something that was not a standard Hammer Horror. Tony Hinds never wanted to do anything else but standard Hammer. So Michael used to get involved in these other kinds of pictures. I honestly don't remember anything about that one at all.

A TASTE OF FEAR

SAM: Your next picture was *A Taste of Fear* (1961), released in America as *Scream of Fear*, executive produced by Michael Carreras, produced and written by Jimmy Sangster, directed by Seth Holt, starring Susan Strasberg, Christopher Lee, and Ann Todd.
IAN: *Taste of Fear*, yes. I was on that one. We shot that on the south coast of France. They needed a Rolls-Royce, so Michael said, "Well, you better go out and find one." So, I found one and we purchased it to resell after the picture was made. I had to drive it down to the South of France where we were filming and then drive it back again when we were done. That was my job.

SAM: (laughs) That's hilarious. If I remember correctly, doesn't that Rolls-Royce roll off the cliff at the climax? How did that work? Did you have to find a double?
IAN: I have no idea how we did that. I don't remember.

SAM: How did Seth Holt compare to say a Terence Fisher?
IAN: Oh, very different. Not the same sort of director. He was more improvisational.

CAPRICORN FILM PRODUCTIONS
[NOTE: In 1961, Michael Carreras and Jimmy Sangster formed their own production company, Capricorn Film

Productions, independent of Hammer Films, even though Michael continued working for Hammer on a non-exclusive basis and Jimmy continued writing and producing projects for Hammer and elsewhere. Capricorn was a short-lived entity, making only two pictures: *The Savage Guns* (1962) and *What a Crazy World* (1963), both directed by Michael Carreras. *The Savage Guns* was a Western shot in Spain in 1961, starring Richard Basehart, Don Taylor and Fernando Rey, written by Edmund Morris and produced by Jimmy Sangster. It was released in the U.S. in 1962 by MGM – but apparently never got released in the UK. It does hold the distinction, however, of being one of the first examples of the "spaghetti western" genre. *What a Crazy World* was a rock 'n' roll musical directed, written and produced by Michael Carreras with Aida Young as the associate producer. It was filmed at Elstree Studios in 1963, released in the UK by Warner-Pathe, but apparently did not get released in the United States.]

SAM: Did you become involved in Michael's independent company Capricorn Film Productions for which he directed *The Savage Guns* and *What a Crazy World*?
IAN: I had very little to do with either *The Savage Guns* or *What a Crazy World* as they were not supposed to have anything to do with Hammer. However, I did help out during pre-production with various tasks unofficially.

THE PIRATES OF BLOOD RIVER
SAM: In between Michael's two Capricorn Film Production ventures, Michael continued his Hammer duties and executive produced *The Pirates of Blood River* (1962) with Kerwin Marthews, Christopher Lee, Oliver Reed and Andrew Kier. Do you remember that one?
IAN: Yes. Tony Nelson-Keys was actually producing it.

SAM: It was directed by John Gilling. How did Gilling compare to Terence Fisher in terms of his style of directing?
IAN: John Gilling was similar to Terry Fisher in that he was the sort of director who knew what his shots were. Tony Nelson-Keys would not have a director who wasn't very, very sure of what he needed to shoot. He knew he had to deliver on time. Val Guest is another director like that – he used to come in with a list of his shots. You knew exactly what the shots were going to be. You could plan for him and it was marvelous. Terry Fisher was the same – but his list wasn't on paper. Terry usually had a blackboard right there on the stage – and he would write the list of shots in chalk, for everyone to see. So, you knew what shots were coming. Seth Holt was a bit more like, "Let's try it and see if it works."

THE EPIC SAGA BEHIND *FRANKENSTEIN: THE TRUE STORY*

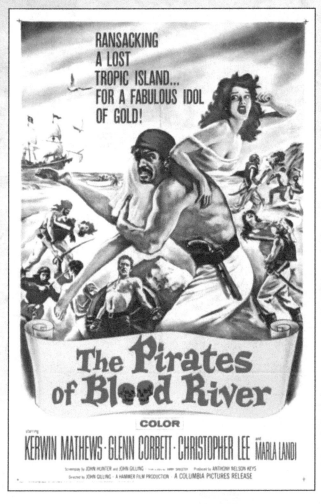

RANSACKING A LOST TROPIC ISLAND... FOR A FABULOUS IDOL OF GOLD!

The Pirates of Blood River

COLOR

KERWIN MATHEWS · GLENN CORBETT · CHRISTOPHER LEE and MARLA LANDI

Screenplay by JOHN HUNTER and JOHN GILLING · Produced by ANTHONY NELSON KEYS
Directed by JOHN GILLING · A HAMMER FILM PRODUCTION · A COLUMBIA PICTURES RELEASE

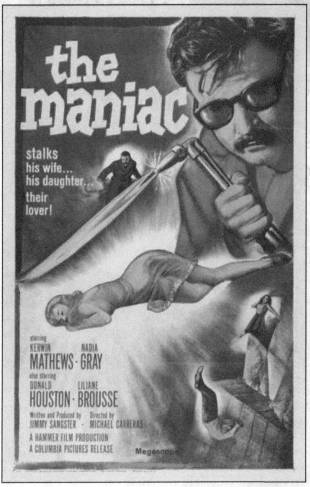

the maniac

stalks his wife... his daughter... their lover!

starring KERWIN MATHEWS · NADIA GRAY
also starring DONALD HOUSTON · LILIANE BROUSSE
Written and Produced by JIMMY SANGSTER · Directed by MICHAEL CARRERAS
A HAMMER FILM PRODUCTION
A COLUMBIA PICTURES RELEASE   Megascope

Jimmy Sangster.

SAM: Oliver Reed had a supporting role. What was he like to work with?

IAN: He was not bad at all at that time. He was quite good. Hammer gave him his opportunity and he behaved himself. It was only later he became a terrible drunk, difficult, throwing tantrums. But even back then, I guess the writing was on the wall and you could see it was coming.

SAM: That's so sad because he was such a good actor.

IAN: Yes, but later on, he was almost impossible to have on a picture. He was out of control.

MANIAC

SAM: The next film you did with Michael Carreras was *Maniac* (1963).

IAN: Yes. *Maniac* was shot in France – a wonderful area called Carmaque where they have wild horses and bulls. Sort of like Spain, actually. Of course, now, there are lots of hotels and things like that, but when we were there, there were hardly any hotels. The only thing there were lots of was mosquitoes. It was a marshy sort of area. Mosquitoes thrived there and loved it.

SAM: Michael Carreras himself directed *Maniac*. It was produced and written by Jimmy Sangster.

[NOTE: This was the fourth feature film directed by Michael Carreras, following *The Steel Bayonet* (1957), *Passport to China* (1961), and the non-Hammer movie *The Savage Guns* (1962). Following *Maniac*, Michael directed the non-Hammer movie *What a Crazy World* (1963) and four more Hammer films: *The Curse of the Mummy's Tomb* (1964), *Prehistoric Women* (1967), *The Lost Continent* (1968), and *Shatter* (1974). Additionally, when director Seth Holt died during the shooting of *Blood from the Mummy's Tomb* (1971), Michael took over and completed directing the film, though he did not take credit.]

IAN: Yes. Aside from the location work in France, we did the stage work out of MGM Studios.

James Carreras.

Anthony Hinds.

SAM: What was the difference between Bray Studios and MGM Studios?

IAN: Well, Bray Studios was owned by Hammer during the years I worked as Michael's assistant. It was a relatively small studio and we would only shoot one picture at a time, so everybody was working for you. It was much easier to handle problems and everything else because everybody was working on that one movie. If you went into MGM Studios, you were one of four or five pictures.

SAM: What is the difference MGM Studios and Elstree Studios?

IAN: MGM Studios was a bigger studio than Elstree Studios. Elstree might have one or two pictures going at the same time.

SAM: So why would Michael Carreras shoot *Maniac* at MGM Studios instead of Bray?

IAN: I don't remember. It could have been an overlap in shooting schedules. Bray may have been tied up on another Hammer film.

SAM: Or maybe Michael wanted to get out from under the watchful gaze of his father, to be more independent?

IAN: Maybe, but I don't think so. I really don't remember the reason.

SAM: Were there problems on the shooting of *Maniac*?

IAN: On the last day of shooting in France, we had some bad weather and Michael shot through for something like 18 or 20 hours, and we caught the plane back. In order to get the crew to do it, we said we'd pay them two days instead of just one day. We'd double up, which was not in the union agreement or anything, but we said that's what we'd do to get them to work. Then, when we got back, we went to MGM Studios. There was a standard three o'clock meeting every day in the studio and all the production managers went there

to discuss what they wanted for the next day, to make sure everything was ready and all that sort of thing. There were three other productions in there at the time. The studio manager stood up and he bollocked Bill Hill, the production manager, and myself in front of everybody in the most appalling way.

SAM: On what grounds?

IAN: Over the payment of extra overtime for the crew. It happened on a weekend. There was nobody working at the studio, so we couldn't discuss what we needed to do with anybody, so we just did it. And we had to make our booked charter flight for the return to England. This studio manager had no right whatsoever to bollock me and Bill in front of all the other production managers and everyone else. All the management people from all the other productions were there at that meeting. It was most appalling. It's something you never, ever, *ever* do. It made Bill and me look like we had no authority whatsoever. He'd undermined us. Mind you, the other people all knew it was wrong. But it was quite an unpleasant experience. So, Bill and I walked out. We went and told Jimmy Sangster [the producer on *Maniac*] what had happened and we stopped shooting for two days because the studio manager wouldn't apologize.

SAM: So, basically, the whole production of *Maniac* went on strike at MGM Studios?

IAN: Yes. In the end, he apologized, and we carried on shooting. But he was one of the most unpleasant people ever.

SAM: How did Michael Carreras compare to the other directors?

IAN: Even though Michael was mostly a producer, he always wanted to direct. He was what you'd call "a frustrated director." So this was one of the few films he ended up directing. As a director, Michael was fairly sure of what he wanted but he always had his editor around him. One of the biggest things of his life, really, was to become a director. But he certainly didn't want to direct a standard Hammer Horror. He was very nice to work with – but he did have, lurking beneath the waves, rather a tough temper if he wasn't getting what he wanted. So you had to be fairly careful with him – but then, I knew that because I had been working with him long enough to know when to back off. You could see what was coming if you knew him well enough. You could see it coming.

SAM: The dynamic of working with Michael Carreras as a director must have been very different than working with, say, Terence Fisher or Val Guest, because Michael was the son of James Carreras, the owner of the company. How could anyone say, "No, you can't have that," to Michael Carreras?

IAN: Well, if Jimmy Carreras had wanted his son to direct, that might have been a problem. But Jimmy really didn't want Michael to direct – and it caused a lot of friction between them.

SAM: Because James didn't think he was a good director?

IAN: I don't know about that, but Jimmy definitely did not agree with the kinds of movies Michael wanted to make. The only thing Jimmy wanted to make was standard Hammer Horrors. Michael didn't want to do that. So Jimmy had to be persuaded by Michael to make these other types of movies.

SAM: And doubly-persuaded to let Michael direct from time to time.

IAN: Yes.

SAM: So, in other words, when Michael finally got his father to agree to let him direct the occasional picture, it was clear that he did not have carte blanche. In fact, quite the opposite. If Michael screwed up, or went over budget, he'd have a very hard time convincing is father to ever let him direct again.

IAN: That's right. So, Michael wasn't about to let things get out of control when he was directing. He could be very tough on his production manager, though. If the production manager came to Michael and said something like, "This prop is going to cost us a lot more money than what we have in the budget," the production manager had to be bloody sure of his facts when he said it. Because if Michael found a cheaper way to do it, the production manager would be in for it.

SAM: Because if Michael didn't like the answer the production manager had given him, he would check on the costs himself?

IAN: Yes. The production manager really didn't have very much authority over him. In fact, he had none.

SAM: So then it sounds like, at certain times, Michael actually *did* throw his weight around because he was the son of the owner. Right?

IAN: No. Michael wasn't difficult in that way – but he knew what he wanted and he was going to get it. He was demanding in that way.

SAM: It seems like Michael was pretty persuasive with his father to get as many non-Hammer Horrors made as he did.

IAN: As long as we had five or six standard Hammer Horrors made during a year, Michael might get one or two out-of-the-ordinary pictures to either produce or sometimes direct. *Camp on Blood Island* was out of the ordinary. *Taste of Fear* was out of the ordinary. *Maniac* was out of the ordinary. And those were Michael. That's what he wanted to do. What happened towards the end of my time there, Tony Nelson-Keys moved up to producing – and he was making the standard Hammer Horrors, just like Tony Hinds had been doing. Michael wanted no part of that. Michael was making his "specials." He tried to make a classier movie than the standard Hammer Horrors. But, unfortunately, Michael's "specials" didn't always do that well.

SAM: How did Anthony Hinds feel about Michael's agenda?

IAN: I don't know. I never knew if Tony Hinds liked what Michael was doing or if he didn't. They went their separate ways and didn't cross paths. Tony Hinds didn't want trouble.

Val Guest.

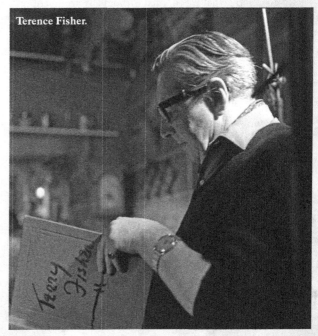

Terence Fisher.

SAM: What was the dynamic between Michael Carreras and Tony Hinds? Did they get along or were they competitive?

IAN: They got along really quite well. I never experienced a row between them in any way. But I wasn't in on board meetings or anything like that. So whether there were rows, I don't know.

SAM: How was Tony Hinds' management style different from Michael Carreras?

IAN: I'll give you an example. When we were at Bray Studios, the sound microphone had to be left on at all times and it was fed through to Tony Hinds' office and the production manager's office. And my office used to be at the back of the sort of entrance to the studios but I could see where Tony Hinds parked his car. I used to see him suddenly come out of his offices, get in his car and drive away. Then I'd see the production manager come out of his office and rush to the stage.

SAM: So, Tony Hinds was avoiding confrontation. He'd send the production manager to be the bad cop.

IAN: Yes. Tony didn't want to get into whatever trouble was going on the set. He'd heard it through the speaker in his office and he would disappear so the production manager had to deal with it.

SAM: If that had been Michael Carreras, he'd have gone right to the set and dealt with the problem himself?

IAN: Yes. That was the difference. Michael didn't mind being confrontational.

SAM: If Michael Carreras really wanted to be a director, would you say that Tony Hinds preferred being a writer, which he did quite often under the pseudonym John Elder?

IAN: Yes. Tony Hinds was very, very keen on writing scripts. He really wasn't that interested in making the movies.

SAM: Do you think that's because Tony Hinds worked better alone at a typewriter than trying to manage the chaos of thirty or forty people on a film set?

IAN: He certainly seemed happiest when he was writing. That's why he loved Terry Fisher because he knew Terry would do exactly what was needed without any argument or trouble. Tony wanted smooth sailing.

SAM: Why didn't Michael work with Terence Fisher more often? Was Fisher considered more like a member of Tony Hinds' camp?

IAN: Maybe. If Michael couldn't direct a picture himself, he would always try to bring in a bigger director of some standing.

SAM: But Terence Fisher had just as big a track record as, say, Val Guest or Seth Holt.

IAN: I think maybe from Michael's point of view, Terry Fisher had typed himself as a Hammer Horror director. Michael preferred using directors who were currently doing other types of pictures.

THE DEVIL-SHIP PIRATES

SAM: You were starting to tell me about the time a galleon nearly capsized during the shooting of *The Pirates of Blood River*, but that accident actually happened during the shooting of *The Devil-Ship Pirates*.

IAN: I must have been transposing the Pirate titles.

SAM: Easy to do, since both movies starred Christopher Lee and Andrew Kier, both were shot at Bray Studios, and both were produced by Anthony Nelson-Keys. In any event, *The Devil-Ship Pirates* does not have a credit for Michael Carreras as executive producer or anything else. So, how did you become involved in a non-Michael Carreras movie?

[NOTE: *The Devil-Ship Pirates* was shot at Bray Studios from August to October 1963.]

IAN: That picture was made on the sand pits that filled up with water and became lakes beside the studio. We nearly killed the whole crew and quite a large number of the stars. The set of the galleon was built on two enormous tanks that could be filled or emptied to make it float properly. They had a naval man who told them how to build it. I believe they were trying to make the boat sink a bit. Actually, I can't remember what they were trying to do because I wasn't there. Anyway, they were emptying water out of the bottom tank and the boat nearly turned turtle. Jimmy Carreras called me into his office and said, "Get down to the studios and sort this out! This is appalling!" And that's when Tony Nelson-Keys and I crossed swords. You see, I actually happened to be a sailor and knew a thing or two about floatation. This mariner that he'd got in to help them build the apparatus – well, he may have been wonderful in submarines but he certainly didn't understand anything about boats floating. And what I had to do was to make sure that they never got into that position again. I think I won Tony Nelson-Keys over in the end because Tony was always very jealous of

THE EPIC SAGA BEHIND *FRANKENSTEIN: THE TRUE STORY*

me. I don't know why. He had the job. I didn't. But he was very, very jealous of me. The fact that I was sent down by the head of the company to sort out what was going on with the boat was almost the last straw. But I went about it in my usual tactful way and I won him round – and in the end he did actually come up to me and say, "Thank you for saving us – because you obviously did." So we got on quite well after that. In fact, I took over as production manager on that one to see it through safely. After I left Hammer, it was Tony Nelson-Keys who hired me back to production manage three of the Hammer pictures he produced – because he wanted me on them and trusted me to do the job right.

SAM: Those pictures would be *Frankenstein Created Woman* (1967), *Quatermass and the Pit* (1967) and *The Devil Rides Out* (1968).
IAN: Precisely.

SAM: Don Sharpe directed *The Devil-Ship Pirates*. What was your impression of him?
IAN: Well, after the scare, he was really quite amiable. He'd been on the boat when it nearly capsized so I think I was rather welcomed because of that.

[NOTE: On IMDB.com, the trivia page for *The Devil-Ship Pirates* offers this similar account of the accident: "According to Christopher Lee, Hammer had built a full-sized galleon in some sand pits on a steel structure under the water. Although warned not to have too many people on board at once, one day the tea boat was lifted onto a platform level with the water with too many people getting their tea. The ship capsized throwing most of the cast and crew in the water. Lee was on the poop deck and luckily managed to hold onto the rail. Thankfully no one was drowned or seriously hurt."]

THE CURSE OF THE MUMMY'S TOMB
SAM: The next picture Michael Carreras did was *The Curse of the Mummy's Tomb* (1964), which was the one time he directed what could be categorized as a "Hammer Horror."
IAN: Are you sure Michael directed that one?

SAM: Yes. He directed, produced – and he even wrote the screenplay, too, under the pseudonym Henry Younger – which was obviously a wink to Hinds' pseudonym John Elder.
IAN: I'm puzzling about it because I don't remember it.

No memory of that one at all. The next picture I did with Michael was *She*.

SHE
SAM: *She* was the biggest picture Michael Carreras had produced to date. It apparently had triple the usual Hammer budget.
IAN: Quite right. It was a much bigger film and Michael was very proud of it.

SAM: The cast was very impressive, too. Peter Cushing, Christopher Lee, John Richardson, Bernard Cribbins and André Morell. But, of course, the main attraction was the actress who played the title role, Ursula Andress, who, at that time, was a very big international star, hot on the heels of *Dr. No* (1962), in which she played Honey Ryder, the very first Bond Girl.
IAN: I've got a very funny little story I can tell you about that. So we were there at Elstree Studios and the costume designer came in and said, "You want to see the costumes that Ursula Andress is going to wear?" Michael said to me, "Come on, we better go have a look at these costumes." So, we went into her dressing room, which had two rooms. Ursula was already in the first costume when we got there. Michael looked at it and said, "That's nice. Let's see the next one." So she's goes into the other room to take it off and put the next one on – but she leaves the door wide open. She undid two things and the dress floated down to the floor. She was absolutely stark naked. My eyes were out in stalks as you can imagine. And she put the next one on, and so forth. She tried four costumes out.

SAM: With a little striptease in-between each one?
IAN: Yes! (laughs) Well, that's one of the most exciting things I think I've ever done.

SAM: There was also an executive producer on *She* named Aida Young [who had previously associate produced *What a Crazy World* for Michael's independent company Capricorn Film Productions].
IAN: Yes. Aida Young was a difficult cookie.

SAM: In what way?
IAN: Let me just say she was a very short lady, dumpy, very opinionated, and could be incredibly difficult. She liked to think that she got along well with everybody, but quite honestly she didn't. She thought she got on very well with

Michael Carreras.

Aida Young on ther set of *The Vengeance of She*.

Michael. But because I was Michael's assistant, there was a certain amount of jealousy that I had Michael's ears. Aida didn't like that. I used to come up against her frequently.

SAM: Aside from the stage work done at Elstree Studios, were you also involved in the location shooting on *She*?
IAN: Yes. We went to Israel. Whatever tasks I was doing for Michael at the time were not enough to keep me busy, so I ended up becoming sort of the location manager on that picture. There wasn't an experienced location manager on the crew so I basically had to take over as location manager.

SAM: On IMDB, I see that a guy named Yoske Hausoorf is credited as the location manager.
IAN: I don't remember if that was his name but the production manager from the Israeli crew didn't have enough experience. At least not experienced in the way a British film crew worked.

SAM: So you had to jump in and pick up the slack.
IAN: Yes. We had a lot of problems because the Arabs came over the border. We were based in Eilat, a very small village with one hotel, which is where we were staying. Before we would be allowed to venture out to the shooting location in the Negev Desert, the Israeli Army had to go out first to repair the telephone line, which went all the way up to Jerusalem. The Arabs used to come across the border and steal the copper telephone wires. So the Army had to go out first. We were not allowed to go out until the phone lines had been repaired and then we'd go out to the location. I

was helping move from location to location. One day, we finished shooting in one area, so we were moving to another area about two-and-a-half miles away – and I was helping with that move. I stayed behind because there were still some things to move and I was basically left out in the desert alone, which was a very spooky experience. You think you hear something and then you don't hear it. It was quite, quite frightening. I had been sitting there waiting, guarding what we had left, and suddenly a Jeep comes up and it was Michael Carreras and Aida Young. Michael gave me the biggest bollocking I'd had for a long while. And I said, "I'm sorry, I was staying here in order to get the stuff back." He said, "Well, the others came back a long time ago." I said, "They were supposed to come back to me to get the final load." He said, "Well, they didn't – and it is very dangerous for you to be out here alone." It was that sort of argument. It was a simple misunderstanding blown out of proportion. But then Aida Young joined in and started yelling at me, too. It was completely unnecessary. Anyway, Michael apologized to me the next day. He was very, very worried about my safety because of what was going on, you know? Anything could happen out there – which is why we had to have the Army.

SAM: Did Aida Young apologize?
IAN: No, she didn't. Now, I have another intriguing little story that happened there that would interest you. We had a wonderful special effects guy from the Israeli Army.

SAM: What was his name?
IAN: I don't recall.

SAM: IMDB lists the special effects department as George Blackwell, Les Bowie, Ian Scoones and Kit West.
IAN: No, none of them. He may not have gotten credit because he was with the Israeli Army. Anyway, this fellow was doing some bullet effects for us by putting detonators just

under the surface of the sand – and setting them off one after another so it looked like bullets going along.

SAM: Rows of squibs?
IAN: Yes, with little electric charges – connected by electrical wires hidden beneath the sand. That's what would fire them off. Well, these detonators were not very good. They were provided by the Israeli Army because we weren't allowed to bring anything like that with us into Israel. It wouldn't have cleared customs. So, we were doing a rehearsal. It was Bernie Cribbins, Peter Cushing and John Richardson, I think. And suddenly, because of the heat of the sand, these detonators started going off – and two of them went off under Bernie Cribbins' bum. He wasn't really very badly damaged, but the special effects guy dashed in and started pulling the detonators out of the sand and they went off in his hand. I had to drive him into Eilat to the hospital and he lost a finger. It was a frightening experience. We corresponded afterwards. And years later I saw him again when I did another picture out there – a miniseries called *Masada*. He didn't work on it. I just looked him up socially.

[NOTE: *Masada* (1981) was a miniseries produced by Universal Television for ABC-TV. Ian is credited as the Production Coordinator but he actually took over the production as Line Producer. The four-part series was directed by Boris Sagal and starred Peter O'Toole, Peter Strauss, Barbara Carrera, Anthony Quayle and David Warner, narrated by Richard Basehart.]

SAM: In *She*, Ursula Andress' voice ended by being dubbed by Nikki Van der Zyl who had previously dubbed Ursula's lines in *Dr. No*.
IAN: Yes. Ursula was Swiss and she had a very heavy Swiss accent. It was very, very difficult to understand her. So, we had to dub her voice. American distributors were very fussy back then about accents. We had to make sure every bit of dialogue could be easily understood by American audiences.

SAM: Nikki Van der Zyl also happened to dub Susan Denberg's part in *Frankenstein Created Woman*. Did you ever meet her?
IAN: No. That was all done by the sound department during post-production.

[NOTE: Nikki Van der Zyl dubbed the voice of Ursula Andress in four pictures: *Dr. No*, *She*, *Casino Royale* and *The Blue Max*. She also dubbed Raquel Welch in *One Million Years B.C.*; Eunice Gayson in *From Russia with Love*; Shirley Eaton in *Goldfinger*; Claudine Auger in *Thunderball*; Eva Renzi in *Funeral in Berlin*; Sylva Coscini in *Deadlier than the Male*; Mie Hama in *You Only Live Twice*; Suzy Kendall in *Fraulein Doktor*; Jenny Hanley in *Scars of Dracula*; Jane Seymour in *Live and Let Die*; Lulu in *The Cherry Picker*; Francoise Therry in *The Man with the Golden Gun*; Corinne Clery in *Moonraker*; among many others. She actually played an on-screen bit part in *Destiny of a Spy* (1969), a Universal Television spy thriller for NBC that Ian associate produced, starring Lorne Greene, Rachel Roberts, Anthony Quayle, James Donald (*Quatermass and the Pit*), Harry Andrews, Patrick Magee, and Angela Pleasence; the TV-movie was directed by Boris Sagal (*The Omega Man*), based on the novel *The Gaunt Woman* by John Backburn (*Nothing but the Night*), with an entire crew of Hammer Film veterans, including director of photography

Arthur Grant, production designer Bernard Robinson, wardrobe supervisor Rosemary Burrows, music supervisor Philip Martell, and assistant director Bert Batt. Nikki later became a lawyer and painter.]

SAM: Peter Cushing and Christopher Lee were starring in *She*, too.
IAN: Yes. They were supporting actors in this one. But they were the professionals. Along with Bernie Cribbins. The *other* two were the amateurs.

SAM: Meaning who?
IAN: Ursula Andress and John Richardson.

SAM: You mean their acting abilities weren't as great as their looks?
IAN: Yes. Of course, Ursula Andress went on to do other things, but she wasn't a great actress. And John Richardson? I don't think he ever did anything else, did he?

SAM: Well, he went on to play Raquel Welch's love interest in *One Million Years B.C.* (1966) – which was Michael Carreras' biggest success ever as a producer. And Hammer's biggest moneymaker.
IAN: But, again, relying on his looks more than his acting.

SAM: He made a lot of B-pictures, a lot of Italian movies. His one big studio picture was Vincente Minnelli's *On a Clear Day You Can See Forever* (1970) starring Barbra Streisand, Yves Montand and Jack Nicholson. Richardson plays a nobleman in 1800s England who was married to Streisand in a former life. But, you're right, he really wasn't called upon to do much more than look drop-dead handsome in a few dream-like flashbacks. Getting back to *She*, though, did Christopher Lee mind playing a supporting role?
IAN: I don't think we had any problems with Christopher Lee on that picture. I don't think we had any problems at all with any of our actors. We had a very happy cast, really. Peter Cushing was always a delight. Bernie Cribbins was lovely.

SAM: What about André Morell?
IAN: Very nice as well – but he wasn't around as much. He had a fairly small part.

SAM: What were your impressions of the director of *She*, Robert Day?

[NOTE: Robert Day had previously directed the celebrated Alistair Sim comedy *The Green Man* (1956); two back-to-back Boris Karloff horror pictures *The Haunted Strangler* (1958) and *Corridors of Blood* (1958); the sci-fi thriller *First Man into Space* (1959); two Tarzan pictures *Tarzan the Magnificent* (1960) and *Tarzan's Three Challenges* (1963); and twelve episodes of *The Adventures of Robin Hood* (1957-1960). His well-rounded resume, with an emphasis on adventure, was just the sort of director that Michael Carreras wanted for *She*. Afterward, Day went on to a very big career as a television director, highlighted by the HBO western *The Quick and the Dead* (1987) starring Sam Elliott, Tom Conti and Kate Capeshaw. When Ian Lewis was Managing Director of Universal Pictures Ltd, he supervised another project directed by Robert Day entitled *Peter and Paul* (1981), the Emmy Award winning Biblical miniseries, produced by

Universal Television for CBS, starring Anthony Hopkins, Robert Foxworth, Jon Finch, Herbert Lom, Raymond Burr, José Ferrer, Eddie Albert, Julian Fellowes and John Rhys-Davies.]

IAN: Oh, Robert Day was a lovely fellow. Lovely man. Very good director. Worked very well with everybody. He did very well on that movie. Very well. The crew liked him. The cast loved him. He was one of those very nice directors. In modern days, you don't often find them.

SAM: How was the rest of the crew?
IAN: It was all a very happy crew, a very happy crew indeed… apart from Aida.

SAM: Did you know the composer James Bernard well?
IAN: No, I didn't. I knew Phil Martell who was the music supervisor was on it.

SAM: Yes. You later hired Philip Martell to be the music supervisor for *Frankenstein: The True Story* (1973).
IAN: Quite right. I was just beginning to get to know Phil back then, but I got to know him very well. He was a marvelous musical director. Composers don't always think about what goes on around their music. And Phil was always one who said, "Look, the music has got to go down under the dialogue." He didn't believe in turning the music down on the volume control. He'd say, "That's the lazy way to do it." He was always very, very insistent about that. He would argue with composers. I remember one time after the first score came in – I can't remember which picture it was on – but the score came in and nobody else had heard it or seen it. He'd just seen it, and he came in to Michael and said, "This is not good at all. It's not gonna work. You won't like it. We can't record it." And after a long discussion, we decided we'd change the composer and redo it because, literally, Phil said, "I've looked at the score. It's no good." And he was always right. Always right.

ONE MILLION YEARS B.C.
SAM: After the tremendous success of *She*, Michael Carreras next produced *One Million Years B.C.*, which became an even bigger success – and turned Raquel Welch into a major international star.
IAN: I'd left Hammer by then.

SAM: So, *She* was the last Hammer film you'd worked on as Michael's assistant?
IAN: It was. I left when *She* was still in post-production. Michael had a huge row with his father. They had a big falling out. Michael left the company for a while, or at least he wasn't involved in any of their pictures for a while.

SAM: It couldn't have been too long because Michael next produced *One Million Years B.C.*, which began shooting in October 1965, about a year after *She* had wrapped principal photography.
IAN: Yes, but in those days at Hammer, a year was a long time not to be shooting something.

SAM: So, *One Million Years B.C.* was a kind of a reunion for Michael to come back into the fold?
IAN: I think it was Jimmy's doing. I don't know, so I'm really surmising here, so I don't wanna be held to it. But I suspect that Jimmy gave him *One Million Years B.C.* in order to bring him back. And *One Million Years B.C.* was not really what Michael wanted to make. It's not his style of movie.

LEAVING HAMMER
SAM: So, why did you end up leaving Hammer?
IAN: I actually left Hammer after this an enormous row between Michael and Jimmy Carreras. It was quite obvious to me that I couldn't stay.

SAM: What exactly happened?
IAN: As we discussed earlier, Michael wanted to direct. He also wanted to make bigger pictures. And *Maniac* was one of the first bigger pictures. It went outside the Hammer recipe. I don't think it did too badly – but I don't think it did all that well. And all Jimmy ever wanted was the Hammer recipe. Those are the pictures he knew he could sell to the major American distribution companies like Universal International. Jimmy knew he'd get the money. He knew how to get the money. And he knew how to get the money before we'd even gone into production. Which was incredible. But he had very strong relationships with American distributors – and he knew exactly what they would buy. Movies like *Maniac* didn't fit in with that pattern. Jimmy didn't want to make the kinds of films that Michael wanted to do, so the relationship between them was always strained.

SAM: So that's what the big blow-up argument was all about?
IAN: Well, this tension between them ended up affecting me in a roundabout way. After I'd been working as Michael's assistant for quite some time, and I was proving myself to be more than just an assistant, it was time for me to start moving up the ladder a little bit and Michael seemed to be promoting that idea. Michael told me that he'd had discussions with Tony Hinds and Jimmy Carreras that I would go down and understudy Jimmy Carreras. Michael and Tony Hinds would carry on making their pictures. But I would basically be groomed to become a salesman, like Jimmy.

SAM: So, in other words, James Carreras wasn't getting any younger and there would come a day when he would either reduce his workload, or perhaps even retire, so the company needed an up-and-comer like yourself to learn the ropes and become like a protégé of James – someone he could introduce to all those major studio relationships?

Someone who could eventually step into that position.
IAN: That's basically it – because Michael didn't want that job. He wanted to *make* movies, not be a *sales* guy. So Michael had been laying the groundwork for me to become a salesman. It would also be a big move up for me. Well, promises had been made but nothing concrete was happening for an awfully long time. I kept on saying to Michael, "Well? When's it gonna happen?" I had also sought the advice of my old neighbor and mentor Jack Goodlatte. I said to Jack, "Look, this what they want me to do." And I took his advice, which was to take it.

SAM: After promises were made, how much time went by with nothing happening?
IAN: This went on for about six months. And I kept on saying, "Is anything happening? When am I going to move downstairs to the second floor?"

SAM: The second floor at Hammer House was where James Carreras and his team were situated.
IAN: Yes. And finally one evening, I said to Michael, "Is anything ever going to happen?" And he stood up in a really bad mood and he said, "I'm going down to see my father about that right now." And we could hear the row up on the fourth floor of Hammer House. And they were down on the second. Finally, Michael came back and said, "My father is now denying that the proposal was ever made to you."

SAM: Wow. That must have been devastating.
IAN: The problem was there was a man called Brian Lawrence who was the company secretary and an accountant. And Brian saw himself as the next Jimmy Carreras. And he had gone in and undermined Michael and Tony Hinds who had talked to Jimmy about me being promoted. Jimmy took Brian's side and basically said the job had never been offered to me. Which was quite untrue. So, I said to Michael, "In that case, I think we'll have to part company – because I can't live in a situation where that sort of thing has happened." And he agreed with me and said, "No, you can't." It was very disappointing and a very emotional parting of the ways.

SAM: I'm sure.
IAN: So, I left. And that's when I became a freelance production manager.

FREELANCE PRODUCTION MANAGING
SAM: How did your career as a freelance production manager get started?
IAN: Well, remember the story I told you about getting into the union on *Sword of Sherwood Forest* – after I'd caught the Irish production manager stealing film stock? Well, as I said, the producer on that movie, Sid Cole. got me into the union and got me my card, so ever since then, I had the legal ability to be a production manager if I'd wanted to. I just hadn't had the opportunity to really do that since then. So, when I left Hammer, I decided it was time to put that union card to use and become a freelance production manager.

SAM: How did you get your first break in that arena?
IAN: It all goes back to *Sword of Sherwood Forest*. We were shooting in a tiny studio in Dublin called Bray Studios, not to be confused with the Bray Studios that Hammer owned in London. There were only two stages, so it was a very small studio. Even so, we were not the only movie shooting there at that time. The other movie based there was being production managed by Bill Hill.

SAM: I just looked up William Hill's credits on IMDB and that other movie must have been *Johnny Nobody* (1961), which was shot at Bray Studios Ireland. Directed by and starring Nigel Patrick.
IAN: That's the one. So, there were days when we needed both stages and there were days when the other film needed both stages, so Bill and I had to work very closely together to carefully schedule this all out like a puzzle, so one company would be out shooting locations while the other company would be at the studio shooting in the stages. And, as a result, we became very friendly.

SAM: And after that, you crossed paths with Bill Hill again on *A Taste of Fear*, *Maniac*, and *Curse of the Mummy's Tomb*.
IAN: Exactly right. Remember the story I told you about *Maniac*? Bill and I were the ones who got bollocked by the studio manager at MGM Studios – and we went on strike for two days.

SAM: So, you and Bill Hill had really bonded through tough times on more than one occasion. Almost like war buddies.
IAN: Yes. Our friendship was very solid.

COURT MARTIAL
SAM: I see that after *Maniac*, the next picture Bill Hill production managed was *From Russia with Love* (1963). That's a pretty nice step up the food chain.
IAN: Indeed. So, when I left Hammer, Bill Hill was production managing a series for Universal Television called *Court Martial* starring Brad Dillman and Peter Graves. He moved up to producing that series and recommended me to George Santoro at Universal Television. George hired me to production manage it and we became great friends.

[NOTE: *Court Marshall*, set during World War II, starred Bradford Dillman and Peter Graves as JAG agents investigating crimes all over Europe. Twenty-six episodes were broadcast in the United States on ABC-TV, April-September 1966, featuring such guest stars as Oliver Reed, Donald Sutherland, Judi Dench, Darren McGavin, Dennis Hopper, Sal Mineo, Mark Lester, Anthony Quayle, Michael Hordern, Dennis Price, Joan Hackett, Diane Cilento, Ferdy Mayne, Kate O'Mara, Bernard Lee and Martine Beswick. Directors included Seth Holt (*The Nanny*, *A Taste of Fear*, *Blood from the Mummy's Tomb*), Sam Wanamaker (*Sinbad and the Eye of the Tiger*) and Silvio Narizzano (*Georgy Girl*, *Die, Die My Darling!*).]

DOCTOR IN CLOVER
SAM: Next, you officially production managed your first feature film, *Doctor in Clover*.
IAN: That was one of the *Doctor* film series produced by Betty Box for the Rank Organisation. Betty was a wonderful producer. It was a family atmosphere like the early days of Hammer.

[NOTE: *Doctor in Clover* (1966), released in the U.S. as *Carnaby, M.D.*, directed by Ralph Thomas and produced by Betty. E. Box for the Rank Organisation. It starred Leslie

Phillips, James Robertson Justice, John Fraser, Joan Sims and Suzan Farmer (*Dracula, Prince of Darkness*; *Rasputin the Mad Monk*; *Die, Monster, Die!*).]

FRANÇOIS TRAUFFAUT'S *FAHRENHEIT 451*

[NOTE: *Fahrenheit 451* (1966), based on the book by Ray Bradbury, directed by François Truffaut, starring Julie Christie, Oskar Werner, Cyril Cusack an Anton Diffring (*The Man Who Could Cheat Death*, and Baron Frankenstein

in Hammer's television pilot *Tales of Frankenstein*). The film was shot January 13 through April 15, 1966, on locations in France and England, with stage work done at Pinewood Studios.]

SAM: Then Universal called you to come and production manage *Fahrenheit 451*, directed François Truffaut. What was he like?
IAN: Well, he didn't speak a lot of English, and bringing him into a big studio picture setup was very difficult because he was used to having a small, intimate crew around him of about six or eight. Also, he didn't get on well with the main actor, Oskar Werner. Oskar didn't tell him that he was afraid of fire. The entire premise is about burning books and his character had to use a flamethrower – which Oskar refused to operate. So we had to use a double.

SAM: Were there any other wrinkles you recall?
IAN: Yes. In the middle of April, I wake up about half-past-five in the morning and everywhere is covered in snow. We *never* have snow in April. So, I got dressed very quickly, dashed out to the location, and sent everybody back to the studio. Truffaut turned up and said, "I've decided that I'm

going to shoot the end sequence in the snow." I said, "But the snow will be gone by tomorrow morning." And he said, "That doesn't matter. I'll do it all today." So we got all the crew back out to the location and he shot it all – the final sequence of all the people reading the books to children, passing the books on. It was an amazing sequence. Next morning, the snow had gone. It was a miracle.

CHARLIE BUBBLES

[NOTE: *Charlie Bubbles* (1967), directed by Albert Finney who also played the title role. The supporting cast included Liza Minnelli, Billie Whitelaw, Colin Blakely, and two future *Frankenstein: The True Story* bit players: Peter Sallis and Yootha Joyce. The film was shot in fall of 1966 on locations around England, with stage work done again at Pinewood Studios.]

SAM: Then you did Universal's *Charlie Bubbles*, directed by Albert Finney, who also starred in the film with Liza Minnelli. After working on these big Universal projects, Hammer asked you back to production manage three of their finest films.
IAN: Yes. *Frankenstein Created Woman*, *Quatermass and the Pit* and *The Devil Rides Out*.

FRANKENSTEIN CREATED WOMAN

[NOTE: *Frankenstein Created Woman* (1967), Hammer Films, produced by Anthony Nelson-Keys and directed by Terence Fisher. Filmed from July 4 to August 12, 1966.]

SAM: Who invited you back to work at Hammer on *Frankenstein Created Woman*?
IAN: Tony Nelson-Keys invited me back.

SAM: Was there residual uneasiness between you, Michael Carreras and James Carreras?
IAN: No. I never saw James. And I basically never saw Michael. I just did the picture. I was a freelance production manager. I did the job and then left. It was just an engagement. Tony Nelson-Keys asked me to do it and it fit in with what I was doing. When you freelance, you take the first job that says they'll give you a contract. And that's what I did.

SAM: Anthony Hinds wrote *Frankenstein Created Woman* – under his usual nom de plume John Elder.
IAN: Quite right.

SAM: Was it common knowledge that John Elder was really Anthony Hinds?
IAN: Oh God, yes. Everyone knew.

SAM: Then why do you think he bothered to use a pseudonym?
IAN: I don't know what the reason for it was. I really have no idea.

SAM: I am assuming that since Anthony Hinds was just the writer on *Frankenstein Created Woman*, he was not around during the shoot.
IAN: Actually, he was around. He was there from time to time, but he didn't come in an awful lot. He used to appear at the studio, come in and we'd all say hello to each other, you know, and all the rest of it. But he wouldn't stay very long. By then, you see, the whole studio was in a totally different situation. There was none of the family atmosphere anymore. Yes, they'd like you to use people that they normally used, but if they were doing something else, then we went with somebody else. The family atmosphere had gone.

SAM: Did Anthony Hinds and Anthony Nelson-Keys get along well?
IAN: Yes, they got on very well. As far as I know there was no problem between them at all.

SAM: Now that you had moved up from being Michael Carreras' assistant to the position of production manager, did Anthony Hinds treat you differently at all?
IAN: No, no. He said, "Oh, it is lovely to see you back," and that sort of thing. Tony Hinds was always very nice to me. Very nice.

SAM: Were there rewrites during the shooting of *Frankenstein Created Woman*?
IAN: No, not that I recall. There weren't a lot of rewrites on Hammer films once they started shooting. The rewrites would happen during pre-production, especially if things were going to be too expensive. Well… there is the *other* story and it's vaguely true, that if we were going over budget on a picture or over schedule, and you went and told Tony Hinds, he'd say, "Well, what haven't we shot?" So, you would show him in the script what hadn't been shot and he'd tear some pages out and say, "Go ahead and shoot that and it will be all right."

SAM: Hilarious. I've heard that before but wondered if it was just legend.
IAN: It did actually happened on one or two occasions. I don't want to downgrade Hammer. That's not my intention. But, of course, the right way to do it would have been to call a meeting and discuss what we didn't need to shoot or how we could re-write a scene so it wouldn't put us over schedule. Tony Hinds just used to take out the pages and throw them away. That was it. It's very funny in retrospect.

SAM: Did something like that happen on *Frankenstein Created Woman*?
IAN: No, no, no. Absolutely not. Because the script was written by John Elder, who we all know is Tony Hinds.

SAM: So, the producer Tony Nelson-Keys wouldn't dare throw away pages of a script by Tony Hinds?

IAN: That's right. Even though Tony Nelson-Keys was the producer, Tony Hinds was in the background all the time.

SAM: Where did you shoot *Frankenstein Created Woman*?
IAN: Bray Studios.

SAM: This was one of the last Hammer films to be shot at Bray Studios.
IAN: That could be. I know *Quatermass and the Pit* and *The Devil Rides Out* were both shot at Elstree Studios, so that would make sense.

[NOTE: The last Hammer film shot at Bray Studios was *The Mummy's Shroud* which wrapped shooting on October 21, 1966. Hammer ceased making their films at Bray Studios after that and sold the studio in 1970.]

SAM: Where did you shoot exterior locations for *Frankenstein Created Woman*? In the early part of the film, Susan Denberg throws herself into a lake and then, at the end, she jumps into a river.
IAN: Well, it was most likely the same lake. I think that was shot at Black Park, right outside Pinewood Studios, not far away from Bray. Every nook and cranny of Black Park has been used by Hammer many times over. I think Hammer shot there more than anybody else.

SAM: What do you recall about Susan Denberg?
IAN: Tricky is how I would describe her. She wasn't easy.

SAM: How so?
IAN: Don't know exactly, but I wouldn't be at all surprised if she was on drugs.

SAM: Sadly, you're intuition is right. It has been well-documented.
IAN: Yes, well, I thought so. But, at that time, I didn't know much about drugs. Drugs in England at that time were really almost non-existent. So, the only time we got any involvement in that sort of thing was when we had an American star who was involved with it.

SAM: Did Susan have mood swings?
IAN: I never had to deal with her directly. But I know we had a lot of problems with her and, in the end, I think we figured out it had to be drugs that were causing the problems.

SAM: Was she difficult on set?
IAN: Yes, and it didn't matter who was around.

SAM: Did she come unprepared?
IAN: I can't tell you this for certain, but I think preparedness came into it.

SAM: As I mentioned earlier, all of Susan's dialogue ended up being dubbed by Nikki Van der Zyl, the same woman who replaced the voice of Ursula Andress in *She*.
IAN: Yes. At Hammer, if they found somebody who did things well, they stuck with them.

SAM: Why was Susan dubbed?
IAN: If I remember correctly, her performance needed enormous assistance.

SAM: She was born in Germany and raised in Austria, so I assumed she must have had a heavy German accent.
IAN: No, no. I don't remember an accent problem. But, honestly, I don't remember an awful lot about her except that she was quite difficult.

SAM: She was the centerfold in *Playboy*, the August 1966 issue, published in July when *Frankenstein Created Woman* was in the middle of shooting.
IAN: Yes. I think Michael fancied the boobs. (laughs) And that's not to be repeated.

SAM: Oh, Ian! Come on! That's hilarious! And if Michael were alive today, he'd admit to that in a heartbeat. Please let me use it.
IAN: Well… I'm probably not the first one to say it, but I said it as a joke. An offhand remark. I really have no idea whether Michael was involved in casting Susan or not. I have no idea. So, don't hold me to it. I really don't know who or why Susan was cast.

SAM: Was Peter Cushing upset about Susan Denberg's behavior?
IAN: I suspect he was, but I don't think he ever showed it. He might have said something to Michael.

SAM: What about Terence Fisher? Did he voice any concerns?
IAN: Terence kept all his problems to himself. But he knew when she was cast that he was going to have problems. So, he did his best to work around them.

SAM: Tell me what you recall about Thorley Walters who played sort of a Dr. Watson-like sidekick to Cushing's Dr. Frankenstein.
IAN: There's not much to tell about him, really. He was very nice and a good actor. Very professional. He did very well.

SAM: Did you know that Martin Scorsese is a fan of *Frankenstein Created Woman*?
IAN: Really? Well, I had no idea.

SAM: Scorsese selected *Frankenstein Created Woman* as part of a National Film Theatre season in London of his favorite guilty pleasures.

[NOTE: Martin Scorsese's exact quote regarding *Frankenstein Created Woman* reads as follows: "I like all Hammer films. If I singled this one out, it's not because I like it the best – it's a sadistic film, very difficult to watch – but because, here, they actually isolate the soul: a bright blue shining translucent ball. The implied metaphysic is close to something sublime."]

SAM: Were you involved at all in post-production on *Frankenstein Created Woman*?
IAN: No. Just prep and shooting. I'm afraid it was just another job and then I moved onto the next one.

QUATERMASS AND THE PIT

SAM: A few months later, Anthony Nelson-Keys hired you again to production manage *Quatermass and the Pit* which was shot February 27 through April 25, 1967.
IAN LEWS: Quite right.

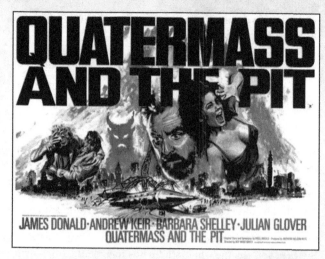

SAM: The director was Roy Ward Baker. How did he compare to Terence Fisher?
IAN: He was a very good, very reliable director. You were not going get anything out of the ordinary from him. He was a very nice man, very easy to work with. If you told him he's only got five crowns, he figured out how to make it work. I got on very well with him.

SAM: Roy Ward Baker was quite well regarded for *A Night to Remember* (1958), the Titanic movie.
IAN: Yes, that was a very big Rank picture made at Pinewood. *Very* big. But don't forget, a decade had passed by then.

SAM: Roy apparently wanted Kenneth More, the star of *A Night to Remember*, to be the star of *Quatermass and the Pit* and wasn't too happy when Hammer cast Andrew Keir instead.
IAN: Yes, well, Andrew Keir was a lot cheaper than Kenneth More. It was purely a matter of money. But Andrew was very good. Not a bad substitute at all. Of course, as I'm sure you know, this wasn't the first Quatermass movie that Hammer made.

SAM: This was the third one, following *The Quatermass Xperiment* (1955) and *Quatermass 2* (1957), both starring Brian Donlevy as Professor Bernard Quatermass.
IAN: Quite right. Hammer got the rights from the BBC.

SAM: It started as a television series in 1953.
IAN: I wasn't around then when Hammer did the first two movies. Hammer still had the movie rights to the character and that's why they wanted to do it, because it didn't cost them any money for the rights.

SAM: What do you recall about the production of *Quatermass and the Pit*? Was it a standard Hammer budget?
IAN: I think it was a little bit over the standard budget because the biggest problem was the alien and how we were going to do that. That was the biggest budget problem. There were many, many discussions about how we were going to do it.

SAM: Where was the underground train station filmed – where they excavate the spaceship?
IAN: On the same stages where we shot the rest of the picture – at MGM Studios.

SAM: Not at Bray Studios.
IAN: That's right.

SAM: Bernard Robinson was the production designer.
IAN: Yes. Bernard Robinson was an absolute master at making things look big. If I remember correctly, the budget was bigger, because we knew the alien and the underground set were going to be a bit more expensive. So we did have a bit more money for that. And, of course, we also had to do the cranes – though a lot of that was model work. Miniatures.

SAM: Were there any problems on that production?
IAN: Not especially – other than figuring out how to make the alien look right. I'm not absolutely certain of this, but I think by the time we got to the model work, we really didn't have an awful lot of money left. I'm trying to remember. Something happened on that picture about the crane sequence. But I can't remember what it was. I've just got it in the back of my mind that we had a problem.

SAM: If my shooting dates are correct, this film had a bit longer schedule than the usual Hammer film – about eight weeks.
IAN: Maybe that's what I'm thinking of – is that we went over schedule because of the troubles we were having with making the alien and all the rest of it work.

SAM: Barbara Shelley was in this. What was she like to work with?
IAN: Very nice. A very nice lady. A very good actress, too.

SAM: And Julian Glover?
IAN: Yes, well, you never could complain about Julian Glover. I worked with him on many occasions. He was a lovely actor.

SAM: Arthur Grant was the director of photography. What was he like?
IAN: Oh, lovely, lovely man. Really lovely man. Never took any more time than absolutely needed. He knew what he had to do. He did an awful lot of Hammer pictures.

SAM: He shot so many of the Hammer films you worked on – including *Hell Is a City, Passport to China, The Pirates of Blood River, Frankenstein Created Woman, Quatermass and the Pit, and The Devil Rides Out.*
IAN: Right. He was great. He wasn't somebody that you would get any finesse with, you know? But a lovely, lovely man to work with. Arthur Ibbetson, who was the DP on *Frankenstein: The True Story*, was another one like that. The same. When you've got to make a picture look big with very little money, you need somebody who's going to be on your side.

THE DEVIL RIDES OUT

SAM: So, the last Hammer film you worked on was *The Devil Rides Out*. You were the production manager.

[NOTE: *The Devil Rides Out* (1968), released in America as *The Devil's Bride*, starring Christopher Lee and Charles Gray, directed by Terence Fisher, screenplay by Richard Matheson from the novel by Dennis Wheatley, produced by Anthony Nelson-Keys.]

IAN: Yes, that was produced by Tony Nelson-Keys again, with Terry Fisher directing.

SAM: What do you remember about this production?
IAN: Well, I remember vividly it had quite a bit of night shooting in Black Park – the ritual scenes with the coven – and the temperature was freezing. We had quite a problem trying to make the people look as though they were warm.

SAM: Why is it that exteriors on movies always seem to be shot when the temperature is the opposite of what you need. I've directed a bunch of winter movies in the dead of summer and there's no visible breath.
IAN: And in this one, we had visible breath that we didn't want.

SAM: Exactly!
IAN: The other funny thing I remember was Rosie Burrows, the wardrobe lady, wanted some flat little pumps for all the coven worshippers to wear. And I remember doing a deal with Marks & Spencer [the famous British department store], because it was one of the shoes they manufactured. I can't remember how many pairs we needed – quite a lot – but I bought all of their rejects, the ones that had minor printing defects or sewing defects that, otherwise, would have been thrown away. I mean, I must have bought 200 pairs. To take the lot, I had to guarantee that nobody would ever know that they were Marks & Spencer shoes.

SAM: And now you're spilling the awful truth? I'm sorry, Ian, but you will have to be killed.
IAN: (laughs) Oh, this was no joke. They were dead serious. They were very fearful that their logo on the inside of the sole would somehow be seen, so we had to print something over it, so it didn't show. They were very concerned that even the extras wearing them should never know they came from Marks & Spencer – because they might talk about it and word would spread.

SAM: Wow. This was a state secret.
IAN: Well... not for long, I'm afraid – because, of course, whatever it was we stamped over the logo on the inner sole immediately wore off when the extras were wearing them.

SAM: Did the people at Marks & Spencer find out?
IAN: No. But anyway, it didn't matter because you never see it in the movie. The extras kept the shoes on, so the inner

soles were never visible. That's all that mattered, really.

SAM: Do you recall anything that strained the budget?
IAN: Yes. We needed several period automobiles from the 1920s – which were quite expensive to hire.

SAM: And there was quite a bit of rear screen projection during the car scenes.
IAN: Yes, but that was standard in those days. I don't recall any problems with that.

SAM: Christopher Lee was a big fan of the Dennis Wheatley novel and campaigned to get this movie made. Do you recall anything about that?
IAN: Unfortunately, no. That would have happened long before I was brought on. Chris did seem to be very happy – always singing opera in his dressing room. He was quite a good singer and it cheered everyone up, as long as we weren't in the middle of shooting a scene.

SAM: What do you recall about Charles Gray – who went on to play Blofeld in *Diamonds Are Forever* (1971) and the criminologist in *The Rocky Horror Picture Show* (1975).
IAN: Nothing in particular except that he was very nice and very professional. Unfortunately, I'm afraid I remember very little else about that picture.

POST-HAMMER

SAM: After these three Hammer projects, what came next?
IAN: In 1969, George Santoro rang me up and asked me to line produce two made-for-TV thrillers for Universal – *Destiny of a Spy* with Lorne Greene and Anthony Quayle, directed by Boris Sagal; and *Run a Crooked Mile* with Louis Jourdan and Mary Tyler Moore, directed by Gene Levitt. Both directors were on long-term contracts with Universal Television in Hollywood and brought over to the UK for these projects.

SAM: The crews of *both* films included such Hammer Film veterans as director of photography Arthur Grant, production designer Bernard Robinson, wardrobe supervisor Rosemary Burrows, music supervisor Philip Martell, and assistant director Bert Batt.
IAN: I wanted to bring on the people I knew and trusted. They were all terrific professionals. They all knew each other

Run a Crooked Mile.

and worked together like a well-oiled machine. I liked working with them and I suppose they liked working for me. After I left Hammer, though, Hammer went into a different sort of persona and didn't seem to be making the same sort of pictures as often. Because Michael Carreras had had the big barney with his father. Everything changed after that. A lot of my favorite crew people weren't working for Hammer anymore, so they were available.

Lorne Greene in *Destiny of a Spy*.

SAM: *Destiny of a Spy* and *Run a Crooked Mile* were both shot on locations around England, with stage work done at Pinewood Studios, right?
IAN: Precisely. Universal always based their UK films out of Pinewood Studios, so I got to know the management at Pinewood. Kip Herron was the Managing Director and one day he asked if I would come and join Pinewood as its Marketing Executive and to look after the technical departments, sound and camera. The whole idea was that I was supposed to eventually take Herron's place. I worked there for three years, 1970 through 1972, but, as time went on, it became quite obvious that there was no way I was going to take Herron's place.

SAM: Were there any Hammer projects they wanted you to production manage but you weren't available?
IAN: I think there was one or two, but I can't remember what they were. I was doing bigger pictures, so I was employed for longer periods. And at that time, I didn't really have much time off between pictures. In fact, I hardly had any. Finished on one on Friday and started on the next one on the Monday. It was wonderful for me. Then I got very heavily involved with Universal – Universal Television, to begin with, then Universal itself.

FRANKENSTEIN: THE TRUE STORY

SAM: So how did you become the Associate Producer on *Frankenstein: The True Story* (1973) – which was made under the working title *Dr. Frankenstein*?
IAN: In late-1972, George Santoro rang up and said, "Look, we need you on *Dr. Frankenstein*. Do you think that Pinewood would release you?" And I said, "I'm sure they will, especially since the picture will be produced at Pinewood." But in the back of my mind, I knew this would mean me leaving my position at Pinewood, which was exactly what I wanted.

SAM: What was your first impression of the movie's producer, Hunt Stromberg Jr.?
IAN: (laughs) I wondered what I was in for. I can tell you some very funny stories. For instance, shortly after Hunt arrived in the UK, I took him to see a set, a big dining room set, which was in the boardroom inside Heatherden Hall at Pinewood Studios because it was lined with beautiful dark wood-paneling. [This was the room used for the dinner scene when Prima feels faint; see photo reference.] It looked absolutely fabulous. But on the floor was a fake carpet, which

THE EPIC SAGA BEHIND *FRANKENSTEIN: THE TRUE STORY*

Art by Oscar Calibos.

The dining room scene when Prima (Seymour) faints; set dressed in the dark wooden paneled boardroom in Heatherden Hall, Pinewood Studios' administration building.

Ian Lewis & Stromberg by the clocktower at Cliveden.

was made of felt with basically the pattern printed onto it with paint. And all the furniture and everything else were reproductions. At first Hunt was quite impressed. Then he suddenly said, "These aren't antiques. I can't have anything but the real thing on my picture." So, I said, "Look, I will borrow the second unit and we will photograph this set as it is now and then we'll go get some real antique furniture to match what we've got here – and we'll photograph the real thing. When I show it to you on the screen, if you can tell me which is the real thing and which is the fake, then I'll get the real stuff." What he didn't know, of course, was I just photographed the reproductions twice with a slightly different arrangement and lighting, and, of course, whatever he said, it was going to be the wrong one. So, I won that battle. [The dining room scene when Prima feels faint was shot in this room.]

SAM: What else do you recall about Hunt?
IAN: Every single night, he went home and got as high as a kite. He drank Bloody Marys, which were 99% vodka and a little coloring of tomato juice. Perhaps a dash of Worcestershire sauce. After he'd had a few of these, he'd ring me up and we'd have a flaming row over some production concern, usually something that was going to cost more money than we had in the budget. And then a little later on, his boyfriend, Jacque Shelton, would ring me up and say, "Hunt's gone to sleep now. I'm sure he'll be very contrite when he wakes up." Then at about one o'clock in the morning, I'd get this phone call with a very contrite Hunt Stromberg on the other end, very sorry that he'd been so unpleasant to me – which, of course, Jacque had made him do. It used to happen most nights.

Jane Seymour surrounded by gay men: Dallas Adams, Stromberg and his lover Jacque Shelton.

SAM: Was Jacque on set a lot?

IAN: Oh yes, absolutely. Jacque was around all the time. He was trying to control Hunt as much as we were.

SAM: Back in 1973, wasn't it unusual for a gay couple to be so open about their relationship?

IAN: Yes, I suppose it was still a bit unusual back then, but we got used to it.

SAM: Was there a good side to Hunt?

IAN: Oh yes. He could be very funny and sociable. He loved dogs and animals of every kind. At that time, my wife Ann and I had a Labrador Retriever – a girl named Fudge. Hunt met her only briefly but would ask me about her every day. I'm very sorry to say that, during the shooting of the film, Fudge became very ill and we had to her put down. When Hunt heard about it, he sent us an arrangement of flowers that was so massive, it wouldn't fit through the front door. Then Hunt wanted to give us a new dog as a gift. We chose an Airedale Terrier puppy, which was wonderful and absolutely marvelous. A girl. My wife and I decided to name her Shelley – after Mary Shelley.

Airedale Terrier that Hunt gave to Ian Lewis. Ian named her Shelley after Mary Shelley.

SAM: Honoring *Frankenstein*?

IAN: Yes. The *Frankenstein* picture that brought us together. Shelley became quite a large dog, black and brown. And she was very willful, rather like Hunt (laughs).

SAM: It sounds like Hunt was more of a creative producer – dealing with script development and casting – while you were more like a line producer, managing the day-to-day business aspects of getting the movie made. Is that an accurate description?

IAN: Yes. That's right. What Hunt *did* have was a very close friendship with James Mason. And that got the ball rolling as far as casting was concerned. Hunt was very determined to put together the greatest cast of all time and he thought he was the cat's whisker of dealing with actors and keeping them happy. I only got involved in casting trying to reign in the costs.

SAM: After James Mason was cast, do you recall who signed on next?

IAN: It was probably Michael Sarrazin. I remember he arrived from America quite early on to have make-up tests.

SAM: Hunt wanted Harry Frampton to do Sarrazin's deterioration makeup because he had done the makeup for *Kind Hearts and Coronets*. Frampton did Sarrazin's prosthetics, but Roy Ashton did the cast of Sarrazin's face that was used as a model.

IAN: Yes. I brought Roy on because of his Hammer experience. He did Jane Seymour's severed head – and the severed arm that comes to life was made by Roy Ashton in collaboration with our special effects team.

SAM: Is it true Stromberg originally wanted singer Neil Diamond to play a thug who cracks a bottle on the Creature's head – a scene that got cut out of the final film?

IAN: Yes! He'd come up with crazy "names" and I'd try to get him off it, but in the end I'd often have to ring George Santoro and tell him, "Hunt won't listen to me. You better get on the phone and stop it."

SAM: That's why you had Sir John Gielgud playing the Chief Constable in a one-scene cameo?

IAN: Yes. It was crazy. Hunt wrote that scene for him. I said, "There's no way you can cast Gielgud. We can't afford him." But Hunt said, "I want him. I'll put up the money." I said, "There's no way Universal will allow you to put up the money." Besides, Gielgud didn't really want to do it. You just got the feeling that he felt it was beneath him. But Hunt offered him quite a lot of money and the studio thought that a name like Gielgud was worth it. So we got him. Hunt and I used to have this same row over and over again, on every cast

Stromberg & Gielgud.

Elsa Lanchester as the mad scientist in *The Man from U.N.C.L.E.*

THE EPIC SAGA BEHIND *FRANKENSTEIN: THE TRUE STORY*

Agnes Moorehead & Stromberg.

member. I remember he wanted Elsa Lanchester to come all the way from California to play the landlady and we tried to get her but she wasn't available – so he got Agnes Moorehead to come all the way from California instead. Which cost a lot of extra money. First class plane tickets and, of course, we had to put her up in a very expensive hotel, either the Dorchester or Grosvenor House, because Hunt insisted on treating his actors like they were kings and queens.

SAM: Was James Mason easy to work with?
IAN: He was very charming but he would alter the script to suit himself. He's a great one for that. He's that sort of person anyway. I worked with him again on *Ffolkes* with Roger Moore.

SAM: How was David McCallum to work with?
IAN: Very nice chap. Very professional. No trouble at all. There was one scene when David had this big round fisheye mirror that he was holding in front of his face. His reflection was huge and distorted. It looked wonderful. Very strange and haunting. Hunt suddenly walked on set and saw David holding this monstrosity. He stopped dead in his tracks and gasped! I thought to myself, "Oh no. He must hate it. Here we go." But, to all our great relief, Hunt loved it. He said, "My God! That's exactly how Boris Karloff was introduced in one of my father's movies."

SAM: *The Mask of Fu Manchu*, to be exact. It's identical. Even the size of the mirror.
IAN: Really? Well, it was either a happy accident or maybe Jack Smight was copying the movie.

SAM: Possibly. Even though *The Mask of Fu Manchu* was released 1932, it had been re-released theatrically in the U.S. in 1972 for its 40th Anniversary, just a few months before *Frankenstein: The True Story* went into production. Someone could have seen it. And, of course, there are photos of that moment that may have appeared in newspapers around that time. It's hard to imagine it was purely by accident – but then again, stranger things have happened.
IAN: I'm sure you are right. There must have been a connection.

[NOTE: According to Wikipedia: "During its initial release, *The Mask of Fu Manchu* was criticized by the Chinese government, and the Chinese embassy in Washington launched a formal complaint against the film for its hostile depiction of the Chinese. The speech where Fu Manchu tells his followers to 'Kill the white man and take his women!' was singled out for strong criticism. Some other critics also objected to the film's depictions of violence and sexuality. The film's re-release in 1972 was met with protest from the Japanese American Citizens League, who stated that 'the movie was offensive and demeaning to Asian-Americans.' Because of the criticism of the film's racism, the 1992 VHS release of the film removed several scenes containing the most criticized lines of dialogue, such as the 'Kill the white man' speech, and the scenes of Myrna Loy in an orgiastic frenzy while witnessing a torture whipping." Modern home entertainment releases of this movie have restored the above scenes. Not long after *Frankenstein: The True Story*, Hunt Stromberg Jr. began to develop a Fu Manchu movie to star Peter Sellers, but producer Zev Braun had already secured the rights which resulted in *The Fiendish Plot of Fu Manchu* (Orion Pictures, 1980), Sellers' final movie. Instead, in 1979, Stromberg developed *Chandu, The Magician* for Peter Sellers but the movie never got made before Sellers died. Stromberg also developed *The Prisoner of Zenda* (1979) for Peter Sellers – a remake of Hunt Stromberg Sr.'s classic movie – which ultimately got made starring Sellers, but for producer Walter Mirisch instead of Stromberg.]

SAM: How about Leonard Whiting?
IAN: He was a bit tricky. Jack Smight had quite a lot of trouble getting a performance out of him. I remember that scenes with Whiting always required more takes than usual. He knew he wasn't giving Jack the performance he wanted and, at times, he got frustrated and became rather moody. But Jack's a very reasonable director. Very patient and kind. They managed to get through it, but it took extra time that we didn't always have.

SAM: Were there other actors who required special handling?
IAN: Well, Sir Ralph Richardson never learned his lines. He *never* did. On any picture. We all knew that. We had to make cue cards.

SAM: Jane Seymour told me she prepared an authentic Irish brogue accent for her role as his granddaughter. But when it came time to shoot the scenes, Richardson played it in "the Queen's English."
IAN: (laughs) Quite right. But, you know, he may have been smart to do it that way because accents were one of the biggest problems between England and America at that time. All our dailies went over to America. If the people at Universal or NBC came across an accent in the dailies that they couldn't understand, we'd have to go back and reshoot the scene – or have the voice post-dubbed by another actor.

SAM: That little farmhouse where Ralph Richardson and Jane Seymour lived? Where was that?
IAN: We built that in Burnham Beeches which is not very far away from Pinewood Studios. Six miles away. But Ralph Richardson still managed to get lost trying to find it on his motorcycle.

SAM: Motorcycle?! Sir Ralph Richardson drove himself to work on a motorcycle?
IAN: Yes! Always. We didn't want him to do it but he

Richardson on motorcycle.

Richardson on motorcycle.

insisted. It worried us because in Burnham Beeches it is incredibly easy to get lost. He said, "I know where I'm going, don't worry." But then, of course, he turned up late because he got lost. He was a great one for doing things like that.

SAM: Did the movie go over budget?
IAN: Yes. But not an awful lot because I had to shift things around and save money in other areas in order to pay for the cast.

SAM: There was a Writers' Strike a week before shooting began.

IAN: Ugh, ugh. I remember that – now that you remind me. This was a disaster because we kept on getting changed scenes from Hunt.

SAM: Do you remember shooting at Cliveden, the mansion used as the Fanshawe estate?
IAN: Indeed I do. But of course, yet again, the reason we went to Cliveden was that Hunt wanted a big "name." Even for the locations! Cliveden was famously owned by Lady Astor and, during the 1960s, was notorious as the setting for the Profumo Affair. Everyone in England knew Cliveden by sight. Did anyone in America know what it was? I doubt it.

SAM: Hunt didn't expect you to shoot scenes at the North Pole, I trust.
IAN: (laughs) I'm surprised he didn't. We created the North Pole at Pinewood, a combination of sets and matte paintings by Peter Melrose who was a very good matte artist. And the set had a forced-perspective backdrop. We also intercut stock shots of the North Pole where the ice was collapsing into the sea.

SAM: The scene where Michael Sarrazin jumps off the chalk cliff must have been tricky, with helicopter shots, a dummy and everything else.
IAN: Yes. We did that at Beachy Head. It wasn't originally scripted that way.

SAM: The script had the Creature walking into a river with rapids that washed him downstream. I thought the visual of jumping off that magnificent cliff was so much more striking and dynamic – especially coming at the climax of Part 1.
IAN: Hunt came up with that idea. And you're right, it's visually striking, absolutely.

SAM: What was it like working with the director of photography, Arthur Ibbetson?
IAN: Arthur was a great cinematographer. I worked with him again later on *The Prisoner of Zenda* with Peter Sellers. I was very lucky to persuade Hunt to have Arthur as the DP. A very, *very* good man. Not one of these hifalutin DPs. He knew what he needed, that's what we got him – and then that was it. There were no surprises.

SAM: The production designer was Wilfrid Shingleton. What was he like?
IAN: Well, it was the first time I'd ever worked with him. He had a very good reputation. He'd worked with Polanski. But he understood the limitations of the budget. He and I collaborated over that dining room set where we had to trick Hunt into letting us use reproductions. He was very amused by that little exercise.

SAM: Let's talk about the ballroom scene when Jane Seymour's head gets ripped off. I'm still surprised NBC allowed that to air in prime time in 1973.
IAN: Everybody was surprised. Amazing that the censor didn't come down on that. I remember it was there in the original script when we started. I asked George Santoro, "Will we get away with that?" And he said, "We're going to try, but just make sure you've got a cover shot for it."

SAM: Were you privy to discussions at Universal about

THE EPIC SAGA BEHIND *FRANKENSTEIN: THE TRUE STORY*

whether it might be bumped up to a theatrical feature in the U.S., rather than TV?

IAN: Hunt thought that if he put together a big enough cast, Universal would have a change of heart. But I knew from George Santoro that Universal had already made the deal with NBC and there was no going back – though it would be released theatrically in the UK to qualify for the Eady Levy.

SAM: For the original television version, the final running time needed to be about 3 hours. While you were shooting, were there concerns that the movie might run longer than that?

IAN: Yes. What's the point of shooting something that's going to end up on the cutting room floor? I kept a close eye on that throughout the making of the picture. The continuity woman, Angela Martelli, who had just worked with Hitchcock on *Frenzy*, would give me the script timing for each scene so we could work out how long the movie was going to be.

SAM: In the original script, after the Creature has ripped the head off Prima, the Creature is arrested and there are several sequences at the police station and the jail where the Creature is tormented by the townsfolk; a jailbreak sequence; loading the ship; the coastguard chasing the ship; among other scenes that were never filmed.

IAN: Yes. All of that was taken out of the script because the movie was becoming too long. And we needed to find ways to save money, too.

SAM: The biggest cuts in the script were in the second half of the film. Did that happen in pre-production or as you were shooting?

IAN: A lot of it got changed as we were shooting. Whenever possible, we tried to film the script in chronological order. Some locations dictated otherwise, but we wanted to have a logical progression for the leading actors – and, of course, Michael Sarrazin's makeup deterioration gets progressively worse as the movie goes along. We couldn't put him through multiple stages of make-up in one day of shooting. So, when we realized that the film was going to be too long, cuts were made in the material left to shoot – which happened to be mostly in the second half.

SAM: I understand that Michael Sarrazin disappeared from the production for about a week, unannounced.

IAN: I can vaguely recall the problem. Sarrazin was inexperienced in the proper behavior that was required of an actor and, if I am right in my recollection, he went off without telling anybody and it took us some time to find out where he had gone.

SAM: First assistant director John Stoneman told me that, about three-quarters of the way through shooting, the powers-that-be at Universal City were considering replacing Jack Smight. Stoneman remembers being asked to take over directing for a few days until a new director arrived. But, out of loyalty to Smight, Stoneman refused – and the next thing he knew, he himself was fired and Smight remained for the rest of the production.

IAN: Unfortunately, I have only a very vague memory of that. I don't remember the specifics.

SAM: During post-production, Gil Mellé's score was recorded in the UK.

IAN: Yes. The composer came to London so it could be recorded by the London Symphony Orchestra. You see, once again, Hunt wanted a big "name" orchestra. I had to take on a little man called Phil Martell.

SAM: From your Hammer Film days. Philip Martell, the great music supervisor.

IAN: That's right. Phil was very, very good at recording music and making it fit the action on film. You'd be surprised how many composers were not good at it. They compose lovely music, but they don't know how to score underneath dialogue or important sound effects. You can always just dip the volume knob in the final sound mix but Phil preferred to rework the score so that the orchestra would swell in the right places and go quiet in the right places. That's the way it should be done.

SAM: Were there problems with the score that needed to be ironed out?

IAN: Yes. Phil argued quite a lot with the composer and insisted on what needed to happen.

SAM: Were there sequences during the shoot that required pre-recorded music for playback on set? Like, for instance, when Sir Ralph Richardson plays a violin.

IAN: Yes. Philip Martell prerecorded a violinist for that. He prerecorded music for the ballroom sequence for the extras and Jane Seymour to dance to. There was a church service with everyone singing a hymn. And there was a sequence where Nicola Pagett plays piano and then Jane Seymour mimics her. That was all prerecorded by Phil.

Nicola Pagett observes as Seymour mimics her piano playing.

SAM: What about the opera that Dr. Frankenstein takes the Creature to see? Mozart's *The Marriage of Figaro*.

IAN: For that we used an existing recording and paid the licensing fee. Much cheaper than recording it because we would have needed to hire a legitimate opera singer.

SAM: Was Hunt very aware of Hammer Films?

IAN: Oh yes. Hammer came up quite frequently. Whenever I'd say, "No, you can't have that because it's not in the budget," he'd glare at me and say, "We're not making a Hammer Film, are we?" That came up many times. Many times.

SAM: Did he dislike Hammer films?

IAN: It wasn't about liking them or disliking them. He just thought of them as B-pictures. And he was insistent that *Dr. Frankenstein* be an A-picture all the way. In fact, when George Santoro suggested that I do the picture, Hunt discovered I had worked for Hammer Films and because of that, he didn't want me to do it.

SAM: So, when you hired crew people who had previously worked on Hammer films, you had to be very quiet about their Hammer credits?
IAN: (laughs) Oh yes. Very hush-hush. I would only mention their other non-Hammer credits.

SAM: What was the difference between *Frankenstein: The True Story* and a Hammer film?
IAN: We had nothing elaborate with Hammer. We got only five or six weeks to shoot. We knew how much we could spend and that was it. With *Frankenstein: The True Story*, we had a lot more money, a fifteen-week shoot, a bigger "name" cast, a much larger crew, and many elaborate sequences that took days to shoot. It was completely different.

JOHN BADHAM'S *DRACULA*
SAM: Having worked for years at Hammer Films and then as the Associate Producer of Universal's *Frankenstein: The True Story*, it seems fitting that when it came time for Universal to do its 1979 version of *Dracula*, you would be involved.
IAN: Yes. By then, I was Managing Director of Universal Pictures Limited and my job was to oversee all the productions that Universal made in the UK, as well as in Europe and Africa. We shot *Dracula* on locations in Cornwall and the stage work was done mostly at Shepperton Studios.

[NOTE: There was also some stage work done at Twickenham Studios.]

SAM: Most of Universal's pictures made in the UK were filmed at Pinewood Studios, like *Frankenstein: The True Story*, for instance. Why was *Dracula* not shot there as well?
IAN: Pinewood may have been too busy to accommodate another picture, but I believe the producer Walter Mirisch preferred to work at Shepperton so that may have been the reason. And Andy Worker, the managing director of Shepperton Studios, was probably offering him a bloody-good deal.

SAM: Had you crossed paths with Walter Mirisch before *Dracula*?
IAN: I can't remember which came first but I also worked with Walter on the Peter Sellers picture, *The Prisoner of Zenda*, when it was shooting in Vienna.

SAM: Both were released in 1979.
IAN: I liked working with Walter. He was a great character. A very, very nice man to work with.

SAM: Walter's brother, Marvin Mirisch, was the Executive Producer. Was he in the UK as well during the shoot?
IAN: Yes. Marvin was a very nice man, too, but I worked most closely with Walter. Tom Pevsner was the Associate Producer, or what you might now call the Line Producer. I worked very well with him. And the Production Manager was Hugh Harlow who was an ex-Hammer Production Manager. I worked very well with him, too. We'd known each other professionally for twenty years.

[NOTE: Hugh Harlow was the Production Manager of two Hammer films: *Crescendo* and *Moon Zero Two*; Third Assistant Director on Hammer's *The Curse of Frankenstein*, *The Revenge of Frankenstein*, *The Hound of the Baskervilles*, and *The Mummy*; Second Assistant Director on *The Brides of Dracula*, *The Kiss of the Vampire*, *The Evil of Frankenstein*, *Dracula: Prince of Darkness*, etc.]

SAM: What was the hierarchy? As the head of Universal UK, were you the boss above Walter and Marvin Mirisch?
IAN: (laughs) If I tried to stop something, Walter and Marvin would immediately go over my head. Immediately. So, I got really quite good at being very tactful about trying to persuade them that they ought not do something or that they ought to do this thing some other way. I knew if I just said, "Sorry, you can't do that," they would call Universal City. I was very lucky that I got on extremely well with Ned Tanen [President of Universal's film division 1976-1982] and Frank Price, who took over immediately after. If I knew a producer was going to go over my head over some disagreement, I would try to get hold of Ned Tanen first, so that he could hear my side of the situation before getting the call from the producer. I didn't always succeed. If Ned wasn't in his office or if he was on another call, I'd leave a message. But if he had a message from someone like Walter Mirisch, he would return his call before he would return mine.

SAM: If a picture was going over budget, how would you go about getting approval from Universal City?
IAN: I dealt with Marshall and Hilton Green who were the two Executive Production Managers at Universal City. The two of them ran the production department. If I had a problem and I couldn't get hold of Ned or Frank, I'd immediately call Marsh or Hilton so they would know what was happening. I always kept them fully advised. They were given the most up-to-date shooting schedules, call sheets every day and cost returns by Wednesday of every week. And if they could find an excuse to come to London, they would come for a visit every now and then. We all became great friends.

SAM: Were you also summoned to Universal City for meetings?
IAN: Yes. I used to go there about eight or nine times a year.

THE EPIC SAGA BEHIND *FRANKENSTEIN: THE TRUE STORY*

SAM: Were you on set much?

IAN: Occasionally. I did my usual thing. If a picture was shooting in the UK, I would go on set at least once a week. When it was a foreign location, I'd go every two weeks. I would sit down with the accountant and find out how accurate the cost return was.

SAM: When Universal decided to make a picture in the UK, what would be your first responsibility?

IAN: During pre-production, the budget would be formulated by the production department at Universal City and then sent to me and I would have to analyze it and give my opinion if the production could be done for that figure. It was an odd system because the way movies were made at Universal City was totally different than the way movies were made in the UK. It would have been more efficient if we had been allowed to formulate our own budgets and get them approved.

SAM: *Dracula* was budgeted at $12 million, the highest ever allocated for a horror film up to that time. Did this production seem significantly different from your experience on a typical Hammer film?

IAN: Oh God yes. Absolutely. It had a *lot* more money spent on it. Much more elaborate on all fronts. I remember Albert Whitlock came over from Universal City for almost the duration of the entire shoot. I had a very good relationship with him. He was a very nice man and a brilliant special effects guy. His glass shots were the best in the business. He was a past master. You couldn't have anybody better and, of course, he worked for Universal full-time.

SAM: What do you remember about John Badham?

IAN: All that I remember about John Badham is that we never had any problems and everything went very smoothly.

SAM: For the DVD release of *Dracula*, John Badham desaturated the color, almost to black and white. Do you recall whether he tried to do this for the original theatrical release?

IAN: He may have. I don't recall. But Universal would never have allowed it. They were very averse to anything out of the ordinary. They wanted to appeal to the average viewer in Middle America. For instance, if a British accent was hard to understand, Sid Sheinberg would insist it be re-voiced. I would get phone calls from Sid saying, "This will not do." So, I am sure, if John Badham had wanted something unusual done with the color of the film, Universal would not have been receptive.

SAM: Was post-production done in England?

IAN: Yes. The editor was very good – John Bloom, who was Claire Bloom's brother. He later went to America and was very successful.

SAM: Did you have to send dailies to Universal City?

IAN: Yes. It was very expensive. We would have to strike two prints from the negative of every selected take – one for the editor in London and one to send to Universal City. And, don't forget, in those days, the sound was on separate 35mm acetate, so we had to order two copies of the sound as well. The sound had to be synched up to the picture by the assistant editors and then one full copy, picture and sound, sent to Universal City. Sometimes, they wanted the dailies flown to California every day but I used to warn them that

the cost was coming out of the budget. It wasn't a cheap process. Occasionally, Universal City would allow us to send dailies every three or four days, to save on shipping costs. They would screen the dailies routinely at Universal City and if they didn't like anything, I can tell you I knew on the phone very quickly.

SAM: Did you watch the dailies on *Dracula*?

IAN: Yes. Once they'd watched the dailies at Shepperton, I'd have the copy sent up to London so I could watch them. We had a small theater at the Universal offices at 139 Piccadilly. And then the dailies would go back to the editor.

SAM: Did the director and editor watch dailies in the evening, after shooting had wrapped?

IAN: Sometimes in the evening, but usually dailies were screened at the beginning of the lunch break. The lab would have the picture ready about 7 or 8 o'clock in the morning and then the assistant editors would synch them up with the sound and be ready to screen them by lunch.

SAM: So, once the director's cut was ready, a copy print would have to be made of the raw work print and sent to Universal City for screening?

IAN: Yes. It was very expensive, so they didn't insist on seeing multiple cuts of the picture unless there was a major problem.

SAM: What do you recall about Frank Langella?

IAN: Nothing specific, I'm afraid. He was very nice. Same with Donald Pleasance who was always a joy to work with. He was always very good. The only actor who stands out in my memory was Laurence Olivier.

SAM: Because?

IAN: Olivier was quite tricky. He was very frail on that picture. We took it upon ourselves to limit the number of hours he worked every day because he just couldn't cope. He had to be helped up out of his chair. But when the camera turned on, he just got up out of a chair quite easily. When it came time to act, his problems seemed to go away. But we always had to have a chair ready for him to flop down into the moment the director said, "Cut."

SAM: Do you recall how much Olivier made for doing the picture?

IAN: No, but considering how much work he did on the picture, it was heavy. It was quite a lot of money at the time. I remember we had a lot of trouble with his contract when we were negotiating it. He and his lawyer were very, very keen to maximize his take on the picture in order to look after his wife, Joan Plowright – because they were very worried about his health.

SAM: Though he did recover and went on making films for another ten years.

IAN: Yes, but at that time, his health seemed so bad, everyone thought *Dracula* would be his last movie. I knew his lawyer very well, a man named Claude Fielding, who was very insistent that Olivier's money be tax-sheltered in some way. Everything perfectly legal, mind you – Universal would not have agreed to it otherwise – but there was tremendous pressure to come up with "creative accounting" that would limit Olivier's tax obligation. Mel Sattler, the head of

Universal's business affairs at Universal City, didn't like it one bit. He thought it smacked of being illegal. But the laws were different in the UK than they were in the U.S., and whatever it was that Fielding wanted, we had to convince Sattler that it was perfectly legal in the UK. So Universal finally agreed to the deal. Reluctantly.

SAM: Do you recall anything funny that happened during the shoot?

IAN: I remember one amusing situation that happened when we were shooting near King Arthur's Castle in Tintagel. There was a scene outside a house in which Jan Francis [as Mina] was going to have her heart cut out. She was on this trestle table and she had a prosthesis on her chest so that the blood would ooze out when Olivier made an incision with a scalpel. Well, Jan kept bursting into laughter and couldn't control herself – which was spoiling take after take and wasting a lot of time and money. John Badham, as you can imagine, was not happy about it and he finally took her aside and said, "What the hell is going on? You can't keep on bursting into laughter." And she said, "Well, you'd burst into laughter, too, if you had Laurence Olivier tickling your tits."

SAM: Seriously?

IAN: Yes. Olivier's hand kept straying underneath the prosthesis and was basically fondling her breasts – and Jan could not keep a straight face. So, John went to Olivier and said, "Behave yourself! Stop fooling around and do the scene properly. Otherwise, we are never going to get it."

SAM: But once one actor starts laughing, it becomes infectious and everybody else starts laughing and then it's very hard to stop.

IAN: Yes, exactly. And that's what was happening. But, you see, we were losing the light or it was Olivier's last day, something like that. So we were quite frantic trying to get it done because it was now or never. It was quite a struggle.

SAM: Was the Eady Levy a prime motivating factor for Universal to make *Dracula* and other films in the UK?

[NOTE: The Eady Levy (1957-1985), named after British Treasury official Sir Wilfred Eady, was a levy on box office receipts in the UK to support the British film industry. The proceeds were divided among qualifying UK films in proportion to each movie's UK box office revenue. To put it simply, to qualify as a British film, at least 85% of the cost of the film had to be spent in the UK, and only up to three non-British individual salaries could be excluded from the costs of the film, encouraging employment of British actors, technicians and film crew.]

IAN: Yes. In fact, the score for *Dracula* had to be recorded in the UK so that the film would qualify for the Eady. John Williams had to come over from America to conduct it. You see, a picture would receive money – sort of a rebate or bonus – from the Eady fund, depending on how well it did at the box office. For something like a James Bond movie, it was a lot of money. It depended on how many UK pictures were exhibited during the calendar year because the fund was allocated among all the pictures, but on a sliding scale based on box office gross.

SAM: Is that why there were so many double-bill movies exhibited in the UK? To increase the number of qualifying UK films?

IAN: Actually, there were two reasons for that. One, there was certainly a proliferation of British films because of the Eady fund. But, two, there was also a quota system for cinemas in the UK. The cinemas had to show a certain percentage of UK-based films each year. So, a lot of small pictures were made called "Quota Quickies" in order to satisfy the quota. There was quite a fight to get one of your "Quota Quickies" on the same bill with something like a Bond movie because that meant it would collect a much bigger chunk of the Eady fund. And, of course, the two big cinema chains were owned by ABPC and Rank, so they made sure that the "Quota Quickies" that went on the double-bills with the big pictures were their own. There was a lot of unhappiness among UK producers because of this bias.

POSTSCRIPT

During Ian Lewis' tenure as Managing Director of Universal Pictures Limited in the UK, he also supervised such films as Herbert Ross' *The Seven-Per-Cent Solution,* William Friedkin's *Sorcerer*, John Schlesinger's *Yanks*, Wilford Leach's *The Pirates of Penzance*, Monty Python's *The Meaning of Life*, Terry Gilliam's *Brazil*, Ridley Scott's *Legend*, Sydney Pollack's *Out of Africa* and Michael Apted's *Gorillas in the Mist*. Another book could be written just on these alone, but I had to draw the line somewhere.

Ian Lewis in more recent years.

Ian's massive impact on the British film industry is being carried forward by his son Tim Lewis who started out as a production runner on *Supergirl* and *Legend*, then worked his way up to Production Manager on the Bond film *Die Another Day*. He worked on six of the seven *Harry Potter* films, starting off as Line Producer/Production Manager and ending as Executive Producer. He Co-Produced the Tom Cruise picture *Edge of Tomorrow*; and was the Executive Producer of *Cinderella*, *Pan* and J.K. Rowling's *Fantastic Beasts and Where to Find Them* (2016), *Fantastic Beasts: The Crimes of Grindelwald* (2018), and *Fantastic Beasts: The Secrets of Dumbledore* (2022). He is also the Executive Producer of *Back in Action* (2023) starring Jamie Foxx and Cameron Diaz.

PART FOUR
BIOGRAPHY OF
THE PRODUCER

Stromberg surrounded by his monsters, artwork by Neil D Vokes; color by Matt Webb.

CHAPTER 17
THE MONSTROUS LIFE & TIMES OF
HUNT STROMBERG JR.

Not to name drop or anything, *but...* Hunt Stromberg Jr. discovered Vampira, got Boris Karloff to wear his Frankenstein monster makeup one last time (and cast him as the Grinch), produced a play with Bela Lugosi, teamed Vincent Price with Peter Lorre, was friends with both Lon Chaney Jr. *and* Sr., met Elsa Lanchester when she was filming *Bride of Frankenstein*, and cast Yvonne De Carlo as Lily Munster. He developed *The Twilight Zone*, expanded *Alfred Hitchcock* to an hour, greenlit *Lost in Space*, settled *The Wild Wild West*, fused Dr. Fu Manchu with Dr. Pretorius, beautified Frankenstein's Creature, got stomped by King Kong and was cursed by the Mummy.

He helped launch the careers of Carol Burnett and Clint Eastwood, escorted Mae West for three decades, got Liberace to perform at his parties, had a cartoon superhero *and* a James Bond supervillain named after him, fired Judy Garland, and was snubbed by Queen Elizabeth (twice). And that's just for starters.

 After growing up on the MGM lot in the 1930s, he conquered Broadway in the 1940s, and became the wunderkind of TV in the 1950s and 1960s. His golden reign as Vice President of Programming for CBS reached its zenith with fourteen of the Top Fifteen highest-rated prime-time shows – a record that has never been broken.

 And then, in a stunning feat of reinvention, Stromberg became an independent producer and created the most daring monster movie of them all – his dream-of-a-lifetime project: *Frankenstein: The True Story*.

 His private life was just as colorful. Openly gay in an era when it was still illegal and classified as a mental illness, Stromberg was a brave and fearless advocate for LGBTQ+ rights. He was the Godfather of television's Gay Mafia – or, as Stromberg dubbed himself, the Kingpin of the Lavender Hill Mob. He also had his demons – alcohol and pills were his poisons of choice. His love life was tumultuous. His Rolls-Royce was torched and exploded. He was his own worst enemy – and collected a few famous ones, too. Nevertheless, he was beloved by most, the life of every party and a world-class eccentric. He had a pet woolly monkey named Wilbur that he brought to work on a leash (and gave Mae West one, too); acquired exotic

A smiling Hunt Stromberg Jr.

birds from around the world; and raised a Bengal tiger. As one does. It would take an encyclopedia to cover every twist and turn of his wild and crazy life – but here are the broad strokes.

FROM CHANEY TO KARLOFF

William Powell, Asta the Dog, Myrna Loy, *The Thin Man.*

Asta, *The Thin Man.*

Stromberg Sr. & William Powell, *The Thin Man.*

produced her first American film *Torrent* (1926). He gave an early break to an unknown actor named Clark Gable in *The Easiest Way* (1931). The young David O. Selznick, who later produced *Gone with the Wind*, started out as Stromberg Sr.'s assistant. At the height of Senior's career at

Hunt Stromberg Sr. (left) is presented with the Oscar for Best Picture for his film *The Great Ziegfeld* (1936).

MGM, he was producing 52 films a year, helping to keep the studio profitable despite the Depression.

Stromberg Sr. was also a shrewd businessman. A horse enthusiast, he was a founding investor in the Santa Anita Park and Hollywood Park racetracks. He also was part-owner

Born in Los Angeles on May 16, 1923, Hunt Stromberg Jr. was the only child of Metro-Goldwyn-Mayer mogul Hunt Stromberg Sr. (1894-1968, Jewish-German descent; born in Louisville, Kentucky) and Katherine Kerwin (1894-1951, Irish-Catholic descent; born in Arcadia, Missouri). His father famously produced *The Thin Man* (1934) and three of its sequels starring William Powell and Myrna Loy; a slew of Jeanette MacDonald / Nelson Eddy musicals; *The Women* (1939); and the Best Picture Oscar winner *The Great Ziegfeld* (1936). He was known as a star-maker, most notably giving Joan Crawford her very first leading role in *Our Dancing Daughters* (1928), the silent film that propelled her to superstardom. He produced all of Jean Harlow's films. He brought Greta Garbo from Germany to Hollywood and

Clark Gable & Hunt Stromberg Sr.

THE EPIC SAGA BEHIND *FRANKENSTEIN: THE TRUE STORY*

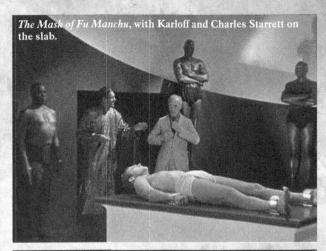

The Mask of Fu Manchu, with Karloff and Charles Starrett on the slab.

Lon Chaney Sr. with his makeup kit.

The Mask of Fu Manchu, Starrett, Loy, Karloff.

of Golden Gate Fields Racetrack in Berkeley, California, where he cross-pollinated commerce by shooting the horserace scenes for *Shadow of the Thin Man* (1941) there.

Stromberg Sr. also owned over one-million shares of stock in the Coca-Cola company, which he had begun acquiring in 1909 at the age of 15. Stromberg Jr. would inherit that fortune upon his father's death in 1968 – which helps explain how Hunt could afford to occasionally pay, out of his own pocket, certain unbudgeted embellishments on *Frankenstein: The True Story* – like the cost of Sir John Gielgud and travel expenses for the composer Gil Mellé.

At a very young age, Stromberg Jr. became a fan of silent horror star Lon Chaney Sr., "the man of a thousand faces," and met him on the set of his father's production of *Where East Is East* (1929), the final collaboration between Chaney and future *Dracula* director Tod Browning (whose films together had included *The Unholy Three*, *London After Midnight*, and *The Unknown*). Stromberg Sr. also produced Chaney's last film *Thunder* (1929). When Chaney died in 1930 of throat cancer and pneumonia (which he contracted during the shooting of *Thunder*), Stromberg Sr. was an honorary pallbearer at his funeral, with Stromberg Jr. by his side.

Stromberg Jr. recalled, "What I remember most about meeting Lon Chaney was his makeup kit and him showing me some of the secrets of his trade. No matter how disguised he made himself, the humanity of his performance always came through." This lesson inspired Stromberg Jr.'s insistence that Michael Sarrazin's Creature in *Frankenstein: The True Story* must *not* be buried under heavy makeup appliances.

The film that made the biggest impression on a 9-year-old Stromberg Jr., however, was his dad's production of *The Mask of Fu Manchu* (1932) starring Boris Karloff as the evil Dr. Fu Manchu, promoted as "The Frankenstein of the Orient!" Karloff's homoerotic stroking and sadomasochistic torturing of the half-naked, exquisitely hunky Charles Starrett took full advantage of the freewheeling pre-code era before censorship would have shut down that "perversion" entirely. (Myrna Loy plays Karloff's wicked daughter and she's practically a BDSM dominatrix!) The movie directly influenced many aspects of *Frankenstein: The True Story*, particularly James Mason's Dr. Polidori character – with an affinity for Chinese houseboys and Oriental décor – a queer fusion of Karloff's Dr. Fu Manchu and Ernest Thesiger's Dr. Pretorius from *Bride of Frankenstein*.

Modern poster tribute for *Bride of Frankenstein* by artist Greg Staples.

Kenneth Strickfaden, artwork by Frederick Cooper.

Kenneth Strickfaden's electrical equipment in *Bride of Frankenstein*.

Kenneth Strickfaden's electrical equipment in *The Mask of Fu Manchu*.

Sam Irvin on the set of *Gods and Monsters*, with Strickfaden equipment.

CHAPTER SEVENTEEN: THE MONSTROUS LIFE & TIMES OF HUNT STROMBERG JR.

Bill Condon & Sam Irvin, *Gods and Monsters*.

James Whale (Ian McKellen) directs Elsa Lanchester (Rosalind Ayres) in *Gods and Monsters*.

Even though Stromberg Jr. grew up at MGM (schooled on the lot at the Little Red Schoolhouse with Judy Garland, Mickey Rooney and Jackie Cooper), the films Hunt loved the most were Universal's horror movies. At the age of 11, Hunt actually met Elsa Lanchester when she was simultaneously filming *Bride of Frankenstein* at Universal *and* his father's production of *Naughty Marietta* at MGM. He already knew Karloff by that time; the actor had become a family friend during the production of *The Mask of Fu Manchu* (less than a year after his breakthrough turn in *Frankenstein*).

And, as any kid would be, Stromberg Jr. was agog over Kenneth Strickfaden's electrical equipment and gizmos that he created for *Frankenstein*, *Bride of Frankenstein* – and *The Mask of Fu Manchu* in between! He spent hours hanging out with the inventor, bombarding him with questions and creating a few copycat devices to play with at home – prompting his father to joke to a journalist that his son "was turning into a juvenile Frankenstein."

[Side note: We borrowed Strickfaden's original electrical equipment when recreating Frankenstein's laboratory for a flashback sequence in Bill Condon's *Gods and Monsters* (1998) starring Sir Ian McKellen as James Whale, for which I very proudly served as a co-executive producer.]

PRINCE OF HOLLYWOOD

Stromberg Jr.'s upbringing was charmed and glamorous, to say the least. His family lived in a beautiful new mansion dubbed "Stromberg Manor" at 144 S. Mapleton Drive in the Holmby Hills neighborhood of Los Angeles, a ritzy residential section of Westwood, west of Beverly Hills. Massive, star-studded parties were thrown there on a regular basis. As an adult, Stromberg Jr. loved to brag, "When I was a kid, my rosy-red cheeks got pinched by every movie star in Hollywood."

When Judy Garland married Sid Luft in 1952, they purchased Stromberg Manor and raised their kids there: Liza Minnelli, Lorna Luft and Joe Luft.

At the age of 8, Stromberg Jr. traveled to Europe with his parents on the RMS Aquitania, the luxury British ocean liner, and got his picture in all the major U.S. newspapers upon their return on September 4, 1931.

The unconditional love that Hunt received from his mother Katherine was much harder to earn from his father – who was demanding, stern, and presumed that his son would obediently follow in his footsteps and work his way up to become an associate producer under his father's tutelage. What he didn't realize was that Hunt Jr. had no interest in being in his father's shadow. Rebellious and independent, Hunt Jr. was determined to forge his own career in show business, on his own terms.

There was also an elephant in the room. Hunt Jr. was obviously gay – and his father was clearly not happy about it and did whatever he could to steer his son in another direction. He tried to "butch him up" by sending him, at age 14, to The Black-Foxe Military Institute on Wilcox Avenue in Hollywood, between the Wilshire Country Club and the Los

Far left: Toddler Hunt, his mother Katherine, and their family dog.
Left: Toddler Hunt with his parents Katherine and Hunt Stromberg Sr.
Above: Young Hunt (right) and an early crush.

THE EPIC SAGA BEHIND *FRANKENSTEIN: THE TRUE STORY*

Hunt, 8, and parents return from European cruise on the RMS Aquitania, photo published in newspapers across the country, September 4, 1931

Hunt, 16, as Ringmaster to his own Circus Party, August 19, 1939.

12-year-old Hunt flamboyantly stylish in jodhpurs and knee-high boots, with his parents Stromberg Sr. and Katherine.

Hunt Stromberg Jr. with parents Stromberg Sr. and Katherine.

Angeles Tennis Club. He studied all four years of high school there, grades 9 through 12, fall of 1937-spring of 1941.

After school each day, Stromberg Sr. demanded that Hunt come straight to MGM where he put him to work as a production assistant on such films as *Idiot's Delight* (shot October-November 1938) starring Norma Shearer and Clark Gable; George Cukor's *The Women* (shot April-July 1939) starring Katharine Hepburn, Norma Shearer and Rosalind Russell; and *Another Thin Man* (shot July-August 1939) reuniting William Powell and Myrna Loy for their third turn as Dashiell Hammett's Nick and Nora Charles solving crimes between cocktails – with the help of their dog Asta. Stromberg was fascinated by the wire fox terrier and his trainers, developing an affinity for animals that became a deep-rooted passion.

Also in the cast of *Another Thin Man* were Otto Kruger (the top-billed star of *Dracula's Daughter*) and a 25-year-old boxer named Tom Neal, who later played the lead in the film noir classic *Detour* (1945).

Hunt Jr., 16, apparently had a major schoolboy crush on Tom whose beefcake photographs, clad in swim-trunks, were floating around town like confetti. It was Tom who introduced Hunt Jr. to George Cukor's notorious weekly Sunday pool parties for men-only. That meant gay men – along with straight men who were either bi-curious or willing to put out for quid pro quo movie gigs.

From most accounts, Tom was primarily a serial womanizer who later, in the 1960s, was convicted of involuntary manslaughter for the death of his wife – and jailed for 6 years. He had a volatile temper and a bad boy reputation – but none of this mattered to Hunt Jr. who worshipped the guy like a moth to a flame.

That same summer, on Saturday, August 12, 1939, Hunt Jr. decided to throw a "Circus Beach Party" to end all parties. As reported in the *Los Angeles Times*, "'Wear circus duds – and eat circus grub' are the main instructions on the gay yellow-and-red invitations extended by 16-year-old Hunt Stromberg Jr. for a dancing and informal supper party this evening at the Miramar Hotel in Santa Monica. A group of the younger set of Los Angeles, Beverly Hills and Bel-Air will congregate in 'the tent' at 8:30 p.m. A floor show of acrobats and trained dogs, a full supply of hotdogs, spaghetti and pink lemonade – and add 200 members of society's younger set – in costume – and you have a GOOD TIME." The following Saturday, a photo of Hunt in a circus ringmaster uniform beating a drum appeared in the papers, with Tom Neal on the guest list.

Above: Three pages from 10-year-old Hunt Stromberg Jr.'s French sketch book. Below: Clark Gable & Norma Shearer meet with their producer Hunt Stromberg Sr. during the making of *Idiot's Delight* in 1938 (on which Hunt Jr. worked as a production assistant).

Hunt with his beloved Cocker Spaniel.

Next, Hunt worked as a production assistant on several more of his father's films, including *Pride and Prejudice* (shot January-April 1940) starring Greer Garson and Laurence Olivier.

The summer of 1940 was highlighted by Hunt's "Old South Party" at the Santa Monica Deauville Club which the *Los Angeles Times* society page described as "strictly southern, with fried chicken, magnolias and plenty of hot music – and no one wants to miss it that can remember Hunt's last circus party." Many more of Hunt's lavish events were reported every few months, with increasing grandiosity – and he became a local celebrity that everyone wanted to befriend.

In 1941, Hunt worked as a production assistant on *They Met in Bombay* (shot February-April 1941) starring Clark Gable, Rosalind Russell and… drum roll please… Peter Lorre, with whom Hunt developed a lasting friendship that resulted in several professional collaborations.

At age 18, the summer before becoming a freshman at UCLA, Stromberg Jr. worked as an assistant on his father's production of *Shadow of the Thin Man* (shot August-September 1941), the fourth film in the franchise. Interestingly, this film was set in the world of horseracing which, as noted earlier, was a side-business of Stromberg Sr. This was followed by the musical *Married an Angel* (shot October-November 1941) with Jeanette MacDonald and Nelson Eddy.

All this gaiety came to a halt, however, when the Japanese attacked Pearl Harbor on December 7, 1941 – signaling the United States' official entry into World War II. Hunt Jr. signed up for Selective Service in the military but only those 20 and older were subject to immediate deployment. The following November 1942, at age 19, Hunt enlisted in the Army for a 2-year stint. To his mother's great relief, he

Bookish Hunt.

The Red Mill on Broadway, produced by Hunt Stromberg Jr.

Silly Hunt, with dress.

to address Senior as "Dad." He always called him "Hunt." Declaring his independence, he moved to New York City. Refusing to rely on daddy's money, he raised financing from private investors – including $3500 secretly invested by his devoted mother, without his father's knowledge.

Hollywood leading ladies Jeanette MacDonald and Joan Leslie sandwich Hunt Stromberg Jr. with congratulatory kisses on the Broadway opening of *The Red Mill*.

never went to battle. Hunt ended up being assigned to the Motion Picture Division as a writer and executive assistant to the head of the Scenario Department which prepared all the Army training films.

GOLDEN BOY OF THE GREAT WHITE WAY

After his Army service was completed, 22-year-old Stromberg decided it was time to cut the umbilical cord with his father. The strain between them was exemplified by Junior's refusal

With that capital, Hunt produced a Broadway revival of the Victor Herbert musical *The Red Mill* which became a smash hit, crowning Stromberg as the Golden Boy of the Great White Way. Follow-up Broadway productions included *The Front Page* (1946) and *Laura* (1946), based on the hit movie, starring Miriam Hopkins and two of the stars he had befriended on *Another Thin Man*: Otto Kruger and, yes, that ubiquitous Tom Neal – one year after his big break in *Detour*. Were they an item? Your guess is as good as mine. But they certainly were chummy.

Stromberg had such a great eye for talent, he ended up hosting a radio show called *Scout About Town* (1945-1947, Mutual Network) on which he would select newcomers to audition their talents, from singing to stand-up comedy routines. The only problem? Another show just like it called

Laura

MIRIAM HOPKINS

OTTO KRUGER

TOM NEAL.

STARRING three outstanding favorites of stage and screen—Miriam Hopkins, Otto Kruger and Tom Neal Hunt Stromberg, Jr.'s stage production of "Laura," the sophisticated comedy-drama by Vera Caspary and George Sklar, becomes the second major theatrical event sponsored by this young producer. His presentation (with Paula Stone) of "The Red Mill" in October, 1945, for a "limited" engagement, turned into the surprise smash hit of last season and promises to continue well into its second year.

Miss Hopkins rose to fame in the theatre in "An American Tragedy," "Lysistrata," "The Affairs of Anatol," "The Skin of Our Teeth," and "The Perfect Marriage." These performances she has alternated with appearances in films, the most outstanding of which include "Becky Sharp" (the first all technicolor picture) "Design For Living," "Trouble in Paradise," "These Three," "The Old Maid," and "Old Acquaintance."

Mr. Kruger's last stage appearance was in "The Moon is Down" in 1942. Other important comedies and dramas in which he has starred are "The Nervous Wreck," "To The Ladies," "Private Lives," "The Royal Family," "Counsellor-At-Law," and "Parnell." He made his motion picture debut in the silent film, "Under the Red Robe," "Ever in My Heart" with Barbara Stanwyck as his co-star, made him a favorite of the talking pictures. His most recent pictures are "Cover Girl," "Murder, My Sweet," "Wonder Man," "The Great John L.," and "On Stage Everybody."

Mr. Neal has been in Hollywood since his appearance in "Daughters of Atreus." Previous to that he was seen in "Love Is Not Triumph" and "Spring Dance." Of the forty-five films he has made, his favorites are "Behind the Rising Sun," "Burn Up O'Connor," "First Yank Into Tokyo," and "Detour."

"Laura" has a unique history. Miss Caspary first conceived the idea as a play, made her notes in the form of three acts, and on these she based the novel. Approached by theatrical producers to dramatize the book, she and her collaborator, George Sklar, wrote the mystery drama. Due to casting difficulties production was postponed and she sold the picture rights. But Hunt Stromberg, Jr. liked the play. He wanted to produce it—and rehearsals got under way.

Above: Program page from *Laura*, featuring bios of stars Miriam Hopkins, Otto Kruger and Tom Neal (with whom Stromberg was infatuated). Below: Stromberg headshot for promoting *Scout About Town*.

Professional headshot of Hunt Stromberg Jr., circa 1947.

Talent Scout was airing on CBS-Radio, hosted by Arthur Godfrey and produced by Irving Mansfield (husband of future *Valley of the Dolls* author Jacqueline Susann). Kind of like *American Idol* and *America's Got Talent* co-existing but not happy about it. Mansfield's persistent threats of legal action eventually spooked the Mutual Network into canceling the series.

BELA LUGOSI

Lugosi & Elaine Stritch, *3 Indelicate Ladies*

Refocusing on stage shows, Stromberg's next Broadway offering was going to be *Three Indelicate Ladies*, a comedy about a trio of secretaries who, after the demise of their boss at a private detective agency, take over the sleuthing themselves and get mixed up with a crook named Francis X. O'Rourke. On January 14, 1947, it was announced in *The New York Times* that Stromberg Jr. had offered the role of O'Rourke to his longtime friend Boris Karloff, who had just finished shooting Hunt Stromberg Sr.'s production of *Lured* with Lucille Ball. Karloff liked the play but wasn't able to commit to a long Broadway run.

Instead, Stromberg offered the part to another one of his horror film idols, Bela Lugosi, who jumped at the chance to do comedy.

Hunt also discovered an ingénue named Elaine Stritch for her first leading role as the main indelicate lady – and would

Lucille Ball & Boris Karloff in *Lured* (1947), produced by dad Stromberg Sr.

later develop her own sitcom for CBS called *My Sister Eileen* (1960-1961). Stritch would go on to become a major Tony Award-winning Broadway star of such shows as Stephen Sondheim's *Company*; and she won three Emmy Awards for her television work, including portraying Alec Baldwin's cranky mother in *30 Rock*.

Stritch loved to tell this anecdote about working with Lugosi on *Three Indelicate Ladies*: "You want to hear a classic line he said to me, over a few drinks? He said to me – in his thick Dracula accent – 'You know, I don't tell this to many people, Elaine. I want you to know that if it hadn't been for Boris Karloff, I would have had a corner at the horror market.'"

Stromberg also cast up-and-comer Ray Walston who had appeared in his production of *The Front Page* the year before – and would later be cast by Stromberg in the hit series *My Favorite Martian* (CBS, 1963-1966).

In April 1947, *Three Indelicate Ladies* had tryout engagements in New Haven and Boston, but reviews were tepid, so the show never made it to New York.

DEAR MONSTER

Speaking of indelicate, around this time, Hunt became romantically involved with at least four men: Thomas Elwell, whom Hunt nicknamed "Boopsie" and hired him to be General Manager and Production Associate on *Three Indelicate Ladies*; Thomas Spengler, a handsome young actor from the cast of Hunt's Broadway production of *The Red Mill* – who would be elevated to business partner on *Three Indelicate Ladies*; *Dark of the Moon* playwright William Berney, one of Tennessee Williams' many boyfriends; and Robert Schuler, a handsome young actor from the cast of *Three Indelicate Ladies*, who would later marry opera star Patrice Munsel and lead a straight life – despite this heartsick "Dear John" letter to Hunt (on file among Stromberg's papers at the USC Library) that demonstrates the intense love they once shared:

Dear Hunt,

You foolishly gave me an opportunity to do a lot of thinking when you left me sitting all day on the park bench without showing up. I have never gone through such hell in my life – remembering. Hunt saying, "Gooood deesguize!" [Good disguise!] Hunt saying, "Gosh I was worried about you down in the Canyon in the storm. You might have been killed!" And the flood of choking emotion I felt to think you really were worried about me – that I was important to you. And again, that wonderful, "Be careful, Bob" in the surf at Laguna and "Come out of that river this minute!" in Winona [Minnesota, where Schuler was born]. Scraps. But I'll never forget the wonder of belonging to someone. That's over now and I'll never be foolish enough to put myself in such a vulnerable position again. You never fooled me Hunt, never for an instant. Each time you double-crossed me, I forgave you because I knew you were driven by some madness that made it impossible for you to shoot straight. And each time, I did what I could to repair the damage you had done to me. But I never left you with any enemies – I always paved the path to keep you from getting bumped. Now, although I don't know what this latest emotional upset is about, I'm finished! I can't go through these crises forever. Nor can I afford to toss another hundred and fifty thousand dollars of my friends' money your way. Nor can I afford to gamble with another year of my life. I'm afraid this time "Popoff" will never return without his blade! I'm looking for a room. Please let me stay here until I find one. I'll try to avoid you. Bob [Robert Schuler]

P.S. I hope *Sally* is a huge success for you, and I do hope that someday, somewhere there'll be a happier day for both of us. You're such a blind fool, Hunt. I'm crying for you – and for me. I'll never really leave you. If you ever need me, just whistle.

B

Opera star Patrice Munsel & Robert Schuler wedding. (Schuler was Hunt's lover.)

Patrice Munsel & Robert Schuler.

Hunt at door that reads "A Popoff Expert." His nickname for lover Robert Schuler was "Popoff" – so he sent this photo to Robert.

Hunt marries Marilyn Elwell.

Hunt seemed more enamored with Thomas Elwell aka "Boopsie," the brother of his wife Marilyn Elwell. She caught them in flagrant delicto and ended their marriage.

True to his word, Robert never did abandon Hunt. They eventually patched up their differences and became close friends for the rest of their lives. Hunt often socialized with Robert and his wife Patrice. In fact, Hunt helped develop *The Patrice Munsel Show*, a variety show that ended up on ABC-TV in 1957, and arranged jobs in television for their son Rhett. In subsequent letters, Schuler always addressed Hunt as "Dear Monster" and signed them as "Popoff."

But in 1947, Hunt was hurt and angry. Clearly on the rebound, after an acquaintanceship of just three days, Hunt, 23, married Marilyn Elwell, 20, on January 26, 1947. Marilyn

just so happened to be the brother of Thomas Elwell, aka "Boopsie," one of Hunt's lovers mentioned above. Awkward. Predictably, the marriage hit the skids two months later when Marilyn unexpectedly came home early and discovered Hunt making whoopie with Boopsie. Oopsie!

A formal separation was filed in June. The divorce was granted October 10, 1949. Hunt was forced to pay alimony for years. The whole drama soured his relationship with Boopsie, too. He would not repeat that mistake. Ever again.

Another mistake he made was adding restauranteur to his hyphenates. Stromberg's East Side Café, a bistro on East 57th Street, opened its doors in February 1947 with Mae West as Hunt's date for the event. (Twenty-six years later, Mae would be Hunt's date to the premiere screening of *Frankenstein: The True Story*.) Mae's presence generated a lot of press and photo ops, but the restaurant got no traction whatsoever and Hunt quickly lost interest. It quietly closed that June.

CARL LAEMMLE JR.

Resuming his Broadway impresario occupation, he mounted a revival of Jerome Kern's *Sally* (1948), a musical-comedy starring Bambi Linn. For about five minutes, Milton Berle was going to be the director – but Billy Gilbert ("Herring" in Chaplin's *The Great Dictator*; and the voice of "Sneezy" in Disney's *Snow White and the Seven Dwarfs*) ended up at the helm.

The hardest part of Hunt's job was raising money from private investors. A fascinating letter from that period, dated May 18, 1948, demonstrates that Hunt had pitched potential investment to one of his closest Hollywood buddies – none other than Carl Laemmle Jr. (1908-1979), the former head of Universal Pictures and the producer of *Dracula, Frankenstein, Bride of Frankenstein, The Invisible Man, The Mummy, The Old Dark House, Murders in the Rue Morgue, The Black Cat,* and countless others. Even though Carl Jr. was fifteen years

Carl Laemmle Jr.

THE EPIC SAGA BEHIND *FRANKENSTEIN: THE TRUE STORY*

older than Hunt (40 and 25, respectively, at the time of this letter), they clearly identified with one another, keenly aware of the mixed blessing of having famous, powerful fathers in the movie business. Hunt certainly idolized and envied Carl for having produced all the films that literally created and defined the horror genre – including Hunt's top two favorite movies of all-time: *Frankenstein* and *Bride of Frankenstein*. The letter reads as follows:

> Dear Hunt,
> I admit I am a long time answering your letter, but answering letters is not one of my virtues. I would have answered sooner if I were interested in participating in *Sally*, but I have never invested in musicals. Furthermore, I won't invest in a show unless I was interested in the property for a motion picture; then again, only if I could have some kind of hold on the picture rights or a chance to meet competitive bids. However, enough of this. I am delighted that you got the show financed, and I hear it is doing very well. I understand it is a hit. When are you coming back to these parts? Please spend more time than you did the last time, when you drove up my driveway at night, honking the horn – and I was in bed, and we only said a quick hello, from the window. I won't even talk about my coming to New York, because it seems when I was away for 26 months in the Army, I realized how much I love California – God knows when I will leave it. I'm too comfortable here. Do you ever see any of the gang, and are you having any fun? What's cooking? Have you seen Jack Wildberg? [John J. Wildberg (1902-1959), producer and choreographer of the Broadway show *Porgy and Bess* (1942-1944).] Haven't run into folks in a long time, but guess I will next week, when Hollywood Park opens. [The horse racetrack co-owned by Hunt Stromberg Sr.] Are you coming out for a stay this summer? Be sure and call me – Crestview 6-7364. Hope you are enjoying good health and are happy. Lots of good luck, and I look forward to seeing you soon.
> All the best.
> Sincerely,
> Junior
> [Carl Laemmle Jr.]

Age was just a number. Hunt seemingly knew everybody in show business, young and old alike. And they all adored him. Regarding *Sally*, however, either Carl Laemmle Jr. was being polite or buying into the publicity hype. The truth was that the box-office was dismal and the show closed after only 36 performances. It was a terrible blow for Hunt – and, after having lost it all on this flop, it meant that he couldn't go back to all those investors for future shows.

ROYAL FLING

Stinging from the failure, Hunt sailed to London where he had an affair with the extremely handsome great-great-grandson of Queen Victoria, 29-year-old David Michael Mountbatten, 3rd Marquess of Milford Haven OBE DSC (1919-1970). Mountbatten had recently been the Best Man at the November 1947 wedding of his first-cousin Prince Philip, Duke of Edinburgh, to Princess Elizabeth (Yup, the future Queen of England!).

While Stromberg was in the throes of this royal fling with Mountbatten, gossip columnist Hedda Hopper published a quote from a July 1948 telegram she had received from Hunt that read, "It looks more like Hollywood and New York over here than cheery old London. At the Caprice, where I lunched today, I saw Freddie March, George Cukor, Tilly Losch, Bill Goetz, Raymond Massey, Jules Stein and Spencer Tracy."

From August 15-20, 1948, Stromberg and Mountbatten vacationed in Cannes on the French Riviera where they shared a room at the Hotel Miramar and rented a Citroen for joy rides along the Boulevard de Croisette. Next stop: Rome, Italy, followed in September with a stay in Zurich, Switzerland.

By the time Hunt returned to New York, Hedda Hopper had apparently gotten wind of the affair and was dropping hints about it, most notably in the following item published coast-to-coast on September 22, 1948: "Lord Milford Haven, who was best man at Princess Elizabeth's wedding in November 1947, will be Hunt Stromberg Jr.'s guest when he arrives in New York."

Nothing overt, of course. Friends can stay with friends. But in those days, this was the kind of sly, winking, coded language that all gossip columnists used to imply scandalous activities – without exposing themselves to legal claims of slander.

This would not have escaped the attention of Hunt's father and it is easy to imagine that there would likely have been some attempt to (Mount)batten down the hatches. Hunt Jr., however, seemed averse to discretion. More and more, he was becoming defiantly "out" about his homosexuality. Everyone in showbiz knew about it, so what was there to hide?

On the other hand, Mountbatten had the full court of the Royal Family to contend with – which no doubt put a damper on the flame. Within two years, Mountbatten would end up marrying a woman, but it wouldn't last. A later marriage in

David Michael Mountbatten. 3rd Marquess of Milford Haven OBE DSC (1919-1970).

the 1960s produced two children. According to Wikipedia, Mountbatten "played a prominent part in the London demimonde of the 1950s, which brought together a colorful mix of aristocrats and shadowy social climbers like osteopath Stephen Ward. This hard-partying set formed the nucleus of the Profumo affair." Mountbatten's fatal heart attack in 1970 at age 50 was attributed to his hedonistic lifestyle of excess.

DEVELOPMENT HELL

Meanwhile, Hunt had to buckle down and get to work. Discouraged with the not-so-Great White Way – and perhaps missing his party days in Hollywood that Carl Laemmle Jr. had waxed nostalgic about in his letter – Stromberg decided to return to his Los Angeles roots and dip his toe back into the movie business. But definitely *not* with his father – who, by then, had left MGM to produce seven films for United Artists (including *Lured* with Boris Karloff). Hunt Jr. set his sights elsewhere. It was good to be home, though, because his mother's health was failing, and he would be able to spend quality time with her. (In less than two years, Katherine would pass away March 15, 1951, at the young age of just 57.)

On June 9, 1949, Hedda Hopper reported, "Hunt Stromberg Jr. tried his hand at producing plays in New York. Now Darryl Zanuck has signed him at 20th Century to develop properties that have been gathering dust. When he finds one to their liking, he'll produce."

On his resume, Stromberg summed up how that went down in flames: "Employed as 'special idea man' for Darryl F. Zanuck, no use was made of me and I sat in a back bungalow for the better part of a year."

On February 20, 1950, a full-page ad in *The Hollywood Reporter* heralded the faltering wunderkind's latest scheme: "Hunt Stromberg Jr., Jack Shaffer, and Peter Shaw announce the opening of the Stromberg-Shaffer-Shaw Agency, for representation of American and English stage successes…

Lansbury and husband Peter Shaw.

Lansbury and husband Peter Shaw.

Lansbury and brothers Bruce and Edgar Lansbury.

Peter Shaw & Joan Crawford.

THE EPIC SAGA BEHIND *FRANKENSTEIN: THE TRUE STORY*

literary properties… and a limited number of directors, writers and artists" to package film and television projects for the major movie studios and TV networks. With a suite of offices at 8506 Sunset Boulevard, Hollywood, development-central opened officially on March 1, 1950.

Jack Shaffer was a guy with deep pockets. Peter Shaw, 32, was a former/failed actor at MGM who happened to be the husband of movie star Angela Lansbury, 24, twice Oscar-nominated for *Gaslight* (1945) and *The Picture of Dorian Gray* (1946) – and would later receive a third Oscar nomination for

Hunt & Eugene at the Leaning Tower of Pisa.

Eugene Banks.

Eugene Banks sits on steps.

Hunt and Eugene in Honolulu.

Eugene & Hunt at hotel.

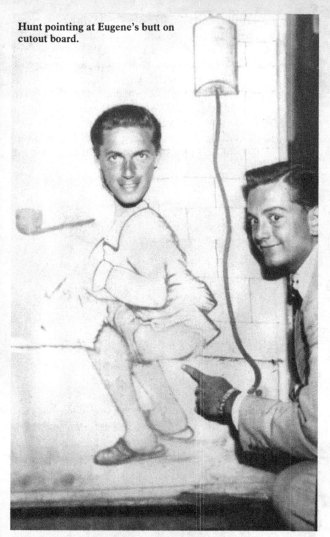
Hunt pointing at Eugene's butt on cutout board.

Hunt & Eugene in amusement park ride.

The Manchurian Candidate (1962).

The new agency's general office assistant, reader and "subagent" was a handsome young dancer named Eugene Banks – who had been a chorus boy in Hunt's Broadway productions of *The Red Mill*, *The Front Page* and *Sally*.

"I met Eugene Banks in drama school in New York in 1941," the late, great Angela Lansbury recalled in a 2016 interview for this book. "Oh, he was a darling, delightful man who really had no business being in acting school. He was *not* an actor. But he had a lovely personality, and he was a fun person to be around."

"Did you know that Eugene was gay?" I asked.

"Yes, yes, of course I did," Angela replied. "I was very sophisticated in that respect. So, yes, I was *well* aware, actually."

"He didn't try to hide it?" I gently prodded further.

"Oh, no, no," Angela said with a laugh. "No, no, no. But Eugene was such a fun person. He was fun with the girls. He was fun with the boys. He was fun with *everybody*, you know? He was just a good, *good* member of the group. We all loved having him around. And he always dressed himself nicely. He wore very stylish clothes. He came from Altoona, Pennsylvania, where Jack Shaffer was also from.

"Tell me about Jack."

"When my husband Peter Shaw teamed up with Hunt Stromberg Jr. to form their company, Jack Shaffer put up the money. That was really all he did. His name was on the shingle – the Stromberg-Shaffer-Shaw Agency – but he

Hunt poses shirtless, arms crossed like statues behind him.

Eugene at pool in bathing suit.

Hunt sunbathes on diving board.

Hunt in G-string in doorway.

Hunt *au naturel.*

Eugene in girl's bikini outside "FRUIT BAR."

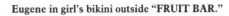

CHAPTER SEVENTEEN: THE MONSTROUS LIFE & TIMES OF HUNT STROMBERG JR.

was never actually there nor did any work. His wife, Patsy Malone, occasionally helped with some secretarial duties, like typing scripts, that sort of thing. But it was really Hunt and Peter, with Eugene as their executive assistant. Hunt gave Eugene a small stake in the company, too.

"So how did you meet Hunt Stromberg Jr.," I asked.

"Well, I was signed to a 7-year contract at MGM in 1944 when I was 17," Angela explained. "You couldn't work at MGM and *not* know the Strombergs. I never did a film for his father, but I always saw him around the lot and at parties and premieres, that sort of thing. And Hunt Jr. was ubiquitous, too. He was everywhere, zigzagging about like a cartoon character. Always full of life and laughing."

"And gay," I added.

"In both senses of the word," Angela said with a giggle. "But I got to know Hunt better when he and Eugene started seeing each other."

"And when was that?"

"It was before my husband formed the company with Hunt," she said. "I remember the four of us socializing together quite often. And that's how the idea came about."

"Were Hunt and Eugene openly a couple?" I asked.

"Oh yes, absolutely," Angela confirmed. "I mean, within a certain circle of friends, it was understood and accepted. And, you know, we just took it for granted."

DRACULA TV SERIES TO STAR LUGOSI

Their agency packaged many film and television proposals, several of them in the horror genre, including a weekly half-hour *Dracula* television series to star Bela Lugosi.

Lugosia as latter day Dracula.

In a letter to Lugosi at 45 Christopher Street, New York, dated June 15, 1950, Hunt made his pitch:

Dear Bela,
I am sorry we have missed each other in our attempted phone calls. It was very kind of you to respond so immediately to my telegram. As you may know I now have a Literary Agency here in Hollywood, our primary function consisting of the packaging of deals for both movies and television. It occurs to me that it might be a good idea to produce a series of half-hour television films, starring you, based on the character of Count Dracula. We would be prepared to finance the first sample film and to act as nominal producers as well as agents for the entire venture. I do not know whether or not the Bram Stoker rights are clear for television. Do you know about this? Does Universal still perhaps own all rights? I hesitate to

make inquiries direct to them inasmuch as I might stir up latent interest. In any event please let me hear from you as soon as possible as to whether or not you would be interested in an association with us for such a project. We have worked well together in the past (if not too successfully!) and I would consider it a great pleasure to get together with you again. My love to your wife.
As ever,
Hunt Stromberg, Jr.

Lugosi's response, dated June 25, 1950, was as follows:

My dear Hunt:
I contacted Brandt & Brandt Agency, 101 Park Ave., who are representing the London Play Company in the United States. They advised their legal department to find out whether the television rights are owned by Universal, John Balderston, the playwright of *Dracula*, or whether they own the rights. They seem to be slow but when I receive the information I will let you know. I am definitely interested in that venture. I will try personally to get lower terms than you would get by breaking their heart with a hard luck story. I will be at St. Michael's Playhouse, Burlington, Vermont, June 27-July 9, 1950. I will be back in New York on July 9th.
With kind regards, I remain,
Sincerely yours,
Bela

Stromberg received a follow-up letter from Lugosi, dated July 19, 1950:

My dear Hunt:
Finally received information from Brandt & Brandt that John Balderston is presently suing Universal in connection with the rights on *Dracula* which both claim and which will not be decided before September. Since I am leaving for a six-week summer tryout of a new play, *The Devil Also Dreams*, I would advise you contact Will Koppelman directly who's [sic] department handles *Dracula*. Enclosed is my itinerary – I do not know what my new address will be on our return to NY in September, the best way to reach me is thru H. Clay Blaney, 1775 Broadway, who is producing the show.
With kindest regards to you, I remain,
Sincerely yours,
Bela

With the rights for *Dracula* tangled up in this legal dispute between Balderston and Universal, Hunt moved on to unencumbered properties.

Hunt himself wrote two pitches for new installments of the Bing Crosby-Bob Hope-Dorothy Lamour "Road" picture franchise: *The Road to Mars*, with spaceships and alien creatures; and *The Road to Cairo*, with mummies rising from the dead and a time-warp that lands the trio in ancient Egypt where they cross paths with Cleopatra and Caesar (more on that later).

CARMILLA IN 3-D

Most intriguing of all, though, was an adaptation of the vampire tale *Carmilla*, based on the novella by Sheridan Le Fanu, from a script by DeWitt Bodeen, screenwriter of several Val Lewton productions, including *Cat People*

Vincent Price.

Simone Simon.

Boris Karloff.

(1942), *The Seventh Victim* (1943) and *The Curse of the Cat People* (1944). Simone Simon (star of *Cat People*), Boris Karloff and Vincent Price were attached to star for director Jacques Tourneur (*Cat People*, *I Walked with a Zombie*, *The Comedy of Terrors*). On February 3, 1953, *The New York Times* reported that *Carmilla* would be filmed in 3-D by Universal-International, produced by Ross Hunter, one of Hunt's gay compadres who would later be Oscar-nominated for producing *Airport*. In fact, Hunter's long-time lover Jacques Mapes, who had just art directed *Singin' in the Rain* (1952), was on board as the production designer.

The 3-D craze of the 1950s had just taken off 9 weeks earlier, on November 26, 1952, with United Artists' release of *Bwana Devil* about a killer-lion, starring Robert Stack. The 3-D / *Carmilla* announcement pre-dated by eleven weeks the 3-D / Vincent Price smash hit *House of Wax*, released by Warner Bros. on April 25, 1953. Sadly, this extremely promising rendition of *Carmilla* was never made. [Of course, several other versions of the source material did come to

fruition, including Hammer Films' surprisingly faithful adaptation *The Vampire Lovers* (1970) starring Ingrid Pitt and Peter Cushing.]

Angela Lansbury, Zachary Scott and Kirk Douglas were attached to *Dark of the Moon*, based on a play by Howard Richardson and his cousin William Berney – the latter gentleman having been Stromberg's lover and producing partner for his Broadway production of *Sally* (not to mention a former boyfriend of Tennessee Williams).

At least two dozen other vehicles were being tailored for Peter Lorre, Claude Rains, Joseph Cotten, Mae West,

CHAPTER SEVENTEEN: THE MONSTROUS LIFE & TIMES OF HUNT STROMBERG JR.

343

Beautiful temptress ...or Bloodthirsty monster ?

...She's the NEW HORROR FROM HAMMER!

THE VAMPIRE LOVERS

A HAMMER-AMERICAN INTERNATIONAL PRODUCTION

INGRID PITT · GEORGE COLE · KATE O'MARA and PETER CUSHING as the General

"THE VAMPIRE LOVERS"x

Also Starring FERDY MAYNE · DOUGLAS WILMER and Guest Star DAWN ADDAMS

Screenplay by TUDOR GATES · Produced by HARRY FINE & MICHAEL STYLE

Directed by ROY WARD BAKER · TECHNICOLOR · Released by MGM-EMI

Director-Producer Cecil B. DeMille & Hunt Stromberg Jr. – Hunt looked up to DeMille for his all-star extravaganzas like *The Greatest Show on Earth* (1952) and *Samson and Delilah* (1949) featuring his friend Angela Lansbury.

Rosalind Russell, Roddy McDowall, Gloria Swanson, Joan Bennett, etc. Although several packages were optioned around town – which generated modest fees – only one project ever made it to the screen: *The Savage* (Paramount, 1952) starring Charlton Heston. Three agonizing years of spinning wheels, with so little to show for it. That's why this process is commonly referred to as "development hell." By the end of 1953, the Stromberg-Shaffer-Shaw Agency was dissolved.

Peter Shaw went on to become a top agent at William Morris where he represented such clients as his wife Angela Lansbury and Elvis Presley – which explains why these two disparate talents starred together in *Blue Hawaii* (1961). He later supervised (without taking any credit) all twelve seasons of his wife's hit series *Murder, She Wrote* (1984-1996) for which she was Emmy-nominated a dozen times.

DISCOVERY OF THE ~~WEEK~~ CENTURY!

The one takeaway that Hunt gleaned from his years in development was that the new frontier of show business was television. The networks and local stations needed daily programming – and Hunt was exactly the right guy at the right time who was bursting with ideas and boundless energy to spare.

On May 18, 1953, on the front page of *Daily Variety*, it was announced that Hunt Stromberg Jr. had landed a job as a producer-writer for KABC-TV, the local ABC affiliate in Los Angeles – which was, at the time, the lowest-rated TV station in Southern California. Hunt must have made a very good impression on his boss, Selig J. Seligman, Vice President

THE EPIC SAGA BEHIND *FRANKENSTEIN: THE TRUE STORY*

Chucko the Clown's Cartoons.

Above: Carol Burnett (standing in rear with "Coach" shirt) in UCLA comedy revue in 1954, seen by Hunt Stromberg Jr.
Right: Detail blow-up of Carol Burnett.

Hunt with singer Margaret Whiting who appeared on *Party at Ciro's.*

of ABC (national) and General Manager of KABC (local), because, after only 9 months, on March 1, 1954, he was promoted to Executive Producer and Programming Director of KABC-TV.

Now Hunt was in the driver's seat, and he wasted no time ramming the pedal to the metal. Within weeks, he introduced a slew of new daytime kids, talk and lifestyle shows, including *Chucko the Clown's Cartoons*, *Little Schoolhouse*, *Glamour Girl*, *Our Famous Husbands*, and *Day in Court* (the precursor of all daytime courtroom shows, from *Divorce Court* to *Judge Judy*) – the latter produced by Hunt's boyfriend Eugene Banks and written by Bruce Lansbury (Angela Lansbury's brother).

For late-night, Hunt created *Party at Ciro's*, "an all-star extravaganza featuring famous guest stars currently appearing

at Ciro's" to be broadcast at 11:00 PM every Saturday night. Ciro's was the most popular nightclub in Hollywood – and the star-studded audience rivaled the Academy Awards. The cabaret had already been made famous in Warner Bros.' *Hollywood Steps Out* (1941), a Merrie Melodies cartoon directed by Tex Avery, that depicts a cavalcade of celebrities whooping it up at Ciro's, including Clark Gable, Greta Garbo, Peter Lorre, Groucho Marx and even FBI Director J. Edgar Hoover.

Each week, *Party at Ciro's* would present the club's current big-name headliner to perform a number or two – which was written into their contracts as a way to promote the engagement. In other words, they were expected to appear for free. The first installment, broadcast Saturday, May 1, 1954, featured the most popular nightclub artist of the era, Kay Thompson (soon to star in *Funny Face* opposite Audrey Hepburn and Fred Astaire, and future author of the *Eloise* children's books). [Side note: I guess now would be as good a time as any to modestly plug my book *Kay Thompson: From Funny Face to Eloise*, published by Simon & Schuster. Now back to our regularly-scheduled text.] Subsequent stars to appear on Party at Ciro's were Nat King Cole, Pearl Bailey and Cary Grant (his first and only live television appearance).

Party at Ciro's also regularly featured the Lester Horton Dancers – a troupe that included Hunt's boyfriend Eugene Banks.

Additionally, for the lineup on *Party at Ciro's*, Hunt insisted on having a "Discovery of the Week," spotlighting up-and-coming talent, from singers to stand-up comics – like what he used to present on his former radio show *Scout About Town*. Hunt's very first "Discovery of the Week" was a young college student whom he had personally spotted in a musical-comedy revue at UCLA. He invited her to be the show's inaugural "Discovery of the Week" which would also be her television debut. This unknown schoolgirl, plucked from obscurity, just so happened to be… wait for it… Carol Burnett. The review in *Daily Variety* by "Kap," dated May 3, 1954, agreed with Stromberg's selection: "Show also included Carol Burnett, a singing comedienne from UCLA who shows definite promise." This was 20 months before her next break when she appeared on *The Walter Winchell Show* (NBC-TV, December 17, 1955) – often erroneously cited as her television debut. Let this set the record straight and give Hunt the credit he is long overdue.

Stromberg's subsequent "Discoveries of the Week" included Kim Novak and Diahann Carroll.

VAMPIRA

But that was not all. Stromberg had another trick up his sleeve. KABC-TV had licensed the rights to a bunch of inexpensive, half-forgotten mysteries and thrillers from Poverty Row studios like Monogram and PRC – including *King of the Zombies* (Monogram, 1941), *Phantom of 42nd Street* (PRC, 1945), *Strangler of the Swamp* (PRC, 1946), and *Detour* (PRC, 1945) starring Hunt's buddy Tom Neal. Stromberg called them "shit-with-sprocket-holes" – and they were being broadcast as filler for the Saturday midnight timeslot. Nobody at the station cared about that wasteland – and neither did viewers. But Hunt sensed a wasted opportunity – and suddenly remembered a person who just might come in handy.

The previous fall, five days before Halloween 1953, Hunt had attended dance choreographer Lester Horton's annual Bal Caribe Masquerade Gala at Moulin Rouge (formerly the Earl Carroll Theatre). As mentioned above, Lester's dance troupe included Hunt's boyfriend Eugene Banks – which would eventually lead to Hunt employing the troupe weekly for *Party at Ciro's* (1954). Lester was gay and attracted a massive capacity crowd of 2,000 – peppered with avant-garde misfits, from beatniks to drag

queens to circus performers. The more unusual, the better. Like something out of *Fellini Satyricon*, long before Fellini was Fellini.

Among the freakshow, Hunt spotted a pale-skinned 30-year-old woman with "a long and mangy-looking black wig," dressed in a form-fitting, tattered black satin gown. She resembled the ghoulish wife of the monster family depicted in Charles Addams' darkly humorous cartoons that regularly appeared in the pages of *The New Yorker* magazine (1937-1988) – collected into a series of very popular books, like *Drawn and Quartered* (1942), and the latest one, *Homebodies*, which would soon be published in January 1954. The characters did not have names back then – but, a decade later, in 1964, when *The Addams Family* was launched as a television series, they called the matriarch "Morticia Addams," and she was played by Carolyn Jones. For shorthand purposes, I will refer to the character as "Morticia" even though that moniker had not yet been coined.

With his affinity for horror, Hunt couldn't take his eyes off this embodiment of "Morticia." In her book *Glamour*

Stromberg's *Vampira* show with Maila Nurmi as the glamour ghoul.

THE EPIC SAGA BEHIND *FRANKENSTEIN: THE TRUE STORY*

Fletcher Jones (Chevrolet dealer who sponsored *The Vampira Show* and appeared on-air); Vampira (Maila Nurmi); and Hunt Stromberg Jr. (Photo of Vampira © Jonny Coffin Collection.)

Ghoul, author Sandra Niemi wrote, "The creepy Cinderella was crowned belle of the ball, and Maila claimed her first-place prize: a portable radio."

Now, five months later, in March 1954, with his new title and power, Hunt was struck with the idea that this macabre femme fatale would be a startling presence on the television screen and could be just the novelty they needed to attract viewers for their weekly late-night horror film broadcasts.

"We needed her as a magnet," Hunt reasoned, in unpublished notes for a memoir he never completed. "The first thing I do when I get my weekly copy of *The New Yorker* magazine is flip through it to find the latest Charles Addams

cartoon. That's the kind of anticipation that was totally lacking with our midnight horror movies. We needed this spooky lady to introduce them!"

To be fair, the idea of a "horror host" was not exactly unchartered territory. There were lots of hosts in radio that would introduce dramas and suspense plays, but many of them were faceless announcers. Raymond Johnson, who hosted the horror anthology radio series *Inner Sanctum* (1941-1945), was certainly a forerunner. He appeared in photographs and newspaper ads dressed in a black cloak and top hat that suggested Bela Lugosi's formal Dracula attire. On air, he spoke in a "mockingly sardonic voice" and made

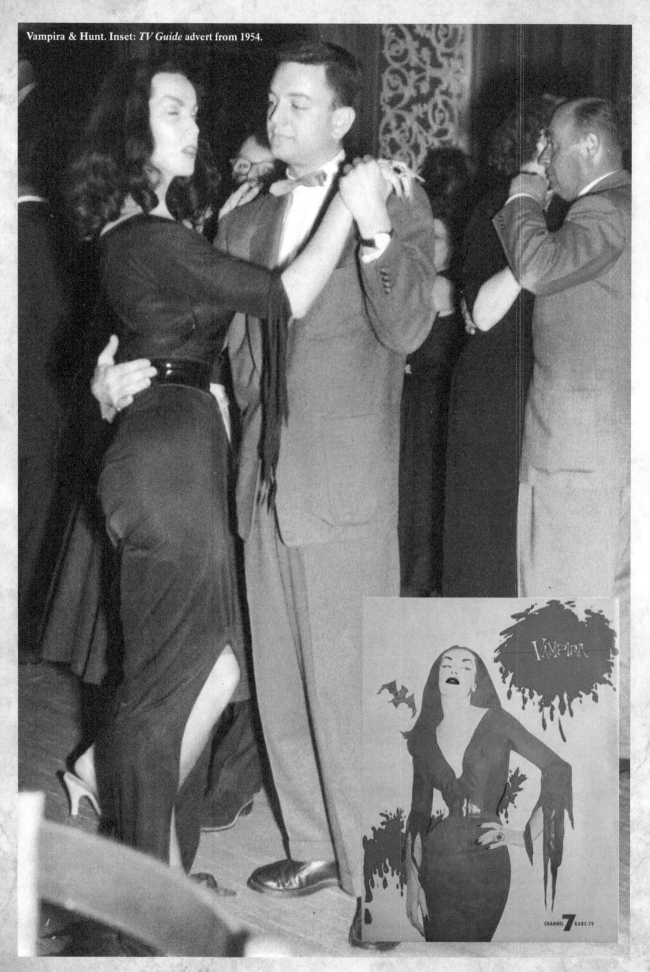

VAMPIRA

CHANNEL 7 KABC-TV

THE EPIC SAGA BEHIND *FRANKENSTEIN: THE TRUE STORY*

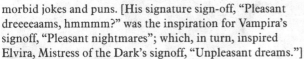

morbid jokes and puns. [His signature sign-off, "Pleasant dreeeeaams, hmmmm?" was the inspiration for Vampira's signoff, "Pleasant nightmares"; which, in turn, inspired Elvira, Mistress of the Dark's signoff, "Unpleasant dreams."]

In Penny Dreadful's Foreword to the book *Vampira and Her Daughters*, she notes, "The lurid EC comic books *Tales from the Crypt*, *Vault of Horror* and *Haunt of Fear* [1950-1955] had their own set of horror hosts. The Crypt Keeper, the Vault Keeper, and the Old Witch took gleeful delight showing readers all manner of grotesque things."

Let's make note that "the Old Witch" is perhaps the first *female* horror host in print – though admittedly an ancient ugly crone, like the witch who gives Snow White the apple in the Disney animated feature.

Horror historian Don Glut and others cite Swami Drana Badour (played by TV announcer Allen Harvey) as the very first *television* horror host. *Murder Before Midnight* (1950-1953) was a local Chicago show on WBKB Channel 4 in which horror movies were broken up into half-hour segments and serialized over three separate broadcasts. The mystical Swami – with exotic turban, robe, and crystal ball – would introduce

them, tongue firmly planted in cheek. There may have been other local horror hosts in those early days of television, but none with any lasting impact.

Out of this witch's brew of influences, Hunt favored going in the direction of the Charles Addams "Morticia" character.

"She had to be backassward," Stromberg explained. "A woman who loved everything ghoulish. Things that gave regular folks the heebie-jeebies. I started making lists of

grotesque one-liners and creepy props she could react to. If the stunt worked, it would give people a reason to tune-in every week, just to see what she did next."

And he'd already seen the perfect woman to play her at the masquerade ball. Unfortunately, he had no idea who she was nor how to get in touch with her.

In practically every profile and bio ever written about this mysterious woman, it has become legend that it took Hunt five excruciating months to find her.

The reality, of course, was that Hunt didn't get the idea until five months later when he had the promotion and power to do something about it.

"Hold on," said his boyfriend Eugene Banks. "I know one of the judges. He's a dancer in my class with Lester Horton. His name is Rudi Gernreich. He'll know."

Born in Vienna, Austria, Rudi Gernreich (1922-1985) was a Jewish refugee who fled the Nazis during World War II and settled in Los Angeles. He was a dancer and costume designer

THE EPIC SAGA BEHIND *FRANKENSTEIN: THE TRUE STORY*

Inset: *Captain Marvel Jr.* (No. 16, December 1952) with "Vampira" banner. Namesake or coincidence?

for Lester Horton's modern dance troupe. He eventually gave up his aspirations to be a choreographer to focus on avant-garde fashion design – for which he was a four-time recipient of the Coty American Fashion Critics Award and was elected to the Coty American Fashion Hall of Fame. He famously created the "monokini" (a topless swimsuit) in 1964 and designed the unisex Moonbase Alpha uniforms worn by the main characters in *Space: 1999* (1975-1976).

Rudi also happened to be gay and was a founding member of the Mattachine Society, one of the first and foremost national gay rights organizations, started in 1950. He was a lover of one of the other founders, Harry Hay.

All it took was one simple phone call to Rudi to ask him for the name of the woman who had won the costume contest. He immediately responded, "Maila Nurmi! She was the first woman in California to wear those backless shoes. She's in the phone book under Mrs. Dean Riesner."

In the authorized book *Vampira: The Original Hollywood Glamour Ghoul 1954-1956* by Jonny Coffin (2021), Maila (pronounced "Myla") is quoted thusly: "It was a Cinderella story. They eventually tracked me down."

Well, I hate to burst the bubble of a fanciful yarn, but it didn't take five months. Hunt's hunt took five *minutes*.

Maila Elizabeth Syrjäniemi, professionally known as Maila Nurmi (1922-2008), was born in Gloucester, Massachusetts; lived in Ohio and Oregon before moving to Los Angeles in 1940 at age 18 to pursue acting. Gaining no traction in Hollywood, she tried her luck in New York and got cast in the play *Catherine Was Great* (1944), produced by Mike Todd (who later produced the movie *Around the World in 80 Days* and was Elizabeth Taylor's third husband). Not long after the opening, however, she got fired by its star Mae West, who was also the playwright, because – according to Maila, Mae felt she was upstaging her.

Mike put Maila into another show he was producing called *Spook Scandals*, a midnight Grand Guignol revue in which

she played a dancing vampire. One night, she was seen by Howard Hawks, director of the films *To Have and to Have Not* (1944) and *The Big Sleep* (1946), both with Humphrey Bogart and Hawks' discovery Lauren Bacall. He brought Maila back to Hollywood, touting her as "the new Lauren Bacall." His proposed movie for her, *Dreadful Hollow*, never got off the ground. Typical showbiz. One minute, you think you've won the jackpot. The next minute, you're kicked to the curb.

In the late-1940s and early-1950s, Maila modeled for Man Ray and cheesecake artist Alberto Vargas, among others, for men's pinup magazines like *Glamorous Models* and *Famous Models*. She also danced as a chorus showgirl at the Earl Carroll Theatre and at Florentine Gardens with burlesque stripper Lili St. Cyr.

Maila became enamored with *Bizarre* (26 issues, 1946-1956; not to be confused with my own *Bizarre* horror fanzine of the 1970s), a BDSM fetish magazine that regularly featured model Bettie Page. She loved all the kinky black attire, the fishnet stockings, the stilettos – and felt it was "the look of the future." She embraced her inner Goth, and it informed her fashion choices throughout her life. The biggest influence from that magazine, though, was the tiny, cinched-in waists depicted in the S&M artwork of John Willie.

Hunt summoned Maila for a meeting at his office. In *Glamour Ghoul*, Sandra Niemi noted, "On a blustery Ides of March 1954, Maila rode the Red Car to meet with Stromberg at KABC at Prospect and Talmadge. Her haircut was short and blonde, and she'd dressed in black from head to toe: sweater, capris, flats, and cape. Inside, she heard the secretaries' whispers. 'That's Hunt's vampire girl.'"

Maila assumed they wanted to do an *Addams Family* sitcom with her as the "Morticia" character. Gently deflating her expectations down to Earth, Hunt explained that they couldn't afford to buy the rights from Charles Addams, and they didn't have the budget for a little local late-night TV show to mount a series of that magnitude with multiple characters. He clarified that he wanted her, and *only* her, to host late-night horror movies, in the style of the Addams character. But, of course, they'd need to come up with their own name – and ever-so-slightly alter the look to avoid any copyright infringement claims.

At first, Maila was concerned about that. But Hunt reassured her that Charles Addams freely admitted his character was inspired by a number of influences, including silent film star Theda Bara (nicknamed "The Vamp"), Edna Tichenor as "Luna" in Tod Browning's silent film *London After Midnight* (1927); Carroll Borland as "Luna" in the remake *Mark of the Vampire* (1935); Gloria Holden as "Countess Zaleska" in *Dracula's Daughter* (1936); the "Evil Queen" in Disney's animated feature *Snow White and the Seven Dwarfs* (1937); and "Dragon Lady" in the *Terry and the Pirates* newspaper comic strip (1934-1973) – played by Sheila Darcy in the 1940 15-episode serial released by Columbia Pictures, and by Gloria Saunders in the then-current 1952-1953 18-episode syndicated television series.

Placated, Maila went home and tweaked her makeup and wardrobe to be a bit more original. And she corseted her waist so tight – like the John Willie illustrations in *Bizarre* – to the point where her measurements were a startling 38-17-36.

Meanwhile, her husband, Dean Riesner (who later wrote the screenplays for two Clint Eastwood movies: *Play Misty for Me* and *Dirty Harry*), came up with the name for the character: "Vampira". This accreditation has seemingly

This Picture and Above: Vampira & Liberace in Las Vegas show.

model for this?"

In any event, there were a lot of influences percolating in this melting pot.

"It was not all my creation," Nurmi admitted in R. H. Greene's documentary *Vampira and Me* (2012). "Like when a chef makes a famous dish… there is inventing and things he knows from history. Everything comes into creation, my inspirations were manifold."

But it was Hunt Stromberg Jr. who spotted the potential and masterminded the platform in which the television horror host Vampira was born.

A special preview show called *Dig Me Later, Vampira* was broadcast live on Friday, April 30, 1954. The following evening, Saturday, May 1, in its regular midnight time slot, *The Vampira Show* was officially launched. Believe it or not, this was the very same night, just one hour earlier, that *Party at Ciro's* was launched with Kay Thompson and Carol Burnett, broadcast live from a studio across the hall. The following week, on Saturday, May 8, Vampira was the "Discovery of the Week" on *Party at Ciro's* – which was easy to do live since she was just steps away from her own set to start her show immediately afterward. Are you with me?

Party at Ciro's did moderately well but the host, Herman Hover, owner of the club, was a deer caught in the headlights. When Stromberg insisted on replacing him with someone more experienced, Hover refused, so the show was canceled in November 1954.

On the other hand, the ratings for *The Vampira Show* went through the frickin' roof. Even though it was just a local program, Vampira became an overnight *national* sensation with spreads in *Life* (June 14, 1954) and *TV Guide* (July 17-23, 1954) – the two most popular magazines in America, read by a quarter of the population. The demand led to guest spots on major network variety shows *The Red Skelton Hour* also with Bela Lugosi and Lon Chaney Jr. (CBS-TV, June 15, 1954); *The Tonight Show* with Steve Allen (NBC-TV, June 18, 1954); and *The George Gobel Show* (NBC-TV, April 2, 1955).

At first, scripts were written by Stromberg himself, peppered with a pastiche of one-liners from a peanut gallery of office mates and social acquaintances. Any clever idea got

been taken at face value and never questioned. However, in my research, I discovered that just 15 months earlier, in December 1952, Fawcett Publications introduced a character named "Vampira: The Korean Queen of Terror!" with her name emblazoned on a banner across the cover of the comic book *Captain Marvel Jr.* No. 16. Coincidence? Perhaps. But when you look at the illustrations in that issue, Vampira has long black hair, a form-fitting black dress, and she is practically a dead ringer for Maila Nurmi! No Korean / Asian facial features whatsoever. With the extraordinary popularity of comic books back then, it is a little hard imagine that somebody didn't show it to Maila and ask, "Were you the

Zsa Zsa Gabor as Vampira.

This picture and Top Right: Vampira & Bela Lugosi guest-starring on *The Red Skelton Hour*.

thrown into the mix. But by Week Three, Hunt was running out of steam and time.

"I found I was devoting far too much time to the Vampira program and neglecting my other duties as overall Program Manager of the station," Stromberg wrote in notes for an intended memoir. "I simply did not have the time to continue writing her material and was desperate for help. One day, while in a particular frenzy as a result of this problem, my secretary told me that a young man was on the telephone who claimed to be a comedy writer from Chicago. He wanted an appointment. His name was Peter Robinson. He was in my office a half-hour later. Under my supervision, Peter now took over the weekly chore of writing the Vampira introductions and sequences of the midnight horror films. We began cutting more and more minutes out of the feature films to allow more and more time for Vampira bits. Our favorite show involved the night Vampira finally decided, after seven years as she said, to take a bath. She got into her tub (or to be more exact, her cauldron), with taps marked 'Scalding' and "Freezing.' Despite the annoyance to her of a live electric eel that also occupied the bathtub, she proceeded to bathe herself with lye. Now and then, because she was thirsty, she would sip some of the murky bathwater through straws provided to her by Rollo, her pet spider."

Bit parts were sometimes added for certain comedy sketches – but these "guests" usually appeared for free, like Fletcher Jones, owner of the local Chevrolet dealership, who sponsored the show. He would appear in his own commercials that were woven into the Vampira show.

"Fletcher was a pompous man with a benign smile," Stromberg explained. "Vampira would introduce him by saying: 'And now, unfortunately, it is my depressing chore to have to inflict upon you Fletcher Jones. He is going to try to get you to buy one of his ridiculously *safe* cars. Frankly, I think you would be much better off buying a more dangerous kind. Then you might get killed.' From the wings, Fletcher

would make his entrance and begin his unctuous pitch. Fletcher Jones' car sales quadrupled within a two-month period."

The Vampira living room set was decorated with cobwebs, a sofa, and a coffin for a coffee-table. "A corpse was glimpsed inside that coffin from time to time," Stromberg noted. "Often, that corpse was played as a lark by Jimmy Dean, a close friend of Maila's."

Of course, no one knew at the time that, the following year, on September 30, 1955, 24-year-old James Dean would tragically die in a car accident. He had just finished shooting *Giant*, opposite Elizabeth Taylor and Rock Hudson. During post-production, Nick Adams had to imitate the late Dean's voice for a few lines that needed to be looped. Dean was posthumously nominated for the Best Actor Oscar.

In the book *Vampira, Dark Goddess of Horror*, author W. Scott Poole describes another typical comedy sketch: "Vampira mimicked the image of the housewife waiting for her husband to come home from work, martini in hand. Wearing an apron over her ragged graveyard gear, she mixed a drink called 'the zombie cocktail' that promised any man walking through the door a quick death rather than a submissive welcome… making it out of 'one jigger of formaldehyde, two jiggers of vulture blood, garnished with a glass eye.'"

On October 29 & 30, 1954, between showings of two horror movies, Vampira headlined a Halloween-themed vaudeville act on stage at The Orpheum in Los Angeles that were sellouts (2,000 fans each night).

And, full-circle, for the 1954 annual Halloween Costume Gala thrown by Lester Horton – that year moved to the much larger Palladium with 4,000 attendees – the announcement read: "Vampira, who was 'discovered' at last year's Bal Caribe by ABC-TV producer Hunt Stromberg Jr., will be a judge at tonight's costume gala." Her escort? Hunt, naturally.

Hunt introduced Maila to his neighbor Liberace which led to her appearing in his Las Vegas revue. And at a February 1955 costume ball thrown at Ciro's, *Daily Variety* reported that Zsa Zsa Gabor stole the show when she entered the joint dressed as Vampira.

"We even managed to sneak a Vampira float into the Pasadena Rose Parade (New Year's Day, Saturday, January 1, 1955)," Stromberg added with mischievous pride. "Midst all of the splendiferous, gorgeous floats, along came Vampira, surrounded by dead lilies and large lettered boxes of manure. Stalid Pasadena is still in a state of shock."

The most unexpected kicker of all? In March 1955, Vampira was honored with an Emmy Award nomination for Most Outstanding Female Personality! On the ballot as "Vampira", not "Maila Nurmi"!

VOLUPTUA

The magnitude of the success of Vampira surprised everyone, including Hunt himself. It was a tough act to follow, but he figured why not see if lightning would strike twice. So, on Wednesday, December 15, 1954, at 9:30 PM, he premiered his latest novelty stunt, *The Voluptua Show* (directed by his boyfriend Eugene Banks) – featuring pin-up model Gloria Pall (who had uncredited walk-ons in *Abbott and Costello Go to Mars* and *20,000 Leagues Under the Sea*). Gloria played a character named "Voluptua, Goddess of Love," a sex kitten "being suggestive with a lot of double entendres, in slinky clothes, and a deep purry voice… slinking around a far-out sex-trap of a room – with a fur-trimmed telephone and a big white bearskin rug – reading intimate stories from a big heart-shaped book of secrets."

All this, of course, served as foreplay for a slate of

Reclined on bed with "Voluptua" pillow.

Voluptua answers the phone.

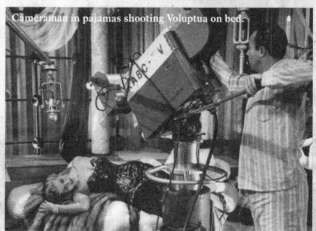

Cameraman in pajamas shooting Voluptua on bed.

Seated on bed with "Voluptua" pillow.

With heart-shaped "Book of Secrets".

Above: *Nightmare Typhoon* with Gloria Pal.
Below: *TV Guide* article on Voluptua & Vampira

Voluptua changes clothes behind a translucent screen.

inexpensive romance movies that the station had licensed. You get the picture. Same formula as Vampira – different genre. If this was a hit, too, Hunt was prepared to install sexy hosts for each night of the week, introducing different types of movies, from Westerns to science fiction. If he could have afforded animation, he'd have created a Jessica Rabbit-style siren to introduce cartoons!

At first, it appeared that Hunt's gambit was going to pay off again – garnering *national* attention. *Life*, *TV Guide* and *Playboy* magazines did Voluptua spreads (no pun intended; well, maybe a little); TV talk show host Arthur Godfrey devoted an entire episode to her; fan mail started rolling in. Even Hunt was getting good press. The January 17, 1955, issue of *Newsweek* put a spotlight on Stromberg as the brains behind the pop culture phenoms of Vampira and Voluptua.

"Hunt decided to have a party," Gloria Pall aka Voluptua explained in her self-published memoir (xeroxed and spiral bound to peddle at her convention appearances). "He'd just bought a home in the Hollywood Hills on Harold Way and was Liberace's neighbor. Hunt's roommate, Gene Banks, was my director. [They also had a pet Schnauzer named Strudel.] Hunt had furnished their home with Hearst Castle splendor; he'd bought almost everything they had at the Hearst auction. Most of the people at the party were gay. In fact, there was only one straight couple there. When Johnny Mathis met me and saw me in a tight purple satin dress, he came over to me and sang, 'Wouldn't it be wonderful if the whole world was purple?' I had never heard that song before or after. Liberace invited some of us to walk over to his home and he took me on a grand tour. It was beyond magnificent."

Then the other shoe dropped. A Catholic newspaper, *The Tidings*, declared that "Voluptua" should be called "Corruptua" and had no business being on television. Next thing they knew, pressure groups filed complaints with the FCC and flooded the show's advertisers with phone calls threatening boycotts. Sponsors of the show began to drop like flies – and with the threat of KABC losing its license, Hunt had no choice but to cancel the show after its seventh broadcast on January 26, 1955.

VAMPIRA RISES FROM THE GRAVE

Bad press and pearl-clutchers shifted their sights on *The Vampira Show* which spooked its sponsor, Fletcher Jones Chevrolet Dealership, to pull the plug at the end of March 1955. Suddenly, Vampira was Kryptonite. This resulted in the cancellation of her show on March 26, 1955, after its 50th broadcast.

Some sources claim that the reason the show was canceled was due to Maila insisting on owning the character. I found very little evidence to support that theory. According to various memos and references in the Hunt Stromberg Jr. Papers at the USC Cinematic Arts Library, the decision to cancel was purely based on the lack of sponsors and the threat of the FCC revoking the station's license. Maila herself didn't blame Hunt at all. According to author W. Scott Poole in his book *Vampira, Dark Goddess of Horror*, "Nurmi always spoke highly of the young producer, especially his willingness to be, as she described him, 'fanatical' – he would try, or let her try, anything."

In the *aftermath* of the cancellation, there was a tense moment or two with Stromberg's crotchety boss Selig J. Seligman clarifying Nurmi's contractual ownership of the character Vampira – but Hunt made sure that she walked away with those rights in her name. There was no bloodshed. The station had absolutely no interest in Vampira anymore,

Vampira in *Plan 9 From Outer Space*.

so the rights were of no value to them. Nobody cared. And because the show was live, there were no videotapes nor films that might have had future licensing value. Only one kinescope had ever been made – strictly for the purpose of showing to potential advertisers. They didn't have the budget to make kinescopes on a regular basis. As for merchandizing, no one had any inkling there would ever be any value in that. Including Maila. There was virtually no such thing in those days – with the exception of Mickey Mouse and other kiddie toys.

"They gave me Vampira," Maila Nurmi wrote in an article she authored for *Fangoria* (Vol. 3, No. 30, 1983). "All of her. I had been leasing 49 percent of her to KABC. Now she reverted back to me 100 percent. But oddly, though we were *hot*, no one would touch us with a hundred-foot pole. That's Hollywood, darlings."

Thusly, when rival Los Angeles TV station KHJ Channel 9 asked Maila to bring the character back from the dead for a trial run of 13 weeks, starting Friday, May 18, 1956, she was a free agent to negotiate her own deal.

Vampira Returns did not make the same sort of splash on KHJ that it had on KABC. "We did not have the inspired courage of my tasteful KABC producer Hunt Stromberg," Nurmi added, "nor the abject genius of my writer Peter Robinson – so far superior in my mind to everyone at KHJ who were aiming at the lowest common denominator."

The novelty had worn thin – and the publicity department did not have a fearless cheerleader like Stromberg beating the drums. Advertisers were hard to come by – and even harder to maintain. The show just didn't set the world on fire. Even the boycott groups were apathetic. There was no cancellation, per se. KHJ simply let the 13-week contract expire after August 10, 1956, without further renewals. Vampira as a horror host was quietly laid to rest.

In November 1956, the Walt Disney Studio used Maila as a model for "Maleficent," the evil witch, in Disney's animated classic *Sleeping Beauty* (1959).

Also in late-1956, director Ed Wood paid Nurmi $200 to make an appearance in her Vampira get-up in his next-to-no-budget horror movie *Grave Robbers from Outer Space*. She would be credited in the opening titles *and* the poster as "Vampira" (no mention of "Maila Nurmi") in second position following Bela Lugosi – who had actually died August 16, 1956, before this movie had started production. "Vampira" would portray a mute character identified as "Vampire Girl" in the cast list. All she does in the film is rise from a grave, hold her arms out and slowly walk forward in a silent trance, like a zombie.

The film included unrelated footage of Lugosi (wearing a Dracula cape from his stage tour) that was filmed in 1955 for an aborted Ed Wood movie called *The Ghoul Goes West*. Wood enlisted his own wife's chiropractor Tom Mason to double for Lugosi holding a matching cape in front of his face in order to flesh out the footage and incorporate it into the new movie – and lay claim to the publicity value of presenting "Bela Lugosi in his last film!" For whatever that was worth. Which was apparently nothing. It took two years to find a distributor desperate enough to release the cringe-worthy film. A fly-by-night company called DCA (Distributors Corporation of America) changed the title to *Plan 9 from Outer Space*, struck a handful of 35mm prints and released it in June 1958 to a few theaters scattered across the country, mostly as filler for the lower-half of double-bills and all-night drive-in marathons. Rentals were negligible. Not long after, the distributor filed for bankruptcy and the film became unavailable for years.

Eventually, *Plan 9 from Outer Space* was licensed for late-night television but never made much of an impact until 1980 when film critic Michael Medved declared it to be "The worst film ever made!" From that moment on, a cult classic was born – and Vampira was suddenly in the spotlight again.

VAMPIRA VS. ELVIRA

Taking notice of this 1980 renewed interest in Vampira, KHJ Channel 9 contacted Maila Nurmi, then 59, about the possibility of reviving Vampira to host horror movies on their station. Maila felt she was too old for the part, recommending instead that they license the name from her, and cast African American singer Lola Falana in her place.

The television management did not agree with the casting idea and, instead, auditioned a slew of actresses for the part, ultimately settling on Cassandra Peterson whose comedic take was a breath of fresh air and got more laughs than anyone else. Unlike all the other candidates, Cassandra boldly ignored the vintage *Vampira Show* script she'd been handed to read for the audition. Her experience in improvisation at the Groundlings Sketch Comedy Theatre & School came in very handy. (Cassandra's contemporaries at the Groundlings included Paul Reubens aka Pee-wee Herman, Phil Hartman of *SNL*, Edie McClurg, John Paragon, Joey Arias, Doug Cox, etc.) Cassandra conjured up one of the characters she had been developing there, an air-headed Valley Girl, and fused it with Morticia Addams and Lily Munster, improvising her own spoofy version of a Goth horror host. Cassandra proposed changing the look to a redhead in a white gown, based on Sharon Tate in *The Fearless Vampire Killers* (1967).

The TV producers, however, insisted on black hair and a black gown so Elvira and her stylist Robert Redding created

a sexier neckline, a dramatic slit from the floor to her upper thigh, and added a "knowledge bump" to the hair, modeled after Ronnie Spector of the Ronettes.

On the day they started shooting the Vampira revival in 1981, Maila suddenly had a change of heart and refused

Figure of Vampira.

Figure of Elvira.

Elvira (Cassandra Peterson) & Sam Irvin promoting the 20th Anniversary Blu-ray of *Elvira's Haunted Hills* (Shout! Factory, 2021).

to sign an agreement to license the name "Vampira." So, everyone on the crew wrote down name suggestions and put them in a hat. At random, Cassandra blindly picked a piece of paper that read, "Elvira." She liked the name because it evoked a female "Elvis," as in Elvis Presley with whom she was acquainted and adored. Thus, she became Elvira, Mistress of the Dark.

The sardonic humor of Vampira was desert dry and funereal, with the morose demeanor of Gloria Holden (in *Dracula's Daughter*) meets Gloria Swanson (in *Sunset Blvd.*). She never cracked a smile. Cassandra Peterson's ebullient, dorky routines of Elvira, Mistress of the Dark, were the complete opposite.

Nevertheless, Nurmi sued Peterson for allegedly copying the Vampira act. On the day of the trial, Nurmi failed to show up in court and the judge ruled in Peterson's favor (though defending herself cost Peterson tens of thousands of dollars in legal fees).

If Nurmi had simply gone along with KHJ's proposal, she could have earned royalties on the character for the rest of her life. Instead, the Elvira franchise filled the void and flourished while Nurmi slid back into obscurity.

A decade later, Maila seemingly did not object to "Vampira" being featured in Tim Burton's wonderful film *Ed Wood* (1994), starring Johnny Depp as "Wood," Martin Landau as "Bela Lugosi" (for which he won the Academy Award for Best Supporting Actor), and Burton's then-girlfriend Lisa Marie as "Vampira." It certainly spurred renewed interest in the character. Even then, Nurmi was slow to respond. Seven years later, in 2001, she finally started an official website and began selling autographed memorabilia on eBay. She died in 2008 at age 85.

[Full disclosure: I have been a personal friend of Cassandra Peterson since 1991 and I directed her in two films: *Acting on Impulse* (1993) and *Elvira's Haunted Hills* (2001). For those who may feel I am biased in Cassandra / Elvira's favor, I can assure you I am a huge fan of Maila / Vampira, too. I have done my homework and read every available account of what happened, including court documents and all biographies, interviews, and unfinished memoir writings of Nurmi and Stromberg, plus meticulous microfilm examination of day-by-day reporting in *Daily Variety* and *Hollywood Reporter*. I stand by my objective conclusions above. I have great empathy for Nurmi whom I adore for what she accomplished. But, very much like one of my other biography subjects Kay Thompson, Maila could be her own worst enemy, and often seemed tone deaf to the prospects that were available to her. Nobody cared about her age other than Maila herself. Cassandra has continued playing Elvira into her 70s. Mae West continued her schtick into her 80s. Nurmi allowed her own vanity to stand in the way of advancing the Vampira franchise.]

Now, let's get back to the subject at hand.

VINCENT PRICE AND PETER LORRE

After developing several more mega-hit shows that raised KABC-TV to the top of the ratings heap, Stromberg was crowned the Golden Boy of Television and, on May 25, 1956, was scooped up by CBS-TV (national) to become its Vice President of Programming.

Hunt's boyfriend, Eugene Banks, who had directed all the episodes of *Voluptua*, *Day in Court* and many others, remained at KABC-TV where he continued to create and direct programs.

Vincent Price and Peter Lorre.

Peter Lorre, Lorre's fake head, and Vincent Price, *Tales of Terror*. Inset: *Collector's Item*.

Stromberg's first order of business at CBS was to develop a series for Vincent Price whose breakthrough hit *House of Wax* (1953) had made him a household name. Stromberg cast the newly anointed King of Horror in two pilots for a series called *Collector's Item*, written by Herb Meadow ("The Left Fist of David" shot January 15, 1957; "Appraise the Lady" shot December 2, 1957), both co-starring Peter Lorre, whom Hunt had gotten to know while working on his father's film *They Met in Bombay* (1941). The series revolved around an art collector (Price) and his assistant (Lorre), a rehabilitated forger, who foil thefts of priceless relics. Directed by Buzz

THE EPIC SAGA BEHIND *FRANKENSTEIN: THE TRUE STORY*

Vincent Price & Alfred Hitchcock.

fame) to write many of the episodes and he got Bernard Herrmann to compose the iconic theme.

HAMMER FILMS' *TALES OF FRANKENSTEIN*

Next, Stromberg wanted CBS to greenlight a proposed Hammer Films/Screen Gems anthology series called *Tales of Frankenstein*. A pilot had been produced in 1958, written and directed by Curt Siodmak (screenwriter of *Frankenstein Meets the Wolfman* and *House of Frankenstein*) with Anton Diffring as Dr. Frankenstein and Don Megowan as the Monster – but reactions among all three networks had been lukewarm. Taking a cue from his Vampira days, Hunt felt that the show needed a host to jazz things up – exactly the same application he had suggested for *The Twilight Zone* (1959-1964), his forthcoming anthology series for CBS, to be hosted by Rod Serling. It had already been a proven success on CBS with *Alfred Hitchcock Presents* (CBS, 1955-1960; NBC, 1960-1962; CBS, 1964-1965) – which was partly inspired by the sardonic deadpan tone of Vampira.

So, to bolster his case that *Tales of Frankenstein* could be a success on CBS, Stromberg wrote the following memo to his immediate superior Hubbell Robinson, Senior V.P. of Programming, dated Monday, November 3, 1958: "What *Tales of Frankenstein* lacks is an identifiable host, like *Alfred Hitchcock Presents*, and there is no one more associated with Frankenstein than Boris Karloff. As it happens, I have known Boris for many years and, informally, I have spoken to him about this. I am happy to report that he is keenly interested and would be happy to discuss it further." Unfortunately,

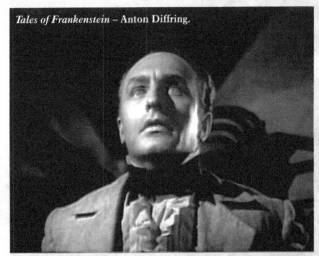

Tales of Frankenstein – Anton Diffring.

Tales of Frankenstein – Don Megowan.

Kulik (*The Twilight Zone*, *Brian's Song*), the two episodes had music scores by the great Bernard Herrmann. Despite lots of tinkering, however, *Collector's Item* did not get picked up for a series, but the undeniable chemistry between Price and Lorre led to three successful motion picture reunions in *The Raven*, *Tales of Terror* and *Comedy of Terrors*. (The first *Collector's Item* pilot, "The Left Fist of David," can be viewed on YouTube.)

Stromberg wasn't done with Vincent Price, however. He cast him as a guest star in an installment of the CBS suspense anthology series *Climax!* ("Avalanche at Devil's Pass," Season 3, Episode 25, April 25, 1957), directed by Jack Smight – who, of course, would later helm *Frankenstein: The True Story*.

Next, he cast Vincent Price to be a guest-star on the smash-hit CBS anthology series *Alfred Hitchcock Presents* ("The Perfect Crime," Season 3, Episode 3, October 20, 1957). Price plays a smug master detective named Charles Courtney whose bubble bursts when John Gregory (James Gregory) tells him he has proof that an innocent man was executed for a murder conviction that Courtney got wrong. Gregory blackmails Courtney, promising to keep quiet about it in exchange for hush money. Hitchcock selectively chose to direct an occasional episode of the series – and Stromberg leaned heavily on him to helm this particular installment because of his ongoing campaign to promote Price as a star commodity on CBS. It was the only time that Price got to be directed by Hitchcock himself. All because of Stromberg.

And, finally, Stromberg cast Vincent Price as a guest-star on the hit CBS Western series *Have Gun—Will Travel* ("The Moor's Revenge," Season 2, Episode 25, December 27, 1957) in which Vincent played a traveling Shakespearean actor who nearly resorts to murder when a heckler gets out of line – foreshadowing *Theatre of Blood* by fifteen years.

Have Gun—Will Travel was Hunt's baby from the get-go, co-created with screenwriter Herb Meadow from the ground up; he hired a young Gene Roddenberry (of later *Star Trek*

Robinson was not interested in pursuing it, so *Tales of Frankenstein* died a second death.

Nevertheless, shortly thereafter, Robinson quit CBS to form Hubbell Robinson Productions at MCA-Revue Productions where he ended up producing an anthology series called *Thriller*, hosted by none other than… WTF… Boris Karloff! *Thriller* was picked up by NBC-

Karloff– *Thriller*.

Alfred Hitchcock hosting his show.

TV for two seasons, 1960-62. Stromberg was furious about the betrayal but had to swallow his pride when Robinson returned to CBS in 1961 as Senior V.P. of Programming, once again Stromberg's immediate superior. By then, however, Stromberg had developed the trust of the infamous network president James T. Aubrey aka the Smiling Cobra – and would routinely go directly to Aubrey to get things done his way.

Hunt & Art Linkletter, *The Linkletter Show*, daytime talk show, CBS-TV 1952-1969.

Danny Kaye signs contract with CBS President James T. Aubrey.

Hunt & Lucille Ball, *The Lucy Show*.

THE HIT PARADE

At CBS, Stromberg helped develop and oversee such iconic hit shows as *The Munsters* (Hunt cast Yvonne DeCarlo as Lily), *The Twilight Zone*, *Alfred Hitchcock Presents* – a half-hour

THE EPIC SAGA BEHIND *FRANKENSTEIN: THE TRUE STORY*

Hunt & Andy Griffith, *The Andy Griffith Show*.

Hunt & Rita Hayworth.

CHAPTER SEVENTEEN: THE MONSTROUS LIFE & TIMES OF HUNT STROMBERG JR.

The Munsters.

Wild Wild West.

Lost in Space.

series that Hunt later expanded to *The Alfred Hitchcock Hour*, *The Wild Wild West*, *Lost in Space*, *My Favorite Martian*, *Living Doll* (with Julie Newmar as a robot), *Have Gun— Will Travel*, *Perry Mason* (Hunt cast Fay Wray of *King Kong* fame in three different episodes, playing different characters), *Gilligan's Island*, *The Beverly Hillbillies*, *Petticoat Junction*, *Green Acres*, *Hogan's Heroes*, *Gomer Pyle: USMC*, *The Andy Griffith Show*, *Dennis the Menace*, *Mister Ed*, *The Dick Van Dyke Show*, *The Danny Kaye Show*, *The Linkletter Show*, *The Garry Moore Show* (Carol Burnett's breakthrough), *The Lucy-Desi Comedy Hour* and *The Lucy Show*. He also imported *Danger Man* from England and retitled it *Secret Agent*.

Above: Pilot for *The Munsters* (1964), with Joan Marshall as Phoebe Munster, wife of Herman Munster (Fred Gwynn) and daughter of Grandpa (Al Lewis). Stromberg replaced Marshall for the series.
Below: Hunt cast his friend Yvonne DeCarlo for the series of *The Munsters* and renamed her character Lily Munster. He changed her look from Vampira / Morticia Addams to a more original concept, adding the two white streaks in her hair as an homage to *Bride of Frankenstein*.

CAROL BURNETT

Hunt continued to champion his 1954 "Discovery of the Week," Carol Burnett. In 1958, he endorsed adding her to the sketch comedy ensemble that performed every week on *The Garry Moore Show* (CBS-TV, 1958-1966). In 1962, she won an Emmy Award for her hilarious performances on the series. America fell head-over-heels in love with Carol. And so did the producer of the show, Joe Hamilton. Toward the end of Season 5, Hamilton and Burnett were married on May 4, 1963.

During her hiatus that followed, rather than go on a honeymoon, Carol accepted an offer to star in a summer stock stage production of *Calamity Jane* for a limited two-week engagement at the Music Hall in Dallas, Texas (June 24-July 7, 1963). When Hunt got word of this, he sent the following congratulatory telegram to her on opening night: "Carol Darling, It's a far cry from the Discovery of the Week on *Party at Ciro's* to the Star of the Decade in *Calamity Jane*. All of us here at CBS West Coast are with you in spirit tonight and wish you all good things always. Love, Hunt."

The next day, Hunt tried to convince CBS president James Aubrey to fund a multi-camera crew to go to Dallas and tape *Calamity Jane* for a TV special. He reasoned, "It's already cast, rehearsed and ready for prime time. All we need to do is videotape it." But once it was determined how much it would cost to wrangle the mobile crew and equipment, Aubrey nixed the idea because he felt Burnett was just a starlet on *The Garry Moore Show*, not yet a star in her own right.

THE EPIC SAGA BEHIND *FRANKENSTEIN: THE TRUE STORY*

Young Carol Burnett.

The Carol Burnett Show: Frankenstein's Monster (Harvey Korman), Dr. Frankenstein (Vincent Price), and the Bride of Frankenstein (Carol Burnett).

Hunt refused to take "no" for an answer. He called Joe Hamilton and said, "How would you like to produce a TV special of *Calamity Jane* starring your new wife?"

"I'd love to do that," Joe responded, enthusiastically. "And I'm sure Carol would be thrilled!"

"Great," said Hunt. "Then figure out a way to bring the mountain to Mohammed. And don't break the bank."

After the final performance of *Calamity Jane* on July 7, 1963, the cast, crew, costumes and sets were transported all the way from Dallas to Studio 50 at CBS in New York where the production was economically taped for a special broadcast that aired November 12, 1963. That week, Carol was featured – by herself – on the cover of *TV Guide*, read by over a quarter of the population of the United States. Ratings went through the roof! And suddenly, the "starlet" from *The Garry Moore*

Show was a national television sensation. Her popularity eclipsed Garry Moore and they had to increase Carol's screen time each week to meet the demand. All of this paved the way for her own spinoff megahit *The Carol Burnett Show* (CBS-TV, 1967-1978), produced by Joe Hamilton, that lasted 11 seasons and garnered three Emmy Awards for Outstanding Variety Series. Carol was a born star and would have somehow made it big, no matter what. But Hunt Stromberg Jr. blew a big gust of wind beneath her wings.

CLINT EASTWOOD

Another up-and-comer championed by Hunt was a tall drink of water named Clint Eastwood. One of Stromberg's close gay associates was Arthur Lubin, known for directing and/or producing talking animal movies and TV shows, from *Francis the Talking Mule* to *Mister Ed*, "the Talking Horse." Arthur had already taken an interest in Eastwood and given him his very first credited role as "Jonesy the Sailor" in *Francis in the Navy* (1955), the sixth film in Lubin's "Francis the Talking Mule" franchise at Universal-International. Stromberg met Eastwood at one of Lubin's parties – and began taking notice of his brief appearances in movies like *Revenge of the Creature* (1955) and *Tarantula* (1955) – and especially his subsequent supporting role the Western *Ambush at Cimarron Pass* (released February 11, 1958).

In the summer of 1958, Hunt personally endorsed the casting of Eastwood, 28, for his first series-regular role in the new CBS Western *Rawhide*. Eastwood's character "Rowdy Yates" was the ever-present sidekick to "Gil Favor" played by Eric Fleming. This turned out to be Eastwood's big break. The series became a major hit on CBS – with 217 episodes spread across 8 seasons (January 1959-December 1965) – propelling Eastwood to stardom.

In late 1963, Eastwood's *Rawhide* co-star Eric Fleming turned down an offer to star in Sergio Leone's Italian-financed Western *A Fistful of Dollars* (1964), to be shot in Spain, because he felt the role was not heroic enough. So, they offered the part to Eastwood, which he readily accepted. "I decided it was time to be an antihero," Clint remarked. *A Fistful of Dollars* was a huge success, not only launching the "Spaghetti Western" craze, but transforming Eastwood into a bankable movie superstar.

Hunt remained social friends with Clint and his first wife Maggie Johnson (married 1953-1984), always including them on his party and gift lists. A thank card from Clint to Hunt, dated Friday, October 2, 1964, demonstrates their camaraderie: "Dear Hunt, Thanks so much for the great champagne celebrating our new season! I know Mag and I will enjoy it. Sincerely, Clint."

SUCCESSION OF BOYFRIENDS

On the subject of *Rawhide*, Hunt also cast Jacque Shelton to play bit parts in four episodes. Why is this significant? Well, in January 1961, Hunt began having an affair with Jacque Shelton, aka John Sterling, 30, a stuntman he'd met in 1960 on the set of *Have Gun—Will Travel*. Jacque dreamed of becoming an actor and had managed to land bit parts in *Annie Oakley* (1954) and *Studio One* (1956) prior to meeting Hunt.

For a while, Hunt and his boyfriend Eugene Banks took Jacque under their wing as a thruple partner. He lived in their house, doing handyman and restoration work in exchange for free room and board. But eventually, three proved to be a crowd. On March 15, 1963, Eugene broke

Title card from *Mister Ed* with the credit for Jacque Shelton.

up with Hunt and moved out from under his shadow, in more ways than one. Fully independent, Eugene thrived as an original producer for two of the longest-running soap operas of all-time: ABC-TV's *General Hospital* (launched in 1963, still running today) and NBC-TV's *Days of Our Lives* (launched in 1965, also still running today). This led to his 1965 appointment as V.P. of TV Development for Chuck Barris Productions where he created and produced such iconic series as *The Dating Game* (ABC-TV, 1965-1986) and *The Gong Show* (ABC-TV, 1976-1980). Eugene died of a sudden heart attack on August 30, 1979. He was just 57.

Smitten with Jacque, Hunt not only arranged bit parts for him in *Rawhide*, but also in a slew of other CBS shows, including *Combat!* (1963), *The Twilight Zone* (1963), *The Great Adventure* (3 episodes, 1963-1964), *Gunsmoke* (3 episodes, 1963-1964), *The Jack Benny Show* (2 episodes, 1964), *Gilligan's Island* (1965), and *The Wild Wild West* (1965). It was quite telling that he never appeared on another network.

When Hunt convinced his dear friend Mae West to be a guest-star on Arthur Lubin's *Mister Ed* on March 24, 1964, he cast Jacque as Mae's hunky assistant who helps give "Mister Ed, the Talking Horse" a bubble bath in her boudoir.

This was one of the extremely rare appearances of Mae West since her retirement from films in 1943. Hunt recognized that there was tremendous media attention whenever a bona fide movie star deigned to appear on television. Nowadays, movie stars jump back and forth between film and television projects, and it is no big deal. Back then, however, there was a serious divide between mediums. It was a rarity for movie stars to appear on television, so when it happened, it was a big event.

JUDY GARLAND

One of the biggest movie stars signed by CBS was Judy Garland to headline *The Judy Garland Show* (1962-1964), a musical variety series pairing her with a dream roster of A-list guest-stars, from Barbra Streisand to Tony Bennett. Hunt had known Judy since they were classmates on the lot at MGM – and she'd lived for years in his former childhood home. He very much wanted the show to work but Judy's erratic behavior made it increasingly difficult. Everyone assumed that his history with Judy would give him the clout to reason with her. But it was his job to be the bad cop and she knew it. After a particularly heated argument during which Judy smashed a cake in his face, Hunt attempted to lighten things up the next day by bringing his monkey Wilbur to set on a leash – but Judy was not amused.

In an October 1963 tape-recorded phone call (reported

Above: Jacque Shelton & Mae West, *Mister Ed* (March 24, 1964). Below: Jacque Shelton and Roger Torrey giving a bubble bath to Mister Ed, the Talking Horse, in Mae West's boudoir.

THE EPIC SAGA BEHIND *FRANKENSTEIN: THE TRUE STORY*

Barbra Streisand & Judy Garland on *The Judy Garland Show*, CBS-TV.

July 8, 1936: Mickey Rooney, Edna Mae Durbin (later known as Deanna Durbin), Judy Garland and Jackie Cooper. Four of Hunt Stromberg Jr.'s classmates at the Little Red School on the MGM Studios lot.

Hunt and old grade school mate Mickey Rooney.

as the heartless corporate villain. The reality, of course, is not so black and white. Insiders were well aware of the complexities, and no one envied his position. It wasn't the first time Garland had been fired because of her addiction issues – and it wouldn't be the last – from *Annie Get Your Gun* (1950) to *Valley of the Dolls* (1967). It was a no-win situation for all concerned.

KARLOFF FOR THE HOLIDAYS

Hunt had a much better rapport with his long-time family friend Boris Karloff. In fact, when Chuck Jones pitched an animated Christmas special based on the popular 1957 book *How the Grinch Stole Christmas!* by Dr. Seuss, Stromberg suggested Boris Karloff to voice the Grinch and to be the narrator. At first, Jones was skeptical until Hunt gave him several LP records of Karloff narrating stories, including *Boris Karloff Reading Rudyard Kipling's Just So Stories and Other Tales* (Caedman Records, 1958) with an abridged version of *The Jungle Book*; *Tales of Mystery and Imagination* (Pickwick Records, 1959) in which Karloff reads "The Legend of Sleepy Hollow" and "Rip Van Winkle"; and *Tales of the Frightened*, Volumes 1 & 2 (Mercury Records, 1963).

Jones was immediately won over: "Boris had this lovely, wonderful voice. Everybody thought of him as being a villain… but didn't know how wonderful a narrator he was."

Boris Karloff and The Grinch.

by Amy Kaufman in the *Los Angeles Times* in 2019), Judy's husband-manager Sid Luft discussed his wife's problems with Hunt.

"Certain people are getting her too much junk," Sid confessed, alluding to Garland's addiction to pills – and the various hangers-on who supplied her with a steady stream of uppers, downers, and everything in between.

Hunt responded, "I'm aware that when you get in that state, you're not responsible for some of the things you do… [but] it just reaches a point where you just say, 'Aw, fuck it!' … If somebody has leprosy, Sid – it is highly regrettable, but you stay away from them."

Ultimately, CBS president James T. Aubrey decided enough was enough and refused to renew the series after 26 episodes. It was Stromberg's unpleasant duty to deliver the blow to Garland. For fans, it was an absolute tragedy that has resounded through the decades as one of the great botched opportunities. And, quite unjustly, Hunt is often portrayed

Lorre, Karloff, Chaney in *Route 66*.

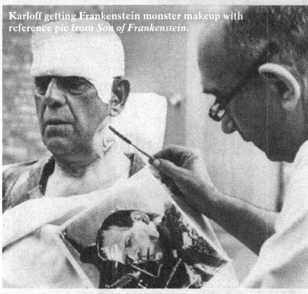

Karloff getting Frankenstein monster makeup with reference pic from *Son of Frankenstein*.

Triple-split-screen phone call from *Route 66*: Lorre, Chaney, Karloff.

Karloff getting makeup and wig as the monster.

Karloff in *Frankenstein* (1931) looks over railing.

Peter Lorre, Boris Karloff and Lon Chaney Jr. (as the Mummy) in *Route 66*.

Karloff in Frankenstein Monster make-up for *Route 66*.

Lorre, Karloff (Monster) and Chaney (Wolf Man) look over railing.

THE EPIC SAGA BEHIND *FRANKENSTEIN: THE TRUE STORY*

Having a name star like Karloff helped Stromberg justify the whopping $315,000 production budget – which was triple the money CBS had allotted to produce the network's other forthcoming animated special *A Charlie Brown Christmas* (1965). Hunt reasoned that the *Grinch* book was already a perennial holiday bestseller, and that a companion TV special could be re-run every year alongside it. Therefore, in the long run, it would easily make its money back ten-fold. CBS president James T. Aubrey agreed. Sadly, by the time the lengthy 14-month animation process was completed, Hunt was no longer at the network and others took credit for its success. *How the Grinch Stole Christmas!* premiered on December 18, 1966 – and CBS repeated it annually for the next 22 years straight. After 1988, it has appeared each year on other networks, never missing a holiday season.

Jones never underestimated Stromberg's contribution. "One of the most important things was my getting Boris Karloff. He was so dear when he read it. He really gave accent to each one and each note."

This wasn't the first time Stromberg got Boris Karloff for a holiday special. For the 1962 Halloween episode of *Route 66*, Hunt wanted to load it up with horror stars, so he got the party started by personally convincing Karloff to wear his Frankenstein monster makeup one last time. He also recruited Lon Chaney Jr. to appear as the Wolf Man, the Mummy, and, as a tribute to the actor's father, Lon Chaney Sr., the Hunchback of Notre Dame. To round out the cast, Hunt added his pal Peter Lorre and the celebrated British actress Martita Hunt, fresh off Hammer Films' *The Brides of Dracula*. This was Stromberg in his element. His mantra was, "Ya go big or ya go home."

GEORGE MAHARIS

It should be noted that Stromberg was a close personal confidante of *Route 66* star George Maharis (1928-2023) who, shall we say "played on his team" – and later posed fully nude in *Playgirl* (July 1973). Discretion was not one of his finer points. It was no secret that Maharis was arrested for lewd conduct. Twice. First, on December 15, 1967, he made a pass at a vice-squad officer in the men's room of a restaurant. And then, on November 21, 1974, Maharis was arrested for engaging in a sex act in the men's room of a Los Angeles gas station – with a male hairdresser aptly named Perfecto Telles. Rumor has it that Stromberg bailed Maharis out of jail on one or perhaps both of those incidents.

George Maharis Arrested In Men's Room

Famous Hollywood actor George Maharis was arrested November 21 and charged with committing a sex act with a hairdresser in the men's room of a gas station in Los Angeles.

The police said that Maharis, 46, best remembered as co-star of the "Route 66" TV series, had been arrested by the vice-squad officers at the gas station.

He was booked on a sex perversion charge along with Perfecto Telles, 33, the hairdresser, and released in $500 bail, according to police.

Maharis was arrested for lewd conduct on Dec. 15, 1967, by a vice-squad officer who said the actor had made a pass at him in the men's room of a Hollywood restaurant. The charge was dismissed when he pleaded guilty to a count of disturbing the peace and was fined $50.

Cast photo from Route 66: Chaney (Wolf Man), Karloff (Monster) and Peter Lorre, with the stars of Route 66: George Maharis (right) and Martin Milner (left).

Top Left: George Maharis, barechested. Top Right: Maharis nude (with car door barely covering) in *Playgirl* (1973). Above: Article about Maharis' 1967 arrest for lewd conduct.

Martin Milner & George Maharis in *Route 66* – with U.S. 66 sign.

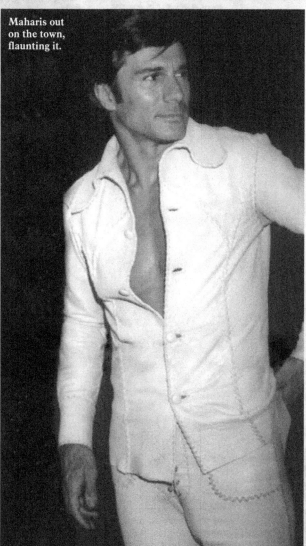

Maharis out on the town, flaunting it.

Miraculously, the scandals did not seem to affect George's ability to get work as a guest-star in over 30 episodes of major series such as *Fantasy Island* (6 episodes, 1978-1982) and *Murder, She Wrote* (2 episodes, 1990). And he was never dropped from Stromberg's party guest and Christmas card lists.

(Full disclosure: In the late-1980s, when George Maharis would have been around 60, my husband Gary Bowers and I had a brief encounter with him at the Meat Rack, 4621 Santa Monica Blvd., in East Hollywood, a "private men's club," not your typical watering hole. We can assure you he was still a heartthrob.)

As incredible as this may sound, I was writing these paragraphs about George Maharis on Wednesday, May 24, 2023. Three days later, on Saturday, May 27, Maharis' friend and caretaker Marc Bahan posted an announcement on Facebook that George had passed away at age 94 – not on Saturday, but three days earlier on Wednesday, May 24, the exact day I had been writing about him! I am not a spiritual person, but this coincidence made the hair on the back of my neck stand on end. I salute you, pal. May you rest in peace.

THE CBS-TV MASSACRE

When it came to business, Stromberg's success rate was unprecedented and, to this day, has never been matched. In the 1963-64 season, all fifteen of the top daytime programs and fourteen of the top fifteen prime-time shows were on CBS. The only exception was *Bonanza* on NBC.

Shockingly, half-way through the 1964-65 season, CBS board chairman William S. Paley fired CBS president James T. Aubrey on Saturday, February 27, 1965. Hunt was

CBS schedule for the new season: September 1964 – May 1965.

Above: CBS stars, 1964-1965 season, group shot: John McGiver (*Many Happy Returns*), Sterling Holloway (*Baileys of Balboa*), Yvonne De Carlo (*The Munsters*), Paul Ford (*Baileys of Balboa*), Fred Gwynn (*The Munsters*), Julie Newmar (*Living Doll*), Cara Williams (*The Cara Williams Show*), Tina Louise (*Gilligan's Island*). Below: Stromberg makes light of his exit from CBS. "YOU'VE BEEN REPLACED."

on holiday in Hawaii when he got the news. He cut his vacation short, jumped on a plane to New York, and met with the newly-appointed CBS president John A. Schneider on Monday, March 1 – a meeting which did not go well. Stromberg resigned Thursday, March 4, 1965.

Dubbed "The CBS-TV Massacre," *The New York Times* wrote that the shake-up "stunned" the industry, particularly in light of the glaring fact that the network was still No. 1, with eleven of the top fifteen primetime shows on television.

No official reason was given but theories abound, including the fact that several new series that season had not done as well as expected; advertising revenue was not as high as it had been the year before; production costs were on the rise; lots more movie stars were being lured to the network with fatter paydays than ever, etc. There was also an attempt by Wall Street syndicates and a group headed by Texas financier Clint Murchison to acquire and merge Paramount and Desilu studios, with firm offers to James Aubrey and Hunt Stromberg Jr. to become President and Head of Production, respectively. The deal eventually fell apart – but the two men were hot commodities throughout the entertainment world, with offers being thrown at them, right and left.

Aubrey and Stromberg were fiercely loyal to one another and ran CBS with a very firm grip. Other executives expressed frustration that their voices were not being heard. There appears to have been a growing feeling that the Aubrey-Stromberg stronghold was becoming too omnipotent – and that their loyalties were to themselves more than the network.

Some also speculated that the stuffier members of the CBS Board of Directors were unhappy with the dumbing down of the overall schedule. In the 1950s, CBS had the reputation of producing sophisticated, prestigious, award-winning dramas like their *Playhouse 90* anthology series. Even the network's sitcoms, like *I Love Lucy* (1951-1957), defined the genre that all others emulated – and critics adored. The Aubrey-Stromberg menu was littered with an increasing number of shows that were often ridiculed or dismissed by highfalutin critics, like *The Munsters*, *Lost in Space*, *My Favorite Martian*, *Mister Ed*, *Hogan's Heroes* and *The Wild, Wild West*. It didn't matter that the great unwashed viewed them in droves. They were an embarrassment to the bigwigs.

In a 1965 interview in *Daily Variety*, Stromberg defended himself thusly: "I don't remember a year when people weren't saying 'what a bad season this is.' I don't think this is as bad a season as they say. I remember years when people said 'what a bad year this is for the picture business. Isn't it a shame pictures aren't like they were in the 40s.' I also remember when people in the 40s said 'what bad pictures – why aren't they like they were in the 30s?' People always seem to think yesterday was better. Five years from now, people will look back and say 'wasn't it fun when we had *The Beverly Hillbillies* and *Gilligan's Island*?' They *are* fun. Yet today there are many detractors of these shows."

In any event, Stromberg's spectacular tenure at CBS had come to a screeching halt.

DEVELOPMENT HELLRAISING

While James Aubrey fielded offers, Stromberg took a job as Executive in Charge of Production at Goodson-Todman Productions, a company that was primarily known for its game shows such as *The Price is Right*, *The Match Game*, *To Tell the Truth*, *Password*, *What's My Line?*, and *Family Feud*. They'd had limited success with dramatic shows, such as two Western series: *The Rebel* (ABC-TV, 1959-1961) starring Nick Adams; and *Branded* (NBC-TV, 1965-1966) starring Chuck Connors (*The Rifleman*). The hiring of Stromberg was an attempt to branch out more in that direction.

Of the myriad projects Stromberg developed for Goodson-Todman, the most intriguing were:

Mastermind, written by Joseph Stefano (*Psycho*), about "the world's greatest and most eccentric detective," to star Michael Dunn, the diminutive actor whom Stromberg had cast as the recurring villain "Dr. Miguelito Loveless" on *The Wild Wild West*. CBS-TV bought the premise by it never got picked up for series.

Uncle Helen, to star Stromberg's discovery Ray Walston (*My Favorite Martian*) as both "a cigar-smoking ex-circus clown named Hal Barker **and** his wealthy sister Helen. When the sister dies, the clown must pose as her in drag in order to gain custody of her young son Robbie." The premise predates *Mrs. Doubtfire* (1993) by twenty-seven years. NBC-TV bought the project for its 1966-67 season, but it never emerged from development hell.

Four Groping Comparison Pics: Ever the jokester, Hunt loved to grope breasts of women at the precise instant a photographer was about to click his camera. Nowadays, of course, this behavior would banish Hunt to the cancel-culture doghouse, but back then, this sort of harmless, nonthreatening tomfoolery between a gay man and a woman was deemed mischievously hilarious and endearing. **Above Top:** Teenage Hunt gropes the breast of female friend to get a laugh. **Right Top:** Hunt pretending to bite the breast of an unidentified friend. **Above:** On set of the ABC-TV / Goodson-Todman Productions pilot for *Rhubarb, The Millionaire Tom-Cat* (1966): Universal Television executive Charlie Engel (with whom Hunt maintained a very jovial and flirtatious relationship), actress Virginia Martin and Hunt Stromberg Jr. (Photo by the late Leigh Wiener; provided exclusively for this book by his son Devik Wiener.) **Right Bottom:** On the set of *Frankenstein: The True Story*, Hunt Stromberg Jr. surprises Nicola Pagett with a cake to celebrate her 28th birthday on June 15, 1973. Hunt also surprised her with a joking breast-grope just as the camera clicked.

Rhubarb, the Millionaire Tom-Cat, a comedy series, based on the book about a wealthy feline who talks. It had previously been adapted into a 1951 movie produced by Arthur Lubin (producer of *Mister Ed*, "the Talking Horse"; and six *Francis the Talking Mule* movies). Lubin was back on board to produce and direct the series. Groucho Marx was attached to star as "J. Paul Greedy," the richest man in the world. ABC-TV financed a pilot, produced by Stromberg and Lubin in November 1966, but the show was never picked up for a series.

Dinosaur Trail, a sci-fi time-travel series, written by Herb Meadow.

Doc Savage, based on the superhero character from pulp magazines and novels, to star Chuck Connors.

All this creativity amounted to nothing. Not one show got picked up for series. After two frustrating years at Goodson-Todman, on October 16, 1967, it was announced that Stromberg was departing the firm to join Aubrey Co., the new production entity founded by his former CBS boss James T. Aubrey. Reunited with his partner-in-crime, Hunt was named V.P. in Charge of Motion Picture and Television Production. Aubrey Co. had a co-production agreement with Columbia Pictures and its television division Screen Gems, with offices on the Columbia lot at 1438 Gower Street in Hollywood. Contractually, Aubrey would receive Executive Producer credit and Stromberg would be the sole Producer on all their projects.

In the 1960s, Hunt Stromberg Jr. appeared on camera in a Civil War uniform for a television series or movie. So far, it's a mystery. If you recognize it, please let us know more about it.

James T. Aubrey.

At that time, Scream Gems V.P. of Program Development just so happened to be former child actor Jackie Cooper (of *Little Rascals* and *Our Gang* fame) – who, fortuitously, was a classmate of Hunt's at the Little Red Schoolhouse at MGM. Maybe this would work to Hunt's advantage. Time would tell. [NOTE: Jackie Cooper would later have a comeback as an actor portraying *Daily Planet* editor Perry White in *Superman* (1978) and its sequels.]

Stromberg's slate of projects developed for Aubrey Co. at Columbia / Screen Gems included:

H-Bomb Beach Party, a broad farce about nuclear disarmament, *Strangelove* meets Mel Brooks, from a script by Paul Mazursky and Larry Tucker, to be directed by Hal Ashby. Laurence Harvey was attached to star in this feature film.

Skye's the Limit, a TV series proposal by Herb Meadow, James T. Aubrey and Hunt Stromberg Jr., about daredevil pilot Sam Skye (Clint Eastwood) and his sidekick (Michael Dunn) who have a twin-engine private jet and accept money from around the world for dangerous assignments that need air transport. Curiously, the last name of the main character was the first name of Aubrey's daughter, actress Skye Aubrey (1945-2020), star of *The Phantom of Hollywood* (1974). In a 2020 interview for this book, shortly before her passing, Skye recalled, "Hunt Stromberg Jr. was a friend of my dad, James Aubrey. I remember as a kid going to Hunt's house and was always fascinated by all the elaborate décor he had acquired from the Hearst Estate – and all the stories he used to tell. And I found if I sat very quietly in the background, Hunt would forget that a kid was there, and go on and on about very adult things. You are probably asking yourself, 'Where

ALBERT FINNEY
"SCROOGE"
A NEW MUSICAL
EDITH EVANS and KENNETH MORE
Also Starring Laurence Naismith · Michael Medwin
David Collings · Anton Rodgers · Suzanne Neve
and ALEC GUINNESS
A Cinema Center Films Presentation
Screenplay by Leslie Bricusse based on Charles Dickens' 'A Christmas Carol' · Music and Lyrics by Leslie Bricusse
Music Conducted and Supervised by Ian Fraser · Executive Producer Leslie Bricusse · Produced by Robert H. Solo
Directed by Ronald Neame · Panavision® Technicolor® · A National General Pictures Release

Soon The Whole World
Will Fall in Love With
OLIVER!

COLUMBIA PICTURES presents The ROMULUS Production of LIONEL BART'S
OLIVER!
—— RON MOODY "Fagin" · OLIVER REED "Bill Sikes" · HARRY SECOMBE "Mr. Bumble"
—— SHANI WALLIS "Nancy"
as "Oliver" played by MARK LESTER · "The Artful Dodger" played by JACK WILD
Book, Music and Lyrics by LIONEL BART · Musical Supervision and Arrangement by JOHN GREEN
Choreography and Musical Sequences staged by ONNA WHITE · Production Designed by JOHN BOX
Photography by OSWALD MORRIS · Screenplay by VERNON HARRIS
Produced by JOHN WOOLF · Directed by CAROL REED · PANAVISION® TECHNICOLOR®

was my dad and why was he allowing me to hear all these things?' Well, he had forgotten I was there, too! Ahhh. Men."

The project-in-development that got the most attention was *A Christmas Carol: A Ghost Story of Christmas*, a two-hour musical for CBS-TV, based on the Charles Dickens classic, from a script by Christopher Isherwood (who, of course, later co-wrote *Frankenstein: The True Story* for Stromberg). Rex Harrison was attached to play "Ebenezer Scrooge," and Stromberg promised to assemble "an all-star cast beyond anything ever seen on television." Seven-time Emmy Award-winner George Schaefer (*Macbeth*) was set to direct. Ray Henderson ("Bye Bye Blackbird", "The Best Things in

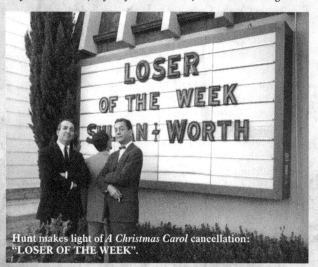

Hunt makes light of *A Christmas Carol* cancellation: **"LOSER OF THE WEEK".**

Life Are Free") was signed to compose the song score. On December 13, 1967, *Variety* reported that the $1 million price tag would be "the fattest budget ever for a telefilm special." Shooting was set to commence spring 1968 in England.

Speaking of England, Hunt extended a formal invitation for Queen Elizabeth to appear in a special introduction of the movie – though she declined. He would repeat the same invitation for *Frankenstein: The True Story*, but Her Highness rebuffed him again. It does beg the question whether the Queen was aware that Stromberg had engaged in a torrid 1948 affair with David Michael Mountbatten, aka Lord Milford Haven, the best man at her 1947 wedding to Prince Philip. Hum. I wonder.

It was not entirely coincidental that another Dickens musical, *Oliver!*, was being made by Columbia Pictures. It would be released later that same year in December 1968 – and go on to win six Academy Awards, including Best Picture. So, this new musical version of *A Christmas Carol* was happening at just the right time and place. And Stromberg knew it. In fact, he had successfully pitched the bright idea of re-using the sets that had been built for *Oliver!* at Shepperton Studios in England to help amortize expenses across both productions. There was always a method to his madness.

But then Screen Gems suddenly got cold feet. On a quiet Sunday morning, February 25, 1968, Jackie Cooper called his friend Hunt Stromberg to inform him that the $1 million budget for *A Christmas Carol* had to be cut in half. Hunt hung up on him and called James Aubrey. An emergency meeting was held that afternoon at Jackie Cooper's Beverly Hills mansion at 804 N. Rodeo Drive – and there must have been blood on the walls (figuratively) before it was over.

On Monday, February 26, 1968, the front-page headline of *Daily Variety* scooped: "Aubrey, Stromberg Exit Columbia!" The trade paper *Broadcasting*, March 4, 1968, screamed: "Stromberg & Aubrey Co. Exit Columbia Pictures and Screen Gems – *A Christmas Carol* Cancelled!" It was another unfathomable turn of events – and yet typical show business.

With considerable irony, two years later, National General Corporation decided to make a theatrical film musical entitled *Scrooge* (1970), based on Charles Dickens' *A Christmas Carol*, starring Oscar-nominee Albert Finney as "Ebenezer Scrooge" and Oscar-winner Alec Guinness as "Jacob Marley's Ghost." Same exact idea as before. Just with different screenwriters, director, composer and producers. The budget? $5 million. But the deepest cut of all? It was filmed at Shepperton Studios… utilizing the existing sets from… no joke… *Oliver!* Hunt's gnashed teeth could have cut diamonds.

Three weeks after exiting Columbia, Aubrey and Stromberg landed on their feet at Warner Bros.-Seven Arts – splashed across the front-page of *Daily Variety*, March 22, 1968.

While setting up their company and developing a number of projects, Hunt's father died of a stroke on August 23, 1968. It was a bittersweet conclusion of a troubled relationship – and yet, in the end, Senior left Junior his Coca-Cola stock and other riches valued in the millions.

MAE WEST

Mae West and her woolly monkey Tricky on the cover of *Life*, April 18, 1969 (photo by Roddy McDowall).

Hunt's passion project for Aubrey Co. at Warner Bros.-Seven Arts was to produce a film starring his dear friend Mae West (to whom he had recently gifted a pet woolly monkey named Tricky – a relative of Wilbur, his own pet monkey). He hired Oscar-nominated screenwriter Leonard Spigelgass (*Gypsy, Silk Stockings*) to adapt West's 1961 stage play *Sextette* for a movie to star the 75-year-old icon – who would be making a comeback after being absent from motion picture screens for 25 years. West hadn't made a movie since *The Heat's On* in 1943. And she had only appeared on television three times during that interim, all on CBS at the behest of Hunt Stromberg Jr. when he was calling the shots at the network: *Person to Person* (1959), *The Red Skelton Hour* (1960) and *Mister Ed* (1964).

Additionally, Hunt was packaging a 90-minute television variety spectacular for West, with a slew of major guest-stars paying homage to the bawdy Queen of the Double-Entendre.

Hunt with his pet woolly monkey Wilbur.

The publicity angle of bringing Mae West out of retirement was explosive. Headlines appeared in newspapers across the country and gossip columns were reporting every tidbit of progress on *Sextette* and the TV special as though it were the Second Coming. Suddenly, Mae West was everywhere, including a lavish photo spread in *Life* magazine on April 18, 1969 – with a special fold-out cover featuring Mae and her monkey Tricky!

[NOTE: The *Life* magazine cover photo and the interior pictorial of Mae West was shot by actor Roddy McDowall (*Planet of the Apes, The Legend of Hell House, Fright Night*), another one of Stromberg's gay pals. The location was West's penthouse suite in The Ravenswood Apartment Building, 570 North Rossmore Avenue, five blocks from the corner of Paramount Studios on Melrose Avenue, in Los Angeles. West lived there for 50 years, from the time the building opened in 1930 until her passing in 1980.]

Sextette was scheduled to begin shooting in early 1969 with Christopher Plummer confirmed as one of Mae West's husbands. On January 28, 1969, however, the movie was suddenly put on hold when it was announced that Warner Bros.-7 Arts was being acquired by Kinney National Service. The new owners halted all projects during the transition. The acquisition was delayed due to antitrust laws prohibiting a company from owning both a production company and a talent agency. Kinney had to sell off its Ashley-Famous Artists division in order for the deal to acquire Warner Bros.-7 Arts to finally close on July 4, 1969 – after five-months of hellish limbo. During this prolonged delay, the option on *Sextette* expired – and the Kinney management team refused to renew it.

Fit to be tied, Aubrey yanked his company from the Warner lot, moving to ABC-TV to set up shop yet again, hoping to get the network to at least commit to the Mae West TV special.

Stromberg, with his newly acquired family fortune, had no financial need nor egotistical desire to continue being the No. 2 guy at a company that did not bear his own name. So, just as he had done with his father back in the 1940s, Hunt declared his independence from Aubrey, and they amicably went their separate ways.

In August 1969, 20th Century-Fox decided to bring Mae West out of her 25-year retirement (Wonder where they got *that* idea?) to be the top-billed star of its high-profile adaptation of Gore Vidal's sensational bestselling book *Myra Breckinridge*, also starring Raquel Welch, John Huston, Rex Reed, Farrah Fawcett, John Carradine and an unknown Tom Selleck. Pre-publicity was sublime but when the film finally premiered on June 22, 1970, the reviews were savage – and it bombed at the box-office. At that point, nobody was going to bankroll *Sextette* nor a Mae West TV special.

Seven years later, without the involvement of Stromberg, Aubrey, or Spigelgass, Crown International, a B-movie distributor, released an independently-produced version of *Sextette* (1977) starring a then 84-year-old Mae West, with a supporting cast that included Timothy Dalton, Alice Cooper, Ringo Starr, Dom DeLuise, Tony Curtis, George Hamilton and Keith Moon. It fared no better than *Myra Breckinridge*. West never made another film nor TV appearance. C'est la vie. She passed away in 1980 at age 87.

On October 21, 1969, James T. Aubrey was appointed President of MGM – ironically, the studio where Stromberg's father had once reigned supreme. During his four-year tenure (1969-1973), Aubrey liquidated assets in an attempt to save the studio from crippling debt – while its new owner Kirk Kerkorian funneled all revenues toward constructing the MGM Grand Hotel in Las Vegas. As a result, MGM's former status as the crown jewel of the major studios became a distant memory.

UNIVERSAL MONSTERS

Produced by
HUNT STROMBERG JR.

Meanwhile, starting May 1, 1970, Hunt Stromberg Productions opened for business at Universal Studios in University City, California – having signed a four-year, non-exclusive deal to develop film and television projects for Universal Pictures and Universal Television. Hunt would draw a salary of $1,000 per week, with negotiable bonus fees as the sole producer of each project that was greenlit by the studio.

Hunt envisioned lavish all-star reboots of classic monsters and horror movies, including *Frankenstein*, *Bride of Frankenstein*, *Dracula*, *Dracula's Daughter*, *The Mummy*, *The Wolf Man*, *The Invisible Man*, *The Phantom of the Opera*, *King Kong*, *The Creature from the Black Lagoon*, a distaff version of *Dr. Jekyll and Mrs. Hyde* to star Ingrid Bergman (from a script by Joseph Stefano, author of *Psycho*), *The Mask of Fu Manchu*, *The Old Dark House*, *Murders in the Rue Morgue*, etc.

When his dream project *Frankenstein: The True Story* was in its early stages of development, Hunt was already confidently planning his follow-up horror reboot for

Stromberg, Whiting and Mason hover over tank with Seymour dummy.

Universal Television and NBC-TV. In April 1971, he asked his *Frankenstein* scribes, Christopher Isherwood and Don Bachardy, to read Bram Stoker's *Dracula* and come up with a fresh treatment.

"Have just finished reading *Dracula*," Isherwood wrote in his diary on May 2, 1971. "It really tells you little or nothing about how it feels to be a vampire."

Isherwood subsequently read Stoker's short story *Dracula's Guest* and discussed the possibility of telling the Dracula saga from the point of view of Jonathan Harker. Given the gay subtext that permeates *Frankenstein: The True Story*, one cannot help but imagine the homoerotic possibilities the authors might have explored between Dracula and Harker – and Bachardy confirmed that was the direction they would have taken.

The proposal, however, was dropped before anything was committed to paper – likely due to an outbreak of at least a dozen vampire movies in just 1970-71 alone. It turned out to be a blessing in disguise because, on February 8, 1974, just two months after *Frankenstein: The True Story* premiered on NBC, the Dan Curtis production of *Dracula* starring Jack Palance premiered in primetime on CBS.

UNWRAPPING THE MUMMY

Instead, Stromberg shifted gears to turf that had been comparatively less traveled – developing a Mummy project (officially assigned Universal production No. 81570).

Since the age of 9, Stromberg had been a fan of Universal's *The Mummy* (1932) starring Boris Karloff. He was fascinated by the mysteries of ancient Egypt; the décor in his home and office featured various Egyptian artifacts.

You will recall that in 1950, when he was developing projects through his literary agency Stromberg-Shaffer-Shaw, Hunt wrote a treatment for Paramount Pictures entitled *Road to Cairo* as a potential installment of the madcap Bob Hope-Bing Crosby-Dorothy Lamour "Road" movie franchise.

His story begins with Bob and Bing touring Egypt as part of a magic show fronted by Fantasia the Great – a smarmy charlatan who gets arrested for gem smuggling, leaving Bob and Bing high and dry. Penniless, they take jobs as janitors at the Cairo Museum, formerly run by the famous archeologist, Pierre Lamour, who has just died. His glamorous daughter, Dorothy Lamour, "having wearied of Stork Club parties, is on her way to Egypt to take up where her pop left off." Bob and Bing hatch a plan to be her tour guide when she arrives.

"Swathed in furs, Dottie looks stunning as she steps out of the plane into the hot Egyptian sun. Her two eager guides,

Bob and Bing, are there to meet her, loaded with equipment down to the last shovel."

Later, while exploring a pyramid, there is a sudden cave-in and the three adventurers are sent spiraling through space in a time warp. They fall, fall, fall, as a mystic voice echoes through the ancient air: "It is the Pharaoh's Curse, proclaiming death and destruction to any and all who shall violate the great tomb. Revenge! Revenge! Revenge!"

Bob and Bing suddenly find themselves in the desert, but Dottie is gone. Captured by hooded warriors, Bob and Bing are cameled to ancient Thebes where they become servants for Queen Cleopatra – who just so happens to be a dead ringer of Dorothy Lamour. Cleo is all hot 'n heavy about a palooka named Julius Caesar – who, coincidentally enough, looks an awful lot like Fantasia the Great.

One mishap leads to another until Bob and Bing end up in Rome, where Caesar has them thrown to the lions in the coliseum – which they narrowly escape by the skin of their behinds. Naturally, the boys doublehandedly thwart Caesar's scheme to enslave Egypt. Once the dust has settled, Cleo has fallen for Bob who elects to remain her love slave in ancient Egypt. Bing returns to the twentieth century to romance the famous archeologist's daughter Dorothy Lamour. "And they lived happily ever after… over and over again."

It was a clever mashup of ideas and would have fit right in with the loony spirit of the other "Road" comedies – with the unusual twist of both Bob *and* Bing claiming Dorothy for themselves in the end. Sadly, it never went any further – or did it? When Universal made *Abbott and Costello Meet the Mummy* (1955), was it mere coincidence that the movie begins with Bud and Lou similarly stranded penniless in Cairo?

Flash forward to February 1972 when Stromberg invited Isherwood and Bachardy to a screening room on the Universal lot to watch archival prints of Universal's first three Mummy movies: *The Mummy* (1932), *The Mummy's Hand* (1940) and *The Mummy's Tomb* (1942).

On March 10, 1972, in a memo to Universal Television president Sid Sheinberg, Stromberg wrote, "Isherwood and I now have what we feel is a very effective story line. Two books provided us with some very unique and exciting material. These are *The Living Mummy* by Ambrose Pratt (1910) and *The Jewel of the Seven Stars* by Bram Stoker (1903)."

The Living Mummy features a mummy obedient to an evil villain. However, the treatment that Isherwood and Bachardy completed on July 27, 1972, seems more inspired by Stoker's novel which centers on an archaeologist's scheme to revive Queen Tera.

While waiting for the powers-that-be at Universal to evaluate their treatment, Isherwood reported in his diary on August 10, 1972: "Two or three days ago we discovered, with some anxiety, that Hammer Films of England have made a movie based on Bram Stoker's *The Jewel of the Seven Stars*, which is one of the books I read while we were concocting our mummy story. Last night we went to see it. It is called *Blood from the Mummy's Tomb*. There are resemblances between our story and theirs, but I don't think they're serious enough to matter."

While in London finishing last-minute revisions of *Frankenstein: The True Story*, Isherwood and Bachardy went to the new *Treasures of Tutankhuman* exhibit at the British Museum and were sufficiently inspired to hunker down and complete the first draft script on March 1, 1973, five days before the Writers' Strike began (two weeks before

Frankenstein: The True Story commenced shooting).

Titled *The Lady from the Land of the Dead*, Isherwood and Bachardy begin their story in Cairo in the early 1950s where archeologist Dr. Ralph Peterson, 40, and his young wife Laura, 20, and his 12-year-old son Eric (from a previous marriage) travel to Cairo to excavate the newly discovered ancient tomb of Egyptian Princess Naketah (pronounced Na-KAY-tah) who committed suicide on her twentieth birthday. Strange things happen – and, when the mummy of Naketah accidentally catches on fire, Laura has a spasm in her stomach that develops into a baby girl. Laura dies during childbirth and, before Dr. Peterson dies of a heart attack, he names the baby Naketah, or Kay for short.

About a third of the way into the script, the action flashes forward to present day (1970s) when Kay is a few days shy of her twentieth birthday. Kay's mysterious half-brother Eric is now the owner of the Peterson mansion in London – and Eric has managed to acquire the mummy of Am Nar, a male that was found buried in the floor beneath the sarcophagus of Naketah, believed to be her lover. Eric is convinced that Kay is the reincarnation of Princess Naketah and that her soul will take charge of Kay's body on her twentieth birthday.

At the opening exhibit of the mummy of Am Nar, Kay hears Am Nar breathing. Hysterical with fear, she jumps into her car and speeds away – only to be stopped by a cop who commits her to a mental ward under the care of psychiatrist Dr. Hugh McCallister. Kay tries to convince the doctor that she will be possessed by Princess Naketah in three days, when she turns twenty. He does not believe her – but falls in love with her and is determined to cure her mental disorder.

On the fateful night, Eric is making preparations for the possession to take place. Kay almost jumps from a fire escape but is saved by an orderly. Meanwhile, Nurse Williams (Kay's nurse from the hospital) comes to Eric's house. Eric purposefully burns the mummy of Am Nar – and Nurse Williams has a spasm in her stomach that will obviously develop into the reincarnation of Am Nar – who, we learn, was not the lover of Naketah after all, but rather her murderer.

Once Kay has managed to survive her twentieth birthday, Dr. McCallister believes she is cured. But, to his surprise, she now fully believes she is Princess Naketah and, in the final scene, she leaves the doctor, bound for her ancestral home in

Smight with Hunt, pointing to script with a joking look of disapproval.

Stromberg & McCallum (in aborted FTTS prologue Lord Byron wardrobe).

Cairo accompanied by her new assistant, Nurse Williams – who just so happens to be reading a magazine article on the plane about expectant mothers. Sequel, anyone?

A month later, on April 2, 1973, it was reported in *Daily Variety* that Jack Smight would direct *The Lady from the Land of the Dead*.

Stromberg offered the leading roles of Laura/Kay/Princess Naketah to Nicola Pagett – who, in real-life, was born in Cairo, Egypt – but the script wasn't her cup of tea and she turned it down. He also sent the script to David McCallum to consider playing the role of Dr. Hugh McCallister.

On July 5, 1973, McCallum sent a letter to Stromberg: "I agree that there is a good idea here… but I would like

Stromberg getting cheeky with Jane Seymour on the set of FTTS.

to keep the Egyptian piece entirely in Kay's mind, either remembered or imagined and thus keep the piece completely contemporary. Do I make any sense to you? Affectionately, David."

In November 1973, the same month that *Frankenstein: The True Story* premiered, *The Hollywood Reporter* announced that Stromberg had cast Jane Seymour as Laura / Kay / Princess Naketah and that Stromberg had made a deal with the Egyptian government to shoot the film in and around Luxor.

After that, however, radio silence. It is not known exactly what happened. Did Universal and/or NBC lose faith in the script? In any event, the project – at least as it was now written – was dead. And the attachments of Jane Seymour, David McCallum and director Jack Smight quickly evaporated.

Stromberg, however, did not give up easily. Starting from scratch, he hired Joseph Stefano of *Psycho* fame to write an original Mummy script entitled *House of Eternity* which Universal assigned the very same production No. 81570. Technically, Stefano's script was entirely new – though both dealt with the reincarnation of an ancient Egyptian princess whose mummy has been discovered.

Like *The Lady from the Land of the Dead*, Stefano's *House of Eternity* begins in Egypt in the mid-1950s – archeologist Dr. Dominic Allan and his pregnant wife Valerie discover the mummy of the lost Egyptian Princess Izadori Akhenamon and mysterious things happen that the locals attribute to the curse of the mummy's tomb. Nothing new here. The tropes of the genre were checked off, one by one.

At the half-way point, the script jumps forward to the mid-1970s in Hollywood where Dori Allan, daughter of the archeologist and his wife, is now grown up and turned into what can only be described as a train wreck. She parties hard, collects celebrity friends, drives too fast, outruns the police, and tests this reader's nerves. Dori turns out to be – cue eyes to roll – the reincarnation of Princess IzaDORI. Yawn. Hardly surprising, this script went absolutely nowhere.

FROM HITCHCOCK TO LIZA

Other early-1970s projects Hunt was developing for Universal (prior to the 1973 filming of *Frankenstein: The True Story*) included:

1. *The Barford Cat Affair*, based on the book by P.H.H. Bryan, offered to Alfred Hitchcock to direct. A cat is the narrator of this story, told in first-person. It revolves around the British town of Barford, circa 1950s, when there was a paranoid movement known as "The Cat Peril" – a satirical metaphor for "The Red Scare" of the 1950s. In a series of local newspaper articles, cats are increasingly deemed disgusting, conniving, and dangerous. The townspeople's paranoia of cats is whipped up into such a frenzy, cats start disappearing – and feline roadkill is suddenly on the rise. The cats must come together to fight back. The answer? An infestation of rats will remind the townspeople just how valuable cats are – and the plan works like a charm. Alfred Hitchcock sent this *rawther* amusing response:

    Dear Mr. Stromberg,
    I have read the *Cat Affair* story with great amusement and interest, but there is, I think, a slight problem. Back in 1932, I was making a picture where some crooks used to foregather in a room of a deserted old Victorian house.

THE EPIC SAGA BEHIND *FRANKENSTEIN: THE TRUE STORY*

I had what I thought at the time was a rather amusing sidelight to this situation. I would make this deserted house a haven for all the stray cats in the neighborhood. My idea was that in the course of the one or two revolver shots, that the story called for, the loud bangs would cause about one hundred cats to rush up the stairs about three flights into the top room. Then later at the sound of the second shot they would all run down again, and I intended this running gag to happen about four or five times during this particular sequence. ... The moment the prop man shot the gun the cats leapt in every direction, not one went up the stairs, but became scattered all over the studio and for the next two hours we could hear nothing but the sounds of owners calling, "Pussy, Pussy, etc., etc.'" in other words, trying to reclaim their particular pets. At the end of two hours all were gathered together again. This time, however, we had fine chicken wire stretched and nailed to ten feet high frames, which we put around the whole of the lower part of the staircase, and prepared to go again. The cats were assembled at the bottom of the stairs. Bang! Three cats went up the stairs for a few feet, the rest clung to the wire netting causing the netting to fall over and once more they were around the studio. Period.

Sincerely,

Alfred Hitchcock

2. *Pride and Prejudice*, a spoof of Hunt Stromberg Sr.'s 1940 MGM classic. To star Peter Sellers, Peter O'Toole, John Gielgud, Margaret Leighton, plus guest appearances by the stars of the original movie Greer Garson and Laurence Olivier, with narration by Cary Grant. From a script by Jerome Lawrence and Robert E. Lee (*Auntie Mame*), based on the novel by Jane Austen. (As mentioned earlier, young Hunt worked as a production

assistant on his dad's version of *Pride and Prejudice*.) Never got made.

3. *A Tale of Two Cities*, a 2-part miniseries adaptation of the Charles Dickens classic, from a script by Herb Meadow, to star Sean Connery (Sydney Carton), Geneviève Bujold (Lucie), Leonard Whiting (Charles Darney), Alec Guinness (Dr. Manette), Cantinflas (Barsad), James Mason (Marquis St. Evrémonde), Faye Dunaway (Madame Defarge), Margaret Leighton (Miss Pross) and Laurence Olivier (General Lafayette). NBC was gung-ho for a period of time, but then nothing happened.

4. *Lady Luck*, created by Hunt Stromberg Jr., a proposed TV series about a beautiful supernatural woman who assists men and women in need of aid. A 30-minute pilot was actually shot at Universal Studios in California in 1972, directed by James Komack, starring Valerie Perrine – hot off of her film debut in George Roy Hill's *Slaughterhouse-Five* (1972); she would later star opposite Dustin Hoffman in Bob Fosse's *Lenny* (1974) for which she was Oscar-nominated for Best Actress; and she would play "Eve Teschmacher" in *Superman* (1978) and *Superman II* (1980). *Lady Luck* was not picked up for a series, but the pilot was aired anyway as filler on NBC-TV, February 12, 1973, 10:30-11:00 PM. By then, Hunt was in England prepping *Frankenstein: The True Story*.

5. *Peter Pan*, to star Liza Minnelli. Went no further than just an idea.

THE TORCHED ROLLS-ROYCE AFFAIR

In 1974, shortly after *Frankenstein: The True Story* premiered, Stromberg, 51, dumped his boyfriend Jacque Shelton, 43. Both men were heavy drinkers and pill poppers with inevitable mood swings, but Jacque became a particularly mean drunk when he'd had too much. There was one incident in particular that weighed on Hunt's mind.

In early-July 1970, Stromberg took delivery of a $30,000 custom Rolls-Royce and parked it in the garage at the Sunset Marquis Hotel. While inside the hotel, someone sprayed paint remover on the car's interior and ignited it, setting the car ablaze, and causing an explosion. In an interview by columnist Joyce Haber, published July 5, 1970, Stromberg said, "I believe I was targeted. There were a hundred cars in the garage and this was the only one it happened to. I'm a little rattled."

A "little"?! Further disturbing details surfaced in Christopher Isherwood's private diary. A September 2, 1970, entry stated: "Hunt has broken up with Jacque Shelton, whom we liked; said Jacque was impossible to live with and talked vaguely about a car being blown up. As a result, Hunt hired a bodyguard."

Two years later, an August 1, 1972, entry added this: "Dr. Scott Schubach alarmed me by saying that Hunt was 'a prisoner' of Jacque Shelton and Jacque's mother [Doris Shelton], and that Hunt is terrified that Jacque will murder him for his money. He doesn't think Hunt will be allowed by them to [leave their ranch in Texas and] return to Los Angeles or go to England for the [*Frankenstein*] film – unless, of course, he is heavily guarded. This is just the sort of hysterical half-truth which one can't dismiss altogether. Hunt certainly did believe his life was in danger from Jacque; that was when he had that bodyguard."

Just one year later, on July 27, 1971, Isherwood noted in his diary, "Hunt called from Texas... [and] told me that the prefab house he and Jacque Shelton had put up on their

Valerie Perrine in Stromberg's pilot for *Lady Luck*.

Jacque Shelton and tiger at the Double S Ranch.

ranch property was burned to the ground only a couple of nights ago!"

Was Jacque responsible for torching Hunt's Rolls-Royce? And their ranch house, too? Was Hunt under the influence of stimulants that drove his paranoia beyond all reason? We'll never know the answer to any of these questions. But, clearly, by 1974, after a tumultuous series of accusations, threats, breakups and reconciliations, Hunt decided it was time to call it quits with Jacque for good.

To soften the blow – and perhaps to avoid retaliation, Hunt allowed Jacque to continue living at their Double S Ranch in Springtown, Texas, in exchange for taking care of the menagerie of animals. Tellingly, no record could be found of Hunt ever returning to that address the rest of his life; he kept his distance and remained steadfast in Los Angeles.

[Postscript: In 1992, Jacque Shelton was arrested for sexual assault of a 16-year-old boy. According to Wise County, Texas, court documents dated November 10, 1992, "The complainant testified he and Shelton had slept together, in Shelton's bedroom, the entire night of the offense." Shelton's attorney called Shelton's great-niece, Shonya Engel, as a witness at the first trial. "Engel testified she had spent that night at Shelton's home and he had been away the entire night. Engel also testified she heard the complainant's mother attempt to extort money or land from Shelton, by threatening to accuse him of child molestation if he did not give in to her threat." The first trial resulted in Shelton's conviction for the crime – though, on appeal, the proceeding was declared a mistrial and a second jury trial was ordered by the judge. Attorneys for Shelton failed to call Shonya Engel as a witness at the second trial, resulting in another mistrial. Before the *third* trial got underway, however, Jacque was killed in a car accident on April 6, 1998, "while being driven to his routine dialysis appointment at the local hospital in Springtown, Texas." He was 66.]

STROMBERG-KERBY

After breaking up with Jacque, Hunt moved on to an attractive chap named Stoddard William "Joe" Kerby, 39, also professionally known as Joe Kirby with an "i," born Jose Silva Domingues in Cambridge, Massachusetts on October 15, 1935. According to his niece, singer Ava Victoria, both Joe's parents immigrated to Boston from the northern

Portuguese Province of Minho; his father and grandfather were bakers. At the age of 10, Joe and his family moved to Tulare, California. He attended Tulare Union High School where he starred in the musical *Brigadoon*, graduating in 1952. Shortly after, Joe was drafted into the U.S. Army for the Korean War. He was discharged within the year for a health issue. At age 21, Joe tried to conform to societal norms by marrying Eva Cotta on September 8, 1957, but his attraction to men won out, and the union didn't last. He settled in Hollywood to become an actor.

At 25, Joe landed a bit part as a cadet in *The Dark at the Top of the Stairs* (Warner Bros., 1960) starring Robert Preston and Angela Lansbury. I asked Angela if she remembered Joe.

"Oh yes," Angela replied. "Joe was the assistant to the producer of that film, Michael Garrison, who later had a big television success with *The Wild Wild West*. When Michael died from an accident, my brother Bruce took over the producing reigns of that series for the rest of its run. Joe was a very handsome young man. All the girls had eyes for him, but he only had eyes for the boys. And I think his boss Michael was one of them. Anyway, when things were cooling off between Hunt and Eugene, Joe became one of Hunt's boyfriends."

Credited as "Joe Kirby" with an "i," Joe was the Assistant Producer on *The Wild Wild West* when it premiered on CBS in 1965, under Michael Garrison, the founding creator-writer-producer. Garrison front-loaded the series with an undercurrent of homoeroticism. The show's beefcake star, Robert Conrad, 30, wore the tightest pants on television, showcasing a bodacious derriere that had viewers of both sexes swooning – and every opportunity to have his shirt off was exploited to the hilt. It worked. The show became a major hit and Conrad was an instant sex symbol.

Just before the second season began airing in September 1966, however, Garrison fell on the marble stairs of his home during a party on August 17 and died from a head injury. As

Headshot of 25-year-old Stoddard "Joe" Kerby.

THE EPIC SAGA BEHIND *FRANKENSTEIN: THE TRUE STORY*

31-year-old Stoddard "Joe" Kerby when he was President of Robert Conrad Productions, under the name "Joe Kirby."

Headshot of Robert Conrad in *The Wild Wild West*.

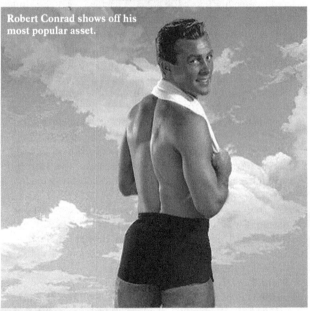

Robert Conrad shows off his most popular asset.

Robert Conrad shirtless in *The Wild Wild West*.

Robert Conrad shirtless in *The Wild Wild West*.

Robert Conrad restrained in *The Wild Wild West*.

CHAPTER SEVENTEEN: THE MONSTROUS LIFE & TIMES OF HUNT STROMBERG JR.

Garrison's assistant, Joe was suddenly out of a job. However, he was immediately taken under the wing of Robert Conrad and, nine days later, was appointed President of Robert Conrad Productions. Out of the multitude of proposed projects developed by the company, only one got made: *The Bandits* (1967), a Western co-written, co-directed and starring Conrad.

There were unsubstantiated rumors that Joe Kirby was Conrad's secret lover. Fiercely private, Conrad was married-slash-divorced twice (to women) and fathered eight children. But, as we all know, statistics don't prove anything.

"I am not gay!" Robert Conrad proclaimed to inquiring members of the media. More than once.

"Bob Conrad doth protest too much," confided Jack "Jimmy Olsen" Larson in an interview I conducted shortly before he died in 2015. "He had flings with lots of men. I should know. I was one of them. So was Nick Adams, Rock Hudson, Tab Hunter, Wally Cox, just to name a few. But don't you dare quote me before Bob kicks the bucket. He'd kill me. Or have me killed." (Robert Conrad passed away at age 84 in 2020; so, the time has come to set the record straight. Or otherwise – as the case may be. You be the judge.)

Hunt was definitely *not* a poster child for monogamy. Christopher Isherwood noted in his diaries several instances of Hunt and his boyfriend Jacque Shelton arguing over infidelity – and based on Stromberg's own financial documents, it is abundantly clear that Joe Kirby was romantically involved with Hunt long before they made it official in 1974.

Immediately after Joe moved into Stromberg's Los Angeles home, they opened a joint personal bank account and Hunt made Joe a minority partner in his newly christened Stromberg-Kerby Productions. Stromberg would receive two-thirds of the earnings; Kerby one-third. They would share credit as producers or executive producers on any projects that got made – with Hunt getting top billing and Joe credited as "Stoddard W. Kerby" with an "e." It sounded

Jack "Jimmy Olsen" Larson and his friend-with-benefits Tab Hunter.

very Ivy League. Which was precisely the point. Publicly, Hunt simply referred to Joe as his "partner," which could be interpreted as business, personal or both, depending on the level of acceptance.

They immediately began developing a torrent of ambitious projects for Universal, including:

1. *Around the World Again*, the sequel to the Best Picture Oscar winner *Around the World in 80 Days* (1956), to star Elizabeth Taylor as "Philena Fogg," daughter of "Phileas Fogg", the lead character in the first film, played by David Niven who would reprise his role in the new one. Sean Connery would portray Philena's fiancé. Elizabeth Taylor would also serve as Executive Producer because she just so happened to own the rights to *Around the World in 80 Days*, inherited from her third husband Mike Todd (1907-1958), Oscar-winning producer of the original movie. The script was written by Leonard Spigelgass (*Gypsy*, *Silk Stockings*) whose real-life lover was Miles White, Oscar-nominated costume designer of *Around the World in 80 Days* who would repeat his duties on the new film. Hunt described the plot as follows: "Philena goes around the world in search of her fiancé, who mysteriously disappeared just before their wedding. An ominous note warns her that she has only 30 days in which to find him. Thus, this time, we are going around the world not for the sake of a bet, but in search of love – and to save her love's life. This is what we have in mind – a big, gaudy, star-studded fun adventure."

2. *The Royal Family of Broadway*, to star 70-year-old Greta Garbo as "Fanny Cavendish," bringing her out of reclusive retirement for a comeback. Script was by Leonard Spigelgass based on the play by George Kaufman and Edna Farber. Stromberg's father had produced Garbo's first American film and they had been friends for decades. She had not made a film since *Two-Faced Woman* in 1941. And she had never appeared on television. Considering Mae West's disastrous comeback in *Myra Breckinridge* (1970), it was doubtful that Garbo would have taken the risk. And she didn't. She would pass away in 1990 at age 84.

3. *The Trials of Norma Desmond*, a sequel to *Sunset Blvd.*, to star 76-year-old Gloria Swanson – who had just been featured in Universal's *Airport 1975*, directed by Jack Smight. It never got off the ground. Swanson passed away in 1983 at the age of 84.

4. *World War III*, based on the book by John Stanley, in the satiric vein of *Catch 22*, to be scripted by Larry Gelbart (*M*A*S*H*, *Tootsie*) and directed by Jack Smight. Never happened.

5. *The Prisoner of Zenda*, a comedic remake, to star Peter Sellers.

None of the above proposals got any further than first base – with the one exception of *The Prisoner of Zenda* that did actually complete a home run at Universal in 1979 starring Peter Sellers, but with Walter Mirisch producing, instead of Stromberg-Kerby. Oh, the pain of it.

THE LEGEND OF KING KONG

The first-and-only Stromberg-Kerby project to finally gain traction at Universal was *The Legend of King Kong*, a big-budget theatrical remake of the 1933 RKO classic, faithfully set in the 1930s, to star Robert Redford (Oscar-nominated for

Stromberg, King Kong, Stoddard "Joe" Kerby.

The Sting), from a script by Bo Goldman (Oscar winner for *One Flew Over the Cuckoo's Nest*).

Joseph Sargent (*Colossus: The Forbin Project*, *The Taking of Pelham One Two Three*, and, later, *Jaws: The Revenge*) was attached to direct – after hot-off-of-*Jaws* Steven Spielberg turned it down to do *Close Encounters of the Third Kind* (1977).

Stromberg had begun curating stars for the cast. Aside from Robert Redford as "Jack Driscoll", Peter Falk would play "Carl Denham" and relative newcomer Susan Blakely was cast as "Ann Darrow." At that time, Blakely was all the buzz on the Universal lot, getting pre-broadcast raves for the forthcoming Universal Television miniseries *Rich Man, Poor*

Man (set to begin airing February 1, 1976 on ABC-TV). Nick Nolte, Blakely's costar in *Rich Man, Poor Man*, was also under consideration if Redford backed out.

And in typical Stromberg fashion, he'd gotten an agreement from his friend Fay Wray, 68, star of the original *King Kong*, to make a cameo appearance in the new film. She hadn't made a movie since the 1950s – but, as personal favors to Hunt, had made guest appearances on several CBS television shows in the late-1950s and early-1960s when he was in charge.

This new *King Kong* would be presented in Sensurround, the low-frequency vibrating gimmick Universal developed for

Key art for *The Legend of King Kong*, with shadow over 1930s-era Manhattan skyline.

Jack Smight and Toshirō Mifune on the set of *Midway*.

Right: On Aug. 28, 1975, Mae West autographed actor Kevin Dobson's lifejacket on the set of *Midway*. Stromberg arranged for this outlandish photo op.

Director Joseph Sargent, Stoddard "Joe" Kerby, Hunt Stromberg Jr., during pre-production for *The Legend of King Kong*.

Earthquake (1974) and subsequently used for Jack Smight's *Midway* (1976), the World War II epic starring Charlton Heston, Henry Fonda, James Coburn, Glenn Ford, Robert Mitchum, Robert Wagner and Toshirō Mifune.

Speaking of *Midway*, Hunt dropped by the set of that film on the Universal lot to pay his respects to the stars and, of course, his *Frankenstein: The True Story* director Jack Smight. Stromberg brought along his pal Mae West for shock value – which resulted in some hilariously incongruous publicity photos of West flirting with one of the hunky supporting actors, Kevin Dobson (Telly Savalas' sidekick on *Kojak* – the hit CBS series made by Universal Television, 1973-1978).

Ray Harryhausen protégé Jim Danforth (stop-motion effects animator of *Equinox*, *Flesh Gordon*, and Hammer Films' *When Dinosaurs Rule the Earth* for which he had been Oscar-nominated) was hired to do the special effects for *The Legend of King Kong* – although it turned out that instead of utilizing stop-motion model animation, the plan was to mostly use a guy in an ape suit. Danforth would focus on designing the ape suit, plus a giant mechanical head, arm, and legs for closeups with actors. There would also be men in dinosaur suits for the battle scenes on the island – which Danforth would also design.

Matte paintings would be done by the great Albert Whitlock, on exclusive contract with Universal, who had recently won an Oscar for *Earthquake* (1974) and would soon win a second Oscar for *The Hindenburg* (1975).

Frankenstein: The True Story composer Gil Mellé had agreed to do the music, incorporating the original 1933 themes composed by Max Steiner – which Universal had acquired from Steiner's widow.

Suddenly, however, the Stromberg-Kerby / Universal Pictures project imploded when Paramount Pictures and producer Dino De Laurentiis announced their own remake, to be set in the *present* day, with Kong climbing Manhattan's new World Trade Center (opened in December 1973). Both studios insisted they had acquired the remake rights from RKO but, upon closer examination, a verbal agreement with Stromberg versus the written agreement with De Laurentiis put Universal at a disadvantage. But then it was discovered that the copyright on a novelization book had not been renewed in 1960. Universal's lawyers were of the opinion that this allowed them to do the film as long as it adhered to the novelization.

In the book *Kong Unmade: The Lost Films of Skull Island*, author John LeMay wrote, "Eventually, a judge ruled that the Kong novelization was in public domain. However, they also decided that the rights to King Kong did indeed belong to the Merian C. Cooper estate after all. Not long after, Richard Cooper sold the rights to Universal."

Yup. I'm as confused as you are. To make a very long story short, the growing mountain of contracts and judicial rulings were a tangled quagmire of contradictions, loopholes and misrepresentations. More lawsuits erupted. In a fury, Team Stromberg took out trade ads insisting they were starting production on January 5, 1976. Spitting-mad, Team De Laurentiis responded by moving up its start date to January 15. The squabbling devolved into a pissing match of one-upmanship.

A 1976 article in *New York* magazine entitled "The Battle for King Kong" by Andrew Tobias, observed, "Unlike the case of *The Towering Inferno*, where two studios with look-alike scripts agreed to join forces, the antagonists in this affair are intractable. Egos are clashing like cymbals."

But eventually, it just made no financial sense to have two competing *Kong* movies in the marketplace at the same time. So, out-of-court settlements were negotiated. Universal *and*

Above: A guy in an ape suit talks to Stoddard "Joe" Kerby and Hunt Stromberg Jr.
Right: A guy in the ape suit clowns around with Stoddard "Joe" Kerby, Hunt Stromberg Jr., unidentified woman, and director Joseph Sargent.

This Picture and next two pages: storyboards for *The Legend of King Kong*

120 KONG —

120 KONG LIFTS A TORCH – FIRES START ON HIS CHEST – HE POUNDS THEM OUT

FORM 2615 (ART 12)

120 HE BREAKS OFF PILLAR WITH HIS HAND

Paramount ended up co-presenting the modern one that got made with Jessica Lange in the big boy's paw. Dino produced.

The loser in all this? Stromberg – who was unceremoniously kicked to the curb. At the risk of career suicide, he sued Universal for a share of the 17.5% box-office gross the studio had negotiated for itself.

"I got so many cold shoulders for doing that, you'd think I was the bad guy," Stromberg wrote in a 1977 letter to a friend. "And now, the supervillain in the new James Bond movie is named after me."

Indeed, Bond's nemesis in *The Spy Who Loved Me* (1977) was a megalomaniac named Stromberg (played by

164 CLOSE KONG'S HAND AND ANN

165 KONG MOVES TOWARD LOG AND MEN
DENHAM CAUGHT ON BRANCH

FORM 2615 (ART-12)

166 KONG POUNDS HIS CHEST—ANN IN B.G.
KONG STARTS TO BEND DOWN

Curd Jürgens). A direct reference? In 2014, screenwriter Christopher Wood replied, "Yes, I knew Hunt and borrowed his name because it sounded Teutonic and powerful. He was highly amused when he saw the movie."

Stromberg was less amused when animator Jay Ward, of *Rocky and Bullwinkle* fame, made a 1966 pilot for *Super Chicken* in which the title character is named Hunt Strongbird Jr. When asked if this was a jab at Stromberg, Ward deadpanned to a reporter, "Merciful heavens, there is absolutely no connection whatsoever between my cartoon character Hunt Strongbird Jr. and the former CBS vice-president Hunt Stromberg Jr. who screwed up my pilot for

CHAPTER SEVENTEEN: THE MONSTROUS LIFE & TIMES OF HUNT STROMBERG JR.

71

246   KONG TEARS AT WINGS OF PETEROSAURS

246   DRISCOLL RUNS BEHIND KONG – ANN AND DRISCOLL START OVER THE SIDE

KONG THROWS THE PETEROSAURS INTO THE AIR.

Nuthouse a few years ago and then rejected it. Why would anyone think such a thing?"

Stromberg had his lawyers send a "cease and desist" letter resulting in the Super Chicken character being renamed Henry Cabot Henhouse III (named after Henry Cabot Lodge Jr., Republican Vice-Presidential nominee on the Richard Nixon ticket for the 1960 Presidential Election) for its segments on *George of the Jungle* (ABC-TV, 1967). Ward alerted the media that the name had been changed "out of professional courtesy to all network programming executives everywhere." (The *Super Chicken* pilot with "Hunt Strongbird Jr." is available on the *George of the Jungle* DVD set.)

386   THE EPIC SAGA BEHIND *FRANKENSTEIN: THE TRUE STORY*

Stromberg-Kerby trade ad announcing that *The Legend of King Kong* would being shooting on January 5, 1976.

Regarding the Stromberg v. Universal case over *King Kong* revenue, it was eventually settled out of court. Stromberg was given $320,000 to go away. Permanently. No more office on the lot for Stromberg-Kerby Productions. All projects under development cancelled, including the two Mummy scripts *The Lady from the Land of the Dead* by Christopher Isherwood and Don Bachardy, and *House of Eternity* by Joseph Stefano – both of which, to this day, remain unproduced properties under Universal's control.

THE CURSE OF KING TUT'S TOMB

Like Bob Hope and Bing Crosby ditched in Cairo, Hunt and Joe had to figure out how they could turn things around for themselves. Stromberg couldn't shake his fixation on Egypt – and now it seemed that all of America was following suit. In 1976, the touring *Treasures of Tutankhamun* exhibit arrived at New York's Metropolitan Museum of Art where it broke all attendance records. This was followed by a six-city tour across America that attracted an astounding eight million visitors through 1979. Every time Stromberg turned on the television, there was another documentary program on King Tutankhamun, the pyramids, mummies, and all things Egyptian.

Even Steve Martin had gotten into the act in 1978 with his *Saturday Night Live* musical routine as King Tut, spoofing the popularity and commercialization of the *Treasures of Tutankhamun* tour. The sketch was so popular, it spawned the hit novelty song *King Tut*, performed by Steve Martin and the Toot Uncommons (members of the Nitty Gritty Dirt Band) – which reached No. 17 on the *Billboard* Hot 100 chart; ranked No. 1 for four weeks in Chicago (where the Tut exhibit was currently on display), and sold over a million copies.

Like the craze that swept Europe during Napoleon's Egyptian Campaign (1798–1801), Egyptomania had been reincarnated in the United States in the late-1970s.

Stromberg also kept thinking about that outstanding deal he'd made with the Egyptian government to shoot a movie in Luxor. Why should that pact go to waste?

So, with renewed resolve that he'd been right all along, Stromberg landed on his feet in 1978 when he signed an exclusive deal for Stromberg-Kerby Productions to develop projects for Columbia Pictures Television. The first project greenlit by this new alliance would be a two-part primetime television movie for NBC-TV entitled *The Curse of King Tut's Tomb*, inspired by the 1973 non-fiction history book *Behind the Mask of Tutankhamen* by Barry Wynne.

According to *Hollywood Reporter*, the venture was "the first coproduction deal between a Hollywood TV production company and the Egyptian government, to be lensed in Luxor and in England."

Hunt Stromberg Jr., Eva Marie Saint, and Stoddard "Joe" Kerby (Stromberg's boyfriend), on set for *The Curse of King Tut's Tomb*.

Stromberg hired an old friend, Herb Meadow, 67, to write the script. Herb had worked on countless projects for Stromberg at CBS, including *Collector's Item* (the Price-Lorre pilot) and the hit series *Have Gun—Will Travel* (1957-1963) which Meadow co-created.

Stromberg then hired Anne Collins, another prolific television writer (*Hawaii Five-O*, *Wonder Woman*, *Buck Rogers in the 25th Century*), to polish the script – though her work went uncredited.

Based on the true story of Egyptologist Howard Carter's 1920s discovery and excavation of the tomb of King Tut, the curses usually prescribed against "grave robbers" befalls many in Carter's team, one by one, starting with Lord George Carnarvon who financed the dig – and died shortly after the tomb was opened from an infected mosquito bite. Fictional characters and situations were added "to enhance the drama."

On November 7, 1979, it was announced in *Daily Variety* that Stromberg-Kerby Productions had made a co-production deal with Harlech Television (HTV) of England – a company founded by Lord Harlech (former British Ambassador to the U.S., appointed by President John F. Kennedy) with a prominent board of directors that included Stromberg's friends Richard Burton and Elizabeth Taylor, stars of HTV's *Divorce His – Divorce Hers* (ABC-TV, 1973), the two-part television movie released theatrically in Europe. HTV had more recently produced a miniseries of Robert Louis Stevenson's *Kidnapped* (1978) starring David McCallum.

To run the day-to-day production duties on *The Curse of King Tut's Tomb*, Stromberg agreed to hire the producers of *Kidnapped*, Peter Graham Scott (director of Hammer Films' *Captain Clegg* starring Peter Cushing and Oliver Reed) and Patrick Dromgoole (*Diagnosis: Murder* starring Jon Finch and Christopher Lee).

To direct, Stromberg selected Emmy-nominee Philip Leacock, 62, who had helmed episodes of numerous television series at CBS under Stromberg's regime (*The Alfred Hitchcock Hour*, *Route 66*, *Secret Agent*). Before all that, Leacock had a sizable career as a theatrical movie director in his native England, including the Oscar-winning film *The Little Kidnappers*.

Additionally, *Frankenstein: The True Story* composer Gil Mellé was hired to provide the orchestral score.

In an interview for the *Los Angeles Times*, Stromberg outlined his manifesto: "I'm not interested in making the straight, modern movie of the week. Holds no interest for me. I like doing the exotica, à la the *Frankenstein* thing. For me this *Tut* film is very fancy, exotic, romantic and suspenseful subject matter."

Stoddard "Joe" Kerby, director Philip Leacock, Stromberg on location for *The Curse of King Tut's Tomb*.

For a period of time during prep, Stromberg hired his *Frankenstein: The True Story* production designer Wilfrid Shingleton (*The Fearless Vampire Killers*). However, Shingleton was soon replaced by John Biggs who regularly worked on HTV projects such as *Kidnapped* – a clear sign that the HTV contingent was determined to control the nuts and bolts of the production. Stromberg was left to do what he did best: curate "names."

And, as usual, Stromberg was thinking big. Just as he'd tried to get Queen Elizabeth to introduce *A Christmas Carol* and *Frankenstein: The True Story*, on November 16, 1979, Stromberg wrote a letter to Anwar Sadat, President of Egypt, with a similar request: "We would consider it an honor if, on camera, from perhaps the Egyptian Museum, you would introduce this film." Sadat respectfully declined.

Then, Stromberg offered the leading role of Egyptologist Howard Carter to Richard Burton and the role of the exotic villainess Giovanna to Burton's ex-wife Elizabeth Taylor. The reunion would have made headlines but neither took the bait. Next, on November 22, 1979, Stromberg offered Giovanna to Sophia Loren. "No, grazie."

Finally, the role of Giovanna was accepted by Joan Collins – only to be rescinded a few days later. "My astrologer told me not to take the part," Collins explained. "I'm very superstitious and always take notice of what my astrologer says. The stars had the right message for me."

Marie-France Pisier, Gayle Hunnicutt and Honor Blackman were the next three candidates to turn down the role of Giovanna until Barbara Murray (*Passport to Pimlico*, *Tales from the Crypt*) accepted. She was a solid character actress but hardly a "name."

Barbara Murray.

Ian McShane was originally cast as "Howard Carter."

THE EPIC SAGA BEHIND *FRANKENSTEIN: THE TRUE STORY*

Harry Andrews.

Oscar winner Eva Marie Saint.

Tom Baker.

Oscar winner Wendy Hiller.

Tom Baker with rifle, surrenders.

Stromberg had a bit more luck attracting stars for the other characters: future Golden Globe winner Ian McShane (*Deadwood, Pirates of the Caribbean: On Stranger Tides*) as Howard Carter; Oscar winner Eva Marie Saint (*North by Northwest*) as American journalist Sarah Morrissey; Oscar winner Wendy Hiller (*Murder on the Orient Express, The Elephant Man*) as the spiritual medium Princess Vilma; BAFTA nominee Harry Andrews (*Theatre of Blood, Superman*) as Lord George Carnarvon; Angharad Rees (*Poldark, Hands of the Ripper*) as Lady Evelyn Herbert, Carter's love interest; and, Oscar winner Paul Scofield (*A Man for All Seasons*) as the narrator.

Angharad Rees.

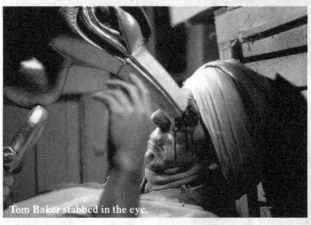
Tom Baker stabbed in the eye.

As the duplicitous antiquities collector Jonash Sabastian, Stromberg called in a favor from one of his longtime gay friends, Emmy winner Raymond Burr (*Rear Window, Perry Mason, Ironside*). They'd originally met when Stromberg was overseeing *Perry Mason* for CBS and become social buddies.

Stromberg also called upon *Frankenstein: The True Story* alumnus Tom Baker – on hiatus from *Doctor Who* (1974-1981) – to play Hassan, the Egyptian henchman for Burr's character.

In his memoir *Who on Earth is Tom Baker?*, Baker recalled the surreal first-class plane ride he took from London to Cairo with Eva Marie Saint and Harry Andrews – plus their tipsy producers Hunt Stromberg Jr. and Joe Kerby who were boisterously arguing about whether they should visit the loo before the service cart blocked the aisle.

"Hunt," said Joe. "It's not my fault that you pour the wine like someone was taking a leak, no wonder it makes me want a wee wee. It would make a horse want a wee wee."

"At that moment," recalled Baker, "the trolley arrived and the stewardess put a bottle of Pouilly-Fumé on the eating desk in front of Hunt who immediately poured some into his glass."

Tom Baker and Raymond Burr.

"That's it," said Joe. "I'll take a wee wee."

"The girl who was in charge of the trolley looked thoughtfully at her carving knife," Baker continued, "as she backed up to let Joe go to the wee-wee house. Hunt apologized for his pal and the girl smiled at his obvious affection for his friend. As she was serving Hunt his beef Wellington or whatever he had chosen, Joe suddenly reappeared on the scene rather annoyed about something."

Joe, who had refused to order any food because he wasn't hungry, now told the flight attendant that he did want something to eat after all.

"The stewardess appeared sometime later," Baker recalled, "with a portion of foie gras and rather frostily offered it to the now-dozing Joe. He looked up at her with incomprehension, saw the round of foie gras on the plate, and thinking it was an ashtray, he muttered, 'Why thank you,' and stubbed out his cigarette in the foie gras. I shall never forget the look on that girl's face. And later, when I got to know Joe, I just adored him."

Budgeted at $5.3 million (touted by the *Los Angeles Times* as the most expensive made-for-TV movie up to that time), *The Curse of King Tut's Tomb* began filming in Egypt on Monday, December 3, 1979. Not long after that, things began to go awry.

In *Raymond Burr: A Biography*, author Ona L. Hill wrote, "Raymond was dressed in flowing robes and a turban as the Arab villain and collapsed one day from exhaustion as well as the extreme desert heat. As he fell from his chair his head struck an object, and he spent the next two days unconscious in the hospital."

Then, on December 7, the fifth day of shooting (and, historically, the same infamous date Pearl Harbor was bombed by Japan in 1941), Ian McShane and Eva Marie Saint were nearly killed in an automobile crash. The lawsuit between the production company and the insurer read as follows: "The scene to be shot was at a site known as Carter's house, near the Nile, Egypt, situated on an unfenced plateau, elevated about 50 feet from the surrounding terrain accessible by dirt track. The scene involved McShane driving a Ford Model A 1928 motor car away from the house toward the dirt track. The handbrake linkage on the said car was not connected. At about 14:30 hours on 7th December 1979, despite his application of the brakes, the vehicle would not stop, but went out of control, over the edge of the plateau."

Miraculously, Eva Marie Saint quickly jumped out the passenger door to safety before the car went over the cliff. "Before the cameras rolled," Saint explained to reporters, "I had difficulty shutting the passenger door. I decided that if it didn't shut, it wouldn't open either, so I left it open. You might say I had a premonition and that's why I kept the door open."

McShane wasn't so lucky. Trapped inside the car as it careened off the plateau, he broke his leg in ten places and had to be flown to a hospital in London. "I am sure it's the mummy's curse," McShane said from his hospital bed. "I was just thankful to get away with what I did. I wouldn't go back to that film even if I was well. The curse is real enough to me." McShane would end up suing the production for $370,000.

Stromberg was scrambling to cast a replacement for McShane when Angharad Rees recommended her *Poldark* costar Robin Ellis.

"I was painting a bedroom in my home in Kensington," Ellis recalled, "when my agent rang and said 'Can you go to Cairo?'"

Ellis jumped on a plane and arrived Sunday, December 9, 1979, to begin shooting the next day. "We stayed in the Winter Palace Hotel in Luxor where Carter stayed," Ellis added, "and we crossed the Nile every morning to go to work."

Raymond Burr in the flowing robes and turban he was wearing when he collapsed and had to be taken to the hospital. With him here are: Stoddard "Joe" Kerby, Hunt Stromberg Jr. and Eva Marie Saint.

THE EPIC SAGA BEHIND *FRANKENSTEIN: THE TRUE STORY*

Darien Angadi and Ian McShane.

Robin Ellis (replacing Ian McShane) and Darien Angadi.

Series of rare photos of Ian McShane as "Howard Carter" before the car accident prevented him from completing the movie. (All his scenes were re-shot with replacement Robin Ellis.)

With high hopes that their streak of bad luck was behind them, the company forged ahead. But then, one member of the production team was hospitalized for an emergency operation; supervising producer Patrick Dromgoole was placed in intensive care with pneumonia; and, the wife of the American publicist was involved in a serious car accident.

Naturally, the international press had a field day pumping up these incidents as proof that the curse of King Tut's tomb was alive and well. And when the company returned to England for location shooting at Highclere Castle of *Downton Abbey* fame – the real-life residence of Lord Carnarvon and his descendants – Eva Marie Saint was almost electrocuted when she accidentally stepped on a live wire.

In an interview for the *Los Angeles Times*, Stromberg stated, "I personally don't believe in curses, however, when we started shooting the picture at the ancestral home of Lord Carnarvon, we had many dinners with the present resident, the son of Carnarvon. When I asked him what does he have on the premises from the Tut tomb, he replied, 'Not one single piece; wouldn't think of it.'"

Stromberg asked if, when the picture was completed, he could meet the elderly Lady Evelyn to have the experience of some real-life link, her brother said he'd arrange it. "The very day Angharad Rees completed her role as Lady Evelyn in the movie," Stromberg said, "the real Evelyn died. Sure, you can say these things are coincidences, but some of it is inexplicable."

Years later, Raymond Burr told Larry King on CNN that he was still fanatically opposed to discussing any details about the film.

On January 8, 1980, unhappy with the look of the dailies, Stromberg threatened to fire director Philip Leacock if he

couldn't give the film the feel of "a big, lush, and flamboyant event." Somehow, they resolved their differences and managed to complete the production with no further bloodshed.

NBC was so enthusiastic about *The Curse of King Tut's Tomb*, they scheduled it to be aired in two parts on its *Big Event* movie series during the all-important "May Sweeps" period when network viewership levels are gaged to set advertising rates for the following television season. Stromberg was extremely pleased by the vote of confidence – but when NBC announced the movie's lead-in programming,

Robin Ellis (who replaced Ian McShane after the car accident that nearly killed McShane and Saint).

his blood ran cold. On Thursday and Friday, May 8 and 9, 1980, *The Curse of King Tut's Tomb*, Parts 1 and 2, would be double-billed with Parts 1 and 2 of a major theatrical film making its television debut – none other than the Dino De Laurentiis production of *King Kong* starring Jessica Lange, the film that had bulldozed Stromberg's planned remake. Was this someone's idea of a cruel joke? Or had King Tut saved the most painful curse of all for Stromberg?

Apparently graced with nine lives, Stromberg had the last laugh when *The Curse of King Tut's Tomb* beat *King Kong* in the ratings both nights – with Part 1 landing at No. 10 for the week. Part 2 not only won its timeslot, it beat the routinely-invincible *Dallas* on CBS.

Eva Marie Saint and Robin Ellis.

Robin Ellis brushing an Egyptian sarcophagus.

Harry Andrews and Robin Ellis investigate a hole in the tomb.

Highclere Castle of *Downton Abbey* fame.

Robin Ellis, Angharad Rees, Barbara Murray, Harry Andrews, on location at Highclere Castle.

Reviews were upbeat, too. The critique in *Daily Variety* read, "Lots of fun. Archeologists and historians will cringe at the whole thing, but all in all, it's a good dig. Produced so ably by Stromberg-Kerby Productions, John Biggs' art direction and Joan Bridge's costumes are smashingly convincing, neither overdone nor understated. Telefilm moves fast and sure."

In England, *The Curse of King Tut's Tomb* premiered on the ITV network on August 31, 1980. Back in the U.S., two years later, *The Curse of King Tut's Tomb* was repeated on August 29, 1982, as a Sunday night *NBC Big Event* (9:00-11:00 pm) with the two parts edited together as one. In 1987, a 98-minute version of the movie was released in the U.S. on VHS video cassette by Columbia TriStar Home Video. In 2011, an 80-minute cut of the movie was released in the UK on DVD by NetworkDVD.co.uk (with a gallery of stills – including a few from Ian McShane's brief stint).

Unfortunately, *The Curse of King Tut's Tomb* has not dated well and seems plodding by today's standards – a far cry

from the bar that was raised with *Frankenstein: The True Story*. Nevertheless, Stromberg proved once again that he had the Midas touch when it came to event television programming – curses be damned.

DEVELOPMENT HELL OR HIGH WATER

After *The Curse of King Tut's Tomb*, Stromberg-Kerby developed many other movie and television projects for Columbia. These included:

1. *The Abominable Dr. Fu Manchu*, a spoof of his father's 1932 Karloff movie *The Mask of Fu Manchu*, to star Peter Sellers. Sellers did end up portraying Fu Manchu in *The Fiendish Plot of Dr. Fu Manchu* (Orion / Warner Bros., 1980), but the film was produced by Zev Braun and *Playboy* magazine editor Hugh Hefner, *not* Stromberg-Kerby.

2. *Chandu, the Magician*, a spoof of the mystery-thriller radio series that was made into three Bela Lugosi movies in the 1930s. To star Peter Sellers.

3. *Rasputin*, a spoof of the mad monk. To star Peter Sellers. To be directed by Jack Smight.

4. *Dashiell Hammett's The Fat Man*, a series to star Raymond Burr. Hammett's widow Lillian Hellman, 75,

Hunt Stromberg Jr. dressed as Fu Manchu for Halloween.

based on a story by Stromberg. A modern urban update of *Cinderella*, with Barbra as the wicked stepmother of Madonna, with two spoiled daughters Radner and Duvall, and Broadway star Christopher Reeve in search of the perfect leading lady for his new show. The "Fairy Godfather" with magical powers would be a former pimp played by Richard Pryor. [This African American sex-role-reversal of the original "Fairy Godmother" predated Billy Porter's African American genderless "Fabulous Godmother" in the modern musical retelling of *Cinderella* (An Amazon Original Movie, 2021) by four decades.]

8. *Guess Who's Having a Baby?*, a sequel to *Guess Who's Coming to Dinner?* (Columbia Pictures, 1967), to reunite Katharine Hepburn (Oscar-winner for the first film), Sidney Poitier and Katharine Houghton, to be directed by Stanley Kramer (Oscar-nominee for the first film).

9. *Mack and Mabel*, to star Liza Minnelli (as silent movie star Mabel Normand) and Frank Sinatra (as silent comedy director / actor Mack Sennett, creator of The Keystone Cops), based on the Broadway musical with a score by Jerry Herman, loosely based on *Father Goose* by Gene Fowler. Leonard Spigelgass was writing the script.

10. *Diamond Lil*, based on the play by Mae West, to star Bette Midler.

11. *Hedda and Louella*, based on the dual biography by George Eells, about the competing gossip columnists Hedda Hopper and Louella Parsons, to star Faye Dunaway (as Hedda) and Bette Midler (as Louella). This same book was eventually produced in 1985 by ITC for the CBS network entitled *Malice in Wonderland*, starring Jane Alexander (as Hedda) and Elizabeth Taylor (as Louella), notably *without* the participation of Stromberg-Kerby.

12. *The Flip of a Coin: The George Raft Story*, based on the book by Lewis Yablonsky, to star John Travolta, produced in association with Robert Stigwood (*Saturday Night Fever*, *Grease*).

13. *Bloomingdale's*, a *Love Boat*-style television series set in the famed department store; later changed to *Macy's* when negotiations stalled. Jerome Lawrence and Robert E. Lee (*Auntie Mame*) were attached to write the pilot.

14. *Noel Coward's Private Lives*, to star Carol Burnett and Dick Van Dyke.

15. *Mother's Boys*, a sex reversal of *Charlie's Angels*, with Bette Davis as the widow of a famous detective who enlists three sexy young hunks to investigate unsolved crimes

was a family friend of Stromberg and she would serve as Executive Producer. His father had produced the first four *Thin Man* movies based on Hammett characters. *The Fat Man* had previously been adapted into a radio series and a 1951 movie for Universal-International, directed by William Castle, starring J. Scott Smart and Rock Hudson. Hellman passed away in 1984 at age 79.

5. *Agatha Christie's The Mousetrap*, to be adapted by Gore Vidal and directed by Hal Ashby, with an all-star cast that Stromberg promised would "rival *Murder on the Orient Express*."

6. *A Christmas Carol: A Ghost Story of Christmas*, resuscitating the musical remake of the Charles Dickens classic, scripted by Christopher Isherwood, that Stromberg had originally developed for Columbia in 1968, now with Rex Harrison, Laurence Olivier and Danny Kaye on the updated wish-list for the role of "Scrooge."

7. *The Cinderella Beat*, a comedy-musical to star Barbra Streisand, Madonna, Christopher Reeve, Gilda Radner, Shelley Duvall and Richard Pryor, to be directed by Herbert Ross (*Footloose*, *Steel Magnolias*, *Pennies from Heaven*, *The Turning Point*, *The Goodbye Girl*) from a screenplay by Carl Reiner (*The Dick Van Dyke Show*),

Hunt & Phyllis Diller.

Letter from Hunt to Phyllis Diller.

Columbia Pictures

VIA MESSENGER

November 25, 1981

Phyllis Diller
163 S. Rockingham Ave
Los Angeles, Ca. 90049

Dear One,

    Herewith the script. Please read carefully the
part of "LIZ."

    Adore your postcards.......and, of course, YOU!

                                        Love,

                                        Hunt

                                        HUNT STROMBERG

HS/nm
enclosure

dictated but not read

A division of Columbia Pictures Industries, Inc.

Columbia Plaza, Burbank, California 91505, Telephone 213-954-6000

Photo of Gypsy Rose Lee, inscribed to Hunt.

each week. When Bette Davis passed, Hunt next went to Lucille Ball. She turned it down, too. Finally, he offered it to Phyllis Diller – who readily accepted – but the show never materialized.

16. *Mario Puzo's Inside Las Vegas*, a television series based on *The Godfather* author's latest book.

17. *Citizen Hearst*, a miniseries to star Burt Lancaster as William Randolph Hearst, based on a book by W. A. Schulberg. With an on-screen introduction by granddaughter Patty Hearst.

18. *Gypsy Rose Lee's The G-String Murders*, to star Loni Anderson (1980 and 1981 two-time Emmy Award-nominee for *WKRP in Cinncinati*). A remake of Stromberg Sr.'s *Lady of Burlesque* (1943), which had starred Barbara Stanwyck.

19. *Night of the Ripper*, based on the 1984 novel by Robert Bloch (*Psycho*), following Inspector Frederick Abberline's attempts to apprehend Jack the Ripper, incorporating Sir Arthur Conan Doyle in its cast of real-life characters. This book was optioned prior to publication in 1983 and was the last project Stromberg was actively developing. To star Michael Caine as "Inspector Frederick Abberline." Stromberg would pass away in 1984 before this project moved forward. A suspiciously similar project, however, did come to fruition in 1988 – a two-part miniseries called *Jack the Ripper* (CBS-TV) starring Michael Caine as "Inspector Frederick Abberline" and Jane Seymour as "Emma Prentiss," filmed at Pinewood Studios. It was not based on the Joseph Stefano book, though. It was directed and co-written by David Wickes – who later wrote and directed *Jekyll & Hyde* (ABC-TV, 1990) starring Michael Caine; and *Frankenstein* (TNT, 1992) starring Patrick Bergin and Randy Quaid. Clearly, Wickes was following in Stromberg's footsteps.

Sadly, none of these projects ever happened with Stromberg-Kerby's involvement – but they sure are interesting insights into the never-ending creativity of Stromberg.

FRANKENSTEIN'S FOLLY

Perhaps the most interesting proposal of all was a half-hour comedy series called *Frankenstein's Folly*, written in 1978 by episodic veteran Shimon Wincelberg (*Lost in Space*, *The Wild Wild West*, *Star Trek*) to team John Ritter (of *Three's Company* fame) with the towering 6' 3½" hunk Tom Selleck (pre-*Magnum P.I.*).

The modern-day story begins with the coda that was cut from *Frankenstein: The True Story* – the hand of the Creature (Selleck) coming out of a crack in a melting glacier. He ends up saving the life of Reverend Norman Caine (Ritter), a mild-mannered preacher who feels a moral obligation to take the Creature under his wing – and decides to name him Adam. Soon, the man of God learns the truth about Adam's origin and, with the help of Dr. Frankenstein's diary, administers shock therapy treatments in his basement to keep Adam from deteriorating and to restore his beauty and strength to that of a Greek god.

In classic sitcom style, however, all this must be kept secret from prying eyes and nosy neighbors. Complicating matters further, Norman's fiancée Sally (tailored for Lucie Arnaz, daughter of Lucille Ball and Desi Arnaz) becomes jealous of the excessive amount of time Norman spends with Adam – and begins "to question her future husband's masculinity." As she gets to know Adam better, however, she finds herself becoming irresistibly attracted to him. The ultimate love triangle – long before Ross, Rachel and Joey.

With Ritter tied to *Three's Company* from 1976 to 1984, and Selleck hitting it big with *Magnum P.I.* from 1980 to 1988, the concept got stalled in development hell.

THE EPIC SAGA BEHIND *FRANKENSTEIN: THE TRUE STORY*

CAUSE OF DEATH

Equally frustrating was the slow progression of basic civil rights for members of the queer community. Because "domestic partnerships," regardless of gender, were not legalized in California until 1999, and gay marriage would not become legal in the U.S. until 2015, gay couples in the Dark Ages had to get creative to ensure that discriminatory laws could be circumvented (like inheritance rights, hospital "family-only" visitation policies, etc.). So, on January 27, 1984, Hunt decided to legally adopt Joe as his "son," establishing a new legal name for him: "Stoddard Joseph Stromberg-Kerby."

Clearly, Hunt had concerns about his own longevity and was getting his affairs in order. On January 16, 1985, he wrote the following hand-written letter to his business manager Michael McShane, to be opened "In Case of Emergency." The cryptic way in which Hunt refers to his "various medical problems" that only his physician or Joe were privy to, begs the question of whether he might have been diagnosed with AIDS but never dared to put it in writing. The AIDS plague was dire during that period, with scores of gay men dropping like flies. Rock Hudson would succumb to AIDS later that very year on October 2, 1985. And Hunt's neighbor and friend Liberace would die of the disease on February 4, 1987. I have not discovered any proof of this theory, but there was so much shame and stigma surrounding AIDS during that period, the disease was often covered-up and rarely reported publicly in obituaries. This letter raises more questions than it answers:

> Dear Mr. McShane,
> As you well know, approximately one year ago I legally adopted Stoddard Kerby, nickname "Joe", my long-term friend, companion and business partner. Should I become ill and/or incapacitated to the degree I am unable to function on my own, I am requesting that you see to it that Joe's needs are met (financially and otherwise) out of my regular monthly income. Also in case Joe himself should be ill or incapacitated in any way, I want you to know that my doctor is Hyman Engelberg (# 275-4366, or 273-9150). [NOTE: This famous Hollywood doctor had been Marilyn Monroe's physician.] Dr. Engelberg is completely familiar with my various medical problems and can and will respond accordingly. Joe's doctor is Jeffrey Grant (# 659-4511) and Dr. Grant could also attend me, but only if Dr. Engelberg is unavailable. Dr. Grant would have to have my medical problems explained to him by either Dr. Engelberg or Joe Kerby. Quite by chance, I discovered, to my horror, that during my father's last days, he was mistreated by a private nurse at St. John's Hospital. While I, too, would want and need private nurses, I hope and pray that what happened to my father never happens to me or Joe. I request that you supervise such matters, should the needs arise, since there is no one else I trust to the extent that I do you. Please never permit me or Joe to suffer in any way.
> Fondly,
> Hunt Stromberg, Jr.

Twenty-two months later, on November 24, 1986, at the relatively young age of 63, Stromberg passed away. According to his obituary in *Daily Variety*, November 26, 1986, "He became ill last Wednesday night, November 19, and it was believed at the time he had suffered a heart attack. Taken to Cedars Sinai, his condition was diagnosed as a ruptured aneurism. He was operated on Thursday morning, November 20, and had been in intensive care until his death on Monday, November 24." Memorial services were held at Pierce Brothers in Hollywood on December 5, 1986.

The "In Case of Emergency" envelope was kept in a safety deposit box at the First National Bank of California in Los Angeles. Four days after Stromberg's memorial, the envelope was mailed to Joe Stromberg-Kerby, postmarked December 9, 1986.

Seven years later, at the young age of just 58, Joe Stromberg-Kerby died on November 9, 1993, in Tulare, California. Cause of death was attributed to "throat cancer" – but as I stated above, obituaries were sometimes sanitized. What I do know is that his tombstone identifies him as "Joe Kerby Domingues," a portmanteau of his professional names and original last name. His connection to Stromberg was laid to rest.

REVERBERATIONS

The primary purpose of this biography of Hunt Stromberg Jr. has been to honor the man and his accomplishments. He was the ultimate Monster Kid. A fanboy who had the clout to be far more than just an observer. He ignited the wildfire of horror hosts everywhere, still going strong today. But that was just for starters.

Lifting the horror genre out of the B-movie ghetto may be Stromberg's most lasting influence. Indeed, the seeds that he planted at Universal bore much fruit – and are still sprouting today. John Badham's big-budget *Dracula* that Universal presented in 1979 with Frank Langella and Laurence Olivier was a direct extension of the path that *Frankenstein: The True Story* pioneered. Universal's reboot of *The Mummy* (1999) with Brendan Fraser (and its sequels) and the monster-mashup *Van Helsing* (2004) with Hugh Jackman were similarly Strombergian in their epic ambitions (even if the results were mixed). The remake of *King Kong* that Peter Jackson made for Universal in 2005 followed the exact same period-set, epic blueprint Stromberg had developed in 1975.

In 2017, Universal began a franchise dubbed "The Dark Universe," a highly-ambitious reimagining all of its classic

Concept art by Dave Elsey of Angelina Jolie for Bill Condon's *The Bride of Frankenstein* remake, before the project was aborted.

monsters, sparing no expense and boasting the kinds A-list actors that would have made Stromberg proud – including Javier Bardem as the Frankenstein Monster, Angelina Jolie as the Bride of Frankenstein (to be directed by Bill Condon), Johnny Depp as the Invisible Man, Channing Tatum as Van Helsing, Russell Crowe as Dr. Jekyll and Mr. Hyde, Dwayne Johnson as the Wolfman, etc. Even Guillermo del Toro was in discussions to direct a re-do of *Creature from the Black Lagoon*.

However, the first movie of the series, *The Mummy* (2017) starring Tom Cruise (featuring Russell Crowe as Jekyll & Hyde) was a critical and box-office dud causing the entire "Dark Universe" to collapse.

Instead, Universal decided standalone reboots would be less risky – resulting in such entries as *The Invisible Man* (2022) starring Elisabeth Moss; and *Renfield* (2023) featuring Nicholas Cage as Dracula.

Instead of his *Creature from the Black Lagoon*, Guillermo del Toro defected to Fox Searchlight for whom he directed his own original Gill-man-inspired masterpiece *The Shape of Water* which won Oscars for Best Picture and Best Director. And, as of this writing, in 2023, del Toro is directing his long-anticipated version of *Frankenstein* for Netflix. Del Toro has been vocal in interviews that both films were partly inspired by *Frankenstein: The True Story*. (See the Afterword in this book by Guillermo del Toro.)

In the wake of Fox Searchlight's extraordinary success with *The Shape of Water*, the studio has followed up with the acclaimed award-winner *Poor Things*, an audacious riff on Frankenstein, directed by Oscar nominee Yorgos Lanthimos. Willem Dafoe stars as mad scientist Dr. Godwin Baxter ("Godwin" derived from Mary Shelley's maiden name) who resurrects from the dead a female creature named Bella (played by Oscar winner Emma Stone, who was also a producer on the movie). The twist is that Godwin has transplanted the brain of Bella's unborn baby into her head, thus she has the innocence of a child in an adult body. Clearly, the Frankenstein mythos lives on — in no small part due to Stromberg's rehabilitation and "sophisticization" of the subject matter.

The Kingpin of the Lavender Hill Mob could not have been prouder of his greatest creation. Shortly before he passed away in 1986, Hunt Stromberg Jr. was asked to talk about his legacy. He responded, "Everything I've done career-wise has been a flamboyant stunt but *Frankenstein: The True Story* was the topper. I hope to be remembered for that."

On the set of *Frankenstein: The True Story*, Michael Sarrazin in Creature makeup gives Hunt Stromberg Jr. the creeps.

THE EPIC SAGA BEHIND *FRANKENSTEIN: THE TRUE STORY*

CHAPTER SEVENTEEN: THE MONSTROUS LIFE & TIMES OF HUNT STROMBERG JR.

Portrait of Guillermo del Toro by Frederick Cooper.

AFTERWORD BY GUILLERMO DEL TORO

The most important figure from English literature for me is, improbably, a teenage author by the name of Mary Shelley. She has remained a figure as important in my life as if she was family. And so many times when I want to give up, when I think about giving up, when people tell me dreaming of the movies and the stories I dream are impossible, I think of her because she picked up the plight of Luigi Galvani and the burden of Prometheus and she conjured the invisible and the bizarre and showed me that sometimes to talk about monsters, we need to fabricate monsters of our own. And parables do that for us.

I've been influenced by three Frankensteins. Once when I saw James Whale's *Frankenstein* (1931), it seemed like Saint Paul's experience on the road to Damascus. I saw a really beautiful figure of pain, of vitality, of existentialism. When Boris Karloff entered through the doorframe, I saw a Messiah that was going to sacrifice himself for me. That's why I live surrounded by life-size Frankenstein creations. The guy who was going to set up my phone didn't want to come in. For me, this really is a church. If the Father, the Son and the Holy Ghost exist, Frankenstein's Creature is the Father of all Monsters to me.

The second time that hit me really hard was when I read Mary Shelley's book, *Frankenstein; or, The Modern Prometheus* (1818). It seemed as if it was speaking to me directly. Everything people find in Milton's *Paradise Lost*, I found in Shelley's novel. The human being's essential questions: What am I doing here? Why? I didn't ask to live, I don't understand the world, it's too big for me, it is too small. What makes me human? Despite the beauty of the novel, nobody has really made it into a film.

The third time was a movie that has nothing to do with Shelley's novel and yet is the one that gets the closest to it. It's the version written by Christopher Isherwood and Don Bachardy that was made into a TV film in two parts. It's called *Frankenstein: The True Story* (1973) and it mixes gothic elements with E.T.A. Hoffman, Oscar Wilde and a lot of other things in a ludic, erudite, fluid way, that captures the character of Frankenstein's Creature from Shelley's novel without looking or seeming like it. It's a elegiac, beautiful jewel that more people need to know about.

I am heartened by this book and Sam Irvin's passionate crusade to shine a long overdue spotlight on this quirky, brilliant, and moving masterpiece.

Caricatures of Sam Irvin by legendary *Vanity Fair* artist Robert Risko.

ABOUT THE AUTHOR

After his teenage years editing and publishing a horror film fanzine called *Bizarre*, Sam Irvin began his filmmaking career as Brian De Palma's assistant on *The Fury* and *Dressed to Kill*. Since then, he has directed over 50 films, including *Elvira's Haunted Hills*, *Guilty as Charged*, *Out There*, *Acting on Impulse*, *Oblivion*, *Backlash: Oblivion 2*, *Magic Island*, *Christmas Land*, *Fatal Acquittal* and *Kiss of a Stranger* (from his own original screenplay).

For television, he directed episodes of Julie Brown's *Strip Mall* on Comedy Central, and all three seasons of the gay supernatural series *Dante's Cove*.

Irvin's 20-plus producing credits include Bill Condon's *Gods and Monsters* (which won the Academy Award for Best Adapted Screenplay), Greg Berlanti's *The Broken Hearts Club: A Romantic Comedy*, and Brian De Palma's *Home Movies*.

Irvin authored the acclaimed biography *Kay Thompson: From Funny Face to Eloise* (Simon & Schuster) which led to him serving as the historical consultant on Broadway's *Liza's at the Palace* starring Liza Minnelli (which won the Tony Award for Best Theatrical Event).

For his own imprint, Knuckle Samwitch Books, Irvin authored the children's book parody *Sam's Toilet Paper Caper!* (2020), illustrated by Dan Gallagher; the novel *ORBGASM: An Erotic Pulp Sci-Fi Satyricon* (2020); and the coming-of-age memoir *I Was a Teenage Monster Hunter! How I Met Vincent Price, Christopher Lee, Peter Cushing & More!* (2022) – which won the 2022 Rondo Award for Best Writer of the Year.

Irvin has won four additional Rondo Awards: 2017 Best Article ("The Epic Untold Saga Behind *Frankenstein: The True Story*" published in *Little Shoppe of Horrors* No. 38); 2018 Best Interview ("Elvira Exposed" published in *Screem* No. 36); 2020 Best Audio Commentary (for Shout! Factory's Blu-ray of *Frankenstein: The True Story*); and 2021 Best Interview

("Sam Irvin Interviews Legendary Horror Hostess Elvira, Mistress of the Dark" published in *The Dark Side* No. 222).

Irvin resides in Horrorwood, Karloffornia, with his husband Gary Bowers.

Rondo Award Winner!
Best Audio Commentary by Sam Irvin!

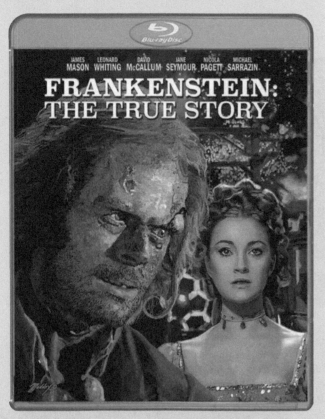

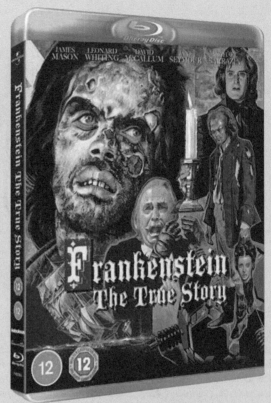

Shout! Factory Region A (USA)
Cover art by Mark Maddox

Fabulous Films Region B (UK)
Cover art by Graham Humphreys

These Blu-ray editions of *Frankenstein: The True Story* include the original two-part U.S. NBC-TV television broadcast in its entirety (over 3 hours), exquisitely remastered from the original 35mm negative in 2K.

- Includes the James Mason Introduction.
- Previews of Part 2.
- Recap of Part 1.
- Special Features produced by Constantine Nasr and Sam Irvin.
- Leonard Whiting interviewed by Sam Irvin.
- Jane Seymour interviewed by Sam Irvin.
- Co-screenwriter Don Bachardy interviewed by Sam Irvin.
- Audio Commentary by Sam Irvin.

Available from Shout! Factory (USA), Fabulous Films (UK), or Amazon in your respective country.

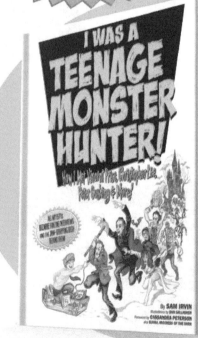

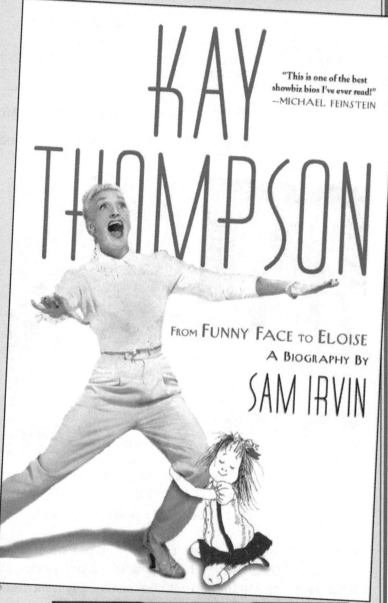

Made in the USA
Las Vegas, NV
17 October 2023

79268932R00223